METHODOLOGICAL AND BIOST
FOUNDATIONS OF
CLINICAL NEUROPSYCHOL<

METHODOLOGICAL AND BIOSTATISTICAL FOUNDATIONS OF CLINICAL NEUROPSYCHOLOGY

Edited by

Byron P. Rourke, Louis Costa,
Domenic V. Cicchetti, Kenneth M. Adams, and
Klaus J. Plasterk

SWETS & ZEITLINGER B.V. AMSTERDAM / LISSE   PUBLISHERS

SWETS & ZEITLINGER INC. BERWYN, PA

Library of Congress Cataloging-in-Publication Data

[applied for]

Cip-gegevens Koninklijke Bibliotheek, Den Haag

Methodological

Methodological and biostatistical foundations of clinical neuropsychology /
ed. by Byron P. Rourke...[et al]. - Amsterdam [etc.] Swets en Zeitlinger.
Met reg.
ISBN 90-265-1165-5 geb.
ISBN 90-265-1245-7 pbk.
NUGI 742
Trefw.: klinische neuropsychologie.

Cover design: Rob Molthoff
Cover printed in the Netherlands by Casparie, IJsselstein
Printed in the Netherlands by Offsetdrukkerij Kanters B.V.,
Alblasserdam

ISBN 90 265 1165 5 geb.
ISBN 90 265 1245 7 pbk.
NUGI 742

Preface

This book was designed to serve as a guide to many of the principal methodological and biostatistical dimensions of the "pure" and "applied" aspects of clinical neuropsychology. We had both advanced graduate students and seasoned researchers in mind as a potential audience for it. Thus, the contents of the book mirror our views regarding those methodological and biostatistical issues that we felt would be of particular importance to this group of individuals.

The papers included in this volume were chosen from the pages of the **Journal of Clinical Neuropsychology**, its successor, the **Journal of Clinical and Experimental Neuropsychology**, and **The Clinical Neuropsychologist**. The commentaries at the beginning and end of the book, as well as those that appear as introductions to each of the sections of the work, were crafted by the editors. These commentaries were felt to be necessary in order to suggest a context for the papers within each section as well as wider issues relating to methodological and biostatistical issues in clinical neuropsychology.

The preparation of this book, of course, would not have been possible without the seminal efforts of the authors of the papers presented herein. Our debt to these persons is immense; our gratitude, of equal dimensions. We would also wish to extend a warm note of thanks to Klaus Plasterk and others among the Editorial staff of Swets Publishing for their prodigious efforts in assembling and indexing the papers contained within this volume. Their efforts serve to make the work easily readable and accessible to the researcher. Of course, any failings or limitations that remain in the work are solely the responsibility of the Editors.

The Editors

CONTENTS

X

CHAPTER I

Introduction

Both Costa (1983, 1988) and Rourke (1991) have commented on the evolution of neuropsychological inquiry in the past quarter century. Twenty-five years ago, the main thrust of neuropsychological investigation was the elucidation of brain-behaviour relationships through the association of discrete neurological lesions with specific behavioural losses. This was true whether the investigator like Benton (see Costa & Spreen, 1985) was one who emphasized the construction of psychometric instruments to measure and increase our understanding of neuropsychological phenomena or like Reitan (see Reitan & Davison, 1974) believed in determining the efficacy of a standardized battery of tests in identifying and localizing neurologic disorders. The approach also characterizes that of Teuber and colleagues in attempting to relate cognitive sensory and motor deficits to lesions resulting from penetrating head injury (see, for example, Semmes, Weinstein, Ghent, & Teuber, 1960). Finally, the clinical examination of Luria (1980) again reflected an attempt to relate observable behavioural deficit to localizable lesions in the context of a specific model of brain and behaviour.

The methodology requisite for such investigations emphasized measurement of the locus, extent, severity, and etiology of cerebral lesions and the necessary statistics most often involved in analysis of variance and t tests. While occasional studies (e.g., Bechtoldt, Fogel, & Benton, 1962) attempted to apply factor-analytic techniques or discriminant function analyses (e.g., Wheeler & Reitan, 1963) to batteries of neuropsychological tests, these were the exception rather than the rule.

Many correlations between the loci of predominantly grey-matter lesions and behavioural deficits have now been established. Furthermore, due to advances in neuroradiological technique, the use of neuropsychological assessment in the localization of discrete neoplastic and vascular lesions is less necessary. Emphasis in patient investigation and research has thus shifted more to issues of management, planning, and rehabilitation. Patients with diffuse lesions (e.g., dementia and closed-head injury) are more commonly subjects for research, and complex and subtle changes in performance resulting from such lesions are more common foci of attention. Understanding patterns of test performance as a function of etiology, demographics, ability, and perhaps treatment variables is what concerns the neuropsychologist of today.

In this context, factor analysis, including confirmatory models, linear discriminant function analysis, canonical correlation, and subtyping methodologies have risen to the fore. The modern neuropsychologist must master a larger variety of statistical and methodological techniques and become increasingly conversant with the basic assumption underlying the application of each.

It is our opinion as editors and reviewers of many excellent and many mundane manuscripts over the years that the typical neuropsychological investigator tends to stick with the statistical methodology she or he learned in graduate school. While there are some significant exceptions to this generalization, it is evident to us that many potentially outstanding investigations are weakened by reliance on outmoded methodological or statistical approaches.

It is our purpose in this volume to provide a collection of articles that explore a broad range of research design issues and data-analytic strategies. Some of the articles deal primarily with methodological theory or research strategy per se and others reflect applications of methodology to specific neuropsychological problems.

This book is meant both for professionals in psychology, neurology, psychiatry, speech pathology, and related disciplines and for students in these areas. It assumes that keeping abreast of methodological advances in neuropsychology will be a life-long endeavour, both for those who simply want to consume neuropsychological literature intelligently and for those who want to contribute to neuropsychological research.

The editors believe that the materials presented herein can form a basic set of readings for a graduate course in neuropsychological research methodology. They can also be used by the advanced professional as a methodological handbook, particularly if the sources cited in many of the articles are also used. It was not our intention to fashion a complete, integrated textbook of neuropsychological statistics or a techniques handbook such as that produced by Hannay (1986).

We hope that the reader who has at least one recent undergraduate course in statistics involving exposure to both ANOVA and multivariate methodology can read it with profit.

REFERENCES

Bechtoldt, H.P., Fogel, M., & Benton, A.L. (1962). An application of factor analysis in neuropsychology. *Psychological Record, 12*, 147-156.

Costa, L. (1983). Clinical neuropsychology: A discipline in evolution. *Journal of Clinical Neuropsychology, 5*, 1-11.

Costa, L. (1988), Clinical neuropsychology: Prospects and problems. *The Clinical Neuropsychologist, 2*, 3-11.

Costa, L., & Spreen, O. (Eds.) (1985). *Studies in neuropsychology: Selected papers of Arthur Benton*. New York: Oxford University Press.

Hannay, H.J. (1986). *Experimental techniques in human neuropsychology*. New York: Oxford University Press.

Luria, A.R. (1980). *Higher cortical functions in man* (2nd ed.). New York: Basic Books.

Reitan, R.H., & Davison, L.A. (1974). *Clinical neuropsychology: Current status and applications*. Washington, DC: V.H. Winston and Sons.

Rourke, B.P. (1991). Neuropsychology in the 1990's. *Archives of Clinical Neuropsychology, 6*, 1-14.

Semmes, J., Weinstein, S., Ghent, L., & Teuber, H.L. (1960). *Somatosensory changes after penetrating brain wounds in man*. Cambridge, MA: Harvard University Press.

Wheeler, L., & Reitan, R.M. (1963). Discriminant functions applied to the problem of predicting cerebral damage from behavior tests: A cross validation study. *Perceptual and Motor Skills, 16*, 681-701.

CHAPTER II

General Methodological and Statistical Issues

The topics in this chapter cover a fairly broad range of issues that are of interest to the researcher in clinical neuropsychology. As with other sections of this book, the introductions to each of the following sub-sections were designed to provide an overview to the topic at hand. Rather than present a general overview of these sections, the reader is referred to their introductions for the specific content dealt with therein.

SECTION II – A: GENERAL

The papers in this section deal with fundamental issues in neuropsychological research. Adams's contribution is a critical commentary concerning a series of methodological papers published in that number of JCEN. Of note is the call for researchers to take advantage of the advances in multivariate statistical measurement that have occurred as a function of the development of computing technology. A central thesis of this paper is that the traditional bivariate experiment analyzed using Analysis of Variance (ANOVA) is an outmoded paradigm that is actually constraining progress in neuropsychology. Moreover, there are dangers inherent for any realm of research when investigations are overly shaped by experimental methods that are familiar, but confining.

In a similar critical fashion, Lezak and Gray describe the ways in which neuropsychological data distributions may violate the basic assumptions of interval-level measurement required by many commonly used techniques. As a constructive general recommendation, these authors suggest the use of nonparametric alternative models to deal with this kind of problem. In the neuropsychological literature in general, only a mere handful of studies have employed nonparametric methods. These nonparametric techniques have appeared with the greatest frequency in the pages of JCEN; but there is a vast and unexplored opportunity to improve the quality of measurement in neuropsychological studies using these powerful methods.

Loring and Papanicolaou address the vital issue of construct validity in memory testing. Employing widely used memory measures in clinical neuropsychology, they analyze the shortcomings of these tests in characterizing memory as a construct. They outline the issues that require consideration in selecting memory measures for use. They quite correctly point to the negative impact on construct and content validity that can result from overconcern with a test's predictive validity in relation to brain damage. Keeping their recommendations in mind, the next generation of memory assessment tools may do a better job of balancing predictive *and* construct validity.

Soper and associates draw attention to a serious problem in neuropsychological research - the abuse of the null hypothesis in the planning and execution of research. They focus on research concerning hemispheric laterality - clearly the realm of neuropsychology with the most egregious and frequent violations of the hypothesis-testing process. Using computer simulation technology, they demonstrate how commonly employed statistical techniques can be misused, with spurious or trivial findings as a result. A key aspect of this paper is a demonstration and discussion of how the *strength* of a research finding may be assessed. This takes the investigator beyond the mere harvesting of "significant" probability test levels into a more thoughtful realm of the consideration of both statistical and clinical significance.

SECTION II – B: SINGLE-CASE DESIGNS

Single-case studies have long been a part of the neurological and psychotherapeutic literature. Their value, however, has been questioned by some who espouse a strongly empirical approach to clinical assessment and treatment validation. The editors are firmly of the opinion that, while some single-case studies may not make a contribution to our understanding of neuropsychological phenomena, diagnostic, or assessment processes, strong arguments *can* be made for the validity of this approach. Indeed, the contributions of Shallice and of Marshall and Newcombe make explicit the many advantages of single-case designs in the study of brain-behaviour relations.

Willmes presents a detailed illustration of the methodology developed by Huber (1973) for the analysis of scores obtained by a single subject on a well-standardized instrument. The methodology is valuable both for assessment and for the evaluation of changes in performance over time. Wilson argues cogently for the value of single-case experimental designs in neuropsychological rehabilitation. If one entertains the premise that patients in rehabilitation manifest different patterns of disability and are best helped by individualized treatment programs, the importance of single-case methodology is self-evident.

REFERENCES

Huber, H.P. (1973). *Psychometrische Einzelfalldiagnostik*. Weinheim: Beltz.

Journal of Clinical and Experimental Neuropsychology
1988, Vol. 10, No. 5, pp. 659-663.

The Right Stuff: Advanced Methods
in Neuropsychology Today*

Kenneth M. Adams

Veterans Administration Medical Center, Ann Arbor, and The University of Michigan

It is highly unlikely that neuropsychologist researchers and clinicians are in much better shape today than their nonneuropsychological scientific contemporaries in terms of the constraints on their progress. That is, merely having the brain and the mind as an investigational focus does not provide us with any particular freedom from the need to gauge our advances carefully against realistic scientific standards of evidence. It would be comforting, but thoroughly misleading, to actually believe Public Television documentaries that tell us how wonderful we have become.

This warning needs saying in the context of the present special presentation of papers - if for no other reason than because there would seem to be a feeling afoot in agencies funding neuropsychological research that high technology instruments and elaborate cognitive theories featured on television networks around the world are the leading edge of progress in neuropsychology. There is certainly room for glamor in our public relations as a science, but this author would submit that it is the present grouping of papers that represents a good sample of what is likely to be tangible and sustainable progress in both theoretical and practical terms. The problems addressed therein have far greater implications for our science than either colorful digital fantasies of putative brain activity having unknown reliability or meaning; or tomes describing new pseudo-breakthroughs on the question of hemispheric lateralization of bizarre abilities not utilized by anyone outside a mental institution (neuropsychology's enduring research equivalent of the "Tastes Great" versus "Less Filling" debate of American television fame).

The fact that some of the elements of the papers are mathematical should not deter the serious student of neuropsychology, since many of the questions and issues described are so eminently qualitative. Further, each of the papers exemplifies the notion that the best of contemporary neuropsychology has long passed the stage of identifying vague syndromes of organicity (Mapou, 1988). The focus here is identifying in objective terms how agreement may exist

---

* This set of comments is based upon original discussion that occurred at the meeting of the International Neuropsychological Society in Denver, CO, in February, 1986.

between experts, or how models can be *tested* instead of debated until their proponents get university tenure, or the observers die of boredom.

The paper by Cicchetti deserves careful scrutiny by any scientist seeking to evaluate the true likelihood of the existence of consensus among expert (or not so expert) clinical judges. The example of dyslexia can be generalized to any number of situations in which agreement represents a "gold standard" of reliability in a research program. The program must include multiple options for replication. However, we note agreement with Cicchetti here and have stated previously (Adams, 1985), that reliability or internal consistency cannot be used to substitute for validity. Nonetheless, the oft-used Kappa statistic turns out in Cicchetti's compelling examples to have more intricacies than first might be obvious in such a beguiling way of mud-wrestling a two-by-two table to the parametric mat. This is not an esoteric issue, since a number of major neuro-psychological projects extending back some years have used this metric as a central test (cf., Russell, Neuringer, & Goldstein, 1970). History may revise itself if we care to do these recalculations.

The reader should note carefully the way in which the prevalence or base rate issue is introduced by Cicchetti's method for dealing with the components of observed agreement. Two issues are important here. First, it might be argued that the reductive comparison of agreement for chance levels of agreement might be irrelevant since no expert would view him/herself as working against chance on an issue such as the identification of dyslexia.

However, this is not the case, however dearly one might wish it to be. A careful reflection on the issues raised by relative agreement and suggested clinical value will remind the experienced reader of a complementary treatment of clinical prediction offered so long ago by Meehl (1954). There is great value in assessing to what degree our assessment procedures have reliability and operate at rates greater than chance. In fact, most medical or neuropsychological laboratories would be very hard pressed to produce data clearly demonstrating this incremental advantage.

This leads to the second issue. Cicchetti aptly notes that the creation of a dichotomy is to some extent an artificial exercise. It also can lead researchers and clinicians to engage in "tunnel vision" with respect to the ultimate goals of neuropsychological assessment. These may extend well beyond any agreement on a diagnosis or syndrome. This has led some investigators, such as Rourke and his associates (Rourke, Fisk, & Strang, 1986), to advocate a complete focus on the full description of behavior to avoid a premature or misleading obsession with diagnostic agreement with syndromes whose definitional accuracy are an order of magnitude less precise and objective than are psychological test instruments.

Finally, it is well worthwhile to become familiar with the various alternative methods (i.e., Cohen's and Chamberlain's) for the evaluation of reliability described by Cicchetti, since the balance of the factors he explores will be played out in different ways. Other methods would appear to have fatal flaws and are to be avoided, although modern statistical consumers can expect to see these printed anyway by mainframe computer programs that are programmed by the statistically promiscuous or those under orders to bring back significant results or else. A brief check reveals that most major packages will produce these suspect indices.

The contribution by Francis provides a very helpful introduction to a very difficult enterprise in neuropsychological research - namely, the building of useful multidimensional models of behavior. The same forces that have been at work to deter scientists in other areas of endeavor (notably anthropology and agriculture) are still arrayed in the field against the would-be model-builder. The epitome of the method rests in the interplay between causation and correlation, the manifest and the latent, and the events of the past and the present. Whether one uses Monte Carlo models or attempts to design special directional correlation metrics, the issues are quite challenging. One very elegant and powerful method (Sonquist, Baker, & Morgan, 1973) dealing with some of the practical problems for neuropsychologists could be usefully restudied in light of some of the advances described by Francis. A study of the dates of his references alone will give the reader some idea of the recency of the explosion of knowledge.

Despite the growth of ways to actually test complex models, there would seem to be a resistance to the adoption of such models in experimental neuropsychology that is difficult to understand. Perhaps the boundaries of the bivariate experiment are known and more comforting; but they are also surely confining. In fact, a dynamic balance of the known and unknown represents much more reasonably the nature of problems as encountered in all of neuropsychology today, whether experimental or not.

Another source of resistance to structural models may rest in the perception that they are too slick or sleazy ways to avoid that familiar parametric test. This is patently false, and the methods advocated by Francis actually encompass all the best elements of the classic experimental method. They also provide ways to estimate the *strength of a relationship or effect;* something almost never done in traditional neuropsychological research.

Herein lies what Cicchetti might well call a paradox too. Before dismissing what Francis suggests we do as too much work, it might be useful to reassess our willingness to stop using the procurement of a statistical probability of less than five in one hundred on a statistical test as permission to stop doubting and thinking. In natural sciences, it is quite often the case that the experimenter finding an effect will make the conditions under which the effect was achieved more difficult, demanding, or circumscribed; thus making it less likely that the result will obtain upon replication. Too often in neuropsychology we shun even replication of our findings, much less a higher hurdle. Structural equation technology does not allow us to as easily fool ourselves, since it encompasses the problem of indeterminacy and builds skepticism into the procedures themselves.

Morris and Fletcher present a primer for the neuropsychologist in understanding classification issues and research as they occur predominantly in child clinical neuropsychology today. This is a very complete compendium of all the sins, without untactful identification of the sinners; this is a research area in which everyone inhabits a glass house at some time or other. At some points this author has taken issue with certain issues concerning the misleading notion that internal consistency is validity. This is a minor semantic point if one just keeps remembering that Ptolemy's *Almagest* had all the internal consistency in the world as an astronomical model. It only fell down on the telling little point that the sun and planets of this solar system do not revolve around the earth.

There is no doubt that the children's literature on the classification of neuropsychological and socio-emotional factors has advanced greatly in recent years. No other area of neuropsychology has made this kind of progress. Researchers using differing testing and assessment approaches are identifying very comparable subtypes and mapping a domain that is intellectually and practically valuable. Faced with a choice of this empirical approach as opposed to group conference *seances* arguing about hemi-semi-demi quavers of difference in attention deficit disorder, there isn't much contest.

The questions and issues of learning disorder are not those of a *nosology,* since it is by no means certain that the full identification of children's learning problems will be predominantly medical in the strict sense. Indeed, the informed deployment of typological methods can actually serve to integrate various domains of knowledge into a *taxonomy* (cf., Fleishman & Quaintance, 1984).

Classification is a broad topic with many applications outside neuropsychology (Adams, 1985), and with issues and problems that very much transcend mathematical considerations. In thinking about a classification approach to any neuropsychological problem, it would probably be best to turn fully away from the problem at hand and conduct some fairly broad inquiries into similar issues that have confronted researchers in other areas of endeavor, such as botany, astronomy, or geology. Fascination with the statistical, mathematical, and computational problems is virtually assured once one concludes that a numerical taxonomy should be attempted. Thus, it behooves the researcher to try to get a good deal of perspective before narrowing the focus.

The papers in this issue of *JCEN* have all the elements of the kind of scientific methodology that can produce lasting advances. It is notable that there is general agreement among researchers who utilize these types of methods and report the results in journals like this one. Interestingly, when investigators do diverge in their conclusions, it is almost always evident that there are major procedural flaws or differences that are evident in comparing the reports. This is to be contrasted with previous lines of work in our field where investigators who are supposedly using the same paradigms cannot get consistent results. Surely, some of this is statistical in nature (Soper, Cicchetti, Satz, Light, & Orsini, 1988), but we should question ourselves constantly as whether our methods are the best possible ones. The approaches reported in the present issue of *JCEN* would appear in the view of this author to be just that.

REFERENCES

Adams, Ķ. M. (1985). Theoretical, methodological and statistical issues. In B. P. Rourke (Ed.), *Neuropsychology of learning disabilities: Essentials of subtype analysis,* (pp. 17-39). New York: Guilford Press.

Fleishman, E. A., & Quaintance, M. K. (1984). *Taxonomies of human performance.* Orlando, FL: Academic Press.

Mapou, R. (1988). Testing to detect brain damage: An alternative to what may no longer be useful. *Journal of Clinical and Experimental Neuropsychology, 10,* 271-278.

Meehl, P. E. (1954). *Clinical versus statistical prediction.* Minneapolis: University of Minnesota Press.

Rourke, B. P., Fisk, J. L., & Strang, J. D. (1986). *Neuropsychological assessment of children: A treatment-oriented approach.* New York: Guilford Press.

Russell, E. W., Neuringer, C., & Goldstein, G. (1970). *Assessment of brain damage: A neuropsychological key approach.* New York: John Wiley and Sons.

Sonquist, J. A., Bakker, E. L., & Morgan, J. N. (1973). *Searching for structure.* Ann Arbor, MI: Survey Research Center, University of Michigan.

Soper, H. V., Cicchetti. D. V., Satz, P., Light, R., & Orsini, D. L. (1988). Null hypothesis disrespect in neuropsychology: Dangers of alpha and beta errors. *Journal of Clinical and Experimental Neuropsychology, 10,* 255-270.

Journal of Clinical Neuropsychology
1984, Vol. 6, No. 1, pp.101-109.

Sampling Problems and Nonparametric Solutions in Clinical Neuropsychological Research*

Muriel D. Lezak and Daniel K. Gray

Veterans Administration Medical Center

Portland, Oregon

ABSTRACT

Research data in clinical neuropsychology frequently do not conform to the requirements for parametric statistical analysis. In some of these cases, data analysis by parametric techniques does not identify existing differences. The usefulness of nonparametric statistical tools in evaluating irregular data sets is demonstrated in three case examples. Methodological considerations arising from these examples are discussed.

Research in clinical neuropsychology can present special problems in data collection and analysis. These problems arise from certain characteristics of neuropsychologically impaired patient-subjects and circumstances associated with their impairments.

In addition to the usual sources of subject variability such as age, sex, and other demographic or psychological attributes, the presence of brain damage introduces additional variables including the site or extent of a lesion, the hemisphere of involvement, and time along a course. Uncontrolled variations in these and other dimensions can dilute the results of data analyses, leaving the investigator with findings that show many tendencies but few characteristics that cannot be explained away by chance.

In many instances, the variable of interest to the neuropsychologist is not normally distributed in the brain-damaged population and its distribution in samples of normal control subjects may be even less likely to satisfy criteria for parametric statistics. Either subject group is liable to contain "sports" or statistical "outliers" on measures of neuropsychological characteristics. Differences between groups may seem apparent to clinical observers or show up in ostensibly husky discrepancies between means. Yet large variances reflecting the scattered distributions of scores obtained by brain-damaged persons may make these discrepancies appear to be insignificant.

Many questions raised in clinical neuropsychological research require the study of conditions or dysfunctional behaviors that do not occur with sufficient frequency to insure a large and steady supply of subjects. If they do happen often enough, they may be prevalent in patient groups subject to confounding disorders (e.g., when studying the effects of industrial toxins, a high incidence of alcoholism among painters may restrict the number of available subjects). As a consequence, research in clinical neuropsychology often must be conducted with relatively small numbers of subjects. When a study requires a longitudinal design, the problem of small numbers is further compounded by missing cases since the behavioral deficits of neurologically impaired patients may make them unreliable, uncooperative, or physically restricted. Furthermore, motor and sensory deficits, and aphasic, apraxic, and perceptual disorders can make it impossible for all patient subjects to take all of the tests in a battery. As a result, data sheets become so riddled with empty cases that few comparisons can be made with subgroups of equal size or equated on the relevant independent variables. By the time a study has progressed to the analysis stage, samples that seemed to have been reasonably large at the outset may shrink to statistically trivial dimensions on many measures.

These problems – small sample sizes to begin with, more variables to be controlled, a wide range of variability on many of the behavioral dimensions of interest, and incomplete samples – tend to work together to decrease the likelihood that the data to be analyzed satisfy the requirements for utilizing parametric statistics. In this field of endeavor it is not uncommon for investigators to complete a parametric analysis, and come up with evaluations of the significance of likely-looking differences that are within the bounds of chance by little more than a hair's breadth. Many investigators give up their struggle with the null hypothesis at this point. They report "tendencies," or no differences, or may simply shelve their data and report nothing at all.

However, the investigator who does not look beyond parametric data analyses may be overlooking positive findings. Nonparametric techniques will sometimes provide the statistical means for identifying differences between groups which size-dependent and variance-sensitive parametric procedures fail to detect. While coarse-grained and often rather simplistic nonparametric techniques lack the conceptual elegance and broad capabilities of their parametric counterparts, they do offer another way of examining probability questions which is sometimes more suited to clinical neuropsychological data analysis than more orthodox parametric approaches. The following three cases illustrate how nonparametric data analysis may be useful.

THE CASE OF THE SKEWED DISTRIBUTION

A study of impaired temporal sequencing in Korsakoff patients compared their performance on several temporal sequencing tasks with those of two matched groups – chronic alcoholics and nondrinkers (Lezak, Howieson, & McGavin, 1983). The average number of errors made by the Korsakoff patients in identifying the year an event occurred (such as the assassination of President Kennedy) was 25 ± 23.27, far greater than the mean error scores of the alcoholic (3.36 ± 6.25) or the nondrinking (1.33 ± 2.56) groups. Despite considerable skewing in the distributions of the latter two groups, the disparity between the Korsakoff group mean and the other two means was so large that analysis of variance resulted in a significant F test ($p < .001$). However, the difference between the means of the alcoholics and the nondrinkers was submerged by the large variances that described the data. Planned contrasts evaluating the difference between these two means did not prove to be significant.

When these data were reviewed and the skewing became apparent, a second analysis, using a nonparametric evaluation was undertaken. In order to dichotomize the data, a cutting score was set at the point which classified 95% of the nondrinking group. Since 20 of the 21 nondrinking subjects made scores of 2 or less, the cut was set between 2 and 3. Eight of the 25 alcoholic patients had error scores above 2. An evaluation of these data by Fisher's exact probability test (Finney, Latscha, Bennett, & Hsu, 1963) resulted in a probability of $p < .05$.

The negative findings in the face of what appeared to be a real difference demonstrates that data with large skew causes parametric analysis to be unduly conservative. Although parametric analyses are said to be robust to skew, the protection afforded by parametric analyses is from making an incorrect assertion, a Type I error. The presence of skewing should always alert one to the possibility that nonparametric data analyses will prove more fruitful in demonstrating a real difference.

THE CASE OF THE FAR-OUT OUTLIERS

A neuropsychologist examined 17 patients who had right temporal lesions and 20 normal control subjects on two administrations of a verbal skill task. The first administration (A) followed standard procedure with no coaching. For the second administration (B), subjects were taught a verbal technique for facilitating performance of the task.

On three trials of Administration A, there were no differences in performance between the two subject groups as their distributions were so close they virtually overlapped. On the coached administration, however, the means of the patient group consistently exceeded those of the control subjects. The author noted that they "performed at a slightly higher level than the control subjects on each of the three trials... The consistent separation of the two groups in the (B condition) is, however, deceptive, because there are large standard deviations at all points of the curve for this difficult task. Analysis of variance comparing the performance of the two groups... revealed no significant differences." Reevaluation of the Administration B data using summed scores for the three trials resulted in a substantial appearing difference, but an insignificant t test value (see Table 1).

Table 1

Statistics for Parametric Comparison of Summed Scores on a Verbal Skill Task

Group	n	M	SD	t
Control	20	15.6	7.45	1.56
Patient	17	18.9	4.63	

Inspection of the raw data, on the other hand, suggested that the apparent difference between these two groups could be demonstrated post hoc by comparing the ratios of cases falling on either side of any cutting score set below the mean of the patient sample (See Table 2). An evaluation of the score distribution, using chi-square, gave statistical support ($\chi^2 = 5.45, p < .025$) to the visual impression that the patients' scores tended to pile up in the 16-22 point range, while the mode of the control group's score distribution was in the 10-12 point range. Several far-flung outliers in the control group had inflated the variance, leading to the author's original acceptance of the null hypothesis. The discrepancy between group variances should have alerted the investigator to the possibility that parametric testing may have been unduly conservative.

THE CASE THAT HAS EVERYTHING

In a study on the cognitive effects of traumatic head injury, relationships between different kinds of deficits were examined by means of a simple one-way analysis of variance design (D. N. Brooks, personal communication 1982). In this example, patients were assigned to three groups according to their memory complaints. Group 1 subjects had no complaints; those in group 2 complained of mild memory problems; and group 3 subjects identified their memory problems as serious. These three groups were compared on 11 measures of cognitive functions at three different time periods, 3, 6, and 12 months. The nature of head injury being what it is, many subjects were unreliable or unavailable so that the number of subjects in each group varied considerably from one test period to the next, and

14

Table 2

Distribution of Summed Scores on a Verbal Skill Task

Score interval	Control subjects	R-lesioned patients
28-30	1	
25-27		2
22-24	6	3
19-21	1	4
16-18	1	5
p<.025*		
13-15	2	1
p<.05*		
10-12	4	2
p>.05*		
7-9	3	
4-6	1	
1-3	1	

*chi-square or Fisher's exact probability test

also varied a little from test to test within each time period. As a result, groups tended to be small. The 16 member "serious" group at time period one, for example, had as few as 9 subjects taking three of the subtests, and never more than 13. Multivariate repeated measures analysis of variance was thus impossible because of gross violations of orthogonality and compound symmetry. The author therefore elected to do one-way analyses of variance at each time period for each variable.

In 25 of the 33 comparisons, the "no problem" group had the highest means; and in all comparisons, the "serious problem" group had the lowest means, suggesting a general performance pattern reflecting severity of damage. Only seven of the 33 F tests proved to be significant beyond the .05 level, however. In nine comparisons, F probabilities were tantalizingly close to the .05 level, ranging from .053 to .10. When reevaluated by nonparametric techniques, six of these nine comparisons exhibited significant differences between subgroups (see Table 3). In three cases, analysis by χ^2 produced probabilities of $p < .01$ (see as one example Table 4). In this example, the probability of a significant difference derived by analysis of variance was .089 (see Table 5). In three other cases in which the probability of F was above .05, significant differences appeared between two subgroups when evaluated by Fisher's exact probability test. In each of these latter cases, t tests of the difference between these subgroups' means were not significant (see Table 6).

Table 3

Evaluations of All Comparisons between Three Groups of Head Trauma Patients

Time	Totals	Significant F[1]	Not Significant F	
			Significant[2]	Not Significant
1	11	3	1	7
2	11	1	2	8
3	11	3	3	5

[1] One-way ANOVA
[2] Nonparametric data analysis

Table 4

Nonparametric Evaluation of 6 Month Performance of Delayed Paragraph Recall by Three Patient Groups

Score Interval	Group 1	Group 2	Group 3
14-15	1		
12-13	1		1
10-11	1	4	3
8-9	5		
6-7	5	2	1
4-5		2	6
2-3	1		1
0-1			2

Score	Group 1	Group 2	Group 3
>6	13	6	5
<5	1	2	10

$\chi^2 = 11.72, p < .01$

Although 13 of the 33 comparisons of this study proved significant, 20 did not, despite the consistency with which means trends showed up throughout the data. In some of these cases, intragroup variability was the culprit; in others, the subgroups were so small that nonparametric evaluations, too, only bordered on significance; and in a few cases, mean differences were practically inconsequential and would have required a battalion of patients to make them statistically significant.

Table 5

Parametric Evaluation of Six-Month Performance on Delayed Paragraph Recall by Three Patient Groups

Group.	n	M	SD	SE
1	14	8.14	3.06	0.817
2	8	7.75	2.87	1.013
3	15	5.53	3.60	0.930
Total	37	7.00	3.40	0.559

ANOVA					
Source	df	SS	MS	F	p
Between	2	55.05	27.53	2.59	0.089
Within	34	360.95	10.61		
Total	36	416.00			

Table 6

Mean Comparisons between Subgroups which Differ Significantly when Evaluated by Chi-square

Variable	Subgroup	M	SD	t
LMI2	1	10.14	3.72	1.983
	3	7.40	3.46	(df,27)
PM3*	2	103.60	19.40	1.6202
	3	92.64	17.82	(df,30)
REY3	1	23.44	6.13	1.982
	3	16.18	9.68	(df,26)

* $t_{1.3} < .05$

DISCUSSION

Scientific methodology is divided into two areas: (1) model building – examination of interrelationships of variables, means, and frequencies with an eye toward fitting the results into a hypothetical model that would account for the relationships; and (2) model testing – the generation of the probability of the truth of a specific hypothesis. Most of a scientist's energy goes toward model building. This process is subjective, and the chief worry is missing something real (Type II errors). Most of the energy involved in producing papers for publication goes into model testing. This process is objective, and the chief concern is the reporting of something false (Type I errors).

The objective-subjective issue is determined by several characteristics of the experimental design (Fisher, 1951). To be classified as objective, (1) all possible experimental outcomes must have been anticipated; (2) each outcome must be interpretable in a theoretical framework; (3) "acceptable" Type I and II error rates must have been chosen; and (4) an appropriate statistical tool must have been selected based upon considerations of distribution, type of data, relationship of variables, and the cost of observation.

Case 1, in which the criterion for dichotomizing the data was determined a priori (by the distribution of scores of the control group) illustrates model testing by means of a nonparametric analysis technique. Cases 2 and 3, in which differences between experimental groups were searched out without regard to an external or theoretical framework, represent an approach to model building. By examining the data in this manner, hypotheses can be generated which can then be tested further in replicative studies.

The choice of statistical techniques for either model building or model testing should depend on the nature of the data and the issue being examined. Parametric tests are usually favored because they are more powerful than nonparametric tests; that is, a smaller sample size is required to achieve the same criterion. Typically a data set which is amenable to both types of analysis can achieve with a parametric test a set Type I error rate (alpha level) with 80% of the number of observations required to achieve the same criterion with the equivalent nonparametric test. Parametric tests are also favored because they are more amenable to multifactorial experimental designs and because they have a reputation for being fairly robust toward violations of assumptions of distribution normality, variance homogeneity, and orthogonality. What is frequently overlooked is that "robust" means that the Type I error rate may actually be overestimated, making the test unnecessarily conservative. The test will have lost its power, giving rise to a high probability of missing something meaningful. The cost of missing a real relationship in clinical neuropsychological research may be quite high. Small sample sizes, high variances, uneven distributions, and missing observations work together to reduce the likelihood that comparisons between groups will be appropriately analyzed with parametric statistics.

Of course, knowing that brain-damaged patients are a highly variable and, for research purposes, unreliable group of subjects, the truly prudent clinical investigator would not begin data analysis until either a statistically suitable number of stable patients had been examined on all the variables for as many times as needed, or data had been collected on an enormous number of subjects. Unfortunately, either goal would take more time to realize than research funding or normal human patience typically allow. Those neuropsychologists whose prudence is limited by patience, money, or other practical considerations, and who will want to do clinical research, must therefore contend with the problems of small and often highly irregular samples. For them, innovation in applying nonparametric techniques to data analysis may provide the best solution to what otherwise can seem to pose an insuperable obstacle to productive research.

REFERENCES

Finney, D. J., Latscha, R., Bennett, B. M., & Hsu, P. (1963). *Tables for testing significance in a 2 x 2 contingency table.* Cambridge, England: Cambridge University Press.

Fisher, R. A. (1951). *Design of experiments.* (6th ed.) Edinburgh: Oliver & Boyd.

Lezak, M. D., Howieson, D. B., & McGavin, J. (1983, February). *Temporal sequencing of remote events task with Korsakoff subjects.* Paper presented at the meeting of the International Neuropsychological Society, Mexico City.

Journal of Clinical and Experimental Neuropsychology
1987, Vol. 9, No. 4, pp. 340-358

Memory Assessment in Neuropsychology: Theoretical Considerations and Practical Utility*

David W. Loring

Medical College of Georgia

and

Andrew C. Papanicolaou

The University of Texas Medical Branch

ABSTRACT

Memory assessment is one of the principal objectives of neuropsychological evaluation. Yet, careful examination reveals very clear shortcomings in the memory tests employed by neuropsychologists. Specifically, most procedures are selected on the basis of their ability to detect structural brain pathology rather than their ability to assess memory performance *per se* or the constituent operations that underlie it. This paper addresses the shortcomings in the structure of several representative memory tests in neuropsychology, how some of these limitations have been overcome with newer scales, and presents practical and theoretical considerations for the development of new clinical memory measures.

With the introduction of sophisticated brain-imaging techniques over the past several decades, the clinical and research functions of the clinical neuropsychologist have shifted from establishing the cerebral localization of lesions and the localization of brain function. Two aspects of this shift, one more theoretical and one largely applied, are seen. Presently, there has been a theoretical shift toward integration with cognitive psychology and analysis of cognitive "components," although localization is still of importance, and an applied shift toward rehabilitation involving the analysis of more pragmatic behavioral "components" (Hart & Hayden, 1986). However, when performing an evaluation of cognitive functioning, the neuropsychologist must first ensure that the tests employed genuinely assess the cognitive operations of interest in order to

* Preparation of this article was supported in part by Department of Education Grant G008435031 to Andrew C. Papanicolaou. We gratefully acknowledge the assistance of George M. Faibish and Tessa Hart, both of whom critically read earlier versions of this manuscript, and the helpful suggestions of our anonymous reviewers. We thank Patricia Downs for her help in manuscript preparation.

avoid making erroneous conclusions regarding the behavioral sequelae associated with brain pathology.

Given the importance of memory evaluation in contemporary neuropsychology, one would expect a considerable degree of sophistication on the part of the professionals performing these assessments, both in their approach to the phenomena of memory and in the assessment procedures they select. Regrettably, however, many neuropsychologists appear to believe tacitly a variant of a familiar theme; that is, memory is that quantity that the Wechsler Memory Scale (WMS) measures. Similarly, when employing newer measures attempting to parcel memory into different components such as storage vs. retrieval (e.g., Selective Reminding Procedure), they fail to remember that an unambiguous operational definition of a psychological construct is completely independent of construct validity.

This paper is not intended as a survey of research performed with various memory tests, since excellent reviews exist already (e.g., Erickson & Scott, 1977; Prigatano, 1978), nor is it meant to update those reports. Similarly, we do not attempt to describe the many techniques available to the neuropsychologist to assess memory since this information is readily available (e.g., Lezak, 1983). Rather, our intention is to evaluate several representative approaches to memory assessment currently in widespread use by clinicians and researchers and to examine their theoretical assumptions and construct validity. These include the Russell and Boston revisions of the WMS and the Selective Reminding Procedure of Buschke. In addition, we discuss the theoretical and practical considerations necessary for the construction of adequate memory tests.

WECHSLER MEMORY SCALE REVISIONS

The Wechsler Memory Scale (WMS) is the most widely used clinical test for memory assessment (Erickson & Scott, 1977). The validity, standardization, and general psychometric properties of the WMS, however, have been extensively criticized (e.g., Erickson & Scott, 1977; Prigatano, 1977, 1978). Briefly, these criticisms refer to inadequate normative information, the assumption that memory is a unitary phenomenon (i.e., the concept of MQ), that the test assesses constructs that, although perhaps necessary for successful memory performance, are not genuine measures of memory (e.g., Orientation and Mental Control), the fact that they correlate highly with intelligence test performance, and their low interscorer reliability for certain subtests.

In an attempt to remedy some of the limitations associated with the WMS, two independent variations of the test have been developed. By evaluating the factor structure of the test, Russell (1975) selected two memory subtests that appeared to be most sensitive to brain damage and, at the same time, differentiated verbal from figural memory (Logical Memory and Visual Reproduction). The remainder of the subtests were discarded for either their inability to discriminate mild brain-damaged patients from a mixed group of non-brain-injured subjects, or for not measuring memory *per se*. In addition, a delayed-recall condition was included for both remaining subtests to evaluate retention over a one-half hour interval.

The Boston revision of the WMS retains all the elements of the original WMS, but has added items to the scale to improve its utility for routine neuropsychological assessment (Milberg, Hebben, & Kaplan, 1986). However, the most important changes from a memory assessment standpoint relate to the Logical Memory, Visual Reproduction, and Paired Associate subtests. Not only were delayed-recall conditions added, but direct questioning and recognition assessment were also included. These changes will be discussed in greater detail later.

Logical Memory

The Logical Memory (LM) subtest has face validity, appearing to tap that aspect of memory of which patients complain when they state that they are "unable to remember things." Two paragraphs are read to the subject, and following each passage, the subject repeats as much of the story as he or she is able. No explicit instructions requesting verbatim recall are provided, however, although some examiners have modified Wechsler's instructions to include a phrase similar to "try to remember as much of the story as you can, using as many of the same words and phrases." The stories are divided respectively into 22 or 24 "memory units," and credit is received for each idea recalled.

The division of the paragraph into memory units results in two interrelated problems. The first is practical, involving both scoring and reliability, whereas the second involves the issue of construct validity. Russell (1975, 1981) states that the paragraphs are administered and scored according to Wechsler's directions, except that a sum rather than an average value is obtained. However, no scoring criteria for correct ideas are presented by Wechsler, nor are descriptions of such criteria found in published reports. Some neuropsychologists require a verbatim response to give credit, others give one-half credit for a "close" response, while many will score an item correct if the essential content of the memory unit is preserved (e.g., "kids" for "little children"). The nature of the closeness is a matter of personal judgement on the part of the neuropsychologist, since responses may be similar on a number of dimensions (e.g., associative, connotative, denotative, referential).

A telling illustration of this problem emerges when one examines the literature on LM performance. Table 1 summarizes the performance of a variety of nonneurologic and control subjects in different studies. As the table clearly shows, there is a great heterogeneity in what has been reported as nonimpaired performance. Therefore, what may be interpreted with one set of norms as impaired performance on this subtest, another set of norms would suggest is acceptable and within the limits of normal variation.

Efforts to remedy this lack of scoring consistency have recently been made. Power, Logue, McCarthy, Rosenstiel, and Ziesat (1979) suggest several rules

Table 1

Means and SDs (in parentheses) of Logical Memory performance reported as normative or control data. Some values have been recomputed based upon information provided in the reports to reflect average performance on the two LM passages.

Study	Age	N	Performance	Note
Bachrach & Mintz (1974)	32.7 (12.9)	42	10.6	3
Cauthen (1977)	30-39	14	7.1	1
Charter (1981)	47 (16.7)	122	8.3 (3.2)	5
Cohen (1950)	29.1 (5.7)	81	8.9 (3.6)	4
Crosson et al. (1984)	53.9	23	8.4 (2.7)	2,5
Dodrill (1978)	27.3 (8.4)	50	11.3 (3.8)	1
Hulicka (1966)	30-39	53	8.0 (3.0)	5
Ivinskis et al. (1971)	16-18	44	7.7 (2.1)	1
Kear-Colwell & Heller (1978)	<35	56	13.6 (3.0)	1
Kear-Colwell & Heller (1978)	>35	60	10.4 (3.1)	1
Kljaic (1975)	46.3 (10.9)	18	5.4 (2.7)	2
Osborne & Davis (1978)	30-39	61	9.4	6
Prigatano (1977)	36.4 (R=20-59)	26	8.6 (2.4)	3
Russell (1975)	36.5 (14.2)	30	11.6 (3.0)	2,5
Wechsler (1945)	20-25	50	9.3 (3.1)	1
Wechsler (1945)	40-49	46	8.1 (2.5)	1

1 = Normal Volunteers
2 = Negative Neurologic Patients
3 = Psychiatric Patients Without Neurologic Evidence
4 = Psychiatric Patients (Nonpsychotic) Without Neurologic Evidence
5 = Medical Patients Without Neurologic or Psychiatric Complaints
6 = Mixed Population of Neurologic and Psychiatric Patients

with which full or half-credit response can be scored, and more recently, Schear (1985) has provided scoring examples that are similar to those used with the WAIS Vocabulary subtest. As these reports indicate, explicit criteria have provided greater scoring reliability, and with sufficient testing, satisfactory normative information can ultimately be obtained.

Even with explicit scoring criteria, a concern regarding adequate construct validity remains. For example, Power et al. (1979) propose that half-credit responses be given if articles, adjectives, or adverbs are omitted since "according them a full credit of one point would equate them with exact reproductions... [and]... half-credit reflects a recognition of the essential accuracy of the response while penalizing to some extent the tendency to modify the idea" (p. 344). However, the process of learning new material is an active one, and involves transformation of the raw input and its incorporation into an existing cognitive schema or framework and is implicitly ignored when verbatim responses for prose passage are required. People abstract the essential features of a story and retain those features rather than the surface structure of the passage in which those features are embedded (e.g., Bartlett, 1932; Brandsford & Franks, 1971; Cofer, 1965; Pompi & Lachman, 1967). Current memory theorists believe that memory is determined by selection, abstraction, interpretation, and integration (see Alba & Hasher, 1983). Therefore, the response of "kids" for "little children" not only indicates that the main idea has been retained, but since it has been transformed, may actually be a better response than a verbatim one since it indicates that the subject has not simply retained an item, but has assimilated it into a representational framework.

In addition to lack of scoring criteria for these paragraphs and the variability in the instructions used by different neuropsychologists, the paragraphs themselves are dated, and consequently, not appropriate for today's subjects. The phrase "made up a purse" is no longer an idiom in American speech, whereas the phrase "liner" is frequently misinterpreted by many younger subjects to refer to an airplane or "airliner". According to Schear's (1985) scoring examples, luxury liner would receive full credit, passenger liner would be scored a half-credit response, while airliner would earn no credit. In each of these examples, it is clear that the information encoded has been guided by different schemata, yet, some responses merit memory credit while others do not. Thus, some subjects are penalized for possessing somewhat different knowledge frameworks with which to interpret information.

Delayed Recall. The inclusion of a delayed-recall component is a genuine improvement since this approach examines retention of material over time, shifting the test from one of comprehension or encoding to one of long-term retention. Although this approach provides valuable information, it is only a partial solution to the problems under consideration since all of the difficulties associated with scoring the paragraphs discussed above are still pertinent. For example, if the response "Annie was a cleaning lady and got mugged. Her kids were hungry so the cops gave her some money" were given, by strict verbatim scoring criteria, no credit would be obtained. If this same response is given after a one-half hour delay, again no credit would be earned, yet the subject would have certainly demonstrated constancy of information retention over time.

Problems specific to the delayed-recall procedure involve the issue of prompting. Russell (1975) states that, if the subject cannot remember the stories at all, a prompt is provided by asking "do you remember a story about a washer woman?" (p. 803). The paragraph is then scored "according to Wechsler's instructions, except that the item used to remind the subject is not counted in the second score" (p. 803). However, if the information of interest is the *retention* of material over time, and not the ability to *retrieve* information (free recall), then the scoring procedure should not penalize those individuals who initially have difficulty remembering the main theme of the story, but who, once prompted (cued), can retrieve information about the story. By attempting to examine both retrieval and retention, which are two distinct operations, neither is genuinely assessed. The nature of the prompts themselves should also be carefully considered, since prompts may be either semantic cues that summarize the story, or associative cues that refer to specific details from it. Accordingly, one may bias the subjects' retrieval depending on the type of cue used and thus affect the patient's score. It is amusing to note that although one full point is subtracted from a patient's score if a prompt is required, if the prompts were themselves scored according to verbatim criteria, no credit would be received, and if scored according to half-credit criteria, would only receive partial credit.

The Boston Revision of the WMS implicitly requests a verbatim response for the LM paragraphs by asking "I want you to tell me everything I said to you." Again, no scoring criteria are presented. However, the Boston version contains an immediate-recall probe asking specific questions regarding story elements (e.g., What kind of work did this person do? Did this person have a family?), attempting to assess retention rather than the ability to retrieve information spontaneously. In the delayed-recall condition, however, it is not indicated whether or not prompts are to be given if the subject fails at free recall. A delayed probe for only the Anna Thompson story is administered, although the format for this probe is multiple choice. A multiple choice format, presumably, was not chosen for the immediate-recall probe in order that additional information provided to the subject with multiple choice would not confound the delayed-recall performance. However, changing the format makes direct comparisons across time more difficult. Moreover, it is likely that delayed-recall performance might be aided with the immediate-recall probe since it provides the opportunity for rehearsal. Therefore, available normative information for delayed recall is not necessarily comparable for the Russell and the Boston revisions. That is, the immediate probe, if it in fact provides rehearsal opportunity, should lead to higher scores for delayed performance and would suggest better retention if compared to norms obtained without probe questioning.

Practical Utility. The above criticisms aside, the LM subtest can still be an effective measure of verbal memory. A clinical neuropsychologist, routinely administering this scale, develops a "feel" for what type of responses are suggestive of either normal or impaired memory abilities. This paper is not intended to discuss the strengths and limitations of the psychometric vs. clinical-intuitive approach to evaluation. It is sufficient to note that, when a patient's memory functioning is determined by clinical acumen and experience, then the particular choice of prose passages used is irrelevant. That is, the LM passages do not provide unique information that could not be obtained by a similarly experienced clinician using different stories that had been routinely used by him or her. There is nothing wrong with this approach; however, it does not fulfill the requirements for objective psychological testing and should not be presented as though it does.

We are not attempting to argue that this test has no value. However, for performance at questionably impaired levels, we must first be sure that low performance is not purely an artifact of our testing procedure. Although experienced neuropsychologists will not examine LM scores out of context, perhaps making some compensation in describing the patient's memory in the clinical report, it is reasonable to expect that these compensations be articulated so that scoring modifications can be developed and made explicit in future revisions of this or other tests or prose passage recall (e.g., Power et al., 1979). In the interim, we suggest that all published reports of LM performance make explicit the scoring procedures used and whether or not verbatim recall is explicitly requested.

Visual Reproduction
The Visual Reproduction (VR) subtest is the only attempt by Wechsler to include a measure of nonverbal memory. In this subtest, subjects are presented with geometric designs for 10 s, and immediately following their presentation, they are requested to draw the designs from memory. In contrast to LM, explicit scoring criteria have been provided which have resulted in greater scoring reliability and greater consistency in reports of normative performance (see Crosson, Hughes, Roth, & Monkowski, 1984).

Unfortunately, factor-analytic studies of this subtest have indicated a principal factor loading in a visual-perceptual-motor ability factor, and only secondarily on memory (e.g., Ivinskis, Allen, & Shaw, 1971; Larrabee, Kane, & Schuck, 1983; Larrabee, Kane, Schuck, & Francis, 1985). This is consistent with some earlier work performed on the Benton Visual Retention Test (Benton, 1962). For example, Silverstein (1962, 1963) found high correlations between copying and immediate-delay performance, and views this test as a measure of visual perception and visual motor ability. As Trahan and Larrabee (1984) have pointed out, however, delayed visual-reproduction performance is more closely related to memory than perceptual motor skills in normal subjects. Further, delayed VR performance has been shown to be superior to immediate recall for discrimination of right unilateral temporal-lobe seizure activity (Delaney, Rosen, Mattson, & Novelly, 1980).

Since immediate reproduction is plagued by concerns regarding construct validity, the only genuine measure of figural memory performance appears to be the delayed component and is included in both the Russell and Boston revisions. However, it must be remembered that visual motor and constructive abilities may be selectively impaired without a corresponding deficit in visual spatial memory. Therefore, recognition assessment should be routinely performed even in the absence of frank visual constructive deficits in order to insure that retention and/or retrieval is not confounded with construction difficulties. The Boston Revision of the WMS adequately addresses this important issue. Immediately following the standard VR administration, patients are presented with a recognition task in which the correct design is displayed with four similar but slightly distorted distractors. After each of the four designs is selected, the patient is asked to copy the designs to examine potential constructional difficulties.

In addition to the standard delayed condition, the Boston version also includes multiple-choice recognition and a matching task requiring the patient to select the correct design from distractor items with the original stimulus present. As with the delayed recall for the Boston modification of LM, caution must be exercised if norms using the Russell version are used given the additional exposure with the immediate multiple choice and copy performance in the Boston procedure.

As with the delayed recall for LM, the scoring compensation required if the subject cannot immediately remember the designs is problematic. Russell states that, if prompting is required (e.g., the picture with the flags), then one point should be subtracted from the patient's score. Again, this confounds free recall with long-term retrieval.

Additional Boston Modifications

The Boston Revision of the WMS has altered the procedure in several additional ways. The Paired-Associate Learning (PAL) subtest of the WMS is a standard paired-associate learning task consisting of three trials. In each trial, 10 word pairs are read to the patient, six of which are easy associations (e.g., north-south) with the remainder being difficult ones (e.g., obey-inch). A subject's performance is measured by summing all the hard associations acquired plus one half the number of easy associations reported. In the Boston version, an additional trial is presented with the pairs reversed; that is, the subject is provided with the second word of the pair and is requested to remember the first. This has the advantage of examining the strength of the association, and tests the ability of the subject to perform an unexpected task. In addition, a delayed free-recall condition is administered in which patients are asked to provide all word-pairs spontaneously. Patients are then cued with the first word for those pairs they failed to recall.

The Cowboy Story (Talland, 1965) is presented as a story comprehension task. Although analogous to LM recall, it differs on one potentially relevant dimension. The patient is able to pace the speed at which the information is provided since it is read by the subject rather than being recited by the examiner. This is an important provision since the ability to encode information depends in part on rate of presentation and since performance of the elderly on at least some tasks is more comparable to that of young adults when the rate of presentation is slowed (e.g., Kinsbourne, 1973). Although each of the 27 memory units must be recalled verbatim in order to be credited, a provision for content ideas is made in which credit is received for synonyms or paraphrases. Probe question are administered for all information not spontaneously recalled.

BUSCHKE SELECTIVE REMINDING PROCEDURE

The selective reminding (SR) procedure is an attempt to ground verbal memory assessment within the context of contemporary information-processing theory (Buschke, 1973; Buschke & Fuld, 1974). Subjects are instructed to learn a list of words in any order. In contrast to standard serial word tests, however, the subject is "selectively reminded *only* of those items he did not recall in the immediately preceding trial" (Buschke & Fuld, 1974, p. 1019). The rationale for this procedure is that the subject is provided the opportunity to recall words spontaneously, presumably demonstrating recall of items from long-term memory. Consequently, this technique has been widely implemented to characterize the verbal memory deficit in a number of clinical populations (e.g., Caine, Ebert, & Weingartner, 1977; Levin, Grossman, Rose, & Teasdale, 1979; Loring, Meador, Mahurin, & Largen, 1986; Muramoto, 1984; Peters & Levin, 1977, 1979; Thal & Fuld, 1983).

It must be remembered that this is a procedure and not a standardized test. Consequently, it must be borne in mind that the information about the test available in the literature is based upon tests of different word lengths with varying number of trials. Further, recent evidence suggests that, even when the composition of the test words is carefully matched on the basis of frequency and length, the difficulty of the lists is not necessary equivalent (Hannay & Levin, 1985).

Hanney and Levin (1985) report test-retest reliabilities ranging from .48 to .65 which, as the authors recognize, are lower than those which are generally acceptable for psychological tests. Further, they report that in their sample of college students, there was a significant practice effect with repeated administration of alternative forms for most of the SR-dependent measures. This practice effect suggests that the ability to learn how to perform a complex task, and not exclusively the ability to remember words, may be accounting for the group differences in research using clinical populations. It is therefore possible that these factors are partially responsible for observed deficits in patients' performances rather than an impairment of memory alone. This point is clearly of paramount importance since SR is becoming a popular technique to investigate the efficacy of pharmacologic intervention (e.g., Mohs, Tinklenberg, Roth, & Koppell, 1980; Yesavage, Lierer, Becker, & Holman, 1980). Researchers have the luxury of administering multiple baseline conditions in order to arrive at a stable level of performance, as is a requirement in single-case experimental designs (see Hersen & Barlow, 1976). However, since the earlier administrations are confounded by task novelty and complexity, SR should not be used clinically as the sole measure of verbal memory.

The SR procedure has found widespread appeal since it purports to parcel verbal memory into long-term storage (LTS), long-term retrieval (LTR), consistent long-term retrieval (CLTR), and short-term recall (STR). However, studies employing the SR procedure have typically found high correlations for memory performance measures in both clinical and control samples (i.e., total recall, LTS, LTR, CLTR), suggesting that these measures are assessing similar constructs (Kenisten, cited in Kraemer, Peabody, Tinklenberg, & Yesavage, 1983; Loring et al., 1986). Further, although the attempt to isolate different components of memory is admirable, the distinction between long-term storage and retrieval is arbitrary. According to Buschke's definition, a word has entered LTS if it has been successfully recalled on two consecutive trials. Therefore, by definition, and definition only, failure to recall is due to retrieval failure. Just as plausible and conceptually appealing, however, is that these "memory traces" have been stored in a weak or degraded form, and that, through the process of additional repetitions from the examiner, the word is encoded more deeply and efficiently, analogous to the way in which a complex motor sequence such as playing music on an instrument is slowly learned with repetition. Therefore, operationally defined retrieval may have in fact little to do with retrieval itself. Although SR appears to offer unique information regarding short- and long-term memory, this distinction can be made using traditional word lists by analyzing both primacy and recency effects (e.g., Brooks, 1972; Glanzer & Cunitz, 1966), or by the number of words, either presented by the examiner or recalled by the subject, between presentation and recall for any particular word (Tulving & Colotla, 1970).

In conclusion, there are important limitations in the use of SR as a technique to assess verbal memory. The standardization for any particular form is limited, forms designed for equivalence differ in their level of difficulty, and there appears to be a significant practice effect with repeated administration. Finally, the operational definitions of storage and retrieval have dubious construct validity.

BRAIN DAMAGE AS A CRITERION

In addition to the psychometric problems of standardization and reliability and the theoretical consideration of construct validity, a problem with these tests is that they have been selected on the basis of their ability to detect brain damage. For example, Russell (1975) states that the subtests selected from the WMS were chosen on the basis of their ability to discriminate mild brain-damage from a mixed group of non-brain-injured subjects. This was obviously important prior to the widespread availability of cerebral imaging techniques. However, since the function of neuropsychologists has shifted, this basis of test selection now assumes a secondary status.

The first decision to be made by neuropsychology is to determine which memory abilities are necessary for independent living and ought to be assessed during the evaluation. Then, on the basis of cognitive theory, operations that mediate the abilities of interest must be defined. Finally, tests must be constructed to assess those operations independently of brain pathology. Ideally, performance on these tests will correlate with different types of cerebral pathology. However, we should not define our constructs of cognitive operations based solely on those tests sensitive to brain damage since sensitivity to brain damage depends on what type of population is included as the criterion group.

The California Verbal Learning Test (CVLT; Delis, Kramer, Ober, & Kaplan, in press), for example, is a memory scale that illustrates strong theoretical grounding in cognitive psychology. Patterned after Rey's Auditory Verbal Learning Test (see Lezak, 1983), the CVLT requires the subject to learn a list of 16 words over five trials in a standard free-recall procedure. The words are from four semantic categories (i.e., spices and herbs, fruits, tools, and clothing). After the fifth trial, a second shopping list is administered and following its free recall, the subject is asked for spontaneous recall of the initial list. For the CVLT, it was decided what information regarding memory performance would be beneficial for clinical assessment, and those techniques available in cognitive psychology were selected (e.g., proactive and retroactive interference, semantic cuing, and prototypic response distractors for recognition memory). In addition, the use of a distractor list allows for the examination of prior list intrusion errors, which may be an important aspect of a patient's neuropsychological status. For example, both alcoholic Korsakoff and Alzheimer's disease patients can be distinguished from those with Huntington's disease by the presence of a higher number of intrusion errors (Butters, 1985).

A related issue to "brain damage as a criterion" is the issue of selective hemispheric damage assessment. With the Russell modification of the WMS, for example, there is a temptation to equate these tests as equivalent on all cognitive dimensions except for the verbal vs. figural distinction. That is, they may be treated as equivalent tests assessing the memory capacity of the left and right hemisphere. However, these tests differ from each other on a number of other potentially relevant dimensions. For example, LM is presented auditorily whereas VR is, by definition, a visual test. As such, differences in basic sensory functioning may produce an apparent difference in memory functioning. Further, the response mode of the two subtests differs. Clearly different cognitive operations mediate verbal recall and still others (i.e., visual constructive) are necessary for reproduction of geometric figures. Therefore, in addition to differences in basic sensory functioning, differences in other nonmemory skills may confound the results. In addition, the differences in the scoring procedures and reliability which, as previously mentioned, exist between these two subtests, may produce an apparent difference in verbal vs. figural memory functioning.

More importantly, LM is a task that is typically experienced in everyday life, whereas VR is a novel task not normally encountered. Therefore, differences in familiarity with the two testing procedures may produce differences that are interpreted only in terms of memory abilities. VR is likely to load heavily on what Cattell (1963) has termed "fluid intelligence," that is, the ability to acquire and manipulate new or novel information. An example of the possible misinterpretation of performance on these two subtests is seen in Logue and Wyrich (1979). These authors concluded on the basis of their aging and dementia study, that the right hemisphere may be more susceptible than the left hemisphere to aging. However, as correctly pointed out by Russell (1981), this is probably a psychometric artifact since the figural test has such a strong fluid intelligence component. Fluid intelligence is highly susceptible to even mild cerebral pathology, such as that observed with the aging process (e.g., Cunningham, Clayton, & Overton, 1975; Reed & Reitan, 1963).

CONCLUSIONS

The imperfections in memory assessment demonstrated in the previous sections of this paper do not constitute proof that these tests are of no value since the obtained scores are usually interpreted with respect to a neuropsychologist's personal experience. Most psychological tests, in fact, do not meet the psychometric criteria to the degree that would satisfy the purist, and compensation is frequently made.

The question becomes one of selection. Among the available methods to assess memory (tests, interviews, etc.), which method is better? To answer the question, we must consider in what contexts memory tests have been used. If the neuropsychologist is asked to evaluate a patient with possible dementia, then it does not matter if the memory tests employed measure a combination of varied abilities, including freedom from distraction, performance on novel tasks, in addition to some memory component; the test needs only be sensitive to cerebral pathology. For example, the rate of accurate differentiation of organic from psychiatric patients using WAIS scores alone has been reported to be equal or better than using the entire Halstead-Reitan or Luria-Nebraska batteries (Kane, Parsons, & Goldstein, 1985; Watson, Thomas, Anderson, & Felling, 1968). Therefore, the critical concern is the referral question. As far as this goes, the original WMS has been reported to be a poor screening test of brain damage (Prigatano, 1977).

If we wish to determine if memory tests offer the advantage of assessing specific aspects of memory over other assessment techniques, we need only consider their construct validity. As we have detailed above, the major tests do not appear to be entirely valid measures of any construct of memory. This is not to say that with low LM, no statement about impaired memory functioning is warranted. Grossly impaired memory ability will be revealed by LM regardless of how it is scored (i.e., full vs. half-credit) and the need for adequate normative information in unnecessary. However, a set of instruments is necessary to help evaluate memory performance in which the ability, or lack of it, is not immediately clear, for example, as in an individual with a grade school education with possible mild anoxia. It is in these borderline cases that the need for clearly identified constructs and adequate tests of those constructs becomes necessary.

With LM, an additional concern is whether the limited normative information in the literature is better than no normative data at all. Specifically, are clinicians in a better position to evaluate memory by relying, in part, on data collected by other laboratories and clinical services than relying solely on personal experience and personal norms? As it currently stands, it is difficult to interpret the literature since the reader knows neither the instructional set provided to the subject nor which scoring approach has been employed for any particular study. That is, one does not know if an average score of 12 responses refers to 12 verbatim responses, 12 "close" responses, or some combination of 12 or more full and half-credit responses, or even whether or not a verbatim response was explicitly requested.

As noted by Crosson et al. (1984), approximately half of both Hulicka's (1966) control subjects in the 15-17 year-old age group and Wechsler's (1945) subjects would be classified as impaired using Russell's (1975) norms. Therefore, we believe that, given the differences in administration and scoring, one must rely either on data that has been personally obtained, or alternatively, on norms that have had the instructions and scoring criteria personally verified. We realize, however, that many neuropsychologists will continue to rely on normative information without the above precautions. Therefore, even the pooled data of Crosson et al. (1984), which is based on several reports, should be used with extreme caution since it is neither clear if explicit instructions requesting verbatim recall were given to the subject nor the precise method of scoring used in the different studies.

Future Directions

What might be the proper direction for test development for clinical memory assessment? First, we suggest that for prose passage recall, the passage should be broken down using a propositional representation network to approximate the story grammar and to arrive at some convention of identifying a memory unit (e.g., Kintsch, 1974, Kintsch & van Dijk, 1975; Mandler & Johnson, 1977). Further, some hierarchy is necessary since all information contained in a story is neither equally important nor equally well remembered (e.g., deVilliers, 1974; Kintsch & Keenan, 1973; Thorndyke, 1975). Verbatim scoring or number of words correctly recalled can never be a sound method given that people transform and abstract the essence of what is presented.

Once the story (or stories) is/are analyzed in terms of propositional representation, allowing for sufficient quantification of the subjects' responses, the basic structure of the test is complete. A title should be provided before reading the story to the patient, to facilitate its interpretation as it is being read, and also to serve as a cue for delayed recall. The title should be provided to all patients when the delayed-recall condition is requested.

The clearest advantage to using paired-associates or the CVLT is the objectivity of the scoring criteria. As illustrated in the literature, there is general agreement in the normative values available for PA. Unfortunately, for the CVLT, there are not yet published norms that would allow the scale to be used immediately for clinical purposes, and differences may exist in patient's ability to appreciate, and thereby benefit from, semantic clustering. For PA performance, we suggest that easy and hard associates be considered separately (e.g., Ivinskis et al., 1971) since the decision to treat the hard associations as twice as valuable as the easy associations was not empirically derived.

Given the various models of verbal memory that appear in the cognitive psychology literature, one is not obliged to assess memory as conceptualized in every memory model nor should one necessarily attempt to assess verbal memory using all the various techniques. However, it must be remembered that these different tests assess different aspects of verbal memory and may be selectively impaired. As previously mentioned, LM passages are more appropriate for the assessment of propositional memory whereas list learning is a test of rote memory. In a patient whose planning and organizational skills are impaired (e.g., frontal-lobe pathology), performance on SR may be impaired. However, on a task that is more highly structured with repeated trials and instructions such as a word list, performance may be at more normal levels. Again, we must carefully define the constructs that we are attempting to assess. We have not discussed nonverbal memory as much since there has been limited clinical research in this area, most of which typically consists of VR type tasks. We would hope to see how performance on VR compares to memory for faces (e.g., Warrington & James, 1967) since the latter is ecologically valid and is more comparable to LM in terms of fluid intelligence.

The basic problem associated with the selection of an instrument to assess memory is the choice of an appropriate criterion variable. In the field of rehabilitation neuropsychology, one approach has been to use either real or simulated job performance or even whether or not a patient is employed (e.g., Ben-Yishay et al., 1980). Of course, many factors in addition to memory functioning are essential for vocational activity. An alternative technique has been to examine the relationship between memory test performance and questionnaires of everyday memory, which are completed by either the patient or their family (see Hermann, 1982, for a review). Unfortunately, the relationship between questionnaires and memory test performances has been poor with the highest correlations observed for test performance and ratings completed by family members (Baddeley, Sunderland, & Harris, 1982; Sunderland, Harris, & Baddeley, 1984).

Given the limitations of directly observing patients' performances in the home, it is clear that we must find some more practical method of assessing or observing everyday memory performance in the laboratory and perhaps use this as our criterion. A recent approach developed by the Rivermead Rehabilitation Centre in Oxford, hopefully, will provide one such ecologically valid criterion (Wilson, in press). The Rivermead Behavioral Memory Test (RBMT) consists of a series of items sampling memory of those behaviors that have been frequently reported to be impaired following brain injury (Sunderland et al., 1983). In addition to conventional assessment of memory, the RBMT examines memory performance using a wide variety of everyday tasks. Some tasks are familiar and consist of associating a name with a photograph, and assessing memory for faces, memory for pictures, and orientation. Several novel memory tasks are administered: (1) A personal possession of the subject is borrowed and hidden from view. The subject is told to ask for its return at the end of the testing session; (2) Patients are informed that they are to ask the examiner a particular question, given to them by the examiner, when an alarm sounds; (3) A short route through five areas of the room is taken, and the patient retraces the route during an immediate and delayed condition; (4) While the route is being shown to the subject, an envelope is left along the route with the subject required to leave the envelope at the same location.

Preliminary results of the RBMT on neurologic patients with and without memory problems, as determined by judgments of occupational therapists based upon patient performance during therapy, suggest that the RBMT does not correlate with intelligence, and correlates most highly with delayed logical memory of the WMS (absolute and percentage of immediate recall) and paired-associate learning. That is, based upon this preliminary report, paired-associate performance and LM, as administered and scored in Oxford, are assessing some abilities that are related to everyday memory performance. This information is encouraging, relating cognitive components to the more pragmatic behavioral components, and we anxiously await replication and extension using other memory tests and procedures.

REFERENCES

Alba, J. W., & Hasher, L. (1983). Is memory schematic? *Psychological Bulletin, 93,* 203-231.

Bachrach, J., & Mintz, J. (1974). The Wechsler Memory Scale as a tool for the detection of mild cerebral dysfunction. *Journal of Clinical Psychology, 30,* 58-60.

Baddeley, A., Sunderland, A., and Harris, J. (1982). How well do laboratory-based psychological tests predict patients' performance outside the laboratory? In S. Corkin, K. L. Davis, J. H. Growder, E. Usdin, & R. J. Wurtman (Eds.), *Alzheimer's disease: A report of progress in research* (pp. 141-148). New York: Raven Press.

Bartlett, F. C. (1932). *Remembering: An experimental and social study.* Cambridge: Cambridge University Press.

Benton, A. L. (1962). The visual retention tests as a construction praxis test. *Confinia Neurologica, 29,* 1-16.

Ben-Yishay, U., Diller, L., Rattok, J., Ross, B., Lakin, P., & Cohen, J. (1980). Relationships between aspects of anterograde amnesia and vocational aptitude in TBD patients: Preliminary findings. Paper presented at the 8th annual meeting of the International Neuropsychological Society, San Francisco, CA.

Bransford, J. D., & Franks, J. J. (1971). The abstraction of linguistic ideas. *Cognitive Psychology, 2,* 331-350.

Brooks, D. N. (1972). Memory and head injury. *Journal of Nervous and Mental Diseases, 155,* 350-355.

Buschke, H. (1973). Selective reminding for analysis of memory and behavior. *Journal of Verbal Learning and Verbal Behavior, 12,* 543-550.

Buschke, J., & Fuld, P. A. (1974). Evaluating storage, retention, and retrieval in disordered memory and learning. *Neurology, 24,* 1019-1025.

Butters, N. (1985). Alcoholic Korsakoff's syndrome. *Journal of Experimental and Clinical Neuropsychology, 7,* 181-210.

Cattell, R. B. (1963). Theory of fluid and crystallized intelligence: A critical experiment. *Journal of Educational Psychology, 54,* 1-22.

Caine, E. D., Ebert, M. H., & Weingartner, H. (1977). An outline for the analysis of dementia: The memory disorder of Huntington's disease. *Neurology, 27,* 1087-1092.

Cauthen, N. R. (1977). Extension of the Wechsler Memory Scale norms to older age groups. *Journal of Clinical Psychology, 33,* 200-211.

Charter, R. A. (1981). Prorating the Wechsler Memory Scale. *Journal of Clinical Psychology, 37,* 183-186.

Cofer, C. N. (1965). On some factors in the organizational characteristics in free recall. *American Psychologist, 20,* 261-272.

Cohen, J. (1950). Wechsler Memory Scale performance on psychoneurotic, organic, and schizophrenic groups. *Journal of Consulting Psychology, 14,* 371-375.

Crosson, B., Hughes, C. W., Roth, D. L., & Monkowski, P. G. (1984). Review of Russell's (1975) norms for the logical memory and visual reproduction subtests of the Wechsler Memory Scale. *Journal of Consulting and Clinical Psychology, 52,* 635-641.

Cunningham, W. R., Clayton, V., & Overton, W. (1975). Fluid and crystallized intelligence in young adulthood and old age. *Journal of Gerontology, 30,* 53-55.

Delaney, R. C., Rosen, A. J., Mattson, R. H., & Novelly, R. A. (1980). Memory function in focal epilepsy: A comparison of nonsurgical unilateral temporal lobe and frontal lobe samples. *Cortex, 16,* 103-117.

Delis, D., Kramer, J., Ober, B. A., & Kaplan, E. (in press). The California Verbal Learning Test: Administration and Interpretation. New York: The Psychological Corp.

deVilliers, P. A. (1974). Imagery and theme in recall of connected discourse. *Journal of Experimental Psychology, 103,* 263-268.

Dodrill, C. B. (1978). A neuropsychological battery for epilepsy. *Epilepsia, 19,* 611-623.

Erickson, R. C. & Scott, M. L. (1977). Clinical memory testing: A review. *Psychological Bulletin, 84,* 1130-1149.

Glanzer, M., & Cunitz, A. R. (1966). Two storage mechanisms in free recall. *Journal of Verbal Learning and Verbal Behavior, 5,* 351-360.

Hannay, H. J., & Levin, H. S. (1985). Selective reminding test: An examination of the equivalence of four forms. *Journal of Clinical and Experimental Neuropsychology, 7,* 251-263.

Hart, T., & Hayden, M. E. (1986). The ecological validity of neuropsychological assessment and remediation. In B. P. Uzzell & Y. Gross (Eds.), *Clinical neuropsychology of intervention* (pp. 21-50). Boston: Kluwer.

Hermann, D. J. (1982). Know thy memory: The use of questionnaires to assess and study memory. *Psychological Bulletin, 92,* 434-452.

Hersen, M., & Barlow, D. H. (1976). *Single case experimental designs: Strategies for studying behavior change.* New York: Pergamon Press.

Hulicka, I. R. (1966). Age difference in Wechsler Memory Scale scores. *Journal of Genetic Psychology, 109,* 135-145.

Ivinskis, A., Allen, S., & Shaw, E. (1971). An extension of Wechsler Memory Scale norms to lower age groups. *Journal of Clinical Psychology, 27,* 354-357.

Kane, R. L., Parsons, O. A., & Goldstein, G. (1985). Statistical relationships and discriminative accuracy of the Halstead-Reitan, Luria-Nebraska, and Wechsler IQ scores in the identification of brain damage. *Journal of Clinical and Experimental Neuropsychology, 7,* 211-223.

Kear-Colwell, J. J., & Heller, M. (1978). A normative study of the Wechsler Memory Scale. *Journal of Clinical Psychology, 34,* 437-442.

Kinsbourne, M. (1973). Age effects on letter span related to rate and sequential dependency. *Journal of Gerontology, 28,* 317-319.

Kintsch, W. (1974). *The representation of meaning in memory.* Hillsdale, N.J.: Lawrence Erlbaum Associates.

Kintsch, W., & Kennan, J. (1973). Reading rate and retention as a function of the number of propositions in the base structure of sentences. *Cognitive Psychology, 5,* 257-274.

Kintsch, W., and van Dijk, T. (1975). Recalling and summarizing stories. *Language, 40,* 89-116.

Kljajic, I. (1975). Wechsler Memory Scale Indices of Brain Pathology. *Journal of Clinical Psychology, 31,* 698-701.

Kraemer, H. C., Peabody, C. A., Tinklenberg, J. R., & Yesavage, J. A. (1983). Mathematical and empirical development of a test of memory for clinical and research use. *Psychological Bulletin,* 367-380.

Larrabee, G. J., Kane, R. L., & Schuck, J. R. (1983). Factor analysis of the WAIS and Wechsler Memory Scale: An analysis of the construct validity of the Wechsler Memory Scale. *Journal of Clinical Neuropsychology, 5,* 159-168.

Larrabee, G. J., Kane, R. L., Schuck, J. R., & Francis, D. J. (1985). Construct validity of various memory testing procedures. *Journal of Clinical and Experimental Neuropsychology, 7,* 239-250.

Levin, H. S., Grossman, R. G., Rose, J. E., & Teasdale, G. (1979). Long-term neuropsychological outcome of closed head injury. *Journal of Neurosurgery, 50,* 412-422.

Lezak, M. D. (1983). *Neuropsychological assessment* (2nd ed.). New York: Oxford University Press.

Loring, D. W., Meador, K. J., Mahurin, R. K., & Largen, J. W. (1986). Neuropsychological performance in dementia of the Alzheimer type and multi-infarct dementia. Manuscript submitted for publication.

Logue, P., & Wyrich, L. (1979). Initial validation of Russell's revised Wechsler Memory Scale: A comparison of normal aging versus dementia. *Journal of Consulting and Clinical Psychology, 47,* 176-179.

Mandler, J. M., & Johnson, N. S. (1977). Remembrance of things parsed: Story structure and recall. *Cognitive Psychology, 9,* 111-151.

Milberg, W. P., Hebben, N., & Kaplan, E. (1986). The Boston process approach to neuropsychological assessment. In I. Grant & K. M. Adams (Eds.), *Neuropsychological assessment of neuropsychiatric disorders* (pp. 65-86). New York: Oxford University Press.

Mohs, R. C., Tinklenberg, T. R., Roth, W. T., & Koppell, B. S. (1980). Sensitivity of some human cognitive functions to effects of methamphetamine and secobarbital. *Drug and Alcohol Dependence, 5,* 145-150.

Muramoto, O. (1984). Selective reminding in normal and demented old people: Auditory verbal versus visual spatial task. *Cortex, 20,* 461-478.

Osborne, D., & Davis, L. J., Jr. (1978). Standard scores for Wechsler Memory Scale subtests. *Journal of Clinical Psychology, 38,* 115-116.

Peters, B. H., & Levin, H. S. (1977). Memory enhancement after physostigmine treatment in the amnesic syndrome. *Archives of Neurology, 34,* 215-219.

Peters, B. H., & Levin, H. S. (1979). Effects of Physostigmine and lecithin on memory in Alzheimer's disease. *Annals of Neurology, 6,* 219-221.

Pompi, K. F., & Lachman, R. (1967). Surrogate processes in the short-term retention of connected discourse. *Journal of Experimental Psychology, 75,* 143-150.

Power, D. G., Logue, P. E., McCarthy, S. M., Rosenstiel, A. K., & Ziesat, H. A. (1979). Inter-rater reliability of the Russell revision of the Wechsler Memory Scale: An attempt to clarify some ambiguities in scoring. *Journal of Clinical Neuropsychology, 1,* 343-345.

Prigatano, G. P. (1977). The Wechsler Memory Scale is a poor screening test for brain dysfunction. *Journal of Clinical Psychology, 33,* 772-777.

Prigatano, G. P. (1978). Wechsler Memory Scale: A selective review of the literature. *Journal of Clinical Psychology, 34,* 816-832.

Reed, H. B. C., & Reitan, R. M. (1963). A comparison of the effect of the normal aging process with the effect of organic brain-damage on adaptive abilities. *Journal of Gerontology, 18,* 177-179.

Russell, E. W. (1975). A multiple scoring method for the assessment of complex memory functions. *Journal of Consulting and Clinical Psychology, 43,* 800-809.

Russell, E. W. (1981). The pathology and clinical examination of memory. In S. B. Filskov & T. J. Boll (Eds.), *Handbook of clinical neuropsychology* (pp. 287-319). New York: Wiley.

Schear, J. M. (1985, February). *Utility of half credit scoring of Russell's revision of the Wechsler Memory Scale.* Paper presented at the meeting of the International Neuropsychological Society, San Diego, CA.

Silverstein, A. B. (1962). Perceptual, motor and memory functions in the Visual Retention Test. *American Journal of Mental Deficiency, 66,* 613-617.

Silverstein, A. B. (1963). Qualitative analysis of performance on the Visual Retention Test. *American Journal of Mental Deficiency, 68,* 109-113.

Sunderland, A., Harris, J. E., & Baddeley, A. (1983). Do laboratory tests predict everyday memory? A neuropsychological study. *Journal of Verbal Learning and Verbal Behavior, 22,* 341-357.

Sunderland, A., Harris, J. E., & Baddeley, A. D. (1984). Assessing everyday memory after severe head injury. In J. E. Harris & P. E. Morris (Eds.), *Everyday memory, actions and absent mindedness* (pp. 191-206). London: Academic Press.

Talland, G. A. (1965). *Deranged memory.* New York: Academic Press.

Thal, L. J., & Fuld, P. A. (1983). Memory enhancement with oral physostigmine in Alzheimer's disease. *New England Journal of Medicine, 308,* 720-721.

Thorndyke, P. W. (1975). Conceptual complexity and imagery in comprehension and memory. *Journal of Verbal Learning and Verbal Behavior, 14,* 359-369.

Trahan, D. E., & Larrabee, G. J. (1984, February). Construct validity and normative data for some recently developed measures of visual and verbal memory. Paper presented at the 12th Annual Meeting of the International Neuropsychological Society, Houston, TX.

Tulving, E., & Colotla, V. A. (1970). Free recall of trilingual lists. *Cognitive Psychology, 1,* 86-98.

Warrington, E. & James, M. (1967). An experimental investigation of facial recognition in patients with unilateral cerebral lesions. *Cortex, 3,* 317-326.

Watson, C. G., Thomas, R. W., Anderson, D., & Felling, J. (1968). Differentiation of organics from schizophrenics at two chronicity levels by use of the Halstead-Reitan organic brain test. *Journal of Consulting and Clinical Psychology, 32,* 679-684.

Wechsler, D. (1945). A standardized memory scale for clinical use. *Journal of Psychology, 19,* 87-95.

Wilson, B. (in press). *Rehabilitation of memory.* New York: Guilford Press.

Yesavage, J. A., Lierer, V., Becker, L., & Holman, C. (1980). Effect of an ergot compound on cognitive ability and depression. *Journal of Psychiatric Treatment and Evaluation, 3,* 14 9-152.

Journal of Clinical and Experimental Neuropsychology
1988, Vol. 10, No. 2, pp. 255-270.

Null Hypothesis Disrespect in Neuropsychology:
Dangers of Alpha and Beta Errors*

Henry V. Soper
University of California, Los Angeles
and
Camarillo State Hospital

Domenic V. Cicchetti
West Haven V. A. Medical Center and
Yale University

Paul Satz, Roger Light, and Donna L. Orsini
University of California, Los Angeles
and
Camarillo State Hospital

ABSTRACT

To understand why there are so many inconsistencies and contradictory findings among hemispheric-asymmetry studies, data were analyzed from a large study of 300 left-handers. These data included information on familial sinistrality (FS), handwriting posture (HPO), a measure of cognitive performance, and five measures of hemispheric specialization. Using computer simulation methodology, 40 independent samples of 36 to 65 subjects each were drawn randomly with replacement. The sample data were analyzed and the results compared to those of the parent "population." Often, the samples poorly reflected the parent "population," and some procedures substantially inflated error rates. These procedures are discussed and specific guidelines suggested. These results are also discussed in the broader context of the necessity for investigators in neuropsychology to differentiate between the statistical and clinical significance of research findings; and to develop a more positive attitude toward the design, execution, and publication of replication studies.

* This research was supported, in part, by the following DHS funds: NIMH Fellowship (1 F32 MH09082) to HVS, NIH (NS-18462) award to PS, and a VA merit review research grant to DVC. The authors would like to thank Wilfred G. Van Gorp, Ph. D., for his very helpful comments on the manuscript and Donna J. Gaier for her general assistance.

Spurious findings, purporting to support relationships which do not in fact exist, present a serious obstacle to scientific progress in neuropsychology. One contributing aspect is that such spurious results often stand a better chance of being published than true "null" results (Greenwald, 1975). Replication should resolve some of this difficulty and is generally recognized as good, standard experimental procedure. In fact, many authors (e.g., Epstein, 1980; Fishman & Neigher, 1982; Lubin, 1957; Sommer & Sommer, 1983) have even gone so far as to suggest that replication be a requirement for publication. However, replication poses another problem. Reports by Kerr, Tolliver, and Petree (1977) and Rowney and Zenisek (1980) indicate strong prejudice among reviewers against publishing replications (and, for that matter, against reanalyses of the data of others, Kerr et al., 1977).

Even though the necessity of reporting results contradictory to previous significant findings has been stressed (e.g., Greenwald, 1975; Sterling, 1959), a further problem arises. Kerr et al. (1977) and Rowney and Zenisek (1980) suggest that reviewers are as or more resistant to agreeing to publish null results than to accepting replication studies (see also McNemar, 1960 and Sterling, 1959). One can imagine the difficulty in publishing studies which fail to find relationships reported by others. Fortunately, this journal recognized some of the implications of null results in the founding issue (Rourke & Costa, 1979).

An illustrative example of this problem involves studies of hemispheric specialization. Levy and Reid (1976, 1978), for example, suggested a strong relationship between handwriting posture (HPO) and cerebral organization. They posited that language dominance is ipsilateral to the writing hand for inverters and contralateral for normal writers. However, critical reviews of the literature (Levy, 1982; Weber & Bradshaw, 1981) indicate that most studies have failed to confirm this relationship.

Another example of this problem concerns the relationship between hemispheric specialization and familial sinistrality (FS). In 1955, Ettlinger, Jackson, and Zangwill reported a robust relationship between FS and crossed dextral aphasia. Later, however, Zangwill (1981) reported a chance FS rate among crossed dextral aphasics. Although the first study may have included more natural sinistrals who became dextrals due to social pressure, it may be that the results of the second study are spurious. Clearly, at least one of these findings misrepresents the true state of affairs, and without attempts to replicate, we are left with only speculation as to which results are truly representative.

There are many probable reasons for the disparity among the results from studies on hemispheric specialization. Certainly, differences in methodologies and in the characteristics of the study samples play a role. Specifically, the small sample sizes used (often less than 50 subjects in a group) would appear to be a significant factor. Frequently such small sizes are required, either by the characteristics of the target population (e.g., crossed dextral aphasics) or the quantity of data to be collected on each subject. However, there would appear to be a high probability of at least some of these small samples seriously misrepresenting the populations from which they were drawn. The chance finding of no relationship when, in fact, one does exist in the parent population (beta error) can impede progress as much as a proposed significant sample-derived relationship that, in fact, does not exist in the population (alpha error). Small samples give rise to a risk of both alpha and beta errors.

The purpose of the present paper is to investigate possible sources of such experimental and statistical biases and to suggest some possible remedies. To examine these issues, data from a large-scale project on laterality were used. The project sought to answer two fundamental questions: first, how do FS+ and FS— subjects compare on both hemispheric and cognitive performance tasks and secondly, do subjects employing an inverted handwriting posture (HPO inverters) perform differently on these same tasks than those subjects with normal handwriting posture (HPO normals)? The data base consisted of 300 left-handers selected from a normal population. The "population" represents the largest sample of left-handers ($N = 300$) selected from the normal population and studied with reference to laterality. Subsets from the large data set were taken to see how well they described the "populations" from which they were drawn. This Monte Carlo (computer simulation) approach of taking random subsamples afforded a unique opportunity to study some of the factors which result in alpha and beta errors. It also afforded the opportunity to look at methods of remediation.

METHODS

Subjects.

The group of 300 left-handers contained 112 males and 188 females. Some of the subjects participated in the study to fulfil part of a requirement for an introductory psychology course at the University of Victoria. Others were enlisted through advertisements, and were paid for their participation. Although the subjects were enlisted initially on the basis of self-report of handedness, this was confirmed through a questionnaire and observation. Only subjects with a history of cerebral damage were excluded from this study. The mean age for all subjects was 28.8 years: for the females it was 29.7 years, and for the males it was 27.7 years. Although an effort was made to collect each assessment from each subject, this was not always possible. Complete data were available on 240 subjects when the classification was based upon HPO status and upon 236 when based upon the FS dichotomy.

Tests

Independent variables. Familial sinistrality (FS) was assessed via questionnaire using the scoring system recommended by Bishop (1980). Higher weights were assigned to siblings and blood parents, with half weights for extended family members. Of the 293 subjects returning the questionnaire, 136 (46%) were designated as showing a positive history for FS, namely, at least one sinistral in the immediate family or two in the extended family. Handwriting posture (HPO) was assessed by having each subject match his/her posture to one of an array of four diagrams, depicting left-handed normal, left-handed inverted, right-handed normal, and right-handed inverted postures (Levy & Reid, 1976, 1978). Of the 300 sinistrals, 134 (45%) wrote with an inverted posture.

Dependent variables. Five of the six dependent variables tapped hemispheric specialization, and one (*embedded figures*) measured cognitive performance. The five hemispheric specialization tasks were: (a) *dichotic listening* word recognition (free recall) and (b) four dual task conditions (*words right, words left, verbal fluency,* and *reading*).

Procedure.
For the *dichotic-listening* task, the 16 trials consisted of three pairs of concrete words. Each pair was presented simultaneously, one stimulus to each ear, and the pairs within a trial were separated by 500 ms. After the stimuli for each trial were presented, the subject was to report all the words heard. The score for this task was the total number of right-ear presented words recalled minus the left-ear total divided into the total number of words recalled. For the *words right* task, the score was the average over two trials of the number of words produced (verbal fluency) beginning with a given target letter while tapping with the right index finger. *Words left* was the average over two trials of the number of words similarly produced while tapping with the left index finger. These latter two assessments were made for244 of the 300 subjects, 240 of whom also returned the familial sinistrality questionnaire. A *verbal fluency* score was determined as the difference between the baseline left-finger tapping rate and the comparable rate under the words left condition divided by the baseline left and the comparable score for the right index finger (i.e., (baseline right - words right)/ baseline right *minus* (baseline left - words left)/ baseline left). For the *reading* task, the subject was asked to read passages while tapping. The score was derived in the same manner as the verbal fluency score (baseline right minus right average score while reading, divided by baseline right, minus the same ratio for the left finger). A more complete description of these variables is given in Orsini, Satz, Soper, Light (1985).

The sixth and final task, *embedded figures,* was used as a measure of cognitive performance, and additionally to determine if inverted HPO, as suggested by Levy (1982), is associated with lower cognitive performance. The embedded-figures task utilizes a figure, identical in size, orientation, and shape to a sample figure, which is embedded in one of three response array figures. The score was the total points over 24 trials, with 3 points for a correct response within 5 s, 2 points for one within 10 s, and 1 point for a correct response within 15 s.

Data analyses
Using computer simulations, 40 random (without restraint to any factor, such as sex), independent samples of 36 to 65 subjects each were drawn, with replacement, from the total "population" of 300 subjects. FS was used as the independent variable for the analyses on half the samples, and HPO on the other half. The data within each sample were analyzed with respect to each of the six dependent measures, usually through a one-way analysis of variance. In the few cases in which the assumption of homogeneity of variance was violated, tests not making such an assumption were used (i.e., as in Dixon, 1981).

Based upon the previous literature, the foci of interest included the six comparisons of mean task performance of FS+ and FS— groups (one per task); and the remaining six comparisons between HPO inverters and HPO normals. In order to control adequately for Type I error, in both sets of analyses, the usual level of alpha (.05) was divided by the number of comparisons (6) to produce a value of .008 (e.g., see Leach, 1979 for justification of this procedure). To test for a trend in the data, the usual level of alpha, or Type I error (.10) was divided by 6 to produce a value of .017. In order to produce consistency in interpretation of any given "population" or sample result, the same data-analytic procedures were used in both.

Because of their rather wide application in the neuropsychology literature, chi square(d) analyses were also performed on each of the samples. Average scores on the embedded-figures task were dichotomized at the mean; for the hemispheric tasks cutoff scores were based upon the shape of the resulting distributions.

RESULTS

"Population" - FS as independent variable
When Type I error rate was properly controlled (i.e., .008 for the .05 level; and .017 for a trend at $p = .10$), there were no statistically significant differences or trends between FS+ and FS— subjects on any of the six tasks. The two groups manifested their largest differences in performance on the embedded-figures task. However, the actual mean scores (based upon 293 of the 300 subjects) were quite similar, namely, an FS+ average score of 59.99 and a corresponding FS—mean score of 58.22. This difference produced an unadjusted p value of .034 with a corresponding p value of .20 (or 6 x .034) when appropriately adjusted for Type I error. It should be noted that such a difference accounts for only 2.4% of the variation in difference scores. To summarize, then, FS+ and FS— subjects could not be significantly differentiated with respect to their performance on either the cognitive task (*embedded figures*) or on any of the five remaining hemispheric tasks (*dichotic listening; words right; words left; verbal fluency;* and *reading*).

"Population" - HPO as independent variable
When the 300 sinistrals were dichotomized into HPO normal or HPO inverted, only one of the six dependent measures significantly differentiated the two groups. Those who wrote with an inverted posture had an average score on the *embedded figures* task of 60.27. Subjects who wrote with a normal posture had a mean score of 58.04. This difference (Table 1) is statistically significant, with $F (1,298) = 7.56$; p unadjusted $= .006$; p adjusted for Type I error, at 6 $p = .036$. Despite its level of statistical significance, the difference itself accounts for only 2.8% of the total variance in scores on the embedded-figures task.

The strength of the relationship between HPO and performance on the embedded figures task can be estimated by the statistic epsilon, which is equivalent to the correlation coefficient squared or the between sums of squares (Cohen & Cohen, 1983). Epsilon for the embedded-figures analysis had a value of .15. Cohen (1977, p. 116) suggested *approximate* single rs of .10, .30, and .50 to define small, moderate, and large effect sizes (ES), respectively. Thus, a value of

Table 1

Results (Anova probabilities)[a]

| Variable | Hemispheric Specialization Tasks Dual Tasks | | | | | Cognitive Performance Task |
	Dichotic Listening	Words Right	Words Left	Verbal Fluency	Reading	Embedded Figures
Familial Sinistrality	.73	.30	.59	.86	.33	.034
Hand Position Orientation	.36	.67	.88	.32	.49	.006

[a] Prior to controlling for Type I error rates. See text for further information.

.15 would be considered small by Cohen's criteria. Consistent with this interpretation, another statistician characterizes an r value of .15 as usually being of trivial consequence (i.e., Fleiss, 1981, p. 60). (It should be noted that levels of clinical significance aside, the obtained results, in fact, argue *against* an hypothesized cognitive impairment associated with a left-handed inverted posture, as suggested by Levy, 1982, and earlier by Gregory and Paul, 1980.)

Samples - FS as independent variable

Type I error was controlled at .05/6 (or .008) for each comparison within a given sample. Eighteen of the 20 samples reflected the "population," by showing no statistically significant relationship between FS status and scores on any of the six dependent measures. In fact p never even reached a level of .10, *prior* to correcting for Type I error. The remaining two samples each produced one result statistically significant at or beyond the .05 level. This compares quite favorably to the (120 x .05/6) or 1 statistically significant comparison expected by chance alone. (Note, however, that if experiment-wise error rate were to be ignored, alpha errors would then appear in one quarter of the samples.)

Samples - HPO as independent variable

Again, Type I error was set at .05/6 (or .008) for each comparison within a given sample. At this level of alpha only one sample mimicked the "population." Specifically, scores on the embedded-figures task differentiated between HPO groups at the .008 level. As in the "population," HPO inverters had higher average scores than those who wrote with a normal posture. Eighteen of the remaining 19 samples showed no group differences at or beyond the .05 level on any of the six variables. One sample showed one significant difference (p at .05) and one near-significant difference (p at .10), but on tasks *other* than embedded figures.

The alpha error rate was just what one would expect, namely, .05/6 x 120 or exactly one occurrence among 20 samples. The beta error, on the other hand, was 95% since 19 of the 20 samples failed to mimic the statistically significant "population" differences on the embedded-figures task. While the beta error rate was rather high, further analysis revealed that 14 of the samples produced mean differences as great or greater than the "population" differences, on the embedded-figures task, in the same direction. Six of these samples produced statistically significant differences (p at .05) and three at near significance (p at .10) *prior* to controlling for Type I error. It is interesting that, if these 14 samples had reached statistical significance, this would have resulted in a beta error of 6/20 or 30%. This approaches the 20% desired beta error (or 80% "desired power convention") suggested by Cohen (1977, p. 56).

DISCUSSION

The "population" HPO group difference on the embedded-figures scores task accounted for only 2.8% of the variance. This reflects a problem of looking for small effects with small sample sizes-the probability of obtaining a difference great enough to be significant is very low. Essentially, one is trying to measure small differences with large variances, and using sample sizes of about 50 is not sufficient to detect relationships which account for about one fortieth of the total variance.

What sample sizes would be sufficient for our purposes? The answer depends in large part on how much intrasubject variability exists on any given measure, relative to the extent of variability between groups on that same measure. While one could have determined by computer simulation exactly at what sample sizes "population" parameters would be consistently mimicked, the exercise would prove futile or cost inefficient. First, and most fundamentally, we do not feel justified in defining our group of 300 sinistrals as a population of all left-handers. Moreover, we are also aware that, even if this assumption were warranted, the required minimal sample sizes would be quite large. The results just presented were based upon the 300 HPO or 293 FS subjects who completed some or all of the six tasks. We also performed identical statistical analyses for both those 236 FS and 240 HPO subjects who provided scores on *each* of the five hemispheric tasks as well as on the cognitive task. These samples were approximately 80% the size of the "population" from which they were drawn. Results based upon FS analyses did mimic the "population" in that there were no statistically significant or near-significant differences between FS+ and FS— subjects on any of the six variables. However, the same was *not* true for the HPO results. Recall that in the "population," HOP inverters had significantly higher average scores on the embedded-figures task than did those who wrote with a normal posture. None of the five hemispheric tasks significantly differentiated the HPO groups. However, when the results were based upon those 240 *sample* subjects who provided scores on each of the six measures, performance on *embedded figures* produced only a near-significant result ($p = .09$), when Type I error was appropriately controlled at $.10/6$ or $.017$. It is even more noteworthy that performance on the *reading task,* which feel far short of significance in the "population" (i.e., $p = .49$ *prior* to correcting for Type I error) differentiated HPO inverters and normals at $p = .038$, *after* Type I error was appropriately controlled.

The results discussed up to this point were based upon parametric analyses, namely, analyses of variance (ANOVAs). However, it is far from unusual for neuropsychologists (as well as other scientists) to define empirical or theoretically derived cutoff points on otherwise dimensionally scaled variables such as those utilized in this research project. Accordingly, the numbers of subjects with scores above or below a given cutoff are then compared using the standard chi square(d) test of significance. Such analyses are then used either to complement or supplant those based upon parametric statistics. It is also not unusual for researchers to employ the chi square test to data deriving from a 2 x 2 table *without* employing the recommended Yates' (1934) correction factor as suggested by a number of prominent statisticians (e.g., Fleiss, 1981; Mosteller & Rourke, 1973). It is the purpose of this section of the discussion to trace some interesting concequences of these approaches when applied to samples deriving from the "population" of 300 sinistrals. This exercise has as its prpose to demonstrate some of the pitfalls that can occur when the chi square(d) statistic is misused.

None of the usual requirements for the appropriate use of the chi square methods was violated (e.g., Siegel, 1956). Results can be briefly summarized as follows: When the correction for continuity was employed, the on-the-average error rates for "significance" and for "trend" or "near significance" very closely matched the nominal values of $.05$ and $.10$ respectively. However, when the correction for continuity was not employed, Type I error rates were, on-the-average, between one and one-half and twice the size of their nominal values of $.05$ and $.10$. More importantly, the simultaneous usage of empirically derived (post-hoc) cutoff points and failing to apply the correction factor can produce results which infer clinically useful relationships which in fact do not exist in the parent "population." We have selected several such results to illustrate further this important point.

In one sample, shown in the upper portion of Figure 1, there was a large ear asymmetry on the dichotic-listening task. In this instance, the basic score was altered, using a difference score rather than a ratio. The results, with an epsilon of $.42$, suggest a difference of moderate clinical relevance. At this level, relatively low "false positive" and "false negative" rates were obtained. However, a different picture emerged when we examined the "population" (lower half of Figure 1). The two groups are effectively identical. In fact, it would appear that FS status and performance on the dichotic-listening task are about as unrelated as two variables can be.

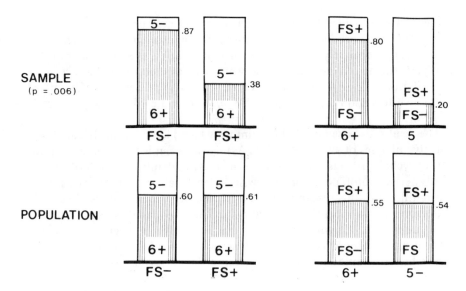

Figure 1. The top portion represents a spurious relationship manifested in one sample between incidence of familial sinistrality among left-handers and performance on a dichotic-listening task. The dichotic-listening task data were dichotomized for this analysis into a relatively proficient group with scores of 6 or greater (6+) and a less proficient group with scores of 5 or less (5—). The bottom portion represents the lack of any relationship found within the "population" sampled.

The HPO analyses provide us with another example of spurious significances, both statistical and clinical. On one of the samples, Sample A, let us say obtained by Over and Under, a mean difference of 3.09 words was found between inverted and normal writers ($p < .001$). The distribution of proportions using a cutoff of 9.5 words is depicted in the top portion of Figure 2. As with the preceding FS example, the rates of false positives and false negatives seem relatively low. With a phi of .66, this would suggest a strong clinical relationship. Another sample, Sample B, let us say found by To and Fro, reveals a moderately strong (phi of .42) relationship opposite to that found by Over and Under (sample A). Here, the mean normal score is 2.95 words higher than the mean score for inverts. The difference To and Fro found is almost as large as the one Over and Under found, although in the *opposite* direction. To and Fro and Over and Under might well be disputing each other's findings, even though, in fact, the same or similar subjects and procedures may have been used by both investigators.

Again, if we focus upon the "population" in the bottom portion of Figure 2, it is, of course, clear that there is no statistically significant relationship between these variables, let alone one of clinical significance.

Similar manipulations can be conducted involving other spurious relation-

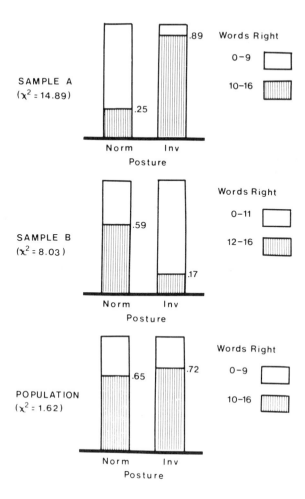

Figure 2. The top and middle portions represent apparently contradictory but spurious findings of a relationship between handwriting position (normal or inverted) and performance on a verbal-fluency task while tapping with the right hand. The subjects were placed into relatively more proficient (lined box) and less proficient (open box) groups. The bottom portion represents the true lack of any such relationship within the "population" from which the samples were drawn.

ships, but the results would be as meaningless as those just presented. If one group of investigators obtained results comparable to those found in one of these examples, it would be easy to see why they would feel that others, whose results might match those of the other samples (or even the "population"), must be doing something wrong. The proportion of such apparently contradictory relationships as in these two cases would increase as further manipulations were conducted on the data. Half these spuriously significant pairs would disagree, and the proposed relationship between the variables would be brought into question. Unfortunately, the other half of these pairs would agree, and the erroneous proposed relationship might prove very resistant to disproof.

CONCLUSIONS AND RECOMMENDATIONS

What conclusions can be drawn from the preceding analyses in which repeated samples were selected from a finite "population" whose parameters were known? When a true relationship exists, but one which accounts for a relatively small proportion of the total variance, the chance of detecting this relationship is somewhat low. A sample may have to be quite large before the test is powerful enough to be assured of a good chance of detecting relatively small, but real, differences between groups. How large a sample is required to determine if a relationship between groups exists? The answer, of course, lies in the analysis of the power of the tests to be used. This, in turn, is a function of the expected variance (often difficult to estimate, but possible with pilot data) and the minimal effect (either in units or proportions of a standard deviation) one is willing to accept as confirming the proposed hypothesis (as well as the desired power and level and directionality of significance). However, as we have just shown, even samples four-fifth the size of the parent "population" do not always guarantee "population" results.

On the other side of the question, *very large* sample sizes may be able to detect a larger number of true relationships, but many of these may account for such small amounts of variance as to be clinically irrelevant. Attempts to confirm these findings with smaller sample sizes may be frustrating. It is, therefore, important to assess the strength of a relationship, *regardless* of the level of significance obtained, through performing an epsilon, phi, or similar analysis. Based upon the earlier work of Rosenthal and Ruben (1982), and consistent with the work of Cohen (1977); Wolf and Cornell (1986) recently demonstrated that correlation coefficients (e.g., epsilon or phi values) of .20 or higher can be regarded as clinically meaningful. One often feels that the reporting of a high level of significance implies a strong relationship. As is evident from the present study, this simply is not true.

It would appear, therefore, that, when designing a study to test a particular hypothesis, several factors should be taken into consideration above and beyond the level of significance desired. One such factor is the magnitude of the difference (or relationship) one wishes to detect. A second is the strength of the obtained effect. This latter consideration should have a great bearing on the theoretical implications of the results. Even when significance is found, it can be fully appropriate not to reject the null hypothesis when the observed strength of the relationship is so trivial as to be meaningless.

When dichotomized at the mean, the chi square analyses of the variable proving significant in the parent "population" resulted in a substantial beta error rate. In fact, the resultant distribution of probability levels was quite similar to that expected when the groups do not differ in the "population." This substantial loss of power is not surprising. As pointed out by Cohen (1983), such a procedure accounts for far less of the variance than procedures which use continuous or dimensionally scaled data. Hence, when the relationship of interest accounts for a relatively small proportion of the total variance, as in the present examples, one should not be surprised that this relationship cannot be detected by dichotomizing at the sample mean.

Correcting for continuity when using the chi square statistic is clearly imperative. Substantial alpha error rates were found using "empirically determined" cutoff scores when no correction was used. These results underscore the need for the correction in order to improve the accuracy of the test (again, see Fleiss, 1981; Mosteller & Rourke, 1973). Thus, when the correction factor was utilized, the alpha error rates were actually quite low. At first this appears to support the contention that the correction factor reduces the power of the test. However, in view of the multiple cutoffs assessed for many of the dependent variables, the resultant alpha error rates compare very well with those found using parametric techniques. This suggests that the observed low rate is a reflection of the data and not the test. In other words, consistent with Fleiss' (1981) recommendations, these results support the use of the correction factor. Unfortunately, our review of the neuropsychology literature indicated that all too often investigators do not apply Yates' appropriate adjustment to the chi square(d) test.

Despite all the caveats, empirically dichotomizing continuous variables could be justified, especially when looking for clinically relevant relationships. The injudicious aspect, however, lies in *applying these cutoff scores to the same sample in which they were found.* Examining a second, independent sample would reduce the chance of a spurious finding being pursued.

The importance of accounting for experiment-wise error rate is obvious. Although increasing the beta error rate, it is clearly warranted when multiple assessments are analysed. This also suggests using care when collapsing data across an independent variable, such as sex, when an analysis shows it has no relationship to the dependent variable.

The data, as they were actually collected, present another potential problem. Not only were repeated measures taken from the subjects, but in order to standardize the data, the same measures were used across several of the dual-task conditions. Using such a procedure could create a dependency between measures. This happened not to be the case for the present data, but had the baseline tapping rate been related to either independent variable, verbal fluency and reading variables might have both appeared to be related to that independent variable. This would suggest that, when such standardized scores are found to be related to another variable, the components of the scores should also be analyzed to determine just where the relationship lies.

The preceding examples demonstrate that contradictory and apparently significant results may emerge from the work of different investigators which are not attributable to differences in subjects or procedures. Again, as Greenwald (1975) and others (e.g., McNemar, 1960; Sterling, 1959) point out, such findings stand a much greater chance of appearing in the literature than (true) null findings, and hence are of greater concern than might appear at first. Replicating ones own work, of course, is always a good idea, but it would appear mandatory when others obtain contradictory results. In view of this, it is worth noting that no investigators have ever replicated their own results of a positive relationship between cerebral organization and HPO. On the other hand, Zangwill (1981), who cast doubt on his own earlier report of a relationship between dextral crossed aphasia and familial sinistrality, represents a refreshingly unprejudiced view of the null hypothesis.

We have argued against the questionable procedure of using multiple, or post hoc, cutoffs since they can result in a substantial increase in the incidence of alpha error. Another example is provided in a recent study by Geschwind (Geschwind & Behan, 1982; Geschwind, 1983), which reports a provocative relationship between sinistrality and dyslexia and/or autoimmune disorder. In a well-controlled portion of the study, a significant relationship was found for only one immune disorder (myasthenia gravis), and even here at only one (the most liberal) of several cutoff points for sinistrality. Obtaining only one such "significant" relationship leaves one suspicious that this may have been an alpha error.

Curiously, some of Geschwind and Behan's (1982) supporting evidence for the proposed relationship points to another difficulty in drawing conclusions based upon small sample sizes. Specifically, the investigators reported that 13 of 247 sinistrals had a history of immune disorders, whereas only 15 of 647 dextrals did, with the resultant chi square significant at the .025 level ($p < .05$, however, when we applied the required correction for continuity). Nonetheless, if only one of the immune disorder subjects was a left-hander due to some factor unrelated to the disorder (e.g., a broken right hand early in childhood), then the altered distribution (i.e., changing the category of one subject out of 894) reduces the chi square value to a level of p at no more than chance significance. The phenomenon just described can occur whenever the number of negative cases far exceeds the number of positive ones. A shift of one or two cases among the *negatives* will have little material affect on the results. However, a similar shift for *positive* cases can make a dramatic difference. Fortunately, there is a straightforward method of protecting against such potential problems. Geschwind and Behan (1982) accurately report finding a relationship, but how *strong* is it? By simply taking the square root of the uncorrected chi square value divided by the number of subjects, one obtains the phi coefficient or Pearson correlation between two dichotomously scored variables (e.g., see Fleiss, 1981, p. 59). One can then apply the criteria of Cohen (1977) to determine the strength of the relationship. The resultant phi value for the Geschwind and Behan data was .08, which, by almost any standards, would be considered a negligible effect. Based upon the data just discussed, Geschwind and Behan (1982, p. 5099) concluded that there is a "markedly elevated frequency of immune disorders in left-handers." Although the relationship found may be of scientific interest, it seems to be of minimal *clinical* importance and should probably not cause undue concern for left-handers. In this specific sense, the Geschwind and Behan conclusion may have been overstated. This example points out the necessity of stating the strength of a relationship (e.g., see Delucchi, 1983, p. 173). It is not surprising that noting the strength of a relationship is often neglected by research investigators. In speaking about one such measure of relationship, namely, the statistic epsilon, Cohen and Cohen (1983, p. 197) remind us that "most textbook treatments do not mention it."

Despite some of the methodological problems noted in the Geschwind and Behan (1982) study, the authors did try to replicate their results. Unfortunately, however, they were not successful in adding confidence to their original findings. In this example, a large data base base was used to investigate a relatively infrequent occurrence. However, many of the populations of interest to neuropsychologists occur infrequently, if not rarely, in nature (e.g., the autistic, people with isolated early left-hemisphere trauma), thus necessitating the use of small sample sizes. In such cases, replicating or otherwise verifying the findings through independent samples is *strongly recommended.*

The results of the present investigation, in sum, strongly suggest that there are several steps neuropsychologists should take to reduce alpha and beta errors. They should replicate or otherwise verify their own findings using independent samples, preferably using different methods and approaches. This will substantially reduce the chance of spurious results affecting one's theory of hemispheric specialization. Presenting the strength of observed relationships, through phi or equivalent analyses, is particularly important, especially when clinical conclusions are to be drawn. Of equal importance, empirically derived (post hoc) or other similar multiple-level assessment analyses should always be verified with an independent sample *prior* to publication, in order to guard against inaccurate categorizations of variables (a caveat issued many years ago by Lewis and Burke, 1949). It is hoped that the preceding comments will engender more concern about hypothesis testing in neuropsychology and perhaps less prejudice against the null hypothesis. More generally, this investigation suggests that computer simulation studies can prove valuable, in their own right, in helping to clarify some of the seemingly contradictory findings published in neuropsychological and other literature.

REFERENCES

Bishop, D. V. M. (1980). Measuring familial sinistrality. *Cortex, 16,* 311-313.
Cohen, J. (1977). *Statistical power analysis for the behavioral sciences.* New York: Academic.

Cohen, J. (1983). The cost of dichotomization. *Applied Psychological Measurement, 7*, 247-253.

Cohen, J., & Cohen, P. (1983). *Applied multiple regression/correlation analysis for the behavioral sciences* (2nd ed.). Hillsdale, NJ: Lawrence Erlbaum Associates, Inc.

Delucchi, K. L. (1983). The use and misuse of chi square: Lewis and Burke revisited. *Psychological Bulletin, 94,* 166-176.

Dixon, W. J. (Ed.). (1981). *BMDP statistical software.* Los Angeles, CA: University of California Press.

Epstein, S. (1980). The stability of behavior II. Implications for psychological research. *American Psychologist, 35,* 790-806.

Ettlinger, G., Jackson, C., & Zangwill, 0. (1955). Dysphasia following right temporal lobectomy in a right-handed man. *Journal of Neurology, Neurosurgery, and Psychiatry, 18,* 214-217.

Fishman, D. B. & Neigher, W. D. (1982). American psychology in the eighties: Who will buy? *American Psychologist, 37,* 533-546.

Fleiss, J. L. (1981). *Statistical methods for rates and proportions* (2nd ed.). New York: Wiley.

Geschwind, N. (1983). Biological associations of left-handedness. *Annals of Dyslexia, 33,* 29-40.

Geschwind, N. & Behan, P. (1982). Left-handedness: Association with immune disease, migraine and developmental learning disorder. *Proceedings of the National Academy of Sciences, USA, 79,* 5097-5100.

Gregory, R. & Paul, J. (1980). The effects of handedness and writing posture of neuro-psychological test results. *Neuropsychologia, 18,* 231-235.

Greenwald, A. G. (1975). Consequences of prejudice against the null hypothesis. *Psychological Bulletin, 82,* 1-20.

Kerr, S., Tolliver, J., & Petree, D. (1977). Manuscript characteristics which influence acceptance for management and social science journals. *Academy of Management Journal, 20,* 132-141.

Leach, C. (1979). *Introduction to statistics: A non-parametric approach for the social sciences.* New York: Wiley.

Levy, J. (1982). Handwriting posture and cerebral organization: How are they related? *Psychological Bulletin, 91,* 589-608.

Levy, J. & Reid, M. (1976). Variations in writing posture and cerebral organization. *Science, 194,* 337-339.

Levy, J. & Reid, M. (1978). Variations in cerebral organization as a function of handedness, hand posture in writing, and sex. *Journal of Experimental Psychology:* General, 197, 119-144.

Lewis, D. & Burke, C. J. (1949). The use and misuse of the chi square test. *Psychological Bulletin, 46,* 433-489.

Lubin, A. (1957). Replicability as a publication criterion. *American Psychologist, 12,* 519-520.

McNemar, Q. (1960). At random: Sense and nonsense. *American Psychologist, 15,* 295-300.

Mosteller, F. & Rourke, R. E. K. (1973). Applying chi-square to counted data: Basic ideas. In F. Mosteller & R. E. K. Rourke (Eds.), *Sturdy statistics* (pp. 159-174). Reading, MA: Addison-Wesley Publishing Co.

Orsini, D. L., Satz, P., Soper, H. V., & Light, R.(1985). Evaluation of familial sinistrality as an indicator of cerebral organization, *Neuropsychologia, 23,* 223-232.

Rosenthal, R. & Rubin, D. B. (1982). A simple, general purpose display of magnitude of experimental effect. *Journal of Educational Psychology, 74,* 166-169.

Rourke, B. P. & Costa, L. (1979). Editorial policy II. *Journal of Clinical Neuropsychology, 1,* 93-96.

Rowney, J. A. & Zenisek, T. J. (1980). Manuscript characteristics influencing reviewers' decisions. *Canadian Psychology, 21,* 17-21.

Siegel, S. (1956). *Nonparametric statistics for the behavioral sciences.* New York: McGraw-Hill.

Sommer, R. & Sommer, B. A. (1983). Mystery in Milwaukee: Early intervention, IQ, and psychology textbooks. *American Psychologist, 38,* 982-985.

Sterling, T. D. (1959). Publication decisions and their possible effects on inferences drawn from tests of significance-or vice versa. *American Statistical Association Journal, 54,* 30-34.

Weber, A. M. & Bradshaw, J. L. (1981). Levy and Reid's neurological model in relation to writing hand/posture? An evaluation. *Psychological Bulletin, 90,* 74-88.

Wolf, F. M. & Cornell, R. G. (1986). Interpreting behavioral, biomedical, and psychological relationships in chronic disease from 2 x 2 tables using correlation. *Journal of Chronic Diseases, 39,* 605-608.

Yates, F. (1934). Contingency tables involving small numbers and the chi square test. *Journal of the Royal Statistical Society, 1,* 217-235.

Zangwill, O. (1981). Crossed aphasia and its relation to cerebral lateralization. In Y. Lebrun & O. Zangwill (Eds.), *Lateralization of language in the child* (pp. 147-154). Lisse: Swets and Zeitlinger.

Journal of Clinical Neuropsychology
1979, Vol. 1, No. 3, 183–211.

Case Study Approach in Neuropsychological Research*

Tim Shallice
Medical Research Council Applied Psychology Unit, Cambridge

ABSTRACT

The contribution of the neurological case study approach for establishing the functional organisation of cognitive subsystems is assessed. A number of potential problems are considered, including "resource artefacts", the nature of the lengthy clinical/experimental procedure used, statistical selection artefacts, reorganisation of function, atypical lateralisation, and the existence of associated deficits. It is argued that, despite these problems, the case study approach is the most promising neuropsychological technique for providing information on the functional organisation of cognitive subsystems.

1. INTRODUCTION

Until the Second World War, studies of the cognitive deficits of neurological patients usually relied on single case studies of patients with intuitively interesting syndromes, or the closely related method of the study of a very small group of patients with apparently similar symptoms. During the inter-war years, criticisms of the inferences derived from such studies were increasingly made (e.g., Head, 1926; Weisenburg & McBride, 1935). These authors relied on the more systematic method of studying a series of patients selected on less arbitrary criteria. Soon after the Second World War, the important methodological approach was developed of comparing the quantitative results of groups of patients with those of appropriate controls. This move to a more rigorous methodology occurred mainly because the study of the cognitive deficits of neurological patients began to be approached from the stand-

*This paper is based on a talk given in the Symposium on Case Study Analysis in Neuropsychology at the Second INS European Conference, Noordwijkerhout, Holland, June 1979. I should like to thank Tony Marcel, Karalyn Patterson, Eleanor Saffran and Elizabeth Warrington for their comments on an earlier draft of the paper.

point of psychology as well as neurology. At the same time, there were continuing criticisms of particular syndromes "established" using the older single case methodology, such as agnosia (see Bay, 1953; Bender & Feldman, 1972) and the Gerstmann syndrome (Benton, 1961).

With the availability of an apparently more rigorous methodology, it might appear that the single case approach would die away in much the same way that nineteenth century methods have been superseded in experimental psychology. Over the last ten years, however, there has instead been a resurgence of the case study methodology, particularly in Europe.

One reason for this resurgence has been that group studies in neuro-psychology continually face the problem of the heterogeneity of the disorders of the neurological patients in a group over which results have to be averaged. In addition to the problems of the enormous range of ages, premorbid intellectual skills and lesion sizes in patients forming a group and the interaction between aetiology and lesion site (see e.g. Zülch, 1965), problems which can be reduced but not eliminated by analysis of covariance, there are even less tractable averaging problems. These problems relate to the difficulties in making inferences about functional systems from group studies. Consider Fig. 1, which represents a simplified flow diagram of one theory of the organization of the functional systems involved in the reading or repeating of individual words, that of Morton and Patterson (in press). The relevance of this particular diagram is that it obtains its justification from outside neuropsychology, being basically derived from experimental studies of normal subjects, and has then been applied to provide one theory of the symptom complex found in a particular form of acquired dyslexia – deep (or phonemic) dyslexia (Marshall & Newcombe, 1966; Shallice & Warrington, 1975). Not all research workers in the area agree with every aspect of the flow diagram (see Shallice & Warrington, in press). However, it appears unlikely, from both research on the acquired dyslexias and on the normal reading process, that any simpler theory of the reading process would be adequate.

If neuropsychological evidence is to be relevant to this class of theory it must relate to the microstructure of the model, for instance, by showing that one subsystem can be operative while another is not. However, it seems likely that many of the functional systems involved will be close to each other anatomically. Therefore any sizeable group of neurological patients, unless selected on extremely precise, and therefore, in practice, unrealisable criteria, will inevitably have a majority of patients who have either both systems or neither damaged. The average results of the group as a whole will therefore tend not to show any interesting differences on two tests, one of which involves only one of these subsystems and the second of which involves only the other. Even cluster analysis of the type recently undertaken for aphasia by Kertesz and Phipps (1977) will be influenced by the anatomical proximity of subsystems as much as by their functional relatedness. Group data may not therefore be able to speak to many aspects of such models.

One way of attempting to avoid this difficulty while keeping groups reason-

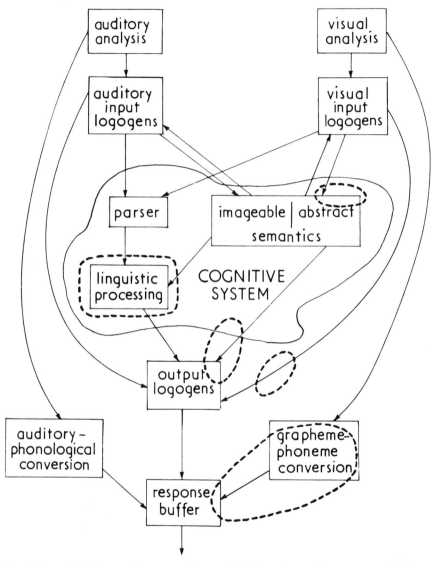

Fig. 1. A typical information-processing model of word repetition and word reading, the logogen model of Morton and Patterson (1980). The hypothesized functional impairments involved in deep dyslexia are indicated by the dotted lines. (From Morton & Patterson, 1980.)

ably large in size is to use broad functional criteria for group selection as is frequently done with the fluent/non-fluent distinction in aphasia. While this distinction is undoubtedly of great clinical importance in the diagnosis of aphasics (Goodglass & Kaplan, 1972; Wagenaar, Snow, & Prins, 1975), it may be correlated with severity (see Mohr, 1976; Kertesz & Phipps, 1977), and its relation to underlying functional sybsystems is most unclear. It shares with the case study method the problem of the uncertainty of the functional adequacy of a particular syndrome classification. However, in the case study approach, this problem has a progressive aspect; it can result in the fractionation of syndromes into "pure" syndromes (see section 3.4). With the group study approach, by contrast, the reification of that classification into a methodological tool and the use of very broad categories to allow reasonable group sizes means that this important progressive aspect of the case study method is lost.

By contrast, information from single case studies should be capable of relating directly to the type of information-processing theory which has become increasingly popular in cognitive psychology. Positive support for the particular fractionation of the total process suggested by the overall model can be obtained from the evidence of dissociations found in individual cases. For instance, from the model depicted in Fig. 1, it should be possible to find patients who can read words which can be transmitted directly to semantics from what Morton and Patterson (in press) call the "visual logogen", but who make many errors in reading nonsense syllables, which require their grapheme-phoneme route. It appears that such patients do exist – the syndrome of phonological alexia (Beauvois & Dérouesné, in press; Dérouesné & Beauvois, 1979; Shallice & Warrington, in press).

Also on this approach, one should be able to predict all the possible types of deficit that can occur within the domain of a theory. Thus, any theory that there is a unitary memory system for verbal material has great difficulty in explaining either the existence of good performance on span tasks and poor performance on supra-span tasks in amnesics (e.g. Drachman & Arbit, 1966) or the complementary specific deficit on span and other tasks requiring only short-term retention in certain patients with posterior left-hemisphere lesions (see Warrington & Shallice, 1969; Saffran & Marin, 1975; Shallice & Warrington, 1977). Nor is this merely a potential programme. In certain areas, such as visual perception, the reading process, and the organization of memory systems, single case studies based on a combination of clinical neuropsychology and cognitive psychology appear to be making considerable advances.

The aim of this paper is not, though, to contrast the group study approach with that of the single case study. It is rather more restricted, namely to assess the single case study method for only one type of use – its potential for providing information relevant to theories of the functional organization of the systems underlying human cognition. Other uses of neuropsychological investigations such as their role in localization of function will not be discussed. Even this more restricted issue gives rise to many questions. Indeed, from the variety of problems to which it gives rise, it might appear that the case study method is so seriously flawed that reliable inferences could not be based on it. However, while this might have seemed a plausible position in, say, 1960, it will be argued that this is now far too pessimistic a view, and that the successes of the methodology since that date far outweigh the undoubted problems to which it is subject.

There is an additional reason for considering the case study methodology in this journal. As a research strategy, the single case approach is far closer in spirit to clinical practice based on the syndrome approach (Walsh, 1978) than are group studies; it also dovetails much more easily with clinical practice. Clinical practice provides the best initial situation for selecting patients appropriate for in-depth investigation. Moreover, the psychometric test performed in clinical assessment are essential baseline tests for any competently conducted case study. Thus, as in medicine in general, the clinician is well placed to undertake or collaborate on single case studies.

In the next two sections, I will discuss the numerous methodological problems of neuropsychological case studies in more detail. By "case studies" are meant studies of individual patients and studies of a very small number of patients who are categorized as exhibiting the same syndrome. Both types of studies present closely related problems. In these sections, I discuss how the methodological problems of the study itself can be diminished, although definitely not eliminated, by the use of appropriate procedures. As I am most familiar with the problems they present, many of the examples are selected from collaborative studies in which I have been involved. In the succeeding section, I will consider how far the inferences to normal function that are drawn from case studies may be strengthened by replication and localization, and by considering the study within a wider neuropsychological context or within the context of other areas of psychology, such as cognitive psychology and physiological psychology.

2. THE PROBLEMS OF NEUROPSYCHOLOGICAL CASE STUDIES: THE INVESTIGATION PROCESS

For clinical reasons, individual case studies vary quite greatly in the detail in which the patient's difficulties can be examined. They may last from a few sessions to a few years. However, they normally pass through four distinct stages:

1. Initially, the selection of the patient as having a pattern of deficits and

intact abilities that are potentially of research interest is made by either a clinician who is part of the research team or one who knows of the interests of the research team.

2. All the baseline tests that are relevant to the syndrome or syndromes which the patient may be exhibiting are performed. These should be quantitative tests for which appropriate norms are available. At the very least they should include all tests necessary for a clinical neuropsychological assessment of the patient, and enable the patient to be assigned to a provisional syndrome category, which may of course be altered as a result of further testing. Much of the problem of the older type of case study lay in the inadequacy with which this stage of the investigation was carried out. Clinical reports lacking quantitative data are of very little use for research purposes; it is impossible for a reader to assess how typical the supposed critical responses were of the patient's behaviour or whether there were crucial associated deficits.

3. Detailed quantitative studies of the specific disabilities of research interest are carried out. At the simplest level, these may involve sketching out the natural history of the syndrome; such studies are normally of value only for novel syndromes. At a more abstract level, they would be orientated towards pinpointing the processing domain(s) or specific functional sub-system(s) that are impaired. At the most complex level, studies can be aimed at questions concerning how these mechanisms operate or how they are organized. On the second, and particularly the third, of these levels the investigation will probably need to involve theories and experimental procedures from other fields, particularly cognitive psychology, psycholinguistics, or physiological psychology.

In the course of these studies, results may well be obtained which show that the provisional diagnosis of the patient was inadequate. In particular, a new deficit may be found which indicates that the deficit of interest arises from a combination of factors, and the study *may* therefore need to be abandoned because it is no longer of research interest.

Studies need to utilize standard experimental methodology, otherwise adequate interpretation of the results may be impossible. In addition, since new tests may well be devised or obtained from experimental psychology practice, many tests may be used for which norms are not available. However, for such tests, when it is unclear whether the patient is performing at or below the normal range, it may well be necessary to compare the patient's performance with that of control subjects matched for age and premorbid intellectual abilities.

4. Finally, the results need to be analyzed statistically and, if of theoretical interest, written up. It is, of course, more convenient if this stage overlaps the previous one, so that further tests can be performed if necessary. However this is frequently not possible for clinical reasons.

The problems that arise in this sort of investigation process are of two main types. First, there are practical problems of the specific methods employed in the second and third stages of the investigation process. Secondly, there are the more abstract problems of how far inferences from the results generalize both to the interpretation of other syndromes and to theories of normal functions. Both of these types of problem can be subdivided into two.

On the practical level, concerning the way the case study is carried out, there are, first, problems of how one establishes the syndrome category into which the patient falls. Then there are the problems of conducting a lengthy experimental investigation in a clinical setting of the disabilities of a patient whose clinical condition and adaptation to his/her disabilities may well not be static.

Questions concerning whether one can generalize from the results of single case studies may also be divided into two types. First, there are the issues concerning the potentially atypical nature of the particular syndrome being investigated. Then there are extremely awkward problems concerning the functional unitariness of the syndrome. Could it, in fact, arise from damage to multiple functional subsystems? In either case, the potential generalizability of the inferences would be much reduced.

2.1 The Specification of the Syndrome

The concept of a 'syndrome' is essential to the usefulness of the case study. Without such a concept, treacherous though it is to apply, there would be no useful meaning to the idea of the replication of findings on any other patient. Results, then, might have considerable curiosity value, but would not be part of a scientific data base.

However, the term "syndrome" has two overlapping meanings. In clinical practice, it is useful and more usual to apply the term to a collection of symptoms that tend to occur together for either functional or anatomical reasons: this means that "partial syndromes" frequently occur (see Kinsbourne, 1971; Strub & Geschwind, 1974; Walsh, 1978). Thus, considering WAIS subtests, a left parietal syndrome would involve deficits on Digit Span, Arithmetic, and Block Design. For the present purposes, though, a syndrome is most usefully given the meaning of a collection of symptoms that occur together because of the presence of a certain type of impairment to a particular functional subsystem or to particular subsystems – "pure" and "mixed" syndromes, respectively. Functional subsystems may be identified with information processing units of the type illustrated in Fig. 1, although it remains possible that any individual unit in a flow diagram may, in turn, be fractionated into more elementary functional subsystems. On this view, there is no such thing as a "partial syndrome", except that "mixed syndromes" can fractionate. I shall use the term in this latter sense.

However one defines a syndrome, in our present state of knowledge, it can only be operationalized as a pattern of associations and dissociations between symptoms. Therefore, it becomes crucial to examine those concepts. Consider, first, the concept of dissociation. In the simplest type of dissociation, performance on one test is in the normal range and is more than n standard deviations better than on the other (n often taken to be 2), where the results of both tests are expressed in terms of age standardized scores. Theoretically, the dissociation should be assessed in terms of the standard deviation of the difference itself $\sqrt{2(1-\rho)}\sigma$. However, since a dissociation would be unlikely to be of theoretical value unless the two tests correlated fairly highly in normal subjects, in interesting situations the expected standard deviation of the difference would be less than that of the tests themselves. (WAIS Verbal subtests, for instance, inter-correlate in the range 0.40 to 0.85 [Wechsler, 1955];) Thus, the simple principle remains appropriate.

Two more complex cases need to be considered. First, in many theoretically interesting dissociations, the better performance is obtained on a task where performance is at ceiling for nearly all normal subjects. This is true for many aphasia tests, such as the Token Test (De Renzi & Vignolo, 1962) and those in the Boston Diagnostic Aphasia Battery (Goodglass & Kaplan, 1972). Secondly, performance on both tests may be below the normal range, with one intuitively far worse than the other. Thus, in deep dyslexia, patients able to read only a very few abstract words, may be able to read most concrete words (Shallice & Warrington, 1975), but still not be able to read all concrete words even at the higher frequency ranges. In such cases, it would be pointless to assess a dissociation in terms of the difference, measured in standard deviations, between the corresponding percentiles of the distribution of normal scores for the two types of word, even if that information were available. Such a measure will be determined by subnormality factors totally irrelevant for the assessment of specific neurological impairment.

In both these cases, the possibility has to be considered that, in the terms of Norman and Bobrow (1975), good performance on one task requires more "resources" of a particular subsystem than the other task does. So an observed dissociation may not actually represent a qualitative difference in the subsystems necessary for adequate performance on the two tasks. It may merely derive from a quantitative difference in the resource requirements of the two tasks. Indeed, this applies even to the first simple case in exceptional circumstances. Thus, a dissociation between the good performance of a particular patient on WAIS Vocabulary and his/her poor performance on another subtest may merely represent the fact that adequate performance on the Vocabulary subtest requires less processing resources.

How does one guard against the problem that different tasks may not only involve different subsystems – their property of theoretical interest – but may also make different resources requirements of a subsystem? At its most basic, how is one to guard against the possibility that the better performed of the two tasks in any of the above cases just has lower resource requirements? The simplest way is to base inferences on a double dissociation (Teuber, 1955; Weiskrantz, 1968; Kinsbourne, 1971), which can be applied to case studies in much the same way as it is applied to group studies. In the simple double dissociation, one patient is significantly better than another on task A and significantly worse on task B. It should be noted, as Kinsbourne (1971) points out, that this does not necessitate that *both* patients have *specific* deficits on different tasks. If one task does require less resources than the other, it may be that only the patient with a deficit on that task has a specific deficit. However, the crucial theoretical point is that the double dissociation does demonstrate that the two tasks make different processing demands on two or more functionally dissociable subsystems.

Are there other methods for dealing with the differential resource requirements of different tasks and, in particular, the potentially lower resource requirement of the better performed of two dissociating tasks? For instance, a double dissociation requires an interaction of the type mentioned above; would any other type of interaction be sufficient? A more complex example occurs when stimuli are used that vary only by being either easy or difficult on one particular dimension – take, for instance, the contrast of script and print in word reading – and patient I is affected by the variable and patient II is not. Can this type of dissociation be confounded by resource factors?

The appropriate method for answering such questions is to consider performance/resource functions as discussed by Norman and Bobrow (1975), and to see whether functions exist that could produce the type of result under consideration from a single subsystem alone. These two cases are considered in the Appendix as examples of how the method would be applied. It is shown that, in both cases, it is possible that the pattern of results might be produced by damage to a single subsystem. However, in the second case, this depends upon making such implausible assumptions about the tasks that, in practice, the method is entirely adequate. Methods other than double dissociation, therefore, do exist for defending a dissociation against the danger of a resource artefact. However, the first case is not always one of them. With that type of interaction, there are real dangers that incorrect conclusions may be drawn. Be that as it may, the same problem would apply to the interpretation of group data. However, in practice, the danger of observed dissociations being attributed to functional separation, when they actually arise from resource artefacts, is not very great if reasonable care is taken in task selection and interpretation. The dissociation remains a very powerful indicator of the existence of functionally separable sub-systems.

The establishment of a theoretically useful association is much more subject to artefacts. It is often advisable to treat an inference based on an association between deficits as tentative, because the association may be caused by contingent damage to anatomically proximal systems. It may, however, be possible to show that the deficits a patient shows on different tasks have similar properties; this greatly increases the likelihood that they derive from the same functional source. An excellent example is the study of classical conduction aphasia in Japanese by Yamadori and Ikumura (1975), where the function relating number of syllables to the probability of a correct naming response was the same whether the stimulus was an auditorily-presented word, a picture, or a Kanji (ideogram) word, thus implicating a common impairment in the same output subsystem for the deficits on the three types of task. Thus, both of the operational defining characteristics of syndromes – dissociations and associations – can be buttressed to greater or less extent against artefacts.

2.2 The Clincial/Experimental Study: Converging Operations

Once it is clear that the syndrome under investigation cannot easily be dismissed as an artefact, the study proper can begin. Different possible flow diagrams of the domain relevant to the syndrome need to be considered and, for any particular flow diagram, hypotheses developed as to which functional subsystem might be impaired so as to produce the syndrome. To test any specific hypothesis, both negative and positive types of investigation need to be carried out. In the negative type of investigation, an attempt is made to demonstrate that *other* subsystems in the overall functional system are operating normally, or at least at a sufficiently good level that they cannot be implicated in the observed deficits; this is, of course, an old established procedure in neuropsychology. Where recent developments in cognitive psychology, physiological psychology or psycholinguistics are more likely to be of use, is in the positive type of investigation. In domains such as reading, where much work has been done on the processes used by normal subjects, one can often develop predictions from the normal literature about what should happen if a particular subsystem were damaged. The possible methods that can be used in such an approach are far too variegated to be discussed. Examples of studies where such importation of techniques or ideas from other areas of psychology has been used include, among others, the following: Wickelgren (1968); Shallice and Warrington (1970); Baddeley and Warrington (1970); Marshall and Newcombe (1973); Weiskrantz, Warrington, Sanders, and Marshall (1974); Warrington (1975); Blumstein, Cooper, Zurif, and Caramazza (1977); Patterson (1978), and Schwartz, Marin, and Saffran (1978). That such "positive" investigations can be carried out in a rigorous way is one important reason why the modern case study is an advance on the older version.

However, an important difficulty with the approach is that the study is not being conducted with randomly selected young subjects in a laboratory for a short interval of time. An individual case study may last for only a few days, but it might last for years. During this period, the neurological and psychological state of the patient may improve, deteriorate or fluctuate. The patient may be easily fatigued during testing sessions, or even have clinical episodes such as seizures. The patient may be tested many times, and even come to rely psychologically on the test sessions. At the very worst, there can be doubt as to whether the patient is hysteric or a malingerer, as in the famous case Schnei of Goldstein and Gelb (1919), (see Bay, Laurenstein, & Cibis, 1949). Then there are problems as to the extent that the observed syndrome represents strategic adaptation by the patient to his or her difficulties, as has been argued by Butterworth (1979) in a case of jargon aphasia. Most important, there may be severe problems due to changes in the neurological or psychological state of the patient.

To a considerable extent, such problems can only be dealt with by clinical as opposed to experimental means. However, some methodological principles do exist. For instance, if the patient's global syndrome changes qualitatively during the recovery process, the results from different phases should not be compared in a theoretical analysis. Secondly, checks should be undertaken, using the more basic tests, that quantitative changes are not occurring, and if they are, allowance must be made for this in comparing results obtained at different times during the investigation. In any case, where a contrast between specific tests is of obvious theoretical relevance, say because they form a key dissociation, they should be performed in the same session using a counter-balanced design.

However, perhaps the most basic principle is that any key test should be repeated on different sessions, if possible well separated in time, to check that the results are not contaminated by day-specific factors such as fatigue. Moreover, any critical inference should, if possible, be checked by different means. As an example, in a recent study of semantic access dyslexia (Warrington & Shallice, 1979) we found to our surprise that the patient who could not read words could judge which of a number of categories they were in (e.g., animal, plant, etc.) well above chance and, in some cases, nearly perfectly. This contrast provided the dissociation which initiated our interest in the patient. The obvious possibility was that this pattern of performance arose from a naming problem possibly specific to the written word. However, we used a number of different experimental procedures to show that this explanation could not account for the dissociation. Thus, the patient could not mime the meanings of the words, although he could do so for auditorily presented words; he could not perform a lexical decision task satisfactorily or match upper and lower case words accurately or do picture-name matching as well with visual as with auditory input. For any of these findings, some alternative explanation could be given. Thus, for the mime dissociation, a highly specific disconnection might have prevented information passing from visual-verbal semantic systems to action control systems. Alternatively, some day-specific factor might have affected this result. However, the combination of results makes the naming hypothesis untenable. This type of procedure is closely related to the converging operations of Garner, Hake, and Eriksen (1956) in experimental psychology, and it can provide strong support for the existence of a particular sort of deficit, even though only one patient is being studied.

3. PROBLEMS OF NEUROPSYCHOLOGICAL CASE STUDIES: GENERALIZATION FROM RESULTS

Even if those aspects of the study that I have discussed so far have been correctly carried out, it may be misleading to generalize from the deficit of the patient being studied to the performance of other patients or of normal subjects. The patient may be, in some way, premorbidly atypical. Crucial in this respect is how the patient is initially selected, which may be because of the observation of an intuitively interesting dissociation, the known presence of an interesting lesion site, or the appearance of a theoretically interesting syndrome. Yet this selection procedure is an unsystematic and highly complex process that is inherently non-random. Three sorts of selection artefact appear possible.

3.1 Statistical Artefacts
In a large number of studies, both the criterion for initial selection and a key part of the eventual results consist of dissociations between performance on one set of tests and those of another set. As the same factors that operate in subject selection form a key element of the theoretical conclusions, a simple statistical artefact appears possible. If we examine the performance of a population of normal subjects on the two tests, there will be a finite probability of the performance of a subject differing by a certain number of standard deviations on the two tasks. Field (1960) has, for instance, produced tables of the "Abnormality of a Discrepancy" probability for pairs of WAIS subtests. Could it not be then that the procedure of selection by dissociation is at least in part confounded by sampling the extreme end of this discrepancy distribution in the normal population? Surely one would not wish to infer that two tests involved different subsystems just because they did not correlate with $p = 1.0$.

In fact this is one of the least important of the artefacts to which the case study method may be liable. To take a simple statistical view, one tends not to be interested in dissociations between tasks if they do not correlate highly in the normal population. Consider the contrast between verbal and performance tasks or between memory and intellectual tasks. We know such pairs of tasks dissociate neuropsychologically. Yet, for tasks which do correlate highly, the standard deviation of the expected Discrepancy in the normal population ($\sqrt{2(1-\rho)}\sigma$) is, as pointed out earlier, small compared with σ. Hence, the rate of such Discrepancies occurring in the normal population is low.

More crucially, many dissociations are so extreme that one would never observe them except in clinical populations. Even where this is not the case, there will often be clinical evidence that the specific impairment arose as a result of a disease process as opposed to, say, a developmental difficulty; thus it is not to be explained as a statistical artefact alone. Finally, if on replication a similar lesion site is observed, this again would be incompatible with the statistical artefact approach. Thus, this sort of selection artefact does not seem a strong reason not to generalize from the basic dissociations found in individual cases.

A related possibility is that there is a qualitative but not a quantitative difference between the way that the cognitive system of the patient was organized pre-morbidly and that of the majority of the population. This is a totally hypothetical possibility. If one leaves aside issues related to handedness and laterality, there are no cognitive syndromes known to me which are plausibly explained in this way. Yet of the potential artefacts of the case study method these are the ones that group studies best guard against!

Where premorbid individual differences in the population may be somewhat more important is in considering the relative pattern of obtained impairments across patients. Thus, from the earlier argument on dissociations it could be concluded that the relative sparing of concrete words by comparison to abstract in deep (or phonemic) dyslexia could only be a reliable indicant of dissociable subsystems mediating the comprehension of abstract and concrete words if a complementary double dissociation syndrome exists (Shallice & Warrington, in press). A patient of this type who reads abstract words better than concrete ones, has indeed been studied by Warrington (in preparation). It could, however, be argued that the relative strengths of the semantic organizations of words of different degrees of abstractness varied across normal subjects depending upon their reading history. Such a factor *might* be a confounding variable in this double dissociation, although it seems very unlikely that it could be responsible for the gross qualitative differences that are observed between patients.

3.2 The Problem of Neurological Reorganization
It is frequently argued by experimental psychologists that extrapolation from neuropsychological data is of uncertain validity (e.g., Postman, 1975). Such arguments are normally premised on the claimed atypical reorganization of cortical mechanisms that might arise after neurological disease.

There is, indeed, one situation where such atypical neural organization may well prevent valid generalizations being made to normal subjects, namely where the crucial lesion whose effects are being investigated occurs in adulthood, but there had been neurological disease since childhood. For instance, Gazzaniga, Le Doux, and Wilson (1977) have argued that most inferences from split-brain patients concerning right-hemisphere language functioning in the normal brain are made dubious by the existence of early left temporal lesions in the most studied split-brain patients, NG and LB.

Yet are such considerations only relevant in generalizing from the study of patients with early neurological disease? Given the different effect of multiple stage and single stage lesions in animals (e.g., Finger, Walbran & Stein [1973]) it could be argued that inferences from the effects of all lesions where the onset is not extremely rapid are similarly vitiated. This would mean excluding nearly all tumour cases and stroke cases in which there were any signs of prior vascular disease.

In fact this is far too extreme a conclusion. The inferences that are made dubious in the split-brain case concern questions of the *extent* to which particular language functions are represented in the right hemisphere and, as Coltheart (in press b) has pointed out, only the positive claims are affected. Those inferences concerned with the more basic issue of functional separation, the main type derived from dissociations, are much less affected by the preceding sort of argument.

Let us assume that a dissociation be observed in a patient which, by arguments such as those discussed in section 2.1, it is reasonable to consider occurs because of damage to a specific subsystem that only one of the tasks uses. Could the results in fact be explained by assuming that, in normal subjects, a common subsystem operates for both tasks, but neurological reorganization accounts for the results in the patient?

Reorganization could result in both tasks being undertaken by a subsystem or two subsystems functionally distinct from the original subsystem and having different properties from it. The dissociation would then reflect the properties of those substitute subsystems rather than the one originally used to perform the task. A possible example of such a situation will be discussed in the next section. However, in general it is not at all clear what such substitute subsystems would consist of, except possibly for systems in the other hemisphere. In any case, with such an explanation it would be extremely difficult to account for normal performance on one of the two tasks of the dissociation, given that reduced resource explanations have been excluded. Such a situation would require the implausible assumption of the perfect substitution of one subsystem for another. Furthermore, it should be noted that objections of this sort could be raised against group studies just as much as against single case studies.

3.3 Atypical Lateralization

A special case of either of the previous artefacts that deserves separate discussion is the problem of atypical lateralization of function. From the statistical point of view, if patients varied premorbidly in their lateralization, then for most syndromes specific deficits would tend to be observed only from the more lateralized patients having unilateral lesions. The less lateralized patients would presumably show less deficits. If one, however, considers particular syndromes, this generalization may not hold. Thus, optic aphasia most plausibly held to occur for failures of transmission *within the left hemisphere* from object meaning to verbal systems (Lhermitte & Beauvois, 1973), as associative object agnosia occurs more with left than right unilateral lesions (De Renzi, Scotti, & Spinnler, 1969; Hecaen et al., 1974; Warrington & Taylor, 1978) which would imply that object semantic categorization systems are more lateralized to the left hemisphere. However, if the degree of lateralization of this function varied, then the syndrome could also occur in patients with splenium lesions and right homonymous hemianopias – the classical explanation (e.g. Freund, 1889; Spreen, Benton, & van Allen, 1966). In this case, though, the preservation of the recognition aspect of object aphasia would be occurring in the right hemisphere of patients with less lateralization of the function. For any particular syndrome the amount of lateralization present in patients being studied as single cases is likely to be different from the average. Yet, if one is concerned with aspects of the functional organization of the human information-processing system, other than lateralization, this apparent artefact would in fact be a virtue of the single case methodology. Only in the more lateralized patients (or alternatively in patients with a particular degree of lateralization), would the functional architecture declare itself in the relevant symptoms. In a group study of unilateral cases, patients with other degrees of lateralization would just add noise. It should also be borne in mind that, if there are major differences in amount of lateralization among right-handers who do not have crossed dominance, this remains to be shown.

The above argument presupposes that a dissociation is occurring and that the critical components of the task on which the better performance is occurring are still being carried out by the hemisphere which originally performed them. If this latter condition is not satisfied and these components of the task are being carried out by the other hemisphere, a situation similar to that discussed in the previous section could apply. The dissociation, then, may in no way reflect normal functioning.

A syndrome where such a possibility has been suggested is that of deep (or phonemic) dyslexia (Marshall & Newcombe, 1966) discussed earlier. This syndrome has been defined by a wide variety of characteristics concerning both the stimuli that patients can and cannot read and the types of errors they make (Coltheart, in press a; Shallice & Warrington, in press). Some authors have argued that this syndrome reflects reliance on right hemisphere reading systems instead of left (Marcel & Patterson, 1978; Coltheart, in press b; Saffran, Bogyo, Schwartz, & Marin, in press). In this case, the observed dissociation between concrete and abstract words could reflect the organization of the compensatory right-hemisphere systems and not the normal reading process at all. In fact in this case the existence of the patient, mentioned earlier, with a specific deficit in reading concrete words (Warrington, in preparation) presents a serious empirical problem for this conclusion, since a double dissociation could not result unless the original subsystems dissociated in the left hemisphere.

As in the previous section, it seems unreasonable to assume that one function of a subsystem should be capable of perfect compensation by the other hemisphere but another should not if the two functions of the subsystem do not differ in their resource requirements. Thus, a dissociation where one task is performed at normal level seems unlikely to be subject to this artefact.

To make this argument more concrete, consider the position of Shallice and Butterworth (1977) that span performance does not depend critically on the stores involved in speech production. This position was derived from the existence of normal spontaneous speech in a patient with severe short-term storage deficit. The normality of her spontaneous speech was inferred from a quantitative comparison of error rates and amount of pausing with those of normal controls. This patient had had a very slow growing meningioma removed at age 24. It might therefore be argued that speech had relateralized in the right hemisphere, and indeed there was a sizable left-ear advantage in dichotic listening. However, even if this were the case, the original inference would still be valid. For, if span performance *were* to depend upon stores whose basic function was to mediate speech production, then *either* span should have been normal because the store relateralized perfectly *or* spontaneous speech should have been abnormal because the store failed to relateralize perfectly. And, of course, the theoretical interest derives from the fact that neither of these happened. Thus, the possibility of a change of lateralization does not alter the functional argument.

Finally, if the type of complex compensatory hypothesis discussed earlier were valid, it is unlikely that it would be satisfactorily demonstrated other than through the comparison of results of single case studies. For instance, if the occurrence of compensation varies across patients, as seems possible (e.g., Czopf, 1972), two qualitatively different states would be being averaged in group studies making them even more difficult to interpret. So, even if this were so, single-case studies would still be crucial.

3.4 Damage to Multiple Functional Systems
Of all the criticisms that can be made of neuropsychological case studies, perhaps the most serious is that the existence of a syndrome does not necessitate that only a single functional subsystem has been damaged. This criticism has been made at two sorts of levels. At the more simple level, it has been argued that certain syndromes of great theoretical interest are in fact merely concatenations of more basic deficits. At the more complex level, it has been argued that the symptoms that together form a syndrome can appear in isolation, thus the syndrome does not reflect a single underlying functional disorder.

A standard example of the first sort of argument is that put forward by Bay

(1953) who argued that, in claimed cases of agnosia, the perceptual deficits arise from a combination of visual deficits and dementia (see also Bender & Feldman, 1972). For such criticisms to be valid, the investigation being assessed must not have established a satisfactory dissociation between performance on the critical tasks and more basic tasks. To show such a dissociation it is, of course, necessary to perform appropriate quantitative background tests. These have now been performed both in individual case studies and in group studies (see Hecaen and Albert [1978] for a review and, for example, the case studies of Rubens and Benson [1971] and Taylor and Warrington [1971]). However, while Bay's criticisms of agnosia have been refuted, his general argument that quantitative background tests are crucial is well taken. Indeed, as the case study methodology becomes increasingly successful, so the set of basic syndromes will increase in number and complexity and the number of background tests it is necessary to perform will increase. While still a potentially valid criticism of particular case studies, this is no longer a substantive objection to the methodology in general.

A much more interesting objection to the syndrome approach concerns the distinction that needs to be drawn between two deficits occurring in a patient due to damage to a common functional subsystem and "associated deficits" that arise due to the impairment of more than one functional subsystem. The presence of associated deficits, if they are treated as such, need in no way invalidate theoretical inferences from a case study, given that the deficit has no effect on performance of theoretically relevant tasks. However, the treatment of an associated deficit as though it were a functional association will almost inevitably lead to incorrect theoretical conclusions. Yet controversy about the status of particular combinations of symptoms occurs repeatedly in neuropsychology.

A classic example is that of the Gerstmann syndrome (Benton, 1961; Heimburger, Demeyer, & Reitan, 1964; Poeck & Orgass, 1966, 1975; Kinsbourne, 1971; Strub & Geschwind, 1974; Geschwind & Strub, 1975). In response to the findings of Benton, of Heimburger, Demeyer and Reitan and of Poeck and Orgass that the elements of the syndrome occur as frequently in combination with other symptoms as with each other, it is often argued that, if the clinical meaning of "syndrome" is used, the syndrome is a useful localizing sign (e.g., Geschwind & Strub, 1975). However, for theoretical uses, it can only be justified as a functional unit if, on all the occasions when a partial Gerstmann syndrome occurs, the functional origin of the observed symptoms is different from when they occur in the setting of the syndrome. As far as I know, no one has ever attempted to substantiate such a strong claim. One additional objection, related to arguments put forward by Kinsbourne (1971), is that measurement of the elements of the Gerstmann syndrome is normally too crude for the apparent absence of an element to be treated as normal performance; thus, an observed partial Gerstmann syndrome might not necessarily indicate that fractionation of the syndrome is occurring.

However, at the very least, the existence of partial Gerstmann syndromes must make the theoretical value of the Gerstmann syndrome highly suspect.

Although one cannot ever be sure that a syndrome is functionally homogeneous, this does not invalidate the syndrome approach, for two separate reasons. First, one can still draw valid theoretical inferences from the properties of "mixed syndromes". Thus, the deep (or phonemic) dyslexic syndrome is now considered by one school of theorists to be a mixed syndrome (see Morton & Patterson, in press; Shallice & Warrington, in press). Yet it is accepted that one element of the syndrome is that the phonological means of reading is not operative in such patients, and it has been shown by Saffran and Marin (1977) that the reading of such patients is very little affected by the visual structure of presented words (such as, vertically instead of horizontally, or with plus signs between adjacent letters). This result provides strong evidence for the "direct route" method of reading being extremely flexible in the type of visual information it can utilize. Moreover, as Saffran (personal communication) points out, if one makes the "worst possible" assumption that reading in deep dyslexia involves an entirely different system from the normal, it is hardly likely that this new mechanism is more flexible than the normal one.

Secondly, and somewhat surprisingly, the problem of mixed syndromes highlights the strength of the individual case study methodology. From a negative point of view, if in single case studies one cannot eliminate the problem of mixed syndromes, how much more is this a difficulty for group studies? In group studies, one must inevitably work with results that are averages of the performance of patients who nearly all have mixed syndromes. Thus, in a recent review of the amnesia literature, Baddeley (note 1) argues that most of the frequent empirical disagreements in the field stem from a difference in methodology, particularly between workers in Boston and those in Britain. Thus, the Boston methodology in the spirit of the group study approach is to study a population of "reasonably intact Korsakoff patients", the primary defining characteristic being aetiology. The British method, in the spirit of the case study approach, has been to ignore aetiology and to attempt to study pure amnesia: namely, to make the defining characteristic of the patient studied the total absence on clinical neuropsychological testing of any evidence of impaired intellectual skills in the context of a severe memory deficit. This means that only a very small number of patients can be studied. Baddeley makes a cogent case that, if one is concerned with functional organization, the latter approach is much more reliable. More positively, the case study approach is inherently progressive. If a patient is observed with less than the defining number of deficits for a syndrome, then the syndrome as a functional entity fractionates into more specific syndromes. The only alternative is to show that the observed deficits arise from different causes in the two cases, which is unlikely to be the case if the deficit can be identified as derived from an impaired internal process rather than just being an observed decrement on a particular test. However, these more specific syndromes, in their turn, become candidates for reflecting an impairment of a basic functional subsystem.

As an example of the fractionation of a previously accepted syndrome, consider the case of simultanagnosia (Wolpert, 1924; Kinsbourne & Warrington, 1962) in which there are three seemingly related types of impairment – letter-by-letter reading, the inability to perceive a whole visual scene, and a reliable tachistoscopic span of no more than one item. In fact the first symptom can occur in the absence of the other two (Warrington & Shallice, in press), and the first and third in absence of the second (Warrington & Shallice, unpublished). Given that the functional origins of the first and third symptoms do not differ between these cases and the original simultanagnosia cases, and there is no reason to believe that they do, then the only way to maintain the functional unity of the syndrome is by means of a varying resource argument. Yet the reading performance of one of the later patients with a single symptom (JDC) was, if anything, worse than those of the earlier patients, so a varying resource argument is not plausible. Thus, it would appear that the syndrome is a mixed syndrome containing three separate functional deficits.

Numerous syndromes appear to be fractionating in this way. Thus, in the aphasias, arguments have been put forward for fractionation of all of Broca's aphasia (Lecours & Lhermitte, 1976), Wernicke's aphasia (Hier & Mohr, 1977) and conduction aphasia (Shallice & Warrington, 1977). In the dyslexias, the old classification in terms of the dysgraphias now seems to be based on associated deficits (Warrington & Shallice, 1979), and even those syndromes in the modern classification introduced by Marshall and Newcombe (1973) are seen to fractionate (Beauvois & Dérouesné, 1979; Dérouesné & Beauvois, 1979; Shallice & Warrington, in press). Nor should this be surprising. If one takes a flow diagram, such as that shown in Fig. 1, every combination of system and transmission pathway could correspond to a potentially occurring disorder. This would provide roughly 30 "pure" syndromes in this domain alone, even if one makes the probable oversimplification of assuming that only one type of deficit can occur as a result of damage to a particular system or transmission pathway. So the number of pure syndromes, even for a very restricted domain, would be expected to be extremely large. And, given the complexity of the domain, the fractionation and isolation afforded by this method are extremely valuable.

4. CORROBORATION OF THE INFERENCES

4.1 Replication and Neurology

In the preceding section, I argued that single case methodology is faced with a number of different types of potential problems, some of which are potentially extremely complicated. Moreover, from the immediately preceding argument, it can be concluded that, if the methodology is successful, the complexity of applying it will arise accordingly. In what ways, then, can the strength of the inferences being made be increased?

The traditional method of strengthening inferences used in neuropsychology has been by replication of the findings on other patients and by the use of neurological correlation. Replication is of great help in reducing the danger of artefacts of the type discussed in section 2.2, namely those of the length and nature of the unusual clinical/experimental procedure used. A psychological adaptation of the patient would, for instance, be expected to be specific to the patient and to the particular testing circumstances. As far as other problems related to normal cognition are concerned, replication has limited value. The selection procedure is further complicated by the social process that arises when a new syndrome is observed. Other investigators will look for it, and so the chance of its being observed again will be increased. However, this does not create any special problems, as selection artefacts of a statistical type are not a major source of error.

The relevance of establishing the lesion site is, if anything, even more limited as regards guarding against the potential artefacts discussed previously. It is, of course, of great interest in its own right. One value for psychological inferences is that, if the same lesion site is found for patients with a common syndrome, any claim that the syndrome arises as a statistical artefact becomes exceedingly implausible. Another is that knowledge of the lesion site may well be relevant if any extrapolation from animal experimentation is being considered. However, these are somewhat limited advantages.

4.2 Parallel Inferences from Different Disciplines

In sections 2 and 3, a number of different possible problems that might arise in using case study information for making more general inferences were considered. However, the arguments against the generalizability of case study inferences were all hypothetical. Whether these potential artefacts cripple the method or are, at worst, minor irritants producing problems in the analysis of the occasional syndrome is an empirical question.

There are two ways in which one could show that the methods do allow for generalization. First, one should be able to assess the validity of syndromes by their relation to other syndromes. Assuming the appropriateness of information processing models of the type illustrated in Fig. 1, one should be able to explain not just single syndromes, but the overall pattern of syndromes that exist in a particular domain. This was, of course, the approach of the diagram-makers and, indeed, their theories (e.g., Lichtheim, 1885) can be viewed as the first information-processing models. This overall pattern approach is only just becoming fashionable again, and it is beginning to appear as though it can be effective in particular domains – the central acquired dyslexias are one example (see Marshall & Newcombe, 1973; Shallice & Warrington, in press). It is too early to assess this approach in such a complex domain.

However, at a simple level, if an intuitively surprising dissociation is discovered within a particular domain and a functional separation between two systems inferred, then the existence of the complementary dissociation is not merely a way of avoiding resource artefact arguments. Rather, on the overall approach, it must be positively predicted that a complementary dissociation should be observable, unless the two systems are in series. Thus, the isolation of a specific deficit of short-term memory almost exactly complementing the pattern of deficit and intact abilities found in pure amnesia, for instance, in free recall tasks (Baddeley & Warrington, 1970; Shallice & Warrington, 1970) is positive evidence that the case study method is working.

The more general way, though, is to compare the inferences that have been made from single case studies with those derived from other areas of psychology, particularly cognitive psychology and physiological psychology. If common inferences are being obtained from very different approaches, this greatly strengthens the plausibility of the single case approach. This indeed appears to be happening.

Consider, for instance, the relation between information-processing studies of reading and the acquired dyslexias. There is now strong support from individual case studies that two reading routes exist. This was argued by Marshall and Newcombe (1973) from the complementary properties of the syndromes, deep and surface dyslexia. From experimental psychology, too, there is much evidence that two routes exist (e.g., Bradshaw, 1975; Baron, 1976).

Moreover, from both fields there is evidence that the direct route to the semantic system can operate for nearly all words without the assistance of the phonological route. In neuropsychology, a syndrome – phonological alexia – exists in which reading of non-words, which depends upon the phonological route, is grossly impaired but the reading of words can be remarkably spared (Beauvois & Dérouesné, 1979); Shallice & Warrington, in press). From experimental psychology, too, there is evidence that individual words are normally read for meaning by the direct route. Manipulations which would be expected to influence the speed of phonological reading have no effect on reading for meaning (Frederiksen & Kroll, 1976; Green & Shallice, 1976; Coltheart, in press c).

Secondly, Weiskrantz (1977) has shown that, in two distinct areas, the use of the case study approach has recently removed certain paradoxes arising from the apparently contrasting abilities of monkeys and humans. Moreover, the deductions one would make from the case studies fit very neatly those derived from physiological psychology. Thus, the properties of 'blindsight' (Weiskrantz et al., 1974; Pöppel, Held, & Frost, 1973; Perenin, 1978; Perenin & Jeannerod, 1978), in which a patient who had a large area of the right occipital lobe removed was able to reach to spots of light that he could not "see", complement beautifully those of "vision" in monkeys with bilateral occipital lobe removal (e.g. Humphrey, 1970). For instance, in neither case could complex patterns be recognized, but simple discriminations depending, say, on intensity could be made. Weiskrantz's other example was of the preserved long-term memory abilities of "pure" amnesic patients, basically those abilities unconnected with episodic memory, which map onto the preserved learning abilities of monkeys with hippocampal lesions.

These are not the only areas in which inferences from single case studies produce similar conclusions to those from experimental psychology. Ratcliff and Cowey (1979) have described correspondences between findings in physiological psychology and neuropsychological syndromes in the area of visual sensation. Within long-term memory itself, Warrington (1975) has shown that Tulving's (1972) distinction between episodic and semantic memory maps on to syndromes. Within short-term memory, I have argued for detailed correspondences between inferences from cognitive psychology and from neuropsychological syndromes (Shallice, 1979). Finally, in considering output speech systems, different linguistic levels of speech production correspond to different types of aphasic syndromes (see, e.g., Lecours & Lhermitte, 1976).

The existence of these converging inferences about normal function strongly support the reliability of the case study method. It would appear that the problems to which the case study method is liable are not, in general, too critical. However, even if these correspondences did not exist, the case study approach would still merit increased usage. In its more modern quantitative form, in which a large number of experimental procedures from other areas of psychology are applied to understand the deficits of a single patient, it is barely 15 years old. Yet, if one considers syndromes such as pure amnesia, the agnosias, blindsight, the short-term memory syndrome, the varieties of acquired dyslexic syndromes now described, and of other language disorders such as specific deficits of the lexical system (e.g., Schwartz et al., 1978), the dissociations obtained are extremely surprising, both intuitively and also often in terms of existing theory. Moreover, it seems most implausible that any of the "simple" artefacts considered in section 2 could account for such syndromes. Thus, whatever explanations are eventually required to account for them, it seems inconceivable that much will not be learned about brain organization in the process. In addition, if the arguments based on Fig. 1 are correct, many further pure syndromes remain to be isolated and explored.

APPENDIX

Performance on any given cognitive task will depend upon the operation of many subsystems. If, however, we consider how performance depends upon a particular critical subsystem, the effectiveness of functioning of that subsystem may be influenced by a number of psychological variables, such as the degree of effort applied by the subject and the demands made by any subsidiary task that is simultaneously utilizing the subsystem. Norman and Bobrow (1975), presupposing that other factors remained constant, argued that the influence of such variables on the subsystem and hence on the performance of the primary task could be usefully characterized in terms of their effect on the "resources" available to the subsystem: the greater the amount of resources available, the better the performance. They argue that the way performance on a particular task depends upon a given subsystem is a function expressible as a performance/resource curve.

This concept of a continuously varying "resource" level can be simply extended to include the effects of neurological or physiological variables. For instance, the time course of dementia can be considered in terms of a reduction in resource levels of cognitive subsystems.

The two examples discussed in section 2.1 can be assessed within this framework. First, consider an interaction which does not take the form of a double dissociation. Can deficits to a single system produce such a pattern of results? Fig. 2 shows hypothetical performance/resource functions in which patient I does significantly better on task A than task B and patient II does significantly better on task B than A. Yet on both tasks patient I performs better than patient II. It is clear that such an interaction does not necessarily

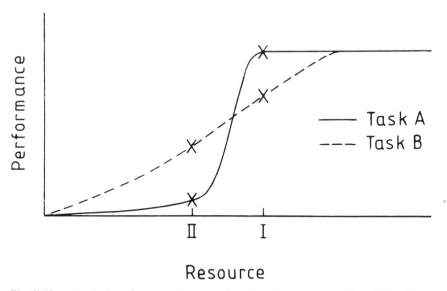

Fig. 2. Hypothetical performance/resource functions for two tasks (A and B) utilizing the same subsystem showing how the results of two patients I and II with different levels of resource, can give rise to an interaction.

mean that two systems are differentially impaired in the two patients and differentially involved in the two tasks. For it is possible that the two tasks involve different performance/resource functions and the two patients merely have different levels of resource. Moreover, to account for some other interactions, the performance/resource functions need not even have to intersect.

Note that this is a quite different situation from the classical double dissociation. Performance/resource functions can be assumed to be continuous monotonically non-decreasing, and determinate (i.e., there are no vertical sections). Hence, in the classical situation, if patient I does better than patient II on task A, then $R(I) > R(II)$ where $R(I)$ is the amount of resource available to patient I. If one assumes the same system is involved for task B, then for it $R(II) > R(I)$ which leads to a contradiction.

In the particular interaction discussed earlier, one has to make relatively specific assumptions about the form of the pair of performance/resource functions to account for the pattern of results assuming only one subsystem to be impaired. This makes a conclusion that two subsystems are involved unlikely to be invalid. A similar conclusion can be obtained from the second more complex example of stimuli being used which vary only by being either easy (E) or difficult (D) on one particular dimension such as the contrast of script and print in word reading – and patient I is affected by the variable, patient II is not, and neither patients' performance is at floor or ceiling. I will assume, for simplicity, that increases in the variable stress only one subsystem (but the argument is not dependent on this assumption). For this subsystem an increase in the variable would mean that a greater amount of resource (R) is required to obtain the same level of performance (P).

Therefore $P_E(R) = P_D(R + L)$, where L is a non-zero positive function of R. In other words, the performance/resource curves for the difficult and easy tasks would be distinct except at floor and ceiling levels. Thus the patient whose deficit was affected by the variable would have damage to the subsystem, and the patient whose deficit is not so affected would have damage to another subsystem.

An exception to this generalization is where the performance/resource function has a flat, non-ceiling, non-floor section, such as that shown in Fig. 3. In this case, for certain levels of resource, there would be no difference between performance on the easy and difficult conditions, at other levels of resource a difference will exist. However, a function like that shown in Fig. 3 would be most atypical for a psychological process; for instance it would be expected for such a function that reaction time for this process would be bimodally distributed. (It is also possible to develop examples where $L = 0$ for certain ranges of R, but these too are very artificial). Therefore this type of inference appears to be less likely to be confounded by resource artefacts, than does a simple dissociation.

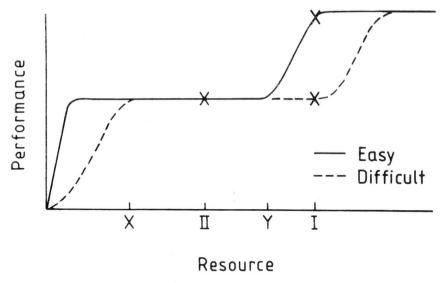

Fig. 3. Hypothetical performance/resource functions with a plateau for easy (E) and difficult (D) tasks. For patients with levels of the resource between X and Y, task difficulty would not affect performance. Yet performance of the task is dependent on the amount of resource available in this subsystem.

REFERENCE NOTE

1. Baddeley, A. D. Amnesia: A minimal model and an interpretation. In L. S. Cermak (Ed.) *Proceedings of the Lake Morey Amnesia Conference*. Hillsdale, N.J.: Erlbaum, in press.

REFERENCES

Baddeley, A. D., & Warrington, E. K. Amnesia and the distinction between long and short-term memory. *Journal of Verbal Learning and Verbal Behavior*, 1970, *9*, 176–189.

Baron, J. Mechanisms for pronouncing printed words: Use and acquisition. In D. Laberge and S. J. Samuels (Eds.), *Basic processes in Reading: Perception and comprehension*. Potomac, Maryland: Erlbaum, 1976.

Bay, E. Disturbances of visual perception and their examination. *Brain*, 1953, *76*, 515–551.

Bay, E., Laurenstein, O., & Cibus, P. Ein Beitrag zur Frage der Seelenblindheit. *Psychiatrie, Neurologie und Medizinische Psychologie*, 1949, *3*, 73–91.

Beauvois, M. F., & Dérouesné, J. Phonological alexia – three dissociations. *Journal of Neurology, Neurosurgery & Psychiatry*, 1979, *42*, 1115–1124.

Bender, M. B., & Feldman, M. The so-called "visual agnosias". *Brain*, 1972, *95*, 173–186.

Benton, A. L. The fiction of the "Gerstmann syndrome". *Journal of Neurology, Neurosurgery & Psychiatry*, 1961, *24*, 176–181.

Blumstein, S. E., Cooper, W. E., Zurif, E. B. & Caramazza, A. The perception and production of voice-onset time in aphasia. *Neuropsychologia*, 1977, *15*, 371–384.

Bradshaw, J. L. Three interrelated problems in reading: A review. *Memory and Cognition*, 1975, *3*, 123–134.

Butterworth, B. Hesitation and the production of verbal paraphasias and neologisms in jargon aphasia. *Brain and Language*, 1979, *8*, 133–161.

Coltheart, M. Deep dyslexia: A review of the syndrome. In M. Coltheart, K. Patterson, & J. Marshall (Eds.), *Deep dyslexia*. London: Routledge, in press.

Colheart, M. Deep dyslexia: a right hemisphere hypothesis. In M. Coltheart, K. Patterson, & J. Marshall (Eds.) *Deep dyslexia*, London: Routledge, in press.

Coltheart, M. Reading, phonological encoding and deep dyslexia. In M. Coltheart, K. Patterson, & J. Marshall (Eds.), *Deep dyslexia*. London: Routledge, in press.

Czopf, J. Über die Rolle der nicht dominanten Hemisphäre in der Restitution der Sprache der Aphasischen. *Archiv für Psychiatrie und Nervenkrankheiten*, 1972, *216*, 162–171.

De Renzi, E., Scotti, G., & Spinnler, H. Perceptual and associative disorders of visual recognition. *Neurology*, 1969, *19*, 634–642.

De Renzi, E., & Vignolo, L. A. The Token Test: A sensitive test to detect receptive disturbances in aphasics. *Brain*, 1962, *85*, 665–678.

Dérouesné, J., & Beauvois, M–F. Phonological processing in reading: data from alexia. *Journal of Neurology, Neurosurgery and Psychiatry*, 1979, *42*, 1125–1132.

Drachman, D. A., & Arbit, J. Memory and the hippocampal complex. *Archives of Neurology*, 1966, *15*, 52–61.

Field, J. G. Two types of tables for use with Wechsler's Intelligence Scales. *Journal of Clinical Psychology*, 1960, *16*, 3–6.

Finger, S., Walbran, B., & Stein, D. G. Brain damage and behavioural recovery: Serial lesion phenomena. *Brain Research*, 1973, *63*, 1–18.

Frederiksen, J. R., & Kroll, J. F. Spelling and sound: Approaches to the internal lexicon. *Journal of Experimental Psychology: Human Perception and Performance*, 1976, *2*, 361–379.

Freund, D. C. Über optische Aphasie und Seelenblindheit. *Archiv für Psychiatrie und Nervenkrankheiten*, 1889, *20*, 276–297.

Garner, W. R., Hake, H. W., & Eriksen, C. W. Operationism and the concept of perception. *Psychological Review*, 1956, *63*, 149–159.

Gazzaniga, M. S., Le Doux, J. E., & Wilson, D. H. Language, praxis and the right hemisphere: Clues to some mechanisms of consciousness. *Neurology*, 1977, *27*, 1144–1147.

Geschwind, N., & Strub, R. Gerstmann syndrome without aphasia: A reply to Poeck and Orgass. *Cortex*, 1975, *11*, 296–298.

Goldstein, K., & Gelb, A. Psychologische Analysen hirnpathologischer Fälle auf grund von Untersuchungen Hirnverletzer. *Zeitschrift für die gesamte Neurologie und Psychiatrie*, 1918, *41*, 1–142.

Goodglass, H., & Kaplan, E. *Assessment of aphasia and related disorders*, Philadelphia: Lea and Febiger, 1972.

Green, D. W., & Shallice, T. Direct visual access in reading for meaning. *Memory and Cognition*, 1976, *4*, 753–758.

Head, H. *Aphasia and kindred disorders of speech*. Cambridge: Cambridge University Press, 1926.

Hécaen, H., & Albert, M. L. *Human neuropsychology*, New York: Wiley, 1978.

Hécaen, H., Goldblum, M. C., Masure, M. C., & Ramiers, A. M. Une nouvelle observation d'agnosie d'object. Déficit de l'association, ou de la categorisation specifique de la modalité visuelle. *Neuropsychologie*, 1974, *12*, 447–464.

Heimburger, R. F., Demeyer, W., & Reitan, R. M. Implications of Gerstmann's syndrome. *Journal of Neurology, Neurosurgery & Psychiatry*, 1964, *27*, 52–57.

Hier, D. B. & Mohr, J. P. Incongruous oral and written naming. *Brain & Language* 1977, *4*, 115–126.

Humphrey, N. K. What the frog's eye tells to the monkey's brain. *Brain Behavior & Evolution*, 1970, *2*, 324–337.

Kertesz, A., & Phipps, J. B. Numerical taxonomy of aphasia. *Brain and Language*, 1977, *4*, 1–10.

Kinsbourne, M. Cognitive deficit: Experimental analysis. In J. L. McGaugh (ed.) *Psychobiology*, New York: Academic Press, 1971.

Kinsbourne, M. & Warrington, E. K. A disorder of simultaneous form perception. *Brain*, 1962, *85*, 461–486.

Lecours, A. R., & Lhermitte, E. The "pure form" of the phonetic disintegration syndrome (pure anarthria): Anatomo-clinical report of a historical case. *Brain and Language*, 1976, *3*, 88–113.

Lhermitte, E., & Beauvois, M. F. A visual-speech disconnexion syndrome – Report of a case with optic aphasia, agnostic alexia and colour agnosia. *Brain*, 1973, *96*, 695–714.

Lichtheim, L. On aphasia. *Brain*, 1885, *7*, 433–484.

Marcel, A. J., & Patterson, K. E. Word recognition and production reciprocity in clinical and normal studies. In J. Requin (Ed.), *Attention and Performance VII*, Hillsdale, N.J.: Erlbaum, 1978.

Marshall, J. C., & Newcombe, F. Syntactic and semantic errors in paralexia. *Neuropsychologia*, 1966, *4*, 169–176.

Marshall, J. C., & Newcombe, F. Patterns of paralexia: A psycholinguistic approach. *Journal of Psycholinguistic Research*, 1973, *2*, 175–200.

Mohr, J. P. Broca's area and Broca's aphasia. In H. Whitacker & H. A. Whitaker (Eds.), Studies in neurolinguistics I. New York: Academic Press, 1976.

Morton, J., Hatan & Patterson, K. E. A new attempt interpretation or an attempt at a new interpretation. In M. Coltheart, K. E. Patterson, & J. C. Marshall (Eds.), *Deep dyslexia*. London: Routledge, in press.

Norman, D. A. & Bobrow, D. G. On data-limited and resource-limited processes. *Cognitive Psychology*, 1975, *7*, 44–64.

Patterson, K. E. Phonemic dyslexia: Errors of meaning and meaning of errors. *Quarterly Journal of Experimental Psychology*, 1978, *30*, 587–607.

Perenin, M. T. Visual function within the hemianopic field following early cerebral hemidecortication in man. II. Pattern Discrimination. *Neuropsychologia*, 1978, *16*, 697–708.

Perenin, M. T., & Jeannerod, M. Visual function within the hemianopic field following early cerebral hemidecortication in man. I. Spatial Localization. *Neuropsychologia*, 1978, *16*, 1–14.

Poeck, K., & Orgass, B. Gerstmann's syndrome and aphasia. *Cortex*, 1966, *2*, 421–437.

Poeck, K., & Orgass, B. Gerstmann's syndrome without aphasia: comments on the paper by Strub and Geschwind. *Cortex*, 1975, *11*, 291–295.

Pöppel, E. Held, R., & Frost, D. Residual visual function after brain wounds involving the central visual pathways in man. *Nature*, 1973, *243*, 295–296.

Postman, L.Verbal learning and memory. *Annual Review of Psychology*, 1975, *26*, 291–335.

Ratcliff, G., & Cowey, A. Disturbances of visual perception following cerebral lesions. In D. J. Oborne, M. M. Gruneberg, & J. R. Eiser (Eds.), *Psychology and Medicine I. Physical Aspects*. London: Academic Press, 1979.

Rubens, A., & Benson, D. F. Associative visual agnosia. *Archives of Neurology*, 1971, *24*, 305–316.

Saffran, E. M., & Marin, O. S. M. Immediate memory for word lists and sentences in a patient with deficient auditory short term memory. *Brain and Language*, 1975, *2*, 420–433.

Saffran, E. M., & Marin, O. S. M. Reading without phonology: Evidence from aphasia. *Quarterly Journal of Experimental Psychology*, 1977, *29*, 515–525.

Saffran, E. M., Bogyo, L., Schwartz, M. F., & Marin, O. S. M. Does deep dyslexia reflect right hemisphere reading? In M. Coltheart, K. E. Patterson, & J. C. Marshall (Eds.), *Deep dyslexia*. London: Routledge, in press.

Schwartz, M. F., Marin, O. S. M., & Saffran, E. M. Dissociations of the language function in dementia: A case study. *Brain and Language*, 1979, *7*, 277–306.

Shallice, T. Neuropsychological research and the fractionation of memory systems. In L. G. Nilsson (Ed.), *Perspectives in memory research*. Hillsdale, N.J.: Erlbaum, 1979.

Shallice, T., & Butterworth, B. Short-term memory impairment and spontaneous speech. *Neuropsychologia*, 1977, *15*, 729–735.

Shallice, T., & Warrington, E. K. Independent functioning of the verbal memory stores: a neuropsychological study. *Quarterly Journal of Experimental Psychology*, 1970, *22*, 261–273.

Shallice, T., & Warrington, E. K. Word recognition in a phonemic dyslexic patient. *Quarterly Journal of Experimental Psychology*, 1975, *27*, 187–199.

Shallice, T., & Warrington, E. K. Auditory-verbal short-term memory and conduction aphasia. *Brain and Language*, 1977, *4*, 479–491.

Shallice, T., & Warrington, E. K. Single and multiple component central dyslexic syndromes. In M. Coltheart, K. E. Patterson, & J. C. Marshall (Eds.) *Deep dyslexia*, London: Routledge, in press.

Spreen, O., Benton, A. L., & Van Allen, M. W. Dissociation of visual and tactile naming in amnesic aphasia. *Neurology*, 1966, *16*, 801–814.

Strub, R., & Geschwind, N. Gerstmann syndrome without aphasia. *Cortex*, 1974, *10*, 378–387.

Taylor, A. M., & Warrington, E. K. Visual agnosia: a single case report. *Cortex*, 1971. *7*, 152–161.

Teuber, H.-L. Physiological psychology. *Annual Review of Psychology*, 1955, *9*, 267–296.

Tulving, E. Episodic and semantic memory. In E. Tulving & W. Donaldson (Eds.) *Organization of Memory*, New York: Academic Press, 1972.

Wagenaar, E., Snow, C., & Prins, R. S. Spontaneous speech of aphasic patients: a psycholinguistic analysis. *Brain and Language*, 1975, *2*, 281–303.

Walsh, K. W. *Neuropsychology: a clinical approach*. Edinburgh: Churchill Livingston, 1978.

Warrington, E. K. The selective impairment of semantic memory. *Quarterly Journal of Experimental Psychology*, 1975, *27*, 635–657.

Warrington, E. K., & Shallice, T. The selective impairment of auditory-verbal short-term memory. *Brain*, 1969, *92*, 885–896.

Warrington, E. K., & Shallice, T. Semantic access dyslexia. *Brain*, 1979, *102*, 43–63.

Warrington, E. K., & Shallice, T. Word-form dyslexia. *Brain* (in press).

Warrington, E. K., & Taylor, A. M. Two categorical stages of object recognition. *Perception*, 1978, *7*, 695–705.

Wechsler, D. *The Wechsler Adult Intelligence Scale*. New York: Psychological Corporation, 1955.

Weisenburg, T., & Bride, K. E. *Aphasia, a clinical and psychological study*. New York: Commonwealth Fund, 1935.

Weiskrantz, L. Some traps and•portifications. In L. Weiskrantz (Ed.) *Analysis of behavioral change*. New York: Harper and Row, 1968.

Weiskrantz, L. Trying to bridge some neuropsychological gaps between monkey and man. *British Journal of Psychology*, 1977, *68*, 431–445.

Weiskrantz, L., Warrington, E. K., Sanders, M. D., & Marshall, J. C. Visual capacity in the hemianopic field following a restricted occipital ablation. *Brain*, 1974, *97*, 709–728.

Wickelgren, W. A. Sparing of short-term memory in an amnesic patient: implications for strength theory of memory. *Neuropsychologia*, 1968, *6*, 235–244.

Wolpert, I. Die Simultanagnosie – Störung der Gesamtauffassung. *Zeitschrift für die gesamte Neurologie und Psychiatrie*, 1924, *93*, 397–415.

Yamadori, A., & Ikumura, G. Central (or conduction) aphasia in a Japanese patient. *Cortex*, 1975, *11*, 73–82.

Zülch, K. J. *Brain tumors: Their biology and pathology*. London: Heinemann, 1965.

Journal of Clinical Neuropsychology
1984, Vol. 6, No. 1, pp. 65-70.

Putative Problems and Pure Progress in Neuropsychological Single-Case Studies*

John C. Marshall and Freda Newcombe

The Radcliffe Infirmary, Oxford, England

ABSTRACT

We consider the logic of basing theories of normal and pathological cognitive functioning upon the selective deficits revealed by single-case studies. Objections to this strategy, concerned with the rarity of pertinent cases, the role of methodological artifacts, and the existence of normal variation in brain functions are refuted. We conclude that, in neuropsychology, a group has no significance over and above the individual members it contains.

Throughout the prehistory of neuropsychology, the analysis of carefully selected single cases provided the driving force behind attempts to understand the relationships between brain and behaviour. The "fractionation" (Shallice, 1979) of higher functions into impaired and preserved categories of performance within and between patients, already implicit in "early descriptions of aphasia" (Benton & Joynt, 1960), eventually led to highly modular theories of cognitive and cerebral organization (Gall, 1791).

For example: In an 18th-century study, Johann Gesner (1770) noted that verbal and articulatory fluency could be retained intact despite the neologistic content of speech, a pattern of performance now known as "jargon aphasia." In the 19th century, Lissauer (1889) reported cases that forced him to distinguish firmly between "apperceptive" and "associative" disorders of object-recognition. In the latter condition, perception is adequate for copying a drawing of an object which nonetheless cannot be identified either by name, mime, or description of use. At the turn of the 20th century, Liepmann (1900) studied a patient who failed to carry out hand movements to command, yet succeeded with whole-body commands. Moreover, the apraxia was unilateral in that the left arm was able to respond appropriately when the right was restrained. More recently, Milner (1958) demonstrated in a single case, H.M., tat many cognitive functions could remain remarkably intact despite gross amnesic impairment.

Further fractionations were discovered *within* "global" faculties. For example, the input and output systems responsible for the use of written language were observed to dissociate, despite the fact that in many aphasic patients, as Head (1926) pointed out, reading and writing are massively and indifferently impaired. Nonetheless, study of individual early cases revealed striking dissociations between these functions. Thus, Schmidt (1676) reported on a patient who, following "apoplexy", could write fluently but could not then read back what he himself had written. Conversely, Gordinier (1899) described a patient with a left frontal glioma which did not perturb spontaneous speech or reading, yet provoked a severe agraphia that could not be "explained away" on peripheral motoric grounds.

THE NATURE OF A RESEARCH PROGRAM

Discovery of such phenomena drove a progressive research program from the late 19th century until the 1920s. The internal structure of the faculties of language, perception, action, and memory was decomposed by study of *selective* deficits observed within the four As of aphasia, agnosia, apraxia, and amnesia. Minimally, the enterprise, conducted in the main by clinical neurologists, looked for correlations between individual symptoms and lesion sites (verified wherever possible at autopsy). Maximally, the enterprise looked for clusters of symptoms ("symptom complexes") that could be interpreted as resulting from anatomo-physiological impairment of an underlying *function* or *component* that "fed" a variety of further subcomponents of the cognitive skill under investigation. One of the clearest accounts of this strategy in full flight can be found in Carl Wernicke's putative explanation of why a severe disorder of comprehension co-occurs with fluent but paraphasic speech (Wernicke, 1874). Damage to a particular functional component (the "store" of auditory word images) impairs verbal comprehension directly, and then indirectly impairs the microstructure of word production because the "articulatory images" of words are checked and controlled by reference to their internal auditory form (Arbib, Caplan, & Marshall, 1982). Wernicke did not conduct a major statistical survey in order to show that the two symptoms co-occurred more frequently than would be expected by the "chance" correlation of any two (or more) deficits consequent upon brain damage. Rather, he boldly conjectured (on the evidential basis of a very small number of patients) that the symptoms *must* co-occur because the functional organization of the *normal* brain is such that the two impairments logically follow from damage to the "auditory lexicon." One very substantial virtue of Wernicke's approach is, of course, that it specifies and hence allows one to recognize counterexamples to any particular theoretical claim.

The structure of the research program thus directed attention to two classes of behavioural phenomena: Surprising double dissociations of function, as in those cases where, for example, reading and writing can each be uniquely impaired; nonobvious associations of symptoms, as in the syndrome of Wernicke's aphasia. Single-case studies supported this program for 50 years or more, and formed the basis of some quite explicit and sophisticated theories of higher cognitive functioning. Why then did the tradition virtually disappear for 40 years? Why did group studies come to be regarded as the royal road to progress, with case studies almost relegated to the realm of anecdote?

RARITY AND SIGNIFICANCE

Many of the phenomena that so excited the early neurologists (alexia without agraphia, pure word deafness, prosopagnosia, ideational apraxia, for example) are undoubtedly rare in clinical practice. It is but a short step from "rare" to "atypical" and then but one more step to the methodological claim that theories should not be built upon atypical cases. This last step, however, is a rather obvious *non sequitur,* despite the frequency with which it has been taken. The theoretical significance (in the nonstatistical sense) of a clinical datum is not logically linked to the number of patients in whom that datum can be observed. If we are discussing the claim that *single* symptoms (e.g., colour anomia) can be seen in pure form without any associated deficits, a single well-described case clearly constitutes an existence-proof. And, indeed, in *human* neuropsychology where we deal in the main with accidents of nature rather than experimental lesions produced by stereotaxic surgery to previously intact animals, one would be considerably surprised to find large numbers of patients displaying closely circumscribed deficits. Similarly, if a universal claim has been made about the *necessary* conjunction of *n* superficial symptoms after damage to a component that purportedly underlies all these manifestations, then a single case in which the symptoms are dissociated suffices to falsify any strong form of the original hypothesis. For example: Wernicke's own account of lexical organization postulated a single "central" word-store that subserves both oral and written naming. Provided that peripheral explanations of the deficit (articulatory difficulties or failure of limb and finger control) can be ruled out, a single case (e.g., Hier & Mohr, 1977) in which these modalities dissociate in naming embarrasses Wernicke's theoretical schema.

Yet, even if the above points are conceded, opponents of the diagram-makers' tradition could, and indeed did (Head, 1926), argue that many of the classical examples of "pure" single-symptom syndromes were so rare as to be nonexistent. Their apparent existence was regarded as artifactual. Thus, a supporter of this position might attempt to dispute the existence of an anomia specific to colours by claiming that a subtle disturbance of colour vision in conjunction with very mild intellectual deterioration has sufficed to create an *illusion* of isolated colour anomia. One could similarly attack the fractionation of a purported multi-symptom syndrome. In the Wernicke-Lichtheim schema, the comprehension and reading aloud of written material is necessarily mediated by the auditory word-store involved in the comprehension and expression of speech. It follows that an alexia, parallel in form to the disorder of repetition and spontaneous speech, must be present in all cases of Wernicke's aphasia. When a case is reported in which reading is apparently preserved (e.g., Heilman, Rothi, Campanella, & Wolfson, 1979) a supporter of Wernicke's theory (as a universal hypothesis) might claim that reading only *appeared* to be intact because, for example, the material presented to the patient was too easy to reveal the dyslexic deficit. There can be no point of *methodological principle* involved in such counterarguments, for they all boil down to the claim that the patient was inadequately examined. No doubt, examples of floor and ceiling effects, failures to match experimental materials, use of too few stimuli, and so forth do find their way into the literature. But the validity of each such attack upon a claim that results from a single-case study must be individually examined on its merits. It cannot surely be a *general* objection to the study of rare syndromes that it is possible to conduct one's investigations badly!

THE RANGE OF NORMAL VARIATION

There is, however, a further, often voiced, objection to building theories upon rare phenomena observed in single cases that are far from representative of the brain-damaged population. The objection is that the patient who displays an uncommon behavioural dissociation *subsequent* to brain injury may have been an atypical individual *prior* to brain injury. Such an individual could presumably differ from his or her fellows in respect of "hard" anatomical wiring or "soft" strategic preferences. In either case, the argument runs as follows: That person cannot be used in constructing accounts of "normal" (where "normal" means "modal") people. In one sense, of course, the argument must be valid: Atypical brains are indeed not typical brains. But nothing much hangs upon this tautology. Obviously, a single case cannot constitute a descriptive statistical generalization. The observation that 5% of the population has right-hemisphere speech does indeed disprove the assertion that *all* people have left-hemisphere speech but unless some theoretical claim has been advanced on the basis of the (purported) universal generalization, little is at stake when one concedes that only 95% of the population is left-dominant for language. If significant individual variation exists within the normal population, it must be described and, ultimately, accounted for by theory. And individual variation is best discovered by comparing and contrasting individuals who have been intensively investigated as single cases. Little progress is likely to be made by constructing theories on a data-base derived from the mean performance of a group of subjects (normal or brain damaged) and dismissing the standard deviation as either "experimental error" or genuine quantitative variation in the efficiency of a single, general mechanism. If we could be sure that all or even the *vast majority* of brains (hardware and software) were built on a solitary unique plan, there would perhaps be little harm in pooling the data from a collection of individuals. But to do so before having an adequate taxonomy of individual variation simply prejudges the issue and makes it less likely that adequate neuropsychological theories will eventually be formulated.

To take a specific example, we have heard it "argued" that data from case studies of deep dyslexia (Marshall & Newcombe, 1966) cannot justifiably be used in the construction of models of "normal" reading because patients who manifest this syndrome in response to left-hemisphere damage may have been at the "far end" of a population continuum; the continuum in question would run from left-hemisphere dominance for semantic aspects of language to bilateral representation of lexical semantics. Such an objection clearly rests upon a pernicious equivocation on the meaning of "normal". If by "normal" we mean "appertaining to the norm", then the argument is obviously valid and the premise (that these subjects had an "above average" dose of right-hemisphere semantics) could be true. But if by "normal" one means "not pathological", then the argument is simply self-contradictory: It claims that these subjects, who were fully literate, competent readers prior to sustaining brain damage (i.e., normal), cannot contribute to the theory of normal reading!

As a final *reductio*, we might note that, if patients with deep dyslexia were not normal (i.e., were not representative of the modal form of brain organization for reading), then perhaps surface dyslexics (Marshall & Newcombe, 1973) were also not, premorbidly, typical. And perhaps phonological dyslexics were not typical either (Beauvois & Dérouesné, 1979). And maybe letter-by-letter readers likewise (Patterson & Kay, 1982). Etc. etc. etc...... This way lies madness. We are about to be left with *no* premorbidly normal readers and hence no population whose capacity to read can be studied, either pre- or post-brain-damage. The fact of the matter is that all the routes and representations implicated in modern theories of reading and reading disorder are, in principle, available to normal adult readers (Newcombe & Marshall, 1981). These routes and representations were very clearly revealed by intensive study of single cases who differed from each other *qualitatively* consequent upon the fractionation of reading skill that resulted from their having sustained brain damage. One dreads to imagine what the data base would look like if these individuals had been coalesced into a group, and students of reading had tried to formulate theories based upon the mean performance of such a group.

CONCLUSION

We end then with an aphoristic moral: There are no useful groups in neuro-psychology; there are only groupings of individuals. And in order to be grouped in a rational, theoretically revealing fashion, the members must first be investigated in highly detailed single-case studies.

REFERENCES

Arbib, M. A., Caplan, D., & Marshall, J. C. (1982). Neurolinguistics in historical perspective. In M. A. Arbib, D. Caplan, & J. C. Marshall (Eds.), *Neural models of language processes.* New York: Academic Press, 5-24.

Beauvois, M.-F., & Dérouesné, J. (1979). Phonological alexia: three dissociations. *Journal of Neurology, Neurosurgery and Psychiatry, 42,* 1115-1124.

Benton, A. L., & Joynt, R. J. (1960). Early descriptions of aphasia. *Archives of Neurology, 3,* 205-221.

Gall, F.-J. (1791). *Philosophisch-medicinische Untersuchungen.* Wien: Gräffner.

Gesner, J. A. P. (1770). *Die Sprachamnesie.* Nördlingen: Beck.

Gordinier, H. C. (1899). A case of brain tumor at the base of the second frontal circonvolution. *American Journal of Medical Science, 117,* 526-535.

Head, H. (1926). *Aphasia and kindred disorders of speech.* New York: Macmillan.

Heilman, K. M., Rothi, L., Campanella, D., & Wolfson, S. (1979). Wernicke's and global aphasia without alexia. *Archives of Neurology, 36,* 129-133.

Hier, D. B., & Mohr, J. P. (1977). Incongruous oral and written naming: Evidence for a subdivision of Wernicke's aphasia. *Brain and Language, 4,* 115-126.

Liepmann, H. (1900). Das Krankheitsbild der Apraxie ("Motorischen Asymbolie"). *Monatsschrift für Psychiatrie und Neurologie, 8,* 15-44, 102-132, 181-197.

Lissauer, H. (1889). Ein Fall von Seelenblindheit nebst einem Beitrag zur Theorie derselben. *Archiv für Psychiatrie, 21,* 222-270.

Marshall, J. C., & Newcombe, F. (1966). Syntactic and semantic errors in paralexia. *Neuropsychologia, 4,* 169-176.

Marshall, J. C., & Newcombe, F. (1973). Patterns of paralexia: A psycholinguistic approach. *Journal of Psycholinguistic Research, 2,* 175-199.

Milner, B. (1958). Psychological defects produced by temporal lobe excision. *Research Publications of the Association for Research in nervous and mental Disease, 36,* 244-257.

Newcombe, F., & Marshall, J. C. (1981). On psycholinguistic classifications of the acquired dyslexias. *Bulletin of the Orton Society, 31,* 29-46.

Patterson, K. E., & Kay, J. (1982). Letter-by-letter reading: psychological descriptions of a neurological syndrome. *Quarterly Journal of Experimental Psychology, 34A,* 411-441.

Schmidt, J. (1676). De oblivione lectionis ex apoplexia salva scriptione. *Miscellanea Curiosa Medico-physica Academiae Naturae Curiosorum, 4,* 195-197.

Shallice, T. (1979). Case study approach in neuropsychological research. *Journal of Clinical Neuropsychology, 1,* 183-211.

Wernicke, C. (1874). *Der aphasische Symptomenkomplex.* Breslau: Cohn and Weigart.

Journal of Clinical and Experimental Neuropsychology
1985, Vol. 7, No. 4, pp. 331-352

An Approach to Analyzing a Single Subject's Scores Obtained in a Standardized Test with Application to the Aachen Aphasia Test (AAT)*

K. Willmes

RWTH, Aachen, Federal Republic of Germany

ABSTRACT

Methods for the analysis of a single subject's test profile(s) proposed by Huber (1973) are applied to the Aachen Aphasia Test (AAT). The procedures are based on the classical test theory model (Lord & Novick, 1968) and are suited for any (achievement) test with standard norms from a large standardization sample and satisfactory reliability estimates. Two test profiles of a Wernicke's aphasic, obtained before and after a 3-month period of speech therapy, are analyzed using inferential comparisons between (groups of) subtest scores on one test application and between two test administrations for single (groups of) subtests. For each of these comparisons, the two aspects of (i) significant (reliable) differences in performance beyond measurement error and (ii) the diagnostic validity of that difference in the reference population of aphasic patients are assessed. Significant differences between standardized subtest scores and a remarkably better preserved reading and writing ability could be found for both test administrations using the multiple test procedure of Holm (1979). Comparison of both profiles revealed an overall increase in performance for each subtest as well as changes in level of performance relations between pairs of subtests.

Although a number of aphasia tests for the English language are available, the objectivity, reliability, and validity of which have been studied more or less extensively, little attention has been given to a psychometrically sound examination of a single subject's total score or profile of subtest scores. Also, the problem of identifying significant changes in performance between two test administrations is neglected in the manuals of these aphasia tests, even if retest reliability estimates are known. For the most part, test authors limit their attention to problems of selection and classification, using either taxonomic approaches or descriptive comparisons with some "typical" profile or mean profile of a syndrome group of aphasic patients. Additionally, it is often the case that only insufficient norm tables from rather small standardization samples are reported.

* The critical reading and helpful suggestions of one of the editors and anonymous reviewers is gratefully acknowledged.

There are at least three major reasons why a detailed and psychometrically sound analysis of single subjects' aphasia test data is of great importance. First, a comprehensive diagnosis cannot be given without a differentiated account of the patient's language disorders in the most relevant language modalities – repetition, naming, reading and writing, and comprehension. That is why the reporting of only a total aphasia score must be replaced by a comparison of performances for different modalities and, if possible, for different components (e.g., phonology, semantics, morphology, syntax). This problem of making decisions based on a given patient's profile of scores obtained in a standardized test is a general one for those engaged in the assessment of certain disorders. Obviously, the clinician/researcher is not satisfied with the mere description of the patient's test scores, be it in a differentiated or in a global manner. He wants to draw inferences about the likelihood of relations between observed and expected test performances within the reference population to which the patient of interest belongs. Consequently, procedures are needed for individual cases which relate diagnostic hypotheses to statistical hypotheses and then statistical decisions based on suitable test statistics back to diagnostic decisions. These diagnostic decisions are thus in turn affected by the same controllable types of errors as statistical decisions.

Secondly, this diagnostic information can have a direct impact on planning a systematic language therapy treatment. As speech therapy has become more elaborate and has been shown to be efficient in recent years (Basso, Capitani, & Zanobio, 1982; Benson, 1979; Reinvang & Engvik, 1980; Springer & Weniger, 1980; Weniger, 1982), evaluation for (longer) periods of routine treatment of single patients also turns out to be helpful. A speech therapist thus can obtain more detailed information regarding the course of recovery of a patient as well as a rational aid to decide on modifications, continuation, or termination of treatment.

Finally, for research purposes, groups of patients can be made more homogeneous and patients used in single-case experimental studies can be made more comparable if they are also tested routinely with some general purpose aphasia test.

One reason for the insufficient use of evaluation methods for single patients in aphasia test manuals may be that no comprehensive collection of procedures is available for standardized test scores in the English literature. The concept of psychometric single case assessment of Huber (1973, in German) provides one solution to the diagnostic problem(s) described above. The procedures are based on the classical test theory model (Lord & Novick, 1968). They can be applied to any test for which norm data from a large sample ($N \geq 400$) and satisfactorily high reliability estimates are available. Contrary to the classical test theory model which was developed for raw scores, these procedures can be applied to standardized scores.

Although not all aspects of Huber's approach can be covered fully, the two most relevant types of inferential comparisons for single (or subsets of) subtests from a test profile will be demonstrated by using two test profiles of one aphasic patient obtained with the Aachen Aphasia Test (AAT; Huber, Poeck, Weniger, & Willmes, 1983, in German; Huber, Poeck, & Willmes, 1984; Willmes, Poeck, Weniger, & Huber, 1983) before and after a period of speech therapy. These inferential procedures are as follows: (i) comparisons between (subsets of) subtest scores on one test application; and, (ii) comparisons between (subsets of) subtest scores from two test applications. For each of these comparisons, two different aspects are of interest: (i) Is there a reliable (significant) difference between scores beyond measurement error? (ii) How likely is the difference obtained or a still larger difference in the reference population of the subject under study? That is, what is the diagnostic validity of the difference between scores?

For the actual analysis of the AAT profile data two FORTRAN computer programs CASE1 and CASE12, written by the author, were used. These are general purpose programs which, after minimal changes, can be used for the analysis of any test for which the single-case assessment procedures are applicable (see the appendix for a description of these requirements). Compared to Huber's treatment of the topic, application of more recent multiple test procedures (Holm, 1979) made possible a unified outline for several of the procedures. The computer output of these programs given in the subsequent figures is used as a basis for explaining the single-case assessment procedures*. For a better understanding of the test procedures, a short description of the AAT and its psychometric properties is necessary (cf. Huber et al., 1984; Willmes et al., 1983).

SHORT DESCRIPTION AND PSYCHOMETRIC PROPERTIES OF THE AAT

The AAT consists of six 6-point spontaneous speech rating scales and five subtests: Token Test (TT), German version of Orgass (1976), Repetition (REP), Written Language (WRIT), Confrontation Naming (NAME), and Comprehension (COMP), in which different units (phonemes, mono- and polysyllabic nouns, sentences) and linguistic rules are incorporated. Each subtest is composed of three to five parts having 10 items each. Except for the Token Test, which has dichotomous scoring, the responses to all items are scored on a 0-3 scale. Although defined more precisely in linguistic terms, for each subtest the scoring is as follows: 3 indicates a correct response; 2, mild or little departure from the stimulus; 1, severe departure from the stimulus; 0, complete error or no response. Thus, scores range from 0-50 for the Token Test, 0-150 for repetition, 0-90 for written language, and 0-150 for confrontation naming and comprehension. In the following, only the five subtests will be of interest.

---

*Copies of the two source programs as well as test data and a technical report describing the mathematical properties of Huber's procedures can be obtained upon request if a computer tape is also provided.

A detailed description of the linguistic structure of the test items is given in Willmes et al. (1983) along with a report on the construct and differential validity of the test. Validity and reliability studies are based on a sample of 120 aphasic patients (30 of each of the four standard aphasic syndromes). Test characteristics of the AAT are reported in Table 1. The standardization sample is comprised of 376 aphasic patients (90 globals, 74 Wernicke's, 79 Broca's, 71 amnesic, 62 nonclassifiable aphasics), almost exclusively with vascular etiology, and 100 control patients (41 left brain-damaged patients without language disorders, 29 right brain-damaged patients, and 30 normal controls).

A nonparametric discriminant analysis program (ALLOC, Habbema, Hermans, & van den Broeck, 1974) is used routinely for the classification of patients with language disorders. It investigates (i) what the (posterior) probability for a new patient is to be aphasic or not and, (ii) if the probability for aphasia is at least 80%, what the probability is of belonging to one of the four standard syndromes. Only if the highest of the four "syndrome" probabilities is above 70% is the patient considered to belong to one of the standard aphasic syndrome groups; otherwise, the patient is taken to be nonclassifiable.

Test-retest reliability was studied in 40 patients (10 of each standard syndrome) over an interval of 2 days. High reliability coefficients and no significant changes in level of performance (no practice or learning effects) were found both for

Table 1

Psychometric Properties of the AAT Needed for Psychometric Single-Case Analysis

AAT subtest	(1) Raw scores scale	M	SD	(2) Consistency coefficient	(3) T score correlations TT	REP	WRIT	NAME	COMP
Token Test (TT)[1]	0- 50	27.13	15.08	.978	—	.702	.831	.835	.772
Repetition (REP)	0-150	96.49	44.67	.989		—	.781	.808	.689
Written Language (WRIT)	0- 90	43.73	29.74	.985			—	.838	.781
Confront. Naming (NAME)	0-120	63.96	38.85	.983				—	.808
Comprehension (COMP)	0-120	73.42	27.00	.928					—

[1] Error scores

(1) Arithmetic means and standard deviations for the AAT standardization sample ($N = 376$ aphasic patients: 90 global, 74 Wernicke's, 79 Broca's, 71 amnesic, 62 nonclassifiable aphasic patients)
(2) Reliability estimates (consistency coefficients X, $n = 120$: 30 global, 30 Wernicke's, 30 Broca's, 30 amnesic aphasic patients)
(3) Intercorrelations (Pearson) between T scores based on the standardization sample

patients with duration of aphasia below and above 3 months. Thus, one can feel safe in attributing substantial (significant) changes in performance to other factors such as spontaneous recovery or language therapy treatment.

Several norm tables have been set up for the AAT. Based on the whole standardization sample of 376 aphasic patients, raw scores for each subtest are transformed into centile ranks first. These centile ranks are then transformed further into T scores. By this 2-step procedure, the nonnormal distributions of raw scores, a problem for all aphasia tests, are turned into (quasi-) normally distributed standard scores (Guilford, 1965, Table 19.3).

For a short description of the patients' level of performance, a stanine scale derived from the centile rank distribution is used. For a still broader categorization, the language impairment is called severe for stanine scores 1-3, medium for 4-5, mild for 6-7, and minimal/not impaired for 8-9. These severity categories are also given as different shades of grey in the T score profile sheet of the AAT (Figure 1).

The lowest raw score equivalent to a stanine score of 8 is in very close agreement with the cut-off score between the aphasic and the nonaphasic control group obtained in nonparametric discriminant analyses for each subtest separately. For each patient assigned to one syndrome group by the ALLOC-procedure, a second impairment grade (severe, medium, or mild) is available. It depends on whether the subtest raw score is below the 33th centile, below the 67th centile or above the 67th centile of the syndrome group's raw score distribution.

BASIC FEATURES OF HUBER'S APPROACH

The mathematical basis for Huber's approach to psychometric single-case analysis is given by the classical test theory model as explicated in Lord and Novick (1968, pp. 30). In order to draw statistical inferences about a single subject's test performance, one needs an estimate of the individual error variance (i.e., variability of test performances in hypothetical replications of assessments with the same test). For a homogeneous population of subjects, one can assume that these individual error variances are approximately equal. In that case, the square of the standard error of measurement, which is computed from the test score variance and the test reliability, can be taken as a good approximation of any subject's error variance within the population of interest.

If one wants to compare a subject's subtest scores from a test profile, this only makes sense if raw scores are converted into standard scores. Using the same standardization for all subtests provides comparability of observed scores. This common approach used for almost all available tests has one drawback: Diagnostic hypotheses about an individual's abilities aim at the identity of true scores and not of observed scores. It can be shown that identity of raw true scores does not imply identity of standardized true scores (cf. Huber, chapter 4.4) unless the reliability parameters of the subtests are identical. Huber suggests τ-standardization (τ indicating true scores) which yields comparability of standardized true scores in all cases. Conversion of a standardized observed score y reported in the norm tables of a test to a τ-standardized score y^τ is accomplished by the following formula using the reliability parameter ρ and mean L of the particular standardization used:

$$y^\tau = y/\sqrt{\rho} + L\,(1 - 1/\sqrt{\rho}).$$

If the test reliability is high (i.e., ρ is close to 1), y and y^τ do not differ much.

For the subsequent test statistics to be distributed as normal or chi square (random) variables one has to assume independent and normally distributed errors and, sometimes (for tests of diagnostic validity), multidimensional normality of true scores (Huber, 1973; Willmes, 1984).

ANALYSIS OF AN INDIVIDUAL AAT T SCORE PROFILE

In the following, the AAT test results of an aphasic patient H.C. are used to demonstrate the application of the single-case analysis estimation and test procedures. Instead of providing a formal derivation of the formulas (Huber, 1973; Willmes, 1984), the respective parts of the computer outputs of CASE1 and CASE12 for H.C. given in Figures 2 to 6 will be explained and discussed.

Case History

H.C., a 56-year old clerk, was admitted to the Neurology department in Aachen on March 10, 1982. On admission there was an aphasia plus a somatosensory impairment of the right arm and leg. No hemiplegia or hemianopia were present. A CT-scan examination on the same day showed a not clearly demarcated hypodense lesion in the territory of the posterior temporal artery.

Because of the patient's good general condition, the AAT could be administered 5 days post onset (first examination). After a 14 days' stay on the ward, during which H.C. received 1 hour of speech therapy every day, the patient was discharged and outpatient speech therapy was continued three times per week, in sessions of 1 hour each.

From the beginning, speech therapy was comprised of structural language training for different language modalities using the better preserved oral reading capacity of the patient. The number of severe semantic and phonemic errors (semantic jargon) in spontaneous speech, repetition, and confrontation naming were reduced to a substantial extent. From May to the end of June, the speech therapy continued in a rehabilitation center, including at this time training of comprehension.

After leaving the rehabilitation center, H.C.'s language was still substantially impaired and control examinations with CT-scan and AAT were done at the Neurology department in Aachen. This time, CT-evaluation revealed a sharply demarcated lesion in the whole superior temporal gyrus as well as small multiple infarcts in the basal ganglia and the posterior white matter.

In Table 2, spontaneous speech ratings, raw scores, centile ranks, stanine scores, and the level of severity assignment compared to the whole aphasic group are listed for both test administrations. The severity grading takes into account 90% confidence intervals for raw scores. Furthermore, the ALLOC classifications, including posterior probabilities, are given.

Although the posterior probability for Wernicke's aphasia falls just short of 70% for the second examination, the neurolinguistic diagnosis is that of a well-recovered Wernicke's aphasia. Qualitative analysis of errors also shows that sentence-semantic and paragrammatical disorders in spontaneous speech, in repetition of sentences (part 5 of the Repetition subtest), and in part 4 of the Confrontation Naming subtest, in which one sentence is

Table 2

AAT Test Results of Patient H.C. for Both Test Administrations,
Including Standardized Scores, Overall Severity Grading,
Psychometric Syndrome Classification with Posterior Classification Probabilities
(ALLOC-Procedure), Syndrome-Specific Severity Grading

	1. EXAMINATION (15.03.1982)				2. EXAMINATION (24.06.1982)			
	Raw Score	Centile Rank	Stanine Score	Severity Grading	Raw Score	Centile Rank	Stanine Score	Severity Grading
TT*	40	28	4	severe - medium	10	81	7	mild - minimal
REP	106	47	5	medium	133	76	6	mild
WRIT	63	65	5	medium - mild	85	95	8	mild - minimal
NAME	38	31	3	severe - medium	95	72	6	medium - mild
COMP	46	35	4	severe	92	70	6	medium - mild
SPONTANE-OUS SPEECH RATINGS	1 5 3 1 2 3				3 5 4 3 4 3			
	COM ART AUT SEM PHO SYN				COM ART AUT SEM PHO SYN			

ALLOC Classification	Syndrome Severity Grading	ALLOC Classification	Syndrome Severity Grading
Aphasia : 100%	TT : severe	Aphasia : 100.0%	TT : mild
	REP : medium		REP : mild
Wernicke's : 100%	WRIT : mild	*Wernicke's* : 66.1%	WRIT : mild
Amnesic : 0%	NAME : severe-medium	Amnesic : 33.4%	NAME : mild
	COMP : severe		COMP : mild

* Error Score

T-SCORE

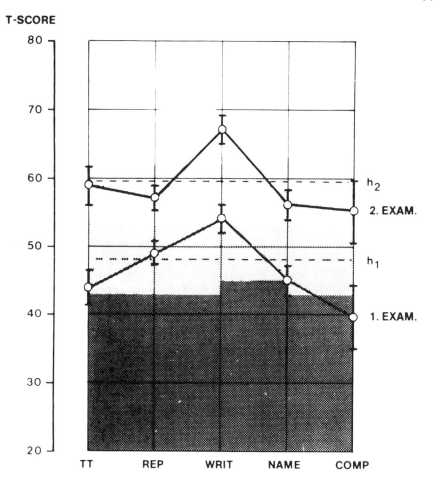

Figure 1. τ-standardized T scores with 90%-confidence intervals for both AAT examinations of patient H.C., and the estimated profile levels, h_1 and h_2 (dashed lines).

required as response, prevailed. Additionally, the severity of naming and comprehension difficulties is very similar. The syndrome-specific level of severity also given in Table 2 is a mild one for all subtests.

For the psychometric single-case analyses, only the T scores for the five subtests of both test administrations are needed (Figure 1). Because the computer programs used are general-purpose programs, instead of AAT subtest labels, only numbers 1 (Token Test), 2 (Repetition), 3 (Written Language), 4 (Confrontation Naming), 5 (Comprehension) are given in the printouts.

Standard Scores and Confidence Intervals

Using the formula for τ standardization given above, first the (point) estimates of the T-standardized true scores are given (Figure 2). Because of the high reliability estimates (Table 1), the estimates are very close to the T scores; only for comprehension is there a somewhat larger difference. For a diagnostic judgement concerning the subject's ability level, the 90%-confidence intervals covering the τ-standardized true score with 90% probability have to be considered. This leads, for example, to the diagnosis of a severe to medium naming disorder, the observed score itself indicating a severe disturbance. In general, the gradation aids reported in test manuals for scores standardized in the usual way (e.g., "below average", "average", etc.) are also valid for τ-standardized scores.

Global Profile Characteristics

The profile level is used as a global index of the overall level of performance. It is computed as a weighted sum of τ-standardized subtest scores, with the weights summing to unity and being functions of the reliability coefficients of the subtests. The more reliable a subtest is, the more weight the actual score obtained in that subtest gets. If the reliabilities of a test battery are identical, the profile level is, simply, the arithmetic mean of the subtest scores.

For H.C., the profile level estimate is $h = 48.08$ (Figure 2) as compared to an arithmetic mean of 46.31. Again, a 90%-confidence interval must be computed for the τ-standardized true profile level. For an aphasia test like the AAT, which is composed of subtests for various language modalities, reporting a profile level as an overall measure of the language disorder is not very useful. Although aphasia is usually viewed as being multi-modal, there is no reason to assume that all modalities must be impaired to the same degree. The scatter of the individual profile is thus an indicator of "real" differences between subtest performances, i.e., differences which cannot be accounted for by measurement errors alone. In order to test whether numerical score differences are beyond chance, one computes the sum of squared deviations of subtest scores from the profile level. These are again weighted with a function of the respective subtest reliability (i.e., the inverse of the square of the subtest's standard error of measurement for τ-standardized scores). To prevent too large a Type II error, the profile is judged to be real if the value of the test statistic is above the 90%-quantile of the χ^2 distribution, with the number of degrees of freedom being one less than the number of subtests. For H.C., the first profile is clearly real.

A real profile calls for a more detailed analysis of the shape of the individual profile to reveal differences between pairs or groups of subtests. If no diagnostic hypotheses are specified in advance, systematic (post hoc) comparisons are useful. For the AAT, all pairwise comparisons of subtests are of interest. Planned comparisons are performed if one or several diagnostically relevant contrasts of subtest groups, specified before the global, overall analysis of the individual profile, are of interest. For example, for an intelligence test like the WAIS, one linear contrast of verbal versus non-verbal subtests might be useful.

```
***********************************************************
*                                                         *
*            STANDARD  SCORES  &  CONFIDENCE  INTERVALS    *
*                                                         *
***********************************************************

    SUB-  STANDARD  TAU-STANDARD.   90 0 %-CONF   INTERVAL
    TEST   SCORE       SCORE        LOWER   -     UPPER


     1       44        43.73        41. 47   -    46. 40

     2       49        48.99        47. 26   -    50. 73

     3       54        54. 03       52. 00   -    56. 06

     4       45        44. 96       42. 79   -    47. 12

     5       40        39. 62       35. 04   -    44. 20

***********************************************************
*                                                         *
*               GLOBAL  PROFILE  CHARACTERISTICS           *
*                                                         *
***********************************************************

      (1)  PROFILE  LEVEL:

      LEVEL  ESTIMATE            =        48. 08

      (2)  90. 0%-CONF. -INTERVAL.

      LOWER  LIMIT               =        47. 08
      UPPER  LIMIT               =        49. 08

      (3)  TEST  FOR  REAL  PROFILE.

      TEST  STATISTIC            =        46. 51
      90. 0%-CHISQUARE  QUANTILE  =        7. 78     DF=   4

      DECISION   THE  PROFILE  IS  REAL.
```

Figure 2. Results of single-case analysis procedures for the first AAT examination of
patient H.C. (output of program CASE1):
Upper part: confidence intervals for τ-standardized T scores.
Lower part: analysis of global profile characteristics.
(The AAT subtests are numbered in the following way: 1 Token Test, 2 Repetition, 3 Written Language, 4 Confrontation Naming, 5 Comprehension)

All Pairwise Comparisons of Subtest Scores

The results are given in Figure 3. Each pairwise difference has to be divided by the standard deviation of that difference. For the resulting standard normal z value, the two-sided p value is computed. In order to decide which of the 10 differences are significant for an overall Type I error of 10%, one of the following two multiple-test procedures can be adopted. With the Bonferroni approach, each individual p value from a pairwise contrast is compared to a Type I error of 10%, divided by the total number of pairwise comparisons, which equals 1% for the AAT. In the computer printout, a "1"

```
•••••••••••••••••••••••••••••••••••••••••••••••••••••••••••••••••••••••••••••••
•                                                                             •
•                ALL PAIRWISE COMPARISONS OF SUBTEST SCORES                   •
•                                                                             •
•••••••••••••••••••••••••••••••••••••••••••••••••••••••••••••••••••••••••••••••
```

SUBTESTS	DIFF	Z-VALUE	RELIABILITY ASPECT BONFERRONI P-VALUE (IN %) TWO-SIDED	DECISION	HOLM RANK	DECISION	VALIDITY ASPECT P-VALUE (IN %, ONE-SIDED)
1 - 2	-5 06	-2 76	0 5769	1	5	1	25 7788
1 - 3	-10 10	-5 20	0 0000	1	10	1	4 2659
1 - 4	-1 02	-0 51	60 7682	0	1	0	42 9944
1 - 5	4 3:	1 36	17 2719	0	2	0	26 6637
2 - 3	-5 04	-3 10	0 1920	1	6	1	22 4838
2 - 4	4 04	2 40	1 6615	0	4	1	25 8828
2 - 5	9 38	3 1:	0 1645	1	7	1	12 2504
3 - 4	9 07	5 03	0 0001	1	9	1	5 6913
3 - 5	14 41	4 73	0 0002	1	8	1	1 6711
4 - 5	5 34	1 73	8 3123	0	3	0	20 0205

```
    ••• DECISION FOR OVERALL TYPE-1 ERROR =10 0 %
    ••• (1  SIGNIFICANT; 0  NOT SIGNIFICANT)
```

```
•••••••••••••••••••••••••••••••••••••••••••••••••••••••••••••••••••••••••••••••
•                                                                             •
•                      PLANNED LINEAR CONTRASTS                               •
•                                                                             •
•••••••••••••••••••••••••••••••••••••••••••••••••••••••••••••••••••••••••••••••
```

THE SUBTESTS COMPARED IN THE LINEAR CONTRASTS ARE

CONTRAST	SUBTEST - GROUPS
1	3 - 1 2 4 5
2	1 5 - 2 3 4

TEST RESULTS

CONTRAST	CONTRAST-VALUE	RELIABILITY ASPECT Z-VALUE	P-VALUE (IN %) ONE-SIDED	DECISION	DIAGNOSTIC VALIDITY ASPECT Z-VALUE	P-VALUE (IN %) ONE-SIDED	DECISION
1	7 86	5 54	0 0000	1	1 63	5 1711	1
2	-6 49	-4 36	0 0007	1	-1 28	9 9777	1

```
    ••• DECISION FOR OVERALL TYPE-1 ERROR
    ••• RELIABILITY ASPECT =10 0 %  DIAGNOSTIC VALIDITY =20 0 %
    ••• (1  SIGNIFICANT; 0  NOT SIGNIFICANT)
```

Figure 3. Results of single-case analysis procedures for the first AAT examination of patient H.C. (output of program CASE1):
Upper part: all pairwise comparisons,
Lower part: planned linear contrasts, both for the reliability aspect and the diagnostic validity aspect.

indicates that the scores of two subtests are judged to be significantly different: that is, the difference in performance cannot be attributed to measurement errors alone but indicates a reliable difference in level of aphasic language disturbance.

Holm (1979) provides a more powerful procedure. The p values for the 10 pairwise comparisons are ordered with the lowest p value obtaining the highest rank. The test procedure is a sequentially rejective one. If the product of the lowest p value and rank 10 is below the overall Type I error, the two subtests are reliably different and the product of the second lowest p value and rank 9 is again compared to the 10% level. If the value of the product is below 10%, the two respective subtests are also judged to be reliably different, etc. The procedure stops as soon as the product of a p value and its rank is above the overall Type I error level.

From the printout in Figure 3, one can see that one more pairwise comparison (repetition vs. confrontation naming) is judged to be significant if Holm's procedure is applied. Arranging subtests according to increased T^τ values, and underlining subtests which are not significantly different, is a good means of visualizing the test results:

COMP   TT   NAME   REP   WRIT.

Written Language abilities are obviously better preserved in this patient, especially reading aloud which is at the 78th centile. Putting together words and sentences (centile rank = 59) and writing to dictation (centile rank = 61) are above average. Auditory and reading comprehension, however, are both equally low.

The better preserved performance in the subtest Written Language can be investigated further for its diagnostic validity. To demonstrate that written language is better preserved, the diagnostic validity of all four pairwise comparisons with the other four subtests must be computed. The probabilities (p values, one-sided) for obtaining still larger pairwise T-score differences are given in the right-hand side column of Figure 3. Applying Holm's procedure for the four comparisons of interest at an overall Type I error of 20% (as suggested by Huber, 1973, p. 116), only the contrast of written language and repetition performance is not diagnostically valid. Such a high Type I error is recommended because diagnostic decisions usually are different from decisions in experimental psychology. In experimental psychology it is widely accepted that one should be hesitant to reject a null hypothesis. That is, the Type I error is usually kept low. With diagnostic decisions, one mostly tries not to overlook "real" symptoms. Symptoms in aphasia testing are often related to differences in true level of performance among subtests. This implies using a rather liberal Type I error level of 10% or even 20% in order to prevent large Type II errors. If for some particular diagnostic problem a large Type I error is critical, a smaller Type I error level could be used. One only has to change the relevant parameter values in the computer programs CASE1 and CASE12.

Planned Linear Contrasts

For an aphasia test having different subtests that assess different language modalities, it is not the most adequate procedure to compare two subgroups of subtests in order to delineate overall profile differences (e.g., to detect particularly well preserved or strongly impaired language modalities). Thus, only for demonstration purposes, written language is compared to the subprofile composed of the other four subtests.

The subprofile level is 46.17, leading to a linear contrast value of 7.86, which indicates a reliable difference of performance (cf. Figure 3, p value = .0000). More interestingly, the diagnostic validity p value = 5.17% is also well below the required level of 20%.

Another reasonable planned linear contrast might be to compare receptive and expressive subtest performances (contrast 2 in the printout). Expressive abilities are significantly better preserved than receptive ones: the diagnostic validity p value of 9.98% is just below 10%, which is the Type I error level per comparison if the Bonferroni procedure is applied to a total of two planned comparisons.

Analysis of the Second Test Profile
The results are given without details. The profile level has risen to 59.55 and the profile is again real. Pairwise comparisons with the p values assessed by Holm's procedure resulted in the following configuration of subtests:

COMP   NAME   REP   TT   WRIT.

All pairwise comparisons of the Written Language subtest and the remaining four subtests are diagnostically valid as well. Similarly, the same planned linear contrasts as used for the first examination reveal better preserved written language ability that is diagnostically valid. However, there are no reliable differences between receptive and expressive modalities.

COMPARISON OF TWO AAT PROFILES OF THE SAME SUBJECT

The procedure used in the following can be applied if either the same subtests or parallel forms of the subtests are compared. The two test administrations may, for example, be before and after some treatment or may follow each of two different treatments. For H.C., AAT performances before and after about 3 months of speech therapy are compared.

Global Profile Comparisons
For a test of overall *profile identity* the sum of (weighted) squared differences of τ-standardized subtest scores is considered (Figure 4). The resulting value of the test statistic (= 187.77) is well above the 90%-quantile of the chi square distribution with 5 d.f. Thus, the two AAT profiles are judged to be significantly different. The two profiles may be nonidentical because of differences in profile levels and/or shapes, each of which can be assessed separately. The difference in *profile level* of 11.45 is highly significant. A one-sided test was performed because there is no reason to assume increase of impairment for an aphasic patient with vascular etiology who also received intensive speech therapy and has a short duration of aphasia. Before testing for *identity of profile shapes*, the two profiles have to be adjusted for differences in level of performance. After subtracting the respective profile level estimate from each subtest score, the weighted sum of squared

(adjusted) subtest scores is again computed. This test statistic value of 10.31 is still above the 90% quantile of the chi square distribution with 4 d.f.

This overall difference in profile shape requires a more detailed analysis of differential changes in relations of subtest performances between the first and second AAT examination. For an aphasia test consisting of one subtest per language modality, again, all 10 pairs of subtests should be analyzed. If diagnostic hypotheses concerning more general changes in relations of subgroups of subtests are of interest, they can be tested as well.

All Comparisons of Pairwise Profile Differences Between Subtest Scores

The difference of each two subtest differences (Figure 5) is divided by the square root of its variance. The resulting standard normal z values are subjected to either

```
*****************************************************************
*                                                               *
*                       GLOBAL  PROFILE  COMPARISONS  *
*                                                               *
*****************************************************************

        (1)  TEST  OF  PROFILE  IDENTITY:

        TEST  STATISTIC           =      187. 77
        90. 0%-CHISQUARE  QUANTILE =        9. 24   DF =   5

        DECISION:  THE  PROFILES  ARE  DIFFERENT.

        (2)  TEST  OF  IDENTICAL  PROFILE  LEVELS:

        PROFILE  LEVEL  DIFFERENCE =       11. 45
        (2ND  EXAM. -1ST  EXAM)
        TEST  STATISTIC  (Z-VALUE) =       13. 32

        ONE-SIDED  TEST:
        P-VALUE  =    0. 0000   (TYPE-1  ERROR  =  10. 0%)

        DECISION:  SIGNIFICANT  CHANGE  IN  PROFILE  LEVEL.

        (3)  TEST  OF  IDENTICAL  PROFILE  SHAPES:

        TEST  STATISTIC           =       10. 31
        90. 0%-CHISQUARE  QUANTILE =        7. 78   DF =   4

        DECISION:  THE  PROFILE  SHAPES  ARE  DIFFERENT.
```

Figure 4. Results of single-case analysis procedures for the comparison of both AAT examinations of patient H.C. (output of program CASE12): global profile comparisons.

```
********************************************************************************
*                                                                              *
*        ALL COMPARISONS OF PAIRWISE DIFFERENCES BETWEEN SUBTEST SCORES        *
*                                                                              *
********************************************************************************
```

						RELIABILITY ASPECT		
							BONFERRONI	HOLM
SUB-	DIFF.	DIFF.	DIFF.	Z-VALUE	P-VALUE	DECISION	RANK	DECISION
TESTS	1ST EXAM	2ND EXAM	1ST-2ND		(IN %)	TWO-SIDED)		
1 - 2	-5.06	2.06	-7.12	-2.75	0.6010	1	10	1
1 - 3	-10.10	-8.03	-2.07	-0.75	45.1263	0	3	0
1 - 4	-1.02	3.05	-4.07	-1.44	14.8779	0	7	0
1 - 5	4.31	3.91	0.40	0.09	92.8180	0	1	0
2 - 3	-5.04	-10.09	5.05	2.20	2.7692	0	9	0
2 - 4	4.04	0.99	3.05	1.28	20.0711	0	6	0
2 - 5	9.38	1.85	7.53	1.79	7.3951	0	8	0
3 - 4	9.07	11.08	-2.00	-0.79	43.2031	0	4	0
3 - 5	14.41	11.94	2.47	0.57	56.6069	0	2	0
4 - 5	5.34	0.86	4.48	1.03	30.4145	0	5	0

```
                                   *** DECISION FOR OVERALL TYPE-1 ERROR =10.0 %
                                   *** (1: SIGNIFICANT; 0: NOT SIGNIFICANT)
```

```
********************************************************************************
*                                                                              *
*                        PLANNED PROFILE COMPARISONS                           *
*                                                                              *
********************************************************************************
```

THE SUBTESTS COMPARED IN THE PROFILE COMPARISONS ARE

COMPARISON	SUBTEST - GROUPS
1	3 - 1 2 4 5
2	1 5 - 2 3 4

TEST RESULTS :

				RELIABILITY ASPECT		
PROFILE	CONTRAST-VALUE		DIFFERENCE	Z-VALUE	P-VALUE	DECISION
COMPARISON	1ST EXAM	2ND EXAM	(1ST - 2ND)		(IN %)	TWO-SIDED)
1	7.86	10.04	-2.18	-1.09	27.7634	0
2	-6.49	-1.65	-4.83	-2.30	2.1609	1

```
                                   *** DECISION FOR OVERALL TYPE-1 ERROR =10.0 %
                                   *** (1: SIGNIFICANT; 0: NOT SIGNIFICANT)
```

Figure 5. Results of single-case analysis procedures for the comparison of both AAT
examinations of patient H.C. (output of program CASE12):
Upper part: all comparisons of pairwise subtest comparisons.
Lower part: planned linear profile contrasts.

Bonferroni's or Holm's multiple test procedure by examining the two-sided p values related to the z values. For H.C., only the relation between the Token Test and the repetition subtest has changed significantly (reliably) for both test strategies. Whereas the T^r score for the Token Test is numerically lower than the one for repetition at the first examination, the opposite relation is found at the second test administration.

Planned Profile Comparisons

The same linear contrast of subgroups is computed for both examinations and the difference of both values is tested to determine if it is significantly different from zero. The rather few changes in the relation of AAT performances for H.C. detected by using pairwise profile comparisons is also reflected in the following result. The profile comparison for the relation of written language performance to the linear combination of the other four subtests is $7.86-10.04 = -2.17$. Thus, it is not significantly different from zero, although the superiority of the written language ability has become more pronounced numerically. The z value of the related test statistic results in a two-sided p value of 27.76%. If one is also interested in a possible change of the relationship between receptive and expressive tasks, one obtains a significant result (cf. the second profile comparison in Figure 5). The distance between receptive and expressive impairment has diminished from a contrast value of -6.49 to a value of -1.65. The two-sided p value of 2.16% indicates that a still larger amount of change is very rare for the reference population of all aphasics.

Comparison of Subtest Performances

If one is not interested in detailed profile comparisons after two profiles were found to be nonidentical, one can also compare performances for the five subtests separately and apply either Bonferroni's or Holm's multiple test procedure. As Figure 6 shows, the z values of the test statistics give rise to very small one-sided p values. Each subtest performance has improved significantly.

If one compares two AAT profiles before and after a period of speech therapy, significant improvement is not necessarily due to the therapeutic treatment alone. Especially if both test administrations are within the first 6 months post onset, spontaneous recovery may have occurred as well. The amount of spontaneous recovery is difficult to estimate, especially for a single patient.

Data on the spontaneous recovery of groups of aphasic patients having received no formal speech therapy are available for the AAT (Willmes & Poeck, 1984). CVA-patients (21 global, 19 Wernicke's, 12 Broca's, 32 amnesic, 12 not classifiable aphasic patients) had been tested 1, 4, and 7 months post onset in that study of spontaneous recovery. The two test administrations for patient H.C. correspond quite well to the first two test occasions of the recovery study. One could use the mean change in T scores for each subtest and the profile level as the best (point) estimate available for the influence of spontaneous recovery. After subtracting

```
********************************************************************************
*                                                                              *
*              COMPARISON OF PERFORMANCES PER SUBTEST                           *
*                                                                              *
********************************************************************************
```

SUB-	STANDARD SCORES		TEST OF DIFFERENCES(2ND-1ST)			DECISION		
TEST	1ST EXAM	2ND EXAM	TAU-DIFF Z-VALUE		P-VALUE(%)	BONF	HOLM	(RANK)
			*** (ONE-SIDED, INCREASE) ***					
1	44	59	15.17	7.15	0.0000	1	1	(4)
2	49	57	8.04	5.39	0.0000	1	1	(2)
3	54	67	13.10	7.51	0.0000	1	1	(5)
4	45	56	11.09	5.97	0.0000	1	1	(3)
5	40	55	15.57	3.95	0.0039	1	1	(1)

```
                        *** DECISION FOR OVERALL TYPE-1 ERROR =10.0 %
                        *** (1: SIGNIFICANT; 0: NOT SIGNIFICANT)
```

Figure 6. Results of single-case analysis procedures for the comparison of both AAT examinations of patient H.C. (output of program CASE12):
All comparisons of subtest performances.

these recovery estimates from the observed differences of τ-standardized T scores the residual differences can be tested for reliable improvement with the same test statistics as for the uncorrected differences. This part of the analysis is not included in the general computer programs and the results are reported without computational details. If one applies Holm's procedure, all residual improvements are still significant at an overall Type I error level of 10%. The residual increase in profile level of 4.40 is also highly significant.

Summing up the psychometric analyses for patient H.C., a detailed account of the considerable improvement could be given. Relative superiority of written language abilities did not decrease. This might also be due to the therapeutic technique of using a better preserved modality to correct mistakes made in other language modalities. It is worth noting that improvement is especially large for the Token Test. There was also substantial improvement in several spontaneous speech ratings, especially for communicative ability and semantic and phonemic structure (Table 2). Continuation of speech therapy was therefore highly recommended; in addition, the decision to allow the patient go on retirement was postponed.

DISCUSSION

Huber's concept of psychometric single-case analysis offers a unified approach to the analysis of profile scores of a single subject obtained in any standardized test, not only in an aphasia test. In principle, the procedures can be applied to all tests constructed and standardized along the lines of the classical test theory model; this is the case for the great majority of assessment procedures available. Once it has been determined that, for a particular test, Huber's methods are applicable, the (profile-)scores of each subject tested can be analyzed. However, the requirements of practical invariance of reliability and correlation estimates (see Appendix) and for standardization samples with at least about 400 subjects may pose difficulties for many tests.

The introduction of τ standardization helps to clarify the diagnostic hypotheses that a test user wishes to test. Only inferences related to true (profile-) scores meet these substantial diagnostic problems. A τ standardization is always possible if standard norms from large samples are reported for a test. However, if reliability estimates are high, the reported standard scores and τ-standardized scores are usually close together.

Huber's approach attempts to follow Zubin's postulates (1950) for the statistical analysis of intraindividual series of observations. These postulates state that (i) each individual must be assumed to be an independent universe characterized by (ii) a given level and (iii) a given degree of variability of performance, both of which characterize the hypothetical distribution of potential scores of the subject and (iv) both of which can be changed by some sort of exogenous factors (treatments) or endogenous changes. The postulate of a characteristic degree of variability of performance is the most crucial one for Huber's approach. Because there is no realistic way of obtaining a good estimate of the error variance of a subject in a specific test by repeated administrations of the same test or several parallel forms of it, the standard error of measurement is used.

A further crucial assumption is that the applications of two subtests of a profile or of parallel tests or two replications of one test form have uncorrelated errors. However, there is evidence (Rozeboom, 1966) that errors can be positively correlated because of illness, fatigue, noise, cheating, etc. Zimmerman and Williams (1977) and Williams and Zimmerman (1977), in deriving the classical test theory model without the assumption of uncorrelated errors, demonstrated that, if the reliability parameters of two tests are high ($>$ .90) and the correlation not much below .50, even rather substantial positive correlations between scores do not affect the true correlation between the two tests to a large extent. But large effects are possible under different circumstances. They also demonstrated that the reliability of a difference score which, according to the classical test theory model can be more fallible than both tests themselves, must not be lower. Again, if errors as well as observed scores are positively correlated ($>$.50), and if reliability parameters are high, the reliability of the difference score may even be considerably higher than the reliability of both tests. Put another way, the standard error of measurement for a difference score (or any linear contrast) may be smaller than for the individual scores so that Huber's test procedures may even be conservative for well-constructed test batteries.

In any case, the choice of an adequate reliability coefficient is an important substantial issue. Although all reliability coefficients can, in principle, be used to estimate the standard error of measurement, the diagnostic problem at hand should guide the choice. If inferences about differences between two parallel tests are of interest, reliability estimates for parallel tests should be used. When testing for score differences within a profile, split-half or consistency coefficients should be preferred. Furthermore, reliability estimates for subpopulations and/or specific age groups should be used although, particularly for clinical subpopulations, they are often not available or are based on very few subjects.

For clinical populations like the aphasic population, there are additional problems. Because raw score distributions often are highly skewed, quasi-normalization by computing T scores from the centile rank distribution may distort the extremes of the scale to some extent. Thus, analyses for patients with very poor or very good performances should be interpreted with some reservation, especially because skewness may be different though high for different subtests contained in the test profile. It may, for example, be impossible to detect a reliable change in performance if the initial score is already quite high. This would also bring into question the model assumption of a constant standard error of measurement over the whole scale of a subtest. The distribution of potential scores of a subject must have a smaller spread at the extremes of a scale. If a clinical population is composed of several subpopulations (e.g., syndrome groups), the normality assumption for true scores is also questionable. The distribution might be bi- or polimodal or may run much flatter than the normal curve. So it would definitely be useful to have normative data for each syndrome group separately. However, for an aphasia test, this will take several more years and the availability of a powerful classification procedure.

The constructional principles of an aphasia test also have consequences for the strategy with which a profile of scores is evaluated. Only if several subtests are assessing the same or a very similar ability is computation of the profile level more than a technical step within the profile analysis procedure. For an aphasia test in which each subtest represents a different modality, pairwise comparisons between subtests should be preferred. With linear contrasts containing several subtests, compensatory effects of some subtest(s) can otherwise disguise substantial differences between some pair of subtests.

Although aphasia is usually taken to be a multimodal deficit, this does not mean that the level of impairment is (almost) identical for all modalities. Consequently, "real" profiles are the rule rather than the exception. Diagnostically valid patterns, on the contrary, are not that frequent. Probably the most interesting kind of profile pattern for an aphasic patient is that of a unimodal deficit or peak in performance. This theoretically based expectation calls for testing the diagnostic validity of the pairwise difference between a certain subtest (modality) and all (several) of the other subtests (modalities). If several subtests for one modality are available in a test, planned comparisons should contain pairwise contrasts of two subgroups of tests, each of the two subgroups assessing one language modality.

The procedures for the detection of a unimodal problem could also help to provide an operational definition for nonstandard aphasias such as transcortical or conduction aphasia. In addition to giving a definition confined to centile rank differences, as do De Bleser, Huber, Willmes, and Blunk (1981) and Reinvang and Engvik (1980), one could also define such an aphasia as follows: "A patient has a transcortical aphasia if his repetition performance, compared to the reference population of aphasic patients, is significantly above his performance on each of the following subtests: Written Language, Confrontation Naming, and Token Test (aspect of diagnostic validity). The repetition score should be at least at the 60th centile rank". For a conduction aphasia, repetition performance should be no better than a T score of 50 and be significantly below all other subtests considering the aspect of diagnostic validity. Also, the patient should have no severe dysarthria and/or speech apraxia.

With the aid of the two computer programs, CASE1 and CASE12, a complete analysis of two AAT test profiles requires only a negligible amount of work. Thus, obtaining detailed diagnostic information on the relative impairment of different language modalities is not restricted to research purposes encompassing only some patients. Rather, it can be used routinely. As has been shown, application of the single-case analysis procedures is also not restricted to diagnostic problems; it can also guide the choice and combination of language therapeutic measures.

APPENDIX

Requirements for the applicability of Huber's procedures
In the derivations of the different test statistics needed for the single-case assessment procedures it is always assumed that the population parameters are known constants. But, for each psychological test, only estimates of them exist. Consequently, one has to assure that sampling errors are negligible in practical applications. The mean and standard deviation of the raw scores are needed for establishing norm scores. The sampling error of both is sufficiently small (cf. Huber's chapters 4.8-4.10) only if the standardization sample size is larger than about $n = 400$ and if the reliability *parameter* is above 0.60. But the reliability parameter itself has to be estimated. Again, it can be demonstrated that a sample size of about 400 is just large enough to yield sufficiently precise reliability estimates. But, for almost all known tests, the reliability studies are based on far less than 400 subjects. Huber suggests that one accept a reliability estimate in case of n less than 400 only if it is *practically invariant*: that is, if the lengh of the 95%-confidence interval of the (true) reliability parameter, ρ, is below 0.1. To examine this property, one first subjects the reliability parameter estimate $\hat{\rho}$, reported for some test, to Fisher's z' transformation, as follows:

$$z' = (\log(1 + \hat{\rho}) - \log(1 - \hat{\rho}))/2;$$

where *log* indicates the natural logarithm.

In terms of the z' scale, the lower z_l and upper z_u 95%-confidence interval boundaries are $z_{l,u} = z' \mp 1.96/\sqrt{(n-3)}$. These have to be transformed back to the original ρ scale again by using the following transformation:

$$\rho_{l,u} = (e^{2z_{l,u}} - 1)/(e^{2z_{l,u}} + 1)$$

In some formulas related to the diagnostic validity aspect, intercorrelations between subtests occur. If they are estimated from samples of less than 400 subjects, their 95%-confidence intervals have to be checked in the same way as the reliability coefficients.

For the AAT, the size of the standardization sample $N = 376$ is just sufficient to guarantee precise enough estimates of the expectation and the standard deviations of the subtests' raw scores. The intercorrelations between subtests are also computed from this sample and are thus practically invariant. Only the reliability estimates are computed from $n = 120$ aphasic patients of the validation sample of the AAT. The Comprehension subtest has the lowest coefficient ($\hat{\rho} = 0.928$). Applying the two formulas given above, one obtains $z_{l,u} = 1.644 \mp 0.1812$ and $\rho_l = .898$, $\rho_u = .949$. The difference between ρ_l and ρ_u clearly is less than .10. Due to the functional form of the above formulas, the other reliability coefficients need not be checked, because higher coefficients result in smaller confidence intervals.

One can also determine, for a given sample size n, what the minimum $\hat{\rho}$ must be in order to guarantee a confidence interval below 0.1. Table A below gives minimum values of $\hat{\rho}$ for several values of n.

Table A

Minimal Reliability Coefficient Values ρ_{min} Which are Practically Invariant for a Given Sample Size n for a Type I Error of 5%

n	ρ_{min}	n	ρ_{min}	n	ρ_{min}	n	ρ_{min}	n	ρ_{min}
10	.975	110	.861	210	.797	310	.745	410	.698
20	.953	120	.853	220	.792	320	.740	420	.693
30	.937	130	.846	230	.786	330	.735	430	.689
40	.924	140	.840	240	.781	340	.730	440	.684
50	.913	150	.833	250	.776	350	.726	450	.680
60	.902	160	.827	260	.770	360	.721	460	.675
70	.893	170	.821	270	.765	370	.716	470	.671
80	.884	180	.815	280	.760	380	.711	480	.666
90	.876	190	.809	290	.755	390	.707	490	.662
100	.868	200	.803	300	.750	400	.702	500	.658

REFERENCES

Basso, A., Capitani, E., & Zanobio, M. E. (1982). Pattern of recovery of oral and written expression and comprehension in aphasic patients. *Behavioral Brain Research, 6,* 115-128.

Benson, F. (1979). Editorial: Aphasia rehabilitation. *Archives of Neurology, 36,* 187-188.

De Bleser, R., Huber, W., Willmes, K., & Blunk, R. (1981, October). Transcortical aphasia. Paper presented at the 19th Annual Meeting of the Academy of Aphasia. London, Ont.

Guilford, J. P. (1965). *Fundamental statistics in psychology and education.* New York: McGraw-Hill.

Habbema, J. D. F., Hermans, J., & van den Broek, K. (1974). A stepwise discriminant analysis program using density estimation. In: G. Bruckmann (Ed.), *COMPSTAT 1974, proceedings in computational statistics,* Wien: Physica.

Holm, S. (1979). A simple sequentially rejective multiple test procedure. *Scandinavian Journal of Statistics, 6,* 65-70.

Huber, H. P. (1973). *Psychometrische Einzelfalldiagnostik.* Weinheim: Beltz.

Huber, W., Poeck, K., Weniger, D., & Willmes, K. (1983). *Der Aachener Aphasie Test (AAT).* Göttingen: Hogrefe.

Huber, W., Poeck, K., & Willmes, K. (1984). The Aachen Aphasia Test (AAT). In F. C. Rose (Ed.), *Progress in aphasiology* (pp. 291-303). New York: Raven.

Lord, F. M., & Novick, M. R. (1968). *Statistical theories of mental test scores.* Reading, MA: Addison-Wesley.

Orgass, B. (1976). Eine Revision des Token Tests. Teil I und II. *Diagnostica, 22,* 70-87 and 141-156.

Reinvang, I., & Engvik, H. (1980). Language recovery in aphasia from 3 to 6 months after stroke. In: M. T. Sarno & O. Höök (Eds.), *Aphasia: Assessment and treatment* (pp. 79-88). Uppsala: Almqvist & Wiksell.

Rozeboom, W. (1966). *Foundations of the theory of prediction.* Homewood, IL: Dorsey Press.

Springer, L., & Weniger, D. (1980). Aphasietherapie aus logopädisch-linguistischer Sicht. In G. Böhme (Ed.), *Therapie der Sprach-, Sprech- und Stimmstörungen* (pp. 190-207). Stuttgart: G. Fischer.

Weniger, D. (1982). Therapie der Aphasien. In: K. Poeck (Ed.), *Klinische Neuropsychologie,* Stuttgart-New York: Thieme.

Williams, R. H., & Zimmerman, D. W. (1977). The reliability of difference scores when errors are correlated. *Educational and Psychological Measurement, 37,* 679-689.

Willmes, K. (1984). An approach to analyzing a single subject's scores obtained in a standardized test: Description of the method. Unpublished manuscript.

Willmes, K., & Poeck, K. (1984). Ergebnisse einer multizentrischen Untersuchung über die Spontanprognose von Aphasien vaskulärer Ätiologie. *Nervenarzt, 55,* 62-71.

Willmes, K., & Poeck, K., Weniger, D., & Huber, W. (1983). Facet theory applied to the construction and validation of the Aachen Aphasia Test. *Brain & Language, 18,* 259-276.

Zimmerman, D. W., & Williams, R. H. (1977). The theory of test validity and correlated errors of measurement. *Journal of Mathematical Psychology, 16,* 135-152.

Zubin, J. (1950). Symposium on statistics for the clinician. *Journal of Clinical Psychology, 6,* 1-6.

Journal of Clinical and Experimental Neuropsychology
1987, Vol. 9, No. 5, pp. 527-544

Single-Case Experimental Designs in Neuropsychological Rehabilitation*

Barbara Wilson

Charing Cross Hospital, London

ABSTRACT

It is becoming accepted that single-case studies can offer important contributions to theoretical aspects of neuropsychology. Such recognition has not been so forthcoming in the field of rehabilitation, where single-case studies can be employed to evaluate neuropsychological treatments. This paper describes behavioural approaches to treatment of the neurologically impaired which include single-case experimental designs that have originated in the field of behavioural psychology. Examples of behaviour programmes for the treatment of apraxia and alexia are provided together with examples of single-case experimental designs used to evaluate memory therapy. The paper concludes with a brief discussion of the role of statistics in single-case studies.

It is often hard to convince doctors and therapists that good research can be carried out with individuals or with small groups of subjects. Even academic psychologists (though not neuropsychologists or behavioural psychologists) find this idea difficult to accept. Although their discipline began with the intensive study of individuals (e.g., Wundt and Ebbinghaus used themselves as subjects for many years), there is a widespread belief amongst psychologists that findings from small-N studies are neither valid nor generalisable. This belief can be traced back to the 1920's when new statistical procedures were developed (e.g., Fisher, 1925). These procedures required large numbers of subjects, the use of randomisation to eliminate secondary variables, and the use of control groups. In many quarters, this kind of research has become the trademark of *acceptable* scientific experimentation.

Despite this general background of scepticism it can be demonstrated quite readily within the field of neuropsychology that valid and generalisable results are obtainable from studies of individual patients. Broca's study of his patient 'Tan', for example (1861), heralded the beginning of modern neuropsychology; and it

* A version of this paper was presented at the Cognitive Neuropsychology Meeting in Venice in March 1985. I should like to thank Dr. Rosamond Gianutsos for her helpful comments on this paper.

can be demonstrated today that, with certain exceptions, damage to 'Broca's' area consistently leads to expressive dysphasia. H.M., the amnesic patient of Scoville and Milner (1957), has probably been written about more than any other individual in the literature of psychology. Studies of H.M.'s memory disorder have contributed enormously to our understanding of normal human memory. Studies of individual patients such as 'Tan', H.M., and others allow us to test theoretical models of normal cognitive functioning.

Single-case designs are also accepted in behavioural psychology. Watson and Rayner (1920) and Skinner (1938, 1956, and 1961) worked with individuals and small groups, realising that valid and generalisable laws of behaviour could be developed from such studies. Behavioural psychology has, in turn, influenced clinical psychology. Shapiro (1966) was an early champion of the single-case approach, and recent years have seen the publication of several books and articles on single-case designs (see, e.g., Gianutsos & Gianutsos, in press; Hersen & Barlow, 1976; Kazdin, 1982; Kratochwill, 1978; and Yule & Hemsley, 1977).

THE IMPORTANCE OF SINGLE-CASE APPROACHES IN TREATMENT

Neuropsychology has tended to pay little attention to the amelioration of cognitive problems, although at last there are signs that a change of outlook is developing within the discipline. Neurologically impaired people and their families are likely to benefit considerably in the future if neuropsychology can strengthen its links with clinical psychology so that the emphasis on intervention strategies, normally practised by the behaviourally orientated clinical psychologists, is shared and informed by the two disciplines.

One criticism often made about the few intervention strategies which are described is that they have not been properly evaluated, and that they are therefore anecdotal. Critics who hold such a view seem to be implying that, because *large scale* evaluation studies have not been carried out, then any findings must be based upon subjective impressions. This is itself a subjective impression; and hopefully readers of this paper will be persuaded that intervention strategies can indeed be subjected to the most rigorous and searching evaluations through behavioural treatment programmes and/or single-case experimental designs. These are rigorous designs not to be confused with single-case descriptions. Furthermore, workers engaged in rehabilitation are interested in individual processes rather than group processes. It is the individual who has to return home, return to work, and cope with his or her life. Findings should therefore be meaningful at an individual level. As Gianutsos and Gianutsos (in press) remind us, individuals risk becoming stuck in the tails of group research designs.

Obviously, large group studies are essential in furthering our understanding of certain areas. Some questions, such as that which seeks to find out whether memory declines with ageing, cannot be answered unless we look at many subjects (and in this particular case, across a wide age range). Group studies are also better able to tease out order or interaction effects. In the evaluation of treatment for individual patients, however, group studies are, at best, of limited value. Individual differences are masked in large-N designs. We are rarely told, for example, how many patients improve, how many remain unchanged, or how many deteriorate under any given condition or treatment. Even when figures are supplied for changes, we do not know whether our particular patient will respond in a way that is similar to any of the groups.

A further complication is that many neurological patients have diverse problems. For example, head injury can lead to a combination of memory, perceptual, and language problems. Group studies are almost always carried out with homogenous groups, which means that, even if an effective treatment is established for the memory problems of such a group, we will not know whether people with additional problems will respond to the treatment in the same way.

Because of the emphasis on statistical significance in group studies, clinical significance is rarely considered. Take, for example, the case of biofeedback for foot drop in stroke patients. It is possible to demonstrate statistically significant improvement in control of a muscle following biofeedback, even though the patients themselves showed no gain in independence or mobility (American College of Physicians, 1985). This is not meant to imply that small changes following biofeedback are never useful but that statistically significant results do not necessarily mean clinical improvement. The converse is also possible: clinical significance can occur without statistical significance. In a study of the effect on memory functioning following treatment in groups (Wilson, in press), no significant difference emerged between training in a problem-solving group and training in a memory group. Nevertheless, some people improved considerably after the training and therefore, for these people, clinical significance had occurred. Ideally, both clinical and statistical significance should result from treatment.

Yet another problem with regard to group studies in neuropsychological rehabilitation is that many of the patients we treat present with rare syndromes. Visual-object agnosia and ideational apraxia are syndromes which would never get treated if we had to wait for large group studies to be completed. Additionally, because group studies tend to take only one or two readings or measurements for each subject, it is not possible to see a pattern of change during treatment, yet identification of such a pattern may be crucial. For example, a patient may respond very well initially only to fall back to pretreatment levels later on. In the large-N design this process would be designated a 'no change' condition. However, should the patient simply need more time to respond or learn later material, then it is only in a single-case design that such an adjustment could be made to allow for the possibility of a successful outcome for treatment. In the latter study we would also have learned more about optimal learning conditions for the particular patient. Any analysis of data during the experiment is rare in large-N studies because of the need to avoid observer bias. In rehabilitation, however, we must be sensitive to the needs of our patients and this calls for close monitoring and responsive adjustments.

Research methods are tools that enable us to answer certain questions. Large-N

and small-N studies simply answer different questions. In rehabilitation one question which should be asked in one form or another of *every* patient treated is "What effect does this particular treatment have on this particular patient?" Furthermore, if the patient improves we usually want to know if improvement is due to the intervention itself or to some other recovery factor such as natural recovery, general stimulation or anything else that is not an essential part of the treatment being assessed. In order to answer these questions satisfactorily, single-case approaches are probably the best research tools for evaluation of treatment. For an excellent discussion on this topic see Gianutsos and Gianutsos (in press).

EXAMPLES OR BEHAVIOURAL TECHNIQUES FOR EVALUATION OF TREATMENT

Behavioural programmes and behavioural assessment techniques are relatively simple ways to evaluate response to treatment. Inherent in behavioural assessment is (a) a precise definition of the behaviour itself, (b) baseline measures of the frequency or severity or rate of occurrence of the behaviour, and (c) a careful monitoring of the effectiveness of the intervention strategy. An example of a behaviour modification approach adapted to a cognitive/neuropsychological problem is shown in Table 1. DPC was a man shot through the head some 3 years earlier who, as a consequence, suffered from total alexia.

Within 6 months DPC had progressed from being untestable on the Schonell Graded Word Reading Rest to having a reading age of over nine years. (Further descriptions of such programmes are given in Wilson and Moffat, 1984a.)

The purpose of the baseline is to obtain a reliable picture of the behaviour prior to treatment and to enable the therapist to determine whether improvement seen after the introduction of treatment is in fact due to the treatment or would have occurred anyway.

A further example of close monitoring of behavioural assessment can be seen in the treatment of S.H., a young woman who was severely brain-injured in an anaesthetic accident. Among other problems, she was left with apraxia of such severity that she could feed herself only with extreme difficulty, and was unable to drink from a cup unaided, despite having the necessary strength to lift and manoeuvre the cup. Observations showed that she was unable to lift the cup to her mouth: when she tried to do so either her hand went to the very top of the cup so that her grasp was unstable, or she found the handle but could not grip it. The task of drinking from a cup was broken down into nine steps:-

(1) Find the table.
(2) Put hand flat on table.
(3) Put thumb through handle.
(4) Grasp handle.
(5) Lift cup to mouth.

Table 1

Two programmes for the remediation of alexia

DPC's first reading programme	
1. Define behaviour.	Inability to read any words or letters. Could tell if stimuli were upside down or not.
2. State goal.	Long term: to teach DPC to read again. Immediate goal: to teach DPC 6 useful words.
3. Obtain baseline.	0/6 words read correctly on 4 occasions.
4. Identify reinforcers.	Success at task. Verbal feedback.
5. Plan treatment.	Three 30-min treatment sessions each week. Errorless learning approach.
6. Begin treatment.	Treatment begun.
7. Monitor and evaluate progress.	Failed to identify reliably or recognise any words after 25 treatment sessions.
8. Change procedure if necessary.	"Look-Say" approach abandoned. Phonetic approach tried.

DPC's second reading programme	
1. Define behaviour.	As above.
2. State goal.	To teach DPC (i) names and (ii) sounds of letters.
3. Obtain baseline.	Maximum of 2/26 correct on 4 occasions.
4. Identify reinforcers.	As above.
5. Plan treatment.	Teach letters and then sounds, one at a time. Practice and feedback daily.
6. Begin treatment.	Treatment begun.
7. Monitor and evaluate progress.	Learned names and sounds in 3 weeks.
8. Change procedure if necessary.	Proceed to identification of vowels, then 2 letter words.

(6) Drink.
(7) Put cup on table.
(8) Open fingers.
(9) Take fingers and thumb out of handle.

Providing S.H. with this structure and prompting her whenever she was unable to successfully complete one of the steps enabled her to improve. However, in step

(5) it was noticed that S.H. often put her mouth to the rim of the cup which was furthest away from her. The liquid therefore spilled down her dress. The answer was to stick a piece of red tape on to the nearer rim and insert an additional step: 'Look for the red rim.' This was an obvious and simple adjustment, made in a closely monitored treatment evaluation. However, its omission could easily have led to failure in a 'before and after' measure typically found in a large group study. This programme illustrates an important feature of behavioural assessment and single-case experimental designs, namely the careful definition of behaviour or task analysis, which makes achievement of treatment goals more likely.

Table 2 shows the way in which S.H. responded to the structured approach.

Table 2

S.H.'s programme to teach her to drink from a cup unaided

		STEP 1	2	3	4	5	6	7	8	9
D	24th FEB.									
	session 1	G	G	G	G	G	*	P	V	V
	2	V	V	V	V	*	*	V	V	V
A	3	*	*	*	*	*	*	*	*	*
	25th FEB.									
	session 1	V	V	V	*	*	*	*	*	*
T	26th FEB.									
	session 1	*	*	V	P	G	*	*	*	*
	2	*	V	V	G	G	*	*	*	*
E	3	*	V	V	*	*+	*	*	V	*
	27TH FEB.									
	session 1	*	V	*	P	G	*	V	*	*
S	2	*	V	*	V	V	*	*	*	*
	3	V	V	V	V	*+	*	V	*	*
	4	V	V	P	V	V	*	*	*	*
	28th Feb. & 1ST MARCH	NO RECORDS - WEEKEND								
	2ND MARCH	*	*	*	*	*	*	*	*	*
	3RD MARCH	*	*	*	*	*	*	*	*	*
	4TH MARCH	*	*	*	*	*	*	*	*	*
	10TH MARCH	*	*	*	*	*	*	*	*	*

+ = additional step inserted

KEY: * = completes step alone
V = verbal prompt
P = physical prompt (touch)
G = physical guidance

SINGLE-CASE EXPERIMENTAL DESIGNS

Single-case experimental designs are invaluable tools for determining whether improvement is a result of treatment or of some other cause such as passage of time, and usually they are more effective than group studies for evaluating treatment. A typical group study would provide different treatments for two or more groups of people, although sometimes an alternative design would subject one group to two or more treatments. Usually, results are described in terms of the average or mean response of each group under each condition. Wide differences are common and findings are often of little value in predicting whether a particular treatment is likely to be effective for a given individual.

Single-case experimental designs avoid many of the problems inherent in group studies. We can tailor treatment to an individual's particular needs and evaluate responses to the treatment or intervention strategies continuously, whilst controlling for the effects of spontaneous recovery or improvements over time. The simplest case design is the reversal or ABAB design where A equals baseline and B equals intervention. An example of this design is shown in Figure 1.

This illustrates an attempt to teach the name of the clinical psychologist to a young man who had received a severe head injury some 2 years earlier. Baselines were taken by telling him the psychologist's name and asking him to recall it after intervals ranging from 5 s to 3 min. The intervals were filled with general conversation. He recalled the name of the psychologist reliably whenever the interval was 30 s or less. After 30 s he made mistakes. This baseline session lasted an hour, following which a timer was introduced in an attempt to shape his behaviour. The timer was initially programmed to sound every 30 s during his

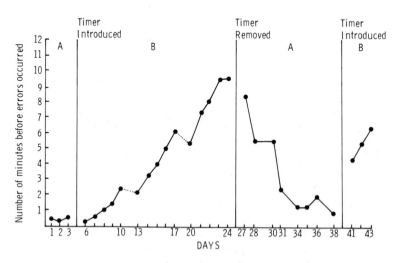

Figure 1. A single-case ABAB design. Evaluating the effect of a timer to recall a name after intervals of gradually increasing length.

daily, hour-long sessions. Each time the alarm sounded he was asked to say the psychologist's name. After four consecutive correct responses the interval was increased by 5 s. In this way, after 3 weeks of the programme, the young man was able to retain the name for $10\frac{1}{2}$ min before making errors. In order to know whether it was the treatment (i.e., the timer) which was effecting the changes or whether the young man had made general progress (i.e., would have remembered the name for longer regardless of treatment), it was necessary to revert to baseline conditions. He was asked to say the name of the psychologist at random intervals during the daily sessions just as he did in the baseline period. Over 2 weeks his recall of the name deteriorated until he was making errors after $1\frac{1}{2}$ min. The second treatment (B) phase began with the re-introduction of the timer, and at this stage the young man's retention span began to increase again.

Variations on the ABAB design are frequently made in behavioural approaches so one might, for example, have included a C phase in the programme, where C equals positive reinforcement in the shape of tokens or money. The design would then have been ABAC or ABABC (see Hersen & Barlow, 1976, for further discussion of these designs).

Although the reversal design is simple, its application to treatment programmes is limited for three main reasons. First, it is often impossible to revert to baseline conditions: if a person has been taught to remember the way from the ward to the occupational therapy department, for example, s/he cannot 'unlearn' this. Second, there are occasions when it is unethical: if an amnesic patient has been taught to check whether s/he has left the gas ring burning, then it would be dangerous to revert back to a time when the gas was not checked! Third, it is often impracticable to revert to baseline conditions. For instance, when it has been possible to stop the constant repetition of a particular question. (Staff and relatives will not view a reversal design very favourably under such circumstances.) However, because of its simplicity, the reversal design is worth having in one's repertoire of evaluation techniques.

Multiple-baseline designs are probably more useful as evaluative procedures, at least as far as cognitive remediation is concerned. There are three main kinds of multiple-baseline design and each will be described below.

(i) *Multiple baseline across behaviours design.* In this design several different behaviours or problems are selected for treatment. Baselines are taken on all the behaviours but only one is treated at a time. Again, this allows the therapist to separate out the effects of general improvement. An illustration of this design is provided in Figure 2. This design was used in the treatment of T.B., a 43-year-old man who was diagnosed as having Korsakoff's syndrome. Three problems were selected for treatment: (1) remembering short routes around the rehabilitation centre, (2) remembering newspaper articles, and (3) learning the names of the staff at the centre. The baseline procedure can be seen in Table 3.

Table 3

Baseline procedures for T.B.'s memory problems

PROBLEM	PROCEDURE	SCORE
1. ROUTES	T.B. was asked: "Take me to the workshops/canteen/office" etc.	1 point if he took the most direct route. (Max. 10 pts.)
2. NEWSPAPER ARTICLES	Article read to T.B. who was asked for immediate and delayed (20 min) recall.	Scoring system adapted from the Wechsler Memory Scale (Max. 20 pts.)
3. NAMES OF STAFF	Photographs of staff were shown one at a time and the name provided. Following presentation of 10 photographs T.B. was asked for immediate and delayed (20 min) recall.	1 point for each correct name. (Max. 20 pts.)

T.B.'s ability to remember his way around the rehabilitation centre improved with rehearsal. No improvement occurred during baseline conditions with regard to newspaper articles or to remembering the names of staff. For one session extra rehearsal was used for both newspaper articles and names, but with little or no effect. A PQRST strategy (Robinson, 1970) was then introduced for the newspaper articles, and the following week a face-name association procedure was used for the names of staff. (PQRST is an acronym for *Preview, Read, Question State and Test,* which comes from the study of field techniques). The results are shown in Figure 2. This figure illustrates that the routes improved with practice, that PQRST helped considerably with newspaper articles, and that face-name association procedure made a dramatic difference to T.B.'s learning of the names of staff. A further example of this approach, with an amnesic patient, is described in Wilson (1982).

The purpose of the multiple-baseline design is that, by staggering the introduction of treatment, we can see if improvement is directly related to the intervention strategy or not. If it is, then there will be a direct relationship between improvement and introduction of treatment. If something other than treatment is responsible for improvement, either all the problems will change simultaneously or there will be no direct relationship between changes and intervention strategies.

(ii) *Multiple baseline across settings design.* In this design only one problem or behaviour is tackled but the effects of treatment are investigated in one *setting* at a time. This particular design is useful when situation specific effects may occur. An illustration may be seen in Figure 3, where the procedure was used with a spinal patient (P.W.) who forgot (or refused) to lift himself from his wheelchair frequently enough (Carr & Wilson, 1983). This resulted in the development of pressure sores. In spite of the reasoning and cajoling of physiotherapists, nurses,

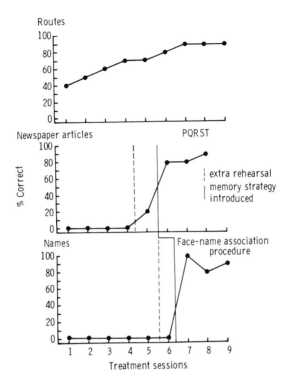

Figure 2. A multiple-baseline-across-behaviours design to evaluate T.B.'s memory therapy programme.

and doctors, P.W. did not lift. A machine was made by Maynard Projects of Oxford and this was attached to the wheelchair to record the number of lifts made. A lift was defined as the man's buttocks leaving the chair for at least 4 s. (He pushed himself up with his arms.) At least one lift every 10 min was considered desirable. Following baselines in four different settings, the workshops, lunch breaks, coffee breaks, and on the ward, the machine was fitted to his wheelchair in one of the settings only (workshops). The rate of lifting increased dramatically. The next stage was to introduce the machine during lunch time, then during coffee breaks, and finally on the ward. P.W. lifted the requisite number of times only *after* the machine had been introduced. Given that generalisation to other settings did not occur during the multiple baselines, it is likely that P.W. would have stopped lifting had a reversal design been used. Thus, despite its desirability from the point of view of research, a reversal design would have been inapplicable to this patient. The most important clinical outcome here, of course, was the condition of P.W.'s skin. His pressure sores began healing almost immediately and he gradually took over the monitoring himself.

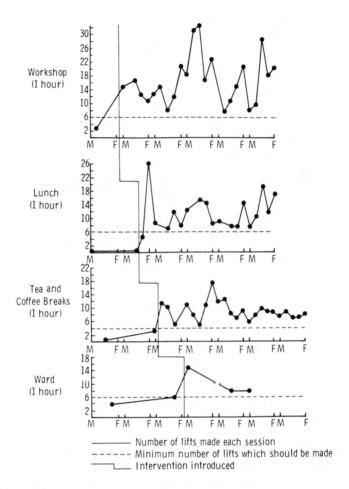

Figure 3. A multiple-baseline-across-settings design. A programme to increase the frequency with which P.W. lifted his buttocks from the wheelchair was introduced successively across different environmental settings.

(iii) *Multiple baseline across subjects design.* Although this is not, strictly speaking, a *single*-case design, it is usually included in single-case methodology because the problems with very small groups of subjects are similar to those encountered when N equals 1 and it yields results that are meaningful at an individual level. This design is illustrated in Figure 4, the results of a study investigating the ability of four men to learn people's names using a visual imagery procedure (Wilson & Moffat, 1984b).

Like T.B. in Figure 2, patients were each asked the names of people at the rehabilitation centre where they were being treated. They were seen individually each day and *all* names were tested on each occasion. However, images were

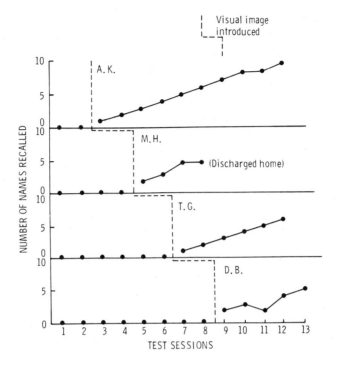

Figure 4. A multiple-baseline-across-subjects design to demonstrate the effectiveness of visual imagery for learning names.

introduced one at a time, thus introducing treatment in a staggered fashion. Again, it can be seen that improvement occurred for each person only with the introduction of the treatment procedure.

The three multiple-baseline designs can be applied to a wide range of patients and problems; they are invaluable tools for monitoring intervention strategies. There are other single-case designs: alternating treatments can be used where two or more treatment strategies are used at the same time (see, e.g., Singh, Beale, & Dawson, 1981, for a discussion of alternating treatments). Embedded designs are further variations of the single-case approach, where reversal and multiple-baseline procedures are used together (see, e.g., Wong & Liberman, 1981).

(iv) *Direct comparison method.* An alternative to the multiple-baseline design is to use a procedure from experimental psychology in which two or more treatments are compared. Usually this design is seen in group studies when several subjects are compared under two different conditions. Each condition is administered to each subject once only. The difference in single-case designs is that one subject receives two treatment procedures on numerous occasions.

An example of this was the procedure adopted for K.J., described by Wilson (1987). An investigation was carried out to see whether the use of a PQRST method (Robinson, 1970) would improve his retention of news items. Each day for a period of 8 days two short paragraphs from the daily newspaper were selected. One paragraph was allocated to the PQRST method and one to the rehearsal or control method. The order of presentation was changed each day. Each PQRST paragraph was read to him and each of the component stages was followed. This took between 7 and 10 min in total. For the control paragraphs, each was read to him four times. After each reading he recalled as much as possible. After the fourth reading K.J. was asked questions about the paragraph. This took between 7 and 10 min in total. Thus, there were five stages in each condition and the total amount of time spent on each paragraph was approximately equal. After 30 min questions from both paragraphs were repeated. The results of immediate and delayed recall can be seen in Table 4.

A Wilcoxon matched-pairs signed ranks test comparing immediate recall in both conditions shows no significant difference ($T = 10$). However, in the delayed-recall condition, there is a significant difference in the amount retained ($T = 2.5$, $p < .05$). Thus, the PQRST procedure would appear to have aided recall of prose material. It should be noted, however, that K.J.'s recall was in response to direct questioning. He could usually remember 50% of the material from the PQRST paragraphs if he was asked the questions. In a free-recall condition, without the prompting provided by questions, he would usually remember nothing from either paragraph. It would appear that the PQRST procedure provided better retrieval cues than rehearsal alone.

Table 4

Percentage of questions answered correctly after PQRST method and rehearsal alone

Test Session	PQRST		REHEARSAL	
	Immediate Recall (%)	30-min Delayed Recall (%)	Immediate Recall (%)	30-min Delayed Recall (%)
1.	75	50	25	0
2.	75	50	100	25
3.	100	50	75	25
4.	75	75	75	50
5.	75	50	75	0
6.	25	0	50	25
7.	100	50	25	0
8.	75	50	75	0
MEAN	77.7	47.1	62.5	15.6

LIMITATIONS OF SINGLE-CASE DESIGNS

Only successful cases have been reported in this paper but obviously single-case designs do not always succeed, so it is perhaps advisable to spend some time here considering reasons why single-case designs might fail. Firstly, natural recovery might be taking place and this would accelerate baselines to the extent that treatment would not need to be introduced. Secondly, the behaviours being treated might be functionally equivalent. Suppose, for example, a patient is being treated for unilateral neglect and the therapist uses a multiple baseline across behaviours design to treat three different behaviours. These might be (a) omitting words on the left-hand side when reading; (b) failing to copy left-hand digits in written arithmetic tasks; and (c) leaving food on the left-hand side of the plate when eating. Following baselines, the first problem is treated by using a scanning procedure and anchor points (described by Diller and his colleagues, Diller & Weinberg, 1977; Weinberg et al., 1979). This proves to be successful but the other problems also improve. The reason may well be due to the fact that the basic underlying difficulty is a scanning problem. Improving scanning therefore improves all three problems. Although this is good as far as the patient is concerned, it makes it harder for the therapist to determine whether improvement is due to treatment or natural recovery. Thirdly, unforseen problems may arise which make the keeping of adequate records extremely difficult or impossible. For instance, a patient may be discharged unexpectedly, or spend more time in other rehabilitation departments than was first expected. Fourthly, the goals or treatment procedures may be inappropriate. Fifthly, the problem behaviour being treated might prove to be resistant to therapy.

GENERALISATION ISSUES

The reason large numbers of subjects are used in most conventional research designs is because experimenters want their results to apply to a wide group of people. Therefore, as large a group as possible is sampled, individual differences are expected and allowances are made for these. Randomisation procedures and control groups ensure that individual variations are fairly equally distributed (or cancelled out) between groups and/or conditions. Furthermore, statistical procedures help the experimenter decide whether findings are due to individual differences or to the variable being tested. In contrast, single-case studies do not need to iron out intersubject variations because only one subject is involved. As a result, control groups and randomisation procedures are unnecessary. Single-case designs use other ways to identify causal relationships. For example, constant and close monitoring replaces the one or two readings from each subject typical in large-N studies. Many measures are taken before, during, and after the introduction of treatment, allowing for *intra*subject comparison of treatment effects (Robinson & Foster, 1979).

How do these two approaches affect generalisation to other patients or subjects? Although many people believe that it is possible to generalise from a large sample, this may not necessarily be true. If, for example, the large sample is heterogenous, then the findings are unlikely to have any relevance for an individual because the *average* response of such a group is unlikely to represent any *one person* within the group. If, on the other hand, the sample is homogenous it will perhaps be possible to generalise from the group to the individual, providing the individual shares the characteristics of the group. However, if it is possible to generalise in this way, then it is equally possible to generalise from one individual whose characteristics are specified to other individuals with the same characteristics. Hersen and Barlow (1976) argue eloquently for such a position, and go on to add:

> "To increase the base for generalisation from a single case experiment, one simply repeats the same experiment several times on similar patients, thereby providing the clinician with results from a number of patients." (p. 57)

Gianutsos and Gianutsos (in press) discuss this further, arguing that generalizability is addressed directly only in single-case designs. Limits of generalization can be established through systematic replication with controlled changes in variables across which generalization might be expected. One problem with single-case designs is that studies failing to show improvement are rarely, if ever, reported. Thus we do not know the failure rate, something that *can* be determined from group studies.

In many cases the solution would seem to lie in discovering as much as possible about the effects of treatment with individuals, including necessary adjustments and optimal learning conditions, before applying the treatment to a more conventional group study. In other words, single-case designs should be regarded as useful pilot studies enabling us to determine through close monitoring what aspects of treatment are important. Once this has been achieved, group studies can throw further light upon the extent to which the treatment is generalisable.

Of course the concept of generalisation can also be applied to different settings, other behaviours and even different therapists, but these applications are usually ignored by both large-N and single-case designs. However, evaluation of the extent to which they occur or ways in which generalisation can be improved, will probably be easier to measure in single-case than in large-group studies. Wilson (1987) considers generalisation in greater detail.

STATISTICS IN SINGLE CASE DESIGNS

Statistics are less often employed in single-case designs than in group studies. There is controversy about their use in single-case studies, with some arguing that, if statistics are needed to determine whether intervention is effective, then clinical significance in unlikely to have occurred. Others argue that there are occasions when statistics are useful. An example which supports the latter argument would be the situation when one is faced with uncontrolled variability in the dependent variable. To illustrate this, let us consider the example of a young man who was unable to learn people's names following a severe head injury. In order to determine whether visual imagery might lead to better learning of names than rehearsal, 16 names of staff were selected, all of whom came into daily contact with the young man, yet he knew none of their names from photographs during four baseline sessions. The 16 names were randomly assigned to one of two conditions, visual imagery or rehearsal. Two new names, one from each condition were introduced in each session and the exposure time for each name was roughly equivalent.

There was a certain amount of variability between test sessions and between conditions, and it was not immediately obvious whether imagery was better than rehearsal. Therefore a Wilcoxon matched-pairs signed ranks test was applied to the data. A nonparametric test was used because such tests do not require a normal distribution. A Wilcoxon was used because the pairs of names were matched (i.e., none were correctly recalled in the baseline and they were introduced for treatment at the same time). Comparisons were made on the basis of the number of occasions each name was successfully recalled. The Wilcoxon test indicated a significant difference in favour of the visual imagery conditions ($T = 2$; $p < .01$).

For further discussion of the arguments for and against statistical analysis, together with descriptions of appropriate statistical techniques, the reader is referred to Edgington (1982), Kazdin (1976), and Yule and Hemsley (1977). It is, perhaps, worth pointing out here that, in a small group study (as opposed to a single-case design), it is necessary to have *all* or almost all of the subjects achieve the desired effect before an acceptable level of significance can be achieved. This is unlike a large-group study where several of the subjects can *fail* to demonstrate the desired effect, yet a significant result can still be obtained provided the majority do not show this pattern. In other words, it can be argued that small-group statistical significance is even more significant than large-group statistical significance or, to put it another way, the effect has to be larger when the Ns are smaller.

CONCLUSIONS

This paper argues for the acceptance of single-case experimental designs in the evaluation of treatment of individual patients. Group studies are important in many investigations and some questions can only be answered by using large samples: for instance, order and interaction effects can be investigated much more readily by using large studies, and some kinds of generalization may also be better answered this way. Furthermore, there are questions which are exclusively in the province of group design. These are typically questions to do with populations: they do not ask whether a particular treatment is effective with a particular patient but whether the effects of a treatment are sufficient to warrant the investment of

Health Service money or to justify a change in a particular institution's rehabilitation policy. In contrast, when we are interested in an individual patient's response to treatment, and when we want to tease out effects of other recovery factors from effects of intervention strategy, then single-case designs are more appropriate.

REFERENCES

American College of Physicians (1985). Biofeedback for neuromuscular disorders. *Annals of International Medicine, 102,* 854-858.

Broca, P. (1861). Nouvelle observation d'aphémie produite par une lésion de la moitié postérieure des deuxième et troisième circonvolutions frontales. *Bulletin de la Société Anatomique de Paris, 6,* 398-407.

Carr, C., & Wilson, B. A. (1983). Promotion of pressure relief exercising in a spinal injury patient: A multiple baseline across settings design. *Behavioural Psychotherapy, 11,* 329-336.

Diller, L. & Weinberg, J. (1977). Hemi-inattention in rehabilitation: the evolution of a rational remediation programme. In E. A. Weinstein & R. P. Friedland (Eds). *Advances in neurology,* Vol. 18 pp. 63-82. New York: Raven Press.

Edgington, E. S. (1982). Nonparametric tests for single-subject multiple schedule experiments. *Behavioural Assessment, 4,* 83-91.

Fisher, R. A. (1925). *Statistical methods for research workers.* London: Oliver and Boyd.

Gianutsos, R., & Gianutsos, J. (in press). Single case experimental approaches to the assessment of interventions in rehabilitation psychology. In B. Caplan (Ed.) *Rehabilitative psychology.* Rockville, MD: Aspen Corp.

Hersen, M., & Barlow, D. H. (1976). *Single case experimental designs: Strategy for studying behaviour change.* Elmsford, New York: Pergamon.

Kazdin, A. E. (1976). Statistical analysis for single case experimental designs. In M. Hersen & D. H. Barlow (Eds.) *Single Case Experimental Designs: Strategy For Studying Behaviour Change.* (pp. 265-316). Elmsford, NY: Pergamon.

Kazdin, A. E. (1982). *Single case research designs.* New York: Oxford University Press.

Kratochwill, T. R. (1978). (Ed.) *Single subject research strategies for evaluating change,* New York: Academic Press.

Robinson, E. P. (1970). *Effective study.* New York: Harper & Row.

Robinson, P. W., & Foster, D. F. (1979). *Experimental psychology: A small-N approach.* New York: Harper & Row.

Shapiro, M. B. (1966). The single case in clinical psychological research. *Journal of General Psychology, 74,* 3-23.

Singh, N. N., Beale, I. L., & Dawson, M. J. (1981). Duration of facial screening and suppression of self-injurious behaviour: analysis using an alternating treatments design. *Behavioural Assessment, 3,* 411-420.

Scoville, W. B., & Milner, B. (1957). Loss of recent memory after bilateral hippocampal lesions. *Journal of Neurology, Neurosurgery and Psychiatry, 20,* 11-21.

Skinner, B. F. (1938). *The behaviour of organisms.* New York: Appleton-Century-Crofts.

Skinner, B. F. (1956). A case history in scientific method. *American Psychologist, 2,* 221-233.

Skinner, B. F. (1961). *Cumulative record.* New York: Appleton-Century-Crofts.

Watson, J. B., & Rayner, R. (1920). Conditioned emotional reactions, *Journal of Experimental Psychology, 3,* 1-14.

Weinberg, J., Diller, L., Gordon, W. A., Gerstman, L. J., Lieberman, A., Lakin, P., Hodges, G., & Ezrachi, O. (1979). Training sensory awareness and spatial organization in people with right brain damage. *Archives of Physical Medicine and Rehabilitation 60*, 491-496.

Wilson, B. A. (1982). Success and failure in memory training following a cerebral vascular accident. *Cortex, 18,* 581-594.

Wilson, B. A. (1987). *Rehabilitation of memory.* New York: Guilford Press.

Wilscn, B. A. (in Press). Identification and remediation of everyday problems in memory impaired adults. In P. Nathan, N. Butters, & O. Parson (Eds.) *Neuropsychology of alcoholism: Implications for diagnosis and treatment.* New York: Guilford Press.

Wilson, B. A., & Moffat, N. (Eds.) (1984a). *Clinical management of memory problems.* London: Croom Helm.

Wilson, B. A., & Moffat, N. (1984b). Rehabilitation of memory for everyday life. In J. Harris & P. Morris (Eds.) *Everyday memory: Actions and absentmindedness* (pp. 207-233). London: Academic Press.

Wong, S. E., & Liberman, R. P. (1981). Mixed single subject designs in clinical research: variations of the multiple baseline. *Behavioural Assessment, 3,* 297-306.

Yule, W., & Hemsley, D. (1977). Single case method in medical psychology. In S. Rachman (Ed.) *Contributions to medical psychology, 1* (pp. 211-229). Oxford: Pergamon Press.

CHAPTER III

Premorbid Risk Factors, Attribute Variables, and Covariance

Grant, Reed, and Adams present a working model for understanding how the natural history of substance abuse may affect the design and interpretation of future research in this area of neuropsychological investigation.

Tupper and Rosenblood argue that attribute or subject variables, because of their putative effect upon brain functioning, are, per force, of more than passing interest to neuropsychologists. The manner in which such variables (e.g., age, gender, socioeconomic status, lateral hemisphere of lesion) affect the underlying assumptions of traditional research designs, the application of standard data-analytic strategies, and the inferences that can be drawn from relevant research investigations are critically examined.

In their comments on inappropriate application of the analysis of covariance (ANCOVA), namely, when the covariate is correlated with the treatment, Tupper and Rosenblood base their arguments on conceptual issues deriving from underlying assumptions of the ANCOVA technique. Adams, Brown, and Grant apply computer-simulation methodology to data deriving from actual patients, in order to provide empirical justification for making decisions about when to employ or not employ ANCOVA in neuropsychological research.

Finally, the last study in this section, undertaken by Adams and Grant, is designed to allow the possible effects of premorbid risk factors on neuropsychological functioning to manifest themselves as specific behavior impairments in matched groups of alcoholics and controls. The investigation has direct implications for possible erroneous conclusions that may have been drawn from earlier studies that have ignored the effects of previous risk variables upon behavioral deficits characterizing the neuropsychological functioning of alcoholics.

Taken together, the four studies in this section have very important implications for a better understanding and appreciation of methodologic and biostatistical issues in behavioral and biomedical research in general and neuropsychological investigations in particular. The major lesson taught here is that the natural history of a given clinical phenomenon, as well as attribute variables and risk factors in general, serve to impose real limitations in each basic area of clinical research, namely: (a) the very design of relevant neuropsychological studies; (b) the results that are obtained; and (c) the meaning these results will have both at a clinical and biostatistical level of interpretation. As such, the selected publications appear to have far-reaching implications for the design, data-analytic strategies, and heuristic value of future clinical investigations of brain-behavior relationships as well as other clinical phenomena.

Journal of Clinical Neuropsychology
1980, Vol. 2, No. 4, 321-331.

Natural History of Alcohol and Drug-Related Brain Disorder: Implications for Neuropsychological Research*

Igor Grant and Robert Reed
V. A. Medical Center, San Diego
and
University of California

Kenneth M. Adams
Henry Ford Hospital

ABSTRACT

Clinical investigations are conducted within limits imposed by the natural history of the phenomena under study. A model for the natural history of alcohol and drug-related brain disorder is presented along with the theoretical arguments and research data which support such a model. The model is then discussed in terms of how it might affect the design and implementation of future studies of the neuropsychological consequences of substance abuse.

Does abuse of drugs cause brain damage? Such a simply phrased question belies the innumerable complexities nested within. Let us say some drug (call it β-neurorgasmine) really does produce irreparable or, at least, long-lasting brain changes. What is involved in unearthing β-neurorgasmine's effect? Figure 1 illustrates the first set of issues in terms of the natural history of β-neurorgasmine induced dementia.

Let us assume a person's existence in time can be represented on a continuum from conception (C) through death (D) and that his chronological age (A) moves along a line from birth (B) to death (D). Let us assume further that the person is born with a healthy brain, and that events do not alter this status between birth (B) and age (X), the time of first exposure to β-neurorgasmine. Time Y then becomes the earliest age at which irreversible neuronal changes begin to occur in relation to use of the drug, and time Z becomes the age at which an abuser of this drug first presents with clinical signs of dementia. Time (Z-Y) can be called the preclinical

* Supported by Medical Research Service of the Veterans Administration
Dr. Adams is also affiliated with Wayne State University and the University of Michigan.

134

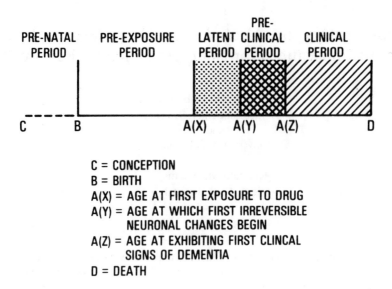

C = CONCEPTION
B = BIRTH
A(X) = AGE AT FIRST EXPOSURE TO DRUG
A(Y) = AGE AT WHICH FIRST IRREVERSIBLE
        NEURONAL CHANGES BEGIN
A(Z) = AGE AT EXHIBITING FIRST CLINCAL
        SIGNS OF DEMENTIA
D = DEATH

Fig. 1. Model for the natural history of neurotoxin induced dementia (1).

stage of drug-induced dementia and the period (D-Z) becomes the clinical course, assuming no recovery potential.

The likelihood of finding drug-induced dementia in a population thus becomes, in part, a function of the age (A) of the subjects studied. If A<X, then no impairments are possible. But even if A>X, no impairment can be found until the subject reaches time Y, the first neurotoxic event. This latent period (Y-X) might be infinite for a relatively nontoxic agent used infrequently; or Y might be virtually concurrent with X for extremely toxic agents, or for moderately toxic ones used in very high doses.

Time Y defines earliest age at which perfectly sensitive neuropsychological (NP) or neurological tests could document a neurotoxic event. In reality, even extremely sensitive tests both extant and yet to be developed can only appraoch Y, since we are unlikely ever to be able to reveal damage only to one or a few neurones. Thus, our research efforts can only find evidence of impairment at some later point in the natural history. This point is termed Y' in Figure 2. The size of the pool occupying the period (Y'-Y) then becomes a reflection of the sensitivity of the neurodiagnostic method in question (i.e., sensitivity in *pre*clinical casefinding).

Let us illustrate some of the points made so far with selected neuropsychological research findings on alcoholism.

In Figure 3 we present some of our own findings with younger alcoholics and controls (Grant, Adams, & Reed, 1979), some work with healthy elderly persons (Grant, Heaton, McSweeny, Adams, & Timms, Note 1) and also show borrowed

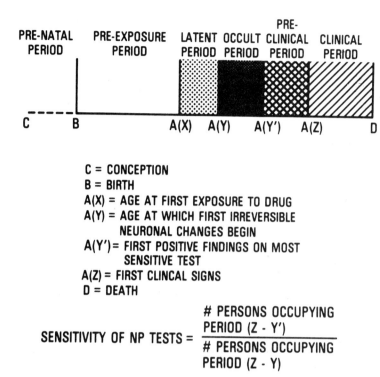

Fig. 2. Model for the natural history of neurotoxin induced dementia (2).

data points from the published works of several other investigators (Blusewicz, Dustman, Schenkenberg, & Beck, 1977; Fitzhugh, Fitzhugh, & Reitan, 1960; 1965; Goldstein & Shelly, 1971; Jones & Parsons, 1971; 1972) who used comparable methods to illustrate changes in Category Test performance in relation to age in alcoholics and nonalcoholics.

Alcoholics in these various studies generally began very heavy drinking in their mid-20s. For our purposes then, X (first clinically important exposure) occurs approximately at age 25. It will be noted that the curves are essentially identical till subjects reach age 40. At this time, alcoholics begin more rapid deterioration than nonalcoholics. Thus, it appears that Y', the age at which a fairly sensitive test begins to find evidence of impairment, is around 40. By age 50, impairment is sufficient that clinical signs are likely. From these data, we would consider that the latent (Y-X) and occult (Y'-Y) periods of alcoholism-related dementia span some 15 years from age 25-40, that the preclinical period (Z-Y) spans another ten years, and that early clinical neurologic signs can be expected when alcoholics who continue active drinking reach age 50 (i.e., Z=50).

The inference that the age (Y) of onset of the preclinical phase is 40 and perhaps

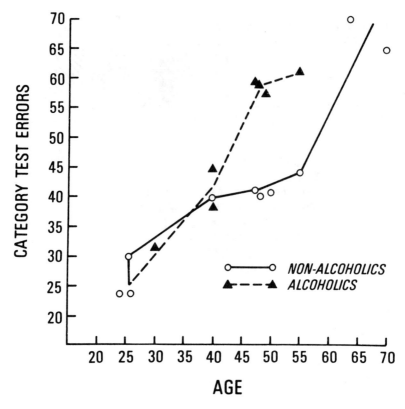

Fig. 3. Natural history of alcoholism - related brain disorder as reflected by the Category Test.

a little younger finds support in some recent work by Ryan and Butters (1980). While finding no significant differences between alcoholics and controls in the 34-49 year old age group on a four-word, short-term memory test, these investigators did note some decrements in alcoholics' immediate learning of verbal-verbal paired associates and more substantial decrements on symbol-digit paired associate learning.

We observed that recently detoxified alcoholics, mean age 37, while appearing normal at initial testing on the Halstead-Reitan Battery augmented by memory tests, at the same time failed to improve at one year retest despite remaining either abstinent or drinking only very modestly (Adams, Grant, & Reed, 1980). This failure to benefit from incidental learning (nonalcoholic controls and long-term abstinent alcoholics *did* improve at retest) may be further evidence that the preclinical period of alcoholism-related cerebral disorder extends back to age 37, perhaps even slightly younger.

Putting these findings together with the Category Test data it looks as though most alcoholics who begin heavy drinking at age 25 can be shown to have some very early deficit by their late thirties. We would, therefore, revise our suggestions above to state that the latent and occult periods (if we call "X" the onset of heavy drinking rather than first drink experience) appear to span a dozen years, and the preclinical period another 12 years. Now, there is also evidence that if X is earlier, then Y' will also be earlier. As an example, Blucewicz et al. (1977) found alcoholics aged 33 to be neuropsychologically impaired. These patients began heavy drinking at around 20 and appeared to abuse alcohol at an unusually heavy level as judged by the frequency of reports of delirium tremens and related signs of severe withdrawal.

We do not know at what age the average alcoholic experiences Y, the earliest irreversible insult. Nor can we estimate the duration of the occult period, since, by definition, it encompasses brain damage too subtle to measure.

To summarize points made so far, if we use a model based on natural history, minimum requirements of a study endeavoring to establish a causal link between drug abuse and brain damage are: a population in which sufficient numbers of cases have traversed time X (began drug taking); a drug which is indeed neurotoxic and which has been taken in an amount and frequency which moves persons to time Y (first neurotoxic event); and tests used to detect brain damage must be sensitive in that the occupants of period Z-Y are largely contained in the preclinical period (Z-Y') and few in the occult period (Y'-Y). Let us turn now to some further issues which impact NP research on substance abuse.

Population mobility complicates efforts to study the relationship between drug abuse and brain function. For example, persons developing organicity are likely to undergo behavior change. Some persons might drift downward in social position and become lost to follow-up either because of their unattached, disorganized life style, or because they have entered a criminal subculture and do not want to be detected. Alternatively, cerebral dysfunction might mimic functional psychopathological syndromes, causing persons to become sequestered in the mental health care delivery system.

As active drug users become inaccessible to examination, population studies of CNS correlates will be prone to underestimate drug-related morbidity. This problem was encountered in the Collaborative Neuropsychological Study of Polydrug Users (CNSP) (Grant, Adams, Carlin, Rennick, Judd, & Schooff, 1978). The patients who could not be traced in a three month follow-up had a tendency to abuse barbiturates more intensively and were less educated than the completers. Although the dropouts and completers were neuropsychologically comparable at the start of the study, it is possible that these groups would ultimately diverge in terms of the incidence of neuropsychological deficit. This serious problem is further complicated by the 50% attrition rates which seem to be typical of longitudinal studies of alcoholics and drug abusers. In the same fashion, death of persons contained in the period Z-Y will serve to lower incidence and prevalence estimates, especially in older populations.

Another issue is *pattern of drug use*. Recreational or dependent drug consumption is not steadily progressive in most instances (Schuckit, 1979). Rather, epochs of intensive use tend to be followed by quiescent periods in which detoxification occurs. Further, a proportion of drinkers and heroin addicts are known to experience permanent spontaneous remissions (Cahalan, 1970; Mulford, 1964; Robins, 1975; Vaillant, 1966) and it is likely that such a pattern is true for the abuse of other substances as well. Such temporary or permanent remissions will tend to lengthen the latent (Y-X) and occult (Y'-Y) periods, leading to further underestimation of possible permanent drug effect.

So far, this discussion has assumed drug effect on the CNS is inexorable, i.e., as various points on the natural history continuum are passed, there is no return. Actually, such a model is overly simplistic. Both the work to be presented here and other studies on alcoholism (Ayers, Templer, Ruff, & Barthlow, 1978; Bergland, Leijonquist, & Horlen, 1977; Page & Linden, 1974; Sharp, Rosenbaum, Goldman, & Whitman, 1977) suggest that there is not a clear separation of acute, reversible and long-term irreversible effects. Alcoholics and polydrug abusers may experience an organic mental disorder of intermediate duration (Grant & Judd, 1976; Judd & Grant, 1978) when they become abstinent. For example, some continuing recovery of neuropsychological functions has been demonstrated as much as a year after stopping heavy drinking among alcoholics (Long & McLachlan, 1974; O'Leary, Radford, Chaney, & Schau, 1977). In the national polydrug study, 25% of the polydrug users judged to be impaired three weeks after entry into treatment improved substantially three months later (Grant et al., 1978). Similar findings were reported earlier by Grant and Judd (1976) using both EEG and neuropsychological assessments. Thus, unless sufficient time has elapsed between last drug taking and neurological or neuropsychological assessment, persons with reversible intermediate duration organic mental disorders might get misclassified as having permanent damage. Using the model in Figure 2, misclassification of cases of intermediate duration disorder as permanent brain damage inflates the toxicity estimate for a drug by inappropriately bringing event Y forward in time.

Up to this point we have made the implicit assumption that polydrug users or alcoholics are a subset of the "normal population", different only in that they have decided to use drugs. It seems unlikely that this is so. Heroin addiction, for example, is over-represented among minority and lower social position groups. There is evidence that very poor people receive inadequate prenatal care, experience more obstetrical difficulty, and have more neonatal morbidity than the general population. Such perinatal variables have been correlated with later cerebral dysfunction (Pasamanick & Knobloch, 1966). Polydrug users from the CNSP, the majority of whom came from lower socioeconomic groups, reported four times as many medical events and symptoms of potential neurological consequence in their medical histories as did controls (Grant et al., 1978). This findings illustrates the point: If drug use and cerebral dysfunction are both more prevalent in a disadvantaged group, and if an association is found between certain drugs and deficit, where is the causality? Are previously dysfunctional people self-medicating? Are drugs causing brain damage? Or is there an interaction between CNS vulnerability and drug toxicity?

There is evidence from the CNSP consistent with each of these causal models (Carlin, Stauss, Grant, & Adams, 1980). Among those polydrug users who were the most promiscuous in their drug taking, an association was noted between lifetime use of opiates and alcohol and neuropsychological impairment, but *not* between neuropsychological deficit and medical history. At the same time, another subset of polydrug users showed a relationship between medical history and impairment. These subjects abused all classes of drugs less, with the exception of barbiturates. The first observation is consistent with (though certainly does not prove) the hypothesis that opiates and alcohol "cause" deficit. The second observation could be consistent with either of two hypotheses: (1) some polydrug users were impaired to start with, and their almost exclusive use of barbiturates either was unrelated to cerebral disorder, or perhaps represented an effort to "medicate" perceived deficits; (2) these polydrug users had marginally compensated cerebral function which began to fail under the impact of barbiturate abuse.

Yet another difficulty in understanding drug-neuropsychological relationships comes from investigators' selection biases, which serve to amplify the inherent "atypicality" (in reference to the "normal population") of the drug user. Studies which try to identify polydrug subjects through survey techniques will be troubled by self-selection on the basis of willingness to cooperate with a survey. Such studies will also suffer the vagaries of response bias, concealment of drug taking, or frivolous and otherwise invalid information. On the other hand, studies based on drug users in treatment must acknowledge that persons who see themselves, or allow themselves to be managed, as patients may be different from nonpatients. For example, Phin (1978) found that multiple drug users *not* in treatment were younger, but better educated than polydrug patients; and Lachar, Schooff, Keegan, and Gdowski (1978) found the former to be psychologically "healthier" on the basis of MMPI testing.

Another consideration is the tendency of the polydrug abuser who is serious about his occupation to use a wide variety of chemicals concurrently or sequentially. There are few people who can legitimately be classified as "pure stimulant users", "pure hallucinogen users" or the like. For example, Judd, Attewell, Riney, and Avery (1978) surveyed drug taking of clients at alcohol treatment programs, mental health clinics, heroin treatment programs, and drug abuse agencies. They found that, irrespective of type of agency studied, approximately 17% of the clients reported substantial use of three major classes of drugs (excluding tobacco and marihuana). Thus, in a naturalistic setting, the separate and joint contributions of drugs to brain disorder can only be appreciated through examination of a large number of subjects with varying drug histories, and evaluation of results with the help of multivariate statistical methods. In one application of this approach, a multivariate analysis of variance was performed to consider simultaneously the potential contributions of life use of seven drugs to impairment (Grant et al., 1978). In this instance, unique contributions of depressants and opiates were noted.

Even if a drug-to-brain damage path can be shown, the question of mechanism remains. Is the drug a neurotoxin? Or does the drug, or conditions of its use, trigger a chain of physiological or behavioral events which make brain damage more likely, for example, heroin and sedative-hypnotic abusers experience hypoxic episodes. If a drug-correlated deficit were found, might it not really be the cumulative result of hypoxic insult? Alcoholics and drug abusers report frequent episodes of head injury and periods of unconsciousness. How might this physical trauma contribute to observed deficit? Unsterile injections introduce foreign matter and microorganisms into the body. The foreign matter can trigger allergic-vascular responses, and certain micro-organisms can infect the brain and meninges. Indeed, there is preliminary evidence that drug use "style", irrespective of specific chemicals used, can be predictive of neuropsychological impairment (Carlin et al., 1980).

Finally, no discussion of neuropsychological research concerning alcohol or drugs can be complete without reminding ourselves of the need to consider age and education in interpreting findings. Although Finlayson, Johnson, and Reitan (1977) and Prigatano and Parsons (1976) have already emphasized this point, perhaps Table 1 will underscore the problem as the data emerge specifically from neuropsychological findings in alcoholism and drug abuse. Here the Halstead-Reitan Battery measured neuropsychological abilities of 96 polydrug users, 83 alcoholics, and 79 controls are represented as four factors. Factor 1 was conceptualized primarily as reflecting verbal-academic skills, factor 2, as attention, factor 3 perceptual-motor skills, and factor 4, spacial-perceptual ability (and trace factor). Readers will observe that a low level, but significant, inverse relationship is found between the last two factors and age, and a positive relationship between the verbal-academic factor and education.

SUMMARY

In this report an attempt has been made to identify concepts and issues critical to designing research programs aimed at understanding the relationship between alcoholism, drug abuse and cerebral disorder. In particular, future research efforts must be placed in the context of the natural history of substance abuse, and samples selected from populations in which sufficient numbers of persons might be expected to have reached the preclinical phase of cerebral disturbance in relation to drug use. In doing so, investigators must be cognizant that persons with serious drug abuse problems are likely to have used at least several drugs in

TABLE 1

Relationship of Age and Education to Neuropsychological Factor Scores in
Combined Alcoholics, Polydrug Users and Controls*

	Factor 1 $r =$	Factor 2 $r =$	Factor 3 $r =$	Factor 4 $r =$
Age	.17 N.S.	−.09 N.S.	−.28 $p < .006$	−.27 $p < .007$
Education	.43 $p < .007$	.21 $p < .03$	−.03 N.S.	.19 $p < .04$

* Mean age and age ranges for subjects were:
   Alcoholics 37.2, 24 to 46; Polydrug users 27.0, 14 to 57; Controls 31.5, 16 to 46.
   Mean education levels and ranges of education were:
   Alcoholics 13.0, 7 to 19; Polydrug users 11.5, 6 to 18; Controls 12.8, 8 to 18.

substantial amounts, and to prepare for this by examining sufficient numbers to permit application of multivariate data analytic techniques. Investigators should remember that polydrug users are an atypical group, probably more apt to have psychiatric disturbance and to have experienced life events that put them at risk for neurological morbidity. Studies must include checks for acute toxicity, and follow-up of abstinent persons must be of sufficient duration to assure that any slowly reversible organic mental disorder has resolved. In this way one can be assured that observed impairment truly represents permanent neurological change. The characteristics of subjects not studied, or studied initially but lost to follow-up, must be of concern. Another way of putting this is that those who are most difficult to recruit in the first place, or those who drop out, might be doing so precisely because their behavior is influenced by brain disorder. Investigators must be alert to the possibility that drug taking and nondrug related neurological insult might be mutually reinforcing, or that drugs, though not being neurotoxic *per se,* might still place people at risk by virtue of the circumstances of their use or their other behavioral effects. This means that careful developmental, medical, and behavrioral histories are essential.

REFERENCE NOTE

1. Grant, I., Heaton, R., McSweeny, A. J., Adams, K. M., & Timms, R. M. Neuropsychological deficits in patients with hypoxemic COPD. Manuscript available from first author.

REFERENCES

Adams, K. M. Grant, I., & Reed, R. J. Neuropsychology in alcoholic men in their late thirties: One year followup. *American Journal of Psychiatry,* 1980, *137,* 928-931.

Ayers, J. L., Templer, D. I., Ruff, C. F., & Barthlow, V. L. Trail Making Test improvement in abstinent alcoholics. *Journal of Studies on Alcohol,* 1978, *39,* 1627-1629.

Bergland, M., Leijonquist, H., & Horlen, M. Prognostic significance and reversibility of cerebral dysfunction in alcoholics. *Journal of Studies on Alcohol,* 1977, *38,* 1761-1770.

Blusewicz, M. J., Dustman, R. E., Schenkenberg, T., & Beck, E. C. Neuropsychological correlates of chronic alcoholism and aging. *Journal of Nervous and Mental Disease,* 1977, *165,* 348-355.

Cahalan, D. *Problem drinkers.* San Francisco: Josey-Bass, 1970.

Carlin, A. S., Stauss, F., Grant, I., & Adams, K. M. The role of streetwise status and drug use in neuropsychological impairment among polydrug abusers. *Addictive Behaviors,* 1980, *5,* 229-234.

Finlayson, M. A. J., Johnson, K. A., & Reitan, R. M. Relationship of level of education to neuropsychological measures in brain-damaged and non-brain-damaged adults. *Journal of Consulting and Clinical Psychology,* 1977, *45,* 536-542.

Fitzhugh, L. C., Fitzhugh, K. B., & Reitan, R. M. Adaptive abilities and intellectual functioning in hospitalized alcoholics. *Quarterly Journal of Studies on Alcohol,* 1960, *21,* 414-423.

Fitzhugh, L. C., Fitzhugh, K. B., & Reitan, R. M. Adaptive abilities and intellectual functioning in hospitalized alcoholics: Further considerations. *Quarterly Journal of Studies on Alcohol,* 1965, *26,* 402-411.

Goldstein, G., & Shelly, C. H. Field dependence and cognitive, perceptual and motor skills in alcoholics: A factor analytic study. *Quarterly Journal of Studies on Alcohol,* 1971, *32,* 29-40.

Grant, I., Adams, K. M., Carlin, A. S., Rennick, P. M., Judd, L. L., & Schooff, K. The collaborative neuropsychological study of polydrug users. *Archives of General Psychiatry,* *35,* 1063-1074.

Grant, I., Adams, K. M., & Reed, R. J. Normal neuropsychological abilities of alcoholic men in their late thirties. *American Journal of Psychiatry,* 1979, *136,* 1263-1269.

Grant, I., & Judd, L. L. Neuropsychological and EEG disturbances in polydrug users. *American Journal of Psychiatry,* 1976, *133,* 1039-1042.

Jones, B., & Parsons, O. A. Impaired abstracting ability in chronic alcoholics. *Archives of General Psychiatry,* 1971, *24,* 71-75.

Jones, B., & Parsons, O. A. Specific vs. generalized deficits of abstracting ability in chronic alcoholics. *Archives of General Psychiatry,* 1972, *26,* 380-384.

Judd, L. L., Attewell, A., Riney, W. B., & Avery, R. F. Response of traditional health care agencies to non-opiate abusers. In D. R. Wesson, A. S. Carlin, K. M. Adams, & G. Beschner (Eds.), *Polydrug abuse: The results of a national collaborative study.* New York: Academic Press, 1978.

Judd, L. L., & Grant, I. Intermediate duration organic mental disorder among polydrug abusing patients. *Psychiatric Clinics of North America,* 1978, *1,* 153-167.

Lachar, D., Schooff, K., Keegan, J., & Gdowski, C. Dimensions of polydrug abuse: An MMPI study. In D. R. Wesson, A. S. Carlin, K. Adams, & G. Beschner (Eds.), *Polydrug abuse: The results of a national collaborative study.* New York: Academic Press Inc., 1978.

Long, J. A., & McLachlan, J. F. C. Abstract reasoning and perceptual motor efficiency in alcoholics: Impairment and reversibility. *Quarterly Journal of Studies on Alcohol,* 1974, *35,* 1220-1229.

Mulford, H. A. Drinking and deviant drinking, U.S.A. 1963. *Quarterly Journal of Studies on Alcohol,* 1964, *25,* 634-650.

O'Leary, M. R., Radford, L. M., Chaney, E. F., & Schau, E. J. Assessment of cognitive recovery in alcoholics by use of the Trail Making Test. *Journal of Clinical Psychology,* 1977, *33,* 579-582.

Page, R. D., & Linden, J. D. Reversible organic brain syndromes in alcoholics: A psychological evaluation. *Quarterly Journal of Studies on Alcohol,* 1974, *35,* 98-107.

Pasamanick, B., & Knobloch, H. Retrospective studies on the epidemiology of reproductive casualty: Old and new. *Merrill-Palmer Quarterly Behavioral Development,* 1966, *12, 7.*

Phin, J. Non-patient polydrug users. In D. R. Wesson, A. S. Carlin, K. M. Adams, & G. Beschner (Eds.), *Polydrug abuse: The results of a national collaborative study.* New York: Academic Press, 1978.

Prigatano, G. P., & Parsons, O. A. Relationship of age and education to Halstead Retian test performance in different populations. *Journal of Consulting and Clinical Psychology,* 1976, *44,* 527-533.

Robins, L. N. History of drug use. In J. Elinson & D. Nurko (Eds.), *Operational definitions in sociobehavioral drug use research.* Rockville: NIDA Research Monograph Series #2, October, 1975.

Ryan, C., & Butters, N. Learning and memory impairment in young and old alcoholics: Evidence for the premature aging hypothesis, *Alcoholism: Clinical and experimental research,* 1980, in press.

Sharp, J. R., Rosenbaum, G., Goldman, M. S., & Whitman, R. D. Recoverability of psychological functioning following alcohol abuse: Acquisition of meaningful synonyms. *Journal of Consulting and Clinical Psychology,* 1977, *45,* 1023-1028.

Schuckit, M. A. *Drug and alcohol abuse: A clinical guide to diagnosis and treatment.* New York and London: Plenum Medical Book Company, 1979.

Vaillant, G. D. A twelve year follow-up of New York narcotic addicts. III. Some social and psychiatric characteristics. *Archives of General Psychiatry,* 1966, *15,* 559-609.

Journal of Clinical Neuropsychology
1984, Vol. 6, No. 4, pp. 441-453

Methodological Considerations in the Use of Attribute Variables in Neuropsychological Research*

David E. Tupper
John F. Kennedy Medical Center

and

Lorne K. Rosenblood
University of Victoria

ABSTRACT

This paper examines the conceptual and statistical difficulties created when neuropsychological research uses attribute variables in traditional orthogonal experimental designs. It is argued that attribute variables, as a result of their statistical and theoretical nonindependence, break the underlying assumptions of these traditional designs, and may lead to incorrect inferences being drawn. These difficulties are illustrated in a consideration of the typical use of analysis of variance designs, matched groups designs, and the analysis of covariance. Finally, a plea is made for the explicit consideration of the assumptions underlying the design models used in neuropsychological research, and a suggestion is made regarding the more appropriate use of correlational techniques in neuropsychology.

Neuropsychological research is concerned with the relationship between behavioral and neural functioning. This research can be roughly divided into two major classes: experimental neuropsychological research, which typically involves the use of normal subjects (or animals) in traditional experimental psychology-like procedures, and clinical neuropsychological research, devoted to the understanding and application of brain-behavior relationships to both normal and brain dysfunctioned subjects in clinical situations.

This paper will discuss an important aspect of research design affecting both experimental and clinical neuropsychological investigations, but which is usually more common in clinical research due to the population of interest. Briefly, the major point is that the use of attribute, or subject, variables in an experimental design can lead to difficulties in the inferences and interpretations that can be

* The authors gratefully acknowledge the editorial comments provided by Louis Costa, Anthony Risser, Holly Tuokko and many others at the University of Victoria.

drawn from the results. The reasons for this state of affairs will be reviewed, examples will be given, and several conceptual and methodological suggestions concerning future neuropsychological research will be suggested.

Attribute Variables in Neuropsychology

Neuropsychologists are interested in a variety of attribute variables that characterize subjects and which may affect performance on brain-related psychological measures. Parsons and Prigatano (1978) have pointed out that the use of attribute variables is very crucial to consider in any research study, since many attribute variables can be related to neuropsychological performance. Weiskrantz (1968) has stressed that behavior is multidetermined by many "causes", only some of which are related to the neural substrate. A representative list of these important attribute variables can be put forth, based upon partial lists given by Lezak (1983), Matarazzo (1972), and Parsons and Prigatano (1978); (1) sex of the subject, (2) age of the subject, (3) level of education of the subject, (4) cerebral status, i.e., brain-damaged versus non-brain-damaged, (5) laterality of lesion (right or left hemisphere), (6) site of lesion within the hemisphere, (7) causal agent creating the lesion, (8) severity and extent of the lesion, (9) time between brain damage and testing, (10) handedness-body laterality of the subject, (11) socioeconomic status of the subject, and (12) condition of the patient at testing (medicated, alert, etc.).

Almost all of the above independent variables and, in fact, most variables that would be of interest to a neuropsychologist can be distinguished as *attribute* variables (Kerlinger, 1973, p. 38). Other authors have referred to them as subject variables (Wood, 1974), organismic variables (Games, 1979) or, in some cases, nuisance variables (Meehl, 1970; 1978). They are characteristics that the subject (patient) brings to the testing procedure that cannot be manipulated — they are "attributes" of the subject. These variables can only be measured; they cannot be changed within each subject for different experimental conditions. For example, except possibly for very unethical researchers, the severity of a lesion cannot be changed in any given human subject in a neuropsychological study.

In contrast to attribute variables stand *active* variables (Kerlinger, 1973; p. 38), which can be manipulated experimentally. Level of blood sugar, for example, can be changed in a person — by giving that person insulin, etc. The distinction between these types of variables is very important in the design of an experiment, since it puts limitations on the types of conclusions and inferences that can be drawn. Neuropsychologists are generally restricted to attribute variables in their research and therefore, need to have knowledge of the effects of using such variables.

Complications of the Research Design When Using Attribute Variables

When an attribute variable is used as an "experimental" variable in a neuropsychological research design, the amount of control over other extraneous influences in the "experiment" is low, due to uncontrolled error variances. Although this may appear to be only a statistical-design problem, it also is a conceptual problem since many neuropsychological variables are correlated with each other. Therefore, any attempt to separate out any specific factor is difficult. In order to understand and look at relationships *between* variables, Goldstein and Shelly (1973) and Crockett, Clark, and Klonoff (1981) suggest that neuropsychology should follow a multivariate, interactional, or factorial approach. However, the nonorthogonal nature of attribute variables limits the type of designs that can be used so that factorial designs, which assume independent (uncorrelated) variables (factors), are not appropriate in many cases.

In order to be able to draw causal inferences to a population from the results of an experiment (especially factorial), it is necessary to have both random sampling of the subjects from the specified population and random assignment of the subjects to treatment conditions (Edgington, 1966). Random sampling and random assignment help to control extraneous influences. This type of control is not possible when using attribute variables. Instead, because the variables the researcher is interested in are characteristics of the subjects, the subjects are not randomly selected and assigned to treatments by the experimenter but rather are *self-selected* (Kerlinger, 1973, p. 381); selected into groups because they differentially possess these characteristics or attributes. For example, many neuropsychological investigations use sex as a factor (independent variable). Since sex is an attribute of the subject, the experimenter cannot randomly assign subjects to conditions. Due to this lack of random assignment any differences found between the sexes cannot be attributed solely to the sex of the subject. The differences could have occurred due to a variable confounded with the sex condition. The investigator usually has little knowledge of, or control over, such confounded variables.

The major problem, therefore, when using attribute variables in neuropsychological research, is that one cannot be sure that the effects found in the study are due to the attribute variables. This is caused by the lack of adequate control over extraneous confounded variables (Kish, 1959). These extraneous variables arise from the nonrandom, self-selection of the subjects into treatment conditions. This is a very important concern for neuropsychological research design and, thus far, has not been seriously considered in the neuropsychology literature. A broader discussion of extraneous and confounded variables can be found in a number of textbooks, for example: Campbell and Stanley (1966), Cook and Campbell (1979), Keppel (1973), Kerlinger (1973), Meyers and Grossen (1974), Wood (1974).

Another major problem with attribute variables, alluded to earlier, is the result of the subject self-selection into conditions. Subject self-selection, due to differing base rates of attributes, usually results in unequal cell frequencies in the design. The unequal cell design tells the researcher that the independent variables are nonorthogonal (Appelbaum & Cramer, 1974; Gorsuch, 1973; Horton, 1978;

Spinner & Gabriel, 1981) or "unbalanced" (Keren, 1982). Thus the basic requirement of orthogonality analysis of variance is violated. Since the factors are confounded, each factor contains variance from the other factors. The consequence of this confounding often makes the interpretation of the factor difficult or impossible.

It should also be noted that the independent variables are related conceptually in the real world. Unequal frequencies in a research design should indicate to the researcher that the "independent" variables involved are not truly independent, cannot be separated uniquely, and they should not be treated in a design as if they were independent.

To summarize, then, research using attribute variables lacks the control over extraneous influences that characterizes experimental research and therefore cannot be interpreted in the same way (Huesmann, 1982). Neuropsychological research which uses attribute variables is a nonexperimental (or ex post facto; Campbell & Stanley, 1966) research design. As Games (1979) succinctly states,

When working with organismic variables, one must face the fact that clear interpretative conclusions are not as easy to come by as when working with manipulative variables. The investigator must recognize that the organismic variables he has used are correlated with many other organismic variables... (pp. 197-198).

This section has discussed some of the conceptual problems seen when using attribute variables in neuropsychological research. The following section will describe some of the statistical difficulties associated with using such variables in experimental research, especially when using traditional analysis of variance designs. Also, two types of "correction" procedures that have been used by researchers to try to correct these shortcomings, matched groups designs and analysis of covariance, will be discussed and the conceptual and statistical problems associated with their use will be presented. Examples of the difficulties will be given from the contemporary neuropsychological literature.

Methodological Complications as a Result of Using Attribute Variables in Neuropsychological Research

Analysis of Variance (ANOVA). The use of attribute variables almost inevitably leads to unequal cell sizes in ANOVA designs. For example, the study by O'Donnell, Kurtz, and Ramanaiah (1983) illustrates the complex relationship between beuropsychological status and sex. Looking at Table 1, it is clear that there are more neurologically impaired males than females (67 males vs. 13 females). This result means that sex and brain damage are not independent of each other, therefore violating the fundamental assumption of ANOVA.

As mentioned earlier, this lack of independence revolves around the difference between experimental and nonexperimental research. In experimental research you can randomly assign treatments to subjects, thus assuring equal number of subjects in each cell. In nonexperimental research the subject's attributes

TABLE 1

An illustration of the nonindependence of sex and neuropsychological status in a
study by O'Donnell, Kurtz, and Ramanaiah (1983).

Neuropsychological Status

	Normal Adolescents	Learning Disabled Adolescents	Brain Damaged Adolescents
Males	$n = 21$	$n = 52$	$n = 15$
Females	$n = 9$	$n = 8$	$n = 5$

determine which cell they will be in. If there is a correlation between the attributes in the population then the cell sizes will be unequal. This is the case in the example above. Sex and neurological status are correlated in the real world. In the experimental equal n situation the inferences that you can draw about the factors are relatively simple. If a factor is found to be significant, then you can assume it is significant. Unfortunately in the unequal n case if a factor is found to be statistically significant in reality it may or may not be significant. The reason for this ambiguity is the correlation between the factors. For example, if one finds the sex effect significant, this significance may be due to the sex effect or in part to the neuropsychological status effect or the interaction of the two factors. In other words the factors are confounded with each other.

There have generally been two proposed solutions to this problem. The first, probably most often used, solution is to select samples not based upon the representative proportions of the attributes in the population but rather selected to give equal cell frequencies. It is quite obvious that this approach is not a solution. While it artificially creates equal cell sizes for the analysis, it still ignores the major conceptual problem underlying the research; that of related independent variables. This type of approach pretends that the variables are not correlated and thus proceeds with the analysis when, in fact, the major important finding should often be that the variables *are* related! While results from such a study can often be used appropriately as a description of the sample, inferences drawn from such a study should be viewed with caution. An example from current neuropsychological research is a study by Kaspar and Sokolec (1980). They used four independent variables: brain damage vs. control, two IQ groups, two age groups, and sex, with equal cell sizes, to investigate the relationship between neurological dysfunction and motor performance. Differences in motor performance were found on the brain damage and IQ variables. These differences should not, however, be used to draw inferences back to the brain-damaged and/or low IQ populations since these variables are conceptually related. (Not many neuropsychologists would disagree with this; brain damage and IQ are not independent —— the "amount" of this relationship is actually what neuropsychologists would like to know.) The use of equal cell sizes, when the reality in the population is unequal proportions, treats the statistical and conceptual nonorthogonality problems as if they do not exist in the sample. This is a frequently abused design in neuropsychological research.

Another proposed approach to the unequal cell frequencies problem is to use any of a variety of statistical "compensation" techniques. These techniques, usually some form of unequal n's analysis of variance, are presumed to "adjust" for the nonorthogonality in the design (Appelbaum & Cramer, 1974; Spinner & Gabriel, 1981). These various techniques each partition the total variance differently. Therefore depending on the technique, a given effect may or may not be significant (see Spinner & Gabriel, 1981, for a discussion of this issue). The use of unequal n's analysis can cause the researcher to overlook both the conceptual and statistical problems of the nonorthogonal design. These designs are often interpreted as if the independent variables are orthogonal. An example of the use of this solution, although it was not explicitly stated, is Fedio, Cox, Neophytides, Canal-Frederick & Chase's (1979) study. They had three groups of subjects: normal ($n = 28$), Huntington's disease ($n = 10$), and at risk for Huntington's disease ($n = 47$) as one "independent" variable. Unequal proportions of males and females from these groups were self-selected into another "independent" variable of sex. Sex and occurrence of Huntington's disease are therefore related. It would seem that this in itself would be an important finding — but it is not mentioned in the paper! Any of the many differences they found on their dependent variables are confounded by this conceptual and/or statistical nonorthogonality between the variables.

Neuropsychological research using attribute variables, therefore, is extremely problematic when using analysis of variance as a technique to analyze the data. Nonorthogonal designs are not an area where ANOVA is robust. Yet a perusal of several recent neuropsychological journals suggests that analysis of variance is probably the most widely used statistical analysis technique in the literature.

A related example is the problem that results from arbitrarily forcing continuous variables into traditional ANOVA designs that require discrete, categorical variables. In practice, some researchers divide up (arbitrarily) a continous independent variable (such as categories of intellectual status based on IQ scores, for example) into discrete categories, i.e., different categories of retardation vs. normals. There are a number of consequences of this categorization of the independent variable. One, the relationship between the variables is usually attenuated. Second, by not using all of the variance contained in the total distribution of the variable, it is not possible to specify relationships in the lost parts. Third, by adjusting the cut-off points for placement into conditions the researcher can create "significant" differences between groups (especially extremes of a distribution; Feldt, 1961) when there are no actual "differences" to be found.

An example of this arbitrary division of an independent variable is a study by Gregory and Paul (1980). They compared three groups of subjects (right-handed, left-handed normal writing postures, and left-handed inverted writing posture) on many neuropsychological variables and found several differences. However, they do not state their exact criteria for inclusion into each of the groups. They say that they measured handedness with a laterality questionnaire which gives a continuous measure. Their criteria for selection into each of the groups therefore had to divide up the continuous measure. Any differences that they found could be due entirely to the way that they divided the scores on the questionnaire. They could have obtained more information about the relationship between their variables by trying to specify and measure the relationship(s) between their continuous handedness variable and their various dependent variables. An appropriate statistical procedure that could have been used is multiple regression.

Analysis of variance techniques with attribute variables suffer several serious problems. Because the independent variables are correlated (due to self-selection), theoretically, conceptually, and statistically, inferences made from neuropsychological studies using this method should be viewed with caution since, at least implicitly, the researchers have ignored major assumptions of the underlying model.

The next two techniques have arisen as methods to gain more control over extraneous influences in a research design. One of these is an attempt at "design control"; trying to hold certain extraneous variables constant, the other is a type of "statistical control"; used to statistically remove an unwanted source of variance. Both of these methods, as compensation techniques, will be shown to be flawed when using attribute variables.

Matched-Groups Design. The purpose behind a matched-groups design is to control extraneous variation by equating the conditions of the independent variable experimentally, prior to the measurement of the dependent variable(s). By doing this, it is thought, other correlated (extraneous) variables can be held constant. This should help the generalizability of the results.

One point concerning the matching itself should be emphasized. All too often matching is done on the basis of group means. That is, as long as groups do not differ on the matching variables, the matching is assumed to be done well. However, this is not the case. As Boneau and Pennypacker (1961) have demonstrated, matching should not be done on groups but on individual subjects, i.e., pairs of subjects should be matched. Otherwise, group matching will artificially restrict the ordinary random variation of the group means and the results will be more difficult to interpret: statistical inference is obviated with group matching.

Matching subjects in an ex post facto design, rather than helping the generalizability of the results actually makes inferences and interpretations more difficult. Meehl (1970) distinguishes three major problems which, even if matching is done properly, create difficulties when using attribute variables in ex post facto-style research. It is worth emphasizing his points here. The first problem he calls *systematic unmatching.* This occurs when pairs of subjects are equated on a "nuisance" (extraneous) variable. By holding this identified nuisance variable constant, the result will generally be to systematically unmatch the pairs with regard to some other (unidentified) nuisance variable(s); thus, actually creating a spurious association. (Of course, the extent of this occurrence depends upon the intercorrelations of the variables.)

The second is the *unrepresentative subpopulation problem.* This occurs when, by matching (pairwise) for a nuisance variable, the matching procedure identifies a sample from the population that differs systematically from the population of interest. This almost automatically affects generalizability. Any inferences to be made can only be made to the sample that has been collected by matching, not to the population.

The third is *causal-arrow ambiguity.* Since a discussion of the notion of "causation" is beyond the scope of this paper, it is sufficient to say here that the distinctions between nuisance variables and experimental variables are not as clear as many people would like to believe. In fact, Meehl's point is that we are not really sure what "nuisance variables" are in a design. Therefore, when we match for them, we may actually be obscuring a relationship that we would be interested in. For anyone interested in matching in nonexperimental research, Meehl's (1970) paper is highly recommended.

An example of a matched-groups design from neuropsychological literature is that of Heaton et al. (1979). They compared four groups of subjects on a variety of neuropsychological measures of impairment. The four groups of subjects (equal $n = 25$) were a schizophrenic group, a normal group, an acutely brain-damaged group, and a chronically brain-damaged group. The four groups were matched (by group mean, not by individual pairs) with respect to age, sex, and years of education — as nuisance variables. Differences between the groups were found on most of the neuropsychological measures with the schizophrenic group showing "milder" impairment than the brain-damaged groups. Other nuisance variables, such as medication, emotional problems, unexplained EEG abnormalities, etc., were not matched and could conceivably be related to the neuropsychological impairment. In any case, the conclusions drawn from the study are obviously flawed based upon all three of Meehl's problems with matched designs presented so far. Matching with attribute variables is a procedure that can easily lead to incorrect inferences.

Analysis of Covariance. Analysis of covariance (ANCOVA) is a technique that is used to "statistically control" confounding effects of a nuisance variable in an experimental design. It removes the variance associated with a possible spurious effect thought due to the confounding variables. There are three principle uses of ANCOVA, as described by Evans and Anastasio (1968) and Wildt and Ahtola (1978), each of which will be discussed in terms of an attribute variable design.

The first use of ANCOVA is to increase the precision of randomized experiments when the covariate (nuisance variable) is statistically independent of the treatment. ANCOVA increases the sensitivity of the analysis by removing the variance of the covariate that is correlated with the dependent variable. The effect is to reduce the size of the error term in the analysis. As Evans and Anastasio (1968) state, "This is the only case in which ANCOVA can be used without serious reservations" (p. 227). The major requirement of a covariance analysis is the independence of treatment (independent variable) and covariate (nuisance variable). In practice this requires random assignment of subjects. A study which uses attribute variables as the "independent" variable is very unlikely to have independence of the treatment and covariate.

The second, more controversial, usage of analysis of covariance is the "adjustment" of treatment means for differences between intact groups when the intact groups themselves have been assigned to the treatments. Many psychological researchers think that this usage would be applicable when attribute variables are concerned (Overall & Woodward, 1977). Evans and Anastasio (1968) accept this application of the analysis of covariance if the covariate is measured before the treatments are administered and the groups are randomly assigned to treatments, i.e., when the covariate is unrelated to treatments. Games (1976), however, thinks that this usage also is *un*likely to lead to interpretable results when used with intact groups (organismic variables). He argues that it is necessary to keep the treatments orthogonal to *all* organismic variables in order to avoid other correlated nuisance variables. The only way to do this, he says, is to randomly assign subjects to treatments. This is not possible when using attribute variables.

A third usage of ANCOVA which has been suggested is removal of some treatment effects when the covariate is linearly correlated with the treatment. That is, when the differences in the covariate means are the result of different treatments. Evans and Anastasio (1968) and Games (1976) say that this is a totally inappropriate use of analysis of covariance since the primary assumption of ANCOVA is that the covariate and treatment are independent of each other. The effect of an ANCOVA in this situation is to artificially increase or decrease the effect (depending on the direction of the correlation).

Lord (1967; 1969) has strongly criticized the conceptual basis of analysis of covariance results when used with preexisting natural groups. He says,

...there simply is no logical or statistical procedure that can be counted on to make proper allowances for uncontrolled preexisting differences between groups.... The usual research study of this type is attempting to answer a question that simply cannot be answered in any rigorous way on the basis of available data (1967, p. 305).

The use of analysis of covariance when nuisance variables are correlated with experimental variables, as in attribute variable research, should therefore be discouraged.

Rubin and Balow (1980) provide an example of the improper use of ANCOVA in a large-scale study of infant neurological abnormalities which they use as indicators of cognitive impairment. As part of the Collaborative Perinatal Research Project they had neuropsychological information available on 1613 infants, which they tried to relate to later cognitive performance. They had three groups of children: group 1 ($n = 1132$) was the neurologically normal group, group 2 ($n = 165$) was neurologically suspect, and group 3 ($n = 22$) was neurologically abnormal. Before they compared these groups on later performance measures, they wanted to "covary out" the effects of two nuisance variables — birthweight and socioeconomic status — thought to also affect later performance. These nuisance variables were measured and found to differ significantly between the three groups. In other words, when using preexisting groups, they had a situation where the covariates (birthweight and SES) and the independent variable (neurological normality-abnormality) were related — in fact, they were significantly related. The necessary assumption of the statistical independence of covariate and treatment was not met in their study. Their subsequent results cannot therefore be interpreted meaningfully since their "adjustment" may well have caused their significant effects.

Conclusions and Suggestions for Future Neuropsychological Research

The preceding sections have discussed the improper use of inappropriate experimental designs in typical neuropsychological research using attribute variables. When using attribute variables, the researcher is in a position where the inferences and interpretations that one normally makes in experimental designs are no longer appropriate. The primary difficulties surrounding the use of attribute variables are: their correlation with many other extraneous variables which cannot be controlled by randomization, matching groups or analysis of covariance, and the nonrandom sampling and assignment of subjects (self-selection) into the "experimental" conditions. It was pointed out that neuropsychological research should (more fruitfully) be considered as a type of ex post facto (correlational) design because of these limitations. The distinction and its implications will now be spelled out more fully.

Correlational, or nonexperimental (Blalock, 1961), research, as traditionally defined, looks at the relationships between several variables, which may or may not be correlated to some degree (Cronbach, 1957; Darlington, 1968; Kerlinger & Pedhazur, 1973). In correlational research the variables used may be continuous or discrete. Because the emphasis is on the relationship (correlation) between variables, it is often not necessary to worry about controlling extraneous variables.

Correlational and experimental research are both based upon the same General Linear Model (Horton, 1978) but their assumptions are different. In general, any "experimental" design could be analyzed with a corresponding correlational technique requiring fewer statistical-model assumptions. The major advantage of a correlational approach for neuropsychology, then, seems obvious — it is not necessary to meet certain assumptions (such as independence of the variables, etc.) which are required when using traditional experimental analyses, and which could not be met in any case. Neuropsychological research, therefore, truly should be viewed as correlational research -- "investigations" instead of experiments. The methodology of the correlational approaches gives just as much, if not more, information for theory-building as does experimental research (see Kenny, 1979 and Kerlinger & Pedhazur, 1973).

Some final suggestions can therefore be made for neuropsychological research when using attribute variables. The major recommendation is to recognize the limitations of these attribute variables since they are so ubiquitous in neuro-psychology — they cannot be manipulated and they force the experimenter into accepting subject self-selection to conditions. The assumptions of experimental research are thus not met. Correction techniques such as matching and analysis of covariance are also not adequate. A better conceptual scheme would be to use correlational techniques which require fewer assumptions and which fit the data better. Correlational techniques, such as the family of multiple regression procedures, can use variables that are multidetermined and continuous, as neuropsychological attribute variables are. That elusive goal of "causation" could even be investigated with certain correlational techniques such as path analysis (Kenny, 1979) or causal modeling.

Another advantage of correlational research is that it does not have to be as artificial (or sterile) as laboratory investigations. Observational studies in most cases should be analyzed by correlational techniques. Whatever type of research design is used, the explicit specification and meeting of the assumptions of that design should be given so that other investigators can judge the appropriateness of the conclusions drawn.

By appropriate choice and careful consideration of the conceptual implications of various research designs, neuropsychologists should be able to meet the requirements of the underlying statistical models. Thus valid inferences and conclusions can be made. The use of attribute variables clouds the design somewhat, but it also makes us more aware of the relationships among various factors that can influence behavior. This increased awareness can give a researcher a better conceptual framework from which to generate better (falsifiable) theories. In the future these theories should help us to understand brain-behavior relationships more fully.

REFERENCES

Appelbaum, M. I., & Cramer, E. M. (1974). Some problems in the nonorthogonal analysis of variance. *Psychological Bulletin, 81*, 335-343.

Blalock, H. M. (1961). *Causal inferences in nonexperimental research.* Chapel Hill, N.C.: The University of North Carolina Press.

Boneau, C. A., & Pennypacker, H. S. (1961). Group matching as a research strategy: How not to get significant results. *Psychological Reports, 8,* 143-147.

Campbell, D. T., & Stanley, J. C. (1966). *Experimental and quasi-experimental designs for research.* Chicago: Rand McNally.

Cook, T. D., & Campbell, D. T. (1979). *Quasi-experimentation: Design and analysis issues for field settings.* Boston: Houghton Mifflin.

Crockett, D., Clark, C., & Klonoff, H. (1981). Introduction — An overview of neuro-psychology. In S. B. Filskov & T. J. Boll (Eds.), *Handbook of clinical neuropsychology* (pp. 1-37). New York: J. Wiley.

Cronbach, L. J. (1957). The two disciplines of scientific psychology. *American Psychologist, 12,* 671-684.

Darlington, R. B. (1968). Multiple regression in psychological research and practice. *Psychological Bulletin, 69,* 161-182.

Edgington, E. S. (1966). Statistical inference and random sampling. *Psychological Bulletin, 66,* 485-487.

Evans, S. H., & Anastasio, E. J. (1968). Misuse of analysis of covariance when treatment effect and covariate are confounded. *Psychological Bulletin, 69,* 225-234.

Fedio, P., Cox, C. S., Neophytides, A., Canal-Frederick, G., & Chase, T. N. (1979). Neuro-psychological profile of Huntington's disease: Patients and those at risk. In T. N. Chase et al. (Eds.), *Advances in neurology, Vol. 23* (pp. 239-255). New York: Raven Press.

Feldt, L. S. (1961). The use of extreme groups to test for the presence of a relationship. *Psychometrika, 26,* 307-316.

Games, P. A. (1976). Limitations of analysis of covariance on intact group quasi-ex-perimental designs. *Journal of Experimental Education, 44,* 51-53.

Games, P. A. (1979). Assessment and statistical control of subject variables in longitudinal designs. In J. R. Nesselroade & P. B. Baltes (Eds.), *Longitudinal research in the study of behavior and development* (pp. 179-198). New York: Academic Press.

Goldstein, G., & Shelly C. H. (1973). Univariate vs. multivariate analysis in neuro-psychological assessment of lateralized brain damage. *Cortex, 9,* 204-216.

Gorsuch, R. L. (1973). Data analysis of correlated independent variables. *Multivariate Behavioral Research, 8,* 89-107.

Gregory, R., & Paul, J. (1980). The effects of handedness and writing posture on neuro-psychological test results. *Neuropsychologia, 18,* 231-235.

Heaton, R. K., Vogt, A. T., Hoehn, M. M., Lewis, J. A., Crowley, T. J., & Stallings, M. A. (1979). Neuropsychological impairment with schizophrenia vs. acute and chronic lesions. *Journal of Clinical Psychology, 35,* 46-53.

Horton, R. L. (1978). *The general linear model.* New York: McGraw-Hill.

Huesmann, L. R. (1982). Experimental methods in research in psychopathology. In P. C. Kendall & J. N. Butcher (Eds.), *Handbook of research methods in clinical psychology* (pp. 223-248). New York: J. Wiley.

Kaspar, J. C., & Sokolec, J. (1980). Relationship between neurological dysfunction and a test of speed of motor performance. *Journal of Clinical Neuropsychology, 2,* 13-21.

Kenny, D. A. (1979). *Correlation and causality.* New York: J. Wiley.

Keppel, G. (1973). *Design and analysis: A researcher's handbook.* Englewood Cliffs, N.J.: Prentice-Hall.

Keren, G. (1982). A balanced approach to unbalanced designs. In G. Keren (Ed.), *Statistical and methodological issues in psychology and social sciences research* (pp. 155-186). Hillsdale, N.J.: Lawrence Erlbaum.

156

Kerlinger, F. N. (1973). *Foundations of behavioral research* (2nd ed.). New York: Holt, Rinehart, and Winston.

Kerlinger, F. N., & Pedhazur, E. J. (1973). *Multiple regression in behavioral research.* New York: Holt, Rinehart, and Winston.

Kish, L. (1959). Some statistical problems in research design. *American Sociological Review, 24,* 328-338.

Lezak, M. D. (1983). *Neuropsychological assessment* (2nd ed.) (Chapter 8, pp. 204-236). New York: Oxford University Press.

Lord, F. M. (1967). A paradox in the interpretation of group comparisons. *Psychological Bulletin, 68,* 304-305.

Lord, F. M. (1969). Statistical adjustments when comparing preexisting groups. *Psychological Bulletin, 72,* 336-337.

Matarazzo, J. D. (1972). *Wechsler's measurement and appraisal of adult intelligence* (5th ed.) (Chapter 13, pp. 377-427). New York: Oxford University Press.

Meehl, P. E. (1970). Nuisance variables and the ex post facto design. In M. Radner & S. Winokur (Eds.), *Minnesota studies in the philosophy of science: Analyses of theories and methods of physics and psychology* (Vol. 4) (pp. 373-402). Minneapolis, MN: University of Minnesota Press.

Meehl, P. E. (1978). Theoretical risks and tabular asterisks: Sir Karl, Sir Ronald, and the slow progress of soft psychology. *Journal of Consulting and Clinical Psychology, 46,* 806-834.

Meyers, L. S., & Grossen, N. E. (1974). *Behavioral research: Theory, procedure, and design.* San Francisco: W. H. Freeman.

O'Donnell, J. P., Kurtz, J., & Ramanaiah, N. V. (1983). Neuropsychological test findings for normal, learning disabled, and brain damaged young adults. *Journal of Consulting and Clinical Psychology, 51,* 726-729.

Overall, J. E., & Woodward, J. A. (1977). Nonrandom assignment and the analysis of covariance. *Psychological Bulletin, 84,* 588-594.

Parsons, O. A., & Prigatano, G. P. (1978). Methodological considerations in clinical neuropsychological research. *Journal of Consulting and Clinical Psychology, 46,* 608-619.

Rubin, R. A., & Balow, B. (1980). Infant neurological abnormalities as indicators of cognitive impairment. *Developmental Medicine and Child Neurology, 22,* 336-342.

Spinner, B., & Gabriel, R. M. (1981). A method to test ANOVA with unequal cell frequencies. *Canadian Psychology, 22,* 260-270.

Weiskrantz, L. (1968). Some traps and pontifications. In L. Weiskrantz (Ed.), *Analysis of behavioral change* (pp. 415-429). New York: Harper and Row.

Wildt, A. R., & Ahtola, O. T. (1978). *Analysis of covariance.* Beverly Hills, CA: Sage Publications.

Wood, G. (1974). *Fundamentals of psychological research.* Boston: Little, Brown, and Co.

Journal of Clinical and Experimental Neuropsychology
1985, Vol. 7, No. 4, pp. 445-462

Analysis of Covariance as a Remedy for Demographic Mismatch of Research Subject Groups: Some Sobering Simulations*

Kenneth M. Adams
Henry Ford Hospital, Detroit, MI

Gregory G. Brown
Henry Ford Hospital, Detroit, MI

Igor Grant
VA Medical Center, La Jolla, CA and
University of California at San Diego

ABSTRACT

Analysis of Covariance (ANCOVA) is often used in neuropsychological studies to effect *ex-post-facto* adjustment of performance variables amongst groups of subjects mismatched on some relevant demographic variable. This paper reviews some of the statistical assumptions underlying this usage. In an attempt to illustrate the complexities of this statistical technique, three sham studies using actual patient data are presented. These staged simulations have varying relationships between group test performance differences and levels of covariate discrepancy. The results were robust and consistent in their nature, and were held to support the wisdom of previous cautions by statisticians concerning the employment of ANCOVA to justify comparisons between incomparable groups. ANCOVA should not be used in neuropsychological research to equate groups unequal on variables such as age and education or to exert statistical control whose objective is to eliminate consideration of the covariate as an explanation for results. Finally, the report advocates by example the use of simulation to further our understanding of neuropsychological variables.

INTRODUCTION

The purpose of this paper is to review the statistical assumptions underlying analysis of covariance (ANCOVA) and to present a set of studies on one common

* The authors are appreciative of reviewers' and editors' helpful recommendations. This research was supported by an award from the Medical Research Service of the Veteran's Administration (MRIS-3240 to Dr. Grant). The project was also supported by grants from the Fund for Henry Ford Hospital (R-35879 to Dr. Adams; R-38839 to Dr. Brown).

usage in neuropsychology. This topic is particularly relevant for neuropsychological investigators, since a large number of studies have employed ANCOVA as a tool for the adjustment of test scores in the analysis of variance. In this paper, the term, "variate", will refer to the dependent variable in ANCOVA, and "covariate" will refer to the concurrently adjusted variable.

ANCOVA is a useful statistical technique designed to reduce error in experimentation due to coexisting characteristics of subjects. While these characteristics may not be central to the study design, they can exert effects upon the dependent variable. ANCOVA adjusts the dependent variable using within-cell regression estimates reflecting the distribution of the covariate in relation to the variate. We should emphasize here that the actual purpose of ANCOVA is to obtain unbiased estimates of true group differences regardless of whether or not initial estimates in ANOVA are biased because of group differences on the covariate.

In psychological research, ANCOVA is most commonly used in three types of design, as follows:

(1) an analysis of posttest performance scores where the pretest score is used as a covariate (e.g., Prokasy, Grant, & Meyers, 1958);

(2) the analysis of test performances where study design groups do *not* differ on any key demographic variable, but covariance is used to adjust test performance scores to attempt artificial diminution of factors such as age or education and increase accuracy of measurement (e.g., Grant et al., 1978);

(3) the analysis of test performance scores where the study design groups differ on some demographic variable or variables (e.g., age, education) and the demographic variable or variables are used as covariates (e.g., Klisz & Parsons, 1979).

It is the intent of this paper to address the third application as it pertains to neuropsychological research. This is important because this particular use of ANCOVA would be attractive to investigators who find that clinically interesting patients have lower education, are older, or are of lower socioeconomic status than their control group counterparts. Given the difficulties and complexities involved in recruiting patients and controls, it happens frequently that researchers find that their study groups differ on some relevant or even important demographic variable.

In their review of methodological considerations in neuropsychological research, Parsons and Prigatano (1978) have recommended ANCOVA to handle age and/or education differences between groups on performance variables. It should be emphasized, however, that this recommendation was made with the admonition that the most unambiguous approach would be to recruit groups comparable on these variables.

Be that as it may, unintended demographic mismatch events do occur and may operate to reduce confidence in research results, since such group differences add a new source of variance to the study design. In some instances, the likely patterns of influence due to the covariate difference are known to a certain degree, as is the case in age and education effects on neuropsychological performance (Finlayson, Johnson, & Reitan, 1977; Heaton, Grant, & Matthews, in press; Parsons & Prigatano, 1978). Stating the case more strongly, some workers have reported data that imply that such demographic variables cannot be viewed as subject variables alone, but actually exert one kind of *causal* influence in the development of neuropsychological deficit (Amante, 1976, 1978; Amante, Van Houten, Grieve, Bader, & Margules, 1977).

Given the importance of the covarying or causal impact of demographic mismatches on the analysis of neuropsychological results, it is clear that investigators would be attracted to techniques which would seem to offer some potential to limit or even correct such unwanted influences.

For example, one report (Brandt, Butters, Ryan, & Bayog, 1983) utilized covariance to align three groups of alcoholic subjects (short-term abstinence, long-term abstinence, and prolonged abstinence) who differed on the following: age; years of abstinence; and, age-corrected WAIS Vocabulary. In this instance, the three variables on which substantial preexisting differences were present were used as simultaneous covariates in a set of ANCOVAs on individual test tasks. It is not evident from this report whether or not all the three covariates were significant in the many analyses. Nevertheless, the investigators seemed assured of the precise interplay of this particular triad of variables with test performances. Based on the ANCOVA, inefficiencies in performance were attributed by Brandt et al. to the effects of alcohol. An alternative and far more likely explanation of their results is that the groups remained biased in their composition, thus eventuating in slowness and error in the older and less bright prolonged abstinence group.

In another context, Klisz and Parsons (1979), in a study of neuropsychological impairment in alcoholics, found that their group of alcoholics who completed the Wisconsin Card Sorting Test required more trials to criterion than did age-matched controls. The alcoholics were less well-educated and an ANCOVA using education as the covariate was used to "adjust" the trials-to-criterion dependent variables so as to compensate for the demographic fault in their design. Since significant ANOVA differences between groups remained after covarying for education, the investigators inferred that alcoholism was associated with worse performance. This attribution was stated with some confidence, since the effects of education had been "controlled" in a statistical fashion.

Can covariance be used correctly in this fashion? This is the principal focus of this paper. It would seem useful to examine next the assumptions governing the appropriate use of ANCOVA.

ASSUMPTIONS UNDERLYING ANCOVA

Winer (1971) has suggested that the statistical assumptions underlying ANCOVA are identical to those for the ANOVA, with some important additional assumptions concerning regression effects. It is assumed, first, that treatment (group) effects and regression effects are additive, and that regressions are homogeneous. In addition, residuals are assumed to be normally and independently distributed with a mean of zero. Residuals are also presumed to be equal across treatment groups. Finally, the correct order of regression (linear versus curvilinear) is assumed to have been applied.

Some internal tests of these assumptions have been suggested (Winer, p. 772-775), but ANCOVA is thought by some to be largely robust in the face of some violations of the above assumptions (Overall & Woodward, 1977). The underlying issue in using covariance as an adjustment is the "intrinsic nature of the concomitance between the variate and the covariate. If the concomitance is predominantly due to a dimension along which adjustment is desired, such an adjustment may be made." (Winer, 1971, p. 753). Put another way, Winer enjoins the ANCOVA user to consider all the *psychological* relationships between the covariate and the dependent variable, rather than merely to consider a potential beneficial statistical impact in "controlling for" the covariate.

More practically, researchers may study correlations between dependent variables and covariates between groups and within groups with particular attention to the existence of the differential existence of significant relationships. While this provides some guidance as to variance patterns between or within groups, these correlations cannot be seen as dependable guideposts on which to base a decision concerning the viability of an ANCOVA. One set of reasons for this lack of dependability is presented by Lord (1967, 1969) who suggests that adjusting for differences between groups is an exercise requiring care, since misinterpretation of results can occur in many ways.

In order to provide a practical demonstration of the use of covariance as an adjustment for demographic mismatch in neuropsychological research, we developed such a mismatch on a simulated basis by a deliberate selection of cases from a previously reported study (Grant, Adams, & Reed, 1984). We created three simulated study situations to examine empirically the possibilities and limitations of covariance procedures.

SIMULATED STUDY SITUATION 1

In this experiment, subjects were selected from a larger pool of alcoholic patients and controls who are described elsewhere (Grant et al., 1984). Extended Halstead-Reitan neuropsychological test batteries were administered to these carefully screened subjects in a large longitudinal study.

We selected subjects by pairwise visual inspection of level of performance test results so as to create two groups whose demographic match would be complete, except for education. At the same time, we selected patients in each group whose neuropsychological performance would make the aggregate groups appear to differ, with less well-educated alcoholic patients performing at levels inferior to those of their better-educated control counterparts. This strategy was selected in order to simulate the frequently occurring situation in which an investigator is concluding a neuropsychological study on alcoholism and finds an educational advantage in the control group.

In the current example, the alcoholic patients ($n = 16$) were recently detoxified (minimum 21 days abstinence) men who were carefully screened for complicating neurological events or disorders such as head injury, diabetes, etc. Their mean age was 44.5 years ($SD = 7.9$); mean education in years was 10.6 ($SD = 1.4$). The control group ($n = 16$) was selected from amongst volunteers who had no evidence of previous history of psychiatric hospitalizations, past or present alcohol abuse, and complicating events or diseases (M age $= 39.3$ years, $SD = 7.1$; M education $= 15.1$ years, $SD = 2.5$). The two groups did not differ significantly on age or on demographic variables other than education, $F(1,30) = 41.1$, $p < .001$.

Two commonly employed neuropsychological tests used in studies of alcoholism were selected for study. These variables were the Halstead Category Test (total number of errors) and time to completion on Part B of the Trail-Making Test (Reitan & Davison, 1974). The distributions of scores on these measures were studied both between and within groups for evidence of undue skewness, kurtosis, or other anomaly. Similarly, within-group regression and slope coefficients of the covariates were found to be homogeneous. No systematic correlations between the two test variables and education were observed within groups.

In the present simulation, a simple inspection of the group means on the Category Test revealed a large difference between the two groups (alcoholics – $M = 83.5$ errors, $SD = 16.8$; controls – $M = 23.9$ errors, $SD = 8.6$). Many investigators would see this difference as compelling, but would also view the educational difference between the group as troubling.

Thus, an ANCOVA would seem to offer an answer. In this exercise, the two-group ANOVA comparison would be "adjusted" or corrected for the portion of variance attributable to education. In this simulation, the assumption of orthogonality between covariate and independent variable was knowlingly violated. Specifically, disparate levels of education were selected so as to create the more accidental situation of demographic mismatch in the literature in which ANCOVA has been used as a correction. An ANCOVA involving the group membership as an independent variable, Category Test errors as the dependent variable, and education as a covariate was conducted. The computational procedure used for this and other analyses throughout this report was the BMDP1V (Dixon, 1983). The results are seen in Table 1 for the ANCOVA and ANOVA. Group means are also displayed for the dependent variable.

Table 1

Analysis of Covariance and Variance on Category Test Errors by Group Membership with Education as a Covariate in Study 1

Source of Variation	Sum of Squares	df	Mean Square	F
Covariate				
Education	14631.7	1	14631.7	81.5**
Main Effect				
Group	13933.3	1	13933.3	77.6**
Explained	28565.0	2	14282.5	79.5**
Residual	5209.9	29	179.7	
Total	33774.8	31	1089.5	
Analysis of Variance (ANOVA)				
Between Groups	28441.1	1	28441.1	160.0**
Within Groups	5333.8	30	177.8	
	Group Means		Adjusted Group Means	
Alcoholics ($n = 16$)	83.5		85.8	
Controls ($n = 16$)	23.9		21.6	

Inequality of Slopes $F(1,28) = 1.8$, n.s.

**$p < .001$

Inspection of Table 1 indicates a robust covariance effect which reduces marginally the strength of the overall group effect (i.e., F ratio reduced from 160.0 to 77.6), and does not alter the group means to any appreciable extent. In fact, a comparison between actual and adjusted group means shows a greater difference between groups in the adjusted case. Study of the ANOVA table confirms the statistically significant nature of the very large difference between groups on the dependent variable.

A parallel analysis could be seen as advisable for Trail Making Test, Part B time for these subjects. Group means are clearly different (alcoholics – $M = 85.1$ s, $SD = 39.0$; controls – $M = 51.2$ s, $SD = 13.3$). Given no violations of assumptions beyond those of reality inherent in a simulation, ANCOVA and ANOVA procedures identical to the ones conducted for Category Test errors were conducted with the substitution of Trail Making Test, Part B time as the dependent variable. The results are shown in Table 2.

Review of Table 2 again reveals a significant covariance effect which reduces noticeably the strength of the overall group effect (i.e., F ratio reduced from 10.9 to 4.4), but does not alter the group means. Comparison of the actual versus adjusted group means reveals nearly identical values. The ANOVA demonstrates a difference between groups on Trail Making Test, Part B that is independent of

Table 2

Analysis of Covariance and Variance on Trail Making Test, Part B Time by Group Membership with Education as a Covariate in Study 1

Source of Variation	Sum of Squares	df	Mean Square	F
Covariate				
Education	5353.9	1	5353.9	6.1*
Main Effect				
Group	3860.2	1	3860.2	4.4*
Explained	9214.1	2	4607.1	5.3**
Residual	25418.0	29	876.5	
Total	34632.2	31	1117.2	
Analysis of Variance (ANOVA)				
Between Groups	9214.0	1	9214.0	10.9**
Within Groups	25418.2	30	847.3	

	Group Means	Adjusted Group Means
Alcoholics ($n = 16$)	85.1	85.1
Controls ($n = 16$)	51.2	51.3

Inequality of Slopes $F(1,28) = 0.2$, n.s.

*$p < .05$
**$p < .01$

education.

Some researchers obtaining the results shown in Tables 1 and 2 would conclude that the group mismatch on education described above could not serve to detract from the overall conclusion that alcoholic patients perform less well than do controls on brain-sensitive neuropsychological tests. The variance that could be seen as attributable to education in the group difference would have been thought to be controlled or even eliminated *via* a rigorous statistical procedure. Further, while the investigators may realize that education does exert an important influence on cognitively rich neuropsychological tasks, an effective correction for education differences would have been thought to have occurred. The maintenance of the magnitude of the group difference in both groups and the small difference in adjusted means would be seen as further proof of the robustness of the group effect and its interpretation.

Is this frequently occurring scenario a reasonable one? Can neuropsychological investigators use covariance in a manner so as to eliminate the complicating fact of an unintended group mismatch on a relevant demographic variable? While the results of this first simulated study would seem to support this usage, we would suggest that the reader suspend judgement as we present a second example. The following simulation – culled from an actual study – will provide further information.

SIMULATED STUDY SITUATION 2

In this experiment, we again selected subjects from a larger study (Grant et al., 1984). In selecting patients for this exercise, we deliberately *reversed* the usual educational disparity so as to make the impaired patient group more highly educated than their neuropsychologically normal control group colleagues. At the same time, we selected the more highly educated patient group so as to have poorer performances (more errors or time to completion) than their less well-educated control counterparts. This made our simulation run counter to the usual event, in that most patient groups in studies of alcoholism are less well-educated than are their control counterparts. The strategy of creating a real, but counter-intuitive, disparity on the intended covariate would seem to offer a challenge to the tactic of *ex-post-facto* group correction. We utilized the same two indices of neuropsychological performance as in Experiment 1 - Category Test errors and Trail Making Test, Part B time. We will describe the analyses used for each in turn.

For Category Test errors, we selected a patient group ($n = 11$) and a control group ($n = 16$) of subjects. The deliberate mismatching of these groups was reflected in the Category Test means as well (alcoholics – $M = 67.1$ errors, $SD = 15.2$; controls – $M = 32.6$ errors, $SD = 12.4$). The two groups of men did not differ on age (alcoholics – $M = 42.0$ years, $SD = 9.6$; controls – $M = 43.2$ years, $SD = 11.1$) or on any other demographic variable except education (alcoholics – $M = 14.9$ years, $SD = 1.8$; controls – $M = 11.3$ years, $SD = 1.1$). The latter difference was significant ($F(1,25) = 41.9, p < .001$), confirming effective case selection for this exercise.

We should note that education correlated in a predictably negative direction with Category Test error score ($r = -.39$), but was not significant in the patient group. This relationship did reach a statistically significant level in the control group ($r = -.62, p < .005$). Within-group regression and slope coefficients were found to be homogeneous, however, allowing the analysis to procede without this violation of the assumptions of ANCOVA.

The actual ANCOVA and ANOVA were conducted with Category Test errors as the dependent variable and education as a covariate. Group membership was the independent variable. The results are presented in Table 3.

Review of Table 3 reveals a robust covariance effect which increases very slightly the group disparity created in the formation of the groups (i.e., F ratio increased from 42.0 to 44.5). Group means reflect some adjustment in the direction of greater group difference. The results for Category Test errors in this exercise, however, do not support the use of ANCOVA to offset a group mismatch. The deliberate mismatch between groups on Category Test errors is confirmed by the ANOVA result which is significant.

Table 3

Analysis of Covariance and Variance on Category Test Errors by Group Membership with Education as a Covariate in Study 2

Source of Variation	Sum of Squares	df	Mean Square	F
Covariate				
Education	2419.2	1	2419.2	16.6**
Main Effect				
Group	6464.2	1	6464.2	44.5**
Explained	8903.4	2	4451.7	30.5**
Residual	3498.9	24	145.8	
Total	12402.3	26	477.0	
Analysis of Variance (ANOVA)				
Between Groups	7771.5	1	7771.5	42.0**
Within Groups	4630.9	25	185.2	
	Group Means		*Adjusted Group Means*	
Alcoholics ($n = 11$)	67.1		77.2	
Controls ($n = 16$)	32.6		25.6	

Inequality of Slopes $F(1,23) = .90$, n.s.

$**p < .001$

A similar analysis was developed for Trail Making Test, Part B time. Alcoholics ($n = 15$, M age $= 43.3$ years, $SD = 8.0$) were matched completely to their control group counterparts ($n = 16$, M age $= 40.0$ years, $SD = 10.1$) with the exception of education (alcoholics - $M = 14.3$ years, $SD = 1.8$; controls - $M = 11.8$ years, $SD = 1.5$). A significant difference between groups in education was confirmed ($F(1,29) = 18.7$, $p < .001$).

In this exercise, time to completion in Part B of the Trail Making Test was also selected to reflect poor performance on the part of the more highly educated patient group ($M = 90.4$ s, $SD = 27.7$). In contrast, better performance was sought in pairwise selection amongst less well-educated controls ($M = 62.5$ s, $SD = 13.1$).

Correlations were computed within groups between education and Trails B time, yielding a significant relationship amongst the patient group ($r = -.50$, $p < .05$) but not within the control group. Within-group regression and slope coefficients were found to be homogeneous, again allowing the ANCOVA to proceed without statistical assumption violations of this restraint.

The ANCOVA was conducted as above, with Trail Making Test, Part B time as the dependent variable, group membership as the independent variable, and education as the covariate. The results of this analysis are seen in Table 4.

Table 4

Analysis of Covariance and Variance on Trail Making Test, Part B Time by Group Membership with Education as a Covariate in Study 2

Source of Variation	Sum of Squares	df	Mean Square	F
Covariate				
Education	16.8	1	16.8	0.1
Main Effect				
Group	9260.1	1	9260.2	11.8*
Explained	9276.9	2	4638.4	5.9*
Residual	21945.1	28	783.8	
Total	31222.0	30	1040.7	
Analysis of Variance (ANOVA)				
Between Groups	6026.4	1	6026.4	6.9*
Within Groups	25195.6	29	868.6	

	Group Means	Adjusted Group Means
Alcoholics ($n = 15$)	90.4	98.9
Controls ($n = 16$)	62.5	59.6

Inequality of Slopes $F(1,27) = .20$, n.s.

*$p < .01$

The findings in Table 4 are somewhat different than those in the previous three ANCOVA tables. The actual effect of the covariate on the ANCOVA analysis here does not reach a level of statistical significance, and the magnitude of the group difference effect is increased as in Table 3 (i.e., F ratio increased from 6.9 to 11.8). In addition, the adjusted group means again are in a direction opposite to one reflecting reduction of the group difference mismatch (confirmed by ANOVA); they are also predictable, given the direction of covariate mismatch. As in the other Category Test example, this result is logical, but does not offer encouragement to investigators who might wish to utilize ANCOVA to correct demographic mismatch.

We should note here that ANCOVA is not generally an appropriate analysis to present in lieu of ANOVA where the effect of the covariate is not significant. We present this analysis for instructional purposes only.

The results of Study 1 and Study 2 can be taken to reflect the ineffective or even misleading effect of using ANCOVA to effect a remedy for group mismatch on demographics. Far from helping investigators to gain confidence in results from such studies, the present findings imply strongly that researchers cannot exclude the mismatched demographic variable as a causative or complicating agent in the emergence of group differences. The strategy of creating a commonly observed mismatch in Study 1 was complemented by the Study 2 simulation, since the direction of the group disparity on the covariate was reversed in the second instance.

It might be argued, however, that the difference between groups on the neuro-psychological variables is so real and robust as to overcome any demographic mismatch or analysis to "fine tune" the results. Put another way, this argument would be congruent with the results from Study 1 and Study 2, providing that neuropsychological differences between recently detoxified alcoholics and controls will exist under almost all conditions and in spite of unwanted design features.

To address this issue, a third study simulation was created to reverse the expected demographic covariate difference as seen in Study 2 *and* create a situation in which group performance levels were reversed as well.

SIMULATED STUDY SITUATION 3

In this final study, patients were again culled from the Grant et al. (1984) study pool. Patients were selected by visual inspection to reflect a situation fully counter-intuitive in relation to the existing literature in that they had significantly higher levels of education and better neuropsychological performance than their control counterparts. As in the previous studies, we employed Category Test errors and Trail Making Part B time as representative neurobehavioral measures very commonly seen in the neuropsychological literature on impairment in alcoholic patients.

In this instance of Category Test errors, the groups ($n = 11$ each) were selected for pairwise mismatch on education (alcoholics – $M = 14.4$ years, $SD = 1.2$; controls – $M = 11.3$ years, $SD = 1.4$) that was statistically significant, $F(1,20) = 30.3$, $p < .001$. Other demographic variables did not differ between groups, including age (alcoholics – $M = 36.7$ years, $SD = 6.8$; controls – $M = 44.0$ years, $SD = 10.5$). Actual Category Test errors differed between groups (alcoholics – $M = 22.5$ errors, $SD = 5.9$; controls – $M = 67.8$ errors, $SD = 19.0$) in a magnitude and direction not seen in studies reported to date. Correlations between Category Test errors and education were calculated within groups, with significant correlations found in the patient group ($r = .54$, $p < .05$), but not in the control group. Within-group regression and slope coefficients were found to be of sufficient homogeneity to permit analysis.

The ANCOVA was conducted as in previous examples, with group membership as the independent variable, Category Test errors as the dependent variable, and years of education as the covariate. The results of this analysis are presented in Table 5.

Inspection of Table 5 reveals a strong covariance effect, which once again serves

Table 5

Analysis of Covariance and Variance on Category Test Errors by Group Membership with
Education as a Covariate in Study 3

Source of Variation	Sum of Squares	df	Mean Square	F
Covariate				
Education	4496.8	1	4496.8	25.4**
Main Effect				
Group	7424.6	1	7424.6	41.9**
Explained	11921.4	2	5960.7	33.7**
Residual	3365.2	19	177.1	
Total	15286.6	21	727.9	
Analysis of Variance (ANOVA)				
Between Groups	11318.2	1	11318.2	57.0**
Within Groups	3958.4	20	198.4	

	Group Means	Adjusted Group Means
Alcoholics ($n = 11$)	22.5	16.0
Controls ($n = 11$)	67.8	74.3

Inequality of Slopes $F(1,18) = .32$, n.s.

**$p < .001$

to decrease the group main effect (i.e., F ratio decrease from 57.0 to 41.9) while increasing the disparity between group means created in the formation of the study groups. In this case, the use of ANCOVA again exaggerates rather than remedies group mismatch.

A a final simulation, we conducted an identical ANCOVA on the same subjects just described, substituting time to completion of Part B of the Trail Making Test for Category Test errors as the dependent variable. We should note that the deliberate mismatch strategy produced a substantial and counter-intuitive result in these subjects on this variable similar to that just described for Category Test errors (alcoholics – $M = 57.3$ s, $SD = 11.4$; controls – $M = 111.2$ s, $SD = 18.3$). That is, the variable means for alcoholics and controls here were at levels which are not usually observed, with patients performing better than controls.

As in previous examples, correlations were computed between the dependent variable, time to completion for Trail Making Test, Part B, and the covariate, education (in years). No significant correlations were found within groups. In the absence of anomalies in distribution and the equality of regression slopes, the ANCOVA was conducted. The results of the ANCOVA are shown in Table 6.

Table 6

Analysis of Covariance and Variance on Trail Making Test, Part B Time by Group Membership with Education as a Covariate in Study 3

Source of Variation	Sum of Squares	df	Mean Square	F
Covariate				
Education	9780.5	1	9780.5	44.3*
Main Effect				
Group	5723.4	1	5723.4	26.0*
Explained	15504.0	2	7752.0	35.1*
Residual	4191.1	19	220.6	
Total	19695.1	21	937.9	
Analysis of Variance (ANOVA)				
Between Groups	15458.8	1	15458.8	73.0*
Within Groups	4236.3	20	211.8	
	Group Means		*Adjusted Group Means*	
Alcoholics ($n = 11$)	57.3		55.6	
Controls ($n = 11$)	111.2		113.8	

Inequality of Slopes $F(1,18) = 2.22$, n.s.

*$p < .001$

Review of Table 6 shows once again the robust effect of the covariate adjustment (reducing the group F ratio from 73.0 to 26.0), with negligible impact on the adjustment of group means; that is, the means again are adjusted to a minimal magnitude and in a counter-intuitive direction.

DISCUSSION

The present results provide empirical support for the cautionary advice proffered by statisticians concerning ANCOVA (Lord, 1967, 1969). In three separate experiments we found that potentially misleading results (as in study 1) or counter-intuitive neuropsychological data (as in study 2 and 3) could not be addressed effectively by the use of ANCOVA to correct demographic mismatch between study groups. That is, when various combinations of intact or impaired performances were associated with greater or lesser levels of education in alcoholic patient or control groups, an *ex-post-facto* ANCOVA correction for education did not adjust the group differences in a reasonable way.

The adjustment of the variate by the covariate in ANCOVA requires knowledge of the full impact of all allied factors of the relationship. In the present experiments, adjustment for education would imply correction for educational experience, opportunity, socio-economic class, and a host of influences. At the present state of knowledge regarding neuropsychological impairment in alcoholic patients, the individual and collective relationships amongst many of these parameters are far from certain.

The present results also suggest that the calculation of within-group correlations between variate and covariate is a less than satisfactory exercise in evaluating likely ANCOVA effects. In Studies 1 and 3, significant correlations in the expected direction were found between education and the neuropsychological variable. In Study 2, a similar significant correlation was found for the control group. The impact of these correlations appears to have been different – reducing group-statistical effect in some cases, while enhancing it in others.

Yet, even if no correlations had been found in within-group analyses, this would or should have had no bearing on the decision concerning the advisability of conducting an ANCOVA. This is particularly true in view of the combination of desired between- and within-group adjustments sought by investigators involved in after-the-fact statistical exercises (e.g., Brandt et al., 1983; Klisz & Parsons, 1979). The reexamination of the central purposes of covariance and some preliminary tests of homogeneity of regression as noted above (Winer, 1971) may have been more productive. In the present studies, heterogeneity of within-cell regression did not influence the results. However, the nature of this simulation did require a violation of the assumption of nonorthogonality between the covariate and independent variable – an unavoidable didactic necessity.

It might be suggested that the present simulations are an extreme example of group neuropsychological differences which represent an unrealistic challenge for the ANCOVA correction. This begs the methodological question, however, because a statistical procedure thought to be as robust as ANCOVA must be able to exert numerical effect across a range of situations. Investigators must take statistical methods as they find them, and not only when the "right" results are produced (Adams, 1979, 1980, 1985; Rourke & Adams, 1984).

Another rejoinder to our report might be that the "real" neuropsychological differences between alcoholics and controls are so powerful that no statistical procedure is likely to influence the outcome. This cannot be seen as an adequate argument, since we have presented actual research results that run directly counter to this "real" neuropsychological difference hypothesis. ANCOVA did not correct outcomes which actually were nonsensical, given the usual state of affairs in which patients perform less well than controls.

The present results suggest that adjustment for education in studies on alcoholism is at present a dubious venture. While our results cannot be used to resolve the issue, it might be useful to know whether or not demographic mismatches on variables whose relationship to alcoholism is marginally better known (e.g., age) could be remedied via ANCOVA.

In trying to understand the influence of chronic alcoholism on behavior, it may be useful to attempt to understand education as one of many explanatory variables, rather than as a nuisance. It may well be that those with less education are more vulnerable to such impairment. Indeed, when considering various medical risk factors (such as birth complications, learning disorders, head injury, etc.), we have reported data reflecting a special neurobehavioral vulnerability for patients having had such events prior to their alcoholism: Specifically, the neuropsychological recovery of such patients from alcoholism is slowed in comparison to similar subjects without such risk histories (Adams & Grant, 1984).

Given the presence of interactions between low education, medical risk, lifestyle, alcoholism, and subsequent impairment, even simple "patient versus control" designs can contain complex effects. An attempt to exert artificial statistical control on one variable (e.g., education) can actually obscure or miss important information. The importance of this point is best illustrated by study of a table that was adapted from a recent comprehensive review of neuropsychological impairment in alcoholic patients (Parsons & Farr, 1981).

Table 7

Mean Education and Halstead Impairment Index of Alcoholic Samples from Studies Reviewed by Parr and Parsons (1981) - Rank Ordered by Education

Studies in Rank Order	Education	Halstead Impairment Index
1	13.8	.42
2	13.7	.30
3	13.6	.30
4	12.6	.27
5	12.6	.75
6	12.6	.27
median split	—	—
7	12.5	.52
8	12.1	.69
9	12.0	.80
10	11.9	.75
11	11.0	.90
12	10.5	.73

* Adapted from Grant, Adams, and Reed (1984). If Halstead Impairment Index $\geq$ .5 is taken as impaired, then the distribution of impairment is significantly different (Fisher's exact test, $p = .03$) between "better" and "less well" educated samples.

In Table 7 it seems abundantly clear that less well-educated alcoholics are more likely to be impaired. Thus, when investigators study groups of alcoholic patients whose educational level is less than about 12 years or whose level is significantly less than control counterparts, very confusing outcomes can occur. Statistical attempts to reduce the influence of education may or may not work, as we have demonstrated here. The important point is that the investigator cannot conclude as a result of the application of ANCOVA that the covariate is eliminated as an alternative explanation for group differences obtained on neuropsychological tests.

On a more general level, the appropriate potential uses of ANCOVA in neuropsychology are many. The present paper has focused on previous ANCOVA studies in the area of alcoholism research, and we discussed a set of simulations using data from an alcoholism project. This focus is not intended to convey an impression that this area is the only one in which ANCOVA was or is incorrectly utilized. The temptation to use ANCOVA as a statistical remedy for "troublesome" variables such as education or age will be greatest when the effect the investigator "knows" is present fails to reach significance on ANOVA, or when we want least to face the fact that our patients of interest, whom we think are differentially impaired, are in fact older, less intelligent, or whatever.

ANCOVA can be used in other areas of neuropsychological research to obtain adjusted estimates of true treatment effects, given careful consideration of the effects to be adjusted (Evans & Anastasio, 1968; Maxwell & Cramer, 1975). Recent Monte Carlo simulation studies have provided further evidence of the relative effect of violations of certain assumptions (Overall & Woodward, 1977). It is clear that ANCOVA can be especially valuable in studies on aging, drug effects, and other treatments having neuropsychological components where unbiased estimates of effects might be obtained.

The present paper is also an example of simulation methods which could be used profitably by neuropsychologists to model performance or outcomes in neuropsychological research. Simulation with data sets is a widely used technique in mathematics; indeed, the Evans and Anastasio (1968) paper makes the same point concerning ANCOVA using imaginary data. Simulation from clinical data sets is not without problems because of the potential for violations of important assumptions. However, given the power and availability of computers, neuropsychologists could gain better understanding of various interactions and nuances of behavior present in their data sets. In turn, modeling of future outcomes and simulation-aided design of new experiments could reduce the all-too-frequent use of statistics to protect cherished hypotheses against numerical realities.

In closing, ANCOVA should not be used (1) to control for covariates in relation to demographically mismatched groups where an initial ANOVA effect is insignificant and the investigator thinks it likely that an effect may be coaxed from an ANCOVA, or (2) to discount the influence of demographic variables where performance differences between demographically mismatched have been obtained. In these instances a significant ANCOVA with a remaining main effect between groups cannot be held out as assurance that the group effect is the sole operative one. As such, our findings and advice can be seen to run counter to that offered by Parsons and Prigatano (1978). At the same time, we see as appropriate their advice to recruit comparable groups in the conduct of such studies.

More important, the appropriate uses of ANCOVA in neuropsychology should be fostered in precise and thoughtful designs where the statistical technique can be used to enhance the accuracy of variance analysis. These uses are most likely to occur when the covariate is employed conceptually and statistically to determine whether mean dependent variable scores in independent groups corresponding to the same level of the covariate are different (Maxwell & Cramer, 1975, p. 189).

Lord (1967, p. 305) may have written the essence of this paper's message most directly, "...there is simply no logical statistical procedure that can be counted on to make proper allowances for uncontrolled preexisting differences between groups."

REFERENCES

Adams, K. M. (1979). Linear discriminant analysis in clinical neuropsychology research. *Journal of Clinical Neuropsychology, 1,* 259-272.

Adams, K. M. (1980, February). The selection of appropriate multivariate analysis techniques. In S. A. Berenbaum (chair), *Methodological and statistical issues in neuropsychological research.* Symposium presented at the 8th annual meeting of the International Neuropsychological Society. San Francisco, CA.

Adams, K. M. (1985). Theoretical, methodological and statistical issues. In B. P. Rourke (Ed.), *Neuropsychology of learning disabilities: Essentials of subtype analysis* (pp. 17-39). New York: Guilford.

Adams, K. M., & Grant, I. (1984, May). Medical risk slows recovery in alcoholism. *New research abstracts (NR175); Proceedings of the 13th annual meeting of the American Psychiatric Association.* Washington, D.C.: American Psychiatric Association.

Amante, D. A. (1976). A neurodiagnostic model. *International Journal of Neuroscience, 6,* 289-295.

Amante, D. A. (1978). Response to psychometric phrenology revisited: Comments on neuropsychological testing. *Journal of Consulting and Clinical Psychology, 46,* 1491-1492.

Amante, D. A., Van Houten, V. W., Grieve, J. H., Bader, C. A., & Margules, P. H. (1977). Neuropsychological deficits, ethnicity and socioeconomic status. *Journal of Consulting and Clinical Psychology, 45,* 524-535.

Brandt, J., Butters, N., Ryan, C., & Bayog, R. (1983). Cognitive loss and recovery in chronic alcohol abusers. *Archives of General Psychiatry, 40,* 435-442.

Dixon, W. J. (1983). *BMDP statistical software.* Berkeley: University of California Press.

Evans, S. H., & Anastasio, E. J. (1968). Misuse of analysis of covariance when treatment effect and covariate are confounded. *Psychological Bulletin, 69,* 225-234.

Finlayson, M. A. J., Johnson, K. A., & Reitan, R. M. (1977). Relationship of level of education to neuropsychological measures in brain-damaged and non-brain-damaged adults. *Journal of Consulting and Clinical Psychology, 45,* 536-542.

Grant, I., Adams, K. M., Carlin, A. S., Rennick, P. M., Judd, L. L., Schooff, K. G., & Reed, R. (1978). Neuropsychological effects of polydrug abuse. In D. Wesson et al. (Eds.), *Polydrug abuse* (pp. 223-261). New York: Academic Press.

Grant, I., Adams, K. M., & Reed, R. (1984). Aging, abstinence and medical risk factors in the prediction of neuropsychological deficit amongst chronic alcoholics. *Archives of General Psychiatry, 41,* 710-718.

Heaton, R. K., Grant, I., & Matthews, C. (in press). Changes in neuropsychological test performance in relation to advancing age. In I. Grant & K. M. Adams (Eds.) *Neuropsychological assessment in neuropsychiatric disorders: Clinical methods and empirical findings.* New York: Oxford University Press.

Klisz, D. K., & Parsons, O. A, (1979). Cognitive functioning in alcoholics: The role of subject attrition. *Journal of Abnormal Psychology, 38,* 268-276.

Lord, F. M. (1967). A paradox in the interpretation of group comparisons. *Psychological Bulletin, 68,* 304-305.

Lord, F. M. (1969). Statistical adjustments when comparing preexisting groups. *Psychological Bulletin, 72,* 336-337.

Maxwell, S., & Cramer, E. M. (1975). A note on analysis of covariance. *Psychological Bulletin, 82,* 187-190.

Overall, J. E., & Woodward, J. A. (1977). Some common misconceptions concerning the analysis of covariance. *Multivariate Behavioral Research, 12,* 171-185.

Parsons, O. A., & Farr, S. P. (1981). The neuropsychology of alcohol and drug use. In S. B. Filskov & T. J. Boll (Eds.), *Handbook of clinical neuropsychology* (pp. 320-365). New York: John Wiley and Sons.

Parsons, O. A., & Prigatano, G. P. (1978). Methodological considerations in clinical neuropsychological research. *Journal of Consulting and Clinical Psychology, 46,* 608-619.

Prokasy, W. F., Grant, D. A., & Meyers, N. (1958). Eyelid conditioning as a function of unconditioned stimulus intensity and intertrial interval. *Journal of Experimental Psychology, 55,* 179-183.

Reitan, R. M., & L. A. Davison (Eds.) (1974). *Clinical neuropsychology: Current status and application.* Washington, D.C.: Winston and Sons.

Rourke, B. P., & Adams, K. M. (1984). Quantitative approaches to the neuropsychological assessment of children. In R. Tarter & G. Goldstein (Eds.), *The neuropsychology of childhood* (pp. 79-108). New York: Plenum.

Winer, B. J. (1971). *Statistical principles in experimental design* (2nd ed.). New York: McGraw-Hill.

Journal of Clinical and Experimental Neuropsychology
1986, Vol. 8, No. 4, pp. 362-370.

III

Influence of Premorbid Risk Factors
on Neuropsychological Performance in Alcoholics*

Kenneth M. Adams
Henry Ford Hospital

Igor Grant
San Diego Veterans Administration Medical Center
and
University of California at San Diego

ABSTRACT

This report provides new evidence that neuromedical risk factors influence levels of behavioral impairment in alcoholics. Using a factorial model, the effects of age, neuromedical risk history, and duration of sobriety were studied in relation to neuropsychological performance. The data showed a consistent interaction between duration of abstinence and risk status: Recently detoxified alcoholics (sober 1 month) with a positive premorbid risk history had worse neuropsychological performance than did those without such historical risk events. By contrast, long-term abstinent alcoholics (sober 4 years) did not demonstrate the interaction between alcohol history and positive premorbid risk history. The present results are held to mean that neuromedical risk factors may exert a differential influence on test scores of recently detoxified men, suggesting a source of variance in neurobehavioral studies of alcoholism requiring attention by investigators.

Many studies have shown that chronic alcoholism is associated with neuro-behavioral, neuroradiological, and a variety of other abnormalities in various clinic populations (Adams, Grant, Carlin, & Reed, 1981; Grant & Reed, 1985; Parsons & Farr, 1981; Ryan & Butters, 1983). However, the causal matrix of these disorders is not clear, and our research program has been attempting to develop a longitudinal and life history model of deficit onset, clinical course, and therapeutic remission to address this issue (Adams & Grant, 1984; Adams, Grant, & Reed, 1980; Grant, Adams, & Reed, 1979, 1984; Grant, Reed, & Adams, 1980).

In this report, we present evidence to suggest that neuromedical risk represents

* Supported by the Medical Research Service of the Veterans Administration (MRIS 3240) and the Project and Human Rights Committee of Henry Ford Hospital (R35679). The authors are appreciative of the editor's and reviewers' constructive commentaries.

an important source of variance which contributes independently to neuro-psychological (NP) deficit, a hypothesis first raised in our recent longitudinal study report (Grant et al., 1984). The implication of this result is that neuromedical risk factors serve to complicate efforts to understand the role of ethanol in the evolution of brain damage. The current report differs from the Grant et al. (1984) report in that a new and intensive analysis of risk factors was conducted especially for the present investigation using a more conservative definition of the subjects at risk.

We hypothesize that alcoholism (as a lifestyle) is associated with reversible brain impairment in some patients, and argue that there are several sources of such impairment, of which the actual neurotoxic effect of ethanol is only one. Other possible sources of deficit in alcoholism include self-selection by persons with subclinical NP impairment into careers of heavy drinking, and the exposure that alcoholics experience to neuromedical risks such as head injuries or illnesses which adversely affect CNS function. In the present report, we examine the interplay of three parameters in the neuropsychological performance of two groups of alcoholic patients and their demographically matched controls.

METHOD

Subjects

In an earlier publication (Grant et al., 1984), we described the details of subject selection in our longitudinal study. Briefly, we recruited two groups of alcoholics and a matched control group. Group 1 ($n = 71$) was composed of inpatient men, aged 25-59, who were abstinent for 3 weeks or more (average, 4 weeks) at a V.A. Alcohol Treatment Program (age in years, $M = 41.5$, $SD = 8.8$; education in years, $M = 12.5$, $SD = 2.6$; years of alcoholic drinking, $M = 13.8$, $SD = 8.6$). Group 2 ($n = 65$) were male alcoholics similar in age, education, and history of alcohol abuse (age in years, $M = 42.6$, $SD = 8.4$; education in years, $M = 12.9$, $SD = 2.5$; years of alcoholic drinking, $M = 15.0$, $SD = 7.4$) to group 1, but continuously abstinent at intake for a minimum of 18 months (average 3.7 years). Group 3 ($n = 68$) consisted of nonalcoholic comparison subjects (age in years, $M = 42.2$; $SD = 9.1$; education in years, $M = 12.9$, $SD = 2.3$). There were no significant differences between these three groups on age or education, and there was no significant difference in years of drinking between alcoholic groups.

All groups were screened to exclude persons who (1) carried a neurological diagnosis unrelated to alcoholism, (2) had medical illnesses which might independently affect NP function (e.g., Chronic Obstructive Pulmonary Disease with hypoxemia), (3) were diagnosed as having schizophrenia or primary major affective disorder, or (4) exceeded preset criteria for nonmedical use of drugs other than alcohol.

With respect to the nonmedical use of drugs, subjects were excluded if (1) they had ingested hallucinogenic substances more than a total of 50 times, (2) they had used amphetamine-like stimulants on more than 20 occasions in any year preceding the study, (3) they had inhaled fumes from glue, paint, or other volatile substances on more than 10 occasions, (4) they had engaged in any intravenous drug use at any time, or (5) had taken hypnotics (including minor tranquilizers) on more than 50 occasions in any year preceding the study. Subjects were asked as well to describe lifetime and recent marijuana use, but few subjects described regular (3 times per week over 52 weeks) usage. Calculation of drug use for all substances for subjects admitted to the study showed that actual drug usage was minimal. No systematic differences between groups emerged in this area.

Although our subjects were thought to be free of obvious and clear-cut sources of NP morbidity, we proceeded to carry out a careful medical and developmental history with all accepted participants. The interviews were conducted by highly experienced staff and were supplemented, where possible, by verification checks of source records and/or inquiry with relatives. Table 1 displays the seven content areas from which a list of 32 critical risk questions was fashioned for our interview. Examples of critical items were as follows: premature birth; hospitalization prior to age 6; febrile convulsions; learning difficulties in school; nonmassive head injury with brief (less than 2 hours) periods of unconsciousness and posttraumatic amnesia not exceeding 48 hours; brief unconsciousness from excessive drinking or asphyxia.

A positive answer to any of the risk items in the various areas caused the subject to receive one credit on the content area score, as well as on the summary score. In our earlier report, we took a positive answer to any of the risk items as contributing one point to both the relevant risk content subscale (see Table 1), as well as summary medical risk score which

Table 1

Content Areas of Neuromedical Risk Studied
in the Life History Questionnaire

1. *Early Risk* (5)* – Based upon affirmative response to questions on prematurity, birth weight, febrile convulsions, and major illness before six years.

2. *Learning Disability Risk* (4) – Based upon affirmative response to questions on learning problems, special education, speech therapy, and grade failures.

3. *Head Injury Risk* (5) – Based upon affirmative response to questions concerning head injuries with loss of consciousness and on duration of posttraumatic amnesia.

4. *Toxicity Risk* (3) – Based upon affirmative response to questions regarding alcohol and drug-related unconsciousness, blackouts, and withdrawal symptoms.

5. *Neurological Risk* (8) – Based upon affirmative response to questions concerning epilepsy, other neurological disease diagnoses, examinations, and neurodiagnostic procedures encountered.

6. *Anoxic Risk* (3) – Based upon affirmative response to questions concerning general anesthesia, cardiopulmonary resuscitation, and carbon monoxide poisoning.

7. *Sick Risk* (4) – Based upon responses to questions concerning other medical conditions not judged severe enough to exclude the subject, but which might have some neuropsychological implications (such as mild hypertension, arthritis, anemia, diabetes and liver disease).

8. *Summary Medical Risk* (32) – The numerical sum of all the above items in the content areas.

* This is the number of questions for each content area.

differentiated the groups from each other at a statistically significant level (Grant et al., 1984, p. 712). However, study of the scale and component items suggested to us that a more conservative treatment of this data might produce more reliable results.

To this end, the present study was conducted by creating two risk groups: (1) those having *no* positive endorsements of any risk items, and (2) those having one or more positive endorsements of any risk items. This methodology, while crude, allowed us to produce an "all-or-none" dichotomy which we felt more confidently reflected the "not at risk" vs. "at risk" independent variable status of the two groups used in this study. Thus, the present study serves as a more rigorous test of the "risk" concept in carefully studied alcoholics with varying degrees of abstinence and controls.

NP assessment involved an extended Halstead-Reitan Battery, augmented by memory measures (i.e., Wechsler Memory Scale, stories and figures, immediate and 30-minute recall; and Rey-Osterrieth Diagram, direct copy and delayed recall). A complete listing of tests and results appears in Grant et al. (1984, p. 713). Beyond considering the usual summary scores (WAIS: VIQ, PIQ, FSIQ; Halstead Impairment Index; Brain Age Quotient), a clinician (I.G) who was blind to group membership rated all protocols on a 6-point impairment scale. Scores for seven ability areas (e.g., attention, abstraction, memory) and a global index of impairment were thus derived. The reliability and validity of the blind clinical rating procedure has been found to be high (Finlayson, 1978; Heaton, Grant, Anthony, & Lehman, 1981; Heaton, Grant, McSweeny, Adams, & Petty, 1983). Specifically, interrater agreement between experienced judges has ranged between 85%-93%, with Kappa statistics and various other indicators of clinician agreement providing strong support of this analytic modality. In previous studies, the clinician ratings proved to be a powerful complement to the numerical analysis of NP protocols. This complementarity of individual and group data analysis is a central feature of this research program (Grant, Adams, Carlin, Rennick, Judd, & Schooff, 1978; Grant, Heaton, McSweeny, Adams, & Timms, 1982). A detailed discussion of the conceptual basis of the clinical rating method can be found in Reitan (1974, 1986).

Data Analysis

We hypothesized that the major sources of NP variability in our sample would be history of alcoholic drinking, length of abstinence, age, and medical risk status. Therefore, we divided our sample so as to create a 3 x 2 x 2 multivariate analysis of variance (MANOVA) design. There were three subject groups (described above), two risk groups (no risk events vs. one or more risk events), and two age groups (under 40 years vs. 40 and above). This division created a fairly balanced design, with no fewer than 10 and no more than 31 subjects per cell.

From the large number of NP scores and ratings, we selected 14 variables to serve as dependent variables in the MANOVA analysis. In selecting these variables, we set the following requirements: (1) coverage of major areas of neurobehavioral functioning, such as memory, abstracting ability, and perceptual-motor skills; (2) selection of test variables known to be sensitive to NP impairment; (3) creation of an amalgam of actual test variables, psychometric summary indices, and blind clinical ratings such that the various major modes of inferring cerebral dysfunction would be represented.

The variables chosen were as follows: (1) WAIS Digit Span scaled score; (2) WAIS Vocabulary scaled score; (3) WAIS Digit Symbol scaled score; (4) WAIS Block Design scaled score; (5) Halstead Category Test errors; (6) Grooved Pegboard time-dominant hand; (7) Grip Strength-dominant hand; (8) Speech-Sounds Perception Test errors; (9) Tactual Performance Test (TPT) location score; (10) Halstead Impairment Index; (11) Brain Age Quotient; (12) blind clinician's rating of overall abstraction capacity; (13) blind clinician's rating of overall memory capacity; and, (14) blind clinician's rating of overall neuropsychological status.

The MANOVA was accomplished using version 9.1 of the Statistical Package for the Social Sciences (Nie, Hull, Jenkins, Steinbrenner, & Bent, 1975). A full factorial model was specified. Study of the within-cell and overall-design homogeneity suggested that the solution was a stable and meaningful one.

RESULTS

The MANOVA produced two main effects and one interaction. The Age factor produced a robust and expected effect (F (14,172) = 8.20, $p < .001$). Study of univariate F ratios revealed eight significant ($p < .05$) contributors to the age effect (Vocabulary, Block Design, Digit Symbol, Category Test, Pegboard time, Impairment Index, Grip Strength, and TPT location score). A Group main effect was identified as well (F (28,344) = 1.96, $p < .01$), with three significant univariate sources (clinician's global rating, dominant Grip Strength, and Speech-Sounds Perception Test errors), and the recently detoxified alcoholics performing worse than abstinent alcoholics and controls in each instance.

The interaction was between Group and Risk main effects (F (28,344) = 1.60, $p < .05$). Five variables contributed significantly ($p < .05$) to this result (Category Test, clinician's abstraction rating, clinician's global rating, Impairment Index, and dominant Grip Strength). In addition, four other variables reflected trends toward significant contribution with univariate F ratio probabilities of .10 or less (Block Design, Pegboard Time, Speech-Sounds Perception Test errors, and TPT location score). Study of test scores revealed that recently detoxified alcoholics who also had positive risk histories performed worse on all 9 of these tests.

To illustrate the influences at work, we present in Tables 2 and 3 a detailed analysis of the results of the Category Test which, as a measure of abstracting ability, has been found to be sensitive to alcoholism effects in more than a dozen studies (Parsons & Farr, 1981).

Looking first at Table 2, which includes data from all subjects, we find the following: (1) older subjects performed significantly worse than younger subjects; (2) a nonsignificant tendency for recently detoxified alcoholics to perform worse than long-term abstinent alcoholics and controls; (3) no significant Risk main effect. Despite the lack of significant Group or Risk main effects, there was a *Group x Risk interaction* ($p < .05$). Inspection of mean scores revealed that risk adversely affected Category Test performance *only* in the recently detoxified alcoholics. Category Test errors for this group are displayed in Table 3 which, for sake of completeness, stratifies this group by age as well as by risk. Table 3 shows that the presence of risk lowered dramatically the achievement level of younger

Table 2

Mean Category Test Error Scores for All Subjects,
Grouped by the Three Independent Variables

Groups	Category Errors	
	M	SD
Recently Detoxified Alcoholics	46.7	25.0
Long-Term Abstinent Alcoholics	41.3	18.8
Nonalcoholic Controls	40.0	22.3
Neuromedical Risk Absent	40.1	22.6
Neuromedical Risk Present	44.1	22.2
Younger ($<$ 40 years)	37.8a	21.4
Older ($\geqslant$ 40 years)	46.9	22.4

$^a p < .01$

Table 3

Detailed Examination of Category Test Errors
in the Recently Detoxified Alcoholics

Risk Group	Age	
	Younger ($<$ 40 years)	Older $\geqslant$ 40 years)
No risk	M = 28.5	M = 44.9
	SD = 20.3	SD = 24.6
Risk	M = 45.0	M = 59.4
	SD = 24.9	SD = 23.5

subjects while exerting a less serious, but nonetheless negative, influence on older subjects, as well. Additionally, older subjects in both risk groups made more errors than did their younger counterparts.

In summary, an ANOVA analysis of Category Test errors identified an expected age main effect, nonsignificant group effect, and a consistent Group by Risk effect. This latter significant effect was observed in five other variables and appeared as trends in an additional four variables as well in the overall MANOVA described above. Specific analysis of this interaction also revealed that risk status exerted a significant detrimental influence on the NP performances of recently detoxified alcoholics in these variables, as described above for the Category Test.

DISCUSSION

The present data indicate that risk factors influence NP functioning in alcoholics. The fact that tests reflecting several ability areas were affected, and that some of these measures (e.g., Category Test) are among the most "brain sensitive" tests, lends support to the notion that neuromedical risk factors pose a special vulnerability for alcoholic patients. Analysis demonstrated that the recently abstinent patient group having previous risk events showed impairment beyond the additive main effects of aging, alcohol status, or risk.

Although we found that both alcoholic groups tended to report increased frequency of certain specific risks, including nonmassive head injury with brief periods of unconsciousness, mild scholastic difficulties in grade school, as well as periods of nontraumatic unconsciousness related to alcohol overdose, our study was not of sufficient size to allow confident identification of the specific neuromedical risks that are operative. An important direction for future research will be to study larger groups of alcoholics, well matched for age, education, and drinking history, but differing in exposure to pretreatment risk events which could serve to disrupt brain-behavior functions when major disorders with CNS impact (such as alcoholism) are introduced into these patients' lives.

Although we believe our findings to have common-sense appeal, we were somewhat surprised that we demonstrated a relatively robust Group X Risk interaction in our alcoholics, who were screened with considerable care to exclude persons with obviously adverse medical backgrounds, and most of whom ended up performing essentially normally on most NP tests. Put another way, we suggest that our study probably had an inbuilt bias *against* finding a significant risk effect. If this is correct, then previous studies which were less restrictive in their selection procedures, and those which actually reported substantial rates of head injury, delirium tremens, or other neurological events (e.g., Bergman, Borg, & Holm, 1980; Blucewicz, Dustman, Schenkenberg, & Beck, 1977; Klisz & Parsons, 1977; Nichols-Hochla & Parsons, 1982), might have inferred inappropriately that the NP change they observed was related primarily to amount of alcohol consumed. That is, failure to identify and treat appropriately any NP variance attributable to neuromedical and developmental history variables may have produced group differences whose sole causal attribution to alcohol consumption may be erroneous.

The possibility that this interaction is a statistically weak effect would seem to be offset in part by its emergence in the MANOVA and its ubiquitous univariate representation among many of the tests held to be most sensitive to cerebral dysfunction.

Finally, the fact that we found a Group X Risk interaction, rather than simply a risk main effect, suggests that history of neuromedical risk might predispose certain patients to manifest NP deficits in the context of recovery from alcoholic drinking. We cannot determine from our data whether NP recovery simply takes longer in alcoholics who have adverse neuromedical backgrounds, or whether the natural history of alcohol-related deficit is actually accelerated by the presence of such background events (Grant et al., 1980).

In summary, these data indicate that future studies should attend more carefully to the issue of patient history. We offer this suggestion as complementary to our previous report (Adams, Brown, & Grant, 1985) showing that insufficient attention to patient group demographic differences or unwarranted statistical attempts to remedy these differences will also produce false "impairment" results in alcoholics. Differential levels of risk might also create uncontrolled error variance unbeknownst to the investigator who might believe that amount and recency of drinking or relative sobriety are uncomplicated selection factors in the formation of alcoholic groups for study.

REFERENCES

Adams, K. M., & Grant, I. (1984). Failure of nonlinear models of drinking history variables to predict neuropsychological performance in alcoholics. *American Journal of Psychiatry, 141,* 663-667.

Adams, K. M., Brown, G. G. & Grant, I. (1985). Analysis of covariance as a remedy for demographic mismatch of research subject groups: Some sobering simulations. *Journal of Clinical and Experimental Neuropsychology, 7,* 445-462.

Adams, K. M., Grant, I., Carlin, A. S., & Reed, R. (1981). Self-reported alcohol consumption in four clinical groups. *American Journal of Psychiatry, 138,* 445-449.

Adams, K. M., Grant, I., & Reed, R. (1980). Neuropsychology in alcoholic men in their thirties: One year followup. *American Journal of Psychiatry, 137,* 928-931.

Bergman, H., Borg, S., Hindmarsh, C., Idestrom, M., & Mutzell, S. (1980). Computed tomography of the brain and neuropsychological assessment of alcoholic patients. In H. Begleiter (Ed.), *Biological effects of alcohol* (pp. 771-786). New York: Plenum Press.

Blusewicz, M. J., Dustman, R. E., Schenkenberg, T., & Beck, C. C. (1977). Neuropsychological correlates of chronic alcoholism and aging. *Journal of Nervous and Mental Disease, 165,* 348-355.

Finlayson, M. A. J. (1978, February). Blind clinician agreement in the rating of the polydrug protocols. In K. M. Adams (Chair), *Cerebral dysfunction in multiple drug users: Conditions affecting the emergence of behavioral impairment,* Symposium presented at the meeting of the International Neuropsychological Society, Minneapolis, Minnesota.

Grant, I., Adams, K. M., Carlin, A. S., Rennick, P. M., Judd, L. L., & Schooff, K. G. (1978). The collaborative neuropsychological study of polydrug users. *Archives of General Psychiatry, 35,* 1063-1074.

Grant, I., Adams, K. M., & Reed, R. (1979). Normal neuropsychological abilities of alcoholic men in their late thirties. *American Journal of Psychiatry, 136,* 1263-1269.

Grant, I., Adams, K. M., & Reed, R. (1984). Aging, abstinence and medical risk factors in the prediction of neuropsychological deficit amongst chronic alcoholics. *Archives of General Psychiatry 41,* 710-718.

Grant, I., Heaton, R. K., McSweeny, A. J., Adams, K. M., & Timms, R. M. (1982). Neuropsychologic findings in hypoxemic chronic obstructive pulmonary disease. *Archives of Internal Medicine, 142,* 1470-1476.

Grant, I. & Reed, R. (1985). The neuropsychology of alcohol and drug abuse. In A. Alterman (Ed.) *Substance abuse and psychopathology* (pp. 289-341). New York: Plenum Press.

Grant, I., Reed, R., & Adams, K. M. (1980). Natural history of alcohol and drug-related brain disorder: Implications for neuropsychological research. *Journal of Clinical Neuropsychology, 2,* 321-331.

Heaton, R. K., Grant, I., Anthony, W. Z., & Lehman, R. A. W. (1981). A comparison of clinical and automated interpretation of the Halstead-Reitan Battery. *Journal of Clinical Neuropsychology, 3,* 121-142.

Heaton, R. K., Grant, I., McSweeny, J., Adams, K. M., & Petty, T. L. (1983). Psychologic effects of continuous and nocturnal oxygen therapy in hypoxemic chronic obstructive pulmonary disease. *Archives of Internal Medicine, 143,* 1941-1947.

Klisz, D. K., & Parsons, O. A. (1977). Hypothesis testing in older and younger alcoholics. *Journal of Studies on Alcohol, 38,* 121-142.

Nichols-Hochla, N. A., & Parsons, O. A. (1982). Premature aging in female alcoholics: A neuropsychological study. *Journal of Nervous and Mental Disease, 170,* 291-245.

Nie, N. H., Hull, C. H., Jenkins, J., Steinbrenner, K., & Bent, D. H. (1975). *SPSS: Statistical Package for the Social Sciences.* New York: McGraw-Hill.

Parsons, O. A., & Farr, S. D. (1981). The neuropsychology of alcohol and drug use. In S. B. Filskov & T. J. Boll (Eds.), *Handbook of clinical neuropsychology* (pp. 320-365). New York: Hohn Wiley & Sons.

Reitan, R. M. (1974). Methodological problems in clinical neuropsychology. In R. M. Reitan & L. A. Davison (Eds.), *Clinical neuropsychology: Current status and applications* (pp. 19-46). New York: V. H. Winston & Sons.

Reitan, R. M. (1986). Theoretical and methodological bases of the Halstead-Reitan neuropsychological test battery. In I. Grant & K. M. Adams (Eds.), *Neuropsychological assessment of neuropsychiatric disorders* (pp. 3-30). New York: Oxford University Press.

Ryan, C. & Butters, N. M. (1983). Cognitive deficits in alcoholics. In B. Kissin & H. Begleiter (Eds.), *The pathogenesis of alcoholism,* Vol. 7, pp. 485-538. New York: Plenum Press.

CHAPTER IV

Biostatistical Techniques

The biostatistical techniques described and analyzed here are, quite arguably, those most commonly utilized in modern clinical neuropsychology. For many investigators, they are the "bread-and-butter" of their research enterprises.

The section on discriminant function analysis begins with a primer on the use of linear discriminant analysis in clinical neuropsychology by Adams. The other contributions to this section detail different manners in which discriminant analysis has been applied to the kindergarten prediction of reading achievement (Fletcher et al.), the prediction of indicators of quality of life in patients with closed-head injury (Klonoff et al.), and prediction of recovery of memory in persons with head injury (Paniak et al.). A careful reading of this section will provide not only the bases for the systematic application of discriminant analysis, but also some very good examples of how, in fact, this type of biostatistical technique has been applied in clinical neuropsychology.

Although not widely applied in our field prior to the last decade, cluster analysis has experienced a "boom" period since that time. As with the previous section, this one begins with a primer on the application of cluster analysis (Morris et al.). The other contribution details the manner in which this set of biostatistical techniques can be applied to problems of classification in clinical neuropsychology. It would behoove anyone who wishes to use cluster techniques to study both of these contributions in a careful, thorough manner. We say this principally because we have seen numerous applications of this set of techniques that fall far short of the criteria envisioned for their use in these two articles.

This chapter closes with a series of papers on common and confirmatory factor analysis. During the formative years of clinical neuropsychology, common factor analysis was among the two or three most commonly employed biostatistical techniques. Its widespread use reflects the early – and, for that matter, continuing – concerns of neuropsychologists regarding the dimensionality of their tests and data sets. More recently, confirmatory factor analysis has emerged as potentially more powerful and adaptable set of techniques for accomplishing this aim. Applications of various forms of factor analysis are offered by Newby et al., Bornstein and Chelune, Roid et al., and Francis et al. For those not completely familiar with the complexities of confirmatory factor analysis, the excellent introduction provided by Francis is thorough and to-the-point.

SECTION IV – A: DISCRIMINANT FUNCTIONS AND PREDICTION

The studies in this section provide the researcher with descriptions and evaluations of a variety of multivariate techniques required to make sense of the numerous dependent measures (and their intercorrelatedness) that would characterize any comprehensive approach to predicting outcome behaviors in neuropsychological research. They include discriminant analysis (Adams and Fletcher, Smidt, & Satz); principal components analysis and canonical correlational analysis (Klonoff, Costa, & Snow); and Hotelling's T^2 criterion (Paniak, Shore, & Rourke). Because the content areas are also of critical concern to clinical neuropsychologists [e.g., early detection of childhood learning disabilities (Fletcher et al.), substance abuse (Adams); prediction of outcome of patients with closed-head injury (Klonoff et al.; Paniak et al.)], it is suggested that the studies be examined in such a way that one neither loses the methodology for the content nor vice versa.

There is much to contemplate concerning these articles. Regarding the research utilizing linear discriminant analysis (LDA), enough specific information is provided to highlight several fundamental problems with the application of this valuable technique prior to the work of Adams and Fletcher et al. Unfortunately, LDA has often been utilized with far too low subject-to-variable ratios. Unless there are at least 5 subjects for every predictor variable of interest, the resulting research is at very high risk for producing invalid results – specifically, prediction rates that are overinflated. It should be noted that because of the mathematical interrelatedness of multivariate techniques, in general, the rule of thumb for subject/variable ratio of 5 to 1 should also be used as a working guideline for multiple regression, factor analysis, and canonical correlational analysis. In the latter regard, note the caveats of Klonoff et al., the third paper in the series.

A second problem with many applications of multivariate techniques is that, often, little or no attempt is made to replicate original findings. To complicate matters further, many journal editors are most reluctant to publish replication studies. But what of those situations in which a satisfactory subject/variable ratio has been achieved and there is almost no likelihood of replication (e.g., a very rare disorder was the focus of study)? One should apply shrinkage methods such as those suggested in Cohen and Cohen (1983) to produce a best estimate of the variability of the predictive accuracy of the phenomenon under investigation.

In concluding this section, it is necessary to consider the issue of prediction in a broader context. When there is a criterion against which to measure the correctness of a prediction, one can speak more generally about the sensitivity-specificity model, namely, the indices of sensitivity, specificity, predicted positive and predicted negative power of a given test. In this specific regard, the valuable conditional probability statistic (Cp) used by Fletcher et al. to predict reading achievement is, in fact, the predicted positive statistic derived from the well-known sensitivity-specificity model.

Finally, since the publication of these four important papers, the sensitivity-specificity model has been considered in yet a still broader context, under the rubric of Receiver Operating Characteristic (ROC) curves. One distinct advantage of ROCs over other multivariate predictive methods is that they allow one to examine a range of possible cut-off scores to define a particular criterion (a point which is quite relevant to the research of Soper, Cicchetti, Satz, Light, and Orsini, 1988, see pages 38-53). This enables the clinical researcher to detect the point at which there is an optimal balance between false positive and false negative errors. In considering this issue further, it is instructive to heed the sage advice of Fletcher et al. (see page 218) who make the valid argument that, in the follow-up evaluation of an initial screening test, "false positive errors may become less costly than false negative errors." Thus, the follow-up evaluation can correct the false positive errors but cannot include those cases lost as false negative errors.

SECTION IV – B: CLUSTER ANALYSIS

Concerns regarding classification of human disorders have been with us since the dawn of psychology as a clinical discipline. These concerns have been reflected in modern clinical neuropsychology, especially with respect to classification in aphasiology and childhood learning disabilities. The methodology for classification has been varied, ranging from clinical techniques to those that involve sophisticated statistical algorithms. The presentations in this section deal primarily with the appplication of one set of biostatistical algorithms, viz., cluster analysis. However, the reader should note that much more than a set of techniques is the focus of inquiry. In addition to demonstrating how these can be applied, the broader – and much more important – issues of the theoretical and hypothesis-testing context within which they should be applied lie at the basis of these inquiries. The interested reader may wish to consult Adams (1985) and Rourke (1985, 1991) for examples of how these issues have been addresssed by other investigators in clinical neuropsychology.

SECTION IV – C: COMMON AND CONFIRMATORY FACTOR ANALYSIS AND STRUCTURAL EQUATIONS

This portion of the book provides some examples of the contemporary usage of factor analysis as both an exploratory technique as well as a confirmatory technique to shed light on questions of theoretical importance. In neuropsychological research, this represents an advance from pioneering investigations that utilized factor analysis as a demonstration tool to reveal the essential dimensionality and relational architecture of neuropsychological test batteries.

Newby and associates present a use of factor analysis that permitted direct and cross-validated comparison of four widely used neuropsychological testing paradigms. The particular strengths of each of the techniques was revealed in the structural model testing; but, surprisingly, no clear ascendency of one method over all others was identified. While this result might be superficially disappointing to some, the advisory outcome of this study in terms of the recommended continuation of neuropsychological test development is as valuable and important as any research finding could be.

Bornstein and Chelune as well as Roid and associates presented data on the factor structure of the Wechsler Memory Scale-Revised in a special issue of TCN soon after the release of the test to the clinical community. The advent of modern software for factor-analytic investigations has made it possible to obtain critical field testing data on new measurement products within a very short period of time. These particular studies are examples of how timely research results may assist clinicians and investigators in the understanding of the advantages and limitations of new tests. Of key importance here are (a) the use of confirmatory technology in the Roid and associates report to verify the measurement model of memory offered by the test publisher, and (b) the employment of new and existing tests in the Bornstein and Chelune report to provide some information on how a new test will "look" in context.

Francis' paper provides the interested reader with an excellent learner's tour of one of the most important statistical techniques developed in the last 20 years. Structural equation techniques are made for neuropsychological research. They offer the investigator virtually limitless power to build and test models of cognitive processes, diagnostic subtypes, or any number of other phenomena of importance in contemporary neuropsychology. The job of learning the intricacies of the software used for structural equations (e.g., LISREL) is miniscule in comparison to the potential benefits to the investigator of actually testing a model as opposed to debating it to death - as has been too often the practice in areas of neuropsychology such as hemispheric specialization.

The practical importance of applying structural equation technology is powerfully demonstrated in the final paper in the section by Francis and associates. Using a structural equation paradigm, these investigators found no evidence for a ubiquitous belief in child neuropsychology - namely that lateralized sensorimotor impairment is a cardinal predictor of neuropsychological impairment in samples such as the one they describe. But that is not all. The results of the structural model actually pointed to a new parameter (namely, skill complexity) as a powerful new predictor of neuropsychological impairment. The reader will share in a demonstration of a method that not only identifies unproductive assumptions, but directs the investigator's attention to new leads and perhaps unexplored realms for future investigation.

REFERENCES

Adams, K. M. (1985). Theoretical, methodological, and statistical issues. In B. P. Rourke (Ed.), *Neuropsychology of learning disabilities: Essentials of subtype analysis* (pp.17-39). New York: Guilford Press.

Cohen, J., & Cohen, P. (1983). *Applied multiple regression/correlation analysis for the behavioral sciences* (2nd ed.). Hillsdale, NJ: Lawrence Erlbaum Assoc., Inc.

Crunch Statistical Package: Vol. II (1991). Oakland, CA: Crunch Software Corporation.

Rourke, B. P. (Ed.). (1985). *Neuropsychology of learning disabilities: Essentials of subtype analysis.* New York: Guilford Press.

Rourke, B. P. (Ed.). (1991). *Neuropsychological validation of learning disability subtypes.* New York: Guilford Press.

Journal of Clinical Neuropsychology
1979, Vol. 1, No. 3, 259–272.

Linear Discriminant Analysis in Clinical Neuropsychology Research*

Kenneth M. Adams
Henry Ford Hospital

ABSTRACT

This paper reviews the use of Linear Discriminant Analysis (LDA) in clinical neuropsychology research. The basic neuropsychological questions addressed by the method, the special problems and requirements for its use, and likely outcomes are described in detail. Recommendations regarding employment of commonly available LDA computer programs are made for the researcher. Careful attention to the assumptions and decisions inherent in LDA programs could enhance its value in clinical research.

The purpose of this paper is to describe the use of Linear Discriminant Analysis in clinical neuropsychology research. The basic process and special problems of the method for the applied researcher are reviewed. When certain assumptions are met, this statistical procedure has great potential value in addressing some central issues in actual practice. While this technique has traditionally been used as a validation/classification tool, its actual place amongst multivariate procedures involves more than "decision-making" alone. We will review here some of the sources of this technique's potential and the problems encountered in its use.

Clinical neuropsychology has evolved as a specialty which seeks to make use of brain-behavior relationships in diagnostic, predictive, and prognostic ways. The use of structured and widely accepted neuropsychological tests in a consistent fashion represents one modality in which neuropsychologists currently operate to answer clinical questions (Costa, 1976). As data accumulates from evaluation of patients, the practitioner with research interests will naturally generate several classes of mathematical questions:

1. Given that comprehensive and accurate data on the state of the subjects' brains (i.e., criterion data) are available, do the behavioral data relate to

* The helpful comments and criticisms by a number of colleagues and reviewers are acknowledged, particularly those of Byron P. Rourke and Gregory G. Brown. This work was assisted by the Fund for Henry Ford Hospital. Dr. Adams is also affiliated with the Department of Psychology, Wayne State University and Department of Psychiatry, University of Michigan.

the criterion data? Can cases be grouped by an independent variable of brain state (e.g., left hemisphere dysfunction, right hemisphere dysfunction, etc.) and can behavioral variables be shown to vary significantly in their level of performance?

2. If differences appear amongst groups, can they be traced to some smaller number of underlying "causes"? Are certain variables more important to, indicative of, or sensitive to the differences? Could the behavioral tests be shortened, or some subtests eliminated and still be expected to generate group differences on criterion variables?

3. Can predictions from behavioral data to group membership be made? Will various indices, weights, or other methods produce accurate classification across samples and settings?

Linear discriminant analysis (LDA) actually relates to all three types of questions. This is not a property of LDA, but rather rests on the relationships between multivariate methods. All multivariate techniques which seek to relate one or more variables to another set of variables in some independent/dependent relationship are special cases of canonical correlation.

In the case of the first questions regarding significant criterion group differences on behavioral variables, the only problem is one of labeling. If one considers the criterion group, or brain measurement variables, as independent, and the behavioral variables from the neuropsychological tests as dependent, the scheme is exactly that of multivariate analysis of variance (MANOVA). In fact, LDA may be seen as a one-factor case of MANOVA. Where only two criterion groups are involved, the multivariate equivalent is Hotelling's T-Squared (Hotelling, 1931). Most LDA computer programs contain the essential information needed to reconceptualize the analysis as MANOVA. The principal device for the investigator is to use the terms "predictor" and "criterion" in the appropriate independent/dependent way.

The second set of questions regarding research also relates to LDA. A good deal of clinical neuropsychological research is devoted to finding the underlying mechanisms of group differences. In turn, the logical questions of how the apparently important or sensitive variables or tests would behave if used alone or on cross-validation arises. In some ways, this process of seeking underlying explanations is similar to that seen in factor analysis. Factor analysis can be used to explore and redefine neuropsychological data in terms of factor scores. However, factor analysis – like LDA – is a procedure whose outcome is indeterminate. That is, the "goodness" of a solution is relative and one selected from amongst many because of some theoretical (neuropsychological) or mathematical (e.g., "simple structure") reason. Factor scores themselves have still other qualities which make their representatives for a particular factor solution far from absolute. Thus, factor analysis may be an important source of understanding of the dimensions and confluences of variance in a matrix. However, direct use of factor scores as predictor variables in LDA should be approached with caution.

The final set of questions – about prediction and classification – has traditionally been seen as the proper goal of LDA. Since clinical prediction is of great interest to neuropsychologists, it would be important to understand the use of the method.

Linear Discriminant Analysis: An Outline

Two-group discriminant analysis for the purpose of classification was first proposed by Fisher (1936), and definitively proven by Anderson (1951). The basic notion of the technique is to look for the optimal separation of the dependent criterion variable groups as defined by the vectors of independent predictor variables. The definition of what is "optimal" separation of groups in a mathematical sense is the subject of considerable research (Bock, 1975; Cacoullos, 1973; Lachenbruch, 1975; Overall & Klett, 1972; Press, 1972; Tatsuoka, 1970).

The interpretation of group differences along these vectors of independent variables may be done visually or mathematically, but the number of points and dimensionality usually make visual plotting of functions inefficient. The actual LDA problem mathematically involves optimizing a matrix algebra equation. Cooley and Lohnes (1971; p. 243) provide a detailed discussion of the calculus of partial differentiation along with the constraints on the solution. Similarly, Finn (1974) provides the same discussion from a slightly different perspective.

Briefly, in solving the equation, a number of pairs of eigenvector–eigenvalue combinations are generated. These can be seen as indicators of the likely robustness of the LDA and are the successive solutions across the data dimensions. Detailed study of some of the references described above is probably the best way to get a thorough understanding of the derivation. The number of pairs generated is the lesser of the number of original variables *or* the number of groups minus 1. These eigenvectors and eigenvalues are arranged in descending order of the value of their eigenvalues. Perhaps the most important point is that the eigenvalues and eigenvectors (also called characteristic roots/characteristic vectors or latent roots/latent vectors) contain the information needed to evaluate the non-stepwise discriminant function solution. It is possible to recombine the eigenvectors with the test scores to produce predicted values whose contribution to *classification* can be evaluated.

For the neuropsychologist, another point is relevant here. First, while the solution of the actual equation involves a "between" to "within" problem similar to that seen in ANOVA, the similarity ends there. Like factor analysis, there is no actual "correct" solution, and the goodness of a particular fit depends upon a variety of compromises or tradeoffs. In effect, differences between criterion groups will be relative, and more than the usual amount of caution is needed in the interpretation of apparent group differences.

The evaluation of the success of a solution in terms of classification can usually be obtained by placing cases in a cross-tabulation table of predicted versus actual group membership. The "hit rate" or degree of success of a particular solution is usually construed as the number of correct group assignments as a *percentage* of the entire sample. Since LDA is an error-minimization technique, this percentage tends to be deceptively high. Cross validation of the eigenvectors with a new sample of behavioral data can produce dramatic shrinkage in accuracy (Fletcher, Rice, & Ray, 1978).

Another aspect of LDA to which we will repeatedly refer in this paper is the assumed base rates for the dependent group variable. In various clinical settings, the probability of certain focal and/or diffuse cerebral damage is not equal. Some LDA programs allow the investigator to set a priori probabilities for the criterion dependent groups before the analysis. Failing to consider this parameter usually will mean that the LDA program will erroneously presume equal base rates.

Types of Linear Discriminant Function Analysis

Most of the description to this point has centered on LDA which is non-stepwise in nature. That is, the analysis is performed with a full set of all predictor variables and the "best" solution selected in relation to the criterion group variable.

A new development in LDA in the last decade is the deployment of computer programs for *stepwise* LDA technique (Nie, Hull, Jenkins, Steinbrenner, & Bent, 1975; Hull & Nie, 1979). A complete discussion of this method as developed for multiple regression appears in Efroymsen's (1960) oft-cited chapter.

A family of techniques now exist which involve successive addition or subtraction of variables. These have been termed step-up, step-down, as well as stepwise.

The stepwise method successively selects or excludes individual predictor variables for membership in some theoretically optimal subset of the original predictors. The entry or exit of variables in this process is, to some degree, under the investigator's control. Yet the entire process is one that lends itself to abuse as every possible source of variance to "improve" separation of groups – and thus increase classification accuracy – is employed. The actual effects of various changes in stepwise LDA parameters are not yet fully understood, and documentation of these methods is incomplete.

Most experts believe that the stepwise method has been oversold or over-simplified in computer manuals. Because of capitalization on chance factors in the stepwise technique, the researcher must take care in the interpretation of the order of the entry of the variables. Lachin and Schachter (1974) have shown, with a psychophysiological data set, that the statistics generated at each step are quite unstable and, in some cases, meaningless. Bock (1966) first suggested a middle strategy whereby groups of variables be ordered for entry by their theoretical importance. In practice, this may be a way of controlling chance results and grounding the analysis on the basis of a theoretical model or previous evidence from the literature.

Because the more recent studies have employed the stepwise method, we will concentrate this report on the stepwise technique. At the same time, we acknowledge the pioneering papers of Wheeler, Burke, and Reitan (1963) as well as Wheeler and Reitan (1963) on the non-stepwise method.

Some Guidelines for Effective Use of Linear Discriminant Functions in Clinical Neuropsychology Research

The three sets of research questions raised earlier in this paper are crucial ones for neuropsychology, although it is important to understand that they are mathematical ones that require a broader and more thorough interpretation. For example, comparison of classification accuracy by a clinician and LDA methods (cross validated or not) must take into account the kinds of information available to each. Actuarial methods have generally been shown to equal or exceed clinical ones (Wiggins, 1973), if simple diagnostic decisions based upon "level of performance" information are involved. More substantial and sophisticated questions in the practice of neuropsychology in the individual case will require different multivariate methods (e.g., profile analysis in configural judgments) against which we may compare the clinician.

In using LDA at present, we can offer the following suggestions in important content areas:

1. *Consider the kinds and types of criterion groups to be discriminated.*
The kinds of criterion groups to be discriminated have an important effect on the outcome of LDA. Variations in level of confidence concerning localization of dysfunction, heterogeneity in disease type, and relative acuity are examples of factors which can obscure classification outcome. Where the objective is to test the clinical utility of a variable set, we have found it wise to create a subject pool similar to our referral population.

Where left hemisphere lesion and right hemisphere lesion groups are to be discriminated alone, for example, a reasonably comprehensive classification using neuropsychological predictors will be high (usually greater than 90%). This is especially true if WAIS or lateralizing motor/sensory tests are involved.

Where a diffuse damage group is to be added to the latter groups, the classification rate will be less. However, the misclassifications and any clinical similarities between the diffuse and lateralized groups will be very useful in understanding why the results emerged. In our experience, left hemisphere dysfunction and diffuse dysfunction will be more difficult to discriminate in younger populations, populations with variations between groups in education, or in populations with mixed language disturbance.

For example, our re-analysis (Adams, Note 1) of previously reported data (Grant, Adams, Carlin, Rennick, Judd, & Schooff, 1978) demonstrates all three of these phenomena nicely. Briefly, the youthful polydrug patients in this study were shown to be neuropsychologically impaired in about one-third of the cases. Clinical and factor analytic analysis of the results showed most impairment to be language-related, and relatively independent of age and education as such. Linear Discriminant Analysis between impaired and unimpaired subjects across large sets of predictor battery data covaried by combinations of age and education did not change the statistical separation of the dependent criterion groups. Restriction of range in age and education may have created this result, and these factors bear watching in accounting for diagnostic disagreements or "off diagonal" cases.

On the other hand, similarities between right hemisphere dysfunction and diffuse impairment groups are the rule in older groups and with certain types of diffuse samples such as are typically seen in neuropsychiatric settings. This was first seen in an older group of subjects in their mid to late forties with carefully defined lesions (Adams, 1975; Adams, Rennick, & Rosenbaum, Note 2; Adams, Sternthal, & Read, Note 3; Adams, Note 4; Adams, Note 5). In brief, these patients created more diagnostic disagreements between right hemisphere and diffusely brain-damaged subjects. This problem changed when age and education were artificially removed from the test scores, creating more left hemisphere/diffuse impairment disagreements. Aging may be the underlying concept which explains these findings.

Again, sampling differences may have created these results. However, the precise nature of the criterion data in these cases eliminates at least one source of uncertainty. The important point of these examples is that one must be aware of alternative sources of explanatory power for results of this nature.

Where criterion groups can be subdivided on the basis of confidence in criterion information, level of CNS involvement, or other relevant factors, care should be taken to see that the accuracy of classification is not spuriously increased by these factors.

Finally, in no case should the normal-abnormal/patient-control distinction be allowed to obscure a simple linear discriminant function. This dimension, when mixed with diagnostic discrimination problems, creates spurious results. Quite simply, one simple LDA analysis cannot adequately and simultaneously handle several dimensions of neurobehavioral impairment.

2. *Select predictor variables carefully and in a representative fashion.*
Various neurobehavioral test variables can be selected as predictors, but they should meet the following criteria (adapted from Wiggins, 1973) for inclusion

in the LDA: (a) the data are available (without missing data), (b) the data are objective (uncontaminated with criterion), (c) the method is public and can be replicated by others, (d) the data are reliable, (e) the data are sufficiently complex to reflect the criterion of brain function, (f) the data are not distributed in some unusual way, and (g) the data are theoretically relevant.

The statistical or actuarial basis of LDA should not detract from the level of thought which needs to go into variable selection. The set should make neuropsychological sense, and the prediction can only be as useful as the variables which are chosen to represent a particular brain model.

In evaluating neuropsychological variables, the researcher must consider other factors. Where several measures of the same test (e.g., latency, errors, etc.) are included. care must be taken to avoid inclusion of too many highly correlated indices of performance. This error of over-inclusion will produce an artificially high level of classification if non-stepwise procedures are used. In factor analytic problems, over-inclusion of indices from the same test can actually produce a spurious factor reflecting methodological variance or the sheer number of such variables entered. In the stepwise case, one of several measures will be selected by the LDA computer algorithm, and perhaps misinterpreted as being "more important" because the high intercorrelation between the several measures resulted in selection of only one of the indices.

For example, Fletcher in one of a series of excellent LDA experiments (Fletcher et al., 1978; Fletcher, Note 6) found that the variable "day of testing" could, artificially, be made to look predictive by virtue of its intercorrelation with other measures. These and other artefacts must be found and their influence eliminated from the prediction.

The missing data problem deserves comment, since many discriminant algorithms cannot operate without complete vectors of scores on each subject. This is a point that deserves attention in the evaluation of clinic studies of very ill patients where testing is incomplete. Regression estimates of missing values based upon other predictors or demographics have been suggested. Group means can also be substituted if the purpose of the LDA is exploratory. However, for classification purposes, the full set of observations must be available on each subject. All of this presumes that the observations are made prior to the formation of the groups, and selection of variables are made without regard to possible group membership.

3. *Provide a suitable number of subjects in relationship to the number of variables to accomplish the analysis.*

This is perhaps the most overlooked requirement in previous neuropsychological work using LDA. In general, ten subjects per variable are required to produce replicable results (Tatsuoka, 1970), although many workers attempt to make do with fewer subjects per variable. The absolute minimum to produce any understandable results, even for exploratory purposes, is three subjects per variable. It is quite unlikely that a complex LDA study with three subjects per variable will replicate. Within limits, a greater number of subjects in relation to variables assures more robust solutions which are likely to be replicated (Fletcher, Note 6).

Where discriminant functions are attempted with more variables than subjects, it is quite likely that the computer program will either break down with error messages or generate actual output which is meaningless. Golden, Hammeke, and Purisch (1978) presented a variant of this error when they included 285 variables on 100 subjects in a discriminant analysis. Not surprisingly, the LDA program (not specified) delivered results identifying 30 variables which separated their clinical groups with 100% accuracy in this invalid exercise.

Even where numbers of subjects and variables are approximately equal, results are likely to emerge which show that a high number of subjects can be correctly classified (Heaton, Smith, Lehman, & Vogt, 1978; Stuss & Trites, 1977). Despite the excellence of the criterion data that define the dependent group membership variables in these studies, the results must be inherently unstable. Discriminant function weights and constants from studies with subject-to-variable ratios of less than 10:1 are not likely to be replicated across larger samples in other centers.

Substitute techniques such as "jacknifing", where subjects or variables are removed one at a time and solutions are averaged, have not been shown to be satisfactory alternatives that will produce reliable results.

4. *Select a computer program for discriminant analysis that is widely-known and well-documented.*

In general, larger numbers of users of computer programs are likely to generate more errors, whose resolution is important to the user. Comprehensive program packages such as The Statistical Package for the Social Sciences (SPSS; Nie et al., 1975), The Biomedical Data Programs (BMD; Dixon, 1977), or The Statistical Analysis System (SAS; Barr & Goodnight, 1972) are good examples. These are routines generally available at university computer centers, and have clear and public algorithms. In addition, the neuropsychological researcher may find it easier to tell others how their analysis and, perhaps, a replication can be done when algorithms from these packages are employed.

5. *Find out the meaning of various parameters of the computer program and their likely effect on the data.*

Progress in the application of multivariate technology is not without its drawbacks. The increased use of multivariate statistical tests has not always been accompanied by equally heightened awareness of the complexity of the procedures involved. Many of the multivariate softwares in "canned" program packages are highly sophisticated routines whose flexibility arises from the number of options and parameters that the user may employ to manipulate data (Adams, Sternthal, & Read, Note 3).

Typically, the user implicitly selects a subset of possible parameters and options that will provide an appropriate test of the hypothesis in question. Often the program documentation provides incomplete or oversimplified information about the effects of particular parameter setting, yet these parameters are set at "default" values even when the user chooses to ignore them. In effect, decisions are made about the analysis whether or not the user knows their likely effect.

Perhaps the worst solution in stepwise programs is to let the "default" parameters control the function. Because of the low statistical barrier that must be exceeded, nearly all variables will ultimately enter the equation and will (falsely) be thought of as meaningful. Early studies (e.g., Goldstein & Shelly, 1972) used default parameters and allowed nearly the entire data set to enter the prediction equation. This modus operandi should be avoided because the entry of variables beyond a very early step in the LDA provides no additional classification power.

Since the principal attractiveness of the stepwise technique rests in the sequential display of the inclusion of the variables which "build" the function, it is worthwhile to describe the information portrayed at an individual "step". As mentioned above, the results should not be taken at face value or interpreted as directly as the computer documentation might imply. The program first displays the action in that particular step for inclusion or deletion of a particular variable. Study of the output of the previous step usually provides information on which variable will be selected on the next step, particularly where the default option of "maximum F to enter" is selected.

Other data (means, standard deviations, co-variances, and correlations) can be displayed initially and characteristics of calculated discriminant functions (eigenvalues, canonical correlations, canonical coefficients, and data coordinates) may be studied as they appear later in the software output (Dixon, 1977). Directly below this are displayed the particular F ratios for variables to be removed or entered, along with appropriate degrees of freedom. These ratios provide an estimate (although not an exact one) of the relative contribution to an overall difference between groups. These ratios have been likened to tests of coefficients in general linear regression (Lachin & Schachter, 1974). They provide a rough idea of the changing importance of particular variables as the function unfolds, and should be studied at each step.

A function parameter that is important in considering these ratios is *tolerance*. In theory, this is a metric that is an estimate of the amount of new variance added by a particular variable. The tolerance metric is discussed in some sources (Dixon, 1977; Nie et al., 1975), but its actual relationship to changes in variable selection seems to be minimal unless it is set quite high (towards 1.0).

The "U statistic" described next in the stepwise output is Wilk's Lambda, which is a general test of the hypothesis that the vector means across the groups on the variables *in the equation at that point* are equal. The "Approximate F" displayed below the Wilk's Lambda is a relation described by Rao (1952), and is one of several alternatives that could have been used to test the hypothesis (Cooley & Lohnes, 1971). Most programs (Dixon, 1977; Nie et al., 1975) provide alternative tests and methods for variable inclusion and tests of significance. Some neuropsychological studies in the literature have pointed to the significance of this F metric in displaying their stepwise results. In a recent and well-reasoned paper, Lachin and Schachter (1974) show that the use of this F ratio as a criterion to "stop stepping" the function or to interpret the results are invalid exercises. In general, the reason for this is that the test of Wilk's Lambda is a "reduced model" test that violates a number of important statistical assumptions when used in a multivariate sequential context. As a remedy, Lachin and Schachter suggest the use of MANOVA on an a priori group of variables screened for collinearity. In effect, the experimenter must make predictions about a best group of discriminator variables for the groups at hand.

Wilkinson (1979) recently provided another method for the evaluation of forward predictor selection in stepwise multiple regression. Based on a Monte Carlo simulation, with least squares smoothing, he generated a table which would allow investigators to compare their results with some objective criterion of significance based upon: (1) the number of predictors, (2) the number of predictors selected, and (3) sample size.

Hull and Nie (1979) recently improved the SPSS LDA algorithm in releases 7 and 8 of their package. Even with the improved program, careful testing of their assertions about the test statistics and LDA parameter output is suggested.

Other methods can be used to evaluate the "value" of the predictors in the equation. Tatsuoka (1970) has recommended direct interpretation of standardized discriminant function coefficients as a guide. Another method has been proposed to determine the value of individual predictors to a full model. Darlington, Weinberg, and Walberg (1973) have described the conditions under which correlations between each predictor and the appropriate canonical variate can be valuable. This correlation for each predictor can be seen as another index (besides entry order) to determine the value of predictors.

Finally, in the step process, a classification matrix can be displayed that shows the actual group membership of the sample displayed against the discriminant function classification. This is computed from a Mahalanobis distance metric and associated probability. It is this matrix that can be useful in calculating the numbers of correct predictions by the discriminant function as it goes through the step process.

There are various problems in parameter settings, such as specification of prior probabilities of group membership, which we mentioned earlier. It is sufficient to emphasize that the possibility of the classification of a case into a particular clinical group (left, right, diffuse, or no damage) is not equal for all groups. In some experiments we have run, we have seen dramatic shifts in classification accuracy when manipulating these "base rate" prior probabilities. Again, further work is needed to fully understand this parameter in neuropsychological research.

6. *Consider the results and examine both the agreements and disagreements between predicted function and actual group membership.*
Various demographic, methodological, or disease variables may appear to explain both on and off diagonal cell results in the prediction summary. Further, some programs provide maps or plots that allow visual inspection of group centroids and sources of group overlap or error. All other probable explanations should be considered before concluding that same subset of variables predicts group membership.

7. *Plan and execute a cross-validation.*
Consider the results in comparison with previous studies which meet the criteria described here. Reanalyze the first solution using another computer program to check accuracy.

Finally, collect a new and independent sample of cases on the same set of variables. Collaboration and close coordination with other investigators could speed the process if the methods are totally comparable. It is the unusual setting that has enough subjects readily available and completely assessed as a "holdout" sample for such a cross-validation. Unfortunately, cases with excellent criterion data and complete neuropsychological assessments usually exist at about the same 1:10 ratio with respect to less completely documented or examined cases. This means a good deal of work must be carried out before an acceptable subject to variable ratio is again achieved.

Overview
Linear discriminant analysis (LDA) is capable of answering certain questions about the significance, structure, and predictability of a set of neuropsychological variables in relation to some brain-related criterion. It does not automatically select the "best" tests to use instead of a more complete set, nor does it prove the predictive effectiveness of this subset over clinical judgment. These uses have been most frequent in the neuropsychological literature. Fletcher et al. (1978) provide a detailed analysis of some of these studies that have serious errors.

However, LDA is probably best seen as one of a variety of methods which can be used under the right conditions to answer questions about brain–behavior relationships. In order to do this effectively and reliably, issues relating to the nature of the subjects and the variables that one wishes to test must be resolved. For the neuropsychologist, this involves questions that computer documentation and consultants cannot answer. The intent of this paper has been to raise these difficult questions so that the researcher can evaluate the effects of various statistical assumptions upon the outcome. The actual psychological explanations for multivariate statistical outcomes are invariably practical and familiar.

REFERENCE NOTES

1. Adams, K. The use of linear discriminant functions in neuropsychological research. Paper presented at the annual meeting of the International Neuropsychological Society, New York, February 1979.
2. Adams, K., Rennick, P., & Rosenbaum, G. Automated clinical interpretation of the neuropsychology battery: An ability based approach. Paper presented at the annual meeting of the International Neuropsychological Society, Tampa, Florida, February 1975.
3. Adams, K., Sternthal, L. & Read, J. The use of linear discriminant functions in neuropsychological research. Paper read at annual meeting of the Canadian Psychological Association, Quebec, P. Q., June 1975.
4. Adams, K. Placing neuropsychological results in perspective. Paper read at the annual meeting of the Canadian Psychiatric Association, Quebec, P. Q., July 1976.
5. Adams, K., & Rennick, P. Early clinical neuropsychology: The data files of Ward C. Halstead. Paper read at the annual meeting of the American Psychological Association, Toronto, Ontario, Canada, September 1978.
6. Fletcher, J. Personal Communication, January, 1979.

REFERENCES

Adams, K. Automated clinical interpretation of the neuropsychology battery: An ability based approach. *Dissertation Abstracts*, 1975, *35*, 75–13, 289.

Adams, K. In search of Luria's battery: A false start. *Journal of Consulting and Clinical Psychology*, in press.

Anderson, T. W. Classification by multivariate analysis. *Psychometrika*, 1951, *16*, 31–50.

Barr, A. J., & Goodnight, J. *A User's Guide to the Statistical Analysis System*. Raleigh, N.C.: North Carolina State University, 1972.

Bock, R. D. Contributions of multivariate experimental designs to educational research. In R. B. Cattell (Ed.), *Handbook of Multivariate Experimental Psychology*. Skokie, Ill.: Rand McNally, 1966.

Bock, R. D. *Multivariate statistical methods in behavioral research*. New York: McGraw-Hill, 1975.

Cacoullos, T. (Ed.) *Discriminant analysis and its applications*. New York: Academic Press, 1973.

Cooley, W., & Lohnes, P. *Multivariate data analysis*. New York: Wiley, 1971.

Costa, L. Clinical Neuropsychology: Respice, adspice, prospice. *INS Bulletin*, March, 1975.

Darlington, R., Weinberg, S. L., & Walberg, H. J. Canonical variate analysis and related techniques, *Review of Educational Research*, 1973, *43*, 433–454.

Dikmen, S., & Reitan, R. M. MMPI correlates of localized cerebral lesions. *Perceptual and Motor Skills*, 1974, *39*, 831–840.

Dixon, W. (Ed.) *BMDP: Biomedical Computer Programs*. Berkeley, California: University of California Press, 1977.

Efroymsen, M. A. Multiple regression analysis. In A. Ralston & H. S. Wilf (Eds.), *Mathematical methods for digital computers*. New York: Wiley, 1960.

Eisenbeis, R. A., & Avery, R. B. *Discriminant analysis and classification procedures: Theory and application*. Lexington, Mass.: Heath, 1975.

Finn, J. *A general model for multivariate analysis*. New York: Holt, Rinehart & Winston, 1974.

Fisher, R. A. The use of multiple measurements in taxonomic problems. *Annals of Eugenics*, 1936, 376–386.

Fletcher, J., Rice, W., & Ray, R. Linear discriminant function analysis in neuropsychology: Some uses and abuses. *Cortex*, 1978, *14*, 564–577.

Golden, C., Hammeke, T., & Purisch, A. Diagnostic validity of a standardized neuropsychological battery derived from Luria's neuropsychological tests. *Journal of Consulting and Clinical Psychology*, 1978, *46*, 1258–1265.

Goldstein, G., & Shelly, C. H. Statistical and normative studies of the Halstead neuropsychological test battery relevant to a neuropsychiatric hospital setting. *Perceptual and Motor Skills*, 1972, *34*, 603–620.

Goldstein, G., & Shelley, C. Neuropsychological diagnosis of multiple sclerosis in a neuropsychiatric setting. *Journal of Nervous and Mental Diseases*, 1974, *158*, 280–290.

Goldstein, G., & Shelly, C. Univariate vs. multivariate analysis in neuropsychological test assessment of lateralized brain damage. *Cortex*, 1973, *9*, 204–216.

Goldstein, G., & Halperin, K. Neuropsychological differences among subtypes of schizophrenia, *Journal of Abnormal Psychology*, 1977, *86*, 34–40.

Grant, I., Adams, K., Carlin, A., Rennick, P., Judd, L., & Schooff, K. The collaborative neuropsychological study of polydrug users. *Archives of General Psychiatry*, 1978, *35*, 1063–1074.

Heaton, R., Smith, H., Lehman, R., & Vogt, A. Prospects for faking believable deficits on neuropsychological testing. *Journal of Consulting and Clinical Psychology*, 1978, *46*, 892–900.

Hotelling, H. The generalization of Student's ratio. *Annals of Mathematical Statistics*, 1931, *2*, 360–378.

Huberty, C. Discriminant analysis. *Review of Educational Research*, 1975, *45*, 543–598.

Hull, C., & Nie, N. *SPSS Update*. New York: McGraw-Hill, 1979.

Lachenbruch, P. A. *Discriminant analysis*. New York: Hafner, 1975.

Lachin, J., & Schachter, J. On stepwise discriminant analysis applied to psychophysiological data. *Psychophysiology*, 1974, *11*, 703–709.

Nie, N., Hull, C., Jenkins, J., Steinbrenner, K., & Bent, D. *SPSS: Statistical Package for the Social Sciences*. New York: McGraw-Hill, 1975.

Neufeld, R. W. J. *Clinical quantitative methods*. New York: Grune and Stratton, 1977.

Overall, J. E., & Klett, C. J. *Applied multivariate analysis*. New York: McGraw-Hill, 1972.

Press, S. J. *Applied multivariate analysis*. New York: Holt, Rinehart, and Winston, 1972.

Purisch, A., Golden, C., & Hammeke, T. Discrimination of schizophrenic and brain injured patients by a standardized version of Luria's neuropsychological tests. *Journal of Consulting and Clinical Psychology*, 1978, *46*, 1266–1273.

Rao, C. *Advanced statistical methods of biometric research*. New York: Wiley, 1952.

Reitan, R., & Davidson, L. (Eds.) *Clinical neuropsychology: Current status and applications*. New York: Wiley-Halstead, 1974.

Stuss, D., & Trites, R. Classification of neurological status using multiple discriminant function analysis of neuropsychological test scores. *Journal of Consulting and Clinical Psychology*, 1977, *45*, 145.

Swiercinsky, D., & Warnock, J. Comparison of the neuropsychological key and discriminant analysis approaches in predicting cerebral damage and localization. *Journal of Consulting and Clinical Psychology*, 1977, *45*, 808–814.

Tatsuoka, M. M. *Discriminant analysis: The study of group differences*. Champaign, Ill.: Institute for Personality and Ability Testing, 1970.

Wheeler, L., Burke, C., & Reitan, R. An application of discriminant functions to the problem of predicting brain damage using behavioral variables. *Perceptual and Motor Skills*, 1963, *16*, 417–440.

Wheeler, L., & Reitan, R. M. Discriminant functions applied to the problem of predicting cerebral damage from behavior tests: A cross validation study. *Perceptual and Motor Skills*, 1963, *16*, 681–701.

Wiggins, J. *Personality and prediction: Principles of personality assessment*. Reading, Mass., Addison-Wesley, 1973.

Wilkinson, L. Tests of significance in stepwise regression. *Psychological Bulletin*, 1979, *86*, 168–174.

Journal of Clinical Neuropsychology
1979, Vol. 1, No. 2, 151–166.

Discriminant Function Strategies for the Kindergarten Prediction of Reading Achievement*

Jack M. Fletcher
Texas Research Institute of Mental Sciences

Robert K. Smidt
California Polytechnical Institute

Paul Satz
University of Florida

ABSTRACT

The present paper evaluates the application of discriminant function analysis to predictive strategies developed for the kindergarten prediction of reading achievement by the Florida Longitudinal Project. In an attempt to optimize the predictiveness of these classification equations, several problems arose that provide important information concerning the application of discriminant analysis to early detection research. These problems highlight the importance of carefully examining (a) statistical assumptions underlying discriminant analysis; (b) the statistical nature of the data and sample employed; and (c) alternative applications of discriminant analysis when certain assumptions cannot be met. Early detection research has considerable relevance for clinical neuropsychology, provided appropriate application of predictive tools is made. The results of the present study show that careful evaluation of the application of discriminant analysis is crucial for reliable prediction. In addition, it is demonstrated that improved prediction can result from optimal use of statistical methods and criterion variables.

The early detection of childhood learning and behavioral disabilities is a problem that is attracting increased research interest. The purpose of this

*This research was supported in part by funds from NIH (NS 08205) and NIMH (MH 19415). The assistance of Jannette Friel and Pona Ott is gratefully acknowledged.

research is the identification of children "at risk" for these disabilities during a period prior to their measurable onset. As such, early detection research can be approached as a prediction problem, where children are classified on the basis of screening instruments according to their degree of risk for potential disabilities. If predictive devices are available which permit screening of large samples of children quickly and at low cost, diagnostic procedures can lead to intervention before these learning and behavioral disabilities are fully manifested and more refractory to treatment (Satz, 1973). While screening is not diagnostic of different disabilities, the successful prediction of risk can lead to optimal use of resources for early intervention.

The methodological problems underlying early detection research are multiple and substantial (Satz, 1973; Satz & Fletcher, 1979). Many of these problems concern the evaluation of the *predictive validity* of the screening instrument. Large and appropriately sampled sets of children must receive the screening instrument during the risk period. These children must then be followed longitudinally over several years until the disabilities are clinically manifested. Only then can prediction strategies be developed and evaluated that address the validity of the screening instrument.

One project that attempted to meet these minimal criteria comprised a seven-year longitudinal study addressed to the early detection of reading problems (Satz, Taylor, Friel, & Fletcher, 1978). This project has attempted to follow the entire population of white males entering kindergarten in Alachua County, Florida in 1970. During kindergarten, each of these children was administered a battery of neuropsychological tests. Reading achievement criteria were obtained on a large proportion of these children at the end of Grade 2 and Grade 5. The longitudinal predictive format of this project made possible careful evaluation of the predictive validity of the screening battery. Preliminary evaluations of the prediction results have been quite promising throughout the seven years of this project (Satz et al., 1978). However, it is always desirable to try to improve these results.

The prediction strategies used in this project were based on discriminant function analysis. Discriminant analysis was selected because the primary use of the screening device was to predict gross achievement levels representative of groups homogeneous in terms of degree of risk. The purpose was not to predict actual reading scores or to specify type or degree of disability. Discriminant analysis is a statistical method that is used to classify individuals into one of several groups. For the prediction of reading achievement, the purpose is to classify children into groups of approximately the same reading level on the basis of previously obtained test scores. Reading achievement is an attribute that is not apparent or measurable during kindergarten. In order to classify a child, information is gathered on variables that can be used as predictors of future reading levels because of their relationship with reading acquisition. Discriminant function analysis combines the predictor variables into a single composite score, the discriminant function, that maximally separates subsequent achievement groups. The function can then be used to classify additional samples of children.

The ultimate goal of discriminant analysis is the selection of a function that minimizes the number of errors in prediction. Overlooking aspects of the data that may produce violations of statistical assumptions can lead to serious difficulties in prediction, especially if the discriminant function is to be employed over a long period of time. Consequently, the adequacy of any given function should be carefully examined with regard to assumptions and types of measurements involved. Neuropsychological research is often lax in applications of multivariate methods (Fletcher, Rice, & Ray, 1978; Adams, Note 1). Sometimes the function used is the one conveniently produced by the computer package at the researcher's disposal. This function is not necessarily the most appropriate one for minimizing the overall number of misclassifications. Unfortunately, evaluative criteria for the adequacy of a discriminant function are purposefully vague, primarily because there are no absolute criteria for a given sample. For each prediction application, the discriminant function must be carefully evaluated in terms of the statistical assumptions underlying its formation and the nature of the data and samples employed.

Early detection research has considerable relevance for clinical neuropsychology, provided that the necessary multivariate methods are applied correctly. Screening can form the first step in early identification, with other clinical and educational procedures specifying type and degree of disability (diagnosis) and subsequent remediation. The present paper presents results from an attempt to evaluate carefully discriminant functions obtained in conjunction with an attempt to develop a screening device for this longitudinal early detection project. In an attempt to optimize the predictiveness of available discriminant functions, several problems arose. The nature of these problems provides some information concerning the application of discriminant analysis to early detection research. In addition, some alternative applications of discriminant analysis are presented that highlight its usefulness for the kindergarten prediction of reading level.

METHOD

Subjects

The prediction results that will be considered comprise the 3-year follow-up of the initial 1970 Sample I (n=497) and 1971 cross-validation Sample II (n=181). Each of these white male children received a battery of 14 neuropsychological tests during the first two months of kindergarten. At the end of Grade 2 (3-year follow-up), criterion information on reading achievement was obtained on 417 children in Sample I (84%) and 151 children in Sample II (84%). It should be noted that no differences emerged on demographic and neuropsychological variables between children in this analysis and those for whom criteria were not available, implying random effects of attrition. Criteria comprised the standardized *IOTA Word Recognition Test* and the teachers' specifications of the child's instructional level in reading (primer, pre-primer, etc.). To form groups based on different reading levels, these criteria were combined and averaged into *T* scores. The resulting distribution was divided according to standard deviation units to form four reading ability groups (Satz et al., 1978): *Severely Disabled, Mildly Disabled, Average,* and *Superior*. Severely Disabled were at least 1 standard deviation below the mean of the distribution. Mildly Disabled readers were from −1 to −.4 standard deviations below the mean. Average readers were from −.4 to 1 standard deviation above the mean. Superior readers were more than 1 standard deviation above the mean. These reading group designations are merely group labels representative of reading level. No distinction among different reading and learning disabilities according to type and specificity was intended.

Predictor Variables
The predictor variables comprised the five tests that revealed the greatest predictive utility of the 14 original variables. The five tests, *Finger Localization, Recognition-Discrimination, Beery Visual-Motor Integration, Alphabet Recitation,* and the *Peabody Picture Vocabulary Test*, have been described in greater detail elsewhere (Satz & Friel, 1973). Selection of these variables was based on the different ranking techniques that select optimal predictors and eliminate unnecessary tests (Fletcher & Satz, Note 2). These techniques are based on methods for interpreting the contribution of individual variables to a discriminant function, including canonical variate analysis, standardization of discriminant function weights, and stepwise ranking techniques. Selection of tests was independent of prediction results. Differences in classification rates using subsets of variables could lead to test selection on the basis of spurious sources of variability. The use of these selection methods and methodological aspects of their application to clinical neuropsychology have been described elsewhere (Fletcher et al., 1978).

RESULTS

Initial Discriminant Function
Table 1 presents the results obtained from the initial three-year follow-up. Potential decisions about risk, which are predictions based on the discriminant functions obtained from the screening battery, are contained in rows. Four levels of risk are designated that represent decisions for potentially Severely Disabled (+ +), Mildly Disabled (+), Average (−), and Superior (− −) readers. Actual group membership is contained in columns. For example, there are 67 children who are Severely Disabled readers. Forty-six of these children were correctly predicted by the discriminant function, while another 12 were placed in the Mildly Disabled group. It was assumed that both Severely and Mildly Disabled children would benefit from intervention, while

TABLE 1
Predictive Classification (Kindergarten to Grade 2) of Sample I[a,b]

Decision	Criterion Reading Groups					
	Severe	Mild	Average	Superior	Total	Cp
+ +	46	25	21	0	71/92	.77 (.76)
+	12	27	40	2	39/81	.48 (.45)
−	8	17	72	17	89/114	.78 (.79)
− −	1	7	80	42	122/130	.94 (.91)
	67	76	213	61	321/417	.77 (.75)

[a]Prior Probabilities = .25, .25, .25, .25
[b]Sample II Cp in parentheses

Average and Superior children would not. Therefore, negatives $(− −, −)$ were combined into one group and positives into a second group $(+ +, +)$ for evaluation of the predictive utility of the discriminant function. For intervention purposes, a $+ +$ classified as a $+$ would be considered a correct decision. The term Cp represents a conditional probability: that is, the probability that an individual prediction is correct (Satz, 1973; Satz & Fletcher, 1979). Conditional probabilities represent the ratio of prior probabilities (base rates) and discriminable test validities (valid positives and negatives). Computation is based on an application of Bayes Theorem (Meehl & Rosen, 1955). The application of statistical decision theory is as important for early detection research as is the use of multivariate statistical methods (Satz & Fletcher, 1979). Conditional probabilities provide direct information concerning the accuracy of "intervention" decisions for the different predictions. Evaluation of this accuracy supersedes indices of predictive accuracy based on the size of the relationship between predictors and criteria since these indices, even when significant, do not necessarily indicate that predictions can be made on an individual basis (Satz & Fletcher, 1979). Consequently, the conditional probability will be used as the evaluative index for all discriminant functions in this paper.

For the present discriminant function, Table 1 shows that a $+ +$ prediction yielded a conditional probability of .77. In other words, a decision to intervene, given a $+ +$ test sign, would be correct for 77% of the possible disabled cases. For a $+$ prediction, the conditional probability dropped to .48. For the $−$ and $− −$ predictions, the conditional probability was .78 and .93, respectively. The overall hit rate was .77. It is important to note that the majority of prediction errors were confined to $+$ and $−$ decisions. These children represented the densest areas of the distribution (65% of the sample). Consequently, more errors were expected for predicted Mildly Disabled and Average children. Fewer errors occurred for the Severely Disabled and Superior children who are at the ends of the distribution. The latter errors were probably more serious, since the consequences of an incorrect decision are more costly for either decision.

Table 1 also contains, for comparative purposes, cross-validation results in parentheses. These results were based on Sample II (n=151), followed since their kindergarten year of 1971 and for whom identical criteria were obtained at the end of 1974 (Grade 2). The discriminant function was cross-validated by classifying Sample II with the function derived from Sample I. Inspection of the predictions revealed only a small reduction in conditional probabilities (within a range of about 3%).

Evaluation of the Discriminant Function

The apparent predictive accuracy of this initial classification equation does not preclude an examination of its workings and assumptions, particularly if improvement can be obtained. The most immediate question concerned the statistical nature of the criterion variable. Because the criterion variable is continuously distributed, the present application represented an atypical use of discriminant analysis. Most applications of discriminant analysis employ criteria that are clearly categorical in nature (e.g., lesion groups). A continuously distributed criterion variable produces subtle changes in the distributional theory underlying discriminant analysis. However, several studies (Flora, Note 3) have shown that results obtained with discriminant analysis do not change when the criterion variable is continuously distributed. Unfortunately, higher misclassification rates must be expected. This occurs because there is no characteristic which would provide distinct, non-overlapping reader groups. Those children near the center of a group will "possess" more of the defining group characteristics than do those nearer a dividing line between two neighboring groups. Consequently, those children who are nearer the dividing line will have a higher probability of misclassification than will those closer to the center of the group. Misclassification rates are automatically higher for groups based on continuously distributed criteria than they are for groups made more homogeneous by discrete criteria. Technically, regression analysis is the most appropriate method for continuously distributed criteria. Discriminant analysis was used because there was no intention to predict individual reading scores. The prediction of primary interest was simple gross achievement levels for screening purposes. Pragmatically, regression analysis may result in slightly improved prediction in the Mild and Average groups. At the same time, it adds the additional problem of determining regression score cutoffs for classification, which again makes the overall results and purpose similar to that involved in the choice of discriminant analysis.

Given the consequences of continuously distributed criteria, the initial function requires further examination according to standard evaluative procedures. The first step is to evaluate the strength of the relationship between predictor and criterion variables. With four groups, it would be possible to employ more than one discriminant function to reach a decision. For example (in the two-variable case), if the groups were oriented as in Figure 1, two discriminant functions would be useful, representing differences in group location along the vertical (X_1) and horizontal (X_2) axes. Classification divisions and decisions would be indicated by the broken lines. If only one discriminant function were used, the decision rule would be based on three parallel lines (i.e., the solid lines in Figure 1). Groups would be linearly related (i.e., discriminated only on the horizontal axis) and would be closer together along the vertical axis.

Although in some instances more than one discriminant function is appropriate, this was not the case in the present study. An examination of the mean values of the variables used for classification revealed that they were linearly related. Consequently, groups were separated only along one dimension. In Figure 1, groups would differ only along the horizontal axis and would not

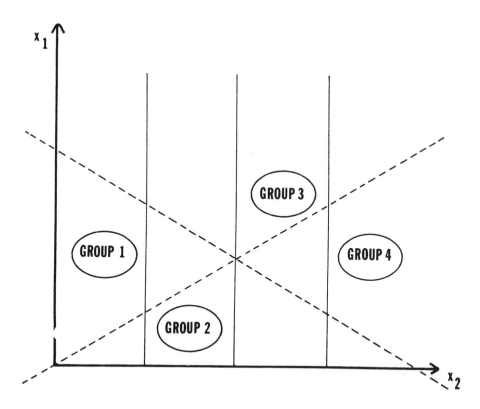

Figure 1. Classification rules for one and two discriminant functions

differ along the vertical axis. The decisions would be made by the three parallel lines in Figure 1. No additional quality in discrimination would be obtained through the use of a second function. This decision was supported when each of the three possible discriminant functions from the four-group study were tested for significance. Only the first discriminant function was significant using F statistics derived from Roy's Greatest Characteristic Root test (Huberty, 1975). Furthermore, using procedures described by Huberty (1975), it was determined that this function accounted for 50% of the variability between predictors and criteria, analogous to a multiple correlation coefficient of about .7 (adjusted for shrinkage). While robust, this relationship does not necessarily mean that individual predictions can be made (Satz & Fletcher, 1979).

The second step in evaluating a discriminant function concerns the covariance structure of the four groups. In Figure 1, the ellipses representing groups were drawn with the same shape, size, and orientation. This configuration was employed to indicate that the predictor variables have equal variance and covariance structures in all groups, one of the assumptions underlying linear discriminant function analysis. In practice, this assumption is difficult to satisfy exactly, and it is commonly assumed that any violation of the assumption is not so serious as to affect the performance of the function. If the violation were serious, it would become necessary to use a quadratic discriminant function (i.e., a function involving second degree terms in the variables, but which does not assume equal covariance). In this study, all of the variances and covariances were not equal. For this reason, a quadratic function was formed and used to classify the sample. Although initial classification results were slightly improved, results upon cross-validation were much poorer. These findings paralleled those of Hubert and Curry (1978), showing that linear classification rules generally have greater replicability in cross-validation than do quadratic rules, even when covariance matrices are unequal. Returning to Figure 1, the effect of using the quadratic instead of the linear function would be the replacement of the parallel straight lines with curves (parabolic sections). This would change the decision rule for observations that are distant from the line connecting the means and close to the original straight lines. In effect, very few such points were found, and few decisions were changed.

Although the quadratic function did not improve prediction results, another alternative is to employ prior probability estimates as part of the classification equation (Morrison, 1976). Prior probabilities can be base rates representing the probability of membership into each group on the basis of estimates of the incidence of group membership in the general population. Applying these estimates to a discriminant function has the effect of adjusting the size of each classifiable group according to the expected probability of potential group membership.

Table 2 contains the prediction results based on prior probability estimates of .15, .20. .50, and .15 for Severe, Mild, Average, and Superior reading groups, respectively. These estimates were based on criterion groupings from the project (Satz et al., 1978) that are in accordance with incidence figures from other epidemiological studies. Although inspection of the conditional probabilities reveals that overall results were improved, closer examination of this Table shows that this improvement is artifactual. The classification equation placed only 25 (of a possible 76) children for the + group and only 6 (of a possible 61) for the − − group. Virtually the entire sample (78%) was predicted for the − group, with an additional 13% classified into the + + group.

TABLE 2

Predictive Classification (Kindergarten to Grade 2) of Sample I[a]

Decision	Criterion Reading Groups					
	Severe	Mild	Average	Superior	Total	Cp
+ +	41	14	15	0	55/70	.79
+	10	10	5	0	20/25	.80
−	16	52	190	58	248/316	.78
− −	0	0	3	3	6/6	1.00
	67	76	213	61	329/417	.79

[a]Prior Probabilites = .15, .20, .50, .15

This artifact can be attributed to the continuously distributed criterion variable. These prior probability estimates made the expected size of the Average group so large that most children received − predictions. Only the poorest performing children (+ +) were far enough away from the center of the distribution to be classified separately. In this sense, it appears that it is easier for a child to do poorly on the battery tests employed in this project than it is for him to do well. In consequence, the potential Superior readers were constrained by the limits (ceilings) of the measures, while potential Severely Disabled readers were more easily distinguishable.

Such a phenomenon suggested that some test scores may not be normally distributed. This necessitated an examination of the distribution of the five predictor variables. It was found that one test, Finger Localization (FL), was not normally distributed. In fact, it appeared to represent a roughly dichotomous variable, with children scoring either low or high. This dichotomy seemed to reflect the nature of the test itself. The Finger Localization task used in this project comprised five hierarchically arranged levels of administration. On the first three levels most children were proficient, regardless of future reading level. Only levels 4 and 5 were predictive of group membership (Fletcher, Taylor, Morris, & Satz, Note 4). However, levels 4 and 5 required children to master a numbering system designating each finger from 1–10. Those children who failed to master this system were not administered levels 4 and 5. As a consequence, scores on these levels were either high or low, depending on the child's mastery of the numbering system. In potentially disabled readers, performance on levels 4 and 5 apparently has less to do with skills specific to the capacity to differentiate the fingers sensorily than to the capacity to adopt a naming strategy (Fletcher et al., Note 4).

Alternative Discriminant Function Strategies

The question that remained was how to best employ FL. To answer this question, it was necessary to return to the basic assumptions of discriminant analysis, which include normality of distribution of the variables. Finger Localization does not satisfy this assumption, which seemed to be met for other variables. However, FL performance has a high predictive relationship with reading achievement (Fletcher et al., Note 4). Improved prediction would necessitate abandoning discriminant function analysis or discarding the predictive information yielded by FL. It was decided to experiment with two discriminant functions, conditional on whether Level 4 and 5 of FL were administered to a child. Consequently, children were divided into two categories according to their mastery of the numbering system. Separate discriminant functions were obtained for children in the two categories.

The formation of the two discriminant functions was a formidable task. With the initial discriminant function, equal prior probabilities provided the best results (Table 1). However, it seemed unreasonable to assign equal prior probabilities after a child had been assigned to the FL categories. It was assumed that children with High FL scores were unlikely to become Severely Disabled readers and that Low FL children were unlikely to become Superior readers. Then, an attempt was made to search for the prior probabilities that yielded the minimum number of classification errors for both categories. For the Low FL category (i.e., those children who were unable to master the scoring system), a prior probability of zero was set for predictions into the Superior group. In the High FL category (i.e., those children who were able to master the numbering system), the zero probability was for the Severe group. The zero prior probability was selected as a short-cut method for precluding classification in the Severe or Superior groups. This procedure for adjusting classification rules can be used only because the variables and groups are linearly related along a single dimension. However, this procedure is not recommended without careful examination of the data base and its representation in discriminant function space. Prior probability estimates for the other groups were determined on a trial-and-error basis, with selection based on estimates that yielded the lowest misclassification rates. This approach combined the information contained in the FL categorization analysis with the possibility of improved classification rates from adjusting prior probability estimates. These estimates were no longer based on the entire sample, and merely represented a convenient way of setting optimal decision lines.

Summaries of these results are contained in Tables 3, 4, and 5. Tables 3 and 4 contain the results for discriminant functions obtained for High and Low FL categories, respectively. Table 5 summarizes Tables 2 and 3 by adding results together, thus permitting direct comparison with the single discriminant function results of Table 1.

An examination of the Tables indicates that the double discriminant functions performed at least as well as, or perhaps superior to, the single discriminant function. In particular, Table 5 shows that the overall hit rate is slightly improved and that the summary table contains correct percentages as accurate as those for the single discriminant function. Virtually identical conditional probabilities were apparent for initial and alternative functions obtained from the High FL category children (Table 3). Improvement was

TABLE 3

Predictive Classification (Kindergarten to Grade 2) of Sample I
(High Finger Localization)[a,b]

Decision	Criterion Reading Group					
	Severe	Mild	Average	Superior	Total	Cp
+ +	0	0	0	0	– –	– –
+	14	26	32	1	40/73	.55 (.48)
–	7	21	84	21	105/133	.79 (.64)
– –	2	5	61	37	98/105	.93 (.89)
	23	52	177	59	243/311	.78 (.68)

[a]Prior Probabilities = 0, .28, .38, .34
[b]Sample II Cp in parentheses

TABLE 4

Predictive Classification (Kindergarten to Grade 2) of Sample I
(Low Finger Localization)[a,b]

Decision	Criterion Reading Group					
	Severe	Mild	Average	Superior	Total	Cp
+ +	34	8	8	0	42/50	.84 (.88)
+	8	11	6	0	19/25	.76 (.67)
–	2	5	22	2	24/31	.77 (.75)
– –	0	0	0	0	– –	– –
	44	24	36	2	85/106	.80 (.78)

[a]Prior Probablities = .42, .34, .24, 0
[b]Sample II Cp in parenthesis

TABLE 5
Summation of Table 3 and Table 4[a]

Decision	Criterion Reading Group					
	Severe	Mild	Average	Superior	Total	Cp
+ +	34	8	8	0	42/50	.84 (.73)
+	22	37	38	1	59/98	.60 (.54)
−	9	26	106	23	129/164	.79 (.79)
− −	2	5	61	37	98/105	.93 (.91)
	67	76	213	61	328/417	.79 (.77)

[a]Sample II Cp in parantheses

entirely due to better classification for the Low FL category children. As the data in Table 4 reveals, intervention would have been appropriate in 84% (42 of 50) of the + + decisions. Cross-validation results on Sample II (in parentheses) show that these results were reliable, despite the relatively small sample from which the discriminant functions were derived.

Comparative Decision Strategies
Since the purpose of these classifications is to select children for early diagnosis and intervention, the two competing ways of making decisions should be compared in this respect. Certain strategies suggest themselves. Strategy I would identify children only if they have been predicted + + (i.e., only those students who are potentially Severely Disabled readers). Strategy II would identify children predicted + + or + (i.e., children at risk for both Severe or Mild disabilities). Strategy III would be identical to Strategy II for the single discriminant function. For the double discriminant function procedure, Strategy III would identify only those children in the low FL category predicted either + + or +.

Comparative results for these 3 strategies are summarized in Table 6. In comparing single and double discriminant functions based on Strategy I, the double discriminant function yielded slightly better decision results than did the single discriminant function. The overall conditional probability was higher, largely because of a reduction in false positive predictions. Indeed, the double discriminant function yielded 18 fewer false positives at a sacrifice of 14 false negatives. Similar results were apparent for Strategy II. The double discriminant function yielded a higher overall conditional probability, with 10 fewer false positives and only 4 more false negatives. The value of the double discriminant function was most apparent for Strategy III. Here, the overall conditional probability was much higher (.81 vs. .65). Although the number of false negatives was higher (82 vs. 38), the reduction in false positives (57 vs. 14) would provide for more optimal use of school resources. Indeed, the

TABLE 6

Comparative Intervention Strategies Based on Single and Double Discriminant Functions for Sample I[a]

| Single Discriminant Function | | Double Discriminant Function | | |

Strategy I

| | | Group | | | | Group | |
		Sev/Mild	Avg/Sup			Sev/Mild	Avg/Sup
Decision	++	69	26	Decision	++	42	8
	other	19	303		other	33	334
		Cp = .73 (.62)				Cp = .84 (.88)	

Strategy II

| | | Group | | | | Group | |
		Sev/Mild	Avg/Sup			Sev/Mild	Avg/Sup
Decision	++/+	105	57	Decision	++/+	101	47
	−/−−	38	217		−/−−	42	227
		Cp = .65 (.60)				Cp = .68 (.64)	

Strategy III

| | | Group | | | | Group | |
		Sev/Mild	Avg/Sup			Sev/Mild	Avg/Sup
Decision	++/+	105	57	Decision	++/+	61	14
	−/−−	38	217		−/−−	82	260
		Cp = .65 (.60)				Cp = .81 (.79)	

[a]Sample II Cp in parentheses

majority of the false negative errors (57) comprised children who eventually had Mild reading disabilities, whilst ensuring sufficient selection of children who eventually manifested Severe disabilities. In this sense, Strategy III would be most useful for school systems with meager intervention resources.

Cross-validation results are also presented in Table 6 (parentheses). Although some shrinkage is apparent (within a range of plus or minus 7%), results generally supported the use of the double discriminant functions. On each of the three possible decision strategies, classification rates and conditional probabilities were better for the double discriminant function strategies. Obtaining new functions on the basis of a larger sample should further improve the reliability of the double discriminant functions, especially for those children who are unable to perform more complex levels of FL.

DISCUSSION

The results of the study illustrate that investigators who employ multivariate statistical procedures should carefully examine data from a variety of standpoints. The appropriateness of the technique employed and the presence and effects of violating the assumptions that underlie the use of the technique are important considerations. In addition, the use of multivariate techniques does not preclude careful examination of the statistical nature of each variable to ensure its appropriateness for analysis. The convenience of computerized packages necessitates even closer perusal of the data base. Neuropsychological research to date is notorious for the careless manner in which discriminant analysis and other multivariate procedures have been employed (Fletcher et al., 1978; Adams, Note 1). As this study illustrates, careful examination of the application of discriminant analysis to a set of data can actually clarify and possibly add to the accuracy of research outcomes.

Turning to the clinical implications of these results, it is clear that evaluation of the data base is especially important for those studies addressed to early detection. Early intervention may have a significant effect on the eventual manifestation of a reading disability. However, intervention based on inadequate or premature analysis of the predictive validity of the screening instrument may have an iatrogenic influence on the developmental course of a reading disability. The present paper addressed only the statistical and decision theory aspects of this validation. Many other methodological factors, including adequate sample definition, longitudinal follow-up, and the validity of predictor and criterion measures must also be assessed (Satz, 1973; Satz & Fletcher, 1979). In addition, screening should not be confused with diagnosis (Silver, 1978). The present results merely specify groups of children that require more specific diagnostic evaluations for school placement and remediation. The early detection device provides for the identification of possible problems early in the child's school career in an efficient, cost-effective manner. Actual intervention should proceed only after a careful diagnostic evaluation of the child by a clinical neuropsychologist (Rourke, in press), educator (Schenk, Fitzsimmons, Bullard, & Satz, 1979), or other qualified person. One advantage of the follow-up evaluation is that false positive errors may become less costly than false negative errors. If the screening device yields a high number of false negative errors, then many children at risk for learning problems may not receive diagnostic evaluations. If the diagnostic evaluation follows screening, then the risk in terms of mislabeling and inappropriate instructions associated with false positive errors can be minimized.

Finger Localization, a commonly used test in clinical neuropsychology, merits special discussion. While Levels 4 and 5 are often included as Finger Localization tasks (Benton, 1978), performance by disabled readers seems quite dependent on the mastery of a numbering system. Furthermore, the statistical properties associated with Levels 4 and 5 provide strong argument for dropping them from the predictive battery. Both these statements require some qualification. An analysis of the Finger Localization subtests reveal that the basic capacity to differentiate the fingers sensorily is less related to reading achievement than are other cognitive variables. In children who master the numbering system, Levels 4 and 5 are strongly related to achievement. However, these subtests are also differentially related to other cognitive skills that are associated with reading achievement and not just to specific Finger Localization skills (Fletcher, et al., Note 4). Consequently, performance on Levels 4 and 5 is not dependent solely on mastery of the numbering system. Furthermore, the present results indicate that the child's capacity to master the numbering system is predictive of future reading achievement. Consequently, Levels 4 and 5 are not merely artifactual variables. They yield information which can lead to improved prediction. Nonetheless, this use of Finger Localization merely represents a demonstration exercise and is not intended to provide guidelines for the clinical use of the test.

More generally, early detection research can represent a useful application of clinical neuropsychological methods. A screening device, followed by a clinical neuropsychological evaluation (Rourke, in press), can lead to accurate diagnosis and specification of remediation methods. When evaluated early in the child's school career (e.g., preschool), the refractory elements of a learning problem can be potentially reduced. At the same time, it should be recognized that, to date, very few screening devices have been adequately validated (Satz & Fletcher, 1979); this precludes the adequate evaluation of the effects of early screening and remediation. While preliminary results have been quite promising (Schenk et al., 1979), considerable research is needed on early remediation methods. This research is not likely to bear fruit if remediation follows inappropriate or incomplete validation of the screening device. The benefits of early detection are possible only with a thorough and careful evaluation of the workings of multivariate methods within the context of the specific sample and variables employed.

REFERENCE NOTES

1. Adams, K. M. Linear discriminant analysis in clinical neuropsychological research. Paper presented at the Annual Meeting of the International Neuropsychological Society, New York, New York, February, 1979
2. Fletcher, J. M., & Satz, P. Developmental changes in the performance correlates of reading achievement. Manuscript submitted for publication, 1979.
3. Flora, R. G. The problem of classifying members of a population into groups. Unpublished doctoral dissertation, Virginia Polytechnical Institute, 1965.

4. Fletcher, J. M., Taylor, H. G., Morris, R., & Satz, P. Developmental and descriptive aspects of finger localization and reading achievement. Paper presented at the Annual Meeting of the International Neuropsychological Society, New York, New York, February, 1979.

REFERENCES

Benton, A. L. The neuropsychological significance of finger recognition. In M. Bortner (Ed.), *Cognitive growth and development*. New York: Bruner & Mazel, 1978.

Fletcher, J. M., Rice, W. J., & Ray, R. R. Linear discriminant function analysis in neuropsychological research: Some uses and abuses. *Cortex*, 1978, *14*, 564–577.

Huberty, C. J. Discriminant analysis. *Review of Educational Research*, 1975, *45*, 543–598.

Huberty, C. J., & Curry, A. R. Linear versus quadratic multivariate classification. *Multivariate Behavioral Research*, 1978, *13*, 237–246.

Meehl, P. E., & Rosen, A. Antecedent probability and the efficiency of psychometric signs, patterns, or cutting scores. *Psychological Bulletin*, 1955, *52*, 194–216.

Morrison, D. F. *Multivariate statistical methods*, second edition. New York: McGraw-Hill, 1976.

Rourke, B. P. Neuropsychological assessment of children with learning disabilities. In S. B. Filskov & T. Boll (Eds.), *Handbook of clinical neuropsychology*. New York: John Wiley, in press.

Satz, P. *Learning disorders and remediation of learning disorders*. Research Task Force, National Institute of Mental Health, Section on Child Mental Illness and Behavior Disorders, 1973.

Satz, P., & Fletcher, J. M. Early screening tests: Some uses and abuses. *Journal of Learning Disabilities*, 1979, *12*, 43–50.

Satz, P., & Friel, J. Some predictive aspects of specific learning disability: A preliminary one year follow-up. In P. Satz & J. Ross (Eds.), *The disabled learner: Early detection and intervention*. Rotterdam, The Netherlands: Rotterdam U. Press, 1973.

Satz, P., Taylor, H. G., Friel, J., & Fletcher, J. M. Some developmental and predictive precursors of reading disabilities: A six-year follow-up. In A. L. Benton and D. Pearl (Eds.), *Dyslexia: An appraisal of current knowledge*. New York: Oxford U. Press, 1978.

Schenk, B. J., Fitzsimmons, J., Bullard P. C., & Satz, P. A prevention model for children at risk for reading failure. In R. M. Knights & D. J. Bakker (Eds.), *Rehabilitation, treatment, and management of learning disorders*. Baltimore: University Park Press, 1979.

Silver, A. A. Prevention. In A. L. Benton & D. Pearl (Eds.), *Dyslexia: An appraisal of current knowledge*. New York: Oxford U. Press, 1978.

Journal of Clinical and Experimental Neuropsychology
1986, Vol. 8, No. 5, pp. 469-485.

Predictors and Indicators of Quality of Life
in Patients with Closed-Head Injury

Pamela S. Klonoff   Louis D. Costa   William G. Snow

Barrow Neurological Institute   University of Victoria   Sunnybrook Medical Centre

Phoenix, AZ   Toronto, Ontario

ABSTRACT

This study examined predictors and indicators of quality of life in 71 patients with closed-head injury (CHI), 2-4 years postinjury. Predictors included premorbid characteristics and acute injury-related data. Indicators included follow-up data, e.g., neuropsychological functioning. Exploratory canonical correlation analyses demonstrated that the combination of the predictor variable, initial Glasgow Coma Scale score, and indicator variables of neuropsychological data in the areas of motor functioning, memory, and constructional ability were related most strongly to quality of life as reported by the patients. Severity of head injury and motor disability also related strongly to quality of life, based on reports by relatives ($n = 68$) on the Katz Adjustment Scale (Relatives' Form). These findings suggest that quality of life is adversely affected by increased severity of head injury and greater residual motor deficits. Implications of these findings for treatment and recovery are discussed.

An important challenge to health care professionals working with patients with closed-head injury (CHI) is to identify those factors which influence or predict the eventual outcome of the patient. If successful, this would enable one to predict the long-term prognosis of the patients and improve methods of patient management (Jennett, Teasdale, & Knill-Jones, 1975).

Some variables which relate to quality of life can be classified as predictors; these include preaccident and acute data (measured at the time of accident). Others are termed indicators or follow-up data, which are measured concurrently with outcome.

One of the premorbid variables which has been evaluated more commonly as a predictor of outcome is age (Field, 1976, for review). As age increases, so does the likelihood of mortality (Becker et al., 1977; Hpay, 1971; Jennett & Teasdale, 1981; Kerr, Kay, & Lassman, 1971), while the probability of favorable prognosis (Jennett et al., 1979; Jennett, Teasdale, Braakman, Minderhoud, & Knill-Jones, 1976), functional independence (Timming, Orrison, & Mikula, 1982), social rehabilitation (Lundholm, Jepsen, & Thornval, 1975), and employment rate (Bruckner & Randle, 1972) decreases.

Other potential premorbid predictors in patients with CHI include the sex of the patient, education, marital status, preinjury employment, and income. To date, however, research in this area is relatively sparse. Of the few studies available, sex has not been identified as an important predictor of outcome, either in adults (Carlsson, von Essen, & Lofgren, 1968) or in children (Klonoff, 1971). Walker (1972) reported that, in patients who sustained head injuries during World War II, and who were followed for 25 years postinjury, marital status was not significantly related to happiness over the latter 10 years of follow-up, based on reports by wives or next-of-kin. Rimel, Giordani, Barth, Boll, and Jane (1981) reported that, in addition to increased age, higher premorbid education, employment, and income were associated with return to work in patients with mild head injuries.

An important acute, injury-related variable which has been evaluated is early Glasgow Coma Scale (GCS) scores (Teasdale & Jennett, 1974). Review of the literature on the role of GCS scores as a predictor of outcome, however, reveals inconsistent findings. Several studies have reported that GCS scores were related to outcome 6 months to 1 year postinjury (Jennett et al., 1979; Minderhoud, Huizenga, van Woerkom, & Blomjous, 1982; Young et al., 1981). However, other studies indicate that GCS is a relatively weak predictor of outcome (Levati, Farina, Vecchi, Rossanda, & Marrubini, 1982) and that such factors as type of lesion (Gennarelli et al., 1982), oculocephalic responses, and age (Choi, Ward, & Becker, 1983) influence the utility of this measure.

Multiple injury and posttraumatic epilepsy are other injury-related variables which have been evaluated as predictors of outcome. Bowers and Marshall (1980) reported that the presence of multiple trauma involving a complicating chest or abdominal injury requiring operation adversely influenced outcome, as measured by the Glasgow Outcome Scale (Jennett & Bond, 1975). Reports have also been made of a relationship between posttraumatic epilepsy and the outcome measures of reduced functional independence (Timming et al., 1980), decreased employ-ability (Bruckner & Randle, 1972; Najenson et al., 1974; Panting & Merry, 1972), and psychiatric disability (Lishman, 1968) in patients with open and closed-head injuries.

In addition to premorbid and injury-related variables, a few studies have evaluated the role of cognitive sequelae in outcome. In these studies, cognitive functioning was measured concurrently with quality of life. Results indicated that a major determinant of outcome in patients with CHI is the severity of cognitive impairment. Levin, Grossman, Rose, and Teasdale (1979) reported that, at a median follow-up period of approximately 1 year, patients who showed a good outcome had Wechsler Adult Intelligence Scale (WAIS) IQ scores within one standard deviation of the population mean. In comparison, patients who showed a poor outcome exhibited profound intellectual impairment on the WAIS. In addition, the latter patients showed increased evidence of aphasic disorders and increased impairment on tasks of learning and memory as compared with patients who showed good recovery. Similarly, Jennett, Snoek, Bond, and Brooks (1981) reported that patients with severe cognitive impairment, as determined by performance on the WAIS and tests of verbal and nonverbal memory, showed poor outcome. In both of the above studies, outcome was assessed using the previously described Glasgow Outcome Scale (Jennett & Bond, 1975). Other researchers have reported a positive relationship between the ability to return to work and performance on tests of memory (Prigatano et al., 1984; Violon, Demol, & Brihaye (1978) and new learning (Prigatano et al., 1984).

Van Zomeren (1981) expanded upon the above investigations by evaluating the role of information processing, using visual choice reaction time (VCRT) as a predictor of outcome. VCRT was measured at 5 months postinjury in a small group of patients, and outcome was assessed at 12 months by neurologists who used a derivation of the Glasgow Outcome Scale (Jennett & Bond, 1975). As the reaction time measures were obtained during an earlier stage of recovery, the predictive relationship between VCRT and outcome could be evaluated. VCRT was found to correlate significantly with clinical outcome (activities of daily living), mental outcome (memory, concentration, apathy, irritability), and, to a lesser extent, social outcome.

Outcome has been evaluated using a series of different criterion measures. However, these have been confined mainly to global indices, e.g., the Glasgow Outcome Scale (Jennett & Bond, 1975), or more simplified versions of the Glasgow Outcome Scale, in which categories were further collapsed, e.g., dichotomous scales of survived/deceased or good/bad outcome (Choi et al., 1983; Jennett et al., 1976, 1979; Levati et al., 1982; Young et al., 1981). Alternatively, researchers have evaluated predictors and indicators of selected aspects of outcome, e.g., employability (Bruckner & Randle, 1972; Najenson et al., 1974; Panting & Merry, 1972; Prigatano et al., 1984; Rimel et al., 1981; Rimel, Giordani, Barth, & Jane, 1982).

Outcome in these studies generally has been rated by interviewers. Although relatives have described CHI patients' postinjury behavioral functioning (Brooks & McKinlay, 1983; McKinlay, Brooks, Bond, Martinage, & Marshall, 1981; Oddy & Humphrey, 1980; Oddy, Humphrey, & Uttley, 1978a, 1978b), no attempt has been made to evaluate predictors and indicators of outcome when outcome is determined by relatives' ratings of patient quality of life.

In summary, previous literature has suggested a role for some premorbid, injury-related, and follow-up variables in outcome. Therefore, this study incorporated a series of premorbid, injury-related, and follow-up variables, which *a priori* were considered as possible predictors/indicators of quality of life. As part of this procedure, a wide spectrum of neuropsychological tests measuring information processing, language, memory, "executive functions," and motor performance were included. These aspects of functioning were selected because areas of the brain thought to be primarily responsible for the mediation of these abilities (e.g., frontal and temporal lobes) are commonly damaged following CHI (Holbourn, 1943; Ommaya & Gennarelli, 1974). As measures of neuropsychological performance were obtained concurrently with quality of life indices, residual neuropsychological impairment was evaluated as an indicator (rather than a predictor) of quality of life. It was hypothesized that residual neuropsychological impairment in these areas would be associated with a reduction in quality of life, 2-4 years postinjury. For example, it was hypothesized that patients with greater neuropsychological impairment would encounter increased difficulty in achieving independence in daily living activities and in the resumption of their preinjury life-styles, i.e., employment, home management, and leisure activities. In addition, it was considered that awareness of these deficits would result in feelings of frustration, irritability, or depression. It was hypothesized that quality of life would vary inversely in proportion to the severity of these neuropsychological sequelae.

This study also attempted to extend previous research findings by using a broader definition of outcome which incorporates the multiple factors determining quality of life. Quality of life was defined according to McSweeney, Grant, Heaton, Adams, and Timms (1982), and encompassed the dimensions of emotional functioning, social role functioning, daily living activities, and recreational activities.

Lastly, as part of the attempt to document fully and clearly the salient variables influencing quality of life, predictors and indicators of patient quality of life as rated by a "significant other" were also evaluated. Relatives' reports on patient quality of life were included in order to compare and contrast their assessment of quality of life with those of the patients. It was considered that identification of a similar subset of important predictors and indicators for both patient and relatives' data would lend concurrent validity to the patients' self-reports.

METHOD

Subjects

This study utilized patients with a diagnosis of CHI who had been admitted to Sunnybrook Medical Centre, Toronto, 2-4 years previous to the time of testing. Participation was limited to patients aged 17-40 years at the time of injury, as this was considered representative of the CHI population (Rimel, 1981). Any individual with a previous head injury involving loss of consciousness or preaccident history of psychiatric institutionalization or alcoholism was excluded.

Initially, 163 patients were sent letters describing the study. Of that number, 123 (75.5%) were located and contacted by telephone regarding participation in the study. Of these, 83 patients (67.5%) agreed to participate. Five patients were excluded from the analysis, 4 because of previous head injuries and 1 who withdrew.

Demographic data were in accord with other recent studies (Annegers, Grabow, Kurland, & Laws, 1980; Rimel et al., 1981; Rimel et al., 1982), in that, at the time of injury, participants were primarily male (82.1%), young (60.3% age 17-25), and single (62.8%). Injuries were most often sustained as a result of motor vehicle accidents (MVA) (62.9%).

Participants showed a range in their severity of head injury (60.3%, mild; 10.2%, moderate; 29.5%, severe) as determined by initial GCS scores (Teasdale & Jennett, 1974) obtained at the time of admission to hospital. Given the retrospective nature of this study, GCS scores were considered the best index of severity of injury, as PTA and duration of coma data were not consistently or reliably available for all patients. Of the sample, 74.4% sustained multiple system injuries. At the time of testing, 78.3% of the sample were employed (vs. 94.9% preinjury).

Other demographic and patient quality of life data are available elsewhere (Klonoff, 1984).

Procedure

Patient participants underwent a neuropsychological assessment in the areas of information processing, language, memory, "executive functions," and motor performance. Table 1 includes the list of neuropsychological tests. Means and standard deviations are included so as to enable the reader to characterize the sample seen. Tests of motor function were not administered for patients with hemiparetic limbs ($n = 2$). However, some of the patients had sustained fractured upper limbs at the time of injury (e.g., 2-4 years previously) and, as there were no frank signs of compromised function, tests of motor function were administered for these patients. Patients also completed a series of quality of life questionnaires. These included the Sickness Impact Profile (SIP; Bergner, Bobbitt, Pollard, Martin, & Gilson, 1976) and the Minnesota Multiphasic Personality Inventory (MMPI; Hathaway & McKinley, 1967).

The SIP is a measure of health-related dysfunction which evaluates a wide range of quality of life domains. It consists of 12 categories of activities, including Ambulation, Mobility, Body Control and Movement, Social Interaction, Communication, Alertness Behaviour, Emotional Behaviour, Sleep and Rest, Eating, Home Management, Recreation and Pastimes, and Work. The MMPI is a self-report measure of psychopathology, which was used to evaluate the emotional functioning of the patients. Patients were administered the 400-item version. For purposes of this study, the MMPI was used as a measure of quality of life. In addition to the above questionnaires, supplemental information was obtained through an interview. This included the presence/absence of employment at the time of testing and subjective report regarding physical and mental recovery.

Relatives and close friends of patient participants were asked to complete the Katz Adjustment Scale - Relatives' Form (KAS-R; Katz & Lyerly, 1963) in order to provide an index of the patient's quality of life as perceived by others. The KAS-R contains five major subscales which measure behavioural symptoms, social adjustment, recreational activities, and social role functioning (Katz & Lyerly, 1963). (Mean data for the KAS-R and SIP are provided elsewhere (Klonoff, Snow, & Costa, in press) and can be obtained by mail from the senior author.)

In order to condense the data from the neuropsychological assessment and the SIP, a Principal Components Analysis (PCA) with Varimax rotation was performed on each set of data ($n = 78$). For missing data on tests of motor function ($n = 2$), mean data were substituted. The performances of each subject on neuropsychological tests and the SIP were expressed in terms of factor scores derived from the PCA.

Five factors with an eigenvalue ≥ 1.0 were derived from the neuropsychological data and were labelled as follows:

Factor 1. *Language*

loadings $\geq .7$ on the Token Test, Stroop A, Stroop B, and Stroop C.

Factor 2. *Laterality*

loadings $\geq .7$ on laterality measures (hand, eye and foot) derived from the Lateral Dominance exam and the handedness score of the Lateral Dominance test.

Table 1
Neuropsychological Test performance
($n = 78$)

Test	M	SD
Laterality		
Lateral Dominance (Harris, 1958)	106.79	39.43
Handedness (Harris, 1958)	58.59	21.79
Motor Tests		
VCRT (preferred; Van Zomeren, 1981)	0.55	0.21
VCRT (nonpreferred)	0.54	0.17
FT (preferred; Reitan & Davison, 1974)	47.26	8.98
FT (nonpreferred)	43.18	8.54
Language		
Token Test (Spellacy & Spreen, 1969)	15.23	1.42
Word Fluency (Spreen & Benton, 1969)	34.01	11.71
Memory		
Wechsler Memory Scale (Wechsler & Stone, 1945)	102.50	17.49
Rey (recall; Rey, 1941)	18.19	6.76
Executive Function		
Stroop A (Esson, Bourke,	50.04	21.84
Stroop B & Yen, 1979)	69.64	37.17
Stroop C	125.26	68.90
Rey (copy)	32.28	3.34
Porteus Mazes (Porteus, 1950)		
Test Age	15.29	2.05
Qualitative Score	32.88	22.36
WCST (Categories; Nelson, 1976)	5.56	0.97
WCST (% Persev.)	21.29	22.20
Luria Christensen	49.94	6.75
Subtests (Christensen, 1975)		

VCRT = Visual Choice Reaction Time; FT = Finger Tapping;
WCST = Wisconsin Card Sorting Test.

Factor 3. *Motor Performance*

    loadings $\geq.7$ on Finger Tapping (dominant and nondominant hands) and VCRT (dominant and nondominant hands) tasks. Given the high correlation between Finger Tapping, a test of motor speed with no information-processing properties, and VCRT, this factor was labelled in the most parsimonious manner as Motor Performance.

Factor 4. *Memory and Constructional Ability*

    loadings $\geq.7$ on the Rey Complex Figure, copy and recall forms; loading $\geq.6$ on the Wechsler Memory Scale Quotient.

Factor 5. *Executive Functions*

    Weak interrelationships between certain tests of executive functions were revealed (loadings $\geq.5$), including the Porteus Maze test (Test Age and Qualitative Score), the Wisconsin Card Sorting Test (Hazel Nelson Modified Version; Percent Perseverations), and the Luria-Christensen (selected subtests). These tests measure motor sequencing and programming, planning behaviour, impulse control, verbal regulation of behaviour, and perseverative behaviour.

Three factors with an eigenvalue ≥1.0 were derived from the SIP and were labelled as follows:

Factor 1. *Physical Well-Being and Social Role Functioning.*
   loadings ≥.7 on the three Physical subscales (Ambulation, Mobility, and Body Control and Movement) and on Home Management and Work.

Factor 2. *Psychosocial Functioning.*
   loadings ≥.7 on the subscales of Social Interaction, Alertness Behaviour, and Emotional Behaviour.

Factor 3. *Oral-Motor Behaviour.*
   loadings ≥.7 on the subscales of Communication and Eating.

   Data from the MMPI ($n = 71$) were expressed as three separate composite scores:
   Sum 1 = T score sum of Hypochondriasis (Hs) + Depression (D) + Hysteria (Hy) (Scales $1 + 2 + 3$).
   Sum 2 = T score sum of Psychopathic Deviate (Pd) + Hypomania (Ma) (Scales $4 + 9$).
   Sum 3 = T score sum of Psychasthenia (Pt) + Schizophrenia (Sc) (Scales $7 + 8$).

   Composite scores are based on *a priori* review of the literature (Black, 1973; Dikmen & Reitan, 1977; Lezak, 1983; Mack, in press). In addition, results of a PCA with varimax rotation of the MMPI data confirmed two of the three groupings (Sum 1 and Sum 2). Although the scales of Sum 3 did not form a separate factor, they are correlated at .83 with each other.

   Identification of the important predictors and indicators of quality of life was conducted using a canonical correlation procedure (SPSSX Canonical Correlation program). This analysis accounts for the maximum amount of relationship between two sets of variables by maximally correlating linear combinations of variables. It is clear that, due to the low subject/variable ratio, results of these canonical correlation analyses should be viewed as hypothesis-generating and in need of future replication.

   The following variables were entered as predictor or indicator variables ($n = 16$):
(a) Demographic variables:
1. sex
2. age at the time of accident
3. preinjury education
4. marital status at the time of testing (married vs. other)
(b) Injury-related variables:
1. presence/absence of multiple trauma
2. presence/absence of other injuries
3. presence/absence of seizures
4. presence/absence of alcohol
5. presence/absence of anatomical evidence of frontal lobe damage (e.g., patients with normal CT scan ($n = 18$), posterior damage on CT ($n = 8$), and patients with mild head injuries for whom a CT scan was not considered necessary ($n = 25$), vs. frontal damage on CT scan ($n = 27$))
6. injury-test interval
7. initial GCS scores
(c) Neuropsychological data:
1. factor scores of neuropsychological data.
   The following variables were entered as criterion variables ($n = 9$):
(a) SIP: factor scores of the SIP
(b) MMPI: 3 separate composite scores:

Sum 1: Hs + D + Hy

Sum 2: Pd + Ma

Sum 3: Pt + Sc

(c) Employment Status: presence/absence of employment at the time of testing.

(d) Subjective Report: subjective report of the patient at the time of testing regarding feeling back to normal physically and mentally (present/absent responses).

The same set of predictor and indicator variables was utilized for a similar analysis which employed relatives' reports of quality of life as the criterion variables. The criterion subset contained the following KAS-R data:

(a) KAS-R.: 13 R1 subscales: Belligerence, Verbal Expansiveness, Negativism, Helplessness, Suspiciousness, Anxiety, Withdrawal and Retardation, General Psychopathology, Nervousness, Confusion, Bizarreness, Hyperactivity and Stability

R2: Performance of Socially Expected Activities

R3: Relatives' Expectations of Performance of Social Role Functioning

R4: Performance of Free-time Activities

R5: Dissatisfaction with Free-time Activities

RESULTS

Table 2 summarizes the results of the canonical correlation utilizing predictor and criterion variables for the patient quality of life data. The analysis was conducted on data from 71 subjects, due to missing or invalid MMPI data. Results indicated one significant canonical correlation ($p < .001$) and a second canonical correlation which approached significance ($p < .06$). Given the exploratory nature of this research, discussion of the second canonical correlation was included for heuristic purposes.

Each canonical correlation is composed of two related sets of canonical variates, one from each subset of variables. The amount of variance shared by the two canonical variates within the first canonical correlation is 77% (eigenvalue). The second set of canonical variates share 61% of their variance. The second set of canonical variates is uncorrelated with the first set, and is selected to account for the maximal amount of relationship left unexplained by the first set. The canonical variates contain correlations between each variable and the canonical variate which, like loadings, reflect the relevance of each variable in describing the canonical variate. Loadings are interpreted both in terms of their magnitude and direction (Tabachnik & Fidell, 1983).

Examination of the loadings of each variable on the first set of canonical variates indicates a high loading ($= .9$) on Factor 3 (motor performance) of the Neuropsychological data and initial GCS scores (loading $= .7$) and a modest loading ($= .4$) on the Presence/Absence of Frontal Lobe Damage variable from the predictor subset. This relates to Factor 1 (Physical Well-Being and Social Role Functioning) and Factor 3 (Oral-Motor Behaviour) of the SIP from the quality of life criterion variables and Presence/Absence of Employment (loadings $> .6$).

The second set of canonical variates loads highly on two predictor variables: Factor 4 (Memory and Constructional Ability) of the Neuropsychological data

Table 2
Canonical Correlation: Relationship of Predictors with Patient
Self-report of Quality of Life
$(n = 71)$

Eigenvalue	Canonical Correlation	Wilks' Lambda	P value
.765	.875	.018	0.001
.607	.779	.075	0.059

Loadings for the canonical variables of the predictor set

Loadings for the canonical variables of the criterion set

	CANVAR 1	CANVAR 2		CANVAR 1	CANVAR 2
Age at accident	184	—078	SIP Factor 1	—681*	436*
GCS	700*	133	SIP Factor 2	—251	—719*
Inj.-test int.	069	394*	SIP Factor 3	—629*	—010
Education	221	409*	MMPI SUM 1	—283	—045
Frontal	393*	207	MMPI SUM 2	—076	—237
Seizures	—136	—210	MMPI SUM 3	—247	—093
Marital Status	161	—199	Employment	—625*	173
Cog. Factor 1	—125	050	Normal Ment.	—280	—653*
Cog. Factor 2	104	—288	Normal Phys.	—148	—538*
Cog. Factor 3	898*	—156			
Cog. Factor 4	250	803*	*Note.* As all the loadings are less than one,		
Cog. Factor 5	—208	012	decimal points have been omitted.		
Sex	138	—154	CANVAR = Canonical Variate; Inj.-test int.		
Alcohol	—142	—070	= Injury-test interval; Cog. = Cognitive;		
Trauma	—293	—511*	Normal Ment. = Normal Mentally; Normal		
Other Injuries	—330	—100	Phys. = Normal Physically;		
			* Loadings discussed in text.		

(loading >.8) and Presence/Absence of Multiple Trauma (loading >.5). Modest loadings were also observed for Education and Injury-Test Interval. This relates to Factor 2 (Psychosocial Functioning) (loading >.7) and to a lesser extent Factor 1 (Physical Well-Being and Social Role Functioning) (loading > .4) of the SIP criterion variables. Moderate loadings were also noted for the variables of Subjective Report of Physical and Psychological Recovery (loadings > .5).

Table 3 summarizes the canonical correlation for the predictor variables and the relatives' reports of patient quality of life, as measured by the KAS-R. Due to missing data, this analysis was conducted on data from 63 subjects. Results indicate one significant canonical correlation ($p < .006$) with 85% of the variance shared between the 2 canonical variates. Examination of the loadings of each variable on the first set of canonical variates (predictors) indicates a high loading (> .7) on Factor 3 (motor performance) of the Cognitive Data and initial GCS scores (loading > .6). Modest loadings are also noted for the variables of Presence/Absence of Frontal Lobe Damage (loading > .4) and Presence/Absence of Seizures (loading > .5). These relate to the KAS-R R5 subscale (Dissatisfaction

Table 3

Canonical Correlation: Relationship of Predictors with Relatives' Reports of Quality of Life ($n = 63$)

Eigenvalue	Canonical Correlation	Wilks' Lambda	p value
.847	.920	.001	0.006

Loadings for the canonical variables of the predictor set		Loadings for the canonical variables of the criterion set	
	CANVAR 1		CANVAR 1
Age at accident	—132	Belligerence	023
GCS	—614*	Verbal Expansive.	—026
Inj.-test int.	—127	Negativism	050
Education	—015	Helplessness	217
Frontal	—407*	Suspiciousness	102
Seizures	511*	Anxiety	—048
Marital Status	—152	Withdrawal/Retard.	659*
Cog. Factor 1	312	General Psychopath.	—025
Cog. Factor 2	—140	Nervousness	420*
Cog. Factor 3	—721*	Confusion	276
Cog. Factor 4	—242	Bizarreness	004
Cog. Factor 5	—305	Hyperactivity	—025
Sex	062	Stability	102
Alcohol	146	R2	—219
Trauma	223	R3	—217
Other Injuries	—012	R4	277
		R5	582*

Note. As all the loadings are less than one, decimal points have been omitted. CANVAR = Canonical Variate; inj.-test int. = injury-test interval; Cog. = Cognitive; Expansive. = Expansiveness; Retard. = Retardation.
* loadings discussed in text.

with Free-Time Activities) (loading $> .5$) and the Rl subscales of Withdrawal/Retardation (loading $> .6$), and to a lesser extent Nervousness (loading $> .4$).

DISCUSSION

The above canonical correlation procedures identify several interesting predictors and indicators of quality of life in CHI patients 2-4 years postinjury. However, before discussing results of the canonical correlation analyses, several cautionary notes regarding interpretation of the findings should be made. First, the statistical analysis procedures employed identify "relationships" between variables and the use of the terms "predictor" or "indicator" is not causative, but rather correlational. Second, the results of the canonical analyses are based on what many would consider to be an unacceptably low subject/variable ratio. Third, to interpret results of a canonical correlation analysis accurately, it should be noted that this analysis reflects the interrelationships between variable subsets based on the series of variables selected for this analysis. Changing the set of variables used may markedly alter the results of the analysis (Tabachnik & Fidell, 1983). Lastly, this analysis procedure is somewhat limited in that each pair of canonical variates is independent of other pairs and no oblique (correlated) solution is available (Tabachnik & Fidell, 1983). Therefore, this data should be viewed as exploratory and hypothesis-generating and all statistical findings to be discussed require future replication.

Results of the canonical correlation employing predictors and patient self-report quality of life data indicate a strong relationship between Factor 3 (Motor Performance) of the neuropsychological data and initial GCS scores and three criterion variables — two factors of the SIP, Factor 1 (Physical Well-Being and Social Role Functioning) and Factor 3 (Oral-Motor Behaviour), and the presence/absence of postinjury employment. Hence, the degree of motor dysfunction (as indicated by performance on the neuropsychological tests of Finger Tapping and VCRT) relates to those aspects of quality of life which involve activities of daily living and social role functioning (e.g., performance in the work and home settings). Those patients with residual motor dysfunction reported more impaired self-care functioning, decreased mobility and more difficulty with ambulation, communication, body control, movement (dressing, washing, and bowel control) and oral-motor (problems swallowing food and dysarthric speech) dysfunction. The degree of motor disability also appears to influence social role functioning, as those patients with motor slowing reported increased dysfunction in the work and home settings. This pair of canonical variates, therefore, represents the physical dimension of postinjury quality of life. This finding confirms the clinical observation that the presence of severe motor dysfunction can be an important limiting factor in returning to work.

It should be noted that the VCRT and Finger Tapping tasks were considered parsimoniously as tests of motor performance, based on the PCA of the neuro-psychological tests. As data for patients with a frank hemiparesis ($n = 2$) were excluded, and no other patients appeared to show significant motor slowing related to peripheral injury, it is felt that poor performance on these tasks primarily reflected central motor impairment. However, the relative contribution of peripherally vs. centrally mediated motor dysfunction cannot easily be discriminated for this patient sample, as a sizeable proportion sustained limb injuries, which could have influenced performance on both of these tests of motor functioning in subtle ways. Less ambiguous interpretation of this data could be provided by another study employing a sample of CHI patients without peripheral injuries. For the purposes of the present study, however, the original intent was to employ as clinically representative a sample of CHI patients as was possible; therefore, CHI patients with multiple trauma were also included.

In addition, the VCRT task has been employed as a measure of information processing, and it is recognized that further research employing measures without a motor component (e.g., the Paced Auditory Serial Addition Task [Gronwall & Wrightson, 1974]) is needed to clarify the role of slowed information processing in outcome.

The finding that initial GCS scores relate to activities of daily living and social role functioning suggests that severity of head injury is also an important predictor of postinjury quality of life. This finding corroborates and expands upon other investigations which identified GCS as a major determinant of outcome when less detailed definitions of outcome were employed (Jennett et al., 1979; Minderhoud et al., 1982; Young et al., 1982). Interestingly, motor slowing, as measured by the neuropsychological tests of VCRT and Finger Tapping, correlates significantly with initial GCS scores ($r = .53$ $p < .0001$). This suggests that those patients with more severe head injuries showed increased motor slowing, which was associated with their relatively poor scores on indices of quality of life.

Concordance with the above findings that Factor 3 (Motor Performance) of the neuropsychological data and initial GCS scores were significantly related to patient self-report quality of life was provided when predictors and indicators of patient quality of life based on relatives' ratings were evaluated. Results of this canonical correlation indicated that motor dysfunction (Factor 3 of the Cognitive Data) and severity of head injury (initial GCS scores) also related strongly to relatives' ratings on the KAS-R. Replication of the variables of initial GCS scores and motor dysfunction as major determinants of quality of life based on two different sets of respondents contributes to the reliability of these findings.

Some support for the role of motor disability in outcome has been reported in the literature. Bruckner and Randle (1972) reported that, although psychological factors most strongly influenced the return to work in patients with severe head injuries, hemiplegia was also associated with persistent unemployment. Jellinek, Torkelson, and Harvey (1982) reported a negative relationship between distress levels and independence of self-care, mobility, and living arrangements in brain-injured individuals. Furthermore, Lezak, Cosgrove, O'Brien, and Wooster (1980) reported that mobility was an important determinant of postinjury independent functioning.

The above studies are based on patient self-report on inventories and interview data. Oddy et al. (1978b) corroborated these results using data obtained from relatives. These authors found that residual physical disability in the form of either limb injuries or hemiplegia was an important factor in severely head-injured patients who, 6 months postinjury, received poor ratings of social adjustment in the areas of work and leisure activities.

Somewhat related findings have been reported by other researchers who have identified motor disabilities, recorded at the acute postinjury stage, as a predictor of eventual cognitive recovery. Dye, Milby, and Saxon (1979) reported that early neurological problems, especially motor abnormalities, were related to poorer neuropsychological performance 3 years postinjury. Zazula, Tabaddor, Mattis, Feiner, and Lynn (1981) reported that, in a small group of head-injury patients, motor dysfunction, measured with the Finger Tapping test during the acute stages of recovery, was a predictor of neuropsychologial outcome 6 months and 1 year postinjury.

The above research and the findings from the present study indicate that motor disabilities in patients detected during the acute postinjury phase, poor long-term neuropsychological recovery, and poor long-term quality of life (particularly in the domains of physical functioning, independence, and social role functioning) are all associated.

It is interesting that, in reviewing the literature, one trend proposed on the basis of research by Bond and his colleagues is the relative subordination of the role of physical disability in outcome, in favor of mental handicaps (Bond, 1975; Jennett et al., 1981). Differences in methodology in the current study which may explain the discrepancy between our findings and those of Bond (1975) and Jennett et al. (1981) include a more limited age range and outcome period, a greater proportion of participants with multiple system injuries, a more inclusive definition of quality of life which incorporates its diversified aspects, and reliance on patients' and relatives' reports of quality of life, as opposed to ratings by neurologists. In addition, careful review of the subjects used by Jennett et al. (1981) indicates that some patients with severe physical deficits who could not perform tests of cognitive functioning were excluded when consideration of the relative contribution of physical vs. mental disability to outcome was made.

In summary, although the role of physical disability in outcome is somewhat controversial in the literature, it is felt that the results of the current study raise the possibility that motor dysfunction is a variable influencing eventual quality of life in CHI patients.

The second canonical correlation for the patient self-report data showed a p value of .06, which approached the standard cutoff of .05; it was included for heuristic reasons. It identified a relationship between Factor 4 of the Cognitive Data (Memory and Constructional Ability) and the Presence/Absence of Multiple Trauma, with Factor 2 (Psychosocial Functioning) and Factor 1 (Physical Well-Being and Social Role Functioning) of the SIP and patient self-report of mental and physical recovery. This pair of linear combinations suggests that impairment of higher order cognitive skills (e.g., memory and constructional ability) relates to psychosocial dysfunction (i.e., decreased mental alertness, increased emotional problems, and increased social isolation) as well as to subjective report of emotional and psychological problems. Patients with cognitive deficits, as measured by neuropsychological testing, reported more emotional distress, social withdrawal, and cognitive confusion. As the first pair of canonical variates was concerned largely with physical dysfunction, and physical dysfunction can occur in the absence of brain damage, this second canonical correlation demonstrates the added effect of cognitive deficits (sustained as a result of brain damage) on quality of life.

The above findings corroborate those of several other groups of investigators who reported a relationship between residual memory deficits and outcome when both were measured at long-term follow-up (Jennett et al., 1981; Levin et al., 1979; Violon et al., 1978). In addition, a relationship between memory deficits and decreased employment has been reported (Bruckner & Randle, 1972; Prigatano et al., 1984).

Lastly, a series of modest predictors/indicators of quality of life based on patient self-report and relatives' reports of quality of life were identified. Lower education, shorter injury-test intervals, as well as the presence of frontal-lobe damage and seizure disorders were associated with poorer quality of life in CHI patients 2-4 years postinjury. These findings corroborate earlier research which has indicated that level of education (Rimel et al., 1981) and presence of seizure disorders (Bruckner & Randle, 1972; Lishman, 1968; Najenson et al., 1974; Panting & Merry, 1972; Timming et al., 1980) relate to aspects of outcome of head injury. The finding that injury-test interval is a modest indicator of quality of life offers supportive evidence to other reports in the literature (Leigh, 1979; Lishman, 1978) that the recovery process is a dynamic one, even 2-4 years postinjury. The finding that frontal-lobe damage, as evidenced by CT-scan data (but not neuro-psychological data), showed a modest negative relationship to quality of life, as rated by both relatives and patients, is an interesting preliminary finding, which requires further investigation.

REFERENCES

Annegers, J. F., Grabow, J. D., Kurland, L. T., & Laws, E. R. (1980). The incidence, causes, and secular trends of head trauma in Olmsted County, Minnesota, 1935-1974. *Neurology, 30,* 912-919.

Becker, D. P., Miller, J. D., Ward, J. D., Greenberg, R. P., Young, H. F., & Sakalas, R. (1977). The outcome from severe head injury with early diagnosis and intensive management. *Journal of Neurosurgery, 47,* 491-502.

Bergner, M., Bobbitt, R. A., Pollard, W. E., Martin, D. P., & Gilson, B. S. (1976). The Sickness Impact Profile: Validation of a health status measure. *Medical Care, 14,* 57-67.

Black, F. W. (1973). Cognitive and memory performance in subjects with brain damage secondary to penetrating missile wounds and closed head injury. *Journal of Clinical Psychology, 29,* 441-442.

Bond, M. R. (1975). Assessment of the psychosocial outcome after severe head injury. *CIBA Foundation Symposium, 34,* 141-157.

Bowers, S. A., & Marshall, L. F. (1980). Outcome in 200 consecutive cases of severe head injury treated in San Diego County: A prospective analysis. *Neurosurgery, 6,* 237-242.

Brooks, D. N., & McKinlay, W. (1983). Personality and behavioural change after severe blunt head injury - a relative's view. *Journal of Neurology, Neurosurgery, and Psychiatry, 46,* 336-344.

Bruckner, F. E., & Randle, A. P. H. (1972). Return to work after severe head injuries. *Rheumatic and Physical Medicine, 11,* 344-348.

Carlsson, C-A., von Essen, C., & Lofgren, J. (1968). Factors affecting the clinical course of patients with severe head injuries. *Journal of Neurosurgery, 29,* 242-251.

Choi, S. C., Ward, J. D., & Becker, D. P. (1983). Chart for outcome prediction in severe head injury. *Journal of Neurosurgery, 59,* 294-297.

Christensen, A.-L. (1975). *Luria's neuropsychological investigation. Text.* Copenhagen: Munksgaard.

Dikmen, S., & Reitan, R. M. (1977). Emotional sequelae of head injury. *Annals of Neurology, 2,* 492-494.

Dye, O. A., Milby, J. B., & Saxon, S. A. (1979). Effects of early neurological problems following head trauma on subsequent neuropsychological performance. *Acta Neurologica Scandinavica, 59,* 10-14.

Esson, M. E., Bourke, R. S., & Yen, J. K. (1979). *Albany developmental assessment of recovery from serious head injury* (DARSHI). Manual. Albany, New York.

Field, J. H. (1976). *Epidemiology of head injury in England and Wales: With particular application to rehabilitation.* Leicester: Printed for H. M. Stationery Office by Willsons.

Gennarelli, T. A., Spielman, G. M., Langfitt, T. W., Gildenberg, P. L., Harrington, T., Jane, J. A., Marshall, L. F., Miller, J. D., & Pitts, L. H. (1982). Influence of the type of intracranial lesion on outcome from severe head injury. *Journal of Neurosurgery, 56,* 26-32.

Gronwall, D. M. A., & Wrightson, P. (1974). Cumulative effect of concussion. *Lancet,* Nov. 22, 995-997.

Harris, A. J. (1958). *Harris tests of Lateral Dominance. Manual of directions for administration and interpretation* (3rd ed.). New York:Psychological Corporation.

Hathaway, S. R., & McKinley, J. C. (1967). *The Minnesota Multiphasic Personality Inventory manual (rev.).* New York: Psychological Corporation.

Holbourn, A. H. S. (1943). Mechanics of head injuries. *Lancet, 2,* 438-441.

Hpay, H. (1971). Psychosocial effects of severe head injury. *Proceedings of an International symposium on Head Injuries* (pp. 110-121). Edinburgh: Churchill Livingstone.

Jellinek, H. M., Torkelson, R. M., & Harvey, R. F. (1982). Functional abilities and distress levels in brain injured patients at long-term follow-up. *Archives of Physical Medicine and Rehabilitation, 63,* 160-162.

Jennett, B., & Bond, M. (1975). Assessment of outcome after severe brain damage. *Lancet, 1,* 480-484.

Jennett, B., Snoek, J., Bond, M. R., & Brooks, B. (1981). Disability after severe head injury: Observations on the use of the Glasgow Outcome Scale. *Journal of Neurology, Neurosurgery and Psychiatry, 44,* 285-293.

Jennett, B., & Teasdale, G. (1981). *Management of head injuries.* Philadelphia: F. A. Davis Company.

Jennett, B., Teasdale, G., Braakman, R., Minderhoud, J., Heiden, J., & Kurze, T. (1979). Prognosis of patients with severe head injury. *Neurosurgery, 4,* 283-289.

Jennett, B., Teasdale, G., Braakman, R., Minderhoud, J., & Knill-Jones, R. (1976). Predicting outcome in individual patients after severe head injury. *Lancet,* May 15, 1031-1034.

Jennett, B., Teasdale, G., & Knill-Jones, R. (1975). Prognosis after severe head injury. Ciba Foundation Symposium, No. 34 (New Series). *Symposium on the outcome of severe damage to the CNS.* Amsterdam: Elsevier, Excerpta Medica.

Katz M. M., & Lyerly, S. B. (1963). Methods for measuring adjustment and social behaviour in the community. I. Rationale, description, discriminative validity and scale development. *Psychological Reports, 13,* 503-535.

Kerr, T. A., Kay, D. W. K., & Lassman, L. P. (1971). Characteristics of patients, type of accident, and mortality in a consecutive series of head injuries admitted to a neurosurgical unit. *British Journal of Preventative and Social Medicine, 25,* 179-185.

Klonoff, H. (1971). Head injuries in children: Predisposing factors, accident conditions, accident proneness and sequelae. *American Journal of Public Health, 61,* 2405-2417.

Klonoff, P. S. (1984). *Quality of life in patients with closed head injury: A comparison of patients with and without frontal lobe damage.* Unpublished Doctoral dissertation, University of Victoria, Victoria.

Klonoff, P. S., Snow, W. G., & Costa, L. D. (in press). Quality of life in patients with closed head injury, 2-4 years post-injury. *Neurosurgery.*

Leigh, D. (1979). Psychiatric aspects of head injury. *Psychiatry Digest,* Aug./Sept., 21-33.

Levati, A., Farina, M. L., Vecchi, G., Rossanda, M., & Marrubini, M. B. (1982). Prognosis of severe head injuries. *Journal of Neurosurgery, 57,* 779-783.

Levin, H. S., Grossman, R. G., Rose, J. E., & Teasdale, G. (1979). Long-term neuropsychological outcome of closed head injury. *Journal of Neurosurgery, 50,* 412-422.

Lezak, M. D. (1983). *Neuropsychological assessment* (2nd Ed.). New York: Oxford University Press.

Lezak, M. D., Cosgrove, J. N., O'Brien, K., & Wooster, N. (1980, February). *Relationship between personality disorders, social disturbance and physical disability following traumatic brain injury.* Paper presented at the meeting of the International Neuropsychological Society, San Francisco, CA.

Lishman, W. A. (1968). Brain damage in relation to psychiatric disability after head injury. *British Journal of Psychiatry, 114,* 373-410.

Lishman, W. A. (1978). *Organic psychiatry. The psychological consequences of cerebral disorder.* New York: Blackwell Scientific Pub.

Lundholm, J., Jepsen, B. N., & Thornval, G. (1975). The late neurological, psychological, and social aspects of severe traumatic coma. *Scandinavian Journal of Rehabilitation Medicine, 7,* 97-100.

Mack, J. L. (in press). The MMPI and neurological dysfunction. In C. S. Newmark (Ed.), *MMPI: Current clinical and research trends.* New York, Praeger.

McKinlay, W. W., Brooks, D. N., Bond, M. R., Martinage, D. P., & Marshall, M. M. (1981). The short-term outcome of severe blunt head injury as reported by relatives of the injured persons. *Journal of Neurology, Neurosurgery, and Psychiatry, 44,* 527-533.

McSweeney, A. J., Grant, I., Heaton, R. K., Adams, K. M., & Timms, R. M. (1982). Life quality of patients with chronic obstructive pulmonary disease. *Archives of Internal Medicine, 142,* 473-478.

Minderhoud, J. M., Huizenga, J., van Woerkom, T.C.A.M., & Blomjous, C.E.M. (1982). The pattern of recovery after severe head injury. *Clinical Neurology and Neurosurgery, 84,* 15-28.

Najenson, T., Mendelson, L., Schechter, I., David, C., Mintz, N., & Groswasser, Z. (1974). Rehabilitation after severe head injury. *Scandinavian Journal of Rehabilitation, 6,* 5-14.

Nelson, H. E. (1976). A modified card sorting test sensitive to frontal lobe defects. *Cortex, 12,* 313-324.

Oddy, M., & Humphrey, M. (1980). Social recovery during the year following severe head injury. *Journal of Neurology, Neurosurgery and Psychiatry, 43,* 798-802.

Oddy, M., Humphrey, M., Uttley, D. (1978a). Stresses upon the relatives of head-injured patients. *British Journal of Psychiatry, 133,* 507-513.

Oddy, M., Humphrey, M., & Uttley, D. (1978b). Subjective impairment and social recovery after closed head injury. *Journal of Neurology, Neurosurgery and Psychiatry, 41,* 611-616.

Ommaya, A. K., & Gennarelli, T. A. (1974). Cerebral concussion and traumatic unconsciousness - correlations of experimental and clinical observations on blunt head injuries. *Brain, 97,* 633-643.

Panting, A., & Merry, P. H. (1972). The longterm rehabilitation of severe head injuries with particular reference to the need for social and medical support for the patient's family. *Rehabilitation* (Stuttgart), *38,* 33-37.

Porteus, S. D. (1950). *The Porteus maze test and intelligence.* Palo Alto, CA: Pacific Books.

Prigatano, G. P., Fordyce, D. J., Zeiner, H. K., Roueche, J. R., Pepping, M., & Wood, B. C. (1984). Neuropsychological rehabilitation after closed head injury in young adults. *Journal of Neurology, Neurosurgery, & Psychiatry, 47,* 505-513.

Reitan, R. M., & Davison, L. A. (1974). *Clinical neuropsychology: Current status and applications.* New York: Hemisphere.

Rey, A. (1941). L'examen psychologique dans les cas d'encéphalopathie traumatique. *Archives de Psychologie, 28,* 286-340.

Rimel, R. W. (1981). A prospective study of patients with central nervous system trauma. *Journal of Neurosurgical Nursing, 13,* 132-141.

Rimel, R. W., Giordani, B., Barth, J. T., Boll, T. J., & Jane, J. A. (1981). Disability caused by minor head injury. *Neurosurgery, 9,* 221-228.

Rimel, R. W., Giordani, B., Barth, J. T., & Jane, J. A. (1982). Moderate head injury; Completing the clinical spectrum of brain trauma. *Neurosurgery. 11,* 344-351.

Spellacy, F. J., & Spreen, O. (1969). A short form of the Token Test. *Cortex, 5,* 390-397.

Spreen, O., & Benton, A. L. (1969). *Neurosensory Center Comprehensive Examination for Aphasia. Manual of instructions.* Victoria: University of Victoria.

Tabachnick, B. G., & Fidell, L. S. (1983). *Using multivariate statistics.* New York: Harper & Row.

Teasdale, G., & Jennett, B. (1974). Assessment of coma and impaired consciousness. A practical scale. *Lancet, 2,* 81-84.

Timming, R., Orrison, W. W., & Mikula, J. A. (1982). Computerized tomography and rehabilitation outcome after severe head trauma. *Archives of Physical Medicine and Rehabilitation, 63,* 154-159.

Van Zomeren, A. H. (1981). *Reaction time and attention after closed head injury.* Lisse: Swets & Zeitlinger.

Violon, A., Demol, J., & Brihaye, J. (1978). Memory sequelae after severe head injuries. In R. A. Frowein, O. Wilcke, A. Karimi-Nejad, M. Brock & M. Klinger (Eds.), *Head injuries* (pp. 105-107). New York: Springer-Verlag.

Walker, A. E. (1972). Longterm evaluation of the social and family adjustment to head injuries. *Scandinavian Journal of Rehabilitation Medicine, 4,* 5-8.

Wechlser, D., & Stone, C. P. (1945). *Manual for the Wechsler Memory Scale.* New York: The Psychological Corporation.

Young, B., Rapp, R. P., Norton, J. A., Haack, D., Tibbs, P. A., & Bean, J. R. (1981). Early prediction of outcome in head-injured patients. *Journal of Neurosurgery, 54,* 300-303.

Zazula, T., Tabaddor, K., Mattis, S., Feiner, C., & Lynn, A. (1981). *Very early bedside neuropsychological evaluations: Predictive efficiency for recovery of moderate and severe head trauma patients at six months and one year.* Unpublished manuscript. Albert Einstein College of Medicine, Comprehensive Central Nervous System Trauma Center, New York.

Journal of Clinical and Experimental Neuropsychology
1989, Vol. 11, No. 5, pp. 631-644

Recovery of Memory after Severe Closed Head Injury: Dissociations in Recovery of Memory Parameters and Predictors of Outcome*

Christopher E. Paniak, Douglas L. Shore,

and Byron P. Rourke

University of Windsor

ABSTRACT

This study examined selective reminding and recognition memory performance of 21 severe closed-head injured patients tested within 6 months of regaining consciousness and then again after at least 1 year. Performances on selective reminding parameters were highly correlated and patients performed significantly worse at both testings than did hospitalized controls matched for age, education, and sex. Patients improved from testing 1 to testing 2 on only four of six memory variables. Average Impairment Rating at testing 1 was a marginally better predictor of memory performance at testing 2 than was length of coma. Results are discussed in terms of (a) utility of selective reminding parameters and predictors of outcome and (b) dissociations in recovery of memory parameters.

Head injury is a major cause of death and disability, especially among adolescents and young adults. Estimates of the incidence of head injury range from 170 to 600 cases for each 100,000 in the population yearly, depending on inclusion criteria (Levin, Benton, & Grossman, 1982). While physical dysfunction is often the most overt consequence of head injury and has historically been the major focus of rehabilitation efforts, cognitive and emotional sequelae are now held to be the more important sources of disability in the vocational, educational, and social domains (Bond, 1975). Although the nature and degree of cognitive impairment following head injury varies considerably, the most commonly reported problem is the disturbance of memory (Levin et al., 1982; Van Zomeren, 1981).

Buschke's (1973) method of selective reminding (SR) has become one of the more widely employed procedures for assessing memory functioning following head injury (e.g., Gronwall & Wrightson, 1981; Levin & Grossman, 1976;

* This project was supported by a Medical Research Council of Canada Studentship to the first author.

McLean, Temkin, Dikmen, & Wyler, 1983). Based on a multitrial free-recall procedure, SR involves practicing the subject on only those list items not recalled on the immediately preceding trial. Buschke described scoring procedures whereby performances could be decomposed to address such familiar information processing-based constructs as short-term recall (STR), long-term storage (LTS), long-term recall (LTR), and a global level of performance measure, total recall (TR). Despite the obvious appeal of such a convenient, face-valid derivation of traditional memory constructs, concern has been raised that these SR scoring parameters may not be measuring discrete processes (Loring & Papanicolaou, 1987). This concern arises from findings of highly significant correlations between the various SR scores in normal subjects (Kenisten, cited in Kraemer, Peabody, Tinklenberg, & Yesavage, 1983) as well as in demented patients (Loring, cited in Loring & Papanicolaou, 1987).

Anticipating that LTS, LTR, and other SR scoring parameters would lend themselves to the uncritical reification of hypothetical stages of information processing, Buschke (1974) stressed that recall is inevitably confounded with adequacy of storage, and suggested the less theoretically encumbered approach of dividing long-term memory into two components: consistent long-term retrieval (CLTR) and random long-term retrieval (RLTR). CLTR simply describes that portion of a subject's performance defined by consistent, unreminded recall, or error-free recall from a given trial until termination of the test. RLTR characterizes those list items in LTS not meeting the criterion for inclusion in CLTR. These items are described by sporadic or intermittent recall, and the consequent need for episodic reminding.

This distinction between CLTR and RLTR in long-term memory is important in that it potentially contains information relating to why a subject's performance is substandard. Specifically, Buschke (1974, 1984) and others (Flavell, 1970; Hasher & Zacks, 1979; Kohl & Brandt, 1985) have stressed the role of attention and cognitive skills that are necessary to execute an efficient strategy in learning and memory. Deficits in these basic cognitive processes do not constitute memory impairment (Buschke, 1984) and are characteristic of the memory test performances of the very young and the retarded (Flavell, 1970) as well as the aged (Hulicka & Grossman, 1967; Hultsch, 1971; Smith, 1977). Such deficits in cognitive processing underlying apparent memory problems would be expected to affect CLTR and RLTR differentially by undermining the various attentional, set-taking, and mnemonic strategy processes that culminate in the primary and secondary organization of material in long-term memory. Adequately processed items would presumably be chunked or associated with one another, and would be more likely to be recalled together, thus enlarging the number of list items meeting the criteria for CLTR. Conversely, words joined by weaker associative bonds resulting from inadequate processing would be more susceptible to omission during recall; this would result in an increase in the number of words characterized by RLTR, and a complementary decrease in CLTR words. Thus, the relative magnitude of

CLTR versus RLTR would appear to reflect an aspect of performance that is specifically sensitive to the adequacy of basic cognitive processing and more meaningfully interpretable than are the LTS, LTR, or TR parameters. The potential diagnostic and prognostic utility of the CLTR-RLTR relationship in cases in which overall level of performance measures such as TR approximate normal but complaints of memory problems persist is considerable.

Although at least one study (Levin & Grossman, 1976) has used the CLTR/LTR parameter in the examination of the performance of head-injured patients, the relationship between CLTR and RLTR has not been emphasized; nor have changes in the relationship between RLTR and CLTR been examined as a function of recovery. The purpose of the present study was to investigate the effects of recovering cognitive processing and memory on the various SR scoring parameters. In keeping with Buschke's (1984) sentiment that processing deficits are at the core of much of what appears to be memory failure, it was hypothesized that CLTR, or the ratio of CLTR to LTR, would best distinguish the performance of closed-head-injury survivors from that of normal controls. Additionally, CLTR and CLTR/LTR should be particulary sensitive and discriminating indices of cognitive processing deficits at follow-up testing, where improvements in TR may create an overly optimistic picture of improvement in memory functioning.

A second goal of this study was to assess the predictive utility of the Average Impairment Rating (AIR), a summary statistic based on the average value of a number of key neuropsychological tests expressed in standard deviation units (Rennick, cited in Russell, Neuringer, & Goldstein, 1970). It seemed reasonable to assume that early test results would more accurately predict later cognitive functioning than would a physical measure (i.e., length of unconsciousness) from which severity of injury is inferred.

METHOD

Subjects and Procedure

Subjects included 21 closed-head-injured (CHI) patients who were tested twice with the SR procedure as part of comprehensive neuropsychological examinations. The majority of the CHI subjects were inpatients at a rehabilitation hospital when tested although many of the followup testings were completed on an outpatient basis. All CHI subjects suffered a loss of consciousness of at least 2 days (range 2-60 days, $M = 27.6$, $SD = 17.0$). Because these subjects were initially admitted to a variety of hospitals in the southeastern Michigan area, coma was variously defined and inconsistently documented, and unconsciousness was medically maintained (with barbiturates) in some cases but not others. Nevertheless, all subjects were reportedly unresponsive for at least 48 hours and were therefore considered to have suffered severe to extremely severe closed head injuries (Jennett & Teasdale, 1981, p. 90). CT and other neurodiagnostic data allowing for the determination of focal lesions in addition to the diffuse involvement characteristic of CHI were inconsistently available and were therefore not considered in the analysis. All of the subjects were judged to be free from aphasia, although some were dysarthric and/or evidenced mild language inefficiencies.

Each of the CHI subjects was tested within 6 months after regaining consciousness

($M = 108$ days, $SD = 43$, range 33-183), and then at least 1 year after return of consciousness ($M = 515$ days, $SD = 133$, range $= 367$-876). Time from return of consciousness to test was used instead of time from injury to test because the latter confounds length of unconsciousness with time since injury. The CHI subjects ranged in age from 14 to 53 years when first tested, had a mean of 12 years of education, and included 12 males and 9 females. Twenty-one inpatient volunteers served as the control group. These subjects had no history of head trauma, neurological disease, substance abuse, or diagnosed psychiatric problems, and were all suffering from chronic, disabling conditions requiring physical therapy. Patients and controls did not differ in terms of sex ratio, age, or years of education (see Table 1).

Table 1
Demographic Variable Comparisons of Patients and Controls

Variable	Patients at Testing 1	Patients at Testing 2	Controls
Sex	M 12 F 9	M 12 F 9	M 13 F 8
Age	M 25.6 SD 10.1	M 26.7 SD 10.1	M 26.4 SD 9.7
Education (years)	M 12.0 SD 1.9	M 12.0 SD 1.9	M 12.6 SD 2.1

Material
The selective reminding (SR) procedure consisted of 12 words and involved a maximum of 9 trials. Instructions were in accordance with the procedure outlined by Buschke (1973). All words were of AA frequency (Thorndike & Lorge, 1944) and were controlled for meaningfulness (Paivio, Yuille, & Madigan, 1968). Six of the words were highly imageable and concrete: bird, girl, door, body, corner, and table. The other six words were more abstract and less imageable: mind, method, interest, chance, position, and history (Paivio et al., 1968).

Following trial 5 of the SR procedure, a yes-no recognition trial was conducted. It was comprised of the 12 list words and 12 distractor words. The distractor words were controlled in a manner similar to the list words in terms of imageability, concreteness, frequency, and meaningfulness (Thorndike & Lorge, 1944; Paivio et al., 1968). The imageable and concrete distractor words were as follows: dress, cat, skin, car, house, and tree. The more abstract and less imageable distractor words were truth, opinion, duty, soul, idea, and knowledge.

Performance on the recognition trial enabled the calculation of signal detection parameters, and subsequent estimation of the average strength of the old (target) words (d') as well as biases in making judgments on the recognition probe (Egan, 1975; Levin et al., 1982). The response bias (RB) measure consisted of subtracting the false alarm rate from the miss (i.e., incorrect rejection) rate. This resulted in all values of response bias falling between $+1$ and -1, with $+1$ indicating the most conservative approach (i.e., saying "no" to all words), and -1 indicating the most uncritical or liberal approach (i.e., saying "yes" to all words). A score of 0 indicated perfect performance on recognition testing (i.e., 12 hits, 12 correct rejections, 0 false alarms, and 0 misses).

To reduce proactive interference effects caused by the recognition probe, all 12 of the target words were read prior to trial 6 of the SR procedure. Testing continued in accordance with SR instructions until the criterion of 12 correct words in a trial was obtained, or until trial 9 was completed. The scoring parameters derived from the data were d', RB, TR, LTS, and CLTR. Additionally, the ratio of CLTR to LTR (CLTR/LTR) was also calculated in order to determine the proportion of LTR that reflected organized list learning (Buschke & Fuld, 1974) independent of subject differences in amount of LTR.

RESULTS

Patients' versus Controls' Performance at Testing 1

A fixed one-way MANOVA using Hotelling's T^2 criterion was performed to compare control and CHI groups at first testing. Group membership was the independent variable and LTS, CLTR, CLTR/LTR, TR, d', and RB were the dependent variables. The analysis indicated that mean vectors of the groups differed significantly, $F(6, 32) = 20.76$, $p < .001$. Average group performances on each dependent variable, as well as t values and associated significance levels

Table 2
Performance of Patients and Controls on Memory Variables at First Testing

Variable	Patients	Controls	t
LTS	M 32.67 SD 22.19	M 85.38 SD 13.26	9.34**
CLTR	M 11.09 SD 11.65	M 73.61 SD 21.97	11.54**
CLTR/LTR	M 0.33 SD 0.22	M 0.86 SD 0.14	8.21**
TR	M 46.33 SD 17.88	M 91.00 SD 10.31	9.91**
d'	M 1.98 SD 1.83	M 5.39 SD 0.92	7.15**
RB	M 0.22 SD 0.33	M 0.03 SD 0.09	-2.35*

Note.
LTS: Words in long-term storage, summed across trials.
CLTR: Words consistently recalled after having entered long-term storage, summed across trials.
CLTR/ CLTR divided by total number of words recalled from long-term storage, both
LTR: consistently and inconsistently.

TR: Total number of words recalled (i.e., total short-term recall plus total long-term recall), summed across trials.

d′: A measure of the ability to distinguish list from distractor words. Values range from -6 to +6, the latter is optimal performance.

RB: Response bias, calculated by subtracting the false alarm rate from the false negative rate. Values range form -1 to +1; the former indicates a totally positive response bias, the latter indicates a totally negative response bias, and a value of 0 indicates no response bias.

$n = 21$ for each of patient and control groups.

*$p < .05$. ** $p < .001$.

are presented in Table 2. Inspection of these data indicates superior performance by the control group on all variables, and a distinctly conservative RB in the recognition memory performance of the CHI group.

Results of a discriminant function analysis on these data are contained in Table 3. This analysis indicated that CLTR best discriminated between the CHI and control groups, and was more strongly correlated with the discriminant function than was the next best discriminator, TR, $t(35) = 2.74$, $p < .01$. Overall, the discriminant function distinguished CHI subjects from controls subjects very well, with χ^2 (6, $N = 39$) = 51.74, $p < .0001$. Twenty of the 21 controls (95.2%) and 19 of the 21 CHI subjects (90.5%) were correctly classified, for a classification rate of 92.7%.

Table 3
Results of a Discriminant Function of Memory Variables at Testing 1

Predictor variable	Correlations of predictor variables with discriminant function	Univariate $F(1,37)$
LTS	.76	82.51
CLTR	.93	124.20
CLTR/LTR	.74	79.28
TR	.83	99.10
d'	.62	56.26
RB	-.21	6.31
Canonical R	.89	
Eigenvalue	3.89	

Pooled within-group correlations among predictors

Predictor variable	LTS	CLTR	CLTR/LTR	TR	d	RB
LTS	1.00	.74	.50	.82	.62	-.13
CLTR		1.00	.68	.77	.48	-.11
CLTR/LTR			1.00	.52	.13	.05
TR				1.00	.68	.01
d'					1.00	.05
RB						1.00

Correlations among the memory variables are also contained in Table 3. Because these correlations were generally quite high, a stepwise discriminant function analysis was performed to determine which variable would contribute to discriminant power once variance associated with the other variables was partialled out. The variables retained by the stepwise analysis, in descending order of discriminatory power were as follows: CLTR, $F(1, 37) = 124.5$; d', $F(2, 36) = 63.38$; and CLTR/LTR, $F(3, 35) = 43.35$.

CHI Group Improvement from First to Second Testing

Paired t tests were performed on each variable to determine if these measures of memory functioning evidenced improvement from first to second testing. Results (Table 4) of these analyses demonstrated significant improvement in LTS, CLTR, TR, and d'. Changes in CLTR/LTR and RB were not significant.

Table 4
Patients' Improvement on Memory Variables from Testing 1 to Testing 2

Variable	Testing 1		Testing 2		t
LTS	M	32.67	M	63.43	5.81**
	SD	22.19	SD	25.80	
CLTR	M	11.09	M	30.57	3.65*
	SD	11.65	SD	29.37	
CLTR/LTR	M	0.33	M	0.47	1.54
	SD	0.22	SD	0.29	
TR	M	46.33	M	68.81	5.60**
	SD	17.88	SD	18.66	
d'	M	1.98	M	4.04	4.06*
	SD	1.83	SD	1.35	
RB	M	0.22	M	0.18	-0.15
	SD	0.33	SD	0.22	

$n = 21$.
*p<.005. **p<.0001.

Patients' Performance at Testing 2 versus Controls' Performance

Since memory test performance improved markedly from first to second testing for the CHI subjects, a comparison of second testing with control group results was performed. The MANOVA indicated significant group differences according to Hotelling's T^2 criterion, F (6, 35) = 5.58, $p<.001$. Mean group performances on each of the memory variables are presented in Table 5, as are t values and associated significance levels. As is evident in these analyses, the CHI group was still significantly inferior to the controls approximately 17 months after regaining consciousness, and continued to evidence a conservative response bias in recognition testing.

Table 5
Memory Performance of Patients at Second Testing versus Controls

Variable	Patients		Controls		t
LTS	M	63.43	M	85.38	3.46*
	SD	25.80	SD	13.26	
CLTR	M	30.57	M	73.61	5.38**
	SD	29.37	SD	21.92	
CLTR/LTR	M	0.47	M	0.86	5.51**
	SD	0.29	SD	0.14	
TR	M	68.81	M	91.00	4.77**
	SD	18.66	SD	10.31	
d'	M	4.04	M	5.39	3.78*
	SD	1.35	SD	0.92	
RB	M	0.18	M	0.03	-2.99*
	SD	0.22	SD	0.10	

$n = 21$ for each of patient and control groups.
* $p < .01$. ** $p < .0001$.

The variables which best discriminated between CHI subjects at testing 2 and the control group were determined by discriminant function analysis. Results of this analysis (Table 6) indicated that CLTR/LTR was marginally more correlated with the discriminant function than was CLTR, $t (39) = .70$, n.s. However, both CLTR/LTR and CLTR were more strongly correlated with the discriminant function than was the third best variable, TR. These differences were significant for CLTR/LTR versus TR, $t (39) = 3.24, p < .01$, as well as for CLTR versus TR, $t (39) = 3.56, p < .001$. It should be noted the second t ratio was larger than the first because the correlation between CLTR and TR was greater (.95) than the correlation between CLTR/LTR and TR (.87).

As in the initial comparison between control and CHI groups at testing 1, the discriminant function distinguished between controls and the patients at second testing quite well, $\chi^2 (6, N = 42) = 24.84, p < .001$. Eighteen of the 21 controls were correctly classified (86%) as were 18 of the 21 CHI subjects (86%).

Correlations among the memory variables are also shown in Table 6. As was the case at testing 1, the correlations among the SR variables were quite high, ranging from .65 to .95. In contrast, the correlation between the recognition memory parameters (d' and RB) was considerably greater (-.63) than that noted at testing 1 (.05). In view of these generally large correlations , a stepwise discriminant function analysis was conducted and only CLTR/LTR, $F (1, 40) = 30.39$, and d', $F (2, 39) = 17.11$, were retained.

Table 6
Results of a Discriminant Function of Memory Variables of
Patients at Testing 2 versus Controls

Predictor variable	Correlations of predictor variables with discriminant function	Univariate $F(1,40)$
LTS	.56	12.03
CLTR	.87	28.98
CLTR/LTR	.89	30.39
TR	.77	22.75
d'	.61	14.26
RB	.48	8.94
Canonical R	.70	
Eigenvalue	.96	

Pooled within-group correlations among predictors

Predictor variable	LTS	CLTR	CLTR/LTR	TR	d'	RB
LTS	1.00	.82	.65	.90	.51	-.51
CLTR		1.00	.90	.95	.45	-.46
CLTR/LTR			1.00	.87	.31	-.38
TR				1.00	.47	-.53
d'					1.00	-.63
RB						1.00

Early Prediction of Later Memory Performance
Duration of unconsciousness was compared to AIR score at first testing as predictors of memory performance at testing 2. CLTR/LTR was used as the criterion because it best distinguished the CHI group from the controls at testing 2. AIR score at testing 1 was more strongly correlated with the criterion than was duration of unconsciousness (-.63 vs. -.50) but this difference was not significant, $t(18) = -.91$, n.s.

Table 7 presents correlations among length of unconsciousness, memory variables, and AIR scores for the CHI group at both testings. Inspection of Table 7 indicates that AIR score was consistently more strongly correlated with the memory variables than was length of unconsciousness.

DISCUSSION

In keeping with the findings of previous research (e.g., Levin, Kalisky, Handel, Goldman, Eisenberg, Morrison, & Von Laufen, 1985; Shore, 1981; Tabaddor, Mattis, & Zazula, 1984), the results of the present study confirmed impaired SR and recognition memory performances within 6 months and after more than 1 year following severe closed-head injury. Earlier studies failing to demonstrate

Table 7

Correlations of Patients' Coma Durations and AIR Scores at each Testing
with their Memory Variable Scores at each Testing

Testing 1

Variable	Length of unconsciousness	AIR score
LTS	-.38*	-.68***
CLTR	-.39*	-.65***
CLTR/LTR	-.26	-.35
TR	-.31	-.64***
d'	-.34	-.45*
RB	.08	.00

Testing 2

Variable	Length of unconsciousness	AIR score
LTS	-.11	-.47*
CLTR	-.46*	-.59**
CLTR/LTR	-.50**	-.60**
TR	-.39*	-.57**
d'	.03	-.17
RB	.10	.43*

* $p < .05$. ** $p < .01$. *** $p < .001$.

impaired SR performance have examined mild head injury cases (e.g., Levin & Eisenberg, 1979; Levin et al., 1982; McLean et al., 1983) or have employed shorter than optimal lists (Kraemer et al., 1983) of unknown difficulty level (e.g., McLean et al., 1983), raising the possibility of ceiling effects.

Consistent with earlier reports (e.g., Kraemer et al., 1983; Loring, cited in Loring and Papanicolaou, 1987), SR parameters were highly correlated in the present data. This high degree of dependence between the various scores has been the basis of criticism that the SR procedure is inadequate to address purportedly distinct memory processes such as storage and retrieval (Kraemer et al., 1983). In fact, the correlated SR scores argue most cogently against simplistic reliance on face-valid scores as sources of inference about underlying processes. These processes are conceptually dependent upon any and all stages preceding them in the temporal course of information flow. Buschke himself has cautioned that retrieval is dependent upon the adequacy of storage. In turn, cognitive processing or encoding deficits may well be the cause of both storage and retrieval deficits (Buschke, 1984).

The present findings strongly support the utility of Buschke's (1974) item (RLTR) versus list (CLTR) learning distinction by demonstrating a preponderance of the less efficient RLTR relative to CLTR in the SR performances of head-injured subjects. While CLTR was shown to improve over the course of the time between first and second testings, a disproportionate amount of essentially unorganized, random long-term retrieval (RLTR) remained. This was evident in the failure of CLTR/LTR to improve significantly between the two testings, despite highly significant improvements in CLTR and the other SR scoring parameters. This stands in marked contrast to the performance of normals who evidenced little RLTR (Buschke & Fuld, 1974; the present study).

Buschke posits that RLTR reflects item learning, which is inefficient and inconsistently recalled because of underlying failure to associate list items together or with material already in LTS. This failure to organize is held to frequently result from cognitive processing deficits (Buschke, 1984) which may be underestimated when summary scores such as TR or percent correct are employed instead of more refined analyses of the various types of learning. In support of this, CLTR best discriminated controls from CHI subjects at first testing, and CLTR and CLTR/LTR were roughly equal in discriminatory power at testing 2 in the current sample. TR had significantly less discriminatory power than CLTR at testing 1, and CLTR and CLTR/LTR at testing 2. This would suggest that TR is a less useful measure of extent of memory dysfunction than are other readily obtainable SR parameters. While the current data are based on a modified version of the standard SR procedure, it is likely that the interpolated recognition probe and subsequent re-reading of the entire list would increase CLTR and consequently attenuate the predictive utility of both CLTR and CLTR/LTR. Nevertheless, future studies that employ the more conventional Buschke procedure are necessary to determine potential limitations in the generalization of these findings to conventional SR procedure contexts.

Improved memory functioning was noted on many SR and recognition memory parameters over the course of the current study. Although practice effects cannot be categorically ruled out, their influence would seem to be minimized by patients' very poor memory at initial testing, as well as by the minimum 6-month test-retest interval. Patients' global level of performance (i.e., TR) improved significantly, as did LTS and CLTR. In the case of LTS, the little research that has been published regarding improvement after head injury (McLean et al., 1983) has yielded results that are consistent with the current data. Only one single-case study (Levin, Handel, Goldman, Eisenberg, & Guinto, 1985) has investigated CLTR changes across serial testings. These authors found little systematic change across five yearly assessments. The fact that the first testing was not completed until 1 year postinjury may have resulted in missing any improvement occurring during the first 12 months.

The present serial testing data demonstrate improved recognition memory performance as reflected in d' and RB changes. These findings are consistent with those of Shore (1981) but at odds with those of Tabaddor et al. (1984) who failed to document improvement in d' following closed-head injury. Possible reasons for this inconsistency include procedural differences as well as subject differences. In the Tabaddor et al. study, the recognition task was not described in detail but was presented to the subjects "every four trials" (p. 702). This raises the possibility of overlearning or practice effects not likely to be encountered in the present study. Additionally, subjects in the Tabaddor et al. study were classified as moderately to severely injured while present study subjects ranged from severely to extremely severely injured. The inherent variability across head injured subjects (Brooks, Deelman, Van Zomeren, Van Harskamp, & Aughton, 1984) may have mitigated against finding significant change in the earlier study.

The previously documented relationship between severity of injury and SR performance (e.g., Levin et al., 1982; Levin & Eisenberg, 1979) was also confirmed in this study, although the present results suggest that AIR is a marginally better predictor of later memory performance than is length of unconsciousness. This finding is of considerable practical significance in that Glasgow Coma Scale scores are sometimes not obtained in the acute care facilities, and length of unconsciousness is commonly reported only anecdotally in patient records. The demonstration of the prognostic utility of test-based measures essentially reduces dependence on sources of information which are not under the neuropsychologist's control, and will hopefully encourage further research in this surprisingly dormant area of investigation. Nevertheless, it is clear that length of unconsciousness remains a useful prognostic indicator, particularly in the initial phase of hospitalization and for patients who are untestable.

Perhaps the most clinically significant finding of the present study was the dissociation between CLTR and CLTR/LTR. While both measures improved over the course of recovery monitored, the change was not significant in the case of CLTR/LTR. The relative stability of this ratio in the face of highly significant improvements in other SR scoring parameters is seen to be the result of increases in RLTR at a rate sufficient to prevent the CLTR/LTR ratio from reflecting any major change. In essence, while summary measures of memory such as TR improve following head injury, a disproportionate amount of this improvement consists of inefficient item learning as reflected in RLTR. This finding lends credence to the often encountered complaints of poor memory from patients whose scores approximate normal on tests which do not lend themselves to a more detailed analysis of underlying mnemonic processes. It is also suggested that commonly employed summary measures such as TR, percent correct, and trials to criterion may be misleading, particularly as these summary measures begin to approximate normal levels. The value of including some index of cognitive processing efficiency, in this case list as opposed to item learning, is highlighted by the present study. While CLTR/LTR is an indirect expression of underlying organizational processes, this ratio provides ready access to the quality and efficiency of memory, and provides information not obtainable from more global measures.

REFERENCES

Bond, M. R. (1975). Assessment of psychosocial outcome after severe injury. In CIBA Foundation Symposium nr. 34, *Outcome of Severe Damage to the CNS* (pp. 141-157). Amsterdam: Elsevier.

Brooks, D. N., Deelman, B. G., Van Zomeren, A. H., Van Harskamp, F., & Aughton, M. E. (1984). Problems in measuring cognitive recovery after acute brain injury. *Journal of Clinical Neuropsychology, 6*, 71-85.

Buschke, H. (1973). Selective reminding for analysis of memory and learning. *Journal of Verbal Learning and Behavior, 12*, 543-550.

Buschke, H. (1974). Retrieval in verbal learning. *Transactions of the New York Academy of Sciences, 36*, 721-729.

Buschke, H. (1984). Control of cognitive processing. In L. R. Squire & N. Butters (Eds.), *Neuropsychology of memory* (pp. 33-40). New York: Guilford Press.

Buschke, H. & Fuld, P. (1974). Evaluating storage, retention and retrieval in disordered memory and learning. *Neurology, 24*, 1019-1025.

Egan, J. P. (1975). *Signal detection theory and ROC analysis*. New York: Academic Press.

Flavell, J.H. (1970). Developmental studies of mediated memory. In H. Reese & L Lipsett (Eds.), *Advances in child development and behavior* (Vol. 5, pp. 181-211). New York: Academic Press.

Gronwall, D. & Wrightson, P. (1981). Memory and information processing capacity after closed-head injury. *Journal of Neurology, Neurosurgery, and Psychiatry, 44*, 889-895.

Hasher, I.M., & Zacks, R.T. (1979). Automatic and effortful processes in memory. *Journal of Experimental Psychology, General, 80*, 356-388.

Hulicka, I., & Grossman, J.L. (1967). Age-group comparisons for the use of mediators in paired associate learning. *Journal of Gerontology, 22*, 46-51.

Hultsch, D.F. (1971). Adult age differences in free classification and recall. *Developmental Psychology, 4*, 338-342.

Jennett, B., & Teasdale, G. (1981). *Management of head injuries*. Philadelphia: F. A. Davis.

Kohl, D., & Brandt, J. (1985). An automatic encoding deficit in the amnesia of Korsakoff's syndrome. In D.S. Olton, E. Gamzu, & S. Corkin (Eds.), *Memory dysfunctions: An integration of animal and human research from preclinical and clinical perspectives* (Vol. 444, pp. 460-462). New York: The New York Academy of Sciences.

Kraemer, H. C., Peabody, C. A., Tinklenberg, J. R., & Yesavage, J. A. (1983). Mathematical and empirical development of a test of memory for clinical and research use. *Psychological Bulletin, 94*, 367-380.

Levin, H. S., Benton, A. L., & Grossman, K. S. (1982). *Neurobehavioral consequences of closed head injury*. New York: Oxford University Press.

Levin, H. S. & Eisenberg, H. M. (1979). Neuropsychological outcome of closed head injury in children and adolescents. *Child's Brain, 5*, 282-292.

Levin, H. S. & Grossman, R. G. (1976). Storage and retrieval. *Journal of Pediatric Psychology, 1*, 38-42.

Levin, H. S., Handel, S. F., Goldman, A. M., Eisenberg, H. M., & Guinto, F. C. Jr. (1985). Magnetic resonance imaging after diffuse nonmissile head injury. *Archives of Neurology, 42*, 963-968

Levin, H. S., Kalisky, Z., Handel, S. F., Goldman, A. M., Eisenberg, H. M., Morrison, D., & Von Laufen, A. (1985). Magnetic resonance imaging in relation to the sequelae and rehabilitation of diffuse closed head injury: Preliminary findings. *Seminars in Neurology, 5*, 221-232.

Loring, D. W., & Papanicolaou, A. C. (1987). Memory assessment in neuropsychology: Theoretical considerations and practical utility. *Journal of Clinical and Experimental*

Neuropsychology, 9, 340-358.

McLean, Jr. A., Temkin, N. R., Dikmen, S., & Wyler, A. R. (1983). The behavioral sequelae of head injury. *Journal of Clinical Neuropsychology, 5*, 361-376.

Paivio, A., Yuille, J. C., & Madigan, S. A. (1968). Concreteness, imagery, and meaningfulness values for 925 nouns. *Journal of Experimental Psychology Monograph Supplement, 76*, 1-25.

Russell, E. W., Neuringer, C. & Goldstein, G. (1970). *Assessment of brain damage: A neuropsychological key approach.* New York: Wiley Interscience.

Shore, D. (1981, February). *Memory impairment following head injury: Differential changes over time in several basic processes.* Paper presented at the meeting of the International Neuropsychological Society, Pittsburgh, PA.

Smith, A.D. (1977). Adult age differences in cued recall. *Developmental Psychology, 13*, 326-331.

Tabaddor, K., Mattis, S. & Zazula, T. (1984). Cognitive sequelae and recovery course after moderate and severe head injury. *Neurosurgery, 14*, 701-708.

Thorndike, E. L. & Lorge, I. (1944). *The teacher's word book of 30,000 words.* New York: Bureau of Publications, Teacher's College.

Van Zomeren, A. H. (1981). *Reaction time and attention after closed head injury.* Lisse: Swets and Zeitlinger.

Journal of Clinical Neuropsychology
1981, Vol. 3, No. 1, 79-99

Neuropsychology and Cluster Analysis:
Potentials and Problems*

Robin Morris and Roger Blashfield
University of Florida

Paul Satz
University of Victoria

ABSTRACT

This report presents a selective overview of the cluster analysis literature and its potential uses in neuropsychology. In addition, an actual problem involving data from the Florida Longitudinal Project is presented to provide a practical example of many of the processes and problems involved in cluster analytic techniques. It is hoped that the reader will gain a theoretical and practical understanding of such methods and their potential usefulness in neuropsychology and other related areas.

Neuropsychology and cluster analysis are two topics which have recently enjoyed increased attention by scientists. There are numerous areas in neuropsychology where subject classification based on multivariate data could be beneficial (laterality, neurolinguistics, aphasic disorders, schizophrenia, etc.). Cluster analysis is a quasi-statistical technique which can be used on multivariate data in order to create such classifications. For example, research by Schwartz, Ramos, and John (1976) has used cluster-analytic techniques to classify evoked potential patterns in cats. Kertesz and Phipps (1977) have used clustering to classify aphasic patients based on their performance on an aphasia examination. Probably the area in neuropsychology that has experienced the greatest use of cluster-analytic techniques has been that of learning disabilities.

Doehring and Hoshko (1977) and Doehring, Hoshko, and Bryans (1979) have used Q-type factor analysis and hierarchical agglomerative clustering techniques in an ongoing research program to identify subtypes of reading-disabled children based on extensive reading-related tests. In related investigations, Petrauskas and

* The authors wish to thank Drs. Kenneth Adams, Jack Fletcher, Byron Rourke and the other journal reviewers for their very helpful criticisms of this paper.

Rourke (1979) and Fisk and Rourke (1979) have used Q-type factor analysis to identify subtypes of learning-disabled children based on the results of an extensive neuropsychological test battery. The use of cluster analysis has been directed to both validating classification systems which have developed clinically and to creating new systems which can then be used for research. Valid and reliable classification systems are needed to strengthen the foundation upon which neuropsychology will build its theoretical basis.

This paper is intended as a tutorial to describe cluster analysis to researchers working in the area of neuropsychology. In order to accomplish this goal, the paper is divided into two sections: (1) an overview of the cluster analytic literature; and (2) an example analysis of multivariate data from a learning-disabled population.

PART 1: CLUSTER ANALYSIS

Cluster analysis is a generic term referring to a loosely connected family of methods which generate classifications.[1] Cluster-analytic methods attempt to form groups of subjects which are relatively homogeneous. Thus, these methods can be used as descriptive techniques in order to explore the structure of multivariate data sets.

The major use of clustering techniques in the biological and social sciences only began in the 1960s with the publication of *Principles of Numerical Taxonomy* by Sokal and Sneath (1963). Since that time, clustering techniques have expanded into the areas of psychology, anthropology, sociology, the humanities, information sciences, pattern recognition, education, and medicine.

A general overview of the literature on cluster analysis leads to the following conclusions. (1) There is a problem with inconsistent terminology, labeling, and thus communication. (2) There are innumerable methods and combinations of methods, some of which have been described but never used, and many of which have been neither critically examined nor widely accepted. (3) Different classification problems can require different methods and create different problems which are not always apparent. (4) There are about as many computer software programs for cluster analysis as there are methods; the algorithms, documentation, and ease of use vary across the many programs. (5) Little attempt has been made to validate and examine cluster results critically, mainly because validation is a

---

[1] The use of the term "classification" in this paper refers to the act of forming categories of subjects or to the resultant act. In contrast, the terms "identification" and "diagnosis" refer to the process of assigning a subject to an existing set of categories. Biologists have consistently recognized this distinction (Simpson, 1961). Unfortunately, statisticians have not. Hence, discriminant analysis, which is actually an identification procedure using this terminology, often has been inappropriately called a classification procedure.

complex process. (6) "Naive empiricism" is increasingly prevalent in applied uses of cluster analysis. (7) Clustering methods are not built upon a firm statistical theory or well-tested foundation; these methods, almost without exception, are heuristic.

In order to introduce the various clustering methods, seven major classes of cluster-analytic procedures will be described. These are: (1) hierarchical agglomerative methods; (2) hierarchical divisive methods; (3) iterative partitioning techniques; (4) density-searching techniques; (5) factor-analysis variants; (6) clumping techniques; and, (7) graphic techniques. Within each of these major clustering classes, there are numerous specific methods. Each of the seven major classes represents different views of how clusters are defined (McQuitty, 1967), and how homogeneous groups can be discovered (Anderberg, 1973).

(1) When using *hierarchical agglomerative methods*, a researcher is faced with three decisions. These are the selection of (a) one, among many, similarity, associational, or distance measures; (b) the method for combining subjects into clusters; and (c) the optimal number of clusters in a data set.

The first step, the choice of the most appropriate similarity measure, is important for both theoretical and practical reasons. Theoretically, similarity is a concept central to the structure of any classification. Hartigan (1967) and Tversky (1977) discuss major theoretical issues surrounding the measurement of similarity. Particular similarity measures are only appropriate for certain data types. An important practical issue is that different similarity measures can lead to different results when the same data and clustering methods are used. Correlation has been shown to be more useful for data where the pattern of the subject's profile is important. A distance measure is more appropriate when elevation across variables is an important consideration and pattern similarity is less crucial. All similarity measures involve a trade-off between profile pattern and elevation (Skinner, 1978). Reviews of similarity/dissimilarity coefficients are provided by Hetler (1976), Carroll and Field (1974), Cormack (1971), and Everitt (1980). Unfortunately, these reviews offer no clear rules about which coefficients are to be preferred.

The second issue involved in using hierarchical agglomerative methods is the choice of a specific method for defining the similarity between groups of subjects. Agglomerative methods begin by combining the most similar pairs of observations into a cluster. The similarity/dissimilarity matrix is recomputed and this cluster is compared to the remaining observations (or other clusters). Again, the most similar entities are combined to form a cluster. Alternative hierarchical agglomerative methods each treat the definition of the distance between two clusters differently. For instance, single linkage methods define the similarity between clusters as the similarity between their closest members. Average linkage methods average the similarities between all members of each cluster. The minimum variance method (Ward, 1963) considers all possible combinations of clusters and combines clusters which minimize the increase in the error sum of squares. It has been shown, as would be expected, that these different methods can yield divergent solutions (Bartko, Strauss, & Carpenter, 1971).

The third basic decision, deciding on the stopping point in the clustering process which provides the most appropriate solution, has attracted little research and will be discussed in more detail at a later point.

Although hierarchical agglomerative methods are the most frequently used, they are not necessarily the best methods. Hierarchical solutions may not be appropriate for many data sets. Also, some statisticians have become disenchanted with the appropriateness of this family of methods (Hartigan, 1975).

(2) The *hierarchical divisive* methods use the reverse process of the hierarchical agglomerative methods. The initial matrix of observations is divided into two subsets. Each set can then be divided into further subsets, and so on. Since all possible divisions of the observations are not possible, except for small data sets, the usual method of forming clusters is through the successive splitting of clusters with the greatest heterogeneity. A problem with both types of hierarchical methods is that an ineffectual division (or grouping) at an early stage in the process is not corrected later.

(3) The *iterative partitioning* methods differ from the hierarchical techniques in that they are able to check cluster groups and relocate any misassigned subjects to a more appropriate cluster. The starting point of this process is a decision on the number of clusters (K = number of clusters) present in the data set. For a given K, estimates of the cluster centroids are found. Some procedures choose the first K subjects in the data set as estimates of the centroids; some choose centroids randomly; others choose K-observations which are furthest apart; and finally, some allow the researcher to specify his/her estimates. Subjects are assigned to the clusters with the most similar centroids, and new centroids are defined as the means of the resulting groupings. This process is repeated iteratively until a stable solution is found. Most iterative partitioning methods find solutions for a fixed number of clusters, although some allow for variability in the number of clusters (see Anderberg, 1973).

After all the observations have been allocated to clusters, each cluster is checked for observations which do not belong. This search is usually performed by the removal of the observations from the cluster, or by its placement into another cluster group. The decision to remove or place a particular observation into a cluster is generally based on optimizing a clustering criterion. Many of these criteria are derived from statistics used in the multivariate analysis of variance.

The major problems associated with iterative partitioning methods are that these methods are often affected by the choice of the initial partition, and that a truly exhaustive search of all partitions of a data set is enormously expensive.

(4) A fourth family of clustering methods is a collection of *density search* techniques. If one considers subjects as points in hyperspace, clusters can be conceptualized as relatively dense areas of points. Density search techniques seek out these dense modal areas. Many of these methods act like the single linkage method, but use various criteria to stop the inclusion of observations into a cluster. The TAXMAP method stops adding observations if the next observation's addition drops the average similarity of a cluster by an amount inconsistent with previous minor drops. Wishart's mode analysis (Wishart, 1969) uses a radius around a point which is gradually increased or decreased depending on "threshold values." Density techniques have been studied theoretically, but have been rarely used with applied data. Hence, the pragmatic characteristics of these methods are not well known.

(5) *Factor-analysis variants*, especially *Q-type factor analysis* (or inverse factor analysis), have been used in psychological research. These methods start by forming a correlation matrix of similarities among subjects. (Note: standard factor analysis, called R-mode, starts by forming a matrix of correlations among variables.) Factors are extracted from the correlation matrix, and various rotational techniques can be used. Subjects are assigned to clusters based upon their factor loadings.

The use of *Q*-type factor analysis has generated much controversy (Burt & Stephenson, 1939). The strongest proponents of its use have been Overall and Klett (1972) and Skinner (1977). These authors have favored the dimensional representation generated by these methods. Categorical representations derived from hierarchical methods are not always useful or appropriate. Criticisms of *Q*-type factoring include the implausible use of a linear model across subjects, the issue of multiple factor loadings, and the double centering of the data (Everitt, 1980; Fleiss, Lawlor, Platman, & Fieve, 1971). Outside of psychology, factor variants are used only rarely. Related ordination techniques which provide alternatives include principal-components analysis, multiple factor analysis, principal-coordinate analysis, nonmetric multidimensional scaling, and seriation (Sneath & Sokal, 1973).

(6) *Clumping* methods are special classification techniques which allow overlapping clusters. Clumping methods can be used in cases such as the classification of word meanings. These methods begin with the similarity-coefficient matrix. Observations are then compared to a randomly chosen observation and certain mathematical functions are used for inclusion criteria. Through the use of various starting points, many large and small groups are formed. These groups are then compared and interconnected. One problem with these methods is that the same groups may be found many times. Another problem is that clumping methods have had only limited usage, hence their characteristics are not well known (Jardine & Sibson, 1968).

(7) The final class of cluster-analytic techniques contains the *graphic* methods. With these methods, the 2-dimensional (sometimes 3-dimensional) representation of distances between observations is mapped. For example, the technique called the minimum spanning tree uses a branching tree in order to represent the structure of similarities among subjects. These methods also have had little applied use, and their potential is generally unknown.

The preceding discussion of cluster analytic methods was very brief and does not describe adequately the characteristics of specific methods. The best resource for further information about cluster analysis is contained in a small but readable book by Everitt (1980). Further information can be found in articles by Cormack (1971), Everitt (1979), Lance and Williams (1967), and in books by Sneath and Sokal (1973), Anderberg (1973), Hartigan (1975) and Clifford and Stephenson (1975).

PART 2: EXAMPLE WITH LEARNING DISABILITY DATA

An example of the application of cluster analysis can be developed from an examination of data studied by Satz, Morris, and Darby (Note 1). Researchers have long expected that a group of children who were exhibiting learning problems in school would constitute different subtypes which were identifiable based on neuropsychological measures (Satz & Morris, in press, a). It was thought that an objective classification of children with learning problems would help to promote better prediction, remediation, and theoretical understanding of learning disabilities. The following example is a methodological description of the use of cluster analysis applied to such data. A review of the specific findings of the particular study in question and their limitations in regard to subtypes of learning-disabled children is beyond the purpose and scope of this report.

In general, there are six major practical steps in any clustering problem: (1) the choice of the population; (2) the selection of variables (attributes); (3) the choice of similarity measure; (4) the determination of the clustering method; (5) the decision about the number of clusters present; and, (6) the validation of the results. Each of these steps will be described for the present example.

(1) *Subjects:* A major area of concern relates directly to subject selection. Subjects were all the white males who entered kindergarten during 1971-1972 in Alachua County, Florida (Satz, Taylor, Friel, & Fletcher, 1978). These subjects were followed during a seven-year longitudinal project and had extensive neuropsychological testing at kindergarten (KG), second (G2), and fifth grades (G5). This sample was felt to be adequate for the purpose of finding subtypes. Local subject characteristics, project attrition, and the use of only white male children are still limitations when making generalizations (Fletcher, Satz, & Morris, in press, b). It should be noted that, without standard randomized sampling techniques, it is

clearly possible to generate "unnatural" subgroups due to a biased sample.

The current problem was more complicated than the average classification problem since two steps of classification were required. The first step, which will be described only briefly, required the identification of those children within the subject population who showed low achievement at grade five. The sample was classified according to achievement levels (Darby, 1978) that were based on Wide Range Achievement Test (WRAT) scores. Those who were classified into the two lowest achievement clusters were identified as learning disabled ($n = 89$) and comprised the sample utilized for subtyping (Satz & Morris, in press, b).

(2) *Variables:* The selection of appropriate variables on which to cluster these learning-disabled subjects was the second consideration. Since all possible variables cannot be used, the purpose of variable selection is to maximize subtype differences. Decisions about variable selection can have a major impact on the results from a clustering study.

One characteristic that has been shown to be important in such choices is whether the frequency distribution of a variable is multimodal and/or skewed. Normally distributed variables do not suggest the presence of multiple populations. Another consideration in variable selection is the psychometric properties of the variables. Finally, theoretical relevance should be a primary concern.

Since this study was preliminary, and because past research has suggested vast numbers of dimensions on which learning-disabled children may be differentiated, only variables related to higher cognitive functions were utilized. These measures loaded highly on factors found in a factor analysis of the test battery used in this project (Fletcher & Satz, 1980). The use of factor scores would appear to be appealing, but such scores are normally distributed and, therefore, thought to be limiting in a clustering problem.

Variables related to abstract verbal conceptualizing, expressive verbal abilities, and visual-motor and visual-spatial abilities were used. These dimensions were represented by the Similarities subtest of the WISC-R (SIM), a Verbal Fluency Test (VF), a Recognition Discrimination Test (R-D), and the Berry Test of Visual Motor Integration (VMI). These measures are well known and have been shown through numerous factor-analytic and predictive studies to be valid measures of children across the ages involved (Fletcher et al., in press, a). Actual reliability coefficients have only been reported for the Similarities subtest and the Berry Test of Visual Motor Integration for children. The variables did deviate significantly from a normal distribution for the learning-disabled sample (Kolmogorov-Smirnov D-Statistic, Stevens, 1974). An additional rationale for these choices was to restrict the number of tests in order to reduce redundancy and random error variance, and to increase cluster (subtype) interpretability.

(3) *Similarity:* The third choice is of an adequate measure of similarity between subjects. As previously described, pattern and elevation are considerations in any

decision. In the present example, it was felt that elevation would be a critical factor and a distance measure would be more appropriate. This was due to the consideration that two children may have the exact same pattern of performances (a correlation of 1.00), but if one performs at a superior level, while the other at a deficit level, they may be very different from a clinical point of view. For this reason, correlation was not chosen. Instead, squared Euclidean distance was selected as the similarity/dissimilarity measure (see Fleiss & Zubin, 1969).

(4) *Cluster Methods:* The next basic step involved the choice of the clustering method. Since this data analysis was intended primarily as a demonstration, the decision was made to use the most popular of the clustering methods – the hierarchical agglomerative techniques. In addition, an iterative partitioning method was used on the results of the hierarchical methods.

The computer software program chosen in this study was CLUSTAN (version IC2, Wishart, 1975). This program is the most versatile of the many software programs for cluster analysis, is reasonably well documented, and is gaining fairly wide distribution (Blashfield, Aldenderfer, & Morey, in press).

(5) *Number of Clusters:* The first actual data analysis was performed using the average linkage, hierarchical agglomerative method, with squared Euclidean distance as the measure of similarity. In order to decide on the number of clusters (subtypes) present in the results, three types of results were examined. These included the hierarchical tree (Figure 1), the clustering coefficient (Table 1), and the cluster profile means for the different clusters (Table 2).

The hierarchical tree can be useful with some experience. If one reviews the trees in Figure 2, a number of important points can be made. In tree 2-A, a process called 'chaining' has occurred. This result is common and suggests that the method has not found clusters, but instead a few outliers. Figure 2-B is an example from the other end of the spectrum of possible results. It clearly shows three clusters in the data. It should be kept in mind that, with hierarchical methods and their trees, there may be more than one level of subgroups (clusters) which may lead to an appropriate classification result. An example of this is shown in Figure 2-C. In this example, one may see results which suggest a two-cluster solution, with males falling in one cluster, and females in the other. If one moves further down the tree a four-cluster solution also looks adequate, with both males and females being broken down further into groups of left- and right-handers.

The clustering coefficients shown in Table 1 represent a metric related to the amount of variance accounted for at each step of the clustering process. If one were to graph these data, it is sometimes possible to see "jumps" in the values which are out of proportion to previous changes. These jumps suggest that the combining of the previous two clusters created a heterogenous cluster with extensive variance within the cluster. Therefore, one needs to look at the cluster

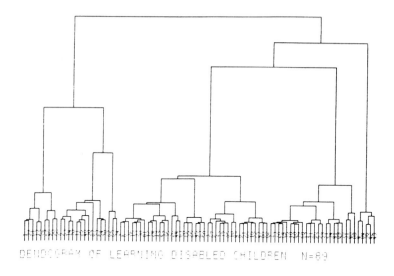

Fig. 1. Hierarchical tree using average linkage on learning disabled children.

TABLE 1

Cluster Coefficients of Four Hierarchical Agglomerative Methods

n of Clusters	Average Linkage	Minimum Variance	Furthest Neighbor	Centroid
13	0.914	2.421	1.938	0.693
12	0.948	2.465	1.955	0.779
11	1.133	3.474	1.997	0.825
10	1.144	3.898	2.205	0.859
9	1.163	4.354	2.858	1.030
8	1.316	4.648	3.062	1.037
7	1.353	4.899	3.263	1.057
6	1.357	4.943	3.292	1.178
5	1.797	8.411	3.310	1.714
4	2.004	14.748	4.838	1.766
3	2.465	15.210	5.911	2.550
2	4.229	22.725	8.565	2.966
1	4.622	49.627	15.496	3.239

solution before such jumps, when the cluster solution appears more homogeneous (small within-cluster variance).

In Table 1, the clustering coefficients for average linkage as well as for three

TABLE 2

Six-Cluster Solution Based on 'Average Linkage Method

Cluster	n	PPVT(a)**	SIM(b)	VF(c)	RD(d)	BVMI(e)	Read	WRAT* Spell	Math
1	32	86.8	6.3	18.1	17.1	88.5	−27.3	−31.0	−20.9
2	14	101.8	10.1	18.5	19.0	110.4	−20.8	−29.3	−20.9
3	5	79.2	5.6	10.6	8.0	71.0	−31.0	−31.8	−22.8
4	23	97.3	9.8	24.2	15.2	83.5	−24.9	−20.3	−28.3
5	12	106.7	11.0	35.8	20.5	99.0	−19.5	−26.7	−20.6
Outliers	3	102.0	10.7	36.3	19.0	145.0	−20.0	−28.3	−17.0
Learning	89	94.4	8.6	22.3	16.6	92.3	−24.4	−29.7	−20.7
Disabled	Std.	14.1	2.7	8.5	3.2	17.6	9.7	6.8	6.9
Total Population	236	103.5	10.9	27.7	18.4	106.2	1.3	−10.6	−10.8
at Grade 5	Std.	16.6	3.6	9.1	3.2	27.9	26.2	22.2	11.9

(a) Peabody Picture Vocabulary Test**
(b) Similarities
(c) Verbal Fluency
(d) Recognition - Discrimination
(e) Berry Visual Motor Integration

* WRAT scores are grade equivalent minus grade level in months.
** Used as an IQ marker and not for clustering.

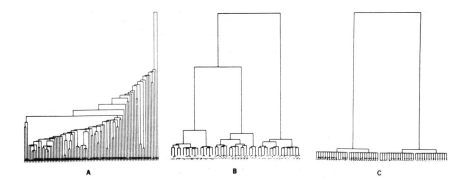

Fig. 2. Example hierarchical trees for demonstration.

other hierarchical methods are shown. From Table 1 and Figure 1, one begins to form some idea of the potential range of cluster solutions. In this example, we considered 3-cluster and 6-cluster results. Notice that this decision was subjective, and the reader may have a different impression. With this information, a review of each cluster's descriptive statistics and interrelationships can be helpful. In this process, one can trace which clusters combine at each step of the clustering process, decide if such combinations make sense, or if the method started to force two very different clusters together. All hierarchical agglomerative methods continue to combine clusters until there is but one cluster remaining. If the agglomerative methods force two clusters together with very unlike profiles, one needs to consider the solutions immediately preceding. From an analysis of the cluster centroids, a six-cluster solution apeared plausible. These six clusters from this first hierarchical agglomerative method were then subjected to a K-means iterative partitioning method.

This additional method took each subject out of its assigned cluster and then compared its similarity to each other cluster in order to determine the one to which it was most similar. The K-means method, therefore, attempts to clarify further a cluster solution. These changes are examined statistically and an attempt is made to reduce within-cluster variance and increase between-cluster variance. It also allows the investigator to examine the number of 'relocated' subjects which could give some idea of the stability of the solution. If many subjects are changing clusters during each iteration, one must wonder about the adequacy of the results. In our example, less than 15% of the subjects were actually placed in a different cluster, and there was very little change in the cluster profiles and make-up.

The six-cluster solution is shown in Figure 3. One will note that only the profiles for five clusters are given. Cluster six had a total of three subjects, but did not become incorporated into any of the larger clusters until a four-cluster solution. Following the recommendation of Everitt (1980), these subjects were considered "outliers" and were dropped from further consideration. "Outliers" may be

264

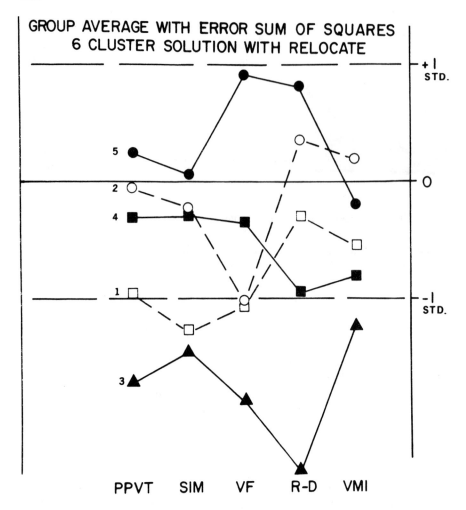

Fig. 3. Cluster patterns based on average linkage method.

viewed as resulting from measurement errors, or as being unique individuals for whom there are few, if any, comparison individuals in a given sample.

To summarize, by using cluster analysis, we have classified a group of 89 learning-disabled 5th-grade boys into five subtypes (clusters) which show different patterns of performance on four variables used to infer brain-behaviour relationships. These five subtypes have been reported by other researchers in the area (Satz, & Morris, in press, a). At this point, five of the general steps in any clustering problem have been completed. In each of these steps, the decisions made were based on subjective criteria where other researchers might have made legitimate alternative choices based on different valuations. The important point is that, without step six, validation, the results could be completely random or simply the self-fulfilling results of our biases.

(6) *Validation:* Internal validation procedures[2] are methods which seek to assess the adequacy and stability of a clustering solution. However, few such validation methods have been developed. The biases that do exist in many of these validation methods require the user to select carefully procedures that are compatible with the research purposes and clustering methodologies.

Three major classes of internal validation procedures have been identified in the literature: statistical measures, data manipulation procedures, and graphical methods. The first class, statistical measures, uses formulae which are designed to: (1) focus on the relationship between similarity matrices (cophenetic measures, Holgerson, 1978); (2) focus on the homogeneity of subjects within the resulting clusters (variance measures); (3) focus on the "tightness" of subjects in the multidimensional space (inter-point distance measures); or, (4) focus on maximum likelihood estimates for parameters of a specific clustering model. It should be noted that many of these statistical measures were not developed for validation, and their adequacy for such purposes is unknown.

Data manipulation procedures represent a wide variety of techniques designed to assess the generality of a clustering result. Manipulations can include the following: (1) cross-sample or split-sample replications; (2) data alteration through the addition or deletion of random variance via subjects or variables; or, (3) the use of external criterion procedures to describe how well a clustering solution discriminates among variables that were not used in the actual clustering. (The latter may also be considered to be concurrent validation.)

The final class of procedures, graphics, represents numerous attempts to allow the researchers to "see" how meaningful a clustering solution is. Examples of graphic techniques include the following: (1) the biplot, which plots clusters in principal component space; and, (2) the discriminant function plot, which graphs the clusters in discriminant space. There have been attempts at three-dimensional graphics. Graphical techniques have limitations due to the number of dimensions in most multivariate data used in cluster analysis and man's limited three-dimensional visual system.

In summary, validation methods can be used to investigate the relationship of a clustering solution to a specific theoretical framework of what a good classification is. At a minimum, some type of internal validation procedure must be used

---

[2] Internal validation refers to the evaluation of a clustering solution in its own right, without influence of subject matter (Dubes & Jain, 1980). Internal validation is the primary focus of the present review, unless otherwise noted. External validation refers to the more traditional forms of content, concurrent, and predictive validity which are subject-matter dependent and refer to the relevance of a classification.

after postulated cluster results are obtained because of the current limitations and the subjective decisions involved in the clustering process. A more detailed review of internal validation techniques in cluster analysis is provided by Dubes and Jain (1980). Unfortunately, most cluster-analytic studies in psychology and neuro-psychology have failed to use validation procedures of any type. Thus, the following step is discussed in some detail.

In the present example, the five clusters (outliers excluded) were used as a standard against which data manipulation, graphics, and statistical validation procedures were performed. Everitt (1980) suggests that a good solution should reappear under different clustering methods. This is not to imply that the exact results should be replicable under all types of cluster analysis. For our purposes, three additional hierarchical agglomerative methods were used: complete linkage, centroid, and minimum-variance.

The results showed that less than 11% of the subjects, using any of the methods, were placed in a different cluster. Two distance measures (Squared Euclidean Distance and Error Sum of Squares) yielded the same results within any specific hierarchical method. Even with this small number of subjects changing between solutions, it is important to look at the actual cluster descriptions, since a few subjects may greatly influence the mean profiles of small clusters and possibly change interpretations.

As a second procedure, a split-sample design was employed which randomly assigned the 89 children into two subsamples. The expectation was that the same subjects should cluster together, and that the subsamples should yield similar results as the standard. Fifteen percent of the subjects changed from their original clusters in split-samples 1 and 2. Due to the small number of subjects in some of these clusters, the actual cluster profiles did show some differences in their characteristics.

In the third procedure, a question was asked about the effect on the standard clusters if additional subjects were added and the data were reclustered. In the first addition, 12 children in an achievement subgroup (based on the original WRAT classifications) which showed a specific arithmetic deficit, but average ability in both reading and spelling skills, were added to the original 89 children. These 101 subjects were then subjected to the original procedure used for clustering.

All five of the original standard clusters maintained their original profiles, and only four percent of the original 89 subjects changed clusters. The 12 added children clustered into two clusters, with 33% going into cluster five while 50% went into cluster four. This result again supported the stability of the original cluster solution and also provided interesting information about possible processes involved in arithmetic deficits.

In the second addition, 25 children who averaged one standard deviation above the population norm on WRAT reading, spelling, and arithmetic were added to the original 89 children. These 114 children were clustered using the original procedures. On the basis of diagnostic and theoretical considerations, it was expected that average or above-average children would form a new cluster. These subjects did not fall into any deficit cluster and did form a new cluster of average or above-average abilities. Only 10% of the subjects from the original 89 changed clusters.

Next, it was asked what would happen if other variables were added to the four originally used in clustering. The two variables which loaded next highest on the factor analysis of the test battery at fifth grade, the Peabody Picture Vocabulary Test (PPVT) and the Embedded Figures Test (EF), were added to the original four variables. This resulted in a six-variable, 89-subject problem that was clustered using the original standard procedure. Less than 12% of the subjects changed clusters and the cluster means did not change appreciably. This result was expected due to the highly redundant nature of these two variables. Most of the other variables that were available were less reliable and were expected to add error variance and decrease the stability of the standard solution.

A more involved, but potentially useful method, a Monte Carlo simulation, was also utilized. Since clustering methods will find clusters even in random data, the development of a data set which mimics the known parameters of the original data, but includes randomly generated subject profiles, could provide useful information. With such a "random" data set, cluster results are compared to the original results. If the results from the randomly generated data set and from the real data set are very similar, one would begin to question the rejection of a null hypothesis of no clusters.

The creation of appropriate Monte Carlo data sets is a complex process. Data sets were generated that had the same number of subjects, variables, means and standard deviations, and the same covariance matrix as the original data set. The actual "subjects" within these data sets were generated through multivariate random numbers. Note that no actual cluster existed in these artificial data sets.

Table 3 presents a summary of the similarities between the cluster centroids generated on the actual child data and those generated on the Monte Carlo data. High similarity values (i.e., large correlation values [similar pattern] *and* small distances [similar elevation]) would suggest that the results could be based on a random clustering of the data. Three learning-disability clusters do have significant correlations (pattern) with a Monte Carlo cluster. Only one of these highly correlated clusters (LD cluster 5) also has a small Euclidean distance (elevation) with its Monte Carlo counterpart. These results do not support fully the null hypothesis that these clusters are based on a random clustering of the learning-disabled data. However, based on pattern similarities, they would tend to introduce some skepticism about the total cluster solution.

The use of external variables as criteria was the final validation method utilized. In this approach, clusters are tested with parametric (MANOVA, ANOVA, Duncan's) and nonparametric (Chi-square) procedures using various measures not used in the original clustering process as the dependent variables. Due to their redundancy, variables that are highly correlated with variables in the actual

TABLE 3

Relationship Between Learning Disability Clusters and Monte Carlo Clusters

Cluster From LD Sample	Highest Correlation with any Monte Carlo Cluster	Euclidean Distance between LD Cluster and Monte Carlo Cluster	Correlation/Euclidean Distance between LD Cluster and Sample Mean ($n = 89$)
1	.61	0.14	.78/0.16
2	.97*	2.28	.57/0.33
3	.97*	4.12	.03/2.54
4	.48	0.35	—.76/0.11
5	.89*	0.34	—.60/1.72
6	.85	1.62	.71/1.72

* $p < .05$.

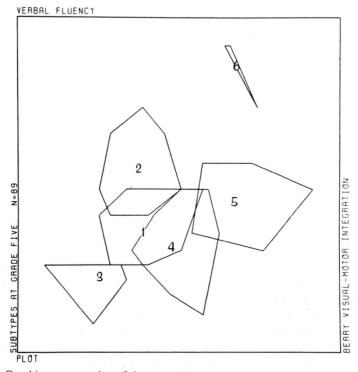

Fig. 4. Graphic representation of cluster results.

clustering process should not be selected for the sole validation criteria. The reliability and validity of the external measures are also important, since unreliable variables could lead to Type 2 errors. In the learning disability example, it was important for one subtype to be distinguishable from other subtypes on a wide variety of neuropsychological, neurological, or behavioral measures. Such differences speak directly to the clinical, experimental, and theoretical external validity of such a classification.

The five clusters were shown to differ statistically on a wide variety of measures and attributes. These included cluster differences on parental achievement levels (WRAT reading and spelling), socioeconomic status, neurological soft signs, various stigmata, and most of the neuropsychological measures from the battery given at kindergarten, second, and fifth grades. These clusters were additionally shown to follow different patterns of development over the six-year investigation. In summary, the five clusters were shown to be different on a large majority of the variables obtained in the Florida Longitudinal Project. A more detailed description of these findings is in preparation.

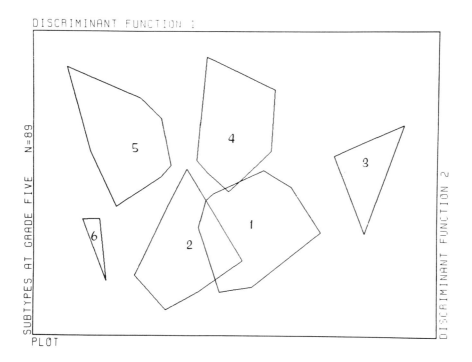

Fig. 5. Graphic representation of cluster results.

Figure 4 and 5 represent two visual-graphic attempts for validation purposes. The degree of overlapping clusters is of prime interest. In Figure 4, the two variables used in the original clustering phase with the least intercorrelation (VMI, VF) are used as the axis for graphing the six-cluster solution. Figure 5 represents the discriminant function plot for the cluster results.

In summary, all but one of the validation procedures appear to support the results of the clustering procedures. The clusters consistently appear in these data, even after some alterations in the data set and cluster methods. On split-sample replication, nearly identical results were found. External validation on independent variables was positive. The only unclear result was from clustering randomly generated data, which yielded similarities with the actual data. Therefore, the results must be considered with caution. An important further step would be the acquisition of comparable data at different research centers in order to attempt to test the generality of the clusters and to explore their external validity.

DISCUSSION

Classification is a fundamental topic in all sciences. A classification system forms the conceptual basis upon which a theory of a science can be developed. For example, the Linnean classification of living organisms was developed during the mid 1700s. About one century later, this classification system became th₂ conceptual foundation upon which Darwin built his theory of evolution.

In the science of neuropsychology, good classification systems are still in the process of being developed. Cluster analysis is a generic term which refers to a wide variety of quasi-statistical procedures used to create new classifications. The goal of most clustering methods is to form descriptive classifications in which the classificatory categories are relatively homogeneous. This paper has discussed cluster-analytic methods and demonstrated how these methods can be applied to neuropsychological research.

Cluster analysis has some major advantages for use in research regarding classification. These advantages include the following:

(1) Cluster-analytic methods are objective and empirical.

(2) Clustering techniques can be used to form descriptive classifications from large data sets whose size might overwhelm a human researcher.

(3) Cluster analysis, factor analysis, and multidimensional scaling are techniques which can help a researcher understand the multivariate structure of the data.

On the other hand, cluster analysis has some important problems of which any user should be aware.

(1) The methods for performing cluster analysis have been developed during the last two decades. The statistical characteristics of the various methods grouped under this generic title are not well known.

(2) Different clustering methods often generate strikingly different classifications

for the same data and require many subjective decisions.

(3) The literature on cluster analysis is varied and can be found in the journals of a wide range of sciences. The jargon associated with this literature is also quite varied and is difficult to learn.

In the light of these problems, researchers need to be careful in the application of cluster analysis. A researcher must approach this methodology systematically. In the demonstration of its use on data about learning-disabled children, there were six major steps in the process: (1) sampling of subjects, (2) choice of variables, (3) choice of similarity measure, (4) choice of cluster-analytic measure, (5) determination of the number of clusters existing in the data, and (6) validation. The last step is particularly important. The application of a cluster-analytic method should not stand alone. Cluster analysis will always find a classification solution of a data set, even if no homogeneous group exists in the data. Internal validation methods are important because they allow the researcher to test a clustering solution in a skeptical fashion. It is essential to be able to discriminate between a cluster solution in which a natural classification system has been found versus a solution in which an artificial classification has been forced on the data. Without adequate internal validation, the more important goal of external validation would seem destined to failure.

REFERENCE NOTE

1. Satz, P., Morris, R., & Darby, R. O. Subtypes of learning disabilities: A multivariate search. International Year of the Child Symposium. Vancouver, B. C., Canada, 1979.

REFERENCES

Anderberg, M. R. *Cluster analysis for applications.* New York: Academic Press, 1973.

Bartko, J. J., Strauss, J. S., & Carpenter, W. T. An evaluation of taxometric techniques for psychiatric data. *Classification Society Bulletin,* 1971, *2,* 2-28.

Blashfield, R. K., Aldenderfer, M. S., & Morey, L. C. Cluster analysis software. In P. R. Krishnaih (Ed.), *Handbook of statistics.* Vol 2, North-Holland, in press.

Burt, C., & Stephenson, W. Alternative views on correlations between persons. *Psychometrika,* 1939, *4,* 269-281.

Carroll, R. M., & Field, J. A comparison of the classification accuracy of profile similarity measures. *Multivariate Behavioral Research,* 1974, *9,* 373-380.

Clifford, H. T., & Stephenson, W. *An introduction to numerical classification.* New York: Academic Press, 1975.

Cormack, R. M. A review of classification. *The Journal of the Royal Statistical Society* (Series A), 1971, *134,* 321-367.

Darby, R. O. *Learning disabilities: A multivariate search for subtypes.* Doctoral Dissertation, University of Florida, 1978.

Doehring, D. G., & Hoshko, I. M. Classification of reading problems by the Q-techniques of factor analysis. *Cortex,* 1977, *13,* 281-294.

Doehring, D. G., Hoshko, I. M., & Bryans, A. Statistical classification of children with reading problems. *Journal of Clinical Neuropsychology,* 1979, *1,* 5-16.

Dubes, R., & Jain, A. K. Validity studies in clustering methodologies. *Pattern Recognition,* 1980, *11,* 235-254.

Everitt, B. S. Unresolved problems in cluster analysis. *Biometrics,* 1979, *35,* 169-181.

Everitt, B. S. *Cluster analysis* (2nd Edition). London: Heineman Educational Books, 1980.

Fisk, J. L., & Rourke, B. P. Identification of subtypes of learning-disabled children at three age levels: A neuropsychological, multivariate approach. *Journal of Clinical Neuropsychology,* 1979, *1,* 289-310.

Fleiss, J. L., Lawlor, W, Platman, S. R., & Fieve, R. R. On the use of inverted factor analysis for generating typologies. *Journal of Abnormal Psychology,* 1971, *77,* 127-132.

Fleiss, J. L., & Zubin, J. On the methods and theory of clustering. *Multivariate Behavioral Research,* 1969, *4,* 235-250.

Fletcher, J., & Satz, P. Developmental changes in the neuropsychological correlates of reading achievement: A six year longitudinal follow-up. *Journal of Clinical Neuropsychology,* 1980, *2,* 23-37.

Fletcher, J., Satz, P., & Morris, R. The Florida longitudinal project: Theoretical implications. In M. Harway & S. Mednick (Eds.), *U.S. longitudinal projects,* in press. (a).

Fletcher, J., Satz, P., & Morris, R. The Florida longitudinal project: A review. In M. Harway & S. Mednick (Eds.), *U.S. longitudinal projects,* in press. (b).

Hartigan, J. A. Representation of similarity matrices by trees. *Journal of the American Statistical Association,* 1967, *62,* 1140-1158.

Hartigan, J. A. *Clustering algorithms.* New York: Wiley, 1975.

Hetler, J. H. A critical examination of the adequacy of typological analyses provided by several clustering techniques. Doctoral Dissertation, University of Minnesota, 1976.

Holgerson, M. The limited value of cophenetic correlation as a clustering criterion. *Pattern Recognition,* 1978, *10,* 287-295.

Jardine, N., & Sibson, R. The construction of hierarchic and non-hierarchic classifications. *Computer Journal,* 1968, *11,* 177-184.

Kertesz, A., & Phipps, J. B. Numerical taxonomy of aphasia. *Brain and Language,* 1977, *4,* 1-10.

Lance, G. N., & Williams, W. T. A general theory of classificatory sorting strategies. I. Hierarchical systems. *Computer Journal,* 1967, *9,* 373-380.

McQuitty, L. L. A mutual development of some typological theories and pattern analytic methods. *Educational and Psychological Measurement,* 1967, *27,* 21-46.

Overall, J. E., & Klett, C. J. *Applied multivariate analysis.* New York: McGraw-Hill, 1972.

Petrauskas, R., & Rourke, B. P. Identification of subgroups of retarded readers: A neuropsychological, multivariate approach. *Journal of Clinical Neuropsychology,* 1979, *1,* 17-37.

Satz, P., & Morris, R. Learning disability subtypes: A review. In F. J. Pirozzolo & M. C. Wittrock (Eds.), *Neuropsychological and cognitive processes in reading.* New York: Academic Press, in press. (a).

Sats, P., & Morris, R. The search for subtype classification in learning disabled children. In R. E. Tarter (Ed.), *The child at risk.* New York: Oxford University Press, in press. (b).

Satz, P., Taylor, H. G., Friel, J., & Fletcher, J. Some developmental and predictive precursors of reading disabilities: A six year follow-up. In A. L. Benton & D. Pearl (Eds.),

Dyslexia: An appraisal of current knowledge. New York: Oxford University Press, 1978.

Schwartz, E. L., Ramos, A., & John, E. R. Cluster analysis of evoked potentials from behaving cats. *Behavioral Biology,* 1976, *17,* 109- 117.

Simpson, G. G. *Principles of animal taxonomy.* New York: Columbia University Press, 1961.

Skinner, H. A. Differentiating the contribution of elevation, scatter and shape in profile similarity. *Educational and Psychological Measurement,* 1978, *38,* 297-308.

Skinner, H. A. The eyes that fix you: A model for classification research. *Canadian Psychological Review,* 1977, *18,* 142-151.

Sneath, P. H. A., & Sokal, R. R. *Numerical taxonomy: The principles and practice of numerical classification.* San Francisco: W. H. Freeman & Co., 1973.

Sokal, R. R., & Sneath, P. H. A. *Principles of numerical taxonomy,* San Francisco: W. H. Freeman, 1963.

Stevens, M. A. Use of the Kolmogorov-Smirnov, Cramer-Von Mises and related statistics without extensive tables. *Journal of the American Statistical Association,* 1974, *69,* 630.

Tversky, A. Features of similarity. *Psychological Review,* 1977, *84,* 327-352.

Ward, J. H. Hierarchical grouping to optimize an objective function. *Journal of the American Statistical Association,* 1963, *58,* 236-244.

Wishart, D. R. Mode analysis: A generalization of nearest neighbor which reduces chaining effects. In A. J. Cole (Ed.), *Numerical taxonomy.* London: Academic Press, 1969.

Wishart, D. R. *CLUSTAN user manual,* (3rd Edition). London: Computer Center, University of London, 1975.

Journal of Clinical and Experimental Neuropsychology
1988, Vol. 10, No. 5, pp. 640-658

Classification in Neuropsychology:
A Theoretical Framework and Research Paradigm*

Robin D. Morris
Georgia State University

Jack M. Fletcher
University of Houston

ABSTRACT

Classification research is not well understood in neuropsychology. A major purpose of classification research is to establish and investigate inclusion and exclusion criteria for group formation. Therefore, classification represents the foundations of clinical assessment as well as traditional contrasting groups research designs in neuropsychology. Null results in neuropsychological research do not pinpoint the basis for the absence of group differences. The most frequent research focuses on the original theory or the validity of the dependent variables. Classification research focuses on a third potential problem area, which has received little attention: poor subject classifications (invalid independent variables). The purpose of this paper is to describe a general theoretical framework and outline a set of decisions for conducting classification research in neuropsychology.

Recent developments in neuropsychology have converged in identifying classification systems and processes as a fundamental problem area. Although classification issues have arisen most explicitly in child neuropsychology (Dennis, 1985 a,b; Morris, Blashfield, & Satz, 1981; Rourke, 1985), it is readily apparent that classification research is fundamental to all aspects of neuropsychology. Even the placement of a patient into brain-damaged or non-brain-damaged groups is a classification question. In this respect, the process and operational criteria used to establish inclusion or exclusion criteria for the

*This work was supported by a grant from the National Institute of Neurological and Communicative Disorders (NINCDS #1 PO1 NS 20489). The authors are grateful to the other Investigators from the Nosology: Higher Cerebral Function Disorders in Children Project for their input and support. Portions of this paper were presented at meetings of the International Neuropsychological Society in Houston (1984) and Denver (1986).

presence or absence of brain damage (i.e., independent variables) is a classification problem. Hence, classification underlies the development of subject selection criteria for research and incorporates basic diagnostic and assessment questions underlying clinical assessment.

The relationship of classification to neuropsychological research and assessment can be illustrated in the context of contrasting group designs. It has become traditional to compare brain-damaged and non-brain-damaged groups on constructs relevant to a particular hypothesis or theory. If a neuropsychological variable (i.e., dependent variable) not used as part of the subject selection criteria differentiates the brain-damaged patient from other patient groups, the traditional inference is that the neuropsychological variable represents an "empirically meaningful dimension for group separation," validating the hypothesis. However, it can also be inferred from such results that the criteria used to classify patients into groups are valid. If the results comparing groups are *null*, then it is possible that *either* the neuropsychological variable lacks discriminative validity (i.e., is not an empirically meaningful dimension of group separation) or the classification is invalid (i.e., the groups are not correctly selected to maximize their differences on theoretically relevant attributes).

Although it is traditional to focus on the theory or on the dependent variables in neuropsychology, it is not traditional to focus explicitly on the independent variables (i.e., criteria for selecting groups). However, any research employing a contrasting groups design is a study of *both* the validity of the independent and dependent variables or, in classification terms, the classification and external variates, respectively. Similarly, a clinical assessment that utilizes neuropsychological tests to determine the type of disorder provides both an explicit test of the validity of the tests, and an implicit test of the validity of the classification underlying the typing of disorders. Hence, classification issues underlie clinical assessment as well as traditional research designs in neuropsychology.

The determination of pertinent variables for describing patients in various groups is an interactive process representing a search for theoretically meaningful measurement constructs, operations, and salient criteria for defining the various disorders of interest. Research and clinical assessment progress through the interaction of the development of theory, valid measurement tools, and valid classification systems.

The need for theory and valid measurement tools is well understood in neuropsychology. In fact, there is an explicit focus on these operations. Classification issues tend not to receive an explicit focus despite their interactive influence on both theory and measurement development. By way of illustration, amnesia is commonly defined as abnormal forgetting in the face of preserved intellect (*classification* criteria). From this definition, numerous studies of forgetting rates were completed in amnestic patients based on hypotheses (i.e., derived from current *theory*) concerning whether the fundamental deficit involved encoding or retrieval skills (see Squire & Cohen, 1982). Considerable energy was devoted to determining procedures for the measurement of encoding and retrieval. It was subsequently recognized that memory patterns were variable in amnestic patients (i.e., all amnestic patients are not the same), leading Squire (1981) to hypothesize that amnesia was not a unitary phenomenon, but representative of at least two types: medial temporal amnesia, characterized as a disorder of encoding, and diencephalic amnesia, characterized by disorders of both encoding and retrieval skills. This new *classification* of amnestics led to further distinctions (theory) in memory systems (e.g., procedural vs. declarative memory) that, in time, led to additional typing of amnesias (*classification*) according to the pattern of disrupted memory skills. In this example, classification occurred at two levels, one involving the identification of the amnestic patient, and the other depicting the subtype of amnestic patient. This is an example of a dual-level, hierarchical classification system that is often implicit in neuropsychology.

This example clearly illustrates how theory, measurement, and classification developments interact. What is not typically recognized is that the initial problem involved classification, i.e., developing criteria for determining which patients were amnestic as opposed to suffering from some other disorder. Demonstrating problems on memory tests (*assessment*) validates the specification (*theory*) of amnesia as a syndrome (*classification*), just as demonstrating differences in memory functions between Korsakoff and hippocampectomy patients validates the neuroanatomical classification of diencephalon and medial temporal amnesias. A lack of such behavioral differences between these groups of patients would have brought into question the validity of such a classification system even though the patients can be easily grouped based on their neuroanatomical deficits. Butters (1984) observed that amnestic patients can have similar scores on the Wechsler Memory Scale (WMS) but may have very different types of memory deficits, leading him to encourage clinicians to use measures from experimental studies of memory to better characterize those deficiencies. In fact, this example further illustrates the two levels of classification in a clinical framework; the WMS can be used to determine who is amnestic (Level I subgroups), with other assessment procedures permitting a more specific classification (Level II subtypes).

Classification issues are not well understood in neuropsychology. This is unfortunate since classification research can be conceptualized as an area of inquiry with paradigms that make explicit the study of the independent variables underlying research and clinical assessment in neuropsychology. With the increasing capacity and sophistication of neural imaging and other neurodiagnostic procedures to measure parameters of the CNS that may be related to behavior, the next decade may see a burgeoning interest in classification research - or at least greater recognition of the implicit role of classification issues in any neuropsychological study.

Unfortunately, recent attempts at classification research in neuropsychology have often been overly empirical, representing an attempt to take advantage of statistical software packages without adequate methodological or theoretical substance. As with any other area of scientific investigation, atheoretical, exploratory studies that simply dump data into computer programs are not likely to yield beneficial results. Furthermore, classification is often equated with certain statistical approaches to the analysis of large data sets (e.g., cluster analysis) when in fact classification issues can be dealt with rationally, through traditional experimental methods or even single-subject research.

The purpose of this paper is to outline a framework and a set of decisions underlying theory formulation for conducting classification research in neuro-psychology. A major focus is on the analysis of large data sets, but the model also applies to small sample studies. In addition, we provide a set of practical criteria for evaluating classification results that should represent minimal criteria for any classification study.

FORMING CLASSIFICATIONS: AN OVERVIEW

Definitions and Purposes

Classification is the process of forming groups from a large set of entities or units based on the similarities and dissimilarities of the individual entities. Bailey (1973) described classification as the "ordering of concepts into groups (or sets) based on their relationship...their similarities". Classifications place their objects of study into groups so that, in each group, subjects are more similar to each other than they are to subjects in other groups on a set of specified attributes. A fundamental assumption of classification research is that there are subjects who show similarities and/or differences on the variables of interest. By identifying these similarities/differences between groups, it is hypothesized that better understanding of etiology, prognosis, and treatment will result. Classification is fundamental to any scientific endeavor. As Kendall (1975) stated, "Theories and therapeutic claims have no more chance of surviving than buildings if they are not built on secure foundations. Developing reliable diagnostic criteria and a valid classification may be tedious...but provides the foundations on which all else will depend." (p. vii).

Taxonomy, which is the theoretical study of classification, involves the analysis and conceptualization of various approaches to classification. A taxonomy may be composed of several classifications depending on the purpose of the study. Classifications oriented to treatment may differ from classifica-tions oriented to biological etiology, pathology, or behavior.

Sokal (1974) stated that "The *paramount* purpose of a classification is to describe the structure and relationship of the constituent objects to each other and to similar objects and to simplify these relationships in such a way that general statements can be made about classes of objects." (p.1116). Blashfield and Draguns (1976) pointed out that two primary purposes of classification are *communication* and *prediction*. These two purposes are frequently in conflict because they require different attributes from a classification system. The development of a classification, therefore, must be considered a dynamic and continuing process which involves communication and scientific components. The purpose of a specific classification needs to be clearly defined.

For the purpose of communication, the classification should be simple. The variables on which the classification is based should be widely used and operational definitions for placing subjects into a particular group should be easy to use. The communicative utility of any classification will be judged by those who use it. Therefore, a classification system that will facilitate communication among consumers should be simple and should reflect the various clinical, political, and theoretical views within the field being addressed. Most changes in classifications represent slow and conservative processes (Blashfield & Draguns, 1976).

These important aspects of communication are in contrast to the purpose of specific prediction. Here, the evaluation of the classification is based on its empirical validation, especially in relationship to outcome, treatment, or the understanding of etiology. To meet these needs, a classification will probably be complex and reflective of new research findings in an area. These needs may be in direct conflict with the simplicity required for communication and utility (Blashfield & Draguns, 1976).

The sometimes conflicting purposes of communication and prediction represent pragmatic considerations in the development of a classification. These considerations warrant a careful consideration of options in the development of any methodology designed to develop and validate a classification system. In this light, it is important to realize that the development of any classification system is neither a beginning nor an endpoint of the process. This process-oriented view of the formation of classification systems is restricted, not only by practical and socio-political influences, but also by the scientific process involved in developing classification systems. In general, any classification system sets some limits on the theories that may evolve. On the other hand, theories also determine the characteristics of the classification. Neither theory nor classification systems can develop rapidly when they are independent of each other.

Theoretical Framework

All classifications should be developed as hypotheses subject to empirical validation. Goodall (1966) suggested that the most practical null hypothesis in classification research is that there are no useful subgroups in the subject population undergoing classification. There are empirical criteria that can be used to evaluate the adequacy and validity of any classification. Although *measurement* tools have been frequently studied in terms of the reliability and validity of various tests, this evaluative process has not consistently been applied to classification systems or typologies. Indeed, many studies treat the derivation of groups (i.e., types) as the endpoint of the research when, in fact, this derivation represents, at best, a set of beginning hypotheses requiring validation. Showing that subjects can be placed into groups does not validate the groups or show that the emergent criteria are useful or discriminative. However, unless the selection criteria variables themselves are studied and evaluated, classification is only implicitly involved. The frequent confusion of discriminant analysis, which requires a priori groups, and classification methods, which generate potential groups, illustrates the need for a theoretical framework for classification that makes explicit the study of the independent or internal variables versus the processes used to assign subjects to pre-defined groups (i.e., discriminant analysis). Skinner (1981) provides a framework for classification research that integrates the theoretical and empirical components necessary for these studies.

First, Skinner (1981) described a *theory formulation* component. This component involves decisions concerning the variables that are used for a classification, and the specific groups that are hypothesized to exist. Second, the *internal validation* component represents the assessment of reliability, coverage, and replicability of the classification. Third, the *external validity* component involves the evaluation of a reliable classification system against external criteria; this addresses whether the groups forming the classification differ from one another in response to treatment, biological markers, or other indices used to study the groups. By considering each area in turn, examples of how this framework elucidates the nature and purpose of classification research can be provided.

In the theory formulation component, a decision concerning the *content domain* or variables (attributes) to be used must be made. Most classification research in neuropsychology uses psychometric test results and behavioral observations for classification purposes. Alternatives could include classifications on the basis of neuroanatomy, history, treatment response, or other characteristics of the population. A second consideration involves the *theoretical model* used to specify the syndromes and their interrelationships. For example, "ideal types" are hypothetical individuals displaying a characteristic set of attributes exemplifying a subset of the population. There are other classification models that depict various theoretical types. The third component is the *a priori* specification of *hypothesized groups* and the relationship of these groups to external variables. As we will see, the attempt to systematically disconfirm these hypotheses in the external validity component is essential for evaluating the adequacy of a classification.

Internal validity concerns the *reliability* and *replicability* of the classification (Skinner, 1981). External validity studies are not meaningful if the classification has low reliability and is difficult to replicate. Considerations include the number of subjects successfully typed (i.e., coverage), the homogeneity of the groups, the reliability of the individual classification attributes, replicability across techniques, and replication across other samples. Morris et al. (1981) provide descriptions of different types of internal validity studies, including applications in an attempt to derive and validate learning disability subtypes.

The external validity component addresses the degree to which the groups can be differentiated according to variables not used to form the groups. There are relatively few classification studies in neuropsychology that contain an external validity component. The demonstration of a subgroup by remediation, or subgroup by experimental task interaction, is a powerful evaluation of the validity of a classification, its generalizability, prognostic accuracy, descriptive validity, clinical utility, and treatment effects. No one research project can adequately evaluate the external validity of any classification system, although each study can add support to an array of evidence for the validity of the classification.

Morris et al. (1981) and Skinner (1981) provide reviews of the issues involved in internal and external validity, along with empirical demonstrations. Since the primary purpose of this paper is to illustrate the conceptual basis of classification as a research process, the remainder of this paper will focus primarily on the issues involved in the theory formulation component of classification. This component is often ignored in neuropsychological research, despite the fact that the decisions of this component are embedded in any neuropsychological study. Consequently, we will focus primarily on the decisions involved in conducting classification studies.

DECISIONS UNDERLYING CLASSIFICATION RESEARCH

All classification studies involve a series of specific issues and decisions that must be addressed in order to ensure that the classification is reliable and valid. The need for these decisions may vary according to the nature and purpose of the study. Table 1 summarizes the components and decisions underlying most *explicit* neuropsychological studies involving classification. Since *any* contrasting groups study involves an *implicit* test of a classification (i.e., basis for forming groups), these methodological considerations are generally relevant for neuropsychology as a scientific endeavor. As Table 1 indicates, many of the decisions and steps underlying theory in classification are actually methodological. We have deliberately embedded these considerations in the theory formulation component in order to emphasize the need for an interactive relationship between theory and methodology. As Sokal (1974) stated, "in most classification research, theory has frequently followed methodology". The result of this approach is the potentially empty array of unvalidated, overly empirical studies that presently predominate neuropsychology as examples of classification research. In this respect, classification research has become synonymous with the application of cluster analysis to large data sets when in fact such studies represent beginning points. As the following review of decisions underlying classification research demonstrates, the issues are more substantive than simply running a cluster analysis.

Table 1. Decisions Underlying Theory Formulation in Classification Research

A. Theoretical Model
  1. Hypothesized types
  2. Basis for similarity
  3. Relationships with external variables

B. Choice of Populations/Samples
  1. Sampling strategy
  2. Outliers

C. Selection of Variables
  1. Classification attributes
  2. External variables

D. Classification Methods
  1. Rational
  2. Statistical

E. Internal Validity

F. External Validity

Theoretical Models

There are several models for classification. *Categorical* models place subjects into discrete classes. Although they permit ease of description, their main drawback is the expectation that all patients fit neatly into each category, an infrequent situation in neuropsychology. *Dimensional* classifications order subjects along dimensional axes in multidimensional space. The strengths of dimensional classifications are that there is little loss of information and maximal combinations are possible along the dimensions. Weaknesses are the need for algebraic or geometrical methods for description: Most neuropsychologists will prefer reduction to categories. *Hierarchical* classifications place subjects successively into non-overlapping subsets which can be further divided at various levels in the hierarchy, representing a variant of categorical models. *Hybrids* are various combinations of the above models. Hempel (1961) has noted that most sciences begin with dichotomous attributes but then replace them with dimensions as more sophisticated and accurate measurement becomes possible.

Although groups are commonly conceptualized as mutually exclusive and jointly exhaustive, neuropsychology (like other clinical sciences) is oriented around inexact class definitions, attribute measurement, and class assignments. Hence, most groups in the state of nature are *polythetic* rather than *monothetic* in nature. According to Bailey (1973), monothetic classifications have a set of unique features that are necessary and sufficient for each member of the class. In contrast, polythetic classifications represent groups formed on the basis of the number of shared features. No one feature is either necessary or sufficient for group membership and may be shared across groups. In neuropsychology, groups are preferred that share attributes but which reduce group overlap. Polythetic classifications based on hierarchical models may be most useful and, in fact, are implicit in most contrasting groups designs. In this respect, there is usually a selection of patients according to a set of independent variables on which members of the group may overlap on any single variable.

Hypothetical Types

Once the classification model is chosen, a hypothetical classification should be developed. Hypothetical types can take several forms, but generally represent a hypothesized pattern or configuration of attributes referred to as the *ideal type*. Skinner (1981) defined an ideal type as "a hypothetical pattern of attributes...-that is characteristic of a subject or individuals in the population. Ideal types are mental constructs that may be used to summarize observed characteristics among relatively homogeneous groups of individuals." (p. 72). Consequently, a hypothetical classification represents a set of classes epitomized by an ideal member. These types may be hierarchically related and there may be overlap on any single variable. Moreover, no one group member may have the set of ideal characteristics.

Basis for Similarity

A second consideration is the basis for similarity/dissimilarity. Types are typically depicted as profiles representing the classification attributes. Profiles vary according to three characteristics: shape, elevation, and scatter (variability). These components can be visualized in two-dimensional plots or measured by various quantitative indices of similarity. However, quantitative indices measure similarity in different ways, so quantitative similarity measures depend in part on the relative weightings given to these components and the nature of the data. Within a particular group, for example, shape may be less important than elevation, so that a measure of similarity emphasizing shape (e.g., Pearson Product-Moment Correlation) and minimizing elevation may be most useful. If a severity dimension is important so that mean profiles vary up and down, then elevation becomes important, indicating the need for a distance-based measure (e.g., squared Euclidean distance) that includes both shape and elevation. Different similarity measures can lead to various results in the same data set, making the a priori consideration of similarity mandatory. These considerations should be explicit, even when qualitative methods (i.e., visualizing profiles) are used to form types.

There are techniques being developed which partition distance-based measures into the various profile components which can allow more control over these factors (Carter, Morris, & Blashfield, in press). However, even these similarity measures may not provide the final classificatory solutions, as it is entirely possible to have two different groups with the same exact mean profiles, but which have different underlying covariance matrices; this would suggest that there are different interrelationships between the classificatory variates. As an example, take the Verbal IQ and Performance IQ as a simple pair of classificatory attributes. Two groups may have very *similar mean levels* on both scores, but one group has no correlation between the scores while the other has a strong positive correlation dependent on the underlying conditions of the two groups. In other words, in the first group, as VIQ scores go up or down, PIQ may or may not change, whereas in the second group, as VIQ scores go up or down, PIQ follows very closely.

External Variables

When the classification model, ideal types, and basis for similarity are selected, the result should be a hypothetical classification for the population of choice. It is important that the classification be presented on an a priori basis. This permits the delineation of pertinent external validity studies and provides guidelines for analyzing the data. In the absence of a hypothetical classification, the analysis will be excessively exploratory, potentially leading to Type I errors. Moreover, external validity studies will not be hypothesis-driven. By formulating a hypothetical classification, it should be possible to predict subtype differences or external variates and then actually test such predictions in the external validity component of the classification study. It is of utmost importance to design this component of the study in the theory formulation component.

Choice of Population (Sampling)

Without careful sampling, it is clearly possible to generate subtypes that do not reflect the dimensional characteristics of the populations of interest. This consideration is especially pertinent for neuropsychology since many of the syndromes of interest occur infrequently. A classification based only on low base-rate subtypes will lack generalizability but still may be useful. Consequently, the development of a adequate *sampling strategy* is a fundamental component of a classification study. For example, if the goal of the study is to develop a classification of aphasia, the population could be defined on disease characteristics. If the classification addresses consequences of neurological disease, the population would represent all patients with CNS disorders and the classification of aphasias would be part of a more general classification of neurological disorders. In contrast, a classification of aphasia based on characteristic language disorders might employ a population of all patients with language problems regardless of neurological disease, emotional disorders, and other etiologies producing language disorders. These examples show that the selection of the population is critical because this step dictates many other components of the classification, including the classification model, the classification attributes, and its generalizability.

The sampling strategy does not have to be completely randomized provided the criteria for including and excluding subjects are clearly determined and do not create "artificial" groups (e.g., referral source differences). The practical problems of all sampling approaches are multiple. First, a "total" sample approach includes many patients who have disorders known to affect cognitive and behavioral functioning that may not be relevant to the purpose of neuropsychological classification (e.g., psychiatric disorders). For example, there are currently classification systems for psychiatric disorders that are widely accepted although certain components have not been validated. Whether such psychiatric classification systems help to further our understanding of brain-behavior relationships is open to question. The inclusion of all such patients would also be impractical due to considerations regarding the number of subjects required in each hypothesized group, the number of groups possible, and the low base rates of some disorders. On the other hand, it could also be argued that the inclusion of psychiatric patients is necessary if one is interested in forming a generalizable classification of, for example, cognitive dysfunctions. Within this orientation, the etiology of such disorders is unimportant. Again, the sampling strategy is dictated by the nature and purpose of the classification questions. With careful delineation of the inclusion and exclusion criteria, practical sampling strategies can be developed to meet a given classification's purpose.

The inclusion criteria actually represent a set of classification attributes (independent variables). In other words, when a classification is not based on a completely random sample, the criteria used to select subjects should be studied to determine their validity as part of the classification. In neuropsychology, this may suggest a need for multi-level classifications. For example, if we attempt to classify memory disorders with a CNS basis, there are a set of criteria that determine whether the disorder has a CNS basis. In sampling, some patients with memory disorders will enter the study and others will be excluded. This represents a first level of classification, with the subtyping of memory disorders representing a second level of classification. Validation at both levels is a required empirical process, and the lack of attention to either level can result in increased error variance in the hypothesized model.

The memory disorders example described above demonstrates that the explicit validation of selection criteria is not a self-fulfilling prophecy. At the first level, validation occurs by comparing performances on memory tests in memory-impaired patients, with and without a CNS etiology. If differences emerge, the selection criteria represent a more valid classification at this level. If the results are null, further investigation of the similarity and differences in memory performances would be indicated irrespective of etiological group. In addition, reconsideration of the reasons for defining groups based on CNS etiology, or of the specific selection criteria used, would be required. There is no information in null results which pinpoints the basis for the absence of group differences: There may be problems with the original theory predicting group differences, in subject classification (invalid independent variates), or in dependent variate assessment (invalid measurement of dependent variables).

Why traditional research focuses on the first and last of these possibilities, and not the second, is open to question.

When sampling, the patients that are excluded should be placed into explicit contrast groups (e.g., psychiatric patients with memory impairment) and, at the very least, kept for Level I validation studies. Not only should the target population be designated, but appropriate contrast groups should also be determined. When hypotheses concerning external variables are developed, these contrast groups will be essential. If the hypothesized types are not different from relevant contrast groups on the major external variables, the classification may have limited utility, depending on its purpose.

For example, it is common to define reading disorders in children in terms of discrepancies in IQ and achievement in the absence of an overt neurological disorder, low SES, and emotional problems (Fletcher & Morris, 1986). However, if a group with reading disorders fails to differ from children with: (a) reading problems and low IQ; (b) other learning problems; (c) low IQ children; (d) normal reading children; (e) culturally disadvantaged children who are poor readers; and (f) poor reading children with neurological and emotional disorders, then the uniqueness and validity of such a group can be questioned. Indeed, if the *hypothesized* differences between such groups do not emerge, designating children with discrepant reading and IQ as a diagnostic group requiring further investigation is a dubious process (see Taylor, Satz, and Friel, 1979, for an example of such research).

There are other considerations underlying the development of a sampling strategy, including: (a) sample size; (b) number of variables; (c) statistical techniques; and (d) validation methods. Sample size is important because it influences the number of possible types that may be discernible in the population. It is important to obtain sufficient numbers of each type in order to validate the classification. If a large number of variables will be used for classification and validation purposes, the number of subjects per hypothesized groups must be increased. Certain statistical techniques require larger samples. Similarly, the need for cross-validation studies may dictate the need for larger samples. In general, the number of subjects is related to the number of variables or attributes being used for the formation of the classification, the number of expected groups within a sample, the number of subjects within each group (base-rate), and the statistical methods being used.

Outliers

Subjects who show extremely deviant results compared to other subjects are called outliers. They may represent low base-rate cases, subjects who had a bad day, or other potential problems leading to measurement error. The presence of outliers significantly influences variable distributions and can disrupt a classification (Milligan, 1980). Extreme outliers are typically removed. Since there is a negative correlation between the amount of coverage of a classification (percentage of subjects included compared to number of subjects studied) and the reliability of a classification, including outliers leads to an increasing probability of reducing the reliability, and therefore the validity, of the classification. We typically use multiple criteria for identifying outliers, such as the following: subjects who fall more than 4.0 standard deviations on the distribution of scores on more than two variables; subjects who are more than 1.5 standard deviations below 95% of the subjects; visual inspection techniques. Other outlier identification procedures are also useful. Note that the identification of outliers is a classification problem in and of itself.

Selection of Variables

Classification attributes are *marker variables* used to define the types of interest. Since all possible variables cannot be used, classification attributes should be selected to *maximize* hypothesized differences among the groups forming the classification, while external variables should be relevant dimensions of group discrimination. The basis for variable selection should derive from theory concerning the nature of the relevant types as well as pertinent dimensions of group discrimination.

Classification Attributes

The variables used for classification in neuropsychology are often behavioral, representing measures of cognitive functioning. Variables pertaining to neuroanatomical etiology and pathology can also be used for classifications, with past symptoms, treatment outcomes, or prognosis representing other potential classification attributes. In general, classification attributes should be directly measurable. Etiological or pathology variables that are inferences generally obfuscate the classification process. Similarly, classification variates must be able to be adequately measured, i.e., meeting traditional criteria for reliability and validity. The validity of a classification can generally be no higher than its reliability, which is directly related to the reliability of the attribute measures. When selecting among variables, it is often necessary to select classification variables on the basis of higher reliability, delegating theoretically important but less reliable measured variables as external variables for validation studies. The number of variables measuring each construct must also be carefully considered, as an excessive number of measures of one construct (e.g., language) will bias the classification solution toward group differences on that construct.

Multi-model or skewed variate distributions are actually desirable for classifications, since normally distributed variables do not suggest the presence of multiple populations. Construct redundancy and the number of classification variables are other important considerations. For neuropsychological research, it is desirable to use as few nonredundant measures as possible. This will facilitate external validity studies, since identification of new subjects into types will be simpler.

It should be noted that a classification variable in one study may be an external variable in another study. Similarly, classifications may overlap and change orientations depending on the purpose of the classification. As example, classification based on the etiology of memory disorders may include alcohol-related dementias, whereas another classification focused on the effects of alcohol use may include certain memory deficits. In the former, etiological variables are used as classification attributes, but in the latter, behavioral data are used as classification attributes. A hypothetical classification is needed to determine which variables are most pertinent to the purpose of the classification.

External Variables

In addition to traditional psychometric considerations, external variables should be selected to test hypotheses about the differentiation of types in the classification. These variables should be theoretically related to the types, but generally from a different measurement domain. Using highly intercorrelated variables from the same measurement domain as the classification attributes is likely to produce expected group differences, but will only provide a crude approximation of external validity. For example, demonstrating differences among aphasics on linguistic measures that are similar to the original classification variates (e.g., naming, comprehension) is not particularly meaningful. However, generating a hypothesis about differences in a language system based on variables not used in forming the classification would be meaningful, just as an autopsy, event related potential, or neural imaging differences - all variables from a different measurement domain (i.e., not behavioral) - would provide a more convincing demonstration of external validity. Variations in treatment outcome predicted by the classification would also provide impressive external validation. Consequently, external variables should be selected on the basis of theory in a manner generating falsifiable predictions concerning various dimensions of validity.

Selection of Classification Methods

There are many methods for completing classification studies. Since there is a tendency in neuropsychology to equate classification with Q-type factor or cluster analysis, it is important to recognize that classification issues can be addressed through rational methods and even through single-case designs. Rational methods for classification are common in neuropsychology. The pluralistic theory of the amnesias (Squire & Cohen, 1984) that we discussed earlier is an excellent example. Similarly, historical attempts to classify aphasias based on a theory of language, or on neuroanatomical correlates, have largely been conducted on rational grounds. Single-case studies are very useful for identifying classification attributes and for defining "ideal type" subjects for larger group studies. The study of deep dyslexia is a prime example of the usefulness of this approach in classification research. The use of qualitative methods does not mean that rational approaches should not be subjected to empirical validation.

To reiterate, any comparison of groups is, in part, an evaluation of a classification hypothesis. Classifications can be derived by logic, reason, or research findings and then entered into a validational framework such as that defined by Skinner (1981). Consequently, issues concerning internal and external validity are equally relevant for rational and statistical approaches and can be addressed through similar technical methods. Wilson and Risucci (1985) provide a useful example of the rational derivation of subtypes of language disabled children, with group assignment based on visual inspection of a child's clinical data. However, their internal validity studies were completed using statistical methods. This approach can be useful, even with small samples.

Statistical methods such as Q-type factor analysis and cluster analysis (see Morris et al., 1981) can be used to search data sets for subtypes and to evaluate classification hypotheses. Unfortunately, these techniques are widely abused in neuropsychology largely due to a failure to adequately conceptualize the study according to the issues in Table 1. Such studies typically treat the results of the statistical analysis as a classification despite insufficient validation. Cluster analysis is a useful tool for classification research, particularly when used in a hypothesis-testing framework. It does not yield confirmatory solutions analogous to maximal likelihood methods of factor analysis that would help determine the goodness of fit of a particular solution. Consequently, the selection and application of any statistical techniques in classification must be guided by theory and rationality. If cluster analysis is used, many subjective decisions must be made (Morris et al., 1981).

Design of Internal and External Validity Studies

The final step in developing a classification study is the design of specific studies of the reliability and validity of the classification. These studies should be designed prior to initiating the project, including some idea of the criteria for establishing acceptable levels of reliability and validity. The absence of these criteria can lead to an excessively exploratory study that lacks reliability and, therefore, validity. Specific criteria may vary according to the level of development of the area of study and the stage of classification at which the study is initiated.

Internal Validation/Reliability

The *reliability* of a classification can be determined through a variety of methods illustrated in Morris et al. (1981), some of which are provided in Table 2. The basic problem is to demonstrate that the typology is reliable. Consequently, if the types can be identified by dividing the sample or replicating the results in another sample, then these findings support the reliability of the classification since the results are not sample-specific. It is also possible to vary the techniques used to define subtypes by employing highly correlated measurement/selection instruments, adding additional subjects, or by subjecting the data to alternative statistical techniques. For example, Rourke (1982)

Table 2. Dimensions of Internal Validity

A. Reliability and Cross-Validity
1. Split-sample and alternative sample
2. Multiple technique comparison
3. Data manipulation
4. Graphical procedures
5. Monte Carlo simulations
B. Homogeneity
C. Coverage

proposed a classification of disabled learners based on scores from the Wide Range Achievement Test (WRAT). If this classification is reliable, children should be similarly typed using an achievement test measuring skills similar to the WRAT. Adding an additional variable (e.g., reading comprehension) may introduce new types, but should not alter the fundamental types suggested by the WRAT classification. Similarly, adding nondisabled children should not result in changes in the disabled learner types. Finally, questions concerning the reliability of a classification can be examined by plotting subjects along visually representable measures or by designing Monte Carlo (i.e., random) studies of the data (see Morris et al., 1981). The purpose of these analyses is simply to demonstrate that the results are not sample-specific, similar to random samples, or influenced by the investigator's or methodologic biases.

Homogeneity refers to the degree to which the types are similar to each other. If there are actual types within the data, identification of subjects into types should result in reduced score dimensions on the classification variates (i.e., less variability). Usually, homogeneous subgroups should yield isolated clusters of individuals around group centroids. Another way to describe this process is to minimize within-group variance and maximize between-group variance. If types are not homogeneous, reliability will be low because classification errors are high.

Coverage refers to the number of subjects grouped by the classification. A classification that excludes or places large numbers of subjects into heterogeneous (e.g., mixed) groups is not likely to be beneficial. There is an inverse relationship between coverage and reliability, so that reliability diminishes as coverage increases. This illustrates the importance of carefully considering outliers, small base-rate types, and the trade-off between coverage and reliability.

External Validity
At this point, in the external validation phase, traditional hypothesis-driven experimental designs and methods should be employed to explore group

similarities and differences. Table 3 outlines some of the various types of external validity that a classification may exhibit. Since validity was thoroughly addressed by Skinner (1981), we will simply point out that most comparisons between groups (classic ANOVA designs) represent examples of discriminative validity. However, validity is also demonstrated if the classification shows clinical relevance and leads to specific treatment considerations.

Table 3. Dimensions of External Validity

A. Predictive Validity

B. Descriptive Validity
   1. Convergent
   2. Discriminant

C. Clinical Validity

D. Generalizability

CONCLUSIONS

This overview of the issues involved in the theory formulation component of classification research was designed to illustrate the major point of this paper, which is that classification issues are implicit in virtually any neuropsychological study. It is important to begin to move classification issues out of the background and into the forefront of neuropsychology. The continued development of neuropsychological research and practice depend, in part, on continued refinements in our understanding of the relationship of various disorders among themselves and with the relevant constructs of interest. Historically, classification often seems to be an end-product of research, with classification problems identified only after decades of research. A good example is research on learning-disabled children (Rourke, 1985). In addition, many of the current problems in neuropsychology, such as the controversy over linguistic methods in aphasia, could be re-conceptualized as classification problems. This re-conceptualization could lead to the development of large, multi-center data bases that permit exploration of several potential classifications based on rational and statistical approaches. Such a development would extend beyond the current disagreements, which mainly revolve around theory and various dependent variables. In fact, theory, and our understanding of the relationship of various psychological variables to the CNS, will develop only to the degree that our classification systems become better operationalized, refined, and precise. Presently, many disagreements in the literature that seem theoretically motivated result, in part, from comparisons of overlapping or poorly defined groups.

This paper outlines some of the major considerations involved in bringing classification research under close, objective scrutiny. Designing classification studies on a careful, theoretically motivated basis should eliminate the need for studies based only on visual inspection of multidimensional neuropsychological profiles or the results of a cluster analysis. Such efforts do not represent adequate examples of classification research and may be misleading in the search for reliable and valid neurobehavioral relationships or typologies.

REFERENCES

Bailey, K.D. (1973). Monothetic and polythetic typologies and their relation to conceptualization, measurement and scaling. *American Sociological Review, 38,* 18-33.

Blashfield, R.K., & Draguns, J. (1976). Evaluative criteria for psychiatric classification. *Journal of Abnormal Psychology, 85,* 140-150.

Butters, N. (1984). The clinical aspects of memory disorders: Contributions from experimental studies in amnesia and dementia. *Journal of Clinical and Experimental Neuropsychology, 6,* 17-36.

Carter, R.L., Morris, R., & Blashfield, R.K. (in press). On the partitioning of squared euclidean distance and its application in cluster analysis. *Psychometrika.*

Dennis, M. (1985a). Intellegence after early brain injury I. Predicting I.Q. scores from medical variables. *Journal of Clinical and Experimental Neuropsychology, 7,* 526-554.

Dennis, M. (1985b). Intelligence after early brain injury II. IQ scores of subjects classified on the basis of medical history variables. *Journal of Clinical and Experimental Neuropsychology, 7,* 555-576.

Fletcher, J., & Morris, R. (1986). Classification of disabled learners: Beyond exclusionary definitions. In S. Ceci (Ed.), *Handbook of Cognitive, Social, and Neuropsychological Aspects of Learning Disabilities* (Vol. 1) (pp. 55-80). Hillsdale, NJ: Lawrence Erlbaum Assoc.

Goodall, D.W. (1966). Hypothesis-testing in classification. *Nature, 211,* 329-330.

Hempel, C.G. (1961). Introduction to problems of taxonomy. In J. Zubin (Ed.), *Field studies in the mental disorders* (pp. 3-26). New York: Grune and Stratton.

Kendell, R. E. (1975). *The role of diagnosis in psychiatry.* London: Blackwell Scientific Publications.

Milligan, G.W. (1980). An examination of the effect of six types of error perturbation on fifteen clustering algorithms. *Psychometrika, 45,* 44-54.

Morris, R., Blashfield, R., & Satz, P. (1981). Neuropsychology and cluster analysis: Potentials and problems. *Journal of Clinical Neuropsychology, 3,* 79-99.

Rourke, B.P. (1982). Central processing deficiencies in children: Toward a developmental neuropsychological model. *Journal of Clinical Neuropsychology, 4,* 1-18.

Rourke, B.P. (Ed.). (1985). *Neuropsychology of learning disabilities: Essentials of subtype analysis.* New York: Guilford.

Skinner, H.A. (1981). Toward the integration of classification theory and methods. *Journal of Abnormal Psychology, 90,* 68-87.

Sokal, R.R. (1974). Classification: Purposes, principles, progress, prospects. *Science, 185*(4157), 1115-1123.

Squire, L. (1981). Two forms of human amnesia: An analysis of forgetting. *Journal of*

Neuroscience, 1, 635-640.

Squire, L., & Cohen, N. (1982). Remote memory, retrograde amnesia, and the neurospychology of memory. In L.S. Cermak (Ed.), *Human memory and amnesia.* (pp. 275-303). Hillsdale, NJ: Erlbaum Assoc.

Taylor, H.G., Satz, P., & Friel, J. (1979). Developmental dyslexia in relationship to other childhood disorders: Significance and utility. *Reading Research Quarterly, 15,* 84-101.

Wilson, B., & Risucci, D. (1985). A model for clinical-quantitative classification. Generation 1: Application to language-disordered preschool children. *Brain and Language, 27,* 281-309.

Journal of Clinical Neuropsychology
1983, Vol. 5, No. 2, pp. 115-133.

Confirmatory Factor Analysis of Four General Neuropsychological Models with a Modified Halstead-Reitan Battery*

Robert F. Newby

University of Wisconsin

and

Charles E. Hallenbeck   Susan Embretson (Whitely)

University of Kansas

ABSTRACT

Four theoretical factor models for a modified Halstead-Reitan battery were formulated, drawing from previous work by Swiercinsky, Royce and co-workers, Christensen and Luria, and Lezak. The relative explanatory power of these four models for this particular battery in an adult neuropsychiatric population was examined using confirmatory factor analysis. None of the models was shown to fit adequately in an absolute sense, but three of them represented substantial, statistically reliable improvements over a null model of mutual independence, and a clear pattern of relative fit was observed. Further improvements were achieved by modifying the best fitting initial model in several ways. A cross-validation with an independent sample supported the results of the model development step. Tentative theoretical and clinical implications for the overall organization of the neuro-psychological abilities measured by this battery were drawn, and recommendations were made for further application of this method in neuropsychological research.

The Halstead-Reitan assessment tradition has undergone much technical and empirical advancement during the last several decades, but theory seems to have lagged behind rather than guided this development. Major empirical studies have refined clinical assessment procedures (Reitan, 1966; Russell, Neuringer, &

---

* Support for this project by the Topeka Veterans Administration Medical Center and the University of Kansas is gratefully acknowledged. Suggestions by James M. Schear and Dennis P. Swiercinsky were particularly appreciated. This article was revised from a paper presented at the International Neuropsychological Society Meeting, Bergen, Norway, June 1981.

Goldstein, 1970; Swiercinsky, 1978), have correlated behavioral test data with various brain-damage types and localizations (Reitan, 1966; Reitan & Davison, 1974), and have explored the battery's underlying factor structure (Goldstein & Shelly, 1972; Halstead, 1947; Swiercincsky, 1978, 1979, Note 1). Among these empirical undertakings, Halstead's (1947) original factor-analytic work represented a highlight in theory development, particularly since he performed his multivariate analyses and interpretations in the days before computers. In spite of the subsequent fading of his particular theoretical notions, his attempt to build theory with complex empirical data stands as a benchmark in clinical neuropsychology. The current study attempted to promote theoretical integration in this field by testing the relative adequacy of four broad conceptual models with one current version of the Halstead-Reitan battery (Swiercinsky, 1978), then developing one of these models further. The project intended to synthesize the theoretical values of several clinically based models for the overall organization of neuropsychological functioning (e.g., Lezak, 1976; Luria, 1966, 1973) with the methodological strengths of multivariate analysis, in particular confirmatory factor analysis.

One major goal of this article was to illustrate some of the research processes involved in the recently developed method of confirmatory factor analysis, which is a subset of structural equation modeling (Bentler, 1980; Jöreskog & Sorbom, 1979). This method offers several important advantages over traditional exploratory factor analysis, which have been demonstrated in other clinical problems outside of neuropsychology (e.g., Bentler & Peeler, 1979; Bentler & Speckart, 1979).

First, the researcher must begin with a theory or, better yet, several competing theories that specify the following: (a) the latent factors that underlie a given set of measured variables; (b) the variables that measure each factor; and, (c) how the factors relate to each other. Theory plays a much greater role in this modeling process than in traditional exploratory methods, which rely almost exclusively on mathematical algorithms to search for relationships in the data. Second, the relative adequacy of alternative models can be tested statistically, and poorer models can be rejected on statistical grounds for inadequate fit with the data. This is accomplished by comparing how well the hypothesized models reproduce an observed data correlation matrix. Although no given model can be conclusively proven, clear standardized comparisons can be made among available models. Third, the entire model estimation process is done simultaneously, thereby avoiding the indeterminacy that may arise in selecting rotations and in separately extracting higher-order factors in traditional factor analysis. Finally, this method can be extended to test hypotheses about causal relationships among the underlying factors.

Despite these advantages, researchers should take caution to not plunge into confirmatory factor analysis uncritically. Although these methods have been used in economics and other fields for years, they have only recently been introduced into psychology, and some statistical controversies and unanswered issues remain (Bentler, 1980). Some of these will be addressed in the description of the current study below. Perhaps even more important, major alterations in the way research questions are conceptualized are called for, largely due to the hypothesis-testing nature of this method and its estimation of latent factors as well as measured variables in theoretical models (Embretson, Note 2).

For purposes of the current project, Swiercinsky's (1978) version of the Halstead-Reitan battery was accepted as a reasonable example of comprehensive assessment in clinical neuropsychology. Drawing from previous empirical and theoretical work by others, four alternative conceptual models were contructed for a core set of test variables from this battery (see Table 1).

Table 1

Thirty-Seven Core Variables from the Modified Halstead-Reitan Battery

Variable	Mean	Standard Deviation
1. Aphasia Language Performance Scales-- Listening Subtest (items correct)	9.11	1.12
2. Aphasia Language Performance Scales-- Reading Subtest (items correct)	8.88	1.11
3. Speech-Sounds Perception Test (errors)	12.00	8.06
4. Wechsler Memory Scale-- Semantic Short-Term Score	13.05	7.32
5. Wechsler Memory Scale-- Semantic Delayed Score	8.89	6.94
6. Wechsler Adult Intelligence scale-- Information Subtest (scaled score)	9.68	3.15
7. Wechsler Adult Intelligence Scale-- Vocabulary Subtest (scaled score)	9.67	2.41
8. Shipley Institute of Living Scale-- Abstraction Score	16.90	9.65
9. Wechsler Adult Intelligence Scale-- Similarities Subtest (scaled score)	9.38	3.02
10. Wechsler Adult Intelligence Scale-- Comprehension Subtest (scaled score)	9.68	3.15
11. Wechsler Adult Intelligence Scale-- Arithmetic Subtest (scaled score)	9.53	3.08
12. Aphasia Language Performance Scales-- Talking Subtest (items correct)	9.91	0.34
13. Aphasia Language Performance Scales-- Writing Subtest (items correct)	9.34	1.06
14. Trail Making Test-- Part A (seconds)	43.10	22.65
15. Trail Making Test-- Part B (seconds)	126.68	73.80
16. Graphesthesia-- Right Hand (errors)	3.58	3.68
17. Graphesthesia-- Left Hand (errors)	2.71	3.27

18. Stereognosis-- Right Hand (errors)	0.16	0.46
19. Stereognosis-- Left Hand (errors)	0.12	0.36
20. Finger Gnosis-- Right Hand (errors)	1.70	2.46
21. Finger Gnosis-- Left Hand (errors)	1.62	2.39
22. Seashore Rhythm Test (errors)	7.19	4.41
23. Wechsler Memory Scale-- Figural Short-Term Score	7.47	3.67
24. Wechsler Memory Scale-- Figural Delayed Score	5.99	3.89
25. Tactual Performance Test-- Location Score	2.07	2.09
26. Tactual Performance Test-- Total Time (minutes)	20.51	7.08
27. Wechsler Adult Intelligence Scale-- Picture Arrangement Subtest (scaled score)	8.03	2.67
28. Wechsler Adult Intelligence Scale-- Block Design Subtest (scaled score)	8.73	2.76
29. Wechsler Adult Intelligence Scale-- Object Assembly Subtest (scaled score)	8.54	2.96
30. Wechsler Adult Intelligence Scale-- Digit Symbol Subtest (scaled score)	6.85	2.43
31. Spatial Relations (cross drawings rating)	2.56	0.98
32. Grip Strength-- Right Hand (kilograms)	40.30	11.11
33. Grip Strength-- Left Hand (kilograms)	38.67	10.30
34. Finger Tapping-- Right Hand (taps per 10 seconds)	41.37	9.81
35. Finger Tapping-- Left Hand (taps per 10 seconds)	38.36	8.48
36. Grooved Pegboard-- Right Hand (seconds)	82.55	32.78
37. Grooved Pegboard-- Left Hand (seconds)	87.12	34.81

Note. These tests are described in more detail in Swiercinsky (1978). The signs of variables 3, 14 to 22, 26, 31, 36, and 37 were reversed in computing correlations so that better performance was uniformly indicated by positive correlations.

In response to recent trends expressing a growing interest in rehabilitation (e.g., Diller, 1976; Goldstein, 1979), models that focused on functional description and explanation rather than on topological localization were sought. It was thought that this orientation would ultimately prove most useful in function-and reha-bilitation-oriented clinical work.

Because liberal interpretation necessarily occurred in the process of translating each model into confirmatory factor analysis terms, the four models cannot be said to represent their source theories exactly, although credits to the sources are acknowledged. Partly due to the translation process, and partly because most of these source theories were not formulated in the context of the test variables used here, this project should be conceptualized as a search for the best set of theoretical constructs to explain the relationships among variables in this particular battery, not as fair generalized tests of the four source theories. Furthermore, given the relatively underdeveloped nature of theory in this assessment tradition, several modifications of the originally hypothesized models were anticipated in cases of inadequate fit. A brief outline of each model follows; more complete formulations are available (Newby, Note 3).

The first model (model A) was based on previous factor-analytic work by Swiercinsky's (Note 1) method and his pragmatic reasons in favor of orthogonal rotations in exploratory factor analyses (Swiercinsky, 1979). To enhance the model's conceptual internal consistency, Swiercinsky's interpretive statements were the only model in the current study to postulate uncorrelated factors, following Swiercinsky's (Note 1) method and his pragmatic reasons in factor of orthogonal rotations in exploratory factor analyses (Swiercinsky, 1979). To enhance the model's conceptual internal consistency, Swiercinsky's interpretive statemens were given considerable weight in balance with the actual factor-loading pattern from his analyses. Thus, many cross-factor-loadings that were low and/or could not fit into his interpretive scheme were eliminated for purposes of the current model. The nine hypothesized factors (and associated variables) are outlined below:

 I. Verbal Information Processing (2,4,5,6,7,8,9.10,11)
 II. Verbal Short-Term Memory (4,5,10)
 III. Language Use (1,2,3,12,13)
 IV. Abstract Reasoning (8,11,22,27,28)
 V. Spatial Reasoning (25,26,28,29,31)
 VI. Speed in Visual-Motor Integration (14,15,30,36,37)
 VII. Primary Motor Functioning (32,33,34,35,36,37)
 VIII. Tactile Pattern Recognition (16,17,18,19,20,21)
 IX. Figural Short-Term Memory (23,24,25)

Model B was constructed from factor interpretations in previous exploratory analyses with a similar neuropsychological battery by Royce and his associates (Aftanas & Royce, 1969; Royce, Yeudall, & Bock, 1976) and from concepts in Royce's (1973) more general theory of cognitive structure. Three second-order factors (e.g., A) subsumed eight first-order factors (e.g., I) (and their associated variables):

A. Perceptual Integration
 I. Perceptual Organization (14,15,25,26,27,28,29,31)
 II. Perceptual-Motor Speed (30,35,36,37)
 III. Temporal Resolution (22,34,35)
B. Verbal Memory
 IV. Verbal Comprehension (1,2,3,4,5,6,7,9,10,11,12,13,20,22)
 V. Long-Term Memory (6,10,14,16,17,20)
C. Visualization
 VI. Spatial Orientation (15,21)
No second-order factor:
 VII. Pattern Recognition (23,24,28)
 VIII. Abstraction (8)

Factors VII and VIII were not associated with any second-order factors in the

Royce et al. (1976) study, so they stood independently here. Differences between tests in that study's battery versus the current battery only allowed meaningful identification of second-order factor C by one first order factor (VI) and of factor VIII by one measured variable (8).

These singular identifications presented two theoretical problems that should be avoided when possible by identifying all latent variables with several measured variables. First, unique or error variances cannot be estimated by the program for singular identifying variables. Thus, they have to be set arbitrarily by the researcher. The particular error values chosen may not affect model fit, as in the current example, but the arbitrariness of the process limits later interpretations that can be made. Second, it is good to account for all of the factors in the model with equivalent conceptual confidence; this was clearly not achievable in model B since the number of variables at hand that could be assigned reasonably to each factor requiring definition ranged from 1 to 14. Carefully planning the theoretical models to be tested before choosing which measured variables to use is a good way out of this dilemma, but this strategy was only partially applicable in the current study because a preset test battery was used.

Model C consisted of Christensen's (1975) and Luria's (1966) 10 categories for neuropsychological assessment, with some additional concepts from Luria's (1973) overall theory. This model's applicability to the current battery was tenuous because of substantial differences between the Halstead-Reitan and Luria assessment approaches. However, this model was tried because it was originally derived from one of the most well-developed theories in clinical neuropsychology (Luria, 1966, 1973). Variables from the current battery were assigned to each of the factors primarily on the basis of similarities in content to the examination procedures for each of Christensen's (1975) 10 categories, and secondarily on the basis of other inferences from Luria's (1973) theory. The factors were allowed to correlate because Luria postulated interdependence between categories of brain functioning. Ten single-order correlated factors (with their associated variables) were defined:

    I.   Motor Functioning (1,23,26,31,32,33,34,35,36,37)
   II.   Acoustico-Motor Functions (22,34,35)
  III.   Higher Cutaneous and Kinsthetic Functions (16,17,18,19,20,21)
  IV.   Higher Visual Functions (14,15,25,28,29,30,31,36,37)
   V.   Impressive Speech (1,3)
  VI.   Expressive Speech (7,12)
 VII.   Writing and Reading (2,3,8,13,14,15)
VIII.   Arithmetic Skill (11,14,15)
  IX.   Mnestic Processes (4,5,23,24,25)
   X.   Intellectual Processing (6,7,8,9,10,27)

The basic framework for model D came from Lezak's (1976) brief conceptualization of the intellectual system, which organized verbal and nonverbal activities into receptive, memory, cognitive or thinking, and expressive functional levels. Considerable elaboration of Lezak's skeletal outline with ideas from other work in the field was carried out. For instance, Milner (1970), Russell (1975), and Butters (1979) have documented a distinction between verbal and nonverbal memory processes. On the other hand, Lezak's (1976) conglomeration of both short-term and long-term memory was maintained in factor II in spite of research differentiating anterograde and retrograde amnesia (Butters, 1979). The cognitive or thinking factors (III and VII) were conceptualized in Luria's (1973) terms as mainly tertiary processes, while particularly in the nonverbal half of the model the receptive factors (I and V) and expressive factors (IV and VIII) mainly involved primary and secondary projection. Both expressive aphasia tests and the Trail Making Test were posited to be determined by the verbal expressive factor (IV) because symbolic coding was seen as intimately involved in these tasks. The WAIS Digit Symbol subtest was considered to be nonverbal expressive (VII) because the sequential and symbolic aspects of this task appeared to be less salient. Two sets of four parallel first-order factors were subsumed under verbal and nonverbal second-order factors:

A. General Verbal Ability
    I.   Verbal Receptive Functions (1,2,3)
    II. Verbal Memory and Learning (4,5,6,7)
    III. Verbal Cognitive Processing (6,7,8,9,10,11)
    IV. Verbal Expressive Functions (12,13,14,15)
B. General Nonverbal Ability
    V.   Nonverbal Receptive Functions (16,17,18,19,20,21,22)
    VI. Nonverbal Memory and Learning (22,23,24,25)
    VII. Nonverbal Cognitive Processing (22,26,27,28,29)
    VIII. Nonverbal Expressive Functions (30,31,32,33,34,35,36,37)

METHOD AND RESULTS

Subjects for the main part of the study were 497 adult neuropsychiatric patients who were referred for neuropsychological testing because of suspected brain impairment. This sample's mean age was 43.5 years, and mean years of education was 11.6; 95% were male. Sixty-five percent of the sample received diagnoses of brain damage by physicians at the time of testing, with nonspecific organic brain syndrome, alcoholic encephalopathy, complex partial seizures, and nonpenetrating head trauma representing the most frequent categories. These neurological diagnoses usually implied diffuse rather than focal damage. Seventy-six percent of the sample had psychiatric diagnoses, including nonorganic-nonpsychotic psychiatric problems, schizophrenia, alcoholism, and nonschizophrenic-psychotic disorders. Half of all subjects carried multiple diagnoses. An independent cross-validation sample of 237 additional patients from the same referral population was also compiled.

These samples represented two recent data collection periods (May, 1976 to February, 1980 and February, 1980 to April, 1981) at the Topeka Veterans Administration Medical Center. Previous samples from this setting have been among the most thoroughly studied neuropsychiatric populations reported in the clinical neuropsychology literature (e.g., Goldstein & Shelly, 1972; Russell et al., 1970; Swiercinsky, 1978, 1979, Note 1). Although arguments can be raised that the conglomeration of subpopulations, low proportion of normal subjects, and VA social context make this a difficult data base for research purposes, it should also be borne in mind that this is exactly the kind of population in which it is most relevant to test clinical theories. The clinical characteristics of these samples present a formidable, but valid, challenge to theoretical models. It can be assumed that normal subjects were present in this population at a frequency that is relevant to neuropsychologists who receive clinical referrals; a higher proportion or exclusive sample of normals would risk meaninglessly skewed distributions of many test measures due to ceiling effects.

Each patient in both samples was administered the entire modified Halstead-Reitan neuropsychological battery following routine, controled laboratory procedures (Swiercinsky, 1978). The standard Halstead-Reitan had been modified by subsituting the Aphasia Language Performance Scales (Keenan & Brassell, 1975) for the Halstead-Wepman Aphasia Test, by substituting the brief Shipley Institute of Living Scale (Shipley, 1940) for the Category Test, and by adding the Grooved Pegboard Test (Matthews, Cleeland, & Hopper, 1970) and Russell's (1975) version of the Wechsler Memory Scale.

Analyses proceeded in three steps. In the first step, the relative adequacy of the four hypothetical models in the initial sample was tested. Following this, the best-fitting initial model was modified to improve fit, using both theoretical notions and analysis-based suggestions for changes. The third step was a cross-validation, in which the second sample was used to compare fit among the four initial models and the final modified model. The cross-validation served to test the stability of the parameter estimations and of the data-based model modifications from the first two steps. Exact procedures and results will be presented separately for the three steps.

Initial Model Testing

Thirty-seven key variables were selected from the battery for this study (see Table 1), primarily because most appeared to tap higher neuropsychological processes more than basic neurological functioning, and/or because they related most strongly to the four theoretical models of interest. On all tasks for which right and left hand measures were taken, the two scores were both included, since previous factor analyses have suggested that lateralized differences may be important in some of these models (Royce et al., 1976). Furthermore, it should be pointed out that combining right and left scores in some manner may lead to spurious or questionably interpretable factors (Swiercinsky, Note 1, reviewed by Newby, Note 3).

A Pearson correlation matrix of these variables was subjected to confirmatory factor analysis by translating each of the four models into a set of simultaneous equations then estimating factor loadings, factor covariances, and unique or error variances with the computer program LISREL IV (Jöreskog & Sorbom, 1978). Although there are alternative statistical methods for formulating and estimating parameters under development, the LISREL maximum likelihood method is widely regarded as the most well-developed, adequately reliable program at this time (Bentler, 1980). Rotations are unnecessary in this procedure because variables are typically assigned to a single factor or a small number of factors and all other loadings are fixed at zero, analogous to the simple structure that is characteristically sought in exploratory factor analysis rotations. LISREL's goodness of fit chi-square test was used to compare the relative adequacy of the models in two ways.

The first goodness of fit judgment involved comparisons among the models' chi-square values, which are derived from the maximum-likelihood fitting function. Three models (A, B, and D) were reliably different from the observed data matrix (all $ps < .0001$), indicating inadequate absolute fit at this initial stage. A nonsignificant chi-square in this comparison would indicate that the

Table 2

Indicators of Fit for the Four Initial Models and the
Final Modified Model in the Initial and Model Development Steps

Model	Deviation from Hypothetical Perfect Model	Improvement over Null Model	Index of Fit
	chi-square (df)	chi-square (df)	index
Null Model	11588.97* (666)	—	—
Model A	4334.05* (618)	7254.92* (48)	.63
Model B	4163.47* (621)	7425.50* (45)	.64
Model C[a]	—	—	—
Model D	3234.99* (616)	8353.98* (50)	.72
Final Modified Model	1664.26* (599)	9924.71* (67)	.86

[a]Model C could not converge to a solution, so it was eliminated from further consideration.
*$p < .0001$

model in question is not different from a hypothetical perfectly fitting model. This test has typically been considered the main test of a model's adequacy in confirmatory factor analysis research, but this criterion may be unreasonably or misleadingly strict in some conditions, and alternative tests have been proposed (Bentler & Bonett, 1980) as follows. All three of the testable models represented statistically reliable improvements over a null model-- i.e., the hypothesis that all test variables were uncorrelated or independent. The *relative* fit among models was compared by examining their chi-square values in relation to the degrees of freedom differences between models. Although the lack of exactly nested parameters across the four models precluded strict significance testing in this comparison process, a clear pattern of relative fit among models was observed, with consistently large chi-square differences divided by degrees of freedom differences: Model D ($\chi^2 = 3234.99$ (616)) fit substantially better than model B ($\chi^2 = 4163.47$ (621)), which in turn was substantially superior to model A ($\chi^2 = 4334.05$ (618)).

In part because some of its latent constructs could not be identified by variables from the current battery, model C did not converge to a solution, so it was eliminated from further consideration. In particular, factors I and IV in model C could not be distinguished from each other mathematically, and the numerous language (V, VI, VII) and arithmetic (VIII) factors were judged to be theoretically underidentified with the available test variables. The failure of model C illustrates incidentally the need for overidentifying restrictions in structural modeling equations-- i.e., the need for a sufficient number and an appropriate pattern of fixed parameters in the model so that each latent factor can be mathematically identified.

In situations such as this (where models differ significantly from both the null model and a hypothetically perfect model), a careful, balanced judgment must be made regarding the explanatory value of each of the models in question. In short, we know that we have more than "nothing" and that we have not achieved "everything", but what is the worth of the "something" that we have constructed? The next comparison method was developed to provide an answer to this question.

Bentler and Bonett's (1980) normed incremental index of fit was used to estimate *how much* improvement the three testable theoretical models had achieved over the null model and to compare the models numerically with each other (see Table 2). This index was computed with the formula index $= (Q_o - Q_t)/Q_o$, where Q_o equals the chi-square value for the null model and Q_t equals the chi-square value for the model of interest. This index ranges from zero, which is equivalent to the most restricted or null model, to one, which represents a perfectly fitting model. The exact meaning of increments in terms of variance accounted for is not known at this time, since no statistical theory has been developed for the index. However, Bentler and Bonett (1980) have suggested that models with indices less than .90 could be modified to improve fit. Again, model D showed the best index (.72), followed by model B (.64), then model A (.63).

Model Modification and Development Step

The non-fitting chi-square (criterion of $p < .05$) and low incremental index (.18 lower than Bentler and Bonett's suggested guideline) in even the best of the four initial models suggested that model modifications might improve fit. In order to pursue a model development strategy that would concentrate on the relative strengths among the initial models, and to avoid the computer problems that arose in trying to expand the relatively less successful initial models, only the best-fitting model (D) was modified to improve fit in the current study. A series of modifications on model D yielded a final model with an index of .86 and a significantly improved, but still statistically inadequate, absolute fit (see Tables 2 and 3).

Three modifications improved chi-square fit reliably and increased the incremental index, so they were retained in the final modified model. In order of strength of effect, these were as follows: (a) correlated error terms between most right- and left-hand measures of the same variable; (b) split and/or alternate factor-loading patterns for many variables that had been hypothesized initially to associate with only one factor; and, (c) the addition of a new factor IX corresponding to Lezak's (1976) "mental activity variables." Several other modifications that were attempted did not improve model fit reliably, so they were rejected. Most notable among these was a reconceptualization of the second-order factors to test an alternative interpretation of Lezak's verbal-nonverbal differentiation. In this unsuccessful modification, each of the four intellectual processes (receptive, memory, cognition, and expressive) comprised a second-order factor that subsumed two first-order factors (verbal and nonverbal elements). Further modifications, while hypothetically possible, were hampered by limitations on the size of models that could be processed by the version of LISREL IV that was available. (In general, we found that LISREL ran into serious technical limitations in models with over 100 free parameters.)

Because model D and its final modified model had "nested parameters", (i.e., variations on the same basic structure of measured and latent variables [Bentler & Bonett, 1980]), a statistical test of the reliability of the difference between their chi-square values could be performed. This difference ($\chi^2 = 1570.73$ (17), $p < .0001$) was reliable.

The initial model testing step was a purely confirmatory analysis in this study, while the second step should be conceptualized as a mingling of exploratory and confirmatory use of the structural equation modeling techniques. This process was exploratory in the sense that both information gleaned from prior analyses and alternative ideas derived from theory were used to change the model in an incremental fashion. It was confirmatory in the sense that standardized judgments about the statistical reliability of differences between the fit of successive model modifications were made.

Table 3

Factor Loading Pattern of Final Modified Model

First Order

Variables	Factors									Unique	
	I	II	III	IV	V	VI	VII	VIII	IX	Variances	Covariances
1	.537	0	0	0	0	0	0	0	0	.711	
2	.726	0	0	0	0	0	0	0	0	.473	
3	.706	—.267	.091	0	0	0	0	0	0	.584	
4	0	.941	0	0	0	0	0	0	0	.114	
5	0	.946	0	0	0	0	0	0	0	.104	
6	0	0	.867	0	0	0	0	0	0	.248	
7	0	0	.867	0	0	0	0	0	0	.248	
8	.325	0	.191	0	0	0	.397	0	0	.343	
9	0	.089	.698	0	0	0	0	0	0	.445	
10	0	.280	.585	0	0	0	0	0	0	.421	
11	0	.243	.532	0	0	0	0	0	0	.532	
12	0	0	0	.346	0	0	0	0	0	.880	
13	0	0	0	.562	0	0	0	0	0	.648	
14	0	0	0	.730	0	0	0	0	.370	.346	
15	0	0	0	.831	0	0	0	0	.150	.249	
16	0	0	0	0	.678	0	0	0	0	.540	.300
17	0	0	0	0	.675	0	0	0	0	.544	
18	0	0	0	0	.305	0	0	0	0	.907	.533
19	0	0	0	0	.397	0	0	0	0	.842	
20	0	0	0	0	.592	0	0	0	0	.649	.313
21	0	0	0	0	.677	0	0	0	0	.542	
22	0	0	0	0	.368	0	.198	0	0	.727	
23	0	0	0	0	0	.946	0	0	0	.104	
24	0	0	0	0	0	.895	0	0	0	.199	
25	0	0	0	0	0	0	.655	0	0	.571	
26	0	0	0	0	0	0	.789	0	.104	.360	
27	0	0	0	0	0	0	.709	0	0	.498	
28	0	0	0	0	0	0	.838	0	0	.298	
29	0	0	0	0	0	0	.744	0	0	.446	
30	0	0	0	0	0	0	0	.707	.189	.449	
31	0	0	0	0	0	0	0	.437	0	.809	
32	0	0	0	0	0	0	0	.441	0	.805	.572
33	0	0	0	0	0	0	0	.430	0	.815	
34	0	0	0	0	0	0	0	.507	0	.743	.450
35	0	0	0	0	0	0	0	.510	0	.740	
36	0	—.113	0	0	0	0	0	.535	.604	.347	
37	0	—.120	0	0	0	0	0	.570	.595	.323	

Second Order			
Factors	Factors[a]		Unique Variances
	A	B	
	A	B	
I	.977	0	.045
II	.593	0	.648
III	.624	0	.610
IV	.944	0	.109
V	0	.721	.479
VI	0	.822	.325
VII	0	.948	.102
VIII	0	.943	.111
IX	0	0	1.000

Note. Fixed parameters include all zeros in this table plus one loading per factor to set the scale for each factor. All other parameters are free. See Table 1 for variable names. See text for factor names.

[a] Correlation between second order factors A and B is .865.

Cross-Validation

Cross-validation is advised in confirmatory factor analysis, especially if model modifications have been undertaken. In the current study, the results of the initial and model development steps were confirmed by the crossvalidation– i.e., no model achieved adequate absolute fit, but three represented statistically reliable improvements over the null model, and the same patterns of relative fit among the initial and modified models were observed (see Table 4).

This step employed the same model fitting, statistical testing, and incremental indexing procedures as did the previous step, in two variations suggested by Bentler (1980). In the first variation, model pattern and factor loading values identical to those from the first two steps were used. The second variation used the same model patterns but allowed loadings to be estimated freshly on the new data. Although the same relative fit among models was observed in both variations, reliably better fit in the latter variation for all models indicated that the actual factor loadings (equivalent to beta weights in a regression analysis) were different in the two samples.

Comparing the same model across multiple populations, as in cross-validation, may be done simultaneously in the same LISREL run. It is necessary to use covariance rather than correlation matrices for this procedure, since the equivalence of sample variances as well as covariances is tested. Again, the sheer size of the current models precluded this approach in the cross-validation step, since LISREL would have to estimate twice as many parameters in a single run. Thus, correlation matrices were used throughout this study for easier interpretation of analysis results.

Table 4

Indicators of Fit for the Four Initial Models and the
Final Modified Model in the Cross-Validation Step

Model	Variation 1-- Identical Pattern and Loadings as in Model Development		Variation 2-- Identical Pattern as in Model Development, New Loadings Estimated		Improvement from Variation 1 to Variation 2
	Chi-square (df)	Index of fit	Chi-square (df)	Index of fit	Chi-square (df)
Null	6450.64***	—	—	—	—
Model A	2755.33*** (666)	.57	2682.26*** (618)	.58	73.14* (48)
Model B	2769.39*** (658)	.57	2505.04*** (621)	.61	264.35** (37)
Model C[a]	—	—	—	—	—
Model D	1974.62*** (655)	.69	1908.99*** (616)	.70	65.73* (39)
Final Modified Model	1311.94*** (650)	.80	1242.44*** (599)	.81	69.50* (51)

Note. All comparisons with the null model showed the same pattern of significant differences as in model development (see Table 2).

[a]Since the solution of model C was invalidated by extreme parameter estimates, it was eliminated from further consideration.

*p < .05
**p < .001
***p < .0001

DISCUSSION

In part because of their recent emergence into the research literature, the most reasonable interpretive balance among the absolute chi-square test, null model test, chi-square difference tests, and indices of fit is not clear at this time. In studies such as the current one, which attempted to apply diverse theoretical constructs to results from a preexisting assessment battery, it would appear appropriately cautious to regard the relatively high index in the final modified model as encouraging but not conclusive. Although the current project did not identify an adequately fitting model for the modified Halstead-Reitan battery in the absolute sense, several theoretically relevant suggestions can be made, and an important new methodology for research in clinical neuropsychology has been illustrated. Three of the initial models (D, B, and A) showed reliably and substantially greater explanatory power with this battery than did a null model of mutual independence, and substantial differences in fit were observed among the theoretical models. A series of modifications with the best initial model effected considerable, reliable improvement in fit. All results from the model development process were substantiated in an independent cross-validation. Theoretical modeling for this version of the Halstead-Reitan bettery has not yet reached a culmination, but current efforts appear to be leading in a productive direction.

Several theoretically and clinically relevant suggestions may be drawn from the current study. First, it is encouraging that a structurally simple conceptual scheme of receptive, memory, cognitive, and expressive neuropsychological processes with parallel verbal and nonverbal manifestations (Lezak, 1976) can be developed into a relatively well-fitting model for a global neuropsychological assessment battery. The current project's model modification process would suggest that introducing complexities such as additional factors and split factor loadings are necessary to improve fit. Model fit was enhanced in the current modification process when many important battery measures were reconceptualized as multifactorial (i.e., Speech-Sounds Perception Test, Shipley Abstraction Test, WAIS Similarities Subtest, WAIS Comprehension Subtest, WAIS Arithmetic Subtest, Trail Making Test, parts A & B, Seashore Rhythm Test, Tactual Performance Test (total time), WAIS Digit Symbol Subtest, Grooved Pegboard Test (right and left hand times)), and it is likely that further modeling would identify even more multifactorial tests.

Second, the inclusion of a factor that corresponds to Lezak's (1976, pp. 27-28) mental activity variables or Luria's (1973, pp. 44-67) regulatory unit of brain functioning increased model adequacy, at least in the best model that we tested. Future causal modeling with clinical batteries might attempt to measure this factor with nontest variables such as physiological measures or structured ratings by observers.

Third, many variables in the current battery appear to be composed primarily of unique and/or error variance rather than common factor variance. Many basic sensory and motor variables which are measured for both right and left hands and most of the Aphasia Languange Performance Scales (Keenan & Brassell, 1975) fell into this category with the current data sets. The skewed distributions of these variables may have contributed to their marginal status in the models that were examined here. Current results would suggest that they should be considered to be pathognomonic signs (Reitan, 1966) rather than well-distributed functional descriptors in this battery.

Fourth, as many other researchers have suggested, relatively short-term semantic and figural memory functions seem to be distinguished from each other and from remote memory as separate, though correlated, latent neuropsychological processes.

Fifth, several variables that were initially presumed to measure certain underlying factors tentatively appear more strongly dependent on other factors.

Most outstandingly, the Shipley Abstraction Subtest is more strongly associated with nonverbal than with verbal cognitive processes, and the Location component from the Tactual Performance Test loads significantly with nonverbal cognitive processes but not with nonverbal short-term memory.

Finally, as least in this population, general verbal and nonverbal abilities appear to be very highly correlated (.86) in the final modified model. This finding brings into question the importance of distinguishing between these two higher-order factors in this population with the final model. All of these conclusions should be considered as tentative, but appropriate, hypotheses for further investigation.

The relative success of model D, and of the derivative final modified model, deserves special emphasis because its basic framework was drawn from a conceptual rather than from an empirically derived factor model. The results of the current study suggest that broad theoretical structures can be applied to the Halstead-Reitan battery in spite of its largely atheoretical historical development. One consequence of this history is that many of the battery's component tests need to be conceptualized as multifactorial, a finding that would merit further investigation with the causal modeling methodology. In the meantime, clinicians should avoid interpreting at least the above list of multifactor tests as if they measured a single neuropsychological function. Because the modified Halstead-Reitan battery was not constructed to operationalize any particular theory, it would be inappropriate to reject the less successful conceptual schemes that were tried here solely on the basis of their performance with this particular set of measures. It is possible that these other theories could generate alternative clinical measures that could produce even more satisfactory models for neuropsychological functioning. The concepts underlying model C (Christensen, 1975; Luria, 1966, 1973) might be particularly promising in this regard, for they have already provided a wealth of test measures that could be used in studies similar to the current one.

Several possible reasons for the current models' inadequate absolute fit may be offered. Some reasons concern the application of theory. The nascent status of theoretical developments in the field and/or the project's practical limitations in exploring exhaustively all available theoretical contributions may have rendered the models attempted here simply inadequate. Size limitations in the most widely used currently available confirmatory computer algorithm thwarted attempts to test more complex models that may have fit better. Statistical problems may have hampered model fitting in several ways. Some variables in the current data set violated the statistical assumption that distributions are multinormal, and some important relationships in the data could have been nonlinear. The effects of such violations on the model estimation procedures and the chi-square goodness of fit test are not yet known (Bentler, 1980). It is known that larger sample sizes increase the reliability of population covariance estimates but, paradoxically, make model fitting criteria more strict (Bentler, 1980); the absolute chi-square tests may therefore have been overly conservative in the current study. Larger variable sets, such as the one used here, may also create the same problem. Some combination of these issues was probably operating in the current study. Future theoretical, technical, and statistical developents in neuropsychology and in causal modeling may ameliorate some of these potential interferences in the modeling process.

Confirmatory factor analysis and related causal modeling approaches appear to be valuable tools for neuropsychological research. The current study has yielded several recommendations for future application of this method. Smaller models (e.g., subsections of the global battery that was examined here) may avoid technical limitations in current modeling algorithms and may be more likely to yield positive results. Eventually, large-scale global modeling such as that attempted here would be desirable, but such efforts might have to await further theoretical and statistical advancements. Full use of the latest methodological developments, such as Bentler and Bonett's (1980) null model and indices of fit, is recommended. Structural modeling of relationships among latent variables of the type explored in the second-order factor patterns here will be extremely valuable, but such efforts may best follow the development of more adequate measurement models (i.e., the identification of which measured variables relate best with the latent, underlying variables of interest). Path models of causal influence among latent factors would enhance structural modeling considerably, and are workable in available computer algorithms. Finally, presumably influential nontest variables such as age, educational level, diagnosis, and mental activities (Lezak, 1976) could also be introduced into these models.

Hopefully, the current investigation has illustrated some of the potential that causal modeling methods offer for research in neuropsychology, particularly in examining functional systems in clinical neuropsychology. The capacity to test conceptual models with latent variables seems especially valuable in a field where most important constructs are latent rather than directly measurable, and where more bridges are needed between theory and research.

REFERENCE NOTES

1. Swiercinsky, D. P. Programmatic series of factor analyses for evaluating the structure of neuropsychological test batteries. Paper presented at the meeting of the International Neuropsychological Society, San Francisco, January 1980.
2. Embretson (Whitely), S. Hypothesis testing and drawing inferences. Invited presentation for symposium: Is problem modeling in educational research an art form? American Educational Research Association meeting, Los Angeles, April 1981.
3. A more complete account of this project's conceptual models, methods, and results will be available through University Microfilms as: Newby, R. F. Confirmatory factor analytic application of four general neuropsychological models to a modified Halstead-Reitan battery. Doctoral dissertation, University of Kansas, 1981.

REFERENCES

Aftanas, M. S., & Royce, J. R. A factor analysis of brain damage tests administered to normal subjects with factor comparisons across ages. *Multivariate Behavioral Research,* 1969, *4,* 459-481.

Bentler, P. M. Multivariate analysis with latent variables: Causal modeling. *Annual Review of Psychology,* 1980, *31,* 419-456.

Bentler, P. M., & Bonett, D. G. Significance tests and goodness of fit in the analysis of covariance structures. *Psychological Bulletin,* 1980, *88,* 588-606.

Bentler, P. M., & Peeler, W. H. Models of female orgasm. *Archives of Sexual Behavior,* 1979, *8,* 405-423.

Bentler, P. M., & Speckart, G. Models of attitude-behavior relations. *Psychological Review,* 1979, *86,* 452-464.

Butters, N. Amnestic disorders. In K. M. Heilman & E. Valenstein (Eds.), *Clinical neuropsychology,* New York: Oxford University Press, 1979.

Christensen, A. *Luria's neuropsychological investigation: Text.* New York: Spectrum Publications, 1975.

Diller, L. A model for cognitive retraining in rehabilitation. *The Clinical Psychologist,* 1976, *29,* 13-15.

Goldstein, G. Methodological and theoretical issues in neuropsychological assessment. *Journal of Behavioral Assessment,* 1979, *1,* 23-41.

Goldstein, G., & Shelly, C. H. Statistical and normative studies of the Halstead neuropsychological test battery relevant to a neuropsychiatric hospital setting. *Perceptual and Motor Skills,* 1972, *34,* 603-620.

Halstead, W. C. *Brain and intelligence.* Chicago: University of Chicago Press, 1947.

Jöreskog, K. G., & Sorbom, D. *LISREL IV: Analysis of linear structural relationships by the method of maximum likelihood.* Chicago: National Educational Resources, 1978.

Jöreskog, K. G., & Sorbom, D. *Advances in factor analysis and structural equation models.* Cambridge, Mass.: Abt Books, 1979.

Keenan, J. S., & Brassell, E. G. *Aphasia language performance scales.* Murfreesboro, Tenn.: Pinnacle Press, 1975.

Lezak, M. D. *Neuropsychological assessment.* New York: Oxford University Press, 1976.

Luria, A. R. *Higher cortical functions in man.* New York: Basic Books, 1966.

Luria, A. R. *The working brain.* New York: Basic Books, 1973.

Matthews, C. G., Cleeland, C. S., & Hopper, C. L. Neuropsychological patterns in multiple sclerosis. *Diseases of the Nervous System,* 1970, *31,* 161-170.

Milner, B. Memory and the medial temporal regions of the brain. In K. H. Pribram & D. E. Broadbent (Eds.), *Biology of memory.* New York: Academic Press, 1970.

Reitan, R. M. A research program on the psychological effects of brain lesions in human beings. In N. R. Ellis (Ed.), *International review of research in mental retardation. Vol. 1.* New York: Academic Press, 1966.

Reitan, R. M., & Davison, L. A. (Eds.). *Clinical neuropsychology: Current status and implications.* New York: John Wiley & Sons, 1974.

Royce, J. R. The conceptual framework for a multifactor theory of individuality. In J. R. Royce (Ed.), *Multivariate analysis and psychological theory.* London: Academic Press, 1973.

Royce, J. R., Yeudall, L. T., & Bock, C. Factor analytic studies of human brain damage: I. First and second order factors and their brain correlates. *Multivariate Behavioral Research,* 1976, *11,* 381-418.

Russell, E. W. A multiple scoring method for the assessment of complex memory functions. *Journal of Consulting and Clinical Psychology,* 1975, *43,* 800-809.

Russell, E. W., Neuringer, C., & Goldstein, G. *Assessment of brain damage: A neuropsychological key approach.* New York: Wiley-Interscience, 1970.

Shipley, W. C. A self-administering scale for measuring intellectual impairment and deterioration. *Journal of Psychology,* 1940, *9,* 371-377.

Swiercinsky, D. *Manual for the adult neuropsychological evaluation.* Springfield, Ill.: Charles C. Thomas, 1978.

Swiercinsky, D. P. Factorial pattern description and comparison of functional abilities in neuropsychological assessment. *Perceptual and Motor Skills,* 1979, *48,* 231-241.

The Clinical Neuropsychologist
1988, Vol. 2, No. 2, pp. 107-115

Factor Structure of the
Wechsler Memory Scale-Revised

Robert A. Bornstein

The Ohio State University

and

Gordon J. Chelune

Cleveland Clinic Foundation

ABSTRACT

The factor structure of the Wechsler Memory Scale-Revised (WMS-R) was examined in a large (N=434) sample of patients referred to the neuropsychology laboratories of two large medical centers. The subtests of the WMS-R were subjected to principal-components factor analysis. Some analyses included only the immediate-recall subtests, while other analyses included both immediate- and delayed-recall subtests. Additional analyses included VIQ and PIQ from the WAIS-R. Initial analyses of immediate-recall subtests indicated a two-factor solution similar to that reported in the standardization sample. Inclusion of IQ scores also revealed a two-factor solution with IQ scores and most memory subtests loading on separate factors. Inclusion in the analysis of delayed-recall subtests revealed three-factor solution with factors interpreted as representing verbal memory, nonverbal memory, and attention/IQ. These results are discussed in terms of factor- analytic studies of the earlier Wechsler Memory Scale, and the implications of the current data for research and clinical practice.

The Wechsler Memory Scale-Revised (WMS-R) may be conceptualized as a battery of tests of particular aspects of memory function. This revision of the previous test (Wechsler Memory Scale) includes tests of verbal and nonverbal paired-associate learning, recall of verbal and nonverbal material, nonverbal recognition memory, mental control, orientation, and delayed-recall trials of the associate learning and recall subtests. Factor-analytic studies of such test batteries are useful in helping to define the underlying constructs which appear to be represented in the test. When such factor- analytic studies are employed with other types of tests (such as IQ), information may be derived which addresses the independence of the constructs included in the different tests.

Numerous studies have examined the factor structure of the Wechsler Memory Scale (WMS). Some of these have included subtests from the Wechsler Adult Intelligence Scale (WAIS) or the revision of that test (WAIS-R). Skilbeck and Woods (1980) reviewed five factor-analytic studies of the WMS. Four of those studies yielded a three-factor solution with the first factor in all studies interpreted as a general learning, and recall factor, based on loadings of Logical Memory, Visual Reproduction, and Associate Learning subtests. In three of these four studies, the second factor was interpreted as an attention/concentration factor based on loadings on Mental Control and Digit Span subtests. The third factor has been interpreted as an information/orientation factor with loadings on Information and Orientation subtests. In one study (Bachrach & Mintz, 1974), the order of the second and third factors was reversed. The study by Davis and Swenson (1970) revealed a two-factor solution in which the initial learning and recall factor also incorporated the information/orientation subtests. Skilbeck and Woods (1980) reported an analysis in neurological and geriatric samples. In the neurological sample, the typical three-factor solution was obtained. In the geriatric sample, the initial factor was somewhat different with loadings from the Information, Orientation, Logical Memory, and Associate Learning subtests. The second factor was the typical attention/concentration factor, and the third factor was comprised by the Visual Reproduction subtest.

Addition of data from the Wechsler Intelligence Scales modifies the factoral relationship of the WMS subtests. Two studies have used data from the WAIS-R (Heilbronner, Buck, & Adams, 1987; Ryan, Rosenberg, & Heilbronner, 1984) and one study has used the WAIS (Larrabee, Kane, & Schuck, 1983). Heilbronner et al. (1987) reported a three-factor solution. The first factor was composed of the VIQ subtests, and Logical Memory, Mental Control, and Digit Span subtests of the WMS. The second factor included the PIQ subtests and the Visual Reproduction subtest from the WMS. The third factor received loadings from the Orientation, Logical Memory, and Associate Learning subtests of the WMS. Ryan et al. (1984) reported a four-factor solution but included the Digit Span scores from both WAIS and WMS, and did not include the Information and Orientation subtests. In addition, the subject-to-variable ratio of less than 4 to 1 raises questions about the reliability of these data. In this study the first factor obtained was a perceptual factor similar to the second factor in Heilbronner et al. (1987). The second factor was an attention/concentration factor, while the third factor obtained its loadings from the VIQ subtests. The fourth factor received its loadings from the Logical Memory and Associate Learning subtests. Larrabee et al. (1983) used the WMS and the WAIS and reported a five-factor solution. The studies by Ryan et al. (1984) and Heilbronner et al. (1987) also reported analyses with the WAIS. Ryan found similar factorial relationships, whereas Heilbronner et al. (1987) found somewhat different relationships.

With the introduction of the WMS-R it becomes important to study the factorial relationship of the test itself as well as the factorial structure of the test when examined in the context of other tests. The present study reports a factor-analytic study of the WMS-R alone and also in the context of the VIQ and PIQ scores from the WAIS-R.

METHOD

Subjects

The sample consisted of 434 (244 males, 190 females) patients who had been referred for neuropsychological evaluation at either the Ohio State University or the Cleveland Clinic Foundation. The majority of patients reported in this study were examined at the latter institution. The mean age of the sample was 44.7 years (SD = 18.1) and the mean educational level was 12.4 years (SD = 3.2). The mean VIQ was 90.6 (SD = 14.6) and the mean PIQ was 89.2 (SD = 15.2). The principal diagnostic groups included: seizure disorder (n=106), dementia (n=64), depression (n=53), alcohol/drug abuse (n=48), head injury (n=28), tumor (n=26), stroke (n=20), encephalitis (n=8), aneurysm/arteriovenous malformation (n=6). There were numerous other diagnoses included in the sample which represented the range of patients referred to the two laboratories (both of which are based in large medical centers).

RESULTS

The primary method of data analysis was Principal Components factor analysis. Various combinations of WMS-R subtests were examined, and some analyses included the VIQ and PIQ from the WAIS-R. The latter analyses employed VIQ and PIQ rather than FSIQ in the interest of examining the relationship between tests which appeared to tap similar content domains. That is, it was of interest to determine if VIQ would load with verbal memory subtests, and PIQ with nonverbal memory subtests.

The inital analysis employed the eight WMS-R subtests which are not delayed-recall trials. The results of this analysis, and the comparable analysis from the WMS-R standardization sample are presented in Table 1. As can be seen in Table 1, the results in the two samples are very similar. In both samples, the strongest loadings on factor 1 occur from Logical Memory, Visual Reproduction, Verbal Paired-Associate Learning, and Visual (nonverbal) Paired-Associate Learning. This could be interpreted as a general memory factor. The strongest loadings for the second factor appear with the Digit Span, Visual Memory Span (Block Tapping), and Mental Control subtests. This could be interpreted as an attentional factor. In the clinical sample, the two factors account for 65.5% of the variance. In addition to the similarities there are some differences between the two samples. In the clinical sample, the Figural Memory and Logical Memory subtests loaded more strongly on the general memory factor (as opposed to the

Table 1. Factor Structure of WMS-R Immediate Recall Subtests in Clinical and Standardization Samples.

	Standardization Sample ($n = 316$)[2]		Clinical Sample	
	I	II	I	II
Mental Control	.03	.80	.19	.79
Figural Memory	.30	.25	.62	.29
Logical Memory	.52	.43	.78	.15
Visual P.A.L.[1]	.72	.16	.79	.20
Verbal P.A.L.	.75	.18	.83	.18
Visual Reproduction	.74	.09	.74	.38
Digit Span	.23	.75	.17	.83
Visual Memory Span	.27	.65	.53	.64

1) P.A.L. = Paired Associate Learning
2) Standardization data Copyright © 1987 The Psychological Corporation. All rights reserved.

more equal loading seen in the standardization sample). In contrast, the Visual Memory Span subtest loads on both factors in the clinical sample whereas it loads primarily on the attentional factor in normals.

The next analysis included the VIQ and PIQ scores from the WAIS-R in addition to the WMS-R subtests from the previous analysis. The results of this analysis are presented in Table 2, which also contains some analogous data from the standardization sample. The data are not directly comparable because the analysis of the latter sample used FSIQ rather than VIQ and PIQ. As can be seen in Table 2, the introduction of IQ modifies the factor structure in the two samples in

Table 2. Factor Structure of WMS-R Immediate Recall Subtests and IQ Scores in Standardization and Clinical Samples.

	Standardization Sample[1]		Clinical Sample	
	I	II	I	II
Mental Control	.76	.02	.26	.63
Figural Memory	.22	.31	.67	.22
Logical Memory	.47	.51	.72	.26
Visual P.A.L.	.14	.72	.79	.19
Verbal P.A.L.	.17	.74	.80	.21
Visual Reproduction	.12	.73	.77	.32
Digit Span	.74	.22	.14	.84
Visual Memory Span	.67	.25	.56	.58
Full Scale IQ	.68	.51	–	–
Verbal IQ	–	–	.21	.84
Performance IQ	–	–	.43	.68

1) Standardization data © 1987 The Psychological Corporation. All rights reserved.

different ways. In the normal sample, FSIQ loads on the attentional factor, and that factor becomes the first factor extracted, with the general memory factor appearing second. In the clinical sample, both VIQ and PIQ also load most strongly on the attentional factor, and that factor remains as the second factor (general memory remains as the first factor).

The next step in the factor-analytic study of the WMS-R involved including the four delayed-recall subtests (Logical Memory, Visual Reproduction, Verbal and Visual Paired Associate Learning). This analysis revealed two clear factors, and a weak third factor (eigenvalue = .88) which accounted for 73% of the variance. The results of this analysis are presented in Table 3. The strongest loadings on the first factor were from Logical Memory (Immediate and Delayed), and Verbal Paired-Associate Learning (Immediate and Delayed). This could be interpreted as a verbal memory factor. Strong loadings on the second factor were observed

Table 3. Factor Structure of WMS-R Immediate and Delayed Recall Subtests.

	I	II	III
Mental Control	.11	.25	.74
Figural Memory	.12	.73	.20
Logical Memory I[1]	.85	.19	.25
Visual P.A.L. I	.45	.67	.13
Verbal P.A.L. I	.76	.40	.19
Visual Reproduction I	.31	.79	.28
Digit Span	.18	.11	.86
Visual Memory Span	.20	.57	.59
Logical Memory D[2]	.88	.23	.16
Visual P.A.L. D	.50	.65	.13
Verbal P.A.L. D	.78	.35	.04
Visual Reproduction D	.45	.72	.20

1) Immediate Recall   2) Delayed Recall

from Figural Memory, Visual Reproduction (Immediate and Delayed), Visual Paired-Associate Learning (Immediate and Delayed), and Visual Memory Span; this would be interpreted as a nonverbal memory factor. The third factor had strong loadings from the Mental Control, Digit Span, and Visual Memory Span subtests, and would be interpreted as the attentional factor observed in the previous analyses.

The final step in the factor analysis was to include the VIQ and PIQ with all of the WMS-R subtests included in the previous analysis. In view of the apparent verbal and nonverbal memory factor, it was of interest to determine if the IQ scores would also load on the appropriate material-specific factors. The results of this analysis are presented in Table 4. It can be seen that the factor structure of the WMS-R subtests is very similar to that observed in Table 3. Of particular interest is the fact that both VIQ and PIQ load on the third factor which in previous analyses was described as an attentional factor.

Table 4. Factor Structure of WMS-R and WAIS-R IQ Scores.

	I	II	III
Mental Control	.05	.36	.58
Figural Memory	.14	.69	.22
Logical Memory I	.83	.17	.30
Visual P.A.L. I	.46	.64	.17
Verbal P.A.L. I	.76	.40	.20
Visual Reproduction I	.31	.78	.28
Digit Span	.12	.14	.82
Visual Memory Span	.18	.60	.56
Logical Memory D	.87	.20	.23
Visual P.A.L. D	.51	.64	.15
Verbal P.A.L. D	.78	.36	.03
Visual Reproduction D	.45	.72	.21
Verbal IQ	.27	.05	.86
Performance IQ	.24	.38	.68

DISCUSSION

These results are similar in many respects to factor-analytic studies of the WMS. When only immediate-recall subtests are considered, there appears to be a general memory factor and an attentional factor. This is of some interest since the WMS-R has been constructed to provide a better balance between verbal and nonverbal memory tests. The appearance of a verbal-memory factor and a nonverbal-memory factor that might have been anticipated on this basis was not found when only immediate-recall subtests are used. Furthermore, while there was a strong similarity between these results and those of the normative sample, there were several important differences. In the clinical sample, all of the immediate-recall memory subtests (excluding Mental Control, Digit Span, and Visual Memory Span) loaded strongly on the general memory factor. In addition, the Figural Memory subtest, which is essentially the only recognition memory task, also loaded on the general memory factor. In the normal sample, this test loaded on neither factor, and the Logical Memory subtest loaded on both. This may suggest that, when applied in clinical settings, performance of all of these test may rely on similar neurobehavioral mechanisms.

In addition, the Visual Memory Span task, which is essentially a visual-attention span task, appears in clinical samples to have different demands than the analogous Digit Span task. In the clinical sample, the Visual Memory Span test loaded on both memory and attentional factors, whereas Digit Span loaded only on the attentional factor. This may suggest that the scores from the two subtests are not directly comparable. Based on clinical experience with this test, it would appear to be the case that the difference is attributable to the backward trial of Visual Memory Span. That is, the difference between the forward and backward trials of Digit Span may not be the same as the difference between the forward and backward trials of Visual Memory Span. In the context of the current results, it may be that the Visual Memory Span subtest (particularly the backward trial) may require processing that exceeds the capacity of short-term or immediate memory.

The inclusion of IQ scores in the analysis with immediate-recall subtests had very different effects in the normal and clinical samples. IQ scores loaded on the attentional factor in both samples but, in the normals, addition of FSIQ resulted in the attentional factor being the first factor extracted. In the clinical sample, the general memory factor remained the first extracted factor. This may be interpreted to suggest that, in the normal sample, IQ and attentional factors accounted for more variance than memory performance. Conversely, in the clinical sample, variability in memory performance appeared to explain more variance (52%) than did the IQ/attentional factor (12%). This may suggest that, in normals, variability in performance on intelligence tests overrides the variability observed in memory test performance. The characteristics of the present clinical sample may have resulted in greater variability in memory test performance, and thus resulted in that factor being more prominent. Since the mean IQ level of the clinical sample was below average (VIQ and PIQ approximately 90), these results may simply reflect a more truncated or skewed range of IQ scores. It would be of interest, therefore, to examine the factor structure of the WMS-R with IQ scores in a clinical sample with somewhat higher mean IQ levels.

Clinical use of the WMS has clearly demonstrated the value of delayed- recall trials in elicitation and demonstration of memory deficits (Prigatano, 1978; Russell, 1975). This has been formally addressed in the WMS-R by the incorporation of delayed-recall trials for two verbal tasks and two nonverbal tasks. The inclusion of these four delayed-recall subtests in the factor analysis revealed a clinically and intuitively attractive result. That is, the factor solution was interpreted as representing a verbal memory factor, a nonverbal memory factor, and an attentional factor. This separation of verbal and nonverbal subtests would appear to support generally held theories about hemispheric specialization and the material specificity (i.e., verbal vs. nonverbal) of memory deficits. The appearance of these material-specific factors only following inclusion of the delayed-recall subtests also provides support for the value of these subtests in the demonstration of specific types of memory deficits.

The fact that the Figural Memory subtest loaded on the nonverbal memory factor indicates that this factor represents both recognition and recall types of memory. It is unfortunate that the WMS-R does not include a comparable verbal recognition memory subtest. Clearly, the two verbal delayed-recall subtests load on the verbal memory factor. The two nonverbal delayed tasks load most strongly on the nonverbal memory factor, but also demonstrate secondary loadings on the verbal factor. This might suggest that some amount of verbal mediation may be employed in the coding or storage of this type of material.

The inclusion of VIQ and PIQ in the analysis which also included the delayed-memory WMS-R subtests was of particular interest. Since the latter subtests resulted in what were interpreted as material-specific memory factors, it was possible that the IQ scores would load with the other material-specific tasks (e.g., VIQ with verbal memory). It was seen, however, that both VIQ and PIQ loaded on the attentional factor, and that the verbal and nonverbal memory factors were preserved. This could be interpreted to suggest that constructs measured by these two tests (WMS-R and WAIS-R) are relatively independent.

This would be of considerable interest and importance for research with these tests, and also for clinical practice. For example, the relative independence would argue in favor of examining discrepancies between IQ and Memory Scores similar to the index suggested by Milner (1975). With the WMS-R, it might be possible to go beyond the simple IQ-Memory Quotient used previously. For example, it is possible to compute material-specific scores such as VIQ minus Verbal Memory Index Scaled Score (VerMSS), and PIQ minus Visual Memory Index Scaled Score (VisMSS). This might be developed as an index of a particular type of memory disorder which might have clinical diagnostic or therapeutic value. In the present sample, approximately 30% of patients had VIQ $>$ VerMSS by 10 points or more, and 35% had PIQ $>$ VisMSS by 10 points or more. Of course we are not suggesting that a discrepancy of this magnitude is of any clinical value. Rather, this is simply intended to illustrate that such contrasts are possible.

It will be useful for future studies to determine if such actuarially based criterion scores for the discrimination of specific memory deficits can in fact be derived. It will be particularly important in this pursuit to develop base-rate information from the WMS-R standardization sample. Other scores which may be developed might include discrepancies within the domain of memory (and the WMS-R). For example, it would be possible to examine the disprepancy between VerMSS and VisMSS, analogous to the VIQ-PIQ discrepancy sometimes employed with the WAIS-R. Butters et al. (1988, this issue) have provided evidence of the potential utility of comparisons between scaled scores from the General Memory, Attention/Concentration, and Delayed Memory indexes from the WMS-R. The proportion of material recalled on immediate- vs. delayed-recall trials from the WMS-R has already been shown to be useful in the discrimination of various clinical groups (Bornstein, Drake, & Pakalnis, 1988; Butters et al., 1988). Clinical necessity and the creativity of future investigators will likely produce other potentially useful indexes.

In summary, the WMS-R was revised to include a more balanced examination of verbal and nonverbal memory functions. Although the test may not reflect current theories of memory function (e.g., procedural vs. declarative) and may not be completely balanced (e.g., lack of a verbal recognition memory test), the WMS-R does represent a clear improvement over the previous version. The delayed-recall subtests appear to represent the basis for the determination of material-specific memory deficits, and the consistent separation of verbal and nonverbal memory factors is encouraging for research and clinical practice. It is of considerable importance that IQ (as measured by the WAIS-R) and memory (as measured by the WMS-R) appear to be largely independent. The structure of the WMS-R will provide opportunities for development of relational scores or indexes such as proportion of immediate to delayed recall, or IQ vs. memory scaled score discrepancies. Further research will be needed to establish the clinical utility of such scores.

REFERENCES

Bachrach, H., & Mintz, J. (1974). The Wechsler Memory Scale as a tool for the detection of mild cerebral dysfunction. *Journal of Clinical Psychology, 30,* 58-10.

Bornstein, R.A., Drake, M.E., & Pakalnis, A. (1988). Effects of seizure type and waveform abnormality on memory and attention in seizure disorder patients. (Manuscript submitted for publication).

Butters, N.M., Salmon, D., Cullum, C.M., Cairs, P., Tröster, A.I., Jacobs, D., Moss, M., & Cermak, L.S. (1988). Differentiation of amnesic and demented patients with the Wechsler Memory Scale-Revised. *The Clinical Neuropsychologist, 2,* 133-148.

Davis, L.J., Swenson, W.M. (1970). Factor analysis of the Wechsler Memory Scale. *Journal of Consulting and Clinical Psychology, 35,* 430.

Heilbronner, R.L., Buck, P., & Adams, R.L. (1987, February). Factor analysis of the Wechsler Memory Scale (WMS) with the WAIS and WAIS-R. Paper presented at the meeting of the International Neuropsychological Society, Washington, D.C.

Larrabee, G.J., Kane, R.L., & Schuck, J.R. (1983). Factor analysis of the WAIS and Wechsler Memory Scale: An analysis of the construct validity of the Wechsler Memory Scale. *Journal of Clinical Neuropsychology, 5,* 159- 168.

Milner, B. (1975). Psychological aspects of focal epilepsy and its neurosurgical management. *Advances in Neurology, 8,* 299-321.

Prigatano, G.P. (1978). Wechsler Memory Scale: A selective review of the literature. *Journal of Clinical Psychology, 34,* 816-832.

Russell, E.W. (1975). A multiple scoring method for the assessment of complex memory functions. *Journal of Consulting and Clinical Psychology, 43,* 800-809.

Ryan, J.J., Rosenberg, S.J., & Heilbronner, R.L. (1984). Comparative relationships of the Wechsler Adult Intelligence Scale-Revised (WAIS-R) and the Wechsler Adult Intelligence Scale (WAIS) to the Wechsler Memory Scale (WMS). *Journal of Behavioral Assessment, 6,* 37-43.

Skilbeck, C.E., & Woods, R.T. (1980). The factorial structure of the Wechsler Memory Scale: Samples of neurological and psychogeriatric patients. *Journal of Clinical Neuropsychology, 2,* 293-300.

The Clinical Neuropsychologist
1988, Vol. 2, No. 2, pp. 116-120

Confirmatory Analysis of the Factor Structure of the Wechsler Memory Scale-Revised

Gale H. Roid
Portland, OR

Aurelio Prifitera and Mark Ledbetter
The Psychological Corporation

ABSTRACT

Memory functions are known to be multifaceted. Models of the dimensionality of memory, as measured by the Wechsler Memory Scale-Revised (WMS-R), were investigated. Confirmatory factor analysis was used to explore one-, two-, and three-factor models for the first eight subtests of the WMS-R given to normal subjects in the standardization sample ($N=316$) and a heterogeneous sample of clinical subjects ($N=343$). The best fitting model was a two-factor model with general memory and attention/concentration dimensions.

The assessment of memory functions has long been a key element in the clinical evaluation of patients with neurological conditions (Russell, 1981). A recent survey of expert opinion on the concept and composition of intellectual functioning showed a high degree of consensus among experts that memory is a key, multifaceted domain within cognitive ability (Snyderman & Rothman, 1987). Memory functions have thus been a primary focus of intellectual and neuropsychological assessment for decades.

One of the most widely used clinical instruments for the assessment of memory has been the Wechsler Memory Scale (WMS, Wechsler, 1945). Although widely used, the Scale had a number of recognized limitations (Prigatano, 1977, 1978) including restricted coverage of visual memory and a single summary score. Therefore, the Scale was recently revised (Wechsler, 1987) with the intention of expanding the dimensionality of the instrument. Additional subtests measuring delayed recall and figural and spatial memory were included along with multiple composite scores. The purpose of the present study was to confirm the expected factor dimensionality of the Wechsler Memory Scale-Revised (WMS-R).

Numerous factor analyses of the WMS have appeared in the literature and several of these have been reviewed and summarized in the WMS-R Manual (Wechsler, 1987). Despite the existence of only one summary score on the WMS, previous analyses have shown more than one dimension among the WMS subtests. Exploratory principal components analyses of the new battery are presented in the WMS-R Manual (Wechsler, 1987). Factor analyses of the WMS and the WMS-R have generally shown evidence of two major factors - general memory and attention/concentration. Whether these suggested dimensions could be identified by *confirmatory* factor analysis was the specific research question of the present study.

METHOD

Subjects

A total of 316 nonimpaired subjects, ages 16-74, were given the WMS-R as part of the standardization of the instrument. Subjects were tested by trained examiners (primarily clinical psychologists and neuropsychologists) who volunteered as standardization examiners in specified geographic locations throughout the United States. The details of the sampling plan, demographics of the sample, and testing procedures are included in the test manual (Wechsler, 1987). In addition, 343 clinical subjects having a variety of diagnoses (e.g., dementia, Alzheimer's Disease, alcoholism) were tested with the full WMS-R battery for comparative and validational purposes.

Instruments

A total of 13 tasks in the WMS-R battery were administered to all subjects. Tasks include a brief mental status subtest (Information and Orientation Questions) used as a screener for the subject's ability to complete the remaining tasks, eight subtests covering a variety of short-term learning and recall functions (Mental Control, Figural Memory, Logical Memory, Visual Paired Associates, Verbal Paired Associates, Visual Reproduction, Digit Span, and Visual Memory Span), and delayed-recall repetitions of four of these subtests (Logical Memory, Visual Paired Associates, Verbal Paired Associates, and Visual Reproduction). The subtests are described in detail in another paper in this issue (Herman, 1988).

Statistical Methods

Since it is generally recognized that memory function is related to the age of the subject, partial correlations among WMS-R subtests were calculated controlling for the variable of age (in whole year units). The factor analysis of these partial correlations allowed for the inclusion of full samples of subjects (N=316 normal, N=343 clinical) in comparison to an alternative strategy of factoring age groups separately (e.g., with N=50).

Since previous principal components analyses (Wechsler, 1987) had shown that the delayed-recall subtests of the WMS-R loaded on the same factors as the initial subtest in each pair (e.g., Logical Memory I and Logical Memory II loading together), the four delayed-recall subtests were not included in the present analyses. Similarly, previous analyses that included separate subscores for Digit Span forward and backward and for Visual Memory Span forward and backward resulted in the backward and forward scores loading together. Therefore, separate scores for the forward and backward series of Digit Span and Visual Memory Span also are not included.

Confirmatory factor analyses were computed using the SIMPLIS program of Joreskog and Sorbom (1987), a microcomputer version of LISREL (Joreskog & Sorbom, 1981) employing a two-stage least-squares algorithm, executable on the IBM XT/AT. Input to the program was the partial correlation matrices among the eight subtests of the WMS-R for normal and clinical samples. Fit to the confirmatory model was assessed using a variety of indexes including the ratio of the chi-square to the degrees of freedom, standardized residual differences between observed and reproduced correlation matrices, and other goodness of fit indexes as recommended by Joreskog and Sorbom (1987), Marsh and O'Neill (1984), and Wolfle (1981).

RESULTS

As is standard practice in confirmatory LISREL modeling, multiple models were contrasted. The null model was based on a single general factor in which all subtests were assumed to comprise a single dimension. The second model was a two-factor model with general memory and attention/concentration factors similar to those identified in previous exploratory principal components analyses. Subtests hypothesized as comprising an attention/concentration factor were Digit Span, Visual Memory Span, and Mental Control. Subtests hypothesized on a general memory factor were Figural Memory, Logical Memory I, Visual Paired Associates I, Verbal Paired Associates I, and Visual Reproduction I.

A third model was also hypothesized by splitting the general memory factor into two parts: verbal and visual-spatial memory. This model was based on previous findings suggesting that visual and verbal memory tasks may be tapping different memory functions. Also, after examining the results of the two-factor model, particularly the standardized residuals for all subtests, it was determined that one subtest (Visual Reproduction I) produced the largest residuals between observed and expected correlation in the two-factor model. This suggested the possible existence of a separate visual memory factor.

Table 1 presents the results of the confirmatory factor analyses. Results include the chi-square fit statistic for each model, and its significance level. As with all confirmatory models, a high chi-square indicates poor fit of the model (large discrepancies between observed and expected parameters), and a good fit is indicated by a small chi-square relative to the degrees of freedom. The ratio of the chi-square to its degrees of freedom is also presented in Table 1, along with a goodness of fit index adjusted for the number of parameters estimated (Joreskog & Sorbom, 1987), and root mean square residual.

Although there exists no universally accepted guideline for evaluating goodness of fit in confirmatory factor analysis, the most widely used indicator is the ratio of chi-square to the degrees of freedom. Alwin and Jackson (1981) and Marsh and O'Neill (1984) have recommended that the ratio should be less than 2, although others (e.g., Wolfle, 1981) have suggested that the ratio need only be less than 5. Applying the $X^2 / df < 2$ guideline to Table 1 reveals that a reasonable fit is obtained only by the two-factor model in the normal sample. However, applying the $X^2 / df < 5$ guideline shows the two-factor model is the best fit for both the clinical and normal samples.

Also, the difference between the chi-squares obtained for each successive

Table 1: Results of the Confirmatory Factor Analyses for One- and Two-Factor Models and a Post-Hoc Three-Factor Model for Normal and Clinical Samples.

Model	Chi-Sq	*p*-value	df	Chi/df Ratio	Goodness of Fit	Root Mean Square
NORMAL SAMPLE						
One-Factor	82.38	.001	20	4.12	.883	.070
Two-Factor	36.07	.010	19	1.90	.949	.041
Three-Factor	213.43	.001	17	12.55	.726	.045
CLINICAL SAMPLE						
One-Factor	143.29	.001	20	7.16	.820	.075
Two-Factor	76.52	.001	19	4.03	.905	.047
Three-Factor	89.93	.001	17	5.29	.874	.068

Note. Sample sizes were 316 Normals and 343 Clinical subjects.

model was calculated (e.g., difference between chi-squares of one-factor and two-factor models). This difference statistic indicates the degree of improvement obtained by the subsequent model, with a large reduction in chi-square indicating a closer fit of the subsequent model in comparison to the contrasting model. Applying this guideline to the results in Table 1 shows that very large decreases in chi-square are observed for the two-factor models in relation to the one-factor or three-factor models. With a drop of only one degree of freedom (from 20 to 19) between one-factor and two-factor models, the chi-square drops 46.31 for normals and 66.77 for clinical subjects. Because such differences in chi-square are also distributed as chi-square variables, their significance can be tested in the conventional way, resulting in an extremely significant probability level ($<.0001$). Thus, the two-factor models fit the data much closer than the alternative models. Similar results in favor of the two-factor models were obtained when contrasting the two-factor and three-factor models.

DISCUSSION

The best-fitting model for the dimensionality of memory functions measured by the WMS-R included two factors: attention/concentration and general memory. The attention/concentration factor involves processes of short-term serial recall of digits (Digit Span) or a series of colored squares (Visual Memory Span) and memory for overlearned material (Mental Control). The general memory factor involves processes of verbal and visual short-term memory and paired-associate learning.

As might be expected, the parsimonious two-factor model best fits the data from a standardization sample of normal subjects in comparison to a heterogeneous sample of clinical subjects having a variety of organic and traumatic disorders. However, even in the clinical sample, the two-factor model was superior to one-factor or three-factor models.

The findings of this study are consistent with previous findings from factor analyses of both the WMS and the WMS-R (Wechsler, 1987) which have suggested the existence of two factors similar to those confirmed here. Also, the findings provide support for the reporting of two major scoring indexes (attention/concentration and general memory) on the WMS-R in comparison to the single summary score, the Memory Quotient, on the original WMS.

REFERENCES

Alwin, D.F., & Jackson, D.J. (1981). Applications of simultaneous factor analysis to issues of factorial invariance. In D.D. Jackson & E.F. Borgotta (Eds.), *Factor analysis and measurement in sociological research: A multidimensional perspective* (pp. 249-279). Beverly Hills, CA: Sage.

Herman, D.O. (1988). Development of the Wechsler Memory Scale-Revised, *The Clinical Neuropsychologist, 2,* 102-106.

Joreskog, K.G., & Sorbom, D. (1981). *LISREL V: Analysis of linear structural relationships by the method of maximum likelihood.* Chicago: International Educational Services.

Joreskog, K.G., & Sorbom, D. (1987). *SIMPLIS: Estimating linear structural relationships the easy way using two-stage least squares (Computer program).* Chicago: International Educational Services.

Marsh, H.W., & O'Neill, R. (1984). Self Description Questionnaire III: The construct validity of multidimensional self-concept ratings by late adolescents. *Journal of Educational Measurement, 21,* 153-174.

Prigatano, G.P. (1977). The Wechsler Memory Scale is a poor screening test for brain dysfunction. *Journal of Clinical Psychology, 33,* 772-777.

Prigatano, G.P. (1978). Wechsler Memory Scale: A selective review of the literature. *Journal of Clinical Psychology, 34,* 816-832.

Russell, E.W. (1981). The pathology and clinical examination of memory. In S.B. Filskov & T.J. Boll (Eds.), *Handbook of clinical neuropsychology* (pp. 287-319). New York: Wiley.

Snyderman, M., & Rothmans, S. (1981). Survey of expert opinion on intelligence and apitute testing. *American Psychologist, 42,* 137-144.

Wechsler, D. (1945). A standardized memory scale for clinical use. *Journal of Psychology, 19,* 87-95.

Wechsler, D.A. (1987). *Wechsler Memory Scale-Revised Manual.* New York: Psychological Corporation.

Journal of Clinical and Experimental Neuropsychology
1988, Vol. 10, No. 5, pp. 623-639

An Introduction to Structural Equation Models*

David J. Francis
University of Houston, Houston, TX

ABSTRACT

This paper provides an overview of structural equation models, and their potential for advancing neuropsychological theory and practice. Four topics are covered: (1) an overview of the various classes of models, and an introduction to the terminology and diagrams used to describe them, (2) an outline of the steps involved in applying structural equation modeling to any research problem, (3) an overview of the information used in assessing model fit, and a discussion of the role of significance tests in structural models, and (4) an outline of the advantages and disadvantages of structural equation models, and their potential contribution to neuropsychology. The paper is intended to help researchers (1) assess the relevance of these advanced statistical techniques to their own research, and (2) begin the process of successful application.

Recent advances in multivariate statistics facilitate the process of drawing causal inferences from correlational data. In general these procedures come under the heading of structural equation modeling, or causal modeling. These procedures are not new to the social sciences, although they have become increasingly popular in the past decade. To date there have been few instances of their use in neuropsychology (Francis, Fletcher, Harvey, Maxwell, & Satz, 1983; Francis, Fletcher, & Rourke, 1988; Larrabee, Kane, Schuck, & Francis, 1985; Newby, Hallenbeck, & Embritson(Whitley), 1983). Nevertheless, most neuropsychologists operate with implicit models that describe the phenomena in which they are interested. Furthermore, many neuropsychologists recognize

*This paper is based in part on presentations made at the meeting of the International Neuropsychological Society in Denver, February, 1986, and at the meeting of the American Psychological Association in Washington, DC, August, 1986. The author wishes to thank Jack M. Fletcher, Scott E. Maxwell, and Roger Blashfield for their constructive criticism of previous versions of this paper, and Byron P. Rourke for allowing the use of data collected under his direction in this and other research on structural equation models.

that their current research methods do not allow explicit use of their implicit models. Structural equation models provide one set of methods for bridging this gap between theory and research practice.

This paper does not attempt to develop or promote a particular model for neuropsychological test performance, but instead provides a nontechnical overview of structural equation modeling procedures. The primary objectives of this overview are to facilitate neuropsychologists' understanding of these advanced multivariate techniques, and to stimulate interest among researchers and clinicians in applying these procedures to their work in neuropsychology. More technical and more detailed coverage of certain aspects of this material is available in several sources (Bentler, 1980,1985; Bentler & Weeks, 1980; Jöreskog & Sörbom, 1979,1986; Kenny, 1979) and the interested reader is referred there for additional information. Four topics are explicitly covered in this paper: (1) a description of the various classes of structural equation models and an introduction to the terminology and diagrams used to describe them, (2) an outline of the steps involved in applying structural equation modeling to any research problem, (3) an overview of the various sources of information, and the mechanism for applying that information to the assessment of model fit, and (4) an outline of the advantages and disadvantages of structural equation models.

MODEL TYPES AND TERMINOLOGY

Fundamental to structural equation modeling is the realization that, although correlation does not imply causation, causation implies correlation. As a result, information about causal relationships among variables is contained in their correlations, or more generally, their covariances. Hence, the matrix of covariances is said to possess a structure, i.e. a systematic pattern.

In the most general sense, a causal model is a network of putative causal relationships among variables. This network consists of the variables involved in the network, the relationships among those variables, and the unknown parameters which describe the strength of those relationships. These parameters are referred to nonspecifically as structural parameters, and their estimates as structural coefficients. Factor loadings represent one type of structural parameter, or coefficient.

It is always possible to translate this network of causal relationships into a system of equations involving the variables and the unknown parameters. Using the equations and the laws of covariance algebra (Kenny, 1979, p. 13-21), the variances and covariances of the variables can be expressed in terms of the unknown parameters. The term, structural equation model[1], derives from these facts, namely that any network of causal relationships implies a "structure" to the variances and covariances among the variables, and that the particular structure is implicit in the system of equations. In applications of structural equation models, the goal is to use the observed variances and covariances to estimate (if possible) the unknown parameters, and to determine the empirical support for the model.

Before going any further, it is important to point out that no statistical procedure in and of itself proves that a causal relationship exists between two variables; such is the case no matter how sophisticated that statistical procedure might be. Structural equation models do not "prove" causation any more than a non-zero bivariate correlation proves causation. Structural equation modeling facilitates drawing causal inferences by proposing a network of causal relationships among variables, and determining the extent to which variables would be related if, in fact, such a network were operating.

It is convenient to think of structural equation models as falling into three basic classes: Manifest Variable models (MV), Confirmatory Factor models (CF), and Structural Models with Latent Variables (LV). All three are structural equation models as previously defined. MV models operate strictly at the level of the variables as observed. MV models do not distinguish between what a variable measures and the variable itself, i.e., MV models treat all variables as perfect measures. The major drawback to MV models is their failure to acknowledge the imperfections in observed measures. Estimates of the relationships in a model can be seriously biased when variables that cause other variables are not perfectly measured.

MV and LV models can be either recursive or nonrecursive. Recursive MV models are a direct extension of multiple regression to causal modeling. Recursive models do not allow for reciprocal causation, either directly or indirectly. In nonrecursive models, reciprocal causation is allowed. Nonrecursive models present problems over and above those associated with recursive systems (Koopmans, 1949; Strotz & Wold, 1960). Such problems are sometimes insurmountable in a given data set. Detailed discussion of these problems, and the differences between recursive and nonrecursive systems is outside the focus of this paper. Interested readers are referred to Duncan (1975), Heise (1975), Kenny (1979), Koopmans (1949), and Strotz and Wold (1960).

Path-analytic and simultaneous equation models represent two different types of MV model. Path analysis generally refers to linear, recursive, MV models where all of the variables have been standardized (Kenny, 1979). The practice of standardizing variables stems from the early work of Wright (1921) who introduced the technique, and Duncan (1966) who popularized path

1. The term "simultaneous equation model" has also been used to describe such systems of equations, particularly in the early literature on causal models in the field of econometrics. However, this term represents a particular class of causal model and a particular approach to working with the equations. For that reason, I will avoid its use in preference for the more general "structural equation" or "causal" model. The terms, "structural equation model" and "causal model", are used synonymously in this paper to refer, nonspecifically, to networks of putative causal relations, including, but not limited to, simultaneous equation models.

analysis in the social sciences. Structural coefficients are called path coefficients when variables have been standardized in a recursive MV model; they are called structural regressions or path regressions when variables are left in their original metric. Standardization is not essential in path analysis, but is traditional to the point of being implicit in the name. Standardization eases interpretation and comparison of structural coefficients, but introduces alternative complications (Kenny, 1979), e.g. when between-groups comparisons or equality of structural parameters in a single group are of interest. Wright (1960) discusses the sometimes complementary nature of path coefficients and path regressions. Simultaneous equation models are MV models which are nonrecursive. The name "simultaneous" stems from the early interest in nonrecursive models shown by econometricians, who refer to reciprocal causation as "simultaneity" (Kenny, 1979)

CF models are causal models that attempt to determine the relationships between variables as measured and the unobservable constructs (factors or latent variables) that they are presumed to measure. In other words, CF models are models of the psychometric properties of a system of measures. In CF models, each observed variable is assumed to be caused by one or more common factors and a uniqueness. Thus, observed variables are generally considered linear combinations of the factors, not vice versa (Herting & Costner, 1985).

Estimating the factor loadings, uniquenesses, and factor correlations in CF models is called confirmatory factor analysis. Confirmatory factor analysis differs from traditional methods of factor analysis in that one specifies a priori the measures which are determined by each factor, and which factors are correlated, if any. Given this particular pattern of relationships, factor loadings, uniquenesses, and factor correlations are estimated, and the degree to which the model adequately reproduces the data is assessed. Unlike traditional methods of factor analysis, there is no indeterminacy in confirmatory factor analysis, i.e., there are no communalities to estimate before estimating factor loadings, and there is no angle through which to rotate the resultant factor solution. Variables are constrained to measure only certain factors, and all other factor loadings are forced to be zero.

This method of analysis is extremely flexible and allows the researcher to test specific, and quite complex, hypotheses regarding the psychometric properties of variables. For example, it is possible to test progressively more restrictive hypotheses regarding the psychometric equivalence of a set of tests. In classical test theory, three levels of psychometric equivalence are defined: congenericism, tau-equivalence, and parallelism, or full equivalence (Jöreskog, 1979). Congeneric tests simply measure the same underlying factor, but do not yield the same true scores. Tau-equivalent tests measure the same underlying factor and give true scores which differ only by an arbitrary constant. However, tau-equivalent tests do not have equal reliabilities. Parallel tests, on the other hand, give equal true scores and have equal reliabilities. From the standpoint of CF models, parallel tests have equal factor loadings and equal errors of measurement, while tau-equivalent tests have equal factor loadings but unequal errors of measurement. It is also possible to use CF models to test the equivalence of neuropsychological measures across multiple populations, or developmental stages. Clearly, the central role of measurement in neuropsychology affords considerable potential for the application of CF models.

The third class of structural equation model, namely structural models with latent variables, are actually a combination of path analytic and confirmatory factor models (Kenny, 1979). Structural models with latent variables can be thought of as path analytic models of causal relationships between latent variables, where the latent variables have been defined through confirmatory factor analysis. Thus, structural models with latent variables consist of two distinct parts - (1) a measurement model which stipulates how the variables measure the underlying factors, and (2) a structural model which stipulates the causal relationships among the factors. Structural equation models of this third type are often called LISREL models. LISREL is the name of a widely available computer program (Jöreskog & Sörbom, 1986) used to analyze structural equation models, particularly CF and LV models. LV models are actually the most general class of linear structural models. MV and CF models are actually special cases of this more general model, much like Analysis of Variance and Multiple Regression are special cases of the General Linear Model. In fact, the General Linear Model is a special case of the more general LISREL model. Other researchers (Bentler & Weeks, 1980; McArdle & McDonald, 1984) have derived alternative formulations of this general model of linear structural relationships. For the most part, the differences between these formulations are cosmetic and need not concern us here. Because the LISREL formulation is most common among applications with which neuropsychologists are likely to be most familiar, this paper uses LISREL terminology almost exclusively.

One final note on terminology concerns the variables under investigation. Obviously, a variable may serve as both a cause and an effect in a structural model. As a consequence, the terms dependent- and independent-variable are replaced by endogenous- and exogenous-variable, respectively. An endogenous variable is any variable that is caused by at least one other variable in the system. In contrast, the causes of exogenous variables are assumed to be external to the system under consideration. The researcher assumes that the causes of the exogenous variables do not affect other variables in the system except through the exogenous variables themselves. If this assumption is met, then controlling an exogenous variable is equivalent to controlling its causes, and unbiased estimation of parameters is then possible. If this assumption is not met, then parameter estimates may be biased, regardless of the method used to derive those estimates. Imperfect measurement of exogenous variables amounts to violation of this assumption. In applying the foregoing discussion to LV models, the terms endogenous and exogenous concern the latent variables of the model, as opposed to the observed variables.

PATH DIAGRAMS

The elements in a structural model are often combined into a pictorial representation of the model known as a path diagram (Kenny, 1979). The path diagram is very important because it explicitly conveys all of the information concerning the network of relationships. From the path diagram, one can derive the entire system of structural equations. Figure 1 presents an example path diagram of a CF model. This model provides one possible explanation for

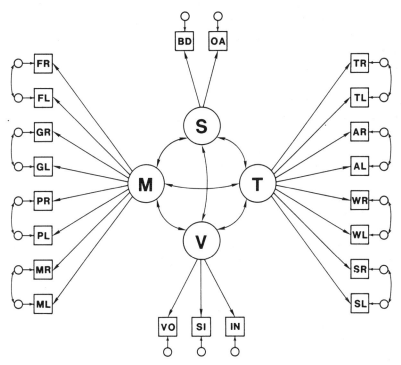

Fig. 1. Hypothetical model for measures of Tactile-Perceptual Skill (T), Motor Skill (M), Verbal Skill (V), and Visual-Spatial Constructive Skill (S). Large open circles are factors; boxes represent individual measures of each factor; small open circles represent errors of measurement in observed test measures. Straight, one-sided arrows indicate causal relationships; curved, two-sided arrows represent correlational relationships. Measures of (T) or (M) with the same first letter represent right- and left-hand versions of the same test, distinguished by the suffix R and L, respectively. Curved arrows between errors of measurement reflect correlation due to common method. Motor tests include finger-tapping (FR,FL), Grip Strength (GR,GL), Grooved Peg-Board (PR,PL), and Mazes (MR,ML). Measures of Tactile-Perceptual Skill include Tactile-Perception (TR,TL), Finger Agnosia (AR,AL), Finger-Tip Number Writing (WR,WL), and Astereognosis (SR,SL). Verbal and Visual Spatial measures are subscales of the WISC.

the variances and covariances among the 21 neuropsychological tests depicted in the figure. It is conventional in path diagrams to designate observed variables with small squares. The letters inside a square identify a particular observed variable. Unobserved variables are generally designated by open circles, of which there are two types: (1) latent variables or common factors are represented by large circles, and (2) disturbances (unmeasured causes of variables) are represented by small circles, e.g., errors of measurement in observed variables. It is conventional to use a straight, one-sided arrow to indicate a causal relationship which operates in the direction of the arrowhead. Thus, in Figure 1, each neuropsychological test is caused by a single common factor, and an error component. Specifically, 8 of the tests measure (are caused by) Tactile-Perceptual Skill, 8 measure Motor Skill, 3 measure Verbal Skill, and 2 measure Visual-Spatial Constructive Skill. In contrast to the straight one-sided arrows, curved two-sided arrows indicate a simple correlational relationship with no causal direction specified. Thus, the four common factors in this particular model are considered mutually intercorrelated.

In LV and CF models, the errors of measurement in observed variables indicate that not all of the variability in a particular observed measure is explained by the common factors. In short, errors of measurement indicate that variables are not perfect measures of their respective factors. However, the error variance in a particular variable may either be systematic or random from the standpoint of the model. For example, the tactile and motor tests depicted in Figure 1 were collected on both the right and left hands. It is possible that left and right versions of the same test share some test specific variance. These relationships are reflected in Figure 1 by the curved arrows which connect the errors of measurement for left- and right-hand versions of the same test. Thus, according to this model, some "error" variance in the tactile and motor tests is systematic, and related to other variables in the model. Although error variance in the measures of Verbal and Visual-Spatial skill may be systematic, it is assumed to be unrelated to other variables in the model. These specifications are testable, and could be altered given sufficient theoretical and empirical grounds. Finally, the model in Figure 1 assumes that errors of measurement are uncorrelated with the factors. This assumption is necessary for CF and LV models to yield unbiased parameter estimates. Researchers should be forewarned that this assumption is sometimes violated when response scales are restricted, such as with questionnaire data (Muthen, 1984).

Path diagrams for LV models are similar to Figure 1 except that some factors would be causally related to one another, and would therefore be joined by one-sided arrows. In addition, those factors which are caused by other factors in the models would have disturbance terms. Disturbance terms for latent variables are similar to errors of measurement for observed variables; the disturbance term indicates that not all of the variability in a particular latent variable is explained by the latent variable(s) in the model which cause it. In LV models, additional assumptions are required beyond those made in CF models.

Specifically, one must assume that latent variables are uncorrelated with the disturbances of other latent variables. Furthermore, one generally assumes that disturbances are uncorrelated. However, this assumption is sometimes testable, much like the assumption of uncorrelated errors of measurement.

STEPS INVOLVED IN CAUSAL MODELING

Making practical use of causal models in one's research consists of several steps. Briefly these steps are as follows: (1) model specification, (2) parameter and model identification, (3) parameter estimation and hypothesis testing, (4) assessment of model fit, and (5) model modification.

There are at least three elements which the researcher must draw on in specifying the relationships in the model. These are substantive theory, experimental design, and measurement theory. Although each area contributes to the overall specification of the model, their relative importance may vary from application to application. For example, Francis et al. (1983) presented a longitudinal, LV model of reading achievement, verbal skills, and nonverbal skills. In that model, substantive theory dictated the relationships among reading, nonverbal skills, and verbal skills. Measurement theory stipulated the relationships between observed and latent variables. Although experimental design dictated the longitudinal nature of the model, the model could have been specified with a single nonverbal and a single verbal skills factor. However, such a specification would have ignored relevant information contained in the temporal characteristics of the design, such as instability in the verbal and nonverbal skills factors. Instability of these factors was of theoretical interest in that study, and consequently played a prominent role in specification of the model.

If the relationships in the model are incorrect, the model is said to be misspecified, or to contain specification errors. Specification error is often considered the major stumbling block to structural equation modeling because of its potential to bias estimates of causal parameters. However, many investigators fail to realize that specification error potentially biases causal inferences in all quasi-experimental or correlational research, whether one analyzes data using ANOVA or structural equation modeling. At least in the structural model, relationships are explicitly stated. Consequently, assumptions and specifications are easier to identify and challenge. Furthermore, as Kenny (1979) points out, it is not sufficient to criticize a model simply because it may contain specification errors. Not all specification errors present equally serious threats to the conclusions reached from a model. One must demonstrate how such specification errors might potentially distort the parameter estimates in a model, and/or bias the conclusions reached from the model.

Model and parameter identification is a critically important and very complex topic. Basically, identification means that a unique solution exists for the parameters in the model. If a parameter is identified, then there is a single estimate for it under a specific estimation criterion, e.g., maximum-likelihood. Alternative estimation criteria may yield different estimates, but only one estimate of each identified parameter optimizes a particular criterion. A model is identified only if all parameters in the model are identified (Jöreskog & Sörbom, 1986). It is possible that not all parameters in a model are identified, and yet the model as a whole can be tested. Kenny (1979, p.38) provides an example of such a situation. Often, when a parameter is not identified, some constraint can be placed on the parameter in order to gain identification, e.g., two parameters can be constrained to be equal to one another.

There are three states of identification for a model - over-, just-, and under-identification. Just-identified models always fit the data perfectly, regardless of the data. They are therefore untestable as models. Changing the data would not alter a just-identified models' ability to reproduce the data. Under-identification means that not enough information is contained in the data to estimate all parameters in the model. Sometimes, the model is under-identified because of empirical relationships. For example, a two-factor model with two variables per factor is identified if the factors correlate, but under-identified if the factors do not correlate. Consequently, if the variables loading on different factors correlate near zero, then the model will be empirically under-identified, and it will not be possible to estimate the factor loadings unless additional constraints are introduced. Basically, over-identification means that the model can be tested, or disconfirmed and the parameters of the model estimated. Consequently, over-identified models are the most interesting substantive models.

No necessary and sufficient conditions exist for a model to be identified, and determining the identification status of complex models can be difficult, if not impossible, to accomplish by hand. In practice, the LISREL computer program checks on the identification status of the model during parameter estimation, and prints a message warning of a possible identification problem. The message is of some help in determining the parameter or parameters that may not be identified (Jöreskog & Sörbom, 1986). Still, in running the program and verifying the results, the researcher will usually find it helpful to have some idea about the identification status of the model prior to parameter estimation.

It is possible to specify minimum conditions for identification of all parameters in a model. Specifically, the number of parameters to be estimated must be less than or equal to the number of variances and covariances in the data matrix. If these minimum conditions are not met, then the model is certainly under-identified. However, even if these minimum conditions are exactly met, the model may be under-identified. Fortunately, the identification problem has been examined for some models, particularly CF and MV models (Jöreskog & Sörbom, 1979; Kenny, 1979). Wheaton, Muthen, Alwin, and Summers (1977) present a readable demonstration of solving the identification problem in a complex longitudinal model, and Kenny (1979) has several readable sections on identification of various models.

Parameter estimation is how numerical values come to be assigned to the relationships in the model. There are many ways to estimate parameters in structural models, but no one method is optimal under all conditions. The most important differences among the various methods concern the distributional theory on which they are based, e.g. normal, elliptical, or arbitrary (distribution free, Browne, 1982) distribution theory. There has been some empirical work that examines the robustness of certain estimators to violations of their distributional assumptions (Boomsma, 1982; Harlow, 1985; Muthen, 1984; Tanaka, 1984). This research generally shows that maximum-likelihood estimators perform well, provided the variable distributions are symmetric. A complete discussion of the issues involved in choosing the best estimator in a given situation would fill an entire article. For an introduction, Bentler (1985) provides some guidelines for choosing an appropriate method of estimation, as do Jöreskog and Sörbom (1986). The latter authors provide considerably less detail because the current release of LISREL (Jöreskog & Sörbom, 1986) only provides normal theory estimates, whereas Bentler's structural equation program, EQS (Bentler, 1985), estimates parameters under elliptical and arbitrary distribution theory as well as under normal theory.

Regardless of the method of estimation chosen, it is most important to keep in mind that one is always trying to assign a numerical value to the same structural parameter. Changing the method of estimation does not change the parameter; it only changes our estimate of its true value. The best estimates will be obtained when the variable distribution conforms to the distribution theory on which the estimator is based. Still, reasonable estimates may be likely even when the distributional assumptions are not met. However, distributional assumptions provide the basis for statistical inferences, and such inferences may be inaccurate when distributional assumptions are not explicitly met.

ASSESSMENT OF MODEL FIT

Structural models may be used because of interest in the model as a whole, or to test an hypothesis involving a specific parameter or set of parameters. Regardless of whether a specific hypothesis is to be tested, or whether the focus is on the model as a whole, it is important to assess the adequacy of the model thoroughly because hypotheses are dependent on the context in which they are evaluated. If the model is grossly inadequate, one must question the meaningfulness of any hypothesis tested within the context of that model.

There are many pieces of information that contribute to the assessment of model fit, and each provides a slightly different view of where the model fits well and where it fits poorly. The indices which assess model fit can be characterized as either global or local. Global indices reflect how well the model as a whole reproduces the relationships among the variables. Local indices reflect more specific aspects of model fit. In assessing model fit, it is important to consider both types of information. It is possible for a model to fit quite well on the whole, and yet poorly reproduce some important relationships among varia-bles. On the other hand, if a model fits poorly in a general sense, global indices do not aid in detecting the source of the problem. The global and local indices often used in assessing model fit are summarized in Table 1.

Table 1. Statistical Assessment of Model Fit

Global Indices

    A) Chi-square test of significance
    B) Chi-square/d.f. (Fit Ratio)
    C) Goodness of Fit Index (GFI)
    D) Adjusted Goodness of Fit Index (AGFI)
    E) Root Mean Square Residual (RMR)
    F) Q-Plot of Normalized Residuals

Local Indices

    A) Acceptability of Parameter Estimates
    B) Significance Tests for Individual Parameters
    C) Squared Multiple Correlations (SMC)
    D) Residuals - Unexplained Relationships
    E) Modification Indices

Descriptions of the indices listed in Table 1 are available in Jöreskog and Sörbom (1986). More detailed discussions of model assessment can be found in Francis and Rourke (1986), Herting and Costner (1985), Maruyama and McGarvey (1980), and Sobel and Bohrnstedt (1985). Anderson and Gerbing (1984), and Gerbing and Anderson (1985) provide information on the empirically derived sampling distributions of several indices in Table 1 whose theoretical distributions are unknown. Although a detailed discussion of model assessment is outside the scope of this overview, some discussion of chi-square and its role in model testing is warranted.

The chi-square test of significance tests the hypothesis that the data were generated by the proposed model. The p value associated with this test corresponds to the probability of obtaining the observed data if, in fact, the covariance matrix has the structure specified by the model, i.e., if in fact the model were "true". This test statistic is produced when either maximum-likelihood (ML) or generalized least squares (GLS) is used to estimate the parameters in the model under normal distribution theory, or when an appropriate generalization of these estimators is used under elliptical or arbitrary distribution theory.

The p value associated with the chi-square test under ML or GLS estimation is only accurate under three conditions. First, analysis must be based on the covariance matrix, as opposed to the correlation matrix. This assumption can be relaxed when the model is invariant under a scaling factor ("scale free")

(Browne, 1982). As a rule of thumb, a model is scale free if it involves a single population, and no parameters are constrained to be equal to one another. Secondly, the observed variables must be multivariate normally distributed in the population. Multivariate nonnormality tends to increase the value of chi-square (Boomsma, 1982) so that it becomes increasingly difficult to find a model that "fits" the data. If the model is "scale free" and the variables are not significantly skewed, then adjusting the chi-square statistic by an estimate of the multivariate kurtosis (Mardia, 1970) results in a more accurate test statistic (Bentler, 1985; Browne, 1982). The computer program EQS (Bentler, 1985) calculates this adjustment, which is the chi-square statistic under elliptical distribution theory. Bentler (1985) provides a discussion of this adjustment, and some guidelines for its use.

Lastly, the sample size must be large. Boomsma (1982) recommends at least 200; Bentler (1985) suggests a ratio of subjects to estimated parameters of at least 5:1. In a large Monte Carlo study, Anderson and Gerbing (1984) found that the chi-square test performed adequately even with small sample sizes, although it did approach its theoretical distribution at $n=300$. Although the chi-square test performed adequately, small sample sizes were more likely to yield improper solutions.[2] Two additional points are worth noting about the Anderson and Gerbing (1984) study. First, the models employed in the study were relatively uncomplicated. Bearden, Sharma, and Teel (1982) reported similar findings as Anderson and Gerbing (1984) for simple models, but also found that Type I error rates were too high when sample size was small and the model was complex (subject to estimated parameter ratios of less than 5:1). Secondly, the data in Anderson and Gerbing (1984) were multivariate normal. It is quite possible that large sample size is more critical when data are not multivariate normal.

Even when the data meet the distributional assumptions associated with the estimation procedure, the chi-square test poses problems. The relationship between the chi-square statistic and sample size is problematic because, with very large samples, even small discrepancies between the model and the observed data will lead to significant values of the test statistic: that is, with very large samples, no model may be adequate in terms of the chi-square test of significance. Paradoxically, when factors are poorly measured, and/or when relationships among the factors are low, the test has very low power, even with large sample sizes (Fornell & Larcker, 1981), thereby increasing the likelihood

---

2. The estimation procedures that yield tests of significance are iterative in nature. If the estimation process does not converge on an optimal solution, or yields inadmissible parameter estimates (e.g. negative variances or correlations exceeding 1.0 in absolute value), the solution is said to be inappropriate. Both of these problems result from models that deviate greatly from the structure of the data. However, in simulations with known data structures, both problems tend to increase in frequency as sample size decreases. This is to be expected because the presence of covariances that deviate greatly from their population values will be most likely when sample sizes are small.

that an incorrect model will be accepted. Even when factors are well measured and highly interrelated, the test has low power when sample sizes are small, such that the value of the chi-square statistic and the associated p value cannot be trusted (Fornell & Larcker, 1981). Finally, unlike simulation studies (where models are constructed to be correct or incorrect), in most applications of structural equations, the model under investigation is known to be false a priori.

Saying that the model can be rejected as false a priori is akin to saying that the null hypothesis is never exactly true in classical hypothesis testing. Hence, statistical confirmation of the model is not necessarily meaningful. In classical hypothesis testing, researchers are only concerned that the null hypothesis be true (or not true) for all practical purposes, not in any strict, or absolute sense. Similarly, whether the model is exactly true is of less consequence than that the model provide better predictions and explanations of behavior than competing or existing models. Thus, these cautions regarding the chi-square test and sample size are analogous to the problem of sample size and power in other statistical tests. Given a sufficiently large sample, one can reject any null hypothesis; given an inadequate sample, the null hypothesis may be retained due to low power. For that reason, researchers distinguish practical from statistical significance in classical hypothesis testing, and structural modelers are wise to do the same. The only difference is that in structural modeling the null hypothesis is typically the hypothesis of scientific interest.

As Jöreskog and Sörbom (1986) have suggested, it is perhaps more reasonable to consider the statistical problem in structural equation modeling to be one of fitting a model to the data and deciding whether or not the fit is adequate, as opposed to testing the statistical significance of a particular model. The problems associated with the use of chi-square as a test statistic have led to the suggestion that chi-square be used instead as a measure of goodness of model fit, where the degrees of freedom serve as a standard against which to evaluate the size of the chi-square statistic (Jöreskog & Sörbom, 1986).

Only three indices listed in Table 1 allow for statistical inferences with regard to the model, namely chi-square, Modification Indices, and the ratios of parameter estimates to their standard errors. While under certain model conditions (Anderson & Gerbing, 1984) approximate 95% confidence intervals are available for other indices in Table 1, all of the remaining indices are generally considered to provide descriptive information. However, any comprehensive assessment of model fit will focus on both descriptive and inferential information. In fact, given that most (if not all) models can be rejected as false a priori, one might argue that previous emphasis on tests of statistical significance in structural equation models has been misplaced. Nevertheless, there is a need for establishing guidelines for model evaluation, and it is desirable to incorporate inferential statistics where possible.

Given the logical inconsistency in attempting to confirm a model which can be rejected a priori as being false, perhaps the most reasonable means for applying structural equations in an area involves the comparison of competing models. Indices in Table 1 can be used to contrast nested[3] and nonnested models for the same data. Additional indices are available for the comparison of nested models. Interested readers should consult Bentler and Bonnett (1980), Francis and Rourke (1986), Maruyama and McGarvey (1980), and Sobel and Bohrnstedt (1985) for details on these indices and the comparison of nested models.

ADVANTAGES AND DISADVANTAGES OF STRUCTURAL MODELS

A primary advantage of structural equations over other statistical methods is that researchers must make their assumptions explicit, rather than implicit (or even totally ignored). Making assumptions explicit allows for more open dialogue about the appropriateness of a particular statistical analysis. Structural models also allow more direct translation of substantive theory into statistical practice. This means that relationships are formulated and tested within a complex network of relationships, not separately.

The distinction between variables and constructs is an important aspect of these networks that has particular relevance for neuropsychology. Structural models allow more precise formulation of measurement models, and can be used to test that such models are invariant across populations of interest. Factorial invariance over populations is essential to the meaningful comparison of different populations on any set of variables. If variables measure different constructs, or the same constructs differently in two populations, then group differences on those variables are not easily interpreted as an index of group differences on a common construct.

As with all statistical procedures, structural equation modeling is not without pitfalls. There is a tendency to disregard assumptions underlying the analysis. While model assumptions are explicit and therefore open to scrutiny, it is doubtful that uninformed consumers of these techniques will be aware of these assumptions and their effect on the model. Secondly, there is a tendency to let the statistics guide the question rather than vice versa. This tendency can lead the unwary to considerable frustration and confusion, and ultimately to meaningless results.

Structural equation modeling has a set of pitfalls unique to it that involve carrying out the analysis. Computer programs used in the analysis have been characterized as "user hostile", and not because they are expensive and time consuming to run, which they are. Fortunately, considerable progress has been made in rendering these programs more useable. In fact, the elimination of matrix algebra in problem setups was one of the major selling features of EQS (Bentler, 1985) when that program was first released. Along these same lines,

---

3. Model A is parameter nested in Model B (Bentler & Bonnett, 1980) if Model A is derived from Model B by placing constraints on the "free" parameters of Model B. A "free" parameter is any parameter not restricted to have a particular value, e.g. 0 or 1.0, and not restricted to be equal to some other parameter.

because these procedures are relatively new, especially to neuropsychologists, there are relatively few places to turn for help when things go wrong, as they seem to do more often than not.

Other problems unique to structural equation modeling include the complexity of model assessment, parameter estimation, and model and parameter identification. Furthermore, much of the research into these problems is not readily available to neuropsychologists without advanced methodological interests. Sample sizes in excess of 200 are probably necessary for most applications, and, if model modification and cross-validation are included, the number should be two to three times larger, or more. Secondly, collecting data that are adequate for use in structural models is difficult, time consuming, and expensive. Structural models involving latent variables require multiple measures of each construct. Four measures of each factor assures over-identification of each factor. However, using multiple items from the same questionnaire is a weak form of multiple indicator model because trait and method variance are confounded, variable on factor regressions may be nonlinear, and factors may correlate with errors of measurement in observed variables. Nevertheless, the unparalleled flexibility of structural equation models for testing complex hypotheses within networks of relationships, and the previously cited advantages far outweigh the disadvantages and difficulties encountered in using these techniques. If mastered, these procedures have tremendous potential for advancing neuropsychological theory and practice, particularly in the area of measurement.

REFERENCES

Anderson, J.C., & Gerbing, D.W. (1984). The effect of sampling error on convergence, improper solutions, and goodness-of-fit indices for maximum-likelihood confirmatory factor analysis. *Psychometrika, 49,* 155-173.

Bearden, W.O., Sharma, S., & Teel, J.E. (1982). Sample size effects on chi-square and other statistics used in evaluating causal models. *Journal of Marketing Research, 19,* 425-430.

Bentler, P.M. (1980). Multivariate analysis with latent variables: Causal modeling. *Annual Review of Psychology, 31,* 419-456.

Bentler, P.M. (1985). *Theory and implementation of EQS: A Structural Equations Program.* Los Angeles: BMDP Statistical Software, Inc.

Bentler, P.M., & Bonnett, D.G. (1980). Significance tests and goodness of fit in the analysis of covariance structures. *Psychological Bulletin, 88,* 588-606.

Bentler, P.M., & Weeks, D.G. (1980). Linear structural equations with latent variables. *Psychometrika, 45,* 289-308.

Boomsma, A. (1982). The robustness of LISREL against small sample sizes in factor analysis models. In K.G. Jöreskog & H. Wold (Eds.), *Systems under indirect observation: Causality, structure, prediction. Part I* (pp. 149-173). Amsterdam: North Holland.

Browne, M.W. (1982). Covariance structures. In D.M. Hawkins(Ed.), *Topics in applied multivariate analysis* (pp. 72-141). London: Cambridge University Press.

Duncan, O.D. (1966). Path analysis: Sociological examples. *American Journal of Sociology, 72,* 1-16.

Duncan, O.D. (1975). *Introduction to structural equation models.* New York: Academic Press.

Fornell, C., & Larcker, D.F. (1981). Structural equation models with unobservable variables and measurement error: Algebra and statistics. *Journal of Marketing Research, 18,* 382-388.

Francis, D.J., Fletcher, J.M., Harvey, D., Maxwell, S.E., & Satz, P. (1983, February). A structural model for developmental changes in the determinants of reading disability. Poster presented at the meeting of the International Neuropsychological Society, Mexico City, Mexico.

Francis, D.J., Fletcher, J.M., & Rourke, B.P (1988). Discriminant validity of lateral tactile and motor skill measures in learning disabled children. *Journal of Clinical and Experimental Neuropsychology, 10,* 00-00.

Francis, D.J., & Rourke, B.P. (1986, August). Structural equation models in neuropsychological research: Assessment of model fit. In J.M. Schear (Chair), *Applications of multivariate methods in neuropsychology.* Symposium conducted at the meeting of the American Psychological Association, Washington, DC.

Gerbing, D.W., & Anderson, J.C. (1985). The effects of sampling error and model characteristics on parameter estimates for maximum-likelihood confirmatory factor analysis. *Multivariate Behavioral Research, 20,* 255-271.

Harlow, L.L. (1985). *Behavior of some elliptical theory estimators with nonnormal data in a covariance structures framework: A Monte Carlo study.* Unpublished doctoral dissertation, University of California, Los Angeles.

Heise, D.R. (1975). *Causal analysis.* New York: Wiley.

Herting, J.R., & Costner, H.L. (1985). Respecification in multiple indicator models. In H.M. Blalock, Jr. (Ed.), *Causal models in the social sciences* (pp. 321-393). New York: Aldine.

Jöreskog, K.G. (1979). Basic ideas of factor and component analysis. In K.G. Jöreskog & D. Sörbom, *Advances in factor analysis and structural equation models* (pp. 5-20). Cambridge, MA: Abt Books.

Jöreskog, K.G.,& Sörbom, D. (1979). *Advances in factor analysis and structural equation models.* Cambridge, MA: Abt Books.

Jöreskog, K.G., & Sörbom, D. (1986). *LISREL VI: Analysis of linear structural relationships by the method of maximum-likelihood.* Chicago: National Educational Resources.

Kenny, D.A. (1979). *Correlation and causality.* New York: Wiley.

Koopmans, T.C. (1949). Identification problems in economic model construction. *Econometrica, 17,* 125-143.

Larrabee, G.J., Kane, R.L., Schuck, J.R.& Francis, D.J. (1985). The construct validity of various memory tests. *Journal of Clinical and Experimental Neuropsychology, 7,* 239-250.

Mardia, K.V. (1970). Measures of multivariate skewness and kurtosis with applications. *Biometrika, 57,* 519-530.

Maruyama, G., & McGarvey, B. (1980). Evaluating causal models: An application of maximum likelihood analysis of structural equations. *Psychological Bulletin, 87,* 502-512.

McArdle, J.J., & McDonald, R.P. (1984). Some algebraic properties of the reticular action model for moment structures. *British Journal of Mathematical and Statistical Psychology, 37,* 234-251.

Muthen, B. (1984). A general structural equation model for dichotomous, ordered categorical, and continuous latent variable indicators. *Psychometrika, 49,* 115-132.

Newby, R.F., Hallenbeck, C.E., & Embritson (Whitley), S. (1983). Confirmatory factor analyses of four general neuropsychological models with a modified Halstead-Reitan Battery, *Journal of Clinical Neuropsychology, 5,* 115-133.

Sobel, M.E., & Bohrnstedt, G.W. (1985). Use of null models in evaluating the fit of covariance structure models. In N. Tuma (Ed.), *Sociological methodology 1985* (pp. 152-178). San Francisco: Jossey-Bass.

Strotz, R.H., & Wold, H.O.A. (1960). Recursive versus nonrecursive systems: An attempt at synthesis. *Econometrica, 28,* 417-427.

Tanaka, J.S. (1984) *Some results on the estimation of covariance structure models.* Unpublished doctoral dissertation, University of California, Los Angeles.

Wheaton, B., Muthen, B., Alwin, D., & Summers, G. (1977) Assessing reliability and stability in panel models. In D.R. Heise (Ed.), *Sociological methodology 1977* (pp. 84-136). San Francisco: Jossey-Bass.

Wright, S. (1921) Correlation and causation. *Journal of Agricultural Research, 20,* 557-585.

Wright, S. (1960) Path coefficients and path regressions: Alternative or complementary concepts? *Biometrics, 16,* 189-202.

Journal of Clinical and Experimental Neuropsychology
1988, Vol. 10, No. 6, pp. 779-799

Discriminant Validity of Lateral Sensorimotor Tests in Children*

David J. Francis[1]   Jack M. Fletcher
University of Houston

Byron P. Rourke
University of Windsor, Windsor, Ontario

ABSTRACT

The discriminant validity of left- (LH) and right-hand (RH) sensorimotor measures from a comprehensive neuropsychological battery was tested using confirmatory factor analysis. A group of children (primarily learning disabled) was divided into analysis ($n = 488$) and cross-validation ($n = 400$) samples and the following measures were taken for both the LH and the RH Tactile Perception, Finger Agnosia, Fingertip Number Writing, Tactile Form Recognition, Finger Tapping, Grip Strength, Grooved Pegboard, and Mazes. RH- and LH scores from these tests, and scores from five WISC subtests (Information, Similarities, Vocabulary, Block Design, and Object Assembly) were analyzed in a series of four nested confirmatory factor models. Models distinguished between LH and RH skill factors, and/or between simple- and complex-skill factors. Models were compared using incremental fit ratios and χ^2 difference tests (Bentler & Bonnett, 1980). Model comparisons revealed little evidence for discriminant validity of LH and RH measures, but strong support for distinctions between measures of simple- and complex- skills. These findings were replicated in the cross-validation sample.

Neuropsychologists are sometimes interested in the measures they collect only in so far as those measures serve as indicators of constructs which cannot be directly observed. Thus, the neuropsychologist is not interested in finger tapping per se, but in speed of motor execution and information-processing efficiency. When the construct of interest is not directly observable, differences on the construct must be inferred from differences on variables presumed to

* A portion of this paper was presented at the meeting of the American Psychological Association, Washington, DC, August, 1986. The authors wish to thank Scott E. Maxwell and Roger Blashfield for their constructive criticism of earlier versions of this paper, and Kevin Davidson for his help in preparing the figures.

measure that construct. Such inferences are limited by the psychometric properties of the tests, and by the consistency of those properties across populations and conditions of interest.

Discriminant validity (Campbell & Fiske, 1959) is a psychometric property which describes the degree to which the constructs measured by a set of tests can actually be distinguished from one another. If two constructs are perfectly correlated, then the two are interchangeable and it is difficult to argue that the tests measure different underlying processes. Although this issue is of less concern in clinical neuropsychological assessment when screening a single patient for nonnormative performance (Maxwell & Niemann, 1984), it is paramount to all other concerns when test performance, nonnormative or otherwise, is interpreted as an indication of hemispheric organization.

In the original Halstead battery, individual tests were included (Halstead, 1947) because of their potential to detect brain damage in adults, not because they measured specific cognitive abilities. Revised by Reitan (Reitan & Davison, 1974), the Halstead-Reitan battery (HRB) is widely used in research on children's abilities (Rourke, Bakker, Fisk, & Strang, 1983), in spite of a general lack of research on the psychometric properties of the battery when used with children, particularly with regard to the cognitive abilities measured by the tests.

The present investigation examines the discriminant validity of the tactile-perceptual, motor, and psychomotor tests commonly included in neuropsychological test batteries. Previous attempts to explicate the psychometric properties of neuropsychological test batteries, such as the HRB, have been hampered by the inclusion of tactile, motor, and psychomotor tests. In most neuropsychological assessment procedures, tests measuring these skills are collected twice, once with the right hand (RH) and once with the left hand (LH). Presumably, LH and RH tests have some level of discriminant validity, that is, the processes measured by LH and RH tests are distinct from one another. If such were not the case, the measures would be redundant, and there would be no reason to include both LH and RH versions of the same test other than to increase the reliability with which the "single" underlying process is measured.

The clinical lore regarding the utility of LH and RH tactile and motor tests for differential diagnosis of lateralized brain damage in children is strong, although the empirical evidence supporting such conclusions is weak. Three studies using comprehensive neuropsychological test batteries to discriminate brain- damaged from normal children have been reported (Boll, 1974; Reed, Reitan, & Kløve, 1965; Reitan, 1971). Both Reed et al. (1965) and Boll (1974) included children aged 9-14, but only Boll (1974) included measures of tactile and motor skill from the LH and the RH. Of the 40 comparisons made by Boll (1974), 32 were significant at $p < .05$ and 19 of those at $p < .001$. In spite of the small sample size ($n = 27$ in each group) relative to the number of comparisons, no attempt was made to control experiment-wise Type-I error. Most striking was the fact that, of the eight measures that did not discriminate between the groups, five were tactile-perceptual measures collected from the two sides of the body. These included Tactile Form Recognition (right and left), Fingertip Number Writing (right and left) and Finger Localization or Finger Agnosia (left hand only). Of the remaining sensorimotor tests, Finger Localization (right hand) was significant at $p < .05$, while Grip Strength and Finger Tapping (dominant hand) were significant at $p < .025$. Nondominant Grip Strength and Finger Tapping were the only sensorimotor tests significant at $p < .005$, which represents a reasonable criterion level in view of the number of variables compared.

Reitan (1971) compared younger (5-8 years old) normal and brain-damaged children on 16 measures, including Finger Tapping and grip strength from the left and right sides of the body. Significant differences were reported for both finger tapping measures and for nondominant grip strength. Dominant grip strength failed to reach significance. Again, there was no attempt to control experiment-wise Type-I error given the large number of comparisons performed. Furthermore, neither Boll (1974) nor Reitan (1971) examined whether the difference between LH and RH performance was the same for brain-damaged and normal children. If LH and RH measures have discriminant validity, then such interaction effects would be expected, although they are not absolutely necessary. Thus, these two studies do not present strong evidence that lateral sensorimotor measures reliably differentiate normal from brain-damaged children, nor that they reliably differentiate left- from right-brain damage in children.

A second source of indirect evidence regarding the discriminant validity of RH and LH tests in children is the wealth of factor-analytic studies involving all or part of the HRB with brain-damaged and/or non-brain-damaged controls (Aftanas & Royce, 1969; Barnes & Lucas, 1974; Goldstein & Shelley, 1972; Grant et al., 1978; Newby, Hallenbeck, & Embritson (Whiteley), 1983; Royce, Yeudall, & Bock, 1976; Ryan, Prifitera, & Rosenberg, 1983; Swiercinsky, 1979; Swiercinsky & Hallenbeck, 1975; Swiercinsky & Howard, 1982). These studies provide indirect evidence because none of the reported factor analyses with the HRB have used children as subjects. Furthermore, only certain of these studies have contained more than two of the tactile and motor tests from the HRB.

Of the studies that have included the tactile and motor measures from the battery, only Goldstein and Shelley (1972), Swiercinsky and Hallenbeck (1975), Royce et al. (1976), Swiercinsky (1979), and Newby et al. (1983) have included both LH and RH tactile and motor measures. These studies employed heterogeneous groups of adult brain-damaged subjects, and four of the five studies were carried out at the V. A. Hospital, in Topeka, Kansas (Goldstein & Shelley, 1972; Newby et al., 1983; Swiercinsky, 1979; Swiercinsky & Hallenbeck, 1975). As a consequence, there is some overlap in the patient samples on which these studies were based.

There is considerable consistency across the results of the five studies with regard to the LH and RH tests. LH and RH versions of the same test loaded on the same factor in virtually every exploratory factor analysis where both versions were included. However, the failure to demonstrate discriminant validity in the exploratory factor studies could reflect the effect of shared method variance on the exploratory factor solutions, and need not imply that the measures lack discriminant validity. Shared method variance simply means that two scores collected with the same measuring device under different conditions (e.g., the same oscillating key in LH and RH finger tapping, or the same examiner testing for finger agnosia on the LH and on the RH) will correlate due to the measuring device as well as the traits being measured by the instrument under the different conditions.

Shared method variance in factor analysis is sometimes indicated by the presence of doublet factors in a factor analysis. A doublet is a factor defined by only two measures, such as a factor with LH and RH finger tapping having the only significant loadings. Studies with LH and RH measures have not generally yielded doublet factors, although some doublets have occurred. However, a failure to find doublet factors does not preclude the possibility that method variance affects the common factors, and subsequent tests of discriminant validity. To assess method variance and discriminant validity of LH and RH measures, Swiercinsky (1979) analyzed LH and RH measures together and then replicated his analysis with only RH measures. The most striking differences that occurred when the LH tests were dropped were the merging of a motor strength (Grip) and motor speed (Finger Tapping, Grooved Pegboard) factor into a single factor, and the merging of a relatively pure tactile skills factor (Finger Agnosia and Graphesthesia) with a complex spatial reasoning, object manipulation factor. These minor differences led Swiercinsky (1979) to reject the hypothesis of discriminant validity for LH and RH tests, and to recommend dropping one set of scores in future factor-analytic studies of neuropsychological tests.

The inclusion of LH and RH tests presents a significant problem for these traditional factor-analytic studies of neuropyschological tests because of shared method variance between any pair of LH and RH tests. As indicated, exploratory factor techniques are inadequate for assessing the discriminant validity of lateral tactile and motor skill measures because test-specific factors seldom emerge with common factors for the same variables. When several other measures of the same skill are included in the data matrix, test-specific factors do not emerge because they do not account for sufficient variance in the overall matrix. When few or no other measures of the same skill are included in the matrix, doublet factors emerge for LH and RH versions of the same test. Consequently, these tests do not load on any common factors because so much of their communality is shared with the analogous measure from the opposite hand. Swiercinsky's (1979) recommendation to eliminate one set of scores is somewhat premature. Although consistent with current evidence, the recommendation was based on an analysis that failed to address the issue of test-specific (method) variance in assessing the discriminant validity of these measures. The present study was designed to address these issues directly.

Confirmatory factor analysis, on the other hand, is well suited to assess the discriminant validity of LH and RH test scores. The confirmatory factor model is a submodel of the more general LISREL (Jörcskog & Sörbom, 1986) or Bentler-Weeks (Bentler, 1985) models of structural relations. In general, a confirmatory factor model is a network of proposed causal relationships between observed variables and unobserved constructs. In exploratory factor analysis, the data determine the pattern of factor loadings, while in confirmatory factor analysis, the experimenter specifies the pattern of factor loadings and the data determine the adequacy of those specifications. Thus, with confirmatory factor analysis, it is possible to model test-specific relationships among pairs of test measures, and simultaneously model relationships with common factors for these same tests. Newby et al. (1983) reported a confirmatory factor analysis designed to compare several competing models for neuropsychological test performance. Unfortunately, it is not possible to apply the results from the models presented by these authors to the question of discriminant validity for lateral tactile and motor skill measures because of the nature of the models tested in that study. Specifically, the current investigation was designed to test the discriminant validity of lateral tactile and motor skill measures through the use of confirmatory factor analysis and nested models (Bentler & Bonnett, 1980), which would allow for the simultaneous inclusion of test-specific relationships for LH and RH pairs of tests, and relationships with common factors.

METHOD

Subjects

Subjects for the study were 888 boys and girls between 9 and 14 years of age who were in the neuropsychology service at the Regional Children's Centre of the Windsor Western Hospital, Windsor, Ontario from June, 1976 to March, 1981. All subjects were right-handed and no child exihibited evidence of (a) mental retardation, (b) frank neurological or unusual childhood illness, (c) emotional disturbance, or (d) environmental deprivation. The sample consisted of 420 children between the ages of 9 and 10, and 468 children between the ages of 11 and 14, including 721 males (81%) and 167 females (19%). Each subject was randomly assigned to either an analysis sample ($n = 488$ or 55%) or a cross-validation sample ($n = 400$ or 45%). The group was split into analysis and cross-validation samples because, as more models are tested, the distinction between confirmatory and exploratory factor analysis becomes blurred. The use of analysis and cross-validation samples allowed for more definitive conclusions to be drawn regarding the final model selected. Furthermore, it is known that the x^2 test of significance is sensitive to sample size (Anderson & Gerbing, 1984; Bentler & Bonnett, 1980; Boomsma, 1982), such that, with very large samples, even minor deviations between the observed and predicted covariances will lead to significant values of x^2. Given these two problems, the sample was split so that the smallest sample would be at least 400.

All children had been referred for neuropsychological assessment, and all diagnoses were made "blind" as described in Rourke, Fisk, and Strang (1986). Diagnoses were

348

made at the time of assessment, and inclusion in the present study was based on information recorded in an archival data base. Children included in this study can be classified into one of three diagnostic categories. The majority of the sample (633 or 71%) received a diagnosis of learning disabled at the time of assessment. This diagnosis required that the child have a WISC FSIQ over 84, at least one WRAT centile score at or below the30th centile, and some evidence of an information-processing or learning-style problem. A second group of 157 (18%) children had WISC FSIQ scores in the range from 71 to 84. The final group of 98 (11%) children had received no diagnosis, i.e., they could not be classified as learning disabled by the above criteria, had WISC FSIQ scores over 84 and no evidence of mental retardation, frank neurological damage, emotional disturbance, or environmental deprivation.

Measures

All measures of tactile and motor skills included in the study were carried out with both the dominant and nondominant hand. A total of 21 neuropsychological tests (8 tactile, 8 motor, 3 verbal, and 2 visual-spatial) were included in all analyses. All tests have been widely employed in clinical neuropsychological assessment over the last three decades (Rourke et al., 1983). Details of test administration are provided in Rourke et al.(1983). Measures of tactile and motor skills were taken from the Halstead-Reitan (Reitan & Davison, 1974) and Kløve (1963) batteries of motor tests as follows (in the test abbreviations, the R and L suffixes indicate RH and LH performance, respectively): Tactile Perception (TACR, TACL), Finger Agnosia (FAGR, FAGL), Finger-Tip Number Writing (FTWR, FTWL), Tactile Forms Test (Astereognosis) (ASTR, ASTL), Finger Tapping (TAPR, TAPL), Grip Strength (GRPR, GRPL), Grooved Pegboard (PEGR, PEGL), and the Maze test (MAZR, MAZL). For all analyses, five measures of Verbal and Visual-Spatial Constructive Skills factors were included in order to increase the opportunity for differential covariation among RH and LH indicators of Tactile, and Motor Skills. TheVerbal Skills factor was measured by the Information, Vocabulary, and Similarities scaled scores from the Verbal subscale of the WISC, while the Visual Spatial Constructive factor was measured by the Block Design and Object Assembly scaled scores from the Performance subscale (Wechsler, 1949).

The inclusion of measures of Verbal and Visual-Spatial Constructive factors can be viewed as increasing the power of the test of discriminant validity. For example, suppose that only the tactile and motor skill measures had been included in the study and there had been no evidence of discriminant validity. One could reasonably question whether discriminant validity would have obtained if additional (non-tactile or -motor) tests had been included that are thought to reflect the (differential) functional integrity of the left and right cerebral hemispheres. However, the converse is not true. That is, if the additional variables were included and there was no evidence for discriminant validity, it is not possible that dropping some of the additional variables would suddenly yield evidence *for* discriminant validity. These relationships must hold because the model of no discriminant validity is a restricted form of the model with discriminant validity. If the restricted model (one without discriminant validity) explains the relationships in a given data matrix, then it is not possible that a more complex model (one with discriminant validity) would be necessary to explain the relationships in a subset of that data matrix. In other words, adding external variables to the data set could only increase the chance of evidencing discriminant validity.

Measures of Verbal and Visual-Spatial Constructive skills were chosen for several reasons. First, these factors would be expected to show differential covariation with measures of right and left hemisphere function. Secondly, these measures are known to be highly reliable. Furthermore, there is considerable knowledge about the factor structure of these measures, which made it possible to include them without seriously complicating the "unknown" aspects of the models under consideration. Also, none of the five measures load on both visual and verbal factors; that is, each measure tends to be a pure indicator of one factor or the other. Lastly, the measures were readily available on virtually the entire sample.

Procedures

To test for discriminant validity of LH and RH test scores, a series of four nested models which differed only in terms of the Tactile and Motor Skills factors were fit and compared within each sample. These models are depicted in Figures 1 thru 4. The large circles in each figure represent factors.

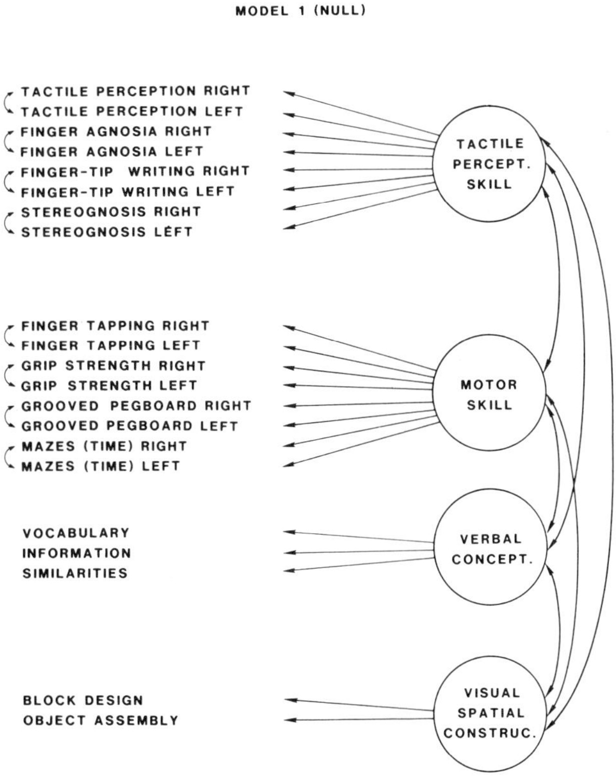

Fig. 1. Path diagram for four factor null model. Large circles indicate latent variables; one sided arrows depict relationships between tests and factors; curved two sided arrows indicate hypothesized non-zero correlations between factors (arrows connecting circles), or test-specific relationships for left- and right-hand versions of the same test.

A straight, one-sided arrow indicates that the variable pointed to loads on the factor from which the arrow leads. The curved two-sided arrows which point to LH and RH versions of the same test indicate that these variables share a test-specific (method) relationship, or correlated errors of measurement. In other words, LH and RH measures of the same test are related above and beyond their respective relationships with the underlying factors. The test-specific relationships do not vary across the four models.

The curved two-sided arrows which adjoin the circles representing the factors signify that the factors are correlated. In each of the four models, all factors are considered correlated with one another. The correlations among the factors provide the test for discriminant validity, and thereby provide the basis for the distinctions among the four models. Because the four models differ only with respect to the Tactile and Motor Skills factors, discussion of the four models will focus only on that aspect of the models.

Model 1 stipulates that the eight Tactile tests measure a single Tactile Skills factor and that the eight Motor tests measure a single Motor Skills factor. Model 1 is considered the

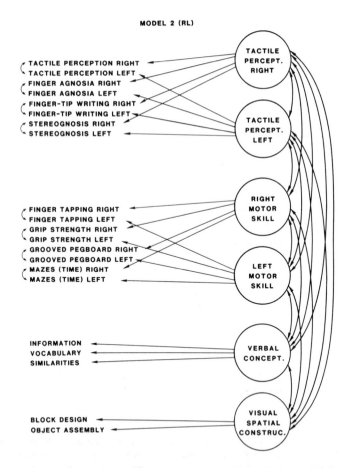

MODEL 2 (RL)

Fig. 2. Path diagram for model with discriminant validity of left- and right- tactile and motor tests. For symbol definitions see Figure 1.

null model because it represents the minimally defensible substantive model for these 21 measures. Given the nature of these 21 tests, a model with fewer factors would seem difficult to justify. Model 2 is presented in Figure 2. Model 2 allows for both RH and LH Tactile and Motor Skills factors, and for that reason is designated Model RL. Note, Model 2 differs from Model 1 in that Model 2 stipulates that RH and LH tests have discriminant validity within each class of measure, i.e., Tactile and Motor. It is often said that Model 1 is "nested" in Model 2 because Model 1 is obtained from Model 2 by placing constraints on the parameters of Model 2. Specifically, Model 1 is obtained from Model 2 by (a) constraining the correlation between LH and RH Tactile Factors in Model 2 to be 1.0, and (b) constraining the correlation between LH and RH Motor Factors in Model 2 to be 1.0. Constraining the correlation between two factors to be 1.0 also implies that their correlations with any third factor must be equal. These equal correlations represent the third set of constraints (c) necessary to produce Model 1 from Model 2.

In terms of parameters, Model 1 differs from Model 2 by nine fewer free parameters: (1) the correlation between LH and RH Tactile factors is constrained to 1.0, (2) the correlation of LH Tactile with Verbal Skills is equal to the correlation of RH Tactile with Verbal Skills, (3) the correlation of LH Tactile with Visual Spatial Skills is equal to the correlation of RH Tactile with Visual Spatial Skills, (4-6) 1 thru 3 are also specified for LH and RH Motor Skills, (7) the correlation with RH Tactile is equal for RH Motor and LH Motor, (8) the correlation with LH Tactile is equal for RH Motor and LH Motor, and (9) 7 and 8 are equal because RH and LH tactile correlate 1.0. In other words, 7-9 imply that there is one correlation between Tactile and Motor Skills instead of the four cross-correlations included in Model 2.

The nested relationship of Models 1 and 2 means that a comparison of these models is a simultaneous test of the constraints that map Model 2 onto Model 1. If Model 2 provides a better fit to the data than Model 1, one would conclude that the distinction between RH and LH Tactile and Motor Factors is an important one, that is, that RH and LH tactile and motor tests have some discriminant validity.

Model 3 differs from Model 1 by specifying that there is not a single type of Tactile or Motor Skills factor (Figure 3). Upon closer examination, the Tactile and Motor Skills tests can be categorized as either Simple or Complex (hence Model 3 is given the designation SC). For example, the tactile Perception and Finger Agnosia tests are simple sensory tests. The subject is administered a tactile stimulus and simply responds as to where the stimulus was felt. On the other hand, the Finger-Tip Number Writing and Stereognosis tests require not only that the subject sense the tactile input, but that they form a complete percept out of that input. That is, these two tests have a higher order perceptive component to them. Similar arguments could be put forth for categorizing Finger Tapping and Grip Strength as simple motor tests, and the Grooved Pegboard and Maze tests as complex motor tests.

In terms of model nesting, Model 1 is again nested in Model 3, while Models 2 and 3 are not nested within each other. In other words, direct comparison of Models 2 and 3 is difficult and any such comparison does not test a clear-cut hypothesis. Because Models 2 and 3 are not nested, it is impossible to compare their χ^2 values statistically even if the degrees of freedom for the two models had been different. On the other hand, comparison of Models 1 and 3 is a test of the discriminant validity of Simple and Complex Tactile and Motor factors. Similar to the relationship between Models 2 and 1, nine constraints map Model 3 onto Model 1. However, in this case the constraints involve correlations for Simple and Complex factors, as opposed to correlations for RH

352

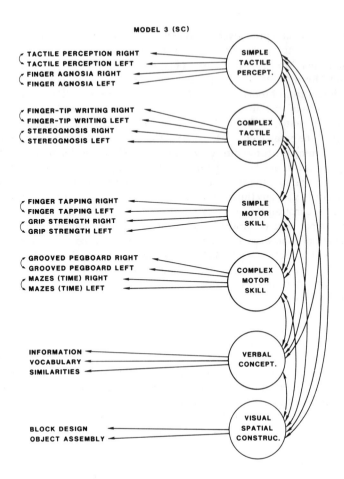

MODEL 3 (SC)

Fig. 3. Path diagram for model with discriminant validity of simple and complex tactile and motor tests. For symbol definitions see Figure 1.

and LH factors. Because the process for identifying these constraints is similar to that carried out for Models 1 and 2, it will not be repeated here.

Model 4 represents the fullest model under consideration (Figure 4). Model 4 combines the distinction of Right and Left from Model 2, and the distinction of Simple and Complex from Model 3 (hence the designation RL,SC). Thus, it is not surprising that Model 1, Model 2, and Model 3 all are nested in Model 4. A comparison of Models 2 (RL) and 4 (RL,SC) tests the contribution of adding Simple and Complex factors to a model that already contains RH and LH factors. Alternatively, a comparison of Models 3 (SC) and 4 (RL,SC) tests the contribution of adding RH and LH factors to a model that contains Simple and Complex factors. Moreover, comparisons among the four models provide two tests for the discriminant validity of RH and LH Tactile and Motor factors: Model 3 (SC) vs. Model 4 (RL,SC), and Model 1 (Null) vs. Model 2 (RL). However, these two comparisons do not test literally the same hypothesis. It is perhaps easiest to think of

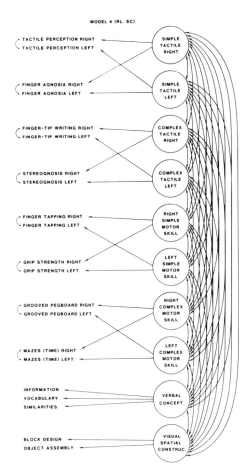

Fig. 4. Path diagram for model with discriminant validity of left- and right-, and simple and complex tactile and motor tests. For symbol definitions see Figure 1.

the difference between these tests as analogous to testing full and reduced models in multiple regression. Comparison of Models 1 and 2 tests the importance of RH and LH factors when no distinctions are made among the eight tactile tests, or among the eight motor tests. That is, comparison of Models 1 and 2 tests the contribution of RH and LH factors to a model with a single Tactile factor and a single Motor factor. On the other hand, comparison of Models 3 and 4 tests the importance of RH and LH factors when covariation among the 21 tests due to the Simple-Complex distinction has already been explained. Analogously, the four models provide two tests for the discriminant validity of Simplex and Complex Tactile and Motor factors: Model 1 (Null) vs. Model 3 (SC), and Model 2 (RL) vs. Model 4 (RL,SC). Following the same logic as for the Right-Left hypothesis, these two comparisons can be seen to test the Simple-Complex hypothesis in two slightly different contexts.

Parameters were estimated for all models using LISREL VI (Jöreskog & Sörbom,

354

1986) running under SPSS[x] 2.1 (SPSS, Inc., 1986) on a National Systems AS9000N computer at the University of Houston. All models were scale free and were therefore analyzed using the sample correlation matrix to facilitate the presentation of residual statistics. If a model is scale free, then analysis based on the correlation matrix is equivalent through a scaling factor to analysis based on the covariance matrix (Browne, 1982).

RESULTS

Global fit indices for all four models for the analysis sample are presented in Table 1. The same data are presented in Table 2 for the Cross-Validation sample. The information in the two tables is very similar, with only slightly greater differences among the four models apparent in Table 2 as compared to Table 1.

Table 1

Summary Fit Statistics for Models 1 thru 4
(Analysis Sample $n = 488$)

Index	Model			
	1	2	3	4
Chi-Square	344.48	328.30	234.07	175.98
DF	175	166	166	136
$p<$	.001	.001	.001	.012
Chi-Square/D.F. (Fit Ratio)	1.969	1.978	1.410	1.287
Goodness of Fit	.934	.937	.957	.967
Adjusted Goodness of Fit	.913	.912	.940	.944
Root Mean Square Residual	.050	.050	.031	.029
Number of Normalized Residuals $\geq \pm 2.0$	15	14	2	3
Largest Normalized Residual	3.7	3.9	2.0	2.0
Q-Plot of Normalized Residuals	Fair	Fair	Good	Good
Normed Fit Index[a,b]	.8356	.8433	.8883	.9160
Nonnormed Fit Index[a,c]	.8967	.8957	.9563	.9694

[a] Values for D and p evaluated with respect to the modified independence null model (see text)

[b] $D = (\chi^2_1 - \chi^2) / (\chi^2_1)$ (Normed Fit Index)

[c] $p = (\chi^2_1 / df_1 - \chi^2/df_f) / [(\chi^2_1 / df_1) - 1]$ (Non-Normed Fit Index)

Table 2

Summary Fit Statistics for Models 1 thru 4
(Cross-Validation Sample $n = 400$)

	Model			
Index	1	2	3	4
Chi-Square	358.95	347.24	212.49	183.81
D.F.	175	166	166	136
$p<$	.001	.001	.009	.004
Chi-Square/D.F. (Fit Ratio)	2.051	2.092	1.280	1.352
Goodness of Fit	.922	.924	.952	.958
Adjusted Goodness of Fit	.897	.895	.933	.929
Root Mean Square Residual	.063	.063	.036	.035
Number of Normalized Residuals $\geq \pm 2.0$	17	18	2	2
Largest Normalized Residual	4.9	4.9	2.0	2.0
Q-Plot of Normalized Residuals	Fair	Fair	Good	Good
Normed Fit Index[a, b]	.7775	.7848	.8683	.8861
Nonnormed Fit Index[a, c]	.8496	.8437	.9599	.9496

[a] See footnote of Table 1

[b] See footnote of Table 1

[c] See footnote of Table 1

Of greater interest is that in both Tables 1 and 2 the indices present conflicting information regarding model fit. For a complete description of the indices presented in Table 1, and their use and interpretation in model assessment see Francis(1986). Using the χ^2 test of significance, none of the models can be considered satisfactory. Even Model 4 (RL,SC), the least restrictive model, yielded a χ^2 with an associated p value of less than the traditional .05 cut-off for well-fitting models. However a model of modified independence yielded $\chi^2 = 2095.61$ and $\chi^2 = 1613.53$ (both with $df = 202$, $p < .001$) in the analysis and cross-validation samples, respectively. The model of modified independence specified that only LH and RH measures of the same test were correlated. Clearly, all four models are considerably better than the model of modified independence. Furthermore, it is more than likely that the χ^2 statistics of Tables

356

1 and 2 are inflated due to multivariate nonnormality.[1]

While the overall χ^2 statistics suggest that the models fit poorly, the Goodness-of-Fit (GFI) and Adjusted Goodness-of-Fit (AGFI) Indices, the root-mean-square residuals (RMRs) (Jöreskog and Sörbom, 1986), fit ratios, and normed and nonnormed fit indices (Bentler & Bonnett, 1980) indicate that all of the models provide a satisfactory fit to the data. RMR, GFI, and AGFI do not have known sampling distributions, but have been studied using Monte Carlo sampling techniques. However, the mixed nature of the models investigated here in terms of the number of indicators per factor and the number of factors, and the use of sample sizes exceeding 300, make it difficult to provide expected values for these indices in this study based on the published Monte Carlo studies (see tables in Anderson & Gerbing, 1984). The normed and nonnormed fit indices are functions of the chi-square statistic and its d.f. These indices are discussed in Bentler and Bonnett (1980), Francis (1986), and Sobel and Bohrnstedt (1985). Basically, they indicate the degree to which the proposed model improves upon some baseline model. Bentler and Bonnett (1980) suggest that models with normed fit indices below .90 can usually be improved substantially. However, Bentler and Bonnett's (1980) recommendation was based on the use of a model of complete independence as the null model. The normed and nonnormed fit indices reported in Tables 1 and 2 are with respect to a null model of modified independence. The model of modified independence must fit at least as well as a model of complete independence, because the latter is nested within the former. The use of this model as the null model necessarily lowers the values for the normed and nonnormed fit indices in this instance where the model of complete independence is strictly inappropriate. A model of complete independence is inappropriate because of the inclusion of LH and RH versions of the same test. Therefore, the normed and nonnormed fit indices in Tables 1 and 2 would appear to be in the acceptable model fit range considering the use of the more stringent null model of modified independence.

[1] Because the models are scale free, it would be possible to adjust the reported values for the multivariate kurtosis (Browne, 1982) of the variables. Multivariate nonnormality increases the value of χ^2, thereby increasing the difficulty of finding a model which fits in a statistical sense. The adjustment to χ^2 is independent of the model being evaluated. Thus, all χ^2s and χ^2 difference tests would be divided by the same value if the adjustment were performed. This adjustment would thus make absolute differences between the models smaller than they are presently, and would make all models fit better from a purely statistical standpoint. However, the adjustment was not attempted because its adequacy has not been thoroughly investigated (Bentler, 1985). Furthermore, sound conclusions can still be reached from the present data based on descriptive (noninferential) information. Adjusting the χ^2 places too great an emphasis on the test of significance which is unwarranted in our opinion. As stated by Bentler: "(in the absence of multivariate normality) the estimates that result from (least squares), (generalized least squares) and (maximum-likelihood), will no doubt be reasonable (see Tanaka, 1984), but the standard errors and χ^2 tests may be incorrect. In such a case, fit indices (Bentler & Bonnett, 1980) become a better guide to the adequacy of a model." (Bentler, 1985, p. 53)

Table 3

Summary Statistics for Tests of Discriminant
Validity (Analysis Sample $n = 488$)

Hypothesis	Models Compared (r	f)[a]	df	$(\chi^2_r - \chi^2_f)$	$p <$	Fit Index D[b]	p[c]
Right/Left	1	2	9	16.18	.10	.047	−.010
	3	4	30	58.09	.005	.169	.120
Simple/Complex	1	3	9	110.41	.001	.321	.577
	2	4	30	152.32	.001	.442	.706

[a] r and f refer to the subscripts for the restricted and fuller models in the formulas for p and D

[b] $D = (\chi^2_r - \chi^2_f) / (\chi^2_1)$ (Normed Fit Index)

[c] $p = (\chi^2_r / df_r - \chi^2_f / df_f) / [(\chi^2_1 / df_1) - 1]$ (Nonnormed Fit Index)

In Tables 1 and 2, the number of normalized residuals exceeding 2.0 and the Q-Plot of normalized residuals suggest that perhaps Models 3 and 4 are preferable to Models 1 and 2. For both samples, Models 1 and 2 yielded many normalized residuals exceeding the 2.0 cutoff. Models 3 and 4 were within the acceptable range with 2-3 residuals (i.e., less than 1% of the 202 residuals not constrained to 0 by the model) exceeding the 2.0 limit. However, the nesting of models allows a more comprehensive comparison of the models which focuses on the specific hypotheses of the discriminant validity of Right/Left and Simple/Complex factors.

Summary statistics for nested model comparisons are presented in Table 3 for theAnalysis sample. Results for the Cross-Validation sample will follow. Recall that comparison of Models 1 and 2, and Models 3 and 4 provide separate tests of the discriminant validity of LH and RH Tactile and Motor factors, while comparison of Models 1 and 3, and Models 2 and 4 provide separate tests of the discriminant validity of Simple- and Complex- Tactile and Motor factors.

The data in Table 3 suggest that the contribution of LH and RH factors to overall model fit is slight. The χ^2 difference test comparing Models 1 and 2 is nonsigificant at $p \leq .05$, suggesting that a model with RH and LH Tactile and Motor factors is not better than a model with single Tactile and Motor factors. On the other hand, the addition of LH and RH factors to a model containing Simple and Complex factors does appear to significantly improve model fit ($\chi^2 = 58.09$, $df = 30$, $p \leq .005$), (disregarding, for the moment, our warnings about significance tests). However, an examination of the parameter estimates in Model 4 shows that the correlations between LH and RH factors are very high, namely $r = .936, .944, .991$, and .896 for Simple Tactile, Complex Tactile, Simple Motor, and Complex Motor, respectively. Thus, while Model 4 may be statistically superior to Model 3 as measured by the χ^2 difference test, the RH and LH factors included in Model 4 do not appear highly discriminant as evidenced by their sizeable correlations.[2]

The discriminant validity of Simple and Complex Tactile and Motor factors is in less doubt. Comparison of Models 1 and 3, and Models 2 and 4 yielded significant results (Table 3). The importance of Simple and Complex factors as opposed to RH and LH factors is further evidenced by the normed and nonnormed incremental fit indices presented in Table 3. Values for p and D in Table 3 are based on Model 1 as the null model, because Model 1 is the minimally defensible model for comparing competing substantive models (Sobel & Bohrnstedt, 1985).

Examining the incremental fit ratios in Table 3, it is clear that there is greater support for the discriminant validity of Simple and Complex factors than for the discriminant validity of LH and RH Tactile and Motor factors. The normed fit indices for including Simple and Complex factors of $D = .321$ and $D = .442$ compare favorably with $D = .047$ and $D = .169$ for including RH and LH factors. A similar comparison is possible for the nonnormed fit index, p. Thus, using the indices and χ^2 difference tests inTable 3, the information from Table 1, and the parameter estimates, the best model is found to be Model 3. Model 3 combines optimum fit with a minimum number of parameters.

Results for the cross-validation sample are presented in Table 4. In this case, the results point even more clearly to Model 3 as the model of choice. The χ^2 difference test for the inclusion of RH and LH factors is nonsignificant on both occasions, while the tests for Simple and Complex factors are both statistically significant. These tests are further supported by the incremental fit ratios using Model 1 as the baseline model.

DISCUSSION

It is common in the neuropsychological assessment of children to infer differences in hemispheric functioning when sensory or motor skills on contralateral hands appear differentially impaired. Although such inferences may be valid for brain-impaired individuals, the present investigation provides no evidence that dominant/nondominant sensorimotor measures possess discriminant validity in children without evidence of frank brain damage. In

---

[2] Violations of the assumption of multivariate normality may inflate the χ^2 difference test, thereby providing a liberal test of the difference in these models. However, violations of this assumption do not systematically bias parameter estimates, and maximum-likelihood will yield good estimates when large sample sizes are used. Thus, the conclusion seems warranted that left-right distinctions are not practically significant in comparison of Models 3 and 4 based on the estimated factor correlations, although the statistical significance of these distinctions cannot be completely ruled out.

Table 4

Summary Statistics for Tests of Discriminant
Validity (Cross-Validation Sample $n = 400$)

| Hypothesis | Models Compared | | df | $(\chi^2_r - \chi^2_f)$ | $p <$ | Fit Index | |
	$(r$	$f)$[a]				D[b]	p[c]
Right/Left	1	2	9	11.71	.250	.033	−.038
	3	4	30	28.68	.600	.080	−.068
Simple/Complex	1	3	9	146.46	.001	.408	.733
	2	4	30	163.43	.001	.455	.705

[a] r and f refer to the subscripts for the restricted and fuller models in the formulas for p and D

[b] $D = (\chi^2_r - \chi^2_f) / (\chi^2_1)$ (Normed Fit Index)

[c] $p = (\chi^2_r / df_r - \chi^2_f / df_f) / [\chi^2_1 / df_1) - 1]$ (Nonnormed Fit Index)

order for such measures to possess discriminant validity, factors for LH and RH tests should have correlated less than 1.0 in the confirmatory factor analyses. In general, no loss of model fit was introduced when LH and RH factors were constrained to correlate perfectly, i.e., when LH and RH factors were considered to have no discriminant validity. In the absence of discriminant validity, inferences concerning differential hemispheric dysfunction based only on contralateral sensorimotor hand performance are suspect, although such conclusions are frequently made for learning-disabled children (e.g., Reitan, 1984). Such inferences disregard the apparent psychometric properties of the tests in this population. It would appear that these tests do not represent unique sources of biological variation as suggested by Reitan (1984), nor are they necessarily more valid as indicators of brain function than performance on other psychometric instruments. In fact, the most appropriate model for the 21 measures in this study distinguished between Simple and Complex Motor and Tactile measures. Furthermore, this distinction was supported in both the validation and cross- validation samples. Greater attention to this distinction may enhance ability- based interpretations of neuropsychological test batteries for children.

It should be noted that these considerations regarding the discriminant validity of lateralized sensory and motor measures apply primarily to modes of interpretation based on levels of performance (Reitan, 1966; Rourke, 1975). In this mode of interpretation, comparisons are made to normative age standards, which could represent scores on various measures for each hand separately, or for differences in hand performance. It is well known that this approach leads to a high rate of false positive errors (Rourke, 1981), which may well be due to the absence of discriminant validity of these measures. However, one cannot conclude that other modes of clinical interpretation that compare performance on the two sides of the body are necessarily invalid. For example, extremely deviant scores may well be a pathognomonic sign of brain dysfunction. Similarly, interpreting lateralized performances in the context of performance on other measures, i.e., a differential score approach, is entirely appropriate. In the latter example, inferences concerning hemispheric dysfunction are based on patterns of performance across motor, tactile, verbal, and visual-spatial tasks, not solely on the basis of right-left discrepancies in motor and tactile performance. The present study does not address the validity of inferences based on either the pathognomonic sign or differential score approaches. Consequently, this study does not indicate that LH and RH test scores do not provide differential information in an individual assessment. However, we can conclude that "on the average" these tests provide no differential information in the types of groups studied here. Furthermore, these data should not be taken to imply that clinicians no longer collect data from both the LH and the RH in clinical assessment. The data of this investigation do not address the question of discriminant validity in individual cases or across patterns of test results, especially as these questions are considered with regard to more diverse patient groups than those studied here.

On the basis of this study, there would appear to be little reason to include LH and RH versions of the same test in future factor-analytic studies of neuropsychological tests with non-brain-damaged individuals. A more efficient strategy to employ in studies not looking at issues of discriminant validity would be to combine LH and RH scores into a single, and more reliable, index. These recommendations follow from the fact that the present study has provided only a limited test of the discriminant validity of lateralized test scores. The conclusions reached on the basis of the models tested in this study are only accurate within the context of these models. Alternative models could well lead to different conclusions. More important, a study involving additional measures might yield different conclusions. In addition, if a study is designed specifically to examine issues of discriminant validity of lateralized test scores, or to examine factor structure in brain-damaged populations, then inclusion of LH and RH scores would be justified. However, researchers should be aware of the potential distorting effects of shared method variance when exploratory factor procedures are used in this situation.

The caution that all models can be considered false a priori must not be overlooked. This is akin to saying that the null hypothesis is never exactly true in classical hypothesis testing. In classical hypothesis testing, we are only concerned that the null hypothesis be true (or not true) for all practical purposes, not in any strict, or absolute sense. Similarly, models are not behavior. Rather, models provide a means for predicting behavior, and for testing complex hypotheses about behavior. Whether the model is exactly true is of less consequence than that the model provide better predictions about behavior than competing, or existing models. In the present case, the model of

Simple and Complex Tactile and Motor Skills factors without LH and RH factors presents a reasonable working model that provided an adequate fit to two sets of sample data. Future studies aimed at identifying alternative models for similar data should incorporate this model as one competing alternative.

The present study also demonstrated that confirmatory factor-analytic methods are powerful tools for explicating the measurement properties of neuropsychological test instruments. However, the successful application of these methods for selecting among competing substantive models is dependent on the identification of an appropriate baseline model (Sobel & Bohrnstedt, 1985). Furthermore, researchers must keep in mind that inferential statistics play only a partial role in the assessment of model fit. Successful applications of structural equation models will focus on descriptive indices of model fit, including Goodness of Fit Indices (GFI, AGFI), residual statistics (RMR, normalized residuals), squared multiple correlations, and the appropriateness of parameter estimates, as well as inferential information where available. The choice of an optimal model must balance tests of statistical significance, descriptive fit criteria, and the rules of parsimony. As with any other statistical method, structural equation models require rational considerations that lead to hypotheses and a basis for interpreting the results. Given a sound prior conceptualization and a thorough understanding of the methods, structural equation models provide a very flexible method for testing complex hypotheses with considerable potential for application in neuropsychology. In the absence of these considerations, structural models can only lead to sterile, uninterpretable results.

REFERENCES

Aftanas, M. S., & Royce, J. R. (1969). A factor analysis of brain damage tests administered to normal subjects with factor score comparisons across ages. *Multivariate behavioral Research, 4,* 459-481.

Anderson, J. C., & Gerbing, D. W. (1984). The effect of sampling error on convergence, improper solutions, and goodness-of-fit indices for maximum-likelihood confirmatory factor analysis. *Psychometrika, 49,* 155-173.

Barnes, G. W., & Lucas, G. J. (1974). Cerebral dysfunction vs. psychogenesis in Halstead-Reitan tests. *Journal of Nervous and Mental Disease, 158,* 50-60.

Bentler, P. M. (1985). *Theory and implementation of EQS: A structural equations program.* Los Angeles: BMDP Statistical Software, Inc.

Bentler, P. M., & Bonnett, D. G. (1980). Significance tests and goodness of fit in the analysis of covariance structures. *Psychological Bulletin, 88,* 588-606.

Boll, T. S. (1974). Behavioral correlates of cerebral damage in children aged 9 through 14. In R. M. Reitan & L. A. Davison (Eds.), *Clinical neuropsychology: Current status and applications* (pp. 91-120). Washington, DC: V. H. Winston & Sons.

Boomsma, A. (1982). The robustness of LISREL against small sample sizes in factor analysis models. In K. G. Jöreskog & H. Wold (Eds.), *Systems under indirect observation: Causality, structure, prediction, Part I* (pp. 149-173). Amsterdam: North Holland.

362

Browne, M. W. (1982). Covariance structures. In D. M. Hawkins (Ed.), *Topics in applied multivariate analysis* (pp. 72-141). London: Cambridge University Press.

Campbell, D. T., & D. W. (1959). Convergent and discriminant validation by the multitrait-multimethod matrix. *Psychological Bulletin, 56,* 81-105.

Francis, D. J. (1986, August). Structural equation models in neuropsychological research: Assessment of model fit. In J. M. Schear (Chair), *Applications of multivariate methods in neuropsychology.* Symposium conducted at the annual meeting of the American Psychological Association.

Goldstein, G., & Shelly, C. H. (1972). Statistical and normative studies of the Halstead neuropsychological battery relevant to a neuropsychiatric hospital setting.*Perceptual and Motor Skills, 34,* 603-620.

Grant, I., Adams, K. M., Carlin, A. J., Rennick, P. M., Judd, L. L., & Schooff, K. (1978). The collaborative neuropsychological study of polydrug users. *Archives of General psychiatry, 35,* 1063-1074.

Halstead, W. C. (1947). *Brain and intelligence.* Chicago: Chicago University Press.

Jöreskog, K. G., & Sörbom, D. (1986). *Lisrel VI: Analysis of linear structural relationships by the method of maximum-likelihood.* Chicago: National Educational Resources.

Kløve, H. (1963). Clinical neuropsychology. In F. M. Forster (Ed.), *The medical clinics of North America* (pp. 1647-1658). New York: Saunders.

Maxwell, J. K., & Niemann, H. (1984). The Fingertip Number Writing Test: Practice effects versus lateral asymmetry. *Perceptual and Motor Skills, 59,* 343-351.

Newby, R. F., Hallenbeck, C. E., & Embritson (Whiteley), S.(1983). Confirmatory factor analyses of four general neuropsychological models with a modified Halstead-Reitan Battery. *Journal of Clinical Neuropsychology, 5,* 115-133.

Reed, H. B. C. Jr., Reitan, R. M., & Kløve, H. (1965). The influence of cerebral lesions on psychological test performances of older children. *Journal of Consulting Psychology, 29,* 247-251.

Reitan, R. M. (1966). A research program on the psychological effects of brain lesions in human beings. N. R. Ellis (Ed.), *International review of research in mental retardation, Vol. 1* (pp. 153-218). New York: Academic Press.

Reitan, R. M. (1971). Sensorimotor functions in brain-damaged and normal children of early school-age. *Perceptual and Motor Skills. 33,* 655-664.

Reitan, R. M. (1984). *Aphasia and sensory-perceptual deficits in children.* Tucson: Neuropsychology Press.

Reitan, R. M., & Davison, L. A. (1974). *Clinical Neuropsychology: Current status and applications.* New York: Winston/Wiley.

Rourke, B. P. (1975). Brain behavior relationships in children with learning disabilities: A research program. *American Psychologist, 30,* 911-920.

Rourke, B. P. (1981). Neuropsychological assessment of children with learning disabilities. In. S. B. Filskov & T. J. Boll (Eds.), *Handbook of clinical neuropsychology* (pp. 453-478). New York: John Wiley.

Rourke, B. P., Bakker, D. J., Fisk, J. L., & Strang, J. D. (1983). *Child neuropsychology: An introduction to theory, research, and clinical practice.* New York: Guilford.

Rourke, B. P., Fisk, J. L., & Strang, J. D. (1986). *Neuropsychological assessment of children: A treatment-oriented approach.* New York: Guilford.

Royce, J. R., Yeudall, L. T., & Bock, C. (1976). Factor analytic studies of human brain damage: I. First and second order factors and their brain correlates. *Multivariate Behavioral Research, 11,* 381-418.

Ryan, J. J., Prifitera, A. P., & Rosenberg, S. J. (1983). Interrelationships between and factor structures of the WAIS-R and WAIS in a neuropsychological battery. *International Journal of Neuroscience, 21,* 191-196.

Sobel, M. E., & Bohrnstedt, G.W. (1985). Use of null models in evaluating the fit of covariance structure models. In N. Tuma (Ed.), *Sociological methodology 1985* (pp. 152-178). San Francisco: Jossey-Bass.

SPSS, Inc. (1983). *SPSSX user's guide.* New York: McGraw Hill.

Swiercinsky, D. P. (1979). A factorial pattern description and comparison of functional abilities in neuropsychological research. *Perceptual and motor skills, 48,* 231-242.

Swiercinsky, D. P., & Hallenbeck, C. E. (1975). A factorial approach to neuropsychological assessment. *Journal of Clinical Psychology, 31,* 610-618.

Swiercinsky, D. P., & Howard, M. E. (1982). Programmatic series of factor analyses for evaluating the structure of neuropsychological test batteries. *Clinical Neuropsychology, 4,* 147-152.

Tanaka, J.S. (1984). Some results on the estimation of covariance structure models. *Dissertation Abstracts International, 45,* 924B.

Wechsler, D. (1949). *Wechsler Intelligence Scale for Children.* New York: Psychological Corporation.

CHAPTER V

Special Topics

This potpourri of special topics covers a fairly broad range of general and specific issues that are of interest to the researcher in clinical neuropsychology. Four contributions to the topic of estimation of premorbid IQ are followed by a single presentation dealing with scaling. Then, several interrelated issues of reliability and stability of measurement are addressed in 11 articles. As with other sections of this book, the introductions to each of the following sub-sections were designed to provide an overview to the topic at hand. Rather than present a general overview of these sections, the reader is referred to their introductions for the specific content dealt with therein.

SECTION V – A: ESTIMATION OF PREMORBID IQ

The estimate of premorbid IQ levels is of importance to clinicians in the identifications of cognitive loss resulting from acute or chronic neurological insult. This is true particularly when repeated neuropsychological testing is not economic or logistically feasible. Researchers wishing to contrast the performance of neurologically impaired groups with appropriate non-neurologically involved control subjects face the problem of equating for premorbid rather than current intellectual ability.

Detailed discussions of the two fundamental approaches to the estimation of premorbid ability may be found in Lezak (1983) and Spreen and Strauss (1991). The approaches involve either (1) inferences from the pattern of performance on tests reputed to be vulnerable or resistant to neurological diseases, or (2) the use of demographic indices as predictor variables. The first three articles in this section, Wilson et al., Karzmark et al., and Goldstein et al. reflect attempts to define and explore the limits of multiple regression techniques applied to demographic variables in IQ estimation. They demonstrate that such approaches offer promise but lose precision at the upper and lower ends of the IQ range. Blair and Spreen attempt to estimate premorbid IQ using the measurement of a skill, reading ability, largely maintained through procedural memory and thus resistant to decline. One would expect, in future, to see the use of combinations of demographic time test variables in premorbid IQ assessment.

SECTION V – B: SCALING

The importance of the adequacy of the scale of measurement used in clinical or research work is difficult to underestimate. However, there are very few studies in the neuropsychological literature that deal specifically with this issue. The effort by Russell in this section should serve as an example of the types of considerations that would be very fruitful in many domains of clinical neuropsychological endeavor.

SECTION V – C: RELIABILITY AND STABILITY

This rather extensive series of articles was selected with a multitude of teaching objectives in mind: (1) to define the general concept of reliability (Cicchetti; Brown, Rourke, & Cicchetti); (2) to differentiate between relative and absolute reliability (Goldstein & Watson; Matarazzo, Carmody, & Jacobs); (3) to distinguish between reliability levels that are statistically significant and those that are both statistically and clinically significant (Cicchetti; Brown et al.; Matarazzo et al.); (4) to explain two classes of paradoxes that occur when the level of interexaminer agreement is high, but reliability levels are low (Cicchetti); (5) to examine the reliability and stability of well-standardized neuropsychological assessment instruments, (i.e., the WISC, WISC-R, WAIS, WAIS-R, McCarthy Scales, and the Halstead-Reitan Battery) in both normal samples (Casey, Ferguson, Kimura, & Hachinski; Matarazzo & Herman, and Matarazzo et al.) and in a wide range of neuropsychologically impaired samples such as children with perceptual, learning, language, behavioral, and information-processing disorders (Brown et al.), normal elderly subjects (Snow, Tierney, Zorzitto, Fisher, & Reid), and adult patients with various physical and neuropsychiatric disorders (Casey, Ferguson, Kimura, & Hachinski; Goldstein & Watson; Sarazin & Spreen; Shatz); (6) to examine the strengths and weaknesses of a number of available data-analytic strategies for making both reliability assessments (Brown et al.; Cicchetti) and validity assessments (Cicchetti, Sparrow, Volkmar, Cohen, & Rourke) of neuropsychological variables; and (7) to present guidelines for establishing the reliability and validity of neuropsychological disorders with low community prevalence (Cicchetti et al.).

There are several unifying principles that serve to provide theoretical, mathematical, and data-analytic bridges to connect the various methodologic and biostatistical information that are presented. Extending what was introduced in Brown et al., the concept of reliability assessment can be subsumed under generalizability theory (most recently, Shavelson & Webb, 1991). Generalizability theory posits and enables the evaluation of several systematic sources of variation (or facets) in the same research design (viz., raters or clinical examiners), test items, and occasions of testing. A given facet (e.g., 2 or more different examiners) or a combination of facets (e.g., 3 examiners, 30 test items, 2 alternate forms of the same test) comprise the "universe" to which test scores can be generalized. Within this unifying framework, the studies presented in this section all focused upon a single, but most important facet, namely, the variability associated with differences in independent ratings of a given neuropsychological measurement (e.g., level of cognitive functioning). In research of this genre, one attempts to control as much as possible for other sources (or facets) of variation (e.g., experience level of the examiners, time between assessments). When this is not possible, generalizability theory enables one to assess the effects that these other sources of variation have upon the ratings.

From a mathematical standpoint, kappa (nominal data), weighted kappa (ordinal data), and the intraclass correlation coefficient (continuous or ordinal data) belong to a family of mathematically related statistics (e.g., Fleiss & Cohen, 1973).

The earlier work of Blashfield (1976) represents what appears to be the first attempt to utilize kappa-type statistics in a broader multivariate framework, namely, applying this data-analytic approach to test the independence of empirically derived groups produced by cluster analysis. The much more recent work of Uebersax (1991) begins to consider kappa statistics in the context of a number of other multivariate techniques that include latent class agreement analysis, latent trait analysis, signal-detection (or ROC) models, item response and Rasch models, log-linear, association, and quasi-symmetry models. The work of Uebersax also focuses upon mathematical similarities and differences among this array of multivariate approaches.

The recent design of computer simulation studies has resulted in important methodologic discoveries pertaining to the proper application of both multivariate statistics (e.g., Adams, Brown, & Grant, see pages 157-174) and the construction of reliable clinical scales (e.g., Cicchetti, Showalter, & Tyrer, 1985). This accumulating corpus of scientific knowledge can be expected to provide further unifying concepts that provide a better understanding of the similarities and dissimilarities among various methodological and biostatistical concepts as these are relevant to biomedical research in general and clinical neuropsychology research in particular.

Finally, Cicchetti and colleagues make available upon request a number of kappa and intraclass correlation coefficient (R_I) computer programs that apply to various examiner and examinee research designs (e.g., same or different sets of examiners; different scales of measurement; varying numbers of assessments per subject). These programs represent various generalizations of Kappa and the R_I statistic to satisfy a variety of different rater reliability research designs.

Given these trends, the future of reliability and validity assessments, both within the field of neuropsychology and more generally, should present a myriad of intellectual challenges. Among the greatest of these challenges will be a comprehensive understanding of those classes of problems to which the new methodologic and biostatistical approaches will best apply, so that the reliability and validity of future assessments of brain-behavior relationships can thereby be enhanced.

REFERENCES

Blashfield, R.K. (1976). Mixture model tests of cluster analysis: Accuracy of four agglomerative hierarchical methods. *Psychological Bulletin, 83,* 377-388.

Cicchetti, D.V., Showalter, D., & Tyrer, P. (1985). The effect of number of rating scale categories upon levels of interrater reliability: A Monte Carlo investigation. *Applied Psychological Measurement, 9,* 31-36.

Fleiss, J.L., & Cohen, J. (1973). The equivalence of weighted kappa and the intraclass correlation coefficient as measures of reliability. *Educational and Psychological Measurement, 33,* 613-619.

Lezak, M.D. (1983). *Neuropsychological assessment* (2nd ed.). New York: Oxford University Press.

Shavelson, R.J., & Webb, N.W. (1991). *Generalizability theory: A primer.* Newberry Park, CA: Sage Publications.

Spreen, O., & Strauss E. (1991). *A compendium of neuropsychological tests.* New York: Oxford University Press.

Uebersax, J.S. (1982). A generalized Kappa coefficient. *Educational and Psychological Measurement, 42,* 181-183.

Uebersax, J.S. (1991). *Quantitative methods for the analysis of observer agreement: Toward a unifying model.* Santa Monica, CA: The RAND Corp.

Journal of Clinical Neuropsychology
1979, Vol. 1, No. 1, 49–53.

The Problem of Premorbid Intelligence in Neuropsychological Assessment*

Robert S. Wilson
Rush University

Gerald Rosenbaum
Wayne State University

Gregory Brown
Henry Ford Hospital

ABSTRACT

The aim of this study was to compare the utility of two methods of estimating premorbid IQ in the assessment of intellectual deterioration secondary to brain dysfunction. One estimate is based on demographic information, and the other is based on measures of present ability thought to be insensitive to brain dysfunction. Demographic and Wechsler Adult Intelligence Scale data were gathered for two groups: (1) 140 neurologic patients and (2) 140 nonneurologic subjects. This diagnostic dichotomy was regressed separately on two deterioration indices which differed only in the method used to estimate premorbid IQ. The index which relied on the demographic estimate was 11% more accurate than the present ability estimate in case classification. The results suggest that demographic information, when applied systematically, can provide a reasonably accurate and useful estimate of premorbid IQ.

There are numerous situations in neuropsychological assessment and research in which knowledge of subjects' premorbid IQ is desirable. Test data from the period preceding disease onset are rarely available, however, forcing clinicians to estimate. These estimates have typically relied on either (a) present ability measures thought to be relatively insensitive to brain dysfunction (e.g., vocabulary) or (b) demographic information known to be related to IQ (e.g., education).

While present ability measures such as vocabulary are highly related to IQ, these measures are not insensitive to brain dysfunction. In fact, neurological patients show a significant decline on all subtests of the Wechsler Adult

* This article is based on a dissertation submitted by the first author under the direction of the second author.

Intelligence Scale (WAIS) (Russell, 1972). Deterioration indices based on this model of estimating premorbid IQ have been ineffective in the assessment of intellectual impairment (e.g., Matarazzo, 1972; Wechsler, 1958; Yates, 1956).

An alternative approach involves the use of demographic information to estimate premorbid IQ. Since adult onset disease should have no effect on premorbid demographic status, the accuracy of such estimates should be limited only by the correlation between IQ and the demographics. In a previous report (Wilson, Rosenbaum, Brown, Rourke, Whitman & Grisell, 1978), we outlined a method for estimating the WAIS Full Scale IQ from demographic information. The Full Scale IQs of the 1955 WAIS standardization sample (n = 1700) were regressed on age, sex, race, education, and occupation. R^2 was .54. We proposed that the resulting regression equation could provide an actuarial method of estimating premorbid IQ in neuropsychological assessment.

The present study was designed to evaluate the clinical utility of this IQ estimate. Specifically, if this equation does provide a useful estimate of premorbid IQ, it should, when combined with present ability measures, aid in the identification of persons who have deteriorated intellectually.

METHOD

Subjects

The sample consists of 140 neurologic patients and 140 nonneurologic subjects. Neurologic patients were selected from the files of the Neurology Department of the Wayne State University School of Medicine. The group is heterogenous with respect to nature, locus, and extent of brain lesion.

The nonneurologic subgroup consists of pseudoneurologic, schizophrenic, and normal subjects. The pseudoneurologic patients (n = 27) were selected from the same files as the neurologic patients. These persons presented with neurologic symptoms (e.g., headache, dizziness), but subsequent investigations proved negative. The majority were discharged with a psychiatric diagnosis.

The schizophrenics (n = 50) were selected from the files of the Lafayette Clinic in Detroit. This is a young group (mean age = 22.6), the bulk of whom were being hospitalized for the first time following an acute psychotic episode. About one-third were unemployed. The pseudoneurologic and schizophrenic patients were included in the nonneurologic group because they often present with neurologic symptoms and are, therefore, often difficult to distinguish from neurologic patients.

The normal subjects (n = 63) were selected from the 1955 WAIS standardization sample (n = 1700) so that their mean age (51.3) would approximate that of the neurologic sample (52.1). Due to the inverse relation between age and education in the WAIS sample, this selection procedure resulted in a relatively poorly educated normal group. The neurological group is older (52.1 versus 37.3, p < .01) and more educated (11.7 versus 10.7, p < .01) than the nonneurological group. There are no sex or race differences.

Procedure

Demographic data and WAIS age-corrected subtest scores were collected. The test of the hypothesis involved regressing the diagnostic dichotomy of neurologic versus nonneurologic on two sets of predictors using discriminant function analysis. One predictor relies on present ability measures to estimate premorbid IQ while the other predictor makes use of demographic information. We assumed that the neurologic patients had deteriorated intellectually and that the nonneurologic patients had not. A comparison of the accuracy with which these two predictors classify cases as way of comparing the utility of the two methods of estimating premorbid IQ.

The first predictor is Wechsler's (1958) deterioration quotient. This formula contrasts performance on four "hold" subtests (Information, Vocabulary, Picture Completion, and Object Assembly) with four "don't hold" subtests (Similarities, Digit Span, Digit Symbol, and Block Design). The "hold" tests in this formula represent, in effect, Wechsler's estimate of premorbid IQ.

The second predictor is a modification of Wechsler's formula, with a demographic estimate of premorbid WAIS Full Scale IQ substituted for the "hold" tests in Wechsler's equation. The demographic estimate was calculated in the following manner:

$$\text{Estimated Full Scale IQ} = .17 \text{ (age)} - 1.53 \text{ (sex)} - 11.33 \text{ (race)} + 2.97 \text{ (education)} + 1.01 \text{ (occupation)} + 74.05.$$

The derivation of this formula is detailed elsewhere (Wilson, et al., 1978). In the equation, male = 1, female = 2, white = 1, nonwhite = 2, and the scores for Wechsler's (1955, page 7) 13 occupational categories are shown in Table 1. Thus, the estimated Full Scale IQ for a 20-year-old, white housewife would be 103.

TABLE 1

Occupation Scores for Wechsler's Thirteen Occupation Categories

Occupation categories	Occupation scores	Occupation categories	Occupation scores
1. Professional, technical, and kindred workers	5	7. Private household workers	3
2. Farmers and farm managers	1	8. Service workers	5
3. Managers, officials, and proprietors	7	9. Farm laborers	0
		10. Laborers	1
4. Clerical, sales, and kindred workers	7	11. Keeping house	4
5. Craftsmen, foremen, and kindred workers	6	12. Students	10
		13. Others (disabled, unemployed, retired, etc.)	0
6. Operatives and kindred workers	3		

After all subjects were classified as deteriorated versus not deteriorated according to the two predictors, a double cross-validation procedure was carried out. All subjects were assigned in a random, stratified manner to one of two groups. Cut-off scores were then derived, for each predictor, on the first subsample and then used to classify the second subsample and vice versa.

RESULTS

On the initial discriminant runs, the rate of correct classification of cases as neurologic versus nonneurologic was 63.2% for Wechsler's formula and 71.8% for the revised formula. On the double cross-validation runs, the hit rates were 61.8% for Wechsler's formula and 72.8% for the revised formula. The revised formula was particularly effective in reducing false positive errors. Specifically, on the double cross-validation runs, the revised formula was 15% more accurate than Wechsler's equation in ruling out intellectual deterioration in the nonneurologic subjects.

DISCUSSION

Substitution of the demographic estimate of WAIS Full Scale IQ for the "hold" tests in Wechsler's deterioration quotient resulted in an 11% improvement in the accuracy with which the formula classified cases as neurologic versus nonneurologic. These results suggest that demographic information may provide a better basis for estimating premorbid IQ than measures of present ability. While Wechsler's deterioration quotient is a rather crude neuropsychological measure, his "hold" tests, however inadequate, represent the most sophisticated attempt to estimate premorbid IQ from present ability measures. The relative failure of the "hold" tests in the present study suggests that present ability measures should not be used to estimate premorbid IQ.

We were also interested in the amount of unique information which the demographics added to this discrimination problem. Therefore, we regressed the neurologic–nonneurologic dichotomy in a stepwise fashion on the WAIS subtests. The hit rate was 71.8% on the initial run and 66.8% on the double cross-validation run. Thus, the demographics only slightly improve on the optimal combination of WAIS subtests in identifying intellectual deterioration in neurologic patients. Nonetheless, the demographics do provide a reasonably accurate measure of premorbid IQ which can be (a) computed readily, (b) combined with Wechsler IQs or other ability measures to aid in the assessment of intellectual deterioration, and (c) used to match experimental subjects on premorbid intellectual ability.

The equation presented here for estimating premorbid IQ from demographic information is based on 1955 data. Given an increase in educational attainment from a mean of 10.1 in the WAIS sample to a median of 12.3 in 1975 (U.S. Bureau of Census, 1976), these equations can be expected to overestimate premorbid IQ. A partial solution to this problem consists of adjusting the education weight in the equation (2.97) to the 1955 level by multiplying by .82 (10.1/12.3).

REFERENCES

Matarazzo, J. *Wechsler's measurement and appraisal of adult intelligence* (5th Ed.). Baltimore: Williams & Wilkins, 1973.

Russell, E. WAIS factor analysis with brain-damaged subjects using criterion measures. *Journal of Consulting and Clinical Psychology*, 1972, *39*, 133–139.

U.S. Bureau of the Census. *Current population reports* (Series P–20, No. 295), Educational attainment in the United States: March, 1975. Washington: U.S. Government Printing Office, 1976.

Wechsler, D. *The measurement and appraisal of adult intelligence* (4th Ed.). Baltimore: Williams & Wilkins, 1958.

Wilson, R. S., Rosenbaum, G., Brown, G., Rourke, D., Whitman, D., & Grisell, J. An index of premorbid intelligence. *Journal of Consulting and Clinical Psychology*, 1978, *46*, 1554–1555.

Yates, A. The use of vocabulary in the measurement of intellectual deterioration – A review. *Journal of Mental Science*, 1956, *102*, 409–440.

Journal of Clinical and Experimental Neuropsychology
1985, Vol. 7, No. 4, pp. 412-420

Use of Demographic Variables to Predict Full Scale IQ: A Replication and Extension

Peter Karzmark and Robert K. Heaton
University of Colorado

Igor Grant
University of California at San Diego

Charles G. Matthews
University of Wisconsin

ABSTRACT

The evaluation of current level of neuropsychological functioning is handicapped by the lack of validated actuarial methods for estimating premorbid intellectual functioning. The present study cross-validated and attempted to improve the one existing method of using demographic variables in a systematic way to predict WAIS Full Scale IQ (Wilson et al., 1978). A sample of 491 neurologically normal subjects was used. The results generally supported the IQ prediction equation, but did reveal systematic differences in accuracy of prediction and direction of prediction error for IQs in the high and low ranges. Also, a simpler IQ prediction formula that uses only years of education was developed and compared with the 5-variable Wilson et al. formula.

Knowledge of premorbid or "expected" level of intellectual functioning is helpful in the evaluation of current neuropsychological status. Several retrospective approaches to the estimation of premorbid intelligence have been used, but each has significant drawbacks. One method, using Wechsler Hold Tests to represent premorbid intelligence, has been called into question by the finding that so-called hold tests are themselves vulnerable to the effects of cerebral dysfunction (Vogt & Heaton, 1977). A second approach involves clinical estimation of expected IQ using demographic variables, and is based on the demonstrated relationships between the latter variables and intelligence (Matarazzo, 1972). However, until recently, there has been little effort devoted to the optimal and systematic combination of variables such as sex, age, race, education, and occupational status in a formal prediction equation, and an informal, clinical approach to their use has prevailed.

In the first comprehensive attempt at actuarial prediction of IQ with demographic variables, Wilson et al. (1978) derived the following equation using the WAIS standardization sample:

$$\text{Estimated Full Scale IQ} = .17 \, (\text{age}) - 1.53 \, (\text{sex}) - 11.33 \, (\text{race}) + 2.97 \, (\text{education}) + 1.01 \, (\text{occupation}) + 74.05.$$

In this equation male $= 1$ and female $= 2$, white $= 1$ and nonwhite $= 2$, and Wechsler's (1955, p. 7) 13 occupation categories are assigned the following respective weights: 5, 1, 7, 7, 6, 3, 3, 5, 0, 1, 4, 10, and 0.

With the above formula, the authors were able to account for 54% of the variance in WAIS FSIQ. However, they did not provide evidence regarding cross-validation of their prediction equation. In addition, there is reason to believe that the predictive accuracy of their approach could be improved in several ways. As the authors noted, their analysis was performed with data collected before 1955 and the relationship between education and intelligence may have changed since that time. Hence, reanalysis employing data that reflect the current relationship between FSIQ and demographic variables would be expected to provide some increment in predictive accuracy. In addition, Wilson et al. (1978) did not use occupational status per se as a predictor. Rather, they empirically generated weightings or scores for occupational categories by using these categories as nominal variables in a regression-based prediction of IQ. There are eight categories, each representing a broad occupational class (e.g., professional, technical, and kindred workers), and scores range from 0 to 10. In its predictive relationship to intelligence, occupation has more traditionally been considered in terms of independently rated occupational status (Matarazzo, 1972). Thus, substitution of an occupational status rating system for the Wilson et al. (1978) approach also may hold potential for improving prediction of FSIQ. Further, the system used by Wilson et al. (1978) categorized together certain occupational groups which are clearly disparate in occupational status at this time, e.g., professionals and technicians. Separation of such groups and assignment of appropriately differential occupational status scores should improve prediction.

With the above issues in mind, the present study was designed: (a) to cross-validate the Wilson et al. (1978) prediction equation and to evaluate its relative predictive accuracy with various demographic subgroups; and, (b) to determine whether the potential improvements discussed above significantly increase accuracy in prediction of FSIQ. Finally, because complex formulas are cumbersome for everyday clinical use, we assessed the adequacy of a much simpler method that uses only education to predict IQ.

METHOD

Subjects

These were 491 control subjects who were recruited for various studies conducted by the neuropsychology laboratories at the University of Colorado School of Medicine ($n = 174$), University of California at San Diego School of Medicine ($n = 152$), and University of Wisconsin School of Medicine ($n = 165$). A detailed and standardized interview (a version of this is available from the second author on request) was conducted with each subject to evaluate prior neurological risk factors. This indicated that none had any history of neurological illness, significant head trauma, or substance abuse. The subjects ranged in age from 15 to 81 ($M = 37.7$, $SD = 16.8$), and their average educational level was 13.3 years ($SD = 3.4$). The sample had 64% males and 9% nonwhite subjects. Mean WAIS FSIQ was 112.8 ($SD = 12.3$). Approximately one-half of the sample was tested before 1975.

Procedure

In the first phase of the study, the regression coefficients generated by Wilson et al. (1978) were used to predict FSIQ for the current sample. Preliminary analyses revealed that accuracy of prediction was not uniform across all levels of selected demographic variables. Therefore, prediction was performed both for the entire sample and for different levels of four subject variables. The variables used were age (less than 40, 40-59, 60 or greater), education (less than 12 years, 12-15 years, 16 or more years), intelligence level (less than 90, deciles in FSIQ from 90 through 129, 130 or greater), and the Wilson et al. (1978) occupational categories. In each case, accuracy of prediction was evaluated in terms of standard error of estimate and direction and magnitude of difference between mean predicted and actual FSIQ[1].

In the second phase of the study, two approaches to the assignment of occupational status, both designed to address the issues discussed previously, were used to generate occupational status scores for each employed subject ($n = 342$). The primary method made use of the Revised Socioeconomic Index (or MSEI2), designed by Stevens and Featherman (1981), to update the Duncan Socioeconomic Index. A second approach used the Hollingshead Occupational Scale (Hollingshead & Redlich, 1958). The MSEI2 coding system does not rate homemakers ($n = 28$), students ($n = 55$), or unemployed persons ($n = 27$) and the Hollingshead system does not rate the former two groups. Hence, these subgroups were not included in subsequent analyses during this phase. The five demographic variables (sex, race, education, age, and occupational status) were then entered in step-wise fashion into two multiple regression analyses to predict FSIQ. The first employed the MSEI2 and the second used the Hollingshead ratings. For both analyses, a subset of approximately 70% of

[1] The standard error of the estimate (*SEE*) is the standard deviation of the actual (criterion) scores around the regression line that predicts such scores. Higher *SEE*s indicate greater prediction error. To judge the value of a regression formula, its *SEE* can be compared with the standard deviation of the variable being predicted (Wiggins, 1973). Consider FSIQ as the variable to be predicted. If there were no relation between FSIQ and the demographic variables used to predict it, the *SEE* would equal the standard deviation of FSIQ (i.e., 15). Therefore, *SEE*s lower than 15 indicate that a regression equation has some predictive value.

the subjects ($n = 265$) was randomly selected as a derivation sample and the remaining subjects ($n = 110$) were used as a cross-validation sample. In order to provide a direct comparison between the efficacy of these regression analyses and the Wilson et al. (1978) prediction equation, prediction accuracy of the latter equation was also computed for the derivation and cross-validation samples.

RESULTS

The intercorrelations among predictor and criterion variables are presented in Table 1. FSIQ correlates significantly with all predictor variables except age. Among the three occupational measures, correlation with IQ is strongest for the MSEI2 and weakest for the Wilson et al. (1978) scores.

Table 1

Intercorrelations Among Predictor and Criterion Variables

Variable	1	2	3	4	5	6	7
1. Sex							
2. Age	—.10*						
3. Race	—.04	.06					
4. Education	—.02	—.21***	—.14***				
5. Occupation 1[a]	.10*	—.46***	.02	.11**			
6. Occupation 2[a, b]	.03	—.11*	.07	.75***	.21***		
7. Occupation 3[a, c]	.01	—.01	.06	—.59***	—.42***	—.88***	
8. FSIQ	—.09*	.01	—.29***	.58***	.13**	.55***	—.46***

[a] Occupation 1 = Wilson et al. (1978) method.   Occupation 2 = MSEI2.
 Occupation 3 = Hollingshead Occupational Scale.
$n = 491$ except: $b_n = 381$. $c_n = 408$.
*$p < .05$.   **$p < .01$.   ***$p < .001$.

The Wilson et al. (1978) regression equation was able to account for 42% of the variance in FSIQ in the present total sample. The resulting standard error of estimate (*SEE*) is 11.4, which compares favorably with the 10.2 obtained by Wilson et al. (1978) in their study. The foregoing *SEE* was computed using Wechsler's IQ standard deviation of 15; if the present sample's standard deviation is employed, the resulting *SEE* is 9.38.

Examination of the variability in *SEE* across different levels of age, education, and intelligence revealed maximum differences of 4%, 13%, and 4% across levels of the three respective factors. The range in *SEE* across occupational categories was somewhat higher, with a 20% difference between the occupation categories with the lowest *SEE* (managers, clerical; *SEE* = 10.5) and highest *SEE* (students; *SEE* = 13.1).

In the total sample, the mean predicted FSIQ was 110.9, in comparison to a mean actual FSIQ of 112.8. The differences between mean predicted and actual FSIQ across levels of education, age, and occupational category were minimal. The maximum difference was 7, 5, and 8 points for each respective variable. However, for intelligence level, a progressive shift from under-estimation of FSIQ at the lower levels of predicted FSIQ to overestimation at the higher levels was found (Table 2). Table 2 also presents the percentage of subjects for whom predicted FSIQ was above or below actual FSIQ by specified limits.

Table 2

Difference Between Mean Predicted and Actual Full Scale IQ, and Probability of Under- and Over-Prediction of Full Scale IQ by Specified Amounts

Predicted Full Scale IQ level	n	Mean predicted minus mean actual IQ	Percent of subjects with IQ over-prediction by[a]			Percent of subjects with IQ under-prediction by		
			>15	11-15	0-10	0-10	11-15	>15
Less than 90	16	−12	0	0	12	32	19	37
90-99	56	− 5	2	4	23	41	14	16
100-109	170	− 3	3	6	29	39	14	9
110-119	158	− 2	4	7	31	41	9	8
120-129	61	1	5	10	36	36	10	3
130 or greater	30	7	17	3	57	20	3	0
Total Sample	491	− 2	4	6	32	38	11	9

[a] Over-prediction is the case in which predicted Full Scale IQ is greater than actual Full Scale IQ.

Table 3 presents the results of the regression analyses using the two alternate approaches to the coding of occupational status. The MSEI2-based and Hollingshead-based regression analyses produced respective R^2s of .50 and .49. In both equations, education was the strongest predictor, accounting for 36% of the variance in FSIQ in each instance. Cross-validation of the MSEI2-based and Hollingshead-based equations resulted in 10 and 7% reductions in R^2, respectively. Application of the Wilson et al. (1978) formula to the derivation and cross-validation samples yielded an R_2 of .46 for each sample.

To investigate the utility of a more parsimonious approach to the prediction of FSIQ, the single predictor most strongly associated with FSIQ, education, was chosen to develop a univariate prediction model. A subset of 50% of the sample

Table 3

R^2 and Standard Error of the Estimate (SEE) for the Prediction of Full Scale IQ, Using
Three Approaches to the Treatment of Occupation

Sample	n	MSEI2		Hollingshead Occupational Scale		Wilson et al. (1978)	
		R^2	SEE	R^2	SEE	R^2	SEE
Derivation	265	.50	10.6	.49	10.7	.46	11.0
Cross-validation	110	.40	11.6	.42	11.4	.46	11.0

was randomly selected as a derivation sample and the following equation was generated:

$$\text{Predicted FSIQ} = 2.10 \,(\text{education}) + 85.34.$$

The remaining 50% of the sample was used to cross-validate this equation. The regression equation was able to account for 34% of the variance in FSIQ in the original sample and 33% in the cross-validation sample. The *SEE* associated with cross-validation is 12.32.

In predicting FSIQ in the cross-validation sample, the Wilson et al. (1978) formula achieved an R^2 which is substantially higher than that achieved by the education-based formula (R^2s = .42 versus .33). Nevertheless, to the clinician a more relevant measure of prediction accuracy may be the likelihood of making prediction errors of various amounts. Table 4 shows that, in the cross-validation sample, the frequencies of four classes of prediction errors were quite similar for the two formulas; in fact, for each formula, the predicted IQ was within 10 points of the actual IQ in 66% of the cases.

Table 4

Distributions of IQ Prediction Errors Achieved by Wilson et al. (1978)
Formula and Univariate Education Formula

Error in predicting Full Scale IQ	% of cross-validation sample ($n = 246$)	
	Wilson et al. (1978) formula	Education formula
0- 5 points	37.4	38.6
6-10 points	28.9	27.6
11-15 points	21.5	18.7
> 15 points	12.2	15.0

DISCUSSION

The results of the present investigation support the predictive utility of the Wilson et al. (1978) formula. Depending upon whether the sample used included various nonemployed subgroups, in our cross-validation there was an 8 to 12% decrease in the predictive accuracy (R^2) that was achieved in the Wilson et al. (1978) study; i.e., percent FSIQ variance accounted for dropped from 54 to 46 for employed subjects, and from 54 to 42 for the full sample. In addition, mean predicted FSIQ was quite similar to mean actual FSIQ (110.9 versus 112.8). The predictive accuracy of the Wilson et al. (1978) formula was relatively stable across different levels of age, education, and occupational category, both in terms of direction and magnitude of the difference between mean predicted and actual FSIQ. However, for intelligence level, there was a trend toward underprediction of FSIQ at lower predicted levels of intelligence and overprediction at higher levels.

Considering that more than 25 years have passed since the data used in the Wilson et al. (1978) formula were gathered, the predictive accuracy of their equation in the present cross-validation is impressive. Wilson et al. (1978) suggested that increases in educational attainment between 1955 and the present should necessitate a downward adjustment of 18% in the education weights in their equation. This was based on an estimated change in educational attainment from 10.1 years to 12.3 years over the period from 1955 to 1975. Mean educational attainment in our sample was 13.4, implying the need for an adjustment of 25%. However, such an adjustment resulted in a less accurate estimate of mean FSIQ (i.e., 103.8 versus 110.9). This would imply either of the following: (1) At least in our sample, the relationship between intelligence and one of the other variables in the equation has changed in a manner that largely offsets the change in educational level; or, (2) the mean level of intelligence as estimated by the WAIS in the 1970s had risen sufficiently to increase the accuracy of the equation through upward "criterion drift" (Wiggins, 1973). Supporting the latter interpretation is the fact that the mean FSIQ in our sample was 112.8 as compared to 100 in the WAIS standardization sample. In any event, our findings argue against an adjustment in education weight when using the Wilson equation to predict current WAIS FSIQ.

The effect of using the Wilson et al. (1978) formula to estimate WAIS-R FSIQ is problematic. When measured by the WAIS-R, FSIQ will be on average about 8 points lower than when assessed by the WAIS (Wechsler, 1981). Thus, assuming that this mean decrease is evenly distributed across IQ levels, estimates made from the Wilson et al. (1978) formula should be reduced by 8 points when the intent is to estimate the equivalent of the WAIS-R FSIQ. It would be important in the future to derive a new prediction equation for use with the WAIS-R.

The Wilson et al. (1978) equation was least effective in estimating WAIS FSIQ at the lower and upper levels of predicted intelligence. Based on our data, it would be appropriate to adjust the estimate in accord with the differences between the means indicated in Table 2.

The results of the current study indicate that the regression analyses using the two proposed occupational coding systems did not have greater predictive accuracy than did the Wilson et al. (1978) formula. The predictive validity of their original regression equation was slightly higher than those of the current analyses. Direct comparison of all three approaches in the cross-validation sample again indicated slight superiority for the Wilson et al. (1978) approach.

In view of the issues raised earlier in this paper, the superiority, however slight, of the Wilson et al. (1978) approach over the current analyses is surprising. The lack of an increment in predictive validity by the use of seemingly more sophisticated occupational status ratings is partially interpretable through examination of the univariate relationships among the variables in the present study (Table 1). The correlations of the MSEI2 and Hollingshead occupational status ratings with FSIQ ($rs = .55$ and $.46$, respectively) are much higher than the correlation for the Wilson occupational ratings ($r = .13$), but the former ratings also correlate much more highly with education ($.75$ and $.59$ versus $.11$). Since education entered the regression process first, the high correlation of the occupational ratings with education effectively removed these ratings as significant independent sources of variance in the prediction process. Thus, although the proposed occupational coding systems provide better univariate predictive power, their inclusion in a multivariate prediction of FSIQ that also uses education does not appear to be warranted.

In conclusion, the Wilson et al. (1978) regression equation would appear to be the most useful *multivariate* approach for the estimation of FSIQ, based upon its performance in comparison with procedures which employ more "sophisticated" measures of occupational status. On the other hand, the univariate prediction formula that uses only education did quite well in this study. It is true that the R^2 between predicted and actual FSIQs was higher for the Wilson et al. (1978) formula than for the education formula. However, Table 4 indicates that, in classifying individual subjects, the magnitude of prediction errors is likely to be comparable for the two formulas. Considering these findings and the education formula's simplicity and ease of use, the busy clinician may prefer it over the more complex Wilson et al. (1978) approach.

REFERENCES

Hollingshead, A. B., & Redlich, F. C. (1958). *Social class and mental illness: A community study*. New York: Wiley.

Matarazzo, J. D. (1972). *Wechsler's measurement and appraisal of adult intelligence* (5th ed.). Baltimore: Williams & Wilkins.

Stevens, G., & Featherman, D. L. (1981). A revised socioeconomic index of occupational status. *Social Science Research, 10,* 364-395.

Vogt, A. T., & Heaton, R. K. (1977). Comparison of Wechsler Adult Intelligence Scale indices of cerebral dysfunction. *Perceptual and Motor Skills, 45,* 607-615.

382

Wechsler, D. (1955). *Manual for the Wechsler Adult Intelligence Scale.* New York: Psychological Corporation.

Wechsler, D. (1981). *WAIS-R Manual: Wechsler Adult Intelligence Scale Revised.* New York: Psychological Corporation.

Wiggins, J. S. (1973). *Personality and prediction: Principles of personality assessment.* Reading, MA: Addison-Wesley.

Wilson, R. S., Rosenbaum, G., Brown, G., Rourke, D., Whitman, D., & Grisell, J. (1978). An index of premorbid intelligence. *Journal of Consulting and Clinical Psychology, 46,* 1554-1555.

Journal of Clinical and Experimental Neuropsychology
1986, Vol. 8, No. 4, pp. 405-412.

Assessment of the Accuracy of Regression Equations Proposed for Estimating Premorbid Intellectual Functioning on the Wechsler Adult Intelligence Scale*

Felicia C. Goldstein, Howard E. Gary, Jr., and Harvey S. Levin

The University of Texas Medical Branch, Galveston, Texas

ABSTRACT

This investigation examined the accuracy of regression equations proposed by Wilson et al. (1978) for estimating premorbid intellectual quotients (IQs) on the Wechsler Adult Intelligence Scale (WAIS). Actual Verbal, Performance, and Full Scale IQs in a sample of 69 neurologically normal adults were compared against their estimated premorbid levels. While the equations provided an adequate overall fit to the data, actual IQ values at the extremes of the WAIS Scales were found to be most susceptible to underestimation (high actual IQ values) or overestimation (low actual IQ values). The clinical importance of this finding and possible applications of the equations are discussed.

The need for an accurate estimate of premorbid intelligence is clearly important for both clinical and research applications since such information is frequently absent for neurologically impaired individuals. One promising method for estimating premorbid intellectual quotient (IQ) has been described (Wilson, Rosenbaum, & Brown, 1979; Wilson et al., 1978). Wilson et al. (1978) derived a regression equation based upon the 1955 standardization sample of the Wechsler Adult Intelligence Scale (WAIS) which included five demographic variables: sex, age, race, occupation, and education. The researchers proposed separate equations to estimate Full Scale, Verbal, and Performance IQs.

This technique for estimation of premorbid IQ has recently appeared in numerous publications as a method for determining comparability of clinical groups (Baird et al., 1984; Bayles & Tomoeda, 1983; Weingartner, 1983), the degree of deterioration in IQ (Hamsher & Roberts, 1985; Kirsher, Webb, & Kelly, 1984), relationship to other clinical tests such as the Halstead-Reitan Battery

* The authors thank Ernest Barratt, Ph.D. for his assistance in allowing us access to the psychometric data used in this study and Beverly Parman for manuscript preparation. This investigation was supported by NIH grants NS 21889 Javits Neuroscience Investigator Award, Neurobehavioral Outcome of Head Injury in Children and NS 07377, A Center for the Study of Central Nervous System Injury.

(Karzmark, Heaton, Grant, & Matthews, 1984) and the WAIS-R (Barona, Reynolds, & Chastain, 1984), and prediction of outcome following closed-head injury (Williams, Gomes, Drudge, & Kessler, 1984). Yet, despite its widespread appeal, accuracy of the equations has been tacitly accepted with no attempt to examine their predictive power with a non-neurologically impaired population. The aim of the present study was to compare predicted IQs using the Wilson et al. (1978) equations with actual obtained IQs in a sample of neurologically normal adults. To the extent that the equations are accurate, one would expect to find little deviation in the estimated versus obtained values.

METHOD

Subjects

The sample included 69 adults referred to the Divisions of Neurosurgery or Psychiatry within the past 8 years for neuropsychological or clinical psychological assessment. The reasons for referral varied, but in most cases entailed cognitive and personality assessment of commercial undersea divers, chronic pain patients, and students desiring career counseling or requests for leaves of absence from school. The patients were between the ages of 18 and 30 and were excluded if there was a previous history of drug or alcohol abuse, major psychiatric illness or developmental disorder (e.g., dyslexia). Evidence for cerebral injury, malformation, or disease on the basis of computed tomographic (CT) and electroencephalographic (EEG) findings, neurologic evaluation, or neuropsychological testing profiles served as further exclusionary criteria. Patients with disturbances judged to compromise performance (e.g., severe depression, psychosis) were excluded.

The demographic characteristics of the sample and reasons for referral are summarized in Table 1. As can be seen, most of the patients were students (41%) or professional/ technical/service workers (35%). All patients received the WAIS (Wechsler, 1955) during the course of their evaluation. The demographic variables necessary to compute the premorbid index of intelligence (age, sex, race, occupation, education) were obtained and coded according to the procedure described by Wilson et al. (1978). Table 2 presents descriptive statistics of actual and estimated IQs for the sample.

RESULTS

The regression equations for estimating IQ would be considered accurate if the estimated IQ differs from the actual IQ only by some random error. The data from this study, then, were analyzed using linear model techniques with the estimated IQ as the outcome variable and the actual IQ as the predictor variable. If the estimated IQ is accurate, the slope for the linear model would be 1.0 and the constant term would be 0. Two main hypotheses were tested for each Scale. The first was the general hypothesis that the estimated and actual IQs are linearly related as indicated by a regression slope different from 0. The second hypothesis was that the slope of the regression line is equal to 1.0. If this is not the case, then the Wilson et al. equation consistently overestimates some values and under-

Table 1
Demographic Characteristics and Reasons for Referral

Occupation	Age (yrs.)	Race White	Non-White	Sex Male	Female	Education (yrs.)	Major Reasons for Referral
Student ($n = 28$)	$M = 22.7$ $SD = 2.8$	26	2	18	10	$M = 15.2$ $SD = 1.9$	Career counseling, leaves of absence, academic difficulty
Professional, Technical Service worker ($n = 24$)	$M = 24.8$ $SD = 4.0$	23	1	16	8	$M = 12.7$ $SD = 2.1$	Undersea diving accidents, adjustment disorders, chronic pain, career counseling
Managerial, Clerical, Sales worker ($n = 8$)	$M = 25.4$ $SD = 2.3$	7	1	4	4	$M = 13.8$ $SD = 2.7$	Depression, chronic pain, career counseling, undersea diving accidents
Unemployed ($n = 5$)	$M = 24.8$ $SD = 4.6$	4	1	4	1	$M = 10.8$ $SD = 1.6$	Adjustment disorders, electrocution
Laborers ($n = 3$)	$M = 23.3$ $SD = 5.5$	3	0	3	0	$M = 12.0$ $SD = 0.0$	Undersea diving accidents, adjustment disorders
Homemakers ($n = 1$)	27	0	1	0	1	16	Adjustment disorder
$N = 69$	$M = 24.0$ $SD = 3.5$	63	6	45	24	$M = 14.0$ $SD = 2.5$	
	Minimum = 18 Maximum = 30					Minimum = 9 Maximum = 19	

Table 2
Descriptive Statistics for Actual and Estimated IQs

	Mean	Standard Deviation	Minimum	Maximum
Actual IQ				
Verbal	109.5	13.99	74.0	138.0
Performance	108.2	14.29	74.0	146.0
Full	109.2	13.42	73.0	137.0
Estimated IQ				
Verbal	112.3	10.50	86.9	130.2
Performance	110.2	9.19	83.5	124.9
Full	112.0	10.51	84.5	129.5

Table 3
Regression Coefficients and Standard Errors of Estimate
for Estimated IQs vs Actual IQs

IQ Scale	Constant	Slope	Standard Error of Estimate
Verbal	54.43	.53	7.50
Performance	67.80	.39	7.35
Full	50.06	.57	7.28

estimates others. This second hypothesis becomes unnecessary if the first is not rejected. The regression coefficients for each IQ Scale are presented in Table 3.

The regression slope of .53 for VIQ was found to be significantly different from 0 ($F = 66.00; p < .01$), with a squared correlation coefficient of .50. In addition, the slope was found to significantly differ from 1.0 ($F = 52.61; p < .01$). This indicates that the estimates were biased with the amount of bias depending on the actual IQ. A scatterplot of the estimated IQs against the actual IQs is presented in Figure 1.

The estimated PIQs were also found to be significantly related to the actual IQs ($F = 39.39; p < .01$), with a squared correlation coefficient of .37. The slope of the regression line was .39, a value significantly different from 1.0 ($F = 95.12; p < .01$). The scatterplot for estimated and actual PIQs is presented in Figure 2.

As would be expected from the results of the other Scales, the estimated FSIQs were significantly related to the actual IQs ($F = 74.36; p < .01$), and the regression slope of .57 was significantly different from 1.0 ($F = 43.21; p < .01$). Figure 3 presents the scatterplot for the FSIQs. In summary, linear relationships between estimated and actual IQs were found for all three Scales. However, since the slopes differed from 1.0, some predicted values were overestimates and others were underestimates of the actual values.

A more direct assessment of the accuracy of the equations would be to perform goodness-of-fit tests for the estimated values. Unfortunately, Wilson et al. (1978) did not provide the variances and covariances of the estimated regression

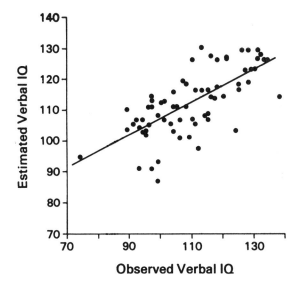

Fig 1. Scatterplot of estimated VIQ vs. observed VIQ with estimated regression line.

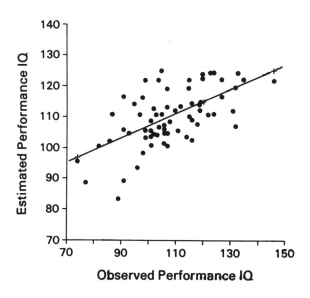

Fig 2. Scatterplot of estimated PIQ vs. observed PIQ with estimated regression line.

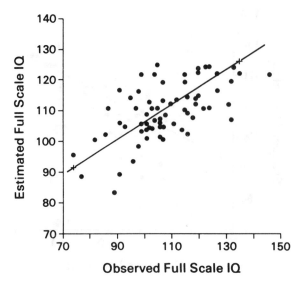

Fig 3. Scatterplot of estimated FIQ vs. observed FIQ with estimated regression line.

coefficients so it was not possible to compute the correct test statistics. However, an approximate chi-square statistic can be computed by disregarding the contributions of these coefficients to the variances of the estimated IQs. The resulting test is biased toward finding a spuriously significant difference between the estimated and observed IQs. When we applied this test to the data, the test for each equation was found to be nonsignificant with all approximate p-values greater than .4. Thus, the equations provided an adequate overall fit to the data.

The analyses described above indicate that the equations of Wilson et al. provide an adequate fit to the data, on average. Finding regression slopes significantly different from 1.0, however, indicates that the average error in the estimated IQ is not the same for all values of the actual IQ. This pattern is frequently seen when applying a regression equation to a new set of data. To provide a better quantification of this error, equations were derived relating the difference between the estimated and actual IQs to the actual IQ. The coefficients for these equations and their standard errors of estimate are presented in Table 4.

Table 4
Regression Coefficients for the Difference Between Estimated
and Actual IQ Against Actual IQ

IQ Scale	Constant	Slope
Verbal	54.43	—0.47
Performance	67.80	—0.61
Full	50.06	—0.43

With these equations, it is possible to approximate the average difference between the estimated and actual score for a given actual IQ. For example, among persons with a VIQ of 80, the average difference between the estimated IQ and the actual IQ is 54.43 - 0.47*80 = 16.7. Furthermore, the standard errors of estimate can be used to get a range of likely errors for a given IQ. For instance, about 90% of the differences are expected to fall within 1.28 standard errors of the mean difference at a given actual IQ. For the example just given, this is the range of values from 7.02 to 26.4.

In addition to the above analyses, tests were performed to determine whether the relationships between the estimated and actual IQs differed by demographic characteristics. No significant differences were found. Also, Wilson et al. (1978) proposed a correction to the education weight in their equations. Although no statistical justification was given for this correction, it is occasionally used. When the corrected estimates were analyzed, each regression slope was closer to 0 than the corresponding slope for the uncorrected scores. Furthermore, the approximate chi-square statistics for goodness of fit were larger than those for the corresponding uncorrected IQs, although they indicated adequate fit. These analyses indicate that the education correction produces poorer estimates for these data, although a direct statistical test of this hypothesis is not possible.

DISCUSSION

The results indicate that the regression equations proposed by Wilson et al. (1978, 1979) provide a reasonable approximation of actual IQs in a sample of neurologically unimpaired adults. While the formulas under- or overestimate extreme IQ values, goodness of fit tests demonstrated that, on average, the differences between the estimated and observed IQs were not significant. Thus, the formulas appear to work well. The practical implications of these under- and overestimates for clinical applications are important to consider. For a patient with a low actual IQ (e.g., 75), the formulas will tend to overestimate the IQ, and the clinician may conclude that there is a greater intellectual deficit than actually exists. On the other hand, for a patient with a high actual IQ (e.g., 120), the formulas generally will underestimate premorbid IQ, leading the clinician to minimize the severity of intellectual impairment. Thus, the formulas may work best in clinical settings with patients whose IQ values are neither extremely high nor unusually low. These shortcomings could be overcome to a large extent if it were possible to estimate a likely range of IQ values rather than a single value. Computation of this range, however, requires information on the variability and covariability of the regression weights. This information was not presented in the Wilson et al. (1978) article.

Although the regression equations were found to be useful, we are cautious in advocating their widespread application pending replication of these procedures in other populations and geographic locations. The current sample included a narrow age range (18-30) and had a high proportion of students and commercial undersea divers. Therefore, additional assessments of the equations are needed.

The coding system for occupation is somewhat vague and may be introducing potentially avoidable errors into the IQ estimates. Given that these equations have enjoyed such widespread application, a more explicit classification scheme is needed to ensure comparability across research studies. Such a scheme, however, may require that the regression coefficients be reestimated. In addition, the findings suggest that the educational correction proposed by Wilson et al. (1978) is not useful and, in fact, leads to a less accurate estimate of IQ.

For research applications, the Wilson et al. (1978, 1979) equations should be most useful for studies requiring comparisons of premorbid IQ or changes in IQ among demographically matched groups. The estimated IQs can also be employed as a convenient substitute for the demographic characteristics used in the equations. The estimates should be particularly useful for group matching and as predictor variables or covariates in regression analyses.

REFERENCES

Baird, A., Adams, K., Shatz, M., Brown, G., Diaz, F., & Ausman, J. (1984). Can neuropsychological tests detect the sites of cerebrovascular stenoses and occlusions? *Neurosurgery, 14,* 416-423.

Barona, A., Reynolds, C. R., & Chastain, R. (1984). A demographicaly based index of premorbid intelligence for the WAIS-R. *Journal of Consulting and Clinical Psychology, 52,* 885-887.

Bayles, K., & Tomoeda, C. (1983). Confrontation naming impairment in dementia. *Brain and Language, 19,* 98-114.

Hamsher, K. deS., & Roberts, R. (1985). Memory for recent U. S. Presidents in patients with cerebral disease. *Journal of Clinical and Experimental Neuropsychology, 7,* 1-13.

Karzmark, P., Heaton, R., Grant, I., & Matthews, C. (1984). Use of demographic variables to predict overall level of performance on the Halstead-Reitan Battery. *Journal of Consulting and Clinical Psychology, 52,* 663-665.

Kirsher, H., Webb, W., & Kelly, M. (1984). The naming disorder of dementia. *Neuropsychologia, 22,* 23-30.

Wechsler, D. (1955). *Manual for the Wechsler Adult Intelligence Scale.* New York: Psychological Corporation.

Weingartner, H. (1983). Forms of memory failure. *Science, 221,* 380-382.

Williams, J. M., Gomes, F., Drudge, O. W., & Kessler, M. (1984). Predicting outcome from closed head injury by early assessment of trauma severity. *Journal of Neurosurgery, 61,* 581-585.

Wilson, R. S., Rosenbaum, G., & Brown, G. (1979). The problem of premorbid intelligence in neuropsychological assessment. *Journal of Clinical Neuropsychology, 1,* 49-53.

Wilson, R. S., Rosenbaum, G., Brown, G., Rourke, D., Whitman, D., & Grisell, J. (1978). An index of premorbid intelligence. *Journal of Consulting and Clinical Psychology, 46,* 1554-1555.

The Clinical Neuropsychologist
1989, Vol. 3, No. 2, pp. 129-136

CLINICAL ISSUES

Predicting Premorbid IQ:
A Revision of the National Adult Reading Test

Jennifer R. Blair and Otfried Spreen
University of Victoria

ABSTRACT

The National Adult Reading Test (NART) has promise as an assessment tool for the determination of premorbid intellectual function, but needs to be modified for current use in a North American population and validated against the WAIS-R. A revision based on American and Canadian pronunciation rules was prepared. Sixty-six unimpaired subjects were tested with a revised NART and all subtests of the WAIS-R. Demographic variables were also recorded. Correlations between actual VIQ, PIQ and FSIQ, and predicted IQs on the basis of revised NART score were .83, .40, and .75, respectively (all $p < .001$). Prediction of IQs was more accurate with equations based on revised NART score than with demographic variable prediction equations developed by Barona, Reynolds, and Chastain (1984).

When assessing neurologically compromised patients, the determination of current general intellectual function is relatively straightforward. Often, an estimate of premorbid intellectual ability is also sought. A determination of the discrepancy between current and premorbid level of function is essential in providing an indication of the degree of deterioration as compared to a pre-injury standard.

The most straightforward method of ascertaining the degree of intellectual deterioration consists of testing the patient before onset of damage or disease and comparing the results to postinjury test results, but premorbid test data are rarely available. Therefore, methods of estimation are needed.

We gratefully acknowledge the support of C.A. Mateer, Ph.D., for assistance in obtaining American subjects, A.M. Weber, Ph.D., for valuable suggestions during the initial development of this project, and S.A. Thomson, for serving as an alternate scorer.

Requests for reprints should be addressed to: Otfried Spreen, Ph.D., Department of Psychology, University of Victoria, P.O. Box 1700, Victoria, BC, V8W 2Y2, CANADA.

Estimation Based on Demographic Variables

The first comprehensive effort to predict premorbid IQ on the basis of demographic variables was made by Wilson, Rosenbaum, Brown, Rourke, Whitman, and Grisell (1978). WAIS Verbal, Performance, and Full Scale IQs were regressed on age, sex, race, education, and occupation. The amount of variance accounted for between all five demographic variables and VIQ, PIQ, and FSIQ was 53%, 42%, and 54%, respectively. Several cross-validation studies of the Wilson et al. equations have been reported. Although initial studies supported the use of these equations (Bolter, Gouvier, Veneklasen, & Long, 1982; Gouvier, Bolter, Veneklasen, & Long, 1983; Karzmark, Heaton, Grant, & Matthews, 1985; Klesges, Sanchez, & Stanton, 1981; Wilson, Rosenbaum, & Brown, 1979), a more recent study by Klesges, Fisher, Vasey, & Pheley (1985) failed to support the use of the Wilson et al. (1978) formulae. The results of the Klesges et al. (1985) study indicated significant, but low correlations between predicted and actual IQ levels in a group of 73 normal adults. In addition, the predicted premorbid IQs failed to discriminate reliably between groups of normal and brain-damaged subjects. Klesges et al. (1985, p. 2) concluded that "... we must temper our previous guarded optimism with the adult prediction formulae. Future uses of the Wilson et al. (1978) formulae should probably be restricted to research purposes for the present time."

Barona, Reynolds, and Chastain developed prediction equations on the basis of the WAIS-R in 1984. In addition to the original demographic variables utilized by Wilson et al. (1978), Barona et al. included region of residence, urban vs. rural (U-R) residence, and handedness as demographic predictor variables. The variance accounted for between the demographic variables and VIQ, PIQ, and FSIQ was 38%, 24%, and 36%, respectively. Clinical validation of these equations has not yet been presented.

The National Adult Reading Test

The National Adult Reading Test (NART) (Nelson, 1982) was developed in Britain in another attempt to provide a reliable measure of premorbid intellectual level in patients who had suffered intellectual deterioration. It was noted in the clinical assessment of demented patients that their ability to read aloud appeared to be surprisingly well-preserved in comparison to other intellectual abilities. Since word reading ability was found to be significantly correlated with general intelligence level in a normal population (Nelson & McKenna, 1975), it was hypothesized that reading ability could be utilized as an indicator of premorbid IQ. When Nelson and McKenna (1975) tested a demented population, they found a larger predicted IQ (on the basis of the Schonell Graded Word Reading Test reading score) than the obtained WAIS IQ.

In 1978, Nelson and O'Connell developed a new word reading test that was composed mainly of "irregular" words that could not be correctly pronounced through the use of common rules of phonetic interpretation. For example, correct pronunciation of "naive" could not be achieved through the application of standard phonetic rules. Since the reading of "regular" words may largely depend on the subject's current ability to apply phonetic rules, the use of "irregular" words was felt to capitalize on the subject's premorbid familiarity with the words and therefore be a more reliable indicator of premorbid ability.

Nelson and O'Connell (1978) standardized the National Adult Reading Test (NART) on a group of 120 normal British subjects. Prediction equations were developed, and standard errors of estimate were 7.6, 9.4, and 7.6 for VIQ, PIQ and FSIQ, respectively.

In a validation study (1978), Nelson and O'Connell compared the performance of 40 subjects with evidence of bilateral cortical atrophy with the 120 subjects utilized in the standardization sample. The demented group had a significantly lower ($p < .001$) WAIS FSIQ than the control group, as was expected. NART score differences between the two groups were not significant, however, suggesting resistance of the NART to the effects of the dementing process.

Hart, Smith, and Swash (1986) recently reported that, in demented subjects, performance on the NART was a better indicator of premorbid function (in terms of size of discrepancy between predicted and obtained IQs) than were VIQ-PIQ discrepancy or Schonell's Graded Word Reading Test (SGWRT). Hart et al. (1986) also reported that, in a preliminary longitudinal study, NART performance appeared stable in the face of intellectual decline. Nebes, Martin, and Horn (1984) reported no statistically significant differences in performance on the NART between 20 mildly demented subjects compared with 20 age-matched controls. In addition, O'Carroll and Gilleard (1986) found no significant relationships between measures of dementia severity and NART performance in 30 demented patients.

While the NART is an extremely promising assessment tool for the determination of premorbid intellectual function in patients who have experienced brain damage or deterioration, it must be modified for current use in the Canadian and U.S. populations. Several items on the NART word list, for example, can be correctly pronounced if they are phonetically decoded according to accepted North American pronunciation rules. In addition, NART performance estimates IQ level on the WAIS rather than the WAIS-R. Therefore, a determination of NART correlation with WAIS-R scores is needed. Lastly, the original NART was standardized on the basis of only seven subtests of the WAIS. Such prorating has been regarded as inadvisable (Matarazzo, 1972), and further research with this test should include administration of all subtests of the WAIS-R.

A normal Canadian and U.S. sample was tested on a revised NART and all subtests of the WAIS-R to explore the estimation of premorbid intellectual level on the basis of performance on the revised NART. Both current level of performance (on the basis of the revised NART) and demographic variables were included in regression equations for the prediction of WAIS-R IQ. It was hypothesized that estimated IQ scores (derived from regression equations based on revised NART performance and demographic variables), and actual IQ scores would be significantly correlated in a group of unimpaired subjects. It was also hypothesized that the correlations between actual VIQ, PIQ and FSIQ, and estimated VIQ, PIQ and FSIQ would be greater than that achieved through the use of the Barona et al. (1984) regression equations.

METHOD

The subjects were 17 unimpaired Americans and 49 unimpaired Canadians. The American subjects consisted of family members of head-injured patients evaluated at Good Samaritan Neuropsychological Services in Puyallup, Washington. The Canadians were volunteers from university and community college (adult basic education) settings. This total group (n=66) consisted of 35 females and 31 males. Sixty-four of the 66 subjects were Caucasian. Ages ranged from 18 to 49 years (M = 27.4 years, SD=8.05).

Demographic data, including age, education, race, occupation, handedness, and residence, were collected. All subtests of the WAIS-R and a revised form of the NART were administered.

Modification of the NART word list included:

(1) Addition of Words: 54 words were added to the original NART word list in an attempt to obtain an adequate sample of items from which to devise the final revised NART.

(2) North American Pronunciations: Pronunciations were obtained from *Webster's Ninth New Collegiate Dictionary* (1985) and the Gage *Dictionary of Canadian English* (1967). Scoring procedures were modified to include Canadian and U.S. pronunciations.*

Table 1. Distribution of Age, Sex, Source, and Education for the Total Sample (n = 66).

Age	25 and above	33
	18-24	33
Sex	Male	31
	Female	35
Source	US	17
	Univ. of Victoria	33
	Community College	16
Education	Above grade 12	37
	Grade 12	18
	Grade 11 and below	11

* Test instructions and word list with acceptable pronunciations are available from the Neuropsychology Laboratory, University of Victoria, P.O. Box 1700, Victoria, B.C., V8W 2Y2.

RESULTS

The distribution of subjects by age, sex, source, and education is found in Table 1.

The correlation between the revised NART-R and FSIQ was calculated separately for American ($r = .66$, $p < .002$) and Canadian ($r = .78$, $p < .001$) groups. Since the difference between the two correlation coefficients was not significant ($p > .05$), the groups were pooled.

A series of item analyses were performed to provide the best group of items for prediction of IQ in this population. Items were correlated with FSIQ, and items with correlations over .2 were considered acceptable (Nunnally, 1978). Items with correlations under .2 were not included in subsequent analyses.

The remaining 61 items were ordered for item difficulty on the basis of total number of errors made on each item. The resulting ordered list of words is presented in Table 2.

Coefficient alpha, a measure of internal consistency, was .935. A measure of interscorer reliability based on the performance of 20 Canadian subjects was virtually perfect ($r = .99$, $p < .001$).

Correlations of the NART-R with VIQ, PIQ, and FSIQ were .83, .40 and .75, respectively; all of these coefficients were statistically significant ($p < .001$).

Step-wise multiple regressions of VIQ, PIQ, and FSIQ on age, sex, education, occupation, source (U.S. vs. Canadian), and NART-R score were calculated to generate prediction equations for the estimation of IQs. The NART-R score was the only variable entered into all three prediction equations. None of the demographic variables accounted for a significant amount of the variance in this sample and were therefore not included as predictors. Prediction equations are as follows:

Estimated VIQ = 128.7 - .89 (NART-R Errors)
Estimated PIQ = 119.4 - .42 (NART-R Errors)
Estimated FSIQ = 127.8 - .78 (NART-R Errors)

The standard errors of estimate are 6.56, 10.67, and 7.63, respectively.

VIQ, PIQ, and FSIQ were estimated with the utilization of the Barona et al. (1984) equations and NART-R equations. Table 3 presents correlations between Barona estimated and actual IQs, and NART-R estimated and actual IQs. Correlations for FSIQ and VIQ were significantly different ($p < .05$); PIQ correlations were not significantly different ($p > .05$).

DISCUSSION

Inspection of the final word list reveals that the distribution of item difficulty, from easy to difficult items, is relatively linear. This linear distribution of item difficulty is essential in order to make fine predictive discriminations.

Table 2. Revised New Adult Reading Test in Order of Level of Difficulty.

Word	Errors	Word	Errors
Debt	02	Cellist	27
Debris	03	Indict	27
Aisle	03	Detente	28
Reign	03	Impugn	30
Depot	04	Capon	31
Simile	04	Radix	32
Lingerie	05	Aeon	32
Recipe	06	Epitome	33
Gouge	06	Equivocal	34
Heir	07	Reify	37
Subtle	07	Indices	38
Catacomb	07	Assignate	39
Bouquet	08	Topiary	39
Gauge	09	Caveat	40
Colonel	09	Superfluous	42
Subpoena	09	Leviathan	43
Placebo	10	Prelate	48
Procreate	11	Quadruped	49
Psalm	12	Sidereal	49
Banal	13	Abstemious	53
Rarefy	15	Beatify	55
Gist	17	Gaoled	56
Corps	19	Demesne	56
Hors D'Oeuvre	21	Syncope	56
Sieve	22	Ennui	57
Hiatus	23	Drachm	59
Gauche	23	Cidevant	59
Zealot	24	Epergne	60
Paradigm	24	Vivace	61
Facade	26	Talipes	61
		Synecdoche	62

Regression equations do not include demographic variables since, once the NART-R score was entered into the step-wise equation, no demographic variable accounted for further significant variance. When all demographic variables were forced into the FSIQ regression equation along with the NART-R score, the percentage of variance accounted for increased by only 3 (56% to 59%). Removal of the NART-R score and utilization of only demographic variables as predictors resulted in a decrease of 49%, 5%, and 41% variance accounted for in VIQ, PIQ and FSIQ, respectively, as compared to variance accounted for by the NART-R score.

It was concluded that demographic variables were not significant predictors of IQ in this sample. This result was not expected given previous success in

Table 3. Correlations of Estimated with Actual IQs.

Barona Equations		
	r	p
FSIQ	.4727	.000
VIQ	.5301	.000
PIQ	.2923	.009
NART-R Equations		
	r	p
FSIQ	.7489	.000
VIQ	.8313	.000
PIQ	.4003	.000

predicting IQ with the use of these variables. Perhaps demographic variables would adequately predict IQ differences for the WAIS 1955 standardization sample (with the utilization of Wilson et al. 1978 equations), but changes in social structure with regard to equal opportunities may have reduced their discriminative efficacy. It is also possible that somewhat limited variability with regard to education and occupational status in our sample reduced the predictive accuracy of the Barona et al. (1984) equations. Further research with the Barona et al. (1984) WAIS-R prediction equations is needed before conclusions regarding accuracy of prediction with demographic variables can be drawn.

Since the NART-R was standardized and validated on the same sample, additional validation studies in a normal population are needed. Validation studies of the NART-R are also needed for a variety of clinical populations, including demented subjects, other neurologically impaired groups such as head injury and stroke victims, and patients with psychiatric diagnoses. Until such additional studies validate the use of the NART-R, it cannot be employed with confidence for the determination of impairment due to brain disease.

The results of this investigation provide preliminary support for the use of the NART-R in the assessment of brain dysfunction.

REFERENCES

Barona, A., Reynolds, C.R., & Chastain, R. (1984). A demographically based index of premorbid intelligence for the WAIS-R. *Journal of Consulting and Clinical Psychology, 52,* 885-887.

Bolter, J., Gouvier, W., Veneklasen, J., & Long, C.J. (1982). Using demographic information to predict premorbid IQ: A test of clinical validity with head trauma patients. *Clinical Neuropsychology, 4,* 171-174.

398

Dictionary of Canadianism on Historical Principles; Dictionary of Canadian English (1967). Toronto: Gage Publishers.

Gouvier, W.D., Bolter, J.F., Veneklasen, J.A., & Long, C.J. (1983). Predicting verbal and performance IQ from demographic data: further findings with head trauma patients. *Clinical Neuropsychology, 5*, 119-121.

Hart, S., Smith, C.M., & Swash, M. (1986). Assessing intellectual deterioration. *British Journal of Clinical Psychology, 25*, 119-124.

Karzmark, P., Heaton, R.K., Grant, I., & Matthews, C.G. (1985). Use of demographic variables to predict full scale IQ: A replication and extension. *Journal of Clinical and Experimental Neuropsychology, 7*, 412-420.

Klesges, R.C., Fisher, L., Vasey, M., & Pheley, A. (1985). Predicting adult premorbid functioning levels: Another look. *International Journal of Clinical Neuropsychology, 7*, 1-3.

Klesges, R.C., Sanchez, V.C., & Stanton, A.L. (1981). Cross-validation of an adult premorbid functioning index. *Clinical Neuropsychology, 3*, 13-15.

Matarazzo, J.D. (1972). *Wechsler's measurement and appraisal of adult intelligence.* Baltimore: Williams and Wilkins.

Nebes, R.D., Martin, D.C., & Horn, L.C. (1984). Sparing of semantic memory in Alzheimer's disease. *Journal of Abnormal Psychology, 93*, 321-330.

Nelson, H.E. (1982). *Nelson adult reading test manual.* London: The National Hospital for Nervous Diseases.

Nelson, H.E., & McKenna, P. (1975). The use of reading ability in the assessment of dementia. *British Journal of Social and Clinical Psychology, 14*, 259-267.

Nelson, H.E., & O'Connell, A. (1978). Dementia: The estimation of premorbid intelligence levels using the new adult reading test. *Cortex, 14*, 234-244.

Nunnally, J. (1978). *Psychometric theory.* New York: McGraw-Hill.

O'Carroll, R.E., & Gilleard, C.J. (1986). Estimation of premorbid intelligence in dementia. *British Journal of Clinical Psychology, 25*, 157-158.

Webster's Ninth New Collegiate Dictionary (1985). Springfield: Merriam-Webster Inc.

Wilson, R.S., Rosenbaum, G., & Brown, G. (1979). The problem of premorbid intelligence in neuropsychological assessment. *Journal of Clinical Neuropsychology, 1*, 49-53.

Wilson, R.S., Rosenbaum, G., Brown, G., Rourke, D., Whitman, D. & Grisell, J. (1978). An index of premorbid intelligence. *Journal of Consulting and Clinical Psychology, 46*, 1554-1555.

Journal of Clinical and Experimental Neuropsychology
1987, Vol. 9, No. 4, pp. 376-392

A Reference Scale Method for Constructing Neuropsychological Test Batteries

Elbert W. Russell

V.A. Medical Center, Miami, FL

ABSTRACT

Scaling of neuropsychological test variables requires knowledge of test parameters. This is a study of the parameters for 12 tests in the Rennick Index of the Halstead-Reitan Battery, using 732 subjects. z-score distributions were plotted. Great variability among test distributions indicated that, for brain-damaged subjects: (1) the range is much greater than for normals; (2) maximum z scores ranged from 3.8 to 27.3 for different tests; (3) the form of the distributions was highly variable, ranging from normal to highly skewed distributions. Thus, the same z scores indicated quite different amounts of impairment on different tests. This raises questions regarding the applicability of z and T scores to a brain-damaged population. The second part of this study demonstrated how scaled scores, indicating equal amounts of impairment, could be constructed. This method used a reference scale produced by averaging control subjects' z scores on 12 tests. Individual scaled scores were obtained through a linear regression prediction.

Almost no adequate research has been directed to scaling problems for neuropsychological tests. There appear to be only three tests or test batteries used extensively in neuropsychology that have an adequate psychometric design. These are the Boston Diagnostic Aphasia Examination (BDAE) (Goodglass & Kaplan, 1983), the Western Aphasia Battery (WAB) (Kertesz, 1979), and the WAIS-R (Wechsler, 1981). The WAIS-R was not designed to be a test of brain-damage impairment and the BDAE and WAB examinations are limited to language disorders. Of the two other extensively used neuropsychological batteries, the Luria-Nebraska Battery (LNB) (Golden, 1981) does not utilize homogeneous scales (Russell, 1980c) and the Halstead-Reitan Battery (HRB) has not been adequately scaled (Russell, 1984a). Age norming is rare. Only a few attempts to create such norms exist (Harley, Leuthold, Matthews, & Bergs, 1980; Pauker, 1977). In fact, with the possible exception of the BDAE and WAB examinations, none of the purely neuropsychological batteries could meet the minimum criteria for a test set forth in the APA Manual *Standards for Education-*

al and Psychological Tests (1974). However, some tests fare better than this as individual scales (Lezak, 1983). One consequence of this lack of study is that the particular problems related to scale construction for a neurological population are largely unknown.

When the only task required of a test is to separate normal from brain-damaged subjects, many problems do not arise. In such a case, scales that are lengthy and sophisticated are not needed. A few items strategically placed near the mentally retarded range are sufficient. This is apparently the basis for the neurological mental examination (Russell, 1980b). Also, sophisticated scales are not needed when dealing with gross focal lesions such as those that make up most of the cases used by Luria and other experimental neuropsychologists who are primarily interested in relating functions to the site of damage (Luria, 1973, 1980). However, when more complex and sophisticated measurement is required, such as that needed in pattern analysis (Russell, 1984b) or in assessing the strengths and weaknesses of a patient for disposition or rehabilitation purposes (Russell, 1985), more adequate scaling is required.

Scaled scores have been used for pattern analysis on the LNB (Golden, 1981) and WAIS (Russell, 1979); probably the most effective use of scale score patterns has been made with the BDAE (Goodglass & Kaplan, 1983). This examination uses patterns from many scales to help determine the type and location of lesions.

It is only in developing adequate scales that problems particularly related to scaling brain-damaged populations are recognized. Goodglass and Kaplan realized some of these problems in developing the BDAE and accordingly changed the method of scaling in the revision of their battery (1972, 1983).

The present study was devised, first, to demonstrate some of the problems related to scaling impairment produced by brain damage and, secondly, to propose a method of alleviating some of these problems. The first part of this investigation is a parametric study of some commonly used neuropsychological tests; the second part describes the development of a reference scale designed to deal with some of these problems.

PARAMETRIC STUDY (PART I)

This study consists of the examination of several test parameters in the Rennick version (Russell, Neuringer, & Goldstein, 1970) of the HRB. This battery was selected because it has been thoroughly studied and sufficient data for stable comparisons could be obtained. It is not considered to be the only good battery in general use.

METHOD

Subjects. The subjects in this study consisted in 732 patients (155 controls and 577 brain-damaged subjects) who were tested with the full HRB. They were examined as part of the ongoing clinical neuropsychological laboratory program at the Cincinnati V.A. Hospital from 1968 to 1971 and at the Miami V.A Medical Center from 1971 to 1982. During this time, the laboratory was directed by the author. All testing was directly supervised by the author and done by one of six thoroughly trained technicians. The Rennick version of the HRB (Russell, Neuringer, & Goldstein, 1970), using the Topeka instructions as written by Shelly (see Swiercinsky, 1978), was generally utilized although modified in some details.

The subjects were carefully selected from a total pool of approximately 1200 cases. All subjects had a neurological examination utilizing those methods that the staff neurologists required for an adequate diagnosis. (Earlier subjects, of course, did not have a CT scan.) The subjects in which there was any doubt concerning the diagnosis of the lesion were rejected. The diagnosis was made separately from the neuropsychological examination so there was no contamination of the criteria. The brain-damaged subjects were all obtained by normal referral procedures from the neurology departments and other sections of the hospitals used in this study. Thus, they represent a typical sample of neuropsychology patients as seen in a VA Medical Center. With the exceptions of a relative lack of women and no children, this population is similar to that which might be expected in any urban medical center.

The control subjects consisted of patients who were suspected of having a neurological condition, but who had negative neurological findings. The test means for the control cases were quite similar to those presented in the studies of Pauker (1977) and Beardsley, Matthews, Cleeland, and Harley (1978), after differences in scoring were resolved. All subjects with severe functional disorders were eliminated; these consisted of patients with a diagnosis of schizophrenia or severe depression. Left-handed subjects were not included if they had lateralized lesions, but were retained in the control and diffusely damaged groups. In almost all cases, a follow-up consisting of a chart review was made at least 1 year after discharge from the hospital to confirm the diagnosis. (One of the advantages of a V.A. Medical Center is that there are relatively good records and patients can be followed.)

For descriptive purposes, the subjects' data were divided into four groups: controls; and right-hemisphere, left-hemisphere, and diffuse brain-damaged groups. However, these groups were not separated in the statistical analysis used in this study. The basic sample statistics for these groups are given in Table 1. The proportion of blacks and females was approximately the same as in the V.A. population as a whole. An ANOVA across the four groups demonstrated that there were no significant differences between the control, right-hemisphere, left-hemisphere, and diffuse damaged groups for age ($F = 2.43[3,728]p > .05$) or education ($F = 1.00[3,724]p > .05$). The mean WAIS scores for the control group were as follows: VIQ, 112.3; PIQ, 109.9; FSIQ, 111.9. The difference between the VIQ and PIQ was not significant ($F = 2.73[1,308]p > .05$). The brain-damaged groups had significantly lower IQs (Mean FSIQ = 93.4). The apparently high IQ for the control group was in line with the usual VA Hospital subject IQ that is about 110 on the original WAIS. The WAIS-R provides IQ scores that are about 7.5 points lower than the WAIS. Thus, if these subjects had taken the WAIS-R their mean IQs would probably have approached 100 (WAIS-R Manual, 1981, p. 47).

Procedure. The tests in the Rennick version of the HRB were selected for two reasons. First, their characteristics of validity and reliability have been more thoroughly examined than have any other tests in neuropsychology (Kiernan & Matthews, 1976; Russell, 1984a; 1984b). As such, they constitute a relatively well-known base from which to begin an exacting parametric study. Secondly, although Rennick never published the basis for his scales,

Table 1

Sample Statistics for Subject Groups used in the Psychometric
and Reference Scale Studies

	Controls	Left	Right	Diffuse	Total	F
			Diagnoses			
No damage	155	0	0	0	155	
Congenital	0	6	2	11	19	
Tumor	0	18	25	6	49	
Trauma	0	25	19	80	124	
CVD	0	62	64	60	186	
MS	0	1	1	12	14	
Degenerative	0	1	4	60	65	
Alcoholic	0	0	0	75	75	
Toxic	0	0	0	17	17	
Infection	0	4	0	3	7	
Other	0	0	1	20	21	
Total	155	117	116	344	732	
			Race			
Caucasian	147	102	111	307	667	
Afro-American	8	13	5	33	59	
Other	0	2	0	4	6	
			Sex			
Male	148	110	114	322	694	
Female	7	7	2	22	38	
			Age (years)			
M	46.19	46.18	50.32	48.06	47.72	2.43*
SD	12.86	15.80	14.42	14.08	14.22	(3,728)
			Education (Years)			
M	12.29	11.86	11.82	11.75	11.89	1.00*
SD	3.00	3.22	3.22	3.40	3.26	(3,728)

* $p > .05$

which are widely used, he apparently utilized a form of z scores (Russell, 1984b). Thus, an examination of the results using z scores would be of interest of the users to this test battery.

The 12 tests that comprise the Rennick Index and the Average Impairment Rating (AIR) (Russell et al., 1970) are as follows: the Category Test; Trail Making Test, Part B (Trails B); Tactual Performance Test (TPT) Total Time, Memory, and Location; Tapping Test; WAIS Digit Symbol; Speech-Sounds Perception Test, Seashore Rhythm Test; the modified Halstead-Wepman Aphasia Screening test; Spatial Relations Test (Russell et al., 1970); and the Perceptual Disorders Examination (Russell et al., 1970). These were generally administrated and scored according to the standard directions given by Russell (1984b; Russell et al., 1970). There were a few changes which are as follows:

(1) A combined score was used for Trails B (Russell, 1984b). This essentially prorated the

unfinished part of the Trails B after the 5-min time limit was reached (Russell, 1984b, p. 67). The prorating method doubled the length of the scale to 600 s.

(2) The Index Tapping test uses whichever hand is worse in the Russell et al. (1970) instructions for computing the AIR. Such a decision is difficult when calculating large numbers of scores. Thus, the Tapping Time for the two hands was averaged. Secondly, Tapping is an attainment test rather than an impairment test. Since for comparison purposes all scores need to be scored in the same direction, the scale was reversed by subtracting the seconds attained score from 70, the highest score any patient obtained.

(3) Renninck's formula (Russell et al., 1970, p. 109) for the WAIS Digit Symbol was not used, since this requires more mathematical manipulation than was warranted. Instead, the unmodified Digit Symbol scale score was utilized. Since this was also an attainment score, it was reversed by subtracting the scale score from 20, the highest obtainable scale score for a WAIS scale.

(4) The TPT Time scores were obtained by prorating blocks into time (Russell, 1985). Then, the scores for the dominant, nondominant, and both hands were summed to produce the Total Time Score. Both TPT Memory and TPT Location are attainment scores so they were reversed by subtracting the score from 10, the maximum obtainable score.

(5) The Speech-Sounds Perception Test and Rhythm Test are scored for errors and were not changed. The Aphasia Screening test scoring has been previously described (Russell et al., 1970). The Cross mentioned in this paper is the same as the Spatial Relations score (Russell et al., 1970), except that the score is not modified by the Block Design score. This makes it an unmodified score of the Cross. The Perceptual Disorders score is unmodified from that described previously by Russell et al., (1970, p.119).

In the first part of this procedure, z scores for each of these scales were obtained using the control subjects' means and standard deviations. The brain-damaged subjects' test scores were then transformed into z scores using the control subjects' means and standard deviations. In a scale derived from z scores, the mean equals zero and one standard deviation equals one.

RESULTS

The results of this study are presented in Table 2 and Figure 1. Table 2 contains several of the statistical characteristics of the Rennick version of the HRB. Since these characteristics were derived from scores obtained from one sample of subjects, the differences represent differences between tests and not between groups of subjects. This table provides the means, standard deviations, z-score means, and the minimum, maximum, range, median, and first and third quartiles for each test for all subjects. Also, the raw z scores and scale scores for a case example are given. This subject (10763) scored at the 75 centile on the AIR. This will be discussed later.

The test distributions in Figure 1 depict four of the major index tests. They were selected for both their diagnostic importance and as illustrations of the variety of distributions found among neuropsychological tests.

These results demonstrated the great variability of distribution characteristics among neuropsychological tests. Three of the characteristics that differed from a

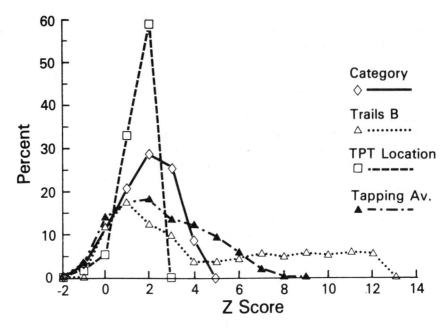

Figure 1. Comparison of four HRB tests using the percent of brain-damaged subjects impaired at each z score on each test.

normal distribution were particularly important. First, the range for brain-damaged subjects is much greater than for normal subjects. Since some brain-damaged subjects have little or no impairment, the range for a neuropsychological distribution includes the normal range. Thus, a neuropsychological scale should begin in the normal range. This insures that the measured impairment on the scale can be compared to the normal person. From the normal range, the scale should extend into the severely or profoundly impaired range: that is, to the point where some subjects can no longer perform the simplest form of this function. Brain-damage impairment extends from the normal range to zero, which is unconsciousness or death. Consequently, neuropsychological scales should reflect this entire range as fully as possible.

Secondly, Table 2 and especially Figure 1 demonstrate the great variability among scales. These scales ranged from 3.82 to 27.27 z scores. As indicated in Table 2, the variability of individual scores was less in the first quartile which included the normal population. However, the third quartile scores showed how great the differences among z scores become when greater impairment was involved. Here the z scores varied from 1.6 to 7.6. If these scores had been given as T scores, the variation would be from 66 to 126 for the same percent of impairment. (Statistics for AIR and AZI are placed in Table 2 only to provide the reader information concerning these scales. Since they are combined scores, their z scores and centiles would be meaningless at this point.)

Table 2

Group Statistics for the Parametric and Reference Scale Studies*

Test	Controls (n=155)		Brain Damaged (n=577)		zScores for all subjects							Case (10763) Scores		
	M	SD	M	SD	M	Minimum	Maximum	Range	Q1	Median	Q3	Raw	z	Scale
Category (errors)	52.11	26.31	88.69	32.30	1.39	−1.68	4.40	6.08	0.53	1.47	2.31	101	1.86	4
Trails B (time)	93.62	42.89	272.48	170.50	4.15	−1.67	11.78	13.45	0.64	2.64	7.58	444	8.14	5
Tapping (Average)	48.48	5.70	37.10	11.64	2.00	−2.54	7.37	9.91	0.44	1.67	3.59	19	5.09	7
Digit Symbol (Scaled Score)	8.84	2.11	5.05	2.94	1.80	−4.36	4.21	8.57	0.88	1.83	2.78	6	1.35	3
TPT Time	14.58	6.18	39.05	16.97	3.96	−1.07	15.50	16.57	1.88	4.06	5.89	35.40	3.37	3
TPT Memory	7.78	1.51	4.91	2.35	1.92	−1.47	5.20	6.67	0.53	1.87	3.20	4	2.53	4
TPT Location	4.18	2.62	1.61	1.85	0.98	−2.22	1.60	3.82	0.45	1.21	1.60	0	1.59	5
Speech (Errors)	7.89	4.44	17.49	10.78	2.18	−1.79	9.80	11.60	0.32	1.62	3.43	28	4.57	5
Rhythm (Errors)	3.95	3.02	7.77	4.77	1.27	−1.32	6.68	8.00	0.02	1.02	2.35	8	1.35	3
Aphasia (Errors)	3.46	3.55	11.56	11.73	2.28	−0.97	19.31	20.28	0.15	1.28	2.97	30	7.48	8
Cross (Errors)	2.44	0.64	3.65	2.09	1.88	−0.68	11.72	12.40	−0.68	0.87	2.42	3	0.87	2
Perceptual (Errors)	5.10	4.41	26.10	24.39	4.77	−1.16	26.11	27.27	0.66	3.16	7.02	30	5.66	3
AIR	1.18	0.43	2.66	0.90								3.33		3
AZI	1.00	0.50	3.38	1.76								4.65		4

* Tapping, Digit Symbol, TPT Memory, TPT Location were reversed for z scores, but not for Means and SDs.

Thirdly, the shapes of the distributions were quite variable, as can be seen in Figure 1. Some of the distributions, such as that for the Category Test, were approximately normal, whereas some were highly skewed, such as that of the Trail Making Test, Part B. In general, the larger the distribution became, the more it tended to be skewed. The distributions for the tests not shown in Figure 1 were plotted but could not be presented here due to space limitations. They tended to be skewed and, in some cases as the Perceptual Disorders Examination, the degree of skewness was extreme.

DISCUSSION

These statistics demonstrate the great variability of almost all characteristics among these HRB tests. Since these tests were probably representative of most tests for brain damage, it is inferred that most tests used in neuropsychological testing exhibit such variability. From the point of view of scaling, the variability in the z scores was particularly important. This variability was highlighted by a comparison with the WAIS subtests. The scaled scores for the WAIS subtests were set with an SD of 3 on the original sample and a mean of 10 (Wechsler, 1981). The impairment range, which is the range from the subtest mean to the lowest score in the test, was a little over 3 SD (in this study the Digit Symbol test had an impairment range of 4.21). By contrast, in this study, the z scores for the Aphasia test extend to 19 SD below the control group mean and the Perceptual Disorders Examination extended to 26 SD below the control group mean.

This being the case, it is evident that the same percentage of impairment on different scales produced quite different z scores. This was particularly evident for the third quartile z scores in Table 2. All of these z scores represented 75% of the total possible impairment for each scale. As such, the amount of impairment in percentage terms was the same. Nevertheless, the z scores varied greatly; thus, the same z score represented quite different amounts of impairment on different scales. This can be understood graphically in Figure 1 when one realizes that 75% is equivalent to a z score of 2.31 for the Category Test, 7.58 for the Trail Making Test, Part B, 1.6 for the Tactual Performance Test, Location and 3.6 for the Average Tapping time.

As an example of the misinterpretation that use of z scores can produce, consider the z scores for the case study subject (10763). His AIR score fell exactly at the third quartile, which represents an overall moderate to severe amount of impairment. His pattern of test scores is given in Table 2. The problem is whether his different z scores represent different amounts of impairment on each test as a result of degree of brain impairment or are they a function of differences among test z score distributions. Is his particular pattern meaningful? His z score for Perceptual Disorders was almost 6, the third highest score that he obtained. Yet, when compared to the sample third quartile scores, one sees that it was, in fact, relatively low. On the other hand, his high Aphasia score compared to the third quartile was actually high, indicating an unusually large amount of aphasic problems. If this subject's scores had been given in terms of T scores, as is the usual practice, a misleading pattern of results would have resulted. Thus, z, T, or any of the other equivalent methods of scaling based on standard deviations evidently do not reflect accurately the relative amount of impairment among these scales that have such different distributions for any but the almost normal subjects.

In their recent revision of the BDAE, Goodglass and Kaplan (1983) abandoned the use of z scores for their scales and began utilizing centiles. They did this for exactly the reasons that are described in this paper. z scores are affected by test distributions, whereas centiles are not. When dealing with such highly deviant populations as aphasics, such test distribution differences become quite important. In addition, they felt it was simpler to read centiles.

Several possible methods of overcoming the difficulty with z and T scores have been proposed. One is to utilize centile scores as did Goodglass and Kaplan (1983). The difficulty with centile scores, however, it that they do not provide equal interval scales (Anastasi, 1982). The advantage of z and T scores is that they do provide equal intervals. In order to utilize the advantages of both of these scaling methods, the centile scores could be normalized. In this procedure, the centile scores are transformed into z scores or any of the z-score equivalents such as T scores (Anastasi, 1982). This normalization would provide one solution to the problem of different test distributions. In fact, it may work as well as the solution proposed in this paper. Certainly, at this point in the development of neuropsychological measurement, all newly developed scales should at least be normalized.

While normalization may be sufficient, there appear to be some difficulties with it. Normalization makes the assumption that the differences in distributions among tests are due to the construction of the tests not to differences in the characteristics of the sample (Anastasi, 1982). In the area of neuropsychological assessment, at least part of the abnormal distributions is evidently due to the pathology of the brain-damaged population.

One effect of brain pathology that has been demonstrated repeatedly (Finlayson, 1977; Reed & Reitan 1963; Russell, 1979; 1980a) is that some functions are more impaired by brain damage than are other functions. Functions that require active mental processing (e.g., "fluid abilities", Cattell, 1963) are generally more impaired by brain damage than are functions that depend on well learned material (e.g., Cattell's "crystallized abilities") (Russell, 1979; 1980a). It should be noted here that this effect is independent of localization and does not imply a holistic theory of brain functioning. Either a fluid or a crystallized function may be related to a limited area of the brain. Fluidity simply represents another way in which mental functions can vary along with the location of the function.

Finally, another major problem in using centiles or normalized scores is that of determining whether to use a normal control group or a brain-damaged

408

group for norming. For many tests, the distribution for the brain-damaged subjects is highly abnormal, while the results for normal subjects produce a normal curve. For example, in this study, only the Category Test had a relatively normal curve for the brain-damaged group (Figure 1). In another study, it was found that the Trail Making Test, Part B and the Speech-Sounds Perception Test have normal distributions for control subjects while having quite abnormal distributions for the brain-damaged subjects (Russell, 1980b). Thus, it would appear that scaled scores based on the normal population do not need to be normalized and do not fit the brain-damaged population, while the normalized scores derived from the brain-damaged population do not fit the normal subjects.

In the second part of this paper, another method of constructing scales is proposed that may overcome these problems, at least to some extent. It utilizes the concept of statistically relating the individual battery scores to a single representative scale so that all scales will have comparable intervals.

Before presenting this reference scale method, one theoretical problem needs to be discussed. This is the question of whether the use of a single reference scale such as the Halstead Index (Halstead, 1947) or the proposed reference scale implies that brain damage has a single dimension (i.e., a holistic theory of brain functioning). In this regard, a composite scale need not imply a single dimension of brain-damage impairment except in the sense that almost any brain damage is likely to impair some functions. A good composite scale samples the various areas of brain function and, as such, it would be a better overall indicator of brain-damage impairment than would any single test that is related to a limited area. In fact, if brain-damage impairment had only one dimension, a composite scale would not be necessary; a single test would do. The proposed reference scale is a composite scale that represents the entire battery in such a way as to provide a constant reference for each of the individual battery scales. It is not a measure of some hypothetical entity called "brain damage."

REFERENCE SCALE CONSTRUCTION (PART II)

The problem for coordinated norming is to create a series of scales such that the same score will indicate the same amount of impairment for all subjects on all scales. In this section, an attempt is made to show that such norming may be done to a great extent by constructing a single representative scale which is then related in a consistent manner to each individual scale in a battery in order to form scaled scores.

METHOD

The procedure for creating a reference scale in this study consisted of three steps: (1) choosing a reference group of tests, (2) combining the results from those tests into a reference scale, and (3) deriving scaled scores from the reference scale.

Subjects.
The subjects used in Part II of this study were the same subjects as were used in Part I.

Procedure.
The procedure for constructing reference scale scores has several steps.

Step 1. Selection of Reference Tests. A reference scale is based on a representative group of tests. In this case, the tests should be selected so as to best represent as wide a range as is possible of impairment resulting from brain damage. At this point, so little is known about how best to represent such a range of impairment that any selection is somewhat arbitrary. However, some guiding concepts are evident. First, it is generally conceded that a single test cannot adequately reflect the wide range of neurological conditions that exist (Boll, 1981; Lezak, 1983). Thus, some sort of index group of tests is required.

The number of tests in an index should follow the general rule for constructing a scale: That is, the more items, or in this case scales, which are utilized, the greater the accuracy of the scale or index. However, the increase in accuracy occurs at a decreasing rate so that, at a certain point, the scale or index reaches a point of diminishing returns. In creating an index, this may occur more rapidly than in creating a scale. The results of an unpublished preliminary investigation, using the same sample of subjects as were in this study, showed that only four scales from the AIR (Trail Making Test, Part B; Tactual Performance Test, Total Time; WAIS Digit Symbol; Speech-Sounds Perception Test) yielded an $r = .94$ with the entire AIR scale. However, selection of scales for a short index would require considerable research that is much beyond the scope of the current study.

One method of creating a reference scale that is representative of all or many brain functions would be to utilize the results of factor analyses. The test that loads most highly on each of the major factors derived from a large neuropsychology battery would be selected for the composite reference scale. Other methods would involve the selection of tests that are theoretically representative of different cognitive functions and different areas of brain involvement.

Since such a procedure would require far more research than was possible for this study, a well-known index, the Rennick Index (Russell et al., 1970; Russell, 1984b) was utilized to provide the group of tests used for this reference scale study. This index has already been well studied (Russell, 1984a, 1984b) and widely utilized. It contains the seven tests from the Halstead Impairment Index that are now employed by the vast majority using the HRB, plus five others. The various index tests were described in Part I of this paper.

While these tests were originally selected before neuropsychological theory had developed to the point which would enable one to know which tests were related to various areas of the brain functioning, they do represent most of the factors found in the HRB and WAIS combination. These and the LNB are the only large general batteries of neuropsychology tests that have been factor-analyzed. The results of these studies indicate that the Rennick Index contains tests that load on almost all of the factors that have been derived from these studies (Goldstein & Shelly, 1972; Newby, Hallenbeck, & Embretson, 1983; Russell, 1971; 1974).

Step 2, Obtaining AZI Scores. The reference scale was produced by combining the reference tests of the Rennick Index. There were two requirements for developing the reference scale. First, as much as possible, it should represent scores for the brain-damaged population as a whole and, second, it should be anchored in the normal population. To meet the first requirement, a large, fairly representative population of brain-damaged subjects was utilized. This consisted of the 577 brain-damaged subjects described in the first part of this study. Brain-damaged subjects were utilized to overcome the difficulty created by using only control subjects to form the scale, as was indicated in the first part of this study and elsewhere (Russell, 1979; 1980a). Such a difficulty can be partly eliminated by norming on brain-damaged subjects, as was done by Goodglass and Kaplan (1983).

However, using only brain-damaged subjects for norms would leave the scales "floating", with no anchor to a normal population. That is, the scaled scores would tell the examiner what were the relative differences between the test scores of brain-damaged subjects but not how impaired a person was in relation to a normal population. Such unanchored scales would also prevent a comparison with other test scales drawn from another group of brain-damaged subjects. There would be no way of determining how much impairment there was in any absolute sense. "Absolute" here is used to mean consistency of measurement for the entire brain-damaged population. The one relatively absolute or stable measure in this area is the average score for the normal population. While not completely invariant, the normal control group with known parameters for age, education, and IQ does provide a fairly stable reference group across most measures used with brain-damaged subjects (Lezak, 1983).

Apparently, one of the very few problems of any consequence with the BDAE is that its scales are not anchored to a normal control group. All of the norming population were aphasics. Thus, there is no way of knowing the severity of the different types of aphasia in relation to normals. For the purpose of the BDAE, the examination of various patterns of aphasia, it may be that such an anchor is not necessary. However, the fact remains that the amount of impairment of various aspects of language as compared to normal language cannot be determined with this instrument. This becomes a disadvantage when examining brain-damaged subjects who are only mildly aphasic.

Thus, in the procedure used in this study, the group reference scales were anchored by obtaining the z scores from a normal control group. As the first step in this procedure, the scores for each subtest of the 155 normal subjects were transformed into z scores. This step was the same procedure as was applied in Part I of this study.

Second, to make the scores representative of the brain-damaged group, the raw scores of the brain-damaged subjects were changed into z score equivalents using the control group z scoring. That is, the brain-damaged raw scores were assigned z scores derived from the means and standard deviations of the control group.

Thirdly, a 1 was added to the scores, changing the mean from 0 to 1 and increasing all the scores by 1. This was done to eliminate minus scores (Russell, 1984a). Finally, all the subjects' index scores were averaged to form the reference scale. Using the z scores, the 12 index scales were summed and divided by 12 for each subject. In this way, the Average z score Index (AZI) was created with a mean of 1 and each interval equivalent to a standard deviation.

Step 3, Deriving Scaled Scores. The scaled scores for individual tests were derived through a regression analysis in which the raw score for a test was predicted from the AZI scores for each AZI interval. All of the subjects were used for scaling, since this provided better scale distributions than attempting to use only the brain-damaged subjects. Restricting the sample to brain-damaged subjects did not provide enough "weight" at the normal end of the scale. That is, scatter diagrams demonstrated that the regression line would not pass as close to the raw score means for each interval at the "normal" end of the scale when the normals were left out as it would when the normals were retained. When all subjects were utilized, the regression line for all of the tests fell close to the test raw score means for each of the AZI intervals, indicating that the test distributions for most of the tests were relatively linear (See figure 2). Scatter diagrams were also plotted for each test in order to verify the linearity of the distributions. The regression line and test score means for each AZI interval are given in Figure 2 for the Speech-Sounds Perception Test.

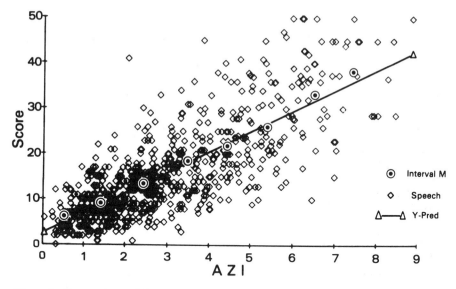

Figure 2. Comparison of the regression line for the Speech-Sounds Perception Test with the mean for each AZI interval.

This demonstrates how close to the interval means the regression line usually fell. Thus, the regression line smoothed the cutting points between the interval means to provide a more consistent scale measure than would have resulted from using individual means for each interval.

Raw score cutting points, representing the beginning point of each scale score interval, were obtained for all of the index tests (See Table 3). The AIR score equivalent (Russell et al., 1970) is provided for those who use the AIR scale scores. The scale scores were obtained for Tapping, dominant and nondominant hands, as well as for the Average Tapping score, since in most testing situations the Average Tapping score is not used. These scale scores are given in Table 3.

The only deviation from this procedure occurred with the Trail Making Test, part B. It was scaled so that the scales could be used with either a time limit of 300 s or with the combined time error formula (Russell, 1984a). Since this distribution was somewhat nonlinear, two regression lines were combined. The first of these lines was the regression line for subjects scoring up to a 2.5 AZI cutting point. The second was a slightly modified regression line derived from subjects with AZI scores above 2.5. When the regression lines were combined, the lower part of the scale closely approximated a scale derived from the time score for the Trail Making Test, Part B when a 300-s time limit is set. With the 300-s time limit, subjects simply cannot obtain a score worse than the scale score of 4. The total scale can be used for the prorated Trail Making Test, part B.

Finally, it should be noted that these scale scores have not been corrected for age and education. The overall mean age for this group is 47.7 years and the educational level is 11.9. Thus, these scales will not necessarily reflect accurately the impairment of subjects who are considerably older and less educated than these limits.

Table 3

Scale scores (AZI intervals) derived from a regression prediction of AZI from test scores

Test	Scale Scores (AZI Intervals)									
	0	1	1.5*	2	3	4	5	6	7	8
AIR	.4	1.2	1.6	2	2.5	3	3.5	4	4.5	5
Category	<52	52	58	64	77	89	101	114	126	138
Trails B	<67	67	92	118	169	247	353	458	564	600
Tapping Average	>49	49	47	45	41	37	33	29	25	21
Tapping, Dom (Males)	>51	51	49	47	43	39	35	31	27	23
Tapping, Non Dom (Males)	>46	46	44	42	38	35	31	27	23	19
Digit Symbol	> 9	9	8	-	6	5	4	2	1	0
TPT Total Time	<15	15	19	23	30	39	46	54	62	70
TPT Memory	> 8	8	7	-	6	5	4	3	2	1
TPT Location	> 4	4	3	-	2	2	1	0	-	-
Speech Perception	< 5	5	7	9	14	18	23	27	32	36
Rhythm (Errors)	< 3	3	4	5	6	8	10	11	13	15
Aphasia	< 1	1	2	5	8	12	16	20	24	28
Cross	2	2	-	3	-	4	5	-	6	7
Perceptual Errors	< 1	1	2	7	18	28	38	48	58	69

* Included in Table, since 1.5 is the usual cutting point for assessment of brain damage.

DISCUSSION

This reference method provides scaled scores which appear to be more accurate than T or z scores and more statistically useful than centiles. An example is provided by the case (10763) mentioned previously that fell at the 75% level for the AIR. This subject's scores are given in Table 2. The comparison of the AZI scale scores to his z scores indicated that they appeared to more accurately reflect his condition than did the z scores. He was a 62-year-old man with a fairly severe chronic (3-year-old) left hemispheric CVA and some bilateral vascular insufficiency. Since many of the "lateralizing" tests were not provided in this study (such as right and left Tapping, right and left Tactual Performance Test times, and the Perceptual Disorders score was a combined score), the severity of the lateralized impairment was not shown. His scale scores did show that all of his scores were in the brain-damaged range. This was particularly striking for the Category Test, Digit Symbol Test and Tactual Performance Test, Memory and Location Measures. While these differences could have been derived by comparing this patient's z scores with the third quartile scores, in practice it would be quite difficult to set up the average z scores at each centile level. In essence, this comparison is built into the AZI scale scores. Thus, this method of creating scale scores should provide a more accurate estimate of a patient's impairment on each test than is now available.

The AZI reference scale can be used to create scale scores not only for the index tests but for any test utilized in the test battery. In fact, one attribute of this method is that temporary scales can be created for a new test based on brain-damaged subjects alone. Thus, when a test is added to the battery, relatively accurate temporary scales can be created after a small number of brain-damaged subjects, 30 or more, have been collected. A large sample of normals is not needed. This is done by predicting their scores from the AZI. As a consequence, new tests can be added to a test battery and scaled relatively quickly. (At this point, age norms cannot be so quickly constructed.)

While this method in its complete form is presented here for the first time, in a less developed form it has been used in several previous studies. The AIR (Russell et al., 1970) essentially used this method for deriving an average score from index tests. The AIR is statistically equivalent to the AZI (Russell, 1984a). This reference scale method, in its AIR form, was used (1) to develop the scales for the revision of the Wechsler Memory Scale (Russell, 1975), (2) for studies of lateralization effects (Russell, 1984b) and (3) to extend the range of the Tactual Performance Test (Russell, 1985). Thus, it has already been utilized in several studies and as such it is evidently workable.

REFERENCES

Anastasi, A. (1982). *Psychological testing* (5th ed.). New York: MacMillan.
American Psychological Association (1974). *Standards for educational & psychological tests.* Washington, D.C.: Author.
Beardsley, J. V., Matthews, C. G., Cleeland, C.S., & Harley, J.P. (1978). *Experimental T-Score norms for CA 35+ on the Wisconsin Neuropsychology Test Battery.* Unpublished manuscript. (Available from C. G. Matthews, 2768 Marshall Parkway, Madison, WI 53713).
Boll, T. J. (1981). The Halstead-Reitan Neuropsychology Battery. In S. B. Filskov & T. J. Boll (Eds.), *Handbook of clinical neuropsychology.* (Vol. 1, pp. 577-609) New York: Wiley-Interscience.
Cattell, R. B. (1963). Theory of fluid and crystallized intelligence: Activated experiment. *Journal of Educational psychology, 54,* 1-22.
Finlayson, M. A. J. (1977). Test complexity and brain damage at different educational levels. *Journal of Clinical Psychology, 33,* 221-223.
Golden, C. J. (1981). A Standardized Version of Luria's Neuropsychological Tests: A Quantitative and Qualitative Approach to Neuropsychological Evaluation. In S. B. Filskov & T. J. Boll (Eds.), *Handbook of clinical neuropsychology* (Vol. 1, pp. 608-644). New York: Wiley-Interscience.
Goldstein, G., & Shelly, C. H. (1972). Statistical and normative studies of the Halstead Neuropsychological test battery relevant to a neuropsychiatric setting. *Perceptual and Motor Skills, 34,* 603-620.

414

Goodglass, H., & Kaplan E. (1972). *The Assessment of Aphasia and Related Disorders.* Philadelphia: Lea & Febiger.

Goodglass, H., & Kaplan E. (1983). *The Assessment of Aphasia and Related Disorders* (2nd ed.). Philadelphia: Lea & Febiger.

Halstead, W. C. (1947). *Brain and intelligence.* Chicago: University of Chicago Press.

Harley, J. P., Leuthold, C. A., Matthews, C. G., & Bergs, L. E. (1980). *T-Score Norms, Wisconsin Neuropsychological Test Battery.* Madison, WI: Kløve-Matthews, Psychological Test Equipment.

Kertesz, A. (1979). *Aphasia and associated disorders: Taxonomy, localization and recovery.* New York: Grune & Stratton.

Kiernan, R. J., & Matthews, C. G. (1976). Impairment Index versus T-Score Averaging in neuropsychological assessment. *Journal of Consulting and Clinical Psychology, 44,* 951-957.

Lezak, M. D. (1983). *Neuropsychological assessment* (2nd ed.). New York: Oxford.

Luria, A. R. (1973). *The working brain.* New York: Basic Books.

Luria, A. R. (1980). *Higher cortical functions in man* (rev. ed.). New York: Basic Books.

Newby, R. F., Hallenbeck, C. E., & Embretson, S. (1983). Confirmatory factor analysis of four general neuropsychological models with a modified Halstead-Reitan battery. *Journal of Clinical Neuropsychology, 5,* 115-133.

Pauker, J. D. (1977, February). Adult norms for the Halstead-Reitan Neuropsychological Test Battery: Preliminary data. Paper presented at the annual meeting of the International Neuropsychological Society, Santa Fe, NM.

Reed, H. B. C., & Reitan, R. M. (1963). A comparison of the effects of the normal aging process with effects of organic brain-damage on adaptive abilities. *Journal of Gerontology, 18,* 177-179.

Russell, E. W. (1971). Reexamination of Halstead's biological intelligence factors. *Proceedings of the 79th Annual Convention of the American Psychological Association, 6,* 461-462.

Russell, E. W. (1974). The effect of acute lateralized brain damage on Halstead's Biological Intelligence Factors. *Journal of General Psychology, 90,* 101-107.

Russell, E. W. (1975). A multiple scoring method for the assessment of complex memory functions. *Journal of Consulting and Clinical Psychology, 43,* 800-809.

Russell, E. W. (1979). Three patterns of brain damage on the WAIS. *Journal of Clinical Psychology, 35,* 611-620.

Russell, E. W. (1980a). Fluid and crystallized intelligence: Effects of diffuse brain damage on the WAIS. *Perceptual and Motor Skills,* 51, 121-122.

Russell, E. W. (1980b). Tactile sensation: An all-or-none effect of cerebral damage. *Journal of Clinical Psychology, 36,* 858-864.

Russell, E. W. (1980c). Theoretical bases of the Luria-Nebraska and the Halstead-Reitan Batteries. Paper presented at The 88th Annual Convention of the American Psychological Association, Montreal, Canada.

Russell, E. W. (1984a). Psychometric parameters of the average impairment rating scale. *Journal of Consulting and Clinical Psychology, 92,* 717-718.

Russell, E. W. (1984b). Theory and development of pattern analysis methods related to the Halstead-Reitan Battery. In P. E. Logue & J. M. Scheer (Eds.), *Clinical neuropsychology, a multidisciplinary approach* (pp. 50-98). Springfield, Il: Charles C. Thomas.

Russell, E. W. (1985). Comparison of the TPT 10 and TPT 6 Hole Form Board. *Journal of Clinical Psychology, 41,* 68-81.

Russell, E. W., Neuringer, C. & Goldstein, G. (1970). *Assessment of brain damage: A neuropsychological key approach.* New York: Wiley-Interscience.

Swiercinsky, D. P. (1978). *Manual for the Adult Neuropsychological Evaluation.* Springfield, Il: Charles C. Thomas.

Wechsler, D. (1981). *Wechsler Adult Intelligence Scale - Revised, Manual.* New York: Psychological Corporation.

Journal of Clinical and Experimental Neuropsychology
1988, Vol. 10, No. 5, pp. 605-622.

V-C

When Diagnostic Agreement is High, but Reliability is Low: Some Paradoxes Occurring in Joint Independent Neuropsychology Assessments*

Domenic V. Cicchetti

VA Medical Center, West Haven,

and Department of Psychiatry, and Child Study Center, Yale University

ABSTRACT

Two paradoxes can occur when neuropsychologists attempt to assess the reliability of a dichotomous diagnostic instrument (e.g., one measuring the presence or absence of Dyslexia or Autism). The first paradox occurs when two pairs of examiners both produce the same high level of agreement (e.g., 85%). Nonetheless, the level of *chance-corrected* agreement is relatively high for one pair (e.g., .70) and quite low for the other (e.g., .32). To illustrate the second paradox, consider two examiners who are in 80% agreement in their overall diagnosis of Dyslexia. Assume, further, that they are in 100% agreement in the proportion of cases they both diagnose as Dyslexic (20%) and as Non-Dyslexic (80%). Somewhat paradoxically, the level of chance-corrected interexaminer agreement for this pair of examiners calculates to only .37. In distinct contrast, a second set of examiners also in 80% overall agreement, is in appreciable disagreement with respect to diagnostic assignments. Thus, the first neuropsychologist: (a) classifies 65% of the cases as Non-Dyslexic, as opposed to 45% so diagnosed by the second neuropsychologist; and (b) classifies the remaining 35% as Dyslexic, as compared to the 55% so classified by the second examiner. Despite these phenomena, this second pair of examiners produces a much higher level of chance-corrected agreement than did the first pair, that is, a value of .61. The underlying reasons for both of these paradoxes, as well as their resolution, are presented.

* The main ideas presented in this paper derive from a two-part series being prepared by the author and Dr. Alvan Feinstein for the more general medical literature. A mathematical resolution to the paradoxes produced by Kappa, in the binary case, is available upon request. Portions of this paper were presented at: (a) The International Neuropsychology Society (INS) meeting, Denver, Co, 1986 (Dr. Byron Rourke, symposium chairman); and at (b) The Joint Meetings of the American Statistical Association, San Francisco, CA, 1987. The author is appreciative of the referees' helpful suggestions. This research was, in part, supported by an award from the Medical Research Service of the Veteran's Administration (MRIS-1416).

When a child neuropsychologist administers a comprehensive battery, such as that developed by Reitan and Davison (1974), one of the multiple tasks that must be accomplished is to apply specific sets of criteria in order to transform certain variables deriving from continuous (or dimensional) scales into the presence or absence of a particular disorder. Some examples include: (1) transforming the number of errors on certain subtraction and multiplication problems into the presence or absence of Dyscalculia; (2) translating the number of errors a child makes copying a square, a triangle, a Greek cross, and a key into the presence or absence of Constructional Dyspraxia; and, finally, (3) ruling in or ruling out a diagnosis of Dyslexia on the basis of the number of errors a child makes while attempting to read specific letters, words, and numbers.

Now, suppose that 100 children have been independently assessed by the same two neuropsychologists, with respect to the presence or absence of Dyslexia. The reliability research design, expressed in *proportions* of cases that were jointly diagnosed, can be illustrated, as in Table 1.

Table 1[1]

Reliability Research Design for Diagnostic
Decisions Expressed as Binary Outcomes

Diagnosis by Neuropsychologist B	Diagnosis by Neuropsychologist A		Total
	Negative	Positive	
Negative	A (F_1G_1)	B (F_2G_1)	G_1
Positive	C (F_1G_2)	D (F_2G_2)	G_2
Total	F_1	F_2	1.00

[1] Note: Unbracketed letters refer to the proportions of actual cases (e.g., A denotes the proportion diagnosed as *negative* by both neuropsychologists; D denotes the proportion diagnosed as *positive* by both neuropsychologists); letters in brackets denote the proportions of cases expected by chance alone in each of the A, B, C, and D cells.

In terms of assessing the level of interexaminer reliability:

PO = A + D, the Proportion of Observed agreement. [1]

PC = $F_1G_1 + F_2G_2$, the Proportion of Chance agreement. [2]

1–PC = the maximum amount of chance-corrected agreement
that is possible. [3]

(PO-PC)/(1-PC) = Kappa (Cohen, 1960; Fleiss, Cohen,
& Everitt, 1969). [4]

A major advantage of Kappa is that it makes a correction or "adjustment" for the amount of agreement that can be expected to occur by chance alone, in ratings expressed as categorical data (Cohen, 1960; Fleiss, 1981). Nonetheless, two clinical examiners who are in high agreement in diagnosing, say, the presence or absence of Dyscalculia, could, in fact, produce a low value of chance-corrected agreement (i.e., Kappa), when the "prevalence" of each examiner's application of the diagnosis of Dyscalculia is either very high or very low (e.g., see Grove, Andreason, McDonald-Scott, Keller, & Shapiro, 1981; Kraemer, 1979; McClure & Willett, 1987). Analogously, diagnostic markers with both high sensitivity and specificity may have low predictive accuracy when the prevalence of the disease is also low.

In order to bring these problems to the attention of neuropsychologists, who will need to apply Kappa-type statistics to reliability assessment problems, the focus of this presentation will be upon two main objectives: (1) to specify those conditions under which the level of interexaminer agreement is high (80% or more), but Kappa is low (less than .40, according to the criteria of Cicchetti & Sparrow, 1981; and Fleiss, 1981); and (2) to offer a rationale for this anomaly, or specific guidelines for resolving the paradox.

Identifying Paradoxes of the First Kind

Consider the apocryphal diagnostic data given in Tables 2 and 3. In both cases, PO = .85. However, the PC value for Table 2 data is .50, resulting in a Kappa of .70 (a value falling into the category of Good chance-corrected agreement (i.e., .60 - .74)). Based upon a much lower "prevalence" of Dyslexia in Table 3, PC becomes .78, so that Kappa now is reduced to a value of .32, which fits the category of Poor chance-corrected agreement (i.e., less than .40, using the clinical criteria of Cicchetti & Sparrow, 1981).

Table 2[1]

Diagnosis by Neuropsychologist B	Diagnosis by Neuropsychologist A		Total
	Non- Dyslexic	Dyslexic	
Non-Dyslexic	.40(.2254)	.09(.2646)	.49
Dyslexic	.06(.2346)	.45(.2754)	.51
Total	.46	.54	1.00

$$PO = .8500$$
$$PC = .5008$$
$$Kappa = (.8500 - .5008)/(1 - .5008)$$
$$= .6995$$
$$= .70$$

[1] Note: Unbracketed numbers refer to *observed* proportions of cases; bracketed numbers denote *expected* proportions of cases.

Table 3[1]

Diagnosis by Neuropsychologist B	Diagnosis by Neuropsychologist A		Total
	Non- Dyslexic	Dyslexic	
Non-Dyslexic	.80(.765)	.10(.135)	.90
Dyslexic	.05(0.85)	.05(.015)	.10
Total	.85	.15	1.00

$$PO = .85$$
$$PC = .78$$
$$Kappa = (.85-.78)/.22$$
$$= .3182$$
$$= .32$$

[1] Note: Unbracketed numbers refer to *observed* proportions of cases; bracketed numbers denote *expected* proportions of cases.

Identifying Paradoxes of the Second Kind

The data in Tables 4 and 5 demonstrate a second paradox. In both instances, the independent clinical assessments are in 80% agreement. Moreover, the examiner marginals (or proportions of cases assigned to each diagnostic category) are in 100% agreement for Table 4 data (.80 - .20 vs. .80 - .20) while they are in moderate disagreement for Table 5 data (.65 - .35 for Examiner A; .45 - .55 for Examiner B). Paradoxically, Kappa based upon Table 4 data is only .37 (reflecting Poor agreement, or less than .40) while Kappa deriving from Table 5 data produces a value of .61, indicating Good agreement.

In the next part of this report, it will be shown how these two paradoxes can be understood and resolved.

Table 4[1]

Diagnosis by Neuropsychologist B	Diagnosis by Neuropsychologist A		Total
	Non- Dyslexic	Dyslexic	
Non-Dyslexic	.70(.64)	.10(.16)	.80
Dyslexic	.10(.16)	.10(.04)	.20
Total	.80	.20	1.00

$$PO = .80$$
$$PC = .68$$
$$Kappa = (.80 - .68)/.32$$
$$= .375$$
$$= .37$$

[1] Note: Unbracketed numbers refer to *observed* proportions of cases; bracketed numbers denote *expected* proportions of cases.

Table 5[1]

Diagnosis by Neuropsychologist B	Diagnosis by Neuropsychologist A		Total
	Non- Dyslexic	Dyslexic	
Non-Dyslexic	.45(.2925)	.00(.1575)	.45
Dyslexic	.20(.3575)	.35(.1925)	.55
Total	.65	.35	1.00

$$PO = .800$$
$$PC = .485$$
$$Kappa = (.800 - .485)/(.515)$$
$$= .6117$$
$$= .61$$

[1] Note: Unbracketed numbers refer to *observed* proportions of cases; bracketed numbers denote *expected* proportions of cases.

Resolving Paradoxes of the First Kind

A key to understanding the anomalous results just presented rests in realizing that there are two ways of defining PO. The first we have already discussed: (1) One simply sums the two cells along the main diagonal. If we consider the data in Table 2, PO becomes $(.40 + .45); = .85;$ (2) An alternate method involves decomposing PO into its two differential statistical indexes, namely, examiner agreement on *positive* (P_{pos}) cases, and examiner agreement on *negative* (P_{neg}) cases, respectively. It is important to stress that the *weighted average* of these two specific indices produces PO (Cicchetti, Lee, Fontana, & Noel-Dowds, 1978; Spitzer & Fleiss, 1974).

It will now be shown that for a given value of PO (e.g., 85%), Kappa (chance-corrected agreement) will be highest when P_{neg}, P_{pos}, and PO are identical (or most similar) in value and will become progressively and predictably lower as the imbalance increases between the values of P_{pos}, and P_{neg}, relative to the size of PO.

While the two methods of defining PO are both valid, the one consisting of summing over the main diagonal (i.e., PO = A+D) *masks* the phenomenon just described. Conversely, the alternate method, whereby PO is expressed as the weighted average of P_{pos} and P_{neg} *identifies* the phenomenon. We shall now apply the principles just discussed in order to both understand and resolve the paradox exemplified by comparing the data deriving from Tables 2 and 3. Recall that in both cases, the clinical neuropsychologists are in high agreement (i.e., PO = 85%). However, the level of Kappa is .70 (good agreement) in case 1 (Table 2) and only .32 (poor agreement) in case 2 (Table 3). This large difference in levels of *clinical significance* of Kappa values (again, see Cicchetti & Sparrow, 1981) occurs because the level of examiner agreement expected by chance alone is .50 in the first case (Table 2) and .78 in the second case (Table 3).

Consider again the decomposition of PO into P_{neg} and P_{pos}, first for the data deriving from Table 2 and then for the data deriving from Table 3. In words, P_{neg} is expressed as the *proportion* of interexaminer agreement on *negative* cases (here, the agreement on cases diagnosed as Non-Dyslexic). Similarly, P_{pos} is expressed as the proportion of interexaminer agreement on *positive* cases (here, agreement on cases diagnosed as Dyslexic). More specifically, P_{neg} refers to the proportion of agreement on *negative* cases (numerator) relative to the *average* proportion of cases to which the two examiners apply a *negative* diagnosis (denominator). Similarly, P_{pos} refers to the proportion of agreement on *positive* cases (numerator) relative to the *average* proportion of cases which the examiners have diagnosed as *positive*. Expressing these relationships with the mathematical notation introduced in Table 1, we can define the formulae for P_{neg} and P_{pos} as follows:

$P_{neg} = A/(F_1+G_1)/2$, in which [5]
A = the proportion of cases for which the two examiners agree on a *negative* diagnosis.
F_1 = the proportion of cases classified as *negative* by Examiner A.
G_1 = the proportion of cases classified as *negative* by Examiner B.
$P_{pos} = D/(F_2+G_2)/2$, in which [6]
D = the proportion of cases for which the two examiners agree on a *positive* diagnosis.
F_2 = the proportion of cases classified as *positive* by Examiner A, and
G_2 = the proportion of cases classified as *positive* by Examiner B.

Applying formulae [5] and [6] to the data deriving from Table 2, we obtain P_{neg} = .84 and P_{pos} = .86, two values which are virtually interchangeable with the PO value of .85. This particular arrangement of overall agreement (.85), and agreement on negative (.84) and positive (.86) cases is associated with a Kappa value of .70, which indicates a good level of agreement (.60 - .74).

In sharp contrast, the data from Table 3 produce a P_{neg} of .91, but a P_{pos} of only .40. These two values do *not* agree closely with the PO value of .85, and are associated with a value for Kappa of .32, reflecting poor agreement (less than .40).

These data suggest that (1) High values of Kappa are associated with P_{neg} and P_{pos} values that are similar to each other and to the value of PO; (2) Low values of Kappa are associated with P_{neg} and P_{pos} values that are quite dissimilar both to each other and to PO.

In order to test the generalizability of these findings, one must hold the examiner marginals for a given binary agreement case constant and then allow PO, P_{neg}, and P_{pos} to vary across all possible values, within this set of constraints.

For the data deriving from Table 2, with marginals fixed at .46 and .54 for Examiner A and at .49 and .51 for Examiner B, there are 47 possible combinations of Negative/Negative, Positive/Positive, Negative/Positive, and Positive/-Negative categories, as given in Table 6.

Table 6

Case	Examiner Pairing A Neg B Neg	Pos Pos	Neg Pos	Pos Neg	PO	PC	Kappa Kappa	Kmax	P_{neg}	P_{pos}	Chamberlain's (1975) P_{pos}
1	46	51	3	0	.97	.50	.94	1.00	.97	.97	.94
2	45	50	4	1	.95	.50	.90	.96	.95	.95	.91
3	44	49	5	2	.93	.50	.86	.91	.93	.93	.87
4	43	48	6	3	.91	.50	.82	.87	.91	.91	.84
5	42	47	7	4	.89	.50	.78	.83	.88	.90	.81
6	41	46	8	5	.87	.50	.74	.79	.86	.88	.78
7	40	45	9	6	.85	.50	.70	.74	.84	.86	.75
8	39	44	10	7	.83	.50	.66	.70	.82	.84	.72
9	38	43	11	8	.81	.50	.62	.66	.80	.82	.69
10	37	42	12	9	.79	.50	.58	.62	.78	.80	.67
11	36	41	13	10	.77	.50	.54	.57	.76	.78	.64
12	35	40	14	11	.75	.50	.50	.53	.74	.76	.62
13	34	39	15	12	.73	.50	.46	.49	.72	.74	.59
14	33	38	16	13	.71	.50	.42	.45	.69	.72	.57
15	32	37	17	14	.69	.50	.38	.40	.67	.70	.54
16	31	36	18	15	.67	.50	.34	.36	.65	.69	.52
17	30	35	19	16	.65	.50	.30	.32	.63	.67	.50
18	29	34	20	17	.63	.50	.26	.28	.61	.65	.48
19	28	33	21	18	.61	.50	.22	.23	.59	.63	.46
20	27	32	22	19	.59	.50	.18	.19	.57	.61	.44
21	26	31	23	20	.57	.50	.14	.15	.55	.59	.42
22	25	30	24	21	.55	.50	.10	.10	.53	.57	.40
23	24	29	25	22	.53	.50	.06	.06	.51	.55	.38
24	23	28	26	23	.51	.50	.02	.02	.48	.53	.36
25	22	27	27	24	.49	.50	−.02	NA	.46	.51	.35
26	21	26	28	25	.47	.50	−.06	NA	.44	.50	.33
27	20	25	29	26	.45	.50	−.10	NA	.42	.48	.31
28	19	24	30	27	.43	.50	−.14	NA	.40	.46	.30
29	18	23	31	28	.41	.50	−.18	NA	.38	.44	.28
30	17	22	32	29	.39	.50	−.22	NA	.36	.42	.27
31	16	21	33	30	.37	.50	−.26	NA	.34	.40	.25
32	15	20	34	31	.35	.50	−.30	NA	.32	.38	.24
33	14	19	35	32	.33	.50	−.34	NA	.29	.36	.22
34	13	18	36	33	.31	.50	−.38	NA	.27	.34	.20
35	12	17	37	34	.29	.50	−.42	NA	.25	.32	.19
36	11	16	38	35	.27	.50	−.46	NA	.23	.30	.18
37	10	15	39	36	.25	.50	−.50	NA	.21	.29	.17
38	9	14	40	37	.23	.50	−.54	NA	.19	.27	.15
39	8	13	41	38	.21	.50	−.58	NA	.17	.25	.14
40	7	12	42	39	.19	.50	−.62	NA	.15	.23	.13
41	6	11	43	40	.17	.50	−.66	NA	.13	.21	.12
42	5	10	44	41	.15	.50	−.70	NA	.11	.19	.11
43	4	9	45	42	.13	.50	−.74	NA	.08	.17	.09

Rank ordering of all possible values of PO, Kappa, P_{pos} and $P_{neg.}$ for marginals of 46% and 54% for Examiner A, and 49% and 51% for Examiner B

424

Table 6 (Continued)

								Kappa			Chamberlain's
	A Neg	Pos	Neg	Pos							
Case	B Neg	Pos	Pos	Neg	PO	PC	Kappa	Kmax	P_{neg}	P_{pos}	(1975) P_{pos}
44	3	8	46	43	.11	.50	−.78	NA	.06	.15	.08
45	2	7	47	44	.09	.50	−.82	NA	.04	.13	.07
46	1	6	48	45	.07	.50	−.86	NA	.02	.11	.06
47	0	5	49	46	.05	.50	−.90	NA	0	.10	.05

Rank ordering of all possible values of PO, Kappa, P_{pos} and P_{neg} for marginals of 46% and 54% for Examiner A, and 49% and 51% for Examiner B

These data indicate that the size of Kappa is directly related to the extent to which P_{neg} and P_{pos} values are similar to each other and to the size of PO. Thus, the maximum values within the marginal constraints of .46 and .54 for Examiner A and .49 and .51 for Examiner B are a Kappa value of .94, associated with P_{neg}, P_{pos}, and PO values of .97. Note also that case 7 represents the data deriving from Table 2. Moreover, the Kappa value of .70 represents the 7th best of the 47 possible Kappa values. Finally, it should be noted that, when examiner marginals are held constant with Kappa, PO, P_{neg}, and P_{pos} allowed to vary, then an exact, mathematical, direct, linear relationship will occur with respect to the levels of Kappa, PO, P_{neg}, and P_{pos}. In the Table 6 data, for every two percentage decrease in the value of PO, there are *corresponding* decreases: in Kappa of .0400; in P_{neg} of .0210; and in P_{pos} of .0190 (when rounding is to 4 decimal places). Put another way, there is a perfect linear regression of Kappa upon PO, P_{neg}, and P_{pos} values.

For comparative purposes, let us now perform the same generalization of the data deriving from the clinical case represented by the data in Table 3. Here, PO is again .85, but Kappa is .32, with marginals of .85 and .15 for Examiner A and .90 and .10 for Examiner B. Note in the generalization of this case (i.e., Table 7) that these marginal constraints are more restrictive than the .46 - .54 and .49 - .51 marginals for Table 2 data, whose generalization produced 47 possible combinations of Kappa, PO, P_{neg}, and P_{pos} values (see again, Table 6).

Thus, there are 11 values possible. However, when one uses the same lower cutoff point of .75 for PO in both Tables 6 and 7, then there remain only 12 possibilities for Table 6 data. The data deriving from Table 3 (shown in Table 7) are represented by the 6th case, which is exactly at the median of all possible values of PO, Kappa, P_{neg}, and P_{pos}. Again, an exact mathematical linear relationship between these four values becomes apparent. For every two percentage point decrease in the value of PO there are corresponding decreases of: .0909 in Kappa values; and .0114 and .0800 in P_{neg} and P_{pos} values, respectively (when carried to 4 decimal places).

As a further relevant comparison let us contrast the *ranges* of PO, Kappa, P_{neg}, and P_{pos} values for the data deriving from Tables 6 and 7 using a PO of 75% as

Table 7

Rank ordering of all possible Kappa values and other indices of agreement, when marginals are set at 85% and 15% for Examiner A, and at 90% and 10% for Examiner B

Case	A Neg B Neg	Pos Pos	Neg Pos	Pos Neg	PO	PC	Kappa	Kappa Kmax	P_{neg}	P_{pos}
1	85	10	5	0	.95	.78	.77	1.00	.97	.80
2	84	9	6	1	.93	.78	.68	.88	.96	.72
3	83	8	7	2	.91	.78	.59	.76	.95	.64
4	82	7	8	3	.89	.78	.50	.65	.94	.56
5	81	6	9	4	.87	.78	.41	.53	.93	.48
6	80	5	10	5	.85	.78	.32	.41	.91	.40
7	79	4	11	6	.83	.78	.23	.29	.90	.32
8	78	3	12	7	.81	.78	.14	.18	.89	.24
9	77	2	13	8	.79	.78	.05	.06	.88	.16
10	76	1	14	9	.77	.78	-.05	NA	.87	.08
11	75	0	15	10	.75	.78	-.14	NA	.86	.00

our lower limit. These can be summarized as:

Ranges of:

Table	PO	P_{neg}	P_{pos}	Kappa
6	75-97	.74-.97	.76-.97	.50- .94
7	75-95	.86-.97	.00-.80	-.14-+.77

Note that the ranges for PO are very similar in both tables. Also, the ranges of P_{neg} and P_{pos} values in Table 6 are almost interchangeable with the range of PO values. There is no such even distribution of PO (.75 - .95), P_{neg} (.86 - .97), and P_{pos} (.00 - .80) ranges of values for Table 7 data. Such disparate values are reflected in the generally higher values of Kappa produced in Table 6 relative to those deriving from Table 7.

These data serve to resolve paradox number 1, namely, why high levels of PO can nonetheless result in low levels of Kappa. They also serve to indict the practice of focusing upon omnibus indices such as PO rather than decomposing them into their respective components (e.g., P_{neg}, and P_{pos}) in this instance.

Resolving Paradoxes of the Second Kind

Recall the second paradox identified earlier, namely, the case for which the same high level of PO (i.e., 80% in both Tables 4 and 5) produced a much lower value of Kappa (.37) when the examiner marginals were *identical* (.80 - .20 for each examiner) than when the examiner marginals were appreciably different (.65 - .35 for Examiner A; .45 - .55 for Examiner B). Kappa in this second case was .61.

In order to resolve this paradox, we shall use the same logic as before, and rank order all possible values of PO, Kappa, P_{neg} and P_{pos}, first for the Table 4 data, then for the data deriving from Table 5. As previously, we will compare these four values both with respect to each other and in relation to all other possible pairings of Negative/Negative, Positive/Positive, Negative/Positive, and Positive/Negative combinations within the designated marginal constraints.

The Table 4 data (identical marginals of .80 - .20 and lower Kappa value of .37) is generalized as Table 8. Note that case 11 reflects Table 4 data and is exactly at the midpoint (median) of all possible values of PO, P_{neg}, and P_{pos}, and Kappa.

Note further that the P_{neg} and P_{pos} values of .87 and .50, respectively, are quite divergent from the PO value of .80.

Let us now contrast these values with those produced by generalizing the Table 5 data. The fourfold interexaminer configuration pattern of this table is exactly reproduced as the first case of Table 9. It represents the highest level that can occur from among 36 possibilities. Note also that the P_{neg} (.82) and P_{pos} (.78) values are quite close in value to that of PO (.80).

Thus Table 5 data represent a PO of .80, a P_{neg} of .82, a P_{pos} of .78, and a Kappa of .61. The Table 4 data, on the other hand, produce a PO of .80, but P_{neg} and P_{pos} values of .87 and .50, respectively, and a Kappa of .37.

It is left for the reader to discover, as previously, that in both Tables 8 and 9, there is a perfect linear regression of Kappa values upon P_{neg} and P_{pos} values.

Table 8

Rank ordering of all possible Kappa values and other indices of examiner agreement when marginals are set at 80% and 20% for both Examiners

Case	Examiner Pairing A Neg B Neg	Pos Pos	Neg Pos	Pos Neg	PO	PC	Kappa	P_{neg}	P_{pos}
1	80	20	0	0	1.00	.68	1.00	1.00	1.00
2	79	19	1	1	.98	.68	.94	.99	.95
3	78	18	2	2	.96	.68	.87	.97	.90
4	77	17	3	3	.94	.68	.81	.96	.85
5	76	16	4	4	.92	.68	.75	.95	.80
6	75	15	5	5	.90	.68	.69	.94	.75
7	74	14	6	6	.88	.68	.62	.92	.70
8	73	13	7	7	.86	.68	.56	.91	.65
9	72	12	8	8	.84	.68	.50	.90	.60
10	71	11	9	9	.82	.68	.44	.89	.55
11	70	10	10	10	.80	.68	.37	.87	.50
12	69	9	11	11	.78	.68	.31	.86	.45
13	68	8	12	12	.76	.68	.25	.85	.40
14	67	7	13	13	.74	.68	.19	.84	.35
15	66	6	14	14	.72	.68	.12	.82	.30
16	65	5	15	15	.70	.68	.06	.81	.25
17	64	4	16	16	.68	.68	.00	.80	.20
18	63	3	17	17	.66	.68	-.06	.79	.15
19	62	2	18	18	.64	.68	-.12	.77	.10
20	61	1	19	19	.62	.68	-.19	.76	.05
21	60	0	20	20	.60	.68	-.25	.75	.00

Table 9

Rank ordering of all possible Kappa values and other indices of examiner agreement when marginals are set at 65% and 35% for ExaminerA, and at 45% and 55% for Examiner B

Case	Examiner Pairing				PO	PC	Kappa	P_{neg}	P_{pos}
	A Neg B Neg	Pos Pos	Neg Pos	Pos Neg					
1	45	35	00	20	.80	.485	.61	.82	.78
2	44	34	01	21	.78	.485	.57	.80	.76
3	43	33	02	22	.76	.485	.53	.78	.73
4	42	32	03	23	.74	.485	.50	.76	.71
5	41	31	04	24	.72	.485	.46	.75	.69
6	40	30	05	25	.70	.485	.42	.73	.67
7	39	29	06	26	.68	.485	.38	.71	.64
8	38	28	07	27	.66	.485	.34	.69	.62
9	37	27	08	28	.64	.485	.30	.67	.60
10	36	26	09	29	.62	.485	.26	.65	.58
11	35	25	10	30	.60	.485	.22	.64	.56
12	34	24	11	31	.58	.485	.18	.62	.53
13	33	23	12	32	.56	.485	.15	.60	.51
14	32	22	13	33	.54	.485	.11	.58	.49
15	31	21	14	34	.52	.485	.07	.56	.47
16	30	20	15	35	.50	.485	.03	.55	.44
17	29	19	16	36	.48	.485	-.01	.53	.42
18	28	18	17	37	.46	.485	-.05	.51	.40
19	27	17	18	38	.44	.485	-.09	.49	.38
20	26	16	19	39	.42	.485	-.13	.47	.36
21	25	15	20	40	.40	.485	-.16	.45	.33
22	24	14	21	41	.38	.485	-.20	.44	.31
23	23	13	22	42	.36	.485	-.24	.42	.29
24	22	12	23	43	.34	.485	-.28	.40	.27
25	21	11	24	44	.32	.485	-.32	.38	.24
26	20	10	25	45	.30	.485	-.36	.36	.22
27	19	9	26	46	.28	.485	-.40	.35	.20
28	18	8	27	47	.26	.485	-.44	.33	.18
29	17	7	28	48	.24	.485	-.48	.31	.16
30	16	6	29	49	.22	.485	-.51	.29	.13
31	15	5	30	50	.20	.485	-.55	.27	.11
32	14	4	31	51	.18	.485	-.59	.25	.09
33	13	3	32	52	.16	.485	-.63	.24	.07
34	12	2	33	53	.14	.485	-.67	.22	.04
35	11	1	34	54	.12	.485	-.71	.20	.02
36	10	0	35	55	.10	.485	-.75	.18	.00

To summarize, the paradox produced by more dissimilar examiner marginals giving higher Kappa values than examiner marginals closer together is also resolved by appropriately generalizing the Tables being contrasted.

The next section of this report will examine the relative usefulness of statistical approaches other than Kappa for assessing levels of agreement deriving from

2x2 (or fourfold) tables.

Some Further Appropriate Reliability Indices

1. *Maximum Possible Agreement*

Cohen (1960, p. 42) noted that the maximum value of Kappa (1.00) cannot be achieved unless both sets of examiner marginals are identical (e.g., the data in Table 8). The maximum possible value of Kappa can be defined as:

$$\text{Kappa}_{max} (PO_{max}\text{-}PC)/(1\text{-}PC), \text{ in which} \tag{7}$$

PO_{max} refers to the maximum value that PO can attain in any given fourfold interexaminer agreement matrix.

PC is defined, as previously, in formula [2].

When the *smallest* of the four examiner marginals (expressed in proportions) is paired with its *opposite* diagonal marginal, the sum of these two proportions produces PO_{max}.

For example, in Table 2, $PO_{max} = (F_1 + G_2) = .97$. Since PC = .50, $\text{Kappa}_{max} = .94$ (see also the first entry of Table 6). In order to produce the maximum possible agreement for a given set of examiner marginals, one simply divides Kappa by Kappa_{max}. *Note:* When Kappa can assume its maximum value of $+ 1$, then both Kappa and Kappa_{max} values are identical. This occurs when both examiner marginals are equal (as in the Table 8 entries). When this is *not* true, one divides a given Kappa by the highest Kappa value possible (here .94). One then obtains the maximum chance-corrected agreement level possible for a given fourfold table with a given set of examiner marginals. For Table 1 data (entry 7, Table 6), $\text{Kappa}/\text{Kappa}_{max}$ is simply $.70/.94 = .74$. Alternatively, this value can be obtained by dividing (PO-PC) by $(PO_{max}\text{-}PC) = (.85\text{-}.50)/(.97\text{-}.50) = .74$. This value occurs for the seventh entry of Table 6 (where all other possible values of $\text{Kappa}/\text{Kappa}_{max}$ also appear). $\text{Kappa}/\text{Kappa}_{max}$ also has a perfect linear regression upon Kappa, PO, P_{neg}, and P_{pos}. When reporting $\text{Kappa}/\text{Kappa}_{max}$ values, it is especially useful to show corresponding Kappa values as well. This will alert the reader of the extent to which the value of Kappa was increased or improved by dividing its value by Kappa_{max}.

For comparative purposes, Tables 6 and 7 both contain all possible $\text{Kappa}/\text{Kappa}_{max}$ values. It should be noted that, as one might conjecture, the more dissimilar the examiner marginals, the greater the increase in $\text{Kappa}/\text{Kappa}_{max}$ values relative to the unadjusted Kappa values.

2. *The Chamberlain et al. (1975) P_{pos} Statistic*

In discussing examiner agreement in the context of a binary diagnosis of breast cancer (present/absent), Chamberlain et al. (1975) noted that, in screening for a disease of relatively low prevalence, most of the diagnoses will, per force, be negative. One might therefore choose to express consensus in terms of the proportion of examiner agreement on positive cases divided by those diagnosed as positive by one or both examiners. Utilizing, once again, the mathematical notation introduced in Table 1:

$$P_{pos\,(Chamberlain)} = D/(B+C+D) \qquad [8]$$

In the context of neuropsychological diagnoses, let us assume that two clinicians wish to establish the reliability of the diagnosis of Dyslexia, preliminary to the establisment of a treatment program for the disorder. Assume further that they are both well trained and work in a community in which the known prevalence of the disorder is about 10%. Consider the following results, based upon the independent, dual diagnoses of 200 children:

Neuropsychologist A

Neuropsychologist B	Dyslexic	Non-Dyslexic	Total
Dyslexic	.09	.01	.10
Non-Dyslexic	.01	.89	.90
Total	.10	.90	1.00

The two examining neuropsychologists decide that, since the negative cases are not of diagnostic interest, Chamberlain's P_{pos} statistic will be used to assess the reliability of the diagnosis of Dyslexia for the sample under study:

$$P_{pos\,(Chamberlain)} = .09/.11 \qquad [9]$$
$$= .8182$$
$$= .82$$

Chamberlain P_{pos} values for the generalization of Table 2 data are given in the last column of Table 6. As is true of PO, PC, Kappa, P_{neg}, P_{pos}, and Kappa/Kappa$_{max}$ values, Chamberlain P_{pos} values steadily decrease from the highest agreement to the lowest agreement case, depending upon the configuration of Neg/Neg, Pos/Pos, Neg/Pos, and Pos/Neg cells. However, there is *not* an exact linear regression of Chamberlain P_{pos} values on the other examiner agreement indices, as was true in the cases of Kappa and Kappa/Kappa$_{max}$ values[1].

Some Inappropriate Statistical Indices
1. Maxwell's RE Statistic
In an attempt to eliminate the phenomenon of high agreement (say 85%) associated with low Kappa values, Maxwell (1977) introduced the Random Error (RE) statistic for assessing observer agreement deriving from a fourfold table. Again using the mathematical notation of Table 1:

$$RE = [(A+D)-(B+C)]$$

[1] As stated, and using the notation of Table 1, Chamberlain's $P_{pos} = D/(B+C+D)$. In addition, Chamberlain's $P_{neg} = A/(A+B+C)$. These two indices, when summed, define PO as:
$$PO = [D/(B+C+D).(B+C+D)]+ [A/(A+B+C).(A+B+C)]$$
$$= A+D.$$

In order to evaluate the RE statistic, consider the data in Table 10. There are 43 cases of all possible combinations of Pos/Pos, Neg/Neg, Pos/Neg and Neg/Pos values when PO $= .85$. These result in: Kappas ranging between .70 and -.08; Kappa/Kappa$_{max}$ values between .74 and .05; P$_{pos}$ values between .85 and .00; and P$_{neg}$ values between .85 and .92.

In each of these 43 cases, RE assumes the *same* value of .85 - .15 or .70 (the size of the *maximum* Kappa value that is possible). This phenomenon occurs because RE is *always* identical to Kappa defined in the restricted sense of (PO - .5)/ (1-.5). Clearly, a statistic which assigns the maximum level of chance-corrected agreement to both the best case (entry 1 of Table 10) and worst case (entry 43 of Table 10) possible is so lacking in discriminatory power as to be quite limited in usefulness as a measure of interexaminer agreement.

2. *Yule's Y Statistic*

In 1985, Spitznagel and Helzer reintroduced Yule's Y statistic, in the binary case, to overcome Kappa's prevalence or "base rate problem." If we continue to use our notation, then (in frequencies)

$$\text{Yule's Y} = (\sqrt{AD} - \sqrt{BC})/(\sqrt{AD} + \sqrt{BC}). \qquad [11]$$

The problems associated with considering Yule's Y as an alternative to Kappa will now be identified. Conceptually, and as correctly noted by Shrout, Spitzer, and Fleiss (1987): (1) Yule's Y, (akin to its odds-ratio sibling) is a measure of association, and *not* a measure of examiner agreement; (2) Unlike Kappa, the Y statistic involves taking a ratio of differences to summations of cross products. This quantity, a function of the odds ratio, has no obvious intuitive appeal, representing a nonlinear square root transformation of both AD and BC.

The inappropriateness of Yule's Y as a measure of observer agreement can be shown in cases in which both Pos/Pos and Neg/Neg values are held constant (i.e., PO), but both Pos/Neg and Neg/Pos values are allowed to vary over all possible values. In such cases the resulting values of PO, P$_{pos}$, P$_{neg}$, and Chamberlain's P$_{pos}$ will remain constant throughout. Kappa values will likewise be very similar across all possible combinations. However, the values of Y will vary across a wide range, equalling Kappa only when the two disagreement cells are identical (or very similar). However, as the imbalance in disagreement cells increases, so will the value of Y relative to Kappa. This discrepancy will reach a zenith when one of the disagreement cells is zero.

This phenomenon can be identified in Table 11. Here both agreement cells are held constant at .42 and .43, respectively, while the two disagreement cells (Pos/Neg and Neg/Pos) are allowed to vary across all 16 possible combinations (0-15 to 15-0). Note that: (a) P$_{pos}$, P$_{neg}$, and Chamberlain's 1975 P$_{pos}$ remain constant at .85, .85 and .74, respectively; and (b) Kappa also remains quite constant (14/16 values at .70; the remaining 2 at .71). However, Yule's Y varies between .70 and .88 with 10/16 values falling beyond the narrow Kappa range of .70 to .71.

These data show that Yule's Y is *not* a useful reliability statistic since it can

Table 10

Rank ordering of all possible values of Kappa, P_{pos} and P_{neg} when PO is held constant at 85%, in the binary case

| | Examiner Pairing | | | | | | | | | | Maxwell's RE |
| | A Pos | Neg | Pos | Neg | | | | *Kappa* | | | |
Case	B Pos	Neg	Neg	Pos	PO	PC	Kappa	Kmax	P_{pos}	P_{neg}	Statistic
1	42	43	9	6	.85	.50	.70	.74	.85	.85	.70
2	41	44	9	6	.85	.50	.70	.74	.85	.85	.70
3	40	45	9	6	.85	.50	.70	.74	.84	.86	.70
4	39	46	9	6	.85	.50	.70	.74	.84	.86	.70
5	38	47	9	6	.85	.50	.70	.74	.84	.86	.70
6	37	48	9	6	.85	.50	.70	.74	.83	.86	.70
7	36	49	9	6	.85	.51	.70	.74	.83	.87	.70
8	35	50	9	6	.85	.51	.69	.74	.82	.87	.70
9	34	51	9	6	.85	.51	.69	.74	.82	.87	.70
10	33	52	9	6	.85	.52	.69	.73	.81	.87	.70
11	32	53	9	6	.85	.52	.69	.73	.81	.88	.70
12	31	54	9	6	.85	.53	.68	.73	.81	.88	.70
13	30	55	9	6	.85	.54	.68	.73	.80	.88	.70
14	29	56	9	6	.85	.54	.68	.72	.79	.88	.70
15	28	57	9	6	.85	:54	.67	.72	.79	.88	.70
16	27	58	9	6	.85	.55	.67	.72	.78	.89	.70
17	26	59	9	6	.85	.55	.66	.71	.78	.89	.70
18	25	60	9	6	.85	.56	.66	.71	.77	.89	.70
19	24	61	9	6	.85	.57	.65	.70	.76	.89	.70
20	23	62	9	6	.85	.58	.65	.70	.75	.89	.70
21	22	63	9	6	.85	.58	.64	.69	.75	.89	.70
22	21	64	9	6	.85	.59	.63	.68	.74	.90	.70
23	20	65	9	6	.85	.60	.62	.68	.73	.90	.70
24	19	66	9	6	.85	.61	.62	.67	.72	.90	.70
25	18	67	9	6	.85	.62	.61	.66	.71	.90	.70
26	17	68	9	6	.85	.63	.60	.65	.69	.90	.70
27	16	69	9	6	.85	.64	.58	.64	.68	.90	.70
28	15	70	9	6	.85	.65	.57	.62	.67	.90	.70
29	14	71	9	6	.85	.66	.56	.61	.65	.90	.70
30	13	72	9	6	.85	.67	.54	.60	.63	.91	.70
31	12	73	9	6	.85	.69	.52	.58	.62	.91	.70
32	11	74	9	6	.85	.70	.50	.56	.59	.91	.70
33	10	75	9	6	.85	.71	.48	.54	.57	.91	.70
34	9	76	9	6	.85	.72	.46	.51	.55	.91	.70
35	8	77	9	6	.85	.74	.43	.48	.52	.91	.70
36	7	78	9	6	.85	.75	.40	.45	.48	.91	.70
37	6	79	9	6	.85	.77	.36	.41	.44	.91	.70
38	5	80	9	6	.85	.78	.32	.37	.40	.91	.70
39	4	81	9	6	.85	.80	.26	.31	.35	.92	.70
40	3	82	9	6	.85	.81	.20	.24	.29	.92	.70
41	2	83	9	6	.85	.83	.13	.16	.21	.92	.70
42	1	84	9	6	.85	.84	.04	.05	.12	.92	.70
43	0	85	9	6	.85	.86	-.08	NA	.00	.92	.70

Table 11

Rank ordering of Kappa and other indices of observer agreement with Yule's Y statistic when the percentage of agreement on positive and negative cases is held constant while the two disagreement cells vary over all possible combinations

	Examiner Pairing									Chamberlain's	Yule's
	A Pos	Neg	Pos	Neg							
Case	B Pos	Neg	Neg	Pos	PO	PC	Kappa	P_{Pos}	P_{neg}	(1975) P_{neg}	Y
1	42	43	0	15	.85	.49	.71	.85	.85	.74	.88
2	42	43	1	14	.85	.49	.70	.85	.85	.74	.84
3	42	43	2	13	.85	.49	.70	.85	.85	.74	.79
4	42	43	3	12	.85	.49	.70	.85	.85	.74	.75
5	42	43	4	11	.85	.49	.70	.85	.85	.74	.73
6	42	43	5	10	.85	.49	.70	.85	.85	.74	.71
7	42	43	6	9	.85	.49	.70	.85	.85	.74	.71
8	42	43	7	8	.85	.49	.70	.85	.85	.74	.70
9	42	43	8	7	.85	.49	.70	.85	.85	.74	.70
10	42	43	9	6	.85	.49	.70	.85	.85	.74	.71
11	42	43	10	5	.85	.49	.70	.85	.85	.74	.71
12	42	43	11	4	.85	.49	.70	.85	.85	.74	.73
13	42	43	12	3	.85	.49	.70	.85	.85	.74	.75
14	42	43	13	2	.85	.49	.70	.85	.85	.74	.79
15	42	43	14	1	.85	.49	.70	.85	.85	.74	.84
16	42	43	15	0	.85	.49	.71	.85	.85	.74	.88

often *over*estimate the extent of interexaminer agreement. This undesirable property would rule out Yule's Y as a valid meaure of interexaminer agreement in the binary case.

A number of other indices of observer agreement are available for the binary case (e.g., see Goodman & Kruskal, 1954, and Armitage, Blendis, & Smyllie, 1966). However, Fleiss (1975) has shown that mostly all of these statistics become methematically equivalent to Kappa with only minor adjustments. Secondly, while the present report has focused upon the binary case, it should be noted that the Kappa statistic is the only one of its genre which has been appropriately generalized to fit reliability designs which vary according to scale of measurement (nominal, ordinal, dimensional (continuous)), number of observers, and whether the same or different sets of observers are employed (Fleiss, 1981).

In closing, some important caveats need to be stressed. First, it is fully realized that there is often a clinically justifiable diagnostic need for neuropsychologists to dichotomize data which originally appeared in a continuous or dimensional scale format. Yet this important clinical task must be accomplished with great sensitivity and should not be applied in a post hoc fashion unless replication is part of the overall analytic strategy. For an estimate of just how much information can be lost when continuous data are inappropriately dichotomized, see Cohen (1983). For the effect the dichotomization procedure can have in raising the incidence of Type I or alpha errors, for other neuropsychological variables, see Soper, Cicchetti, Satz, Light, and Orsini (1988).

As a final caveat, neuropsychologists are strongly urged to present (either in text or in tabular format) the fourfold table of any reliability data they wish to publish. This is especially crucial since, as we have seen, any given overall index of interexaminer agreement can mask and at times even misrepresent the true level of diagnostic reliability. Thus, a Chamberlain P_{pos} value of .94, presented alone, can mask the fact that the corresponding P_{neg} value may be only .67; a Kappa value of .40 associated with a PO value of .70 is quite different in clinical meaning than the same level of kappa associated with a PO value of .95; a PO value of .90 with corresponding P_{pos} and P_{neg} values of .90 is quite different than a PO value of .90 associated with a P_{pos} value of .95 and a P_{neg} value of .55.

At a more general level, and using the data presented in this paper as only a specific instance, it is incumbent upon all of us, as clinical investigators, not only to examine data at the most molar level but also at finer and finer levels of molecular analysis, so that the resulting clinical picture becomes a truer representation of reality than would otherwise be the case.

REFERENCES

Armitage, P., Blendis, L. M., & Smyllie, H. C. (1966). The measurement of observer disagreement in the recording of sighs. *Journal of the Royal Statistical Society, Series A, 129,* 98-109.

Chamberlain, J., Ginks, S., Rogers, P., Nathan, B. E., Price, J. L., & Burn, I. (1975). Validity of clinical examination and mammography as screening tests for breast cancer. *Lancet, 2,* 1026-1030.

Cicchetti, D. V., Lee, C., Fontana, A. F., & Dowds, N. B. (1978). A computer program for assessing specific category rater agreement for qualitative data. *Educational and Psychological Measurement, 38,* 805-813.

Cicchetti, D. V., & Sparrow, S. S. (1981). Developing criteria for establishing the interrater reliability of specific items in a given inventory: Applications to assessment of adaptive behavior. *American Journal of Mental Deficiency, 86,* 127-137.

Cohen, J. (1960). A coefficient of agreement for nominal scales. *Educational and Psychological Measurement, 20,* 37-46.

Cohen, J. (1983). The cost of dichotomization. *Applied Psychological Measurement, 7,* 249-253.

Fleiss, J. L. (1975). Measuring agreement between two judges on the presence or absence of a trait. *Biometrics, 31,* 651-659.

Fleiss, J.L. (1981). Statistical methods for rates and proportions (2nd ed.). New York: Wiley (Chapter 13).

Fleiss, J. L., Cohen, J., & Everitt, B. S. (1969). Large sample standard errors of kappa and weighted kappa. *Psychological Bulletin, 72,* 323-327.

Goodman, L. A., & Kruskal, W. H. (1954). Measures of association for cross classification. *Journal of the American Statistical Association, 49,* 732-764.

Grove, W. M., Andreason, N. C., McDonald-Scott, P., Keller, M. B., & Shapiro, R. W.

434

(1981). Reliability studies of psychiatric diagnosis: Theory and practice. *Archives of General Psychiatry, 38,* 408-413.

Kraemer, H. C. (1979). Ramifications of a population model for kappa as a coefficient of reliability. *Psychometrika, 44,* 461-472.

McClure, M., & Willett, W. C. (1987). Misinterpretation and misuse of the kappa statistic. *American Journal of Epidemiology, 126,* 161-169.

Maxwell, A. E. (1977). Coefficients of agreement between observers and their interpretation. *British Journal of Psychiatry. 130,* 79-83.

Reitan, R. M., & Davison, L. A. (1974). *Clinical neuropsychology: Current status and applications.* Washington, DC: Winston.

Shrout, P. E., Spitzer, R. L., & Fleiss, J. L. (1987). Quantification of agreement in psychiatric diagnosis revisited. *Archives of General Psychiatry, 44,* 172-177.

Soper, H. V., Cicchetti, D. V., Satz, P., Light, R., & Orsini, D. L. (1988). Null hypothesis disrespect in neuropsychology: Dangers of alpha and beta errors. *Journal of Clinical and Experimental Neuropsychology, 10,* 255-270.

Spitzer, R. L., & Fleiss, J. L. (1974). A re-analysis of the reliability of psychiatric diagnosis. *British Journal of Psychiatry, 125,* 341-347.

Spitznagel, E. L., & Helzer, J. E. (1985). A proposed solution to the base rate problem in the kappa statistic. *Archives of General Psychiatry, 42,* 725-728.

Journal of Clinical and Experimental Neuropsychology
1991, Vol. 13, No. 2, pp. 328-338

V-C

Establishing the Reliability and Validity of Neuropsychological Disorders With Low Base Rates: Some Recommended Guidelines*

Domenic V. Cicchetti
West Haven VA Medical Center

Sara S. Sparrow, Fred Volkmar,
and Donald Cohen
Yale Child Study Center

Byron P. Rourke
University of Windsor

ABSTRACT

The issues of low prevalence in the context of the diagnosis of neuropsychological disorders in the larger community is discussed. Guidelines are proposed for producing reliability and validity estimates which are clinically, as well as statistically meaningful.

The recent clinical and biostatistical literature has examined the extent to which low base rates (prevalence, incidence) affect the reliability of diagnosis of specific disorders (e.g., Grove, Andreason, McDonald-Scott, Keller, & Shapiro, 1981; Kraemer, 1979, 1987; McClure & Willett, 1987; and Uebersax, 1987). In fact, if one were to perceive correctly the message inherent in recent biostatistical arguments on this subject (notably the work of Spitznagel & Helzer, 1985), one would conclude that low base rates of a disorder and low reliability of identification of that same disorder, in the manner of the proverbial "love and marriage" or "horse and carriage," must *per force,* always "go together." Spitznagel and Helzer (1985) argue that this so-called "base rate" problem is caused by applying an "invalid" reliability statistic (kappa). The authors reason further that kappa should be replaced by Yule's (1912) Y statistic which they believe is not so affected by base rates.

Several biostatistical workers in the field have seriously challenged the Spitznagel and Helzer assertion that low base rates necessarily produce low kappas. Shrout, Spitzer, and Fleiss (1987) have demonstrated convincingly that

* This research was, in part, supported by an award from the Medical Research Service of the Veterans' Administration (MRIS-1416).

kappa's mathematical properties *define* it as "a true reliability statistic" (p. 175), while Yule's Y cannot be so defended. Shrout et al. (1987) also provided empirical support for the argument that progressively lower base rates do not *of necessity* covary with values of kappa. Specifically, results deriving from each of *two* phases of DSM-III field trials (American Psychiatric Association, 1980) indicate that a number of adult disorders with very low prevalence rates (1.5% to 2.4%) nonetheless show excellent kappa values, namely: .75 and .92 for the diagnostic reliability of Psychosocial Disorder; and .85 and .91 for the diagnostic reliability of Dementias arising in the senium and presenium. On the basis of such data, Shrout et al. (1987, pp. 176-177) conclude correctly that there is "no mathematical necessity for small kappa values with low sample base rates."

Kraemer (1987) also disagrees with Spitznagel and Helzer (1985). She employs a signal (identification of *positive* cases) to noise model (separating out errors of measurement, illness-related factors and other factors) and reasons correctly that "to achieve a high signal to noise ratio in a low-or-high-risk population, the signal must be amplified (multiple or consensus diagnosis, better diagnostic procedures), or the noise attenuated (better diagnostic training, better standardization of testing conditions, better tests, better prescreening of patients). Seeking instead to find a statistic less sensitive to the true situation is a form of avoidance" (Kraemer, 1987, p. 192).

Uebersax (1987) again argues that kappa is *not* "responsible" for low levels of reliability when base rates are correspondingly low. Specifically, Uebersax (1987, p. 194) notes that "to really solve the 'base rate problem,' then, it may be necessary to measure agreement on presence and absence of a disorder separately, as is done, for example, with the proportion of specific agreement discussed by Spitzer and Fleiss (1974)."

Cicchetti (1985) presented data to support the more general hypothesis that across varying base rates (ranging from very low to very high) kappa-type statistics will: (a) produce their highest levels when the disparity between agreement on positive and negative cases is least; and (b) produce progressively lower levels as the extent of specific agreement shifts toward a nadir of 0% on *positive* cases and toward a zenith of 100% on *negative* cases. These arguments were presented more fully in the context of paradoxes in reliability levels which can occur following neuropsychological diagnostic assessments (Cicchetti, 1988). This paper also notes serious deficiencies of Yule's Y as a reliability statistic in its own right.

It should be noted, finally, that in the ideal case in which *the diagnostic assignments of two independent examiners are in complete agreement* (e.g., *both* assign a *positive* diagnosis to 5% of the cases and a *negative* diagnosis to the remaining 95%), the value of kappa, for all logically possible levels of interexaminer agreement, will be mathematically *identical* to those values obtained using other standard statistical approaches:

(1) For the *reliability* case:

Kappa = the phi coefficient = the standard Pearsonian Product Moment Correlation, when applied to dichotomous data.*

(2) In the *validity* case (in which the *accuracy* of the diagnosis is known):
Kappa = [(Sensitivity + Specificity) - 1] (e.g., see Kraemer, 1982, p. 750; and Youden, 1950).

Having said all this, what caveats remain to be discussed when the kappa procedure is applied to determine the reliability of a low prevalence disorder? Shrout et al. (1987) note that one needs to be sensitive to three fundamental issues: (1) "... the demand placed on a procedure when it is used to study rare disorders" (p. 174); (2) "... the real problem of making distinctions in increasingly homogeneous populations" (p. 175); and (3) the fact that "since few true-positive cases are expected, even a small number of false-positives may undermine the overall reliability of the procedure" (p. 176).

In order to appreciate the practical implications of these quotations, one can consider the *ramifications* of the following hypothetical reliability assessment problem, as it was presented in Shrout et al. (1987). Two clinical examiners each diagnose independently 100 cases as either "positive" or "negative." Further, the clinicians: (a) are in complete agreement in their diagnostic assignments, such that 6 of the cases are diagnosed as "positive" and 94 as "negative" by each of the two examiners; (b) agree on a "positive" diagnosis for 3 of 6 cases; (c) agree on a "negative" diagnosis for 91 of the 94 remaining cases; and (d) disagree, in an unbiased fashion, on the 6 positively diagnosed cases, such that 3 receive a "negative" diagnosis from the first examiner and a "positive" diagnosis from the second one, while the remaining 3 cases fit a mirror-opposite disagreement pattern, in which the first examiner assigns a "positive" diagnosis and the second examiner assigns a "negative" diagnosis. These data are presented as Case 4 in Table 1, along with the remaining 6 diagnostic patterns that are logically possible when the agreement on positive cases is allowed to vary between 0% (0/6 cases in agreement) and 100% (6/6 cases in agreement).** It should be noted that

* It should be stressed that the identities presented only hold in the ideal case of 100% interexaminer agreement in diagnostic assignments. To the extent that these vary, the phi coefficient and the Pearsonian Product Moment Correlation should not be used in lieu of kappa (e.g., see Shrout, Spitzer, & Fleiss, 1987). Moreover, the important specific components of kappa (e.g., PO, PC, P_{pos}, and P_{neg}) are not derivatives of phi and the Pearson r.

** While these logical possibilities assume equivalence in interexaminer diagnostic assignments (here, 6% *positive* and 94% *negative* diagnostic assignments for *both* examiners), the results presented will be very similar, even in cases in which the diagnostic assignments for positive cases differ as widely as possible. This will hold, providing only that the examiners assign *on-the-average,* the same number of positive cases as they do in this hypothetical series. As one example, in case 4, if the 6 cases of disagreement on positive cases were all ones in which examiner 1 gave a positive diagnosis and examiner 2 gave a negative diagnosis, the values for PO, PC, kappa, P_{pos}, and P_{neg} would remain identical except that kappa would be .48 as compared to the value of .47 given in Table 1. Note that in the original case *both* examiners diagnose 6 cases as positive. In the most extreme case, examiner 1 assigns a positive diagnosis to 3 cases while examiner 2 assigns 9 cases a positive diagnosis. However, *on-the-average* the two examiners still diagnose 6 cases as positive (i.e., (3 +9)/2 = 6).

while this example is purely apocryphal, it would represent all logically possible interexaminer agreement levels for community diagnosed Developmental Coordination Disorder as detected in 100 five-to eleven-year-old children (i.e., the 6% prevalence rate given in DSM-III-R-American Psychiatric Association, 1987, pp. 48-49).

These data demonstrate that a single-case shift in examiner agreement on positive diagnoses (e.g., 4/6–Case 3 vs. 5/6–Case 4): (1) will, as expected, affect, only minimally, both the overall agreement level (PO) as well as the agreement on negative cases (p_{neg}). Thus, PO will increase from .97 (when there is agreement on 4 of the 6 cases diagnosed as "positive") to .98 (when the examiners agree on 5 of 6 "positive" cases); (2) likewise, p_{neg} will increase only slightly (.98 for the 4/6 case to .99 for the 5/6 case); (3) in bold contrast, both the agreement on "positive" cases and the value of kappa will increase dramatically when agreement on "positive" cases improved from 4/6 to 5/6. Thus, p_{pos} will increase from .67 to .83 and, similarly, kappa will improve from .64 to .82 (increases from "GOOD" to "EXCELLENT" levels of clinical significance, based upon the criteria of Cicchetti & Sparrow, 1981).

Table 1. Rank orderings of all possible Kappa values[1] and other indices of interexaminer agreement when each of two independent examiners assigns 6 of 100 cases a "positive" diagnosis and the remaining 94 a "negative" diagnosis.

Case	A B	Pos Pos	Neg Neg	Pos Neg	Neg Pos	PO	PC	Kappa[2]	p_{pos}	p_{neg}
1		6	94	0	0	1.00	.89	1.00	1.00	1.00
2		5	93	1	1	.98	.89	.82 (E)[3]	.83	.99
3		4	92	2	2	.96	.89	.64 (G)[3]	.67	.98
4		3	91	3	3	.94	.89	.47 (F)[3]	.50	.97
5		2	90	4	4	.92	.89	.29 (P)[3]	.33	.96
6		1	89	5	5	.90	.89	.11 (P)[3]	.17	.95
7		0	88	6	6	.88	.89	−.06	.00	.94

[1] Kappa (Cohen, 1960; Fleiss et al., 1969) is defined as the difference between observed and expected agreement, divided by the maximum difference that is possible between the Proportion of Observed (PO) and the Proportion of Chance (PC) agreement: Kappa = (PO-PC)/(1-PC).

[2] Case 4 derives from the hypothetical data set presented in Shrout et al. (1987, p. 173) and is exactly at the median of all possible levels of agreement when diagnostic assignments are set for each examiner at 6 positive and 94 negative cases.

[3] It should be noted that a kappa value of .40 or greater, based upon a total N of 100 or more cases, will invariably produce statistically significant results at well beyond the conventional .05 level. According to the criteria of Cicchetti and Sparrow (1981), and consistent with those provided by Fleiss (1981), the clinical significance level of kappa values are: below .40 = POOR (P); .40-.59 = FAIR/MODERATE; .60-.74 = GOOD; and .75 and above = EXCELLENT.

In this hypothetical example, the number of cases diagnosed by each examiner as *positive* was 6. Even more dramatic results would have occurred with yet smaller numbers. Suppose there were only 3 cases diagnosed by each examiner as "positive". The only logical possibilities for agreement on positive cases (p_{pos}) would be 3/3 (100%), 2/3 (67%), 1/3 (33%), and 0/3 (0%). For these same data, the corresponding agreement on "negative" cases would be 97/97 (100%), 96/97 (99%); 95/97 (98%); and 94/97 (97%); and finally, the values of kappa would become 1.00 (Perfect, .66 (Good), .31 (Poor) agreement; or –.03 (*below* chance expectancy). These represent a .34 difference in the size of kappa for a one-case shift in agreement on positive cases. Obviously, the reader can verify that reducing the number of cases even more will produce ever more unstable results. The point to be made here is that since one can make such calculations *a priori,* that is to say, before launching into reliability testing of a new instrument, one should judiciously avoid engaging in research that will produce very unstable, likely unreproducible results, since the shifting of a single case or two can result in a diagnostic instrument's reliability level going from "excellent" to "poor", or clinically unacceptable.

These examples suffice to underscore the Shrout et al. (1987) and the Kraemer (1987) caveats concerning the strain that low prevalence disorders can potentially make upon a given reliability assessment, *no matter how valid the statistical approach.* What then to do in such circumstances? One can simply avoid studying those community disorders with very low base rates. However, as we have already shown, low base rates do not guarantee low kappa values (e.g., Shrout et al., 1987; the data in Table 1). Moreover, if one refused to assess the reliability of neuropsychological diagnoses with base rate less than 5% "this would rule out the study of reliability of all but a handful of diagnoses in the community" (Shrout et al., 1987; p. 174). Clearly, then, such a bold strategy is simply *not* a viable alternative. What would qualify as such?

In addition to the aforementioned suggestions of Kraemer (1987), within the context of her signal-detection model (see also Kraemer, 1988 and Swets, 1988), we can also pool research resources in order to increase the number of positive cases for a given rare disorder. Thus, cooperative studies can be designed in which various centers, academic institutions, private organizations, and federal agencies, all using the same protocol, can pool their data. Despite all of these suggestions, there remains the question of what would be a reasonable cut-off level in terms of numbers of positive cases, *below which* it would be hazardous to make the diagnostic venture, but *at and above which* the situation would become more and more potentially fruitful as a research endeavor? Clearly, we have seen that 6 cases out of 100 is arguably too few. But what can we learn from this? Why does this happen? One important issue, which was "evident" in our examples but not identified as such, is what might be referred to as a comparison of denominators which represent, simply, the number of positive or negative cases. When there is a large discrepancy between the two, say, 5 cases diagnosed positive, 95 cases diagnosed negative (on-the-average) by two independent clinical examiners, the six logically possible levels of agreement on *positive* cases decrease by 20 percentage points per subject (i.e., 5/5 = 100%; to 4/5 = 80%; to 3/5 = 60%; . . . 0/5 = 0%). However, the *corresponding* decreases in agreement on *negative* cases are 95/95 = 100%; to 94/95 = 99%; to 93/95 = 98%; to 92/95 = 97%; to 91/95 = 96%; to 90/95 = 95%). Thus, when agreement on *negative* cases is still at 98% (93/95), agreement on *positive* cases is only at 60% (3/5). As noted earlier (Cicchetti, 1988), it is this large discrepancy in agreement on positive and negative cases that favors lower kappa values.

If one were to select an absolute number of *positive* cases, on-the-average, that would (a) be relatively easy to obtain; and (b) not be an absolute strain on any valid reliability statistic, what might that number be? Our suggestion would be a minimum of 10 positive cases which would produce a rather wide range of agreement levels (i.e., 10/10 = 100%; 9/10 = 90%; 8/10 = 80%; . . . 0/10 = 0%).

[Note: This number (N=10) exceeds the $2k^2$ minimal N estimate required for valid application of the kappa statistic, as empirically shown by Cicchetti (1981) and earlier by Cicchetti and Fleiss (1977). In these investigations, the number of k categories of classification ranged between 3 and 10.]

Suppose we were interested in assessing the reliability of Developmental Articulation Disorder, in children under 8 years of age. According to the most recent DSM-III-R guidelines (American Psychiatric Association, 1987), the disorder has an estimated community prevalence of about 10%. In order to meet our criterion of the minimal number of 10 cases, for a given low prevalence disorder, neuropsychologists, interested in assessing the reliability of the presence or absence of Developmental Articulation Disorder (DAD) would obviously require a *minimal* total community sample size of 100 (since 10/.10 = 100). Thus, for every 100 cases of children under 8 years of age, drawn randomly from the general community, we should expect, *"on-the-average"* 90 children to test negatively for the disorder and 10 to test positively for DAD. The minimal *(on-the average)* total community sample sizes required to study prototypic neuropsychological disorders with estimated prevalences ranging between 5% and 1% are given in Table 2. These were determined by dividing 10 by the estimated prevalence (Prev) of each disorder.

In the application of any diagnostic instrument (new or standard), the clinical neuropsychologist is interested in providing answers to the following questions: Is the instrument reliable, both statistically and clinically, for (a) positive cases; (b) negative cases; (c) both; or (d) neither. We shall see how the answer to this question can be found with regard to a 5% prevalence rate disorder such as the Developmental Articulation Disorder in Children under 8 years of age. The data in Table 3 illustrate the rank orderings of all possible kappa values and related indices of interexaminer agreement when each of two clinicians independently assigns 10 of 200 cases (5%) a positive diagnosis and the remaining 190 (95%) a negative diagnosis. Note that for every shift in agreement on positive cases (e.g.,

Table 2. Recommended minimal sample size requirements for prototypic neuropsychological disorders with estimated community prevalences ranging between 1 and 5 percent.

DSM-III-R (1987) Estimated Prevalence[a]	Neuropsychologic Disorder	Diagnostic Group	Age Range	Gender	Recommended Minimal Sample Sizes		
					Number Positive Cases	Number Negative Cases	Total Number of Required Cases (10/prevalence)
5%	Developmental Articulation	Children	8 years	Both	10	190	200
4%	Primary Degeneration Dementia (Alzheimer's)	Adults	65 years	Both	10	240	250
3%	Attention Deficit Hyperactivity	Children	18 years	Both	10	323	333
2%	Conduct Disorder	Children	18 years	Females	10	490	500
1%	Mental Retardation	Children and Adults	All Ages	Both	10	990	1000

[a]Taken from DSM-III-R (American Psychiatric Association, 1987)

Table 3. Hypothetical Reliability Estimates of Developmental Articulation Disorder in Children Under 8 Years of Age (DSM-III-R, 1987).

Rank orderings of all possible Kappa values and other indices of interexaminer agreement when each of two independent examiners (A, B(assigns 10 of 200 cases a "positive" diagnosis and the remaining 190 a "negative" diagnosis).

Case	A B	Pos Pos	Neg Neg	Pos Neg	Neg Pos	PO	PC	Kappa	P_{pos}	P_{neg}	Se	Sp
1	10	190	0	0	1.00	.905	1.00	1.00	1.00	1.00	1.00
2	9	189	1	1	.99	.905	.89 (E)	.90	.99	.90	.99
3	8	188	2	2	.98	.905	.79 (E)	.80	.99	.80	.99
4	7	187	3	3	.97	.905	.68 (G)	.70	.98	.70	.98
5	6	186	4	4	.96	.905	.58 (F)	.60	.98	.60	.98
6	5	185	5	5	.95	.905	.47 (F)	.50	.97	.50	.97
7	4	184	6	6	.94	.905	.37 (P)	.40	.97	.40	.97
8	3	183	7	7	.93	.905	.26 (P)	.30	.96	.30	.96
9	2	182	8	8	.92	.905	.16 (P)	.20	.96	.20	.96
10	1	181	9	9	.91	.905	.05 (P)	.10	.95	.10	.95
11	0	180	10	10	.90	.905	−.05	.00	.95	.00	.95

from 9/10 to 8/10) there is a corresponding shift in kappa values of .1053 (which rounds to between 10 and 11%).

With respect to the question just posed, two neuropsychologists, examining independently the reliability of any DSM-III-R disorder, ranging between 1% and 5% prevalence (or incidence), would require a minimum of 10 positive cases. However, the *total* number of sampled cases would need to vary *on-the-average,* between 200 (for a 5% estimated prevalence disorder such as Developmental Articulation in children under 8 years of age) and 1000 (for assessing a 1% prevalence disorder, such as DSM-III-R diagnosed Mental Retardation).

It should be noted further that at times there may be interest in obtaining samples which are consistent with relevant demographic mixes within given nosologic categories. Thus, for example, in a disorder such as Reading Disability, a reasonable estimate of overall prevalence is about 2%. Thus for every 10 positive cases, on-the-average, one would need to sample randomly from about 500 cases in the community (since 10/500 = 2%). However, if the sample is to be balanced in terms of the estimated 6 to 1 prevalence of Reading Disability, in favor of males, then one would be speaking of an overall 2% prevalence, weighted by 6/7 for males, (or 6/7 x 2% = .017); and weighted by 1/7 for females (or 1/7 x 2% = .003). In recalculating the required numbers of community cases required to study reliably this disorder we would need 10/.017 or 588 males and 10/.003 or 3333 females.

Another important issue which needs to be considered before neuropsychologists embark into the community to study rare disorders is the effect of improved medical technologies which increase the likelihood that persons born with life threatening rare disorders will survive and thereby increase the prevalence of the disorder in question. As one recent example, the changing (developing) medical technologies that have enhanced the probability of survival of children with serious neurological disease has had concomitant impact of increased probability of the incidence of Nonverbal Learning Disorders (NLD) (Rourke, 1987, 1990; Cicchetti, Sparrow, & Rourke, *in press*). Survivors of pediatric head injury (HI), intracranial hemorrhage, lymphocytic leukemia (to name but a few) increase the ranks of persons who have a high probability of exhibiting the NLD syndrome. Hence, we would predict that the incidence will continue to rise as the medical technologies capable of increasing the probability of survival of children with potential for exhibiting NLD rises. Thus, the current estimated probability of 1% for the community prevalence rate of NLD will probably rise to 1.5% or even 2.0% of the school-age population within the next decade or so. Within the context of the present paper, this would mean a decrease in the recommended minimum sample size for studying NLD in the community, from 1000 (10/.01) to 667 (10/.015) to 500 (10/.02), as medical technologies continue to improve.

While the preceding discussion has focused exclusively upon the problem of prevalence and the reliability of diagnosis issue, it should be noted that the same arguments hold for validity. In recent years, there has been an increasing tendency for behavioral scientists to utilize the best available clinical diagnosis as the gold standard (best estimate of "true diagnosis") against which to compare the sensitivity, specificity and related indexes of diagnostic accuracy (e.g., Baldessarini, Finklestein, & Arana, 1983). Two recent examples include the DSM-III diagnosis of dementia (Anthony, LeResche, Niaz, von Korff, & Folstein, 1982), and the DSM-III and DSM-III-R diagnoses of Autism (Volkmar, Bregman, Cohen, & Cicchetti, 1988). It will be recalled that when the independent examiners' diagnostic assignments to positive and negative cases are identical *(or very nearly so)* then:

$$\text{Kappa} = [(\text{Sensitivity (Se)} + \text{Specificity (Sp)}) - 1] \tag{1}$$

When this formula is used to derive Se and Sp (as in the final two columns of data in Table 3) then an interesting finding emerges, namely, Se bears an equivalence to the agreement on positive cases (p_{pos}) and Sp bears an analogous equivalence to the agreement on negative cases (p_{neg}).

In summary, these comments and observations concerning the impact of prevalence upon the reliability and validity of diagnoses of rare disorders will be of use to those clinical research neuropsychologists who are considering testing the psychometric properties of new or existing instruments in the community at large.

REFERENCES

American Psychiatric Association. (1980). *Diagnostic and statistical manual of mental disorders* (3rd ed.). Washington, DC: APA.

American Psychiatric Association. (1987). *Diagnostic and statistical manual of mental disorders* (3rd ed., revised). Washington, DC: APA.

Anthony, J.C., LeResche, L., Niaz, U., von Korff, M.B., & Folstein, M.F. (1982). Limits of the 'Mini-Mental State' as a screening test for dementia and delirium among hospital patients. *Psychological Medicine, 12*, 397-408.

Baldessarini, R.J., Finklestein, S., & Arana, G.W. (1983). The predictive power of diagnostic tests and the effect of prevalence of illness. *Archives of General Psychiatry, 40*, 569-573.

Cicchetti, D.V. (1981). Testing the normal approximation and minimal sample size requirements of weighted kappa when the number of categories is large. *Applied Psychological Measurement, 5*, 101-104.

Cicchetti, D.V. (1985). A critique of Whitehurst's "Interrater agreement for journal manuscript reviews": De Omnibus, Disputandum Est. *American Psychologist, 40*, 563-568.

Cicchetti, D.V. (1988). When diagnostic agreement is high, but reliability is low: Some paradoxes occurring in independent neuropsychological assessments. *Journal of Clinical and Experimental Neuropsychology, 10*, 605-622.

Cicchetti, D.V., & Fleiss, J.L. (1977). Comparison of the null distributions of weighted kappa and the C ordinal statistic. *Applied Psychological Measurement, 1*, 195-201.

Cicchetti, D.V., & Sparrow, S.S. (1981). Developing criteria for establishing the interrater reliability of specific items in a given inventory: Applications to assessment of adaptive behavior. *American Journal of Mental Deficiency, 86*, 127-137.

Cicchetti, D.V., Sparrow, S.S., & Rourke, B.P. (in press). Adaptive behavior profiles of psychologically disturbed and developmentally disabled persons. In J.L. Matson and J. Mulich (Eds.), *Handbook of Mental Retardation*. New York: Pergamon.

Cohen, J. (1960). A coefficient of agreement for nominal scales. *Educational and Psychological Measurement, 20*, 37-46.

Fleiss, J.L. (1981). *Statistical methods for rates and proportions* (2nd ed.). New York: Wiley.

Fleiss, J.L., Cohen, J., & Everitt, B.S. (1969). Large samples standard errors of kappa and weighted kappa. *Psychological Bulletin, 72*, 323-327.

Grove, W.M., Andreason, N.C., McDonald-Scott, P., Keller, M.B., & Shapiro, R.W. (1981). Reliability studies of psychiatric diagnosis: Theory and practice. *Archives of General Psychiatry, 38*, 408-413.

Kraemer, H.C. (1979). Ramifications of a population model for kappa as a coefficient of reliability. *Psychometrika, 44*, 461-472.

Kraemer, H.C. (1982). Estimating false alarms and missed events from interobserver agreement: Comment on Kaye. *Psychological Bulletin, 92*, 749-754.

Kraemer, H.C. (1987). Charlie Brown and statistics: An exchange. *Archives of General Psychiatry, 44*, 192-193.

Kraemer, H.C. (1988). Assessment of 2 x 2 associations: Generalization of signal detection methodology. *American Statistician, 42*, 37-49.

McClure, M., & Willett, W.C. (1987). Misinterpretation and misuse of the kappa statistic. *American Journal of Epidemiology, 126*, 161-169.

Rourke, B.P. (1987). Syndrome of nonverbal learning disabilities: The final common pathway of white-matter disease/dysfunction? *The Clinical Neuropsychologist, 1*, 209-234.

Rourke, B.P. (1990). *Nonverbal learning disabilities: The syndrome and the model*. New York: Guilford Press.

Shrout, P.E., Spitzer, R.L., & Fleiss, J.L. (1987). Quantification of agreement in psychiatric diagnosis revisited. *Archives of General Psychiatry, 44,* 172-177.

Spitzer, R.L., & Fleiss, J.L. (1974). A re-analysis of the reliability of psychiatric diagnosis. *British Journal of Psychiatry, 125,* 341-347.

Spitznagel, E.L., & Helzer, J.E. (1985). A proposed solution to the base rate problem in the kappa statistic. *Archives of General Psychiatry, 42,* 725-728.

Swets, J.A. (1988). Measuring the accuracy of diagnostic systems. *Science, 240,* 1285-1293.

Uebersax, J.S. (1987). Letter to the editor. *Archives of General Psychiatry, 44,* 193-194.

Volkmar, F.R., Bregman, J., Cohen, D.J., & Cicchetti, D.V. (1988). Diagnosis of Autism: DSM-III and DSM-III-R. *American Journal of Psychiatry, 145,* 1404-1408.

Youden, W.J. (1950). Index for rating diagnostic tests. *Cancer, 3,* 32-35.

Yule, G.U. (1912). On the methods of measuring the association between two attributes. *Journal of the Royal Statistical Society, 75,* 579-642.

Journal of Clinical Neuropsychology
1980, Vol. 2, No. 2, pp. 89–105

Test-Retest Reliability and Stability of the WAIS: A Literature Review with Implications for Clinical Practice

Joseph D. Matarazzo, Timothy P. Carmody, and Leo D. Jacobs
University of Oregon Health Sciences Center

ABSTRACT

The literature on the test-retest reliability of the WAIS is reviewed. Included are eleven studies which reported the test-retest reliability or stability of FSIQ, VIQ, and PIQ, and six studies which reported the test-retest stability of the 11 individual subtests. The findings are discussed in relation to their implications for evaluating test-retest changes found in the individual patient by clinical or forensic psychologists who are being asked to evaluate such patients in increasing numbers.

An important byproduct of recent developments in neuropsychology and forensic psychology has been a marked increase in the number of patients being referred to clinical neuropsychologists for psychological assessment following head or other injury, psychopharmacologic treatment, and neurosurgery. Furthermore, in addition to such an initial assessment, it is not unusual for the patient to be referred for reevaluation once (or even twice) in order to document the extent, if any, of the clinical recovery in the months or years following the trauma or medical-surgical intervention. The increasing number of these referrals has stimulated practicing psychologists to a consideration of the test-retest reliability and stability[1] in normal as well as patient

---

[1] Although investigators often have used the term *reliability* in their test-retest studies, test constructors use the term test-retest *reliability* for describing studies conducted over *short intervals* (e.g., 1–2 months) to determine the psychometric property of the *test* itself. Conversely, clinicians, educators, cognitive theorists and others who are interested in test-retest changes which take place in a *single individual* due to a specified intervention (e.g., brain surgery, the administration of drugs) or to a whole *group* of individuals (e.g., following enrichment interventions, or nonspecific matura-

populations of assessment instruments such as the Halstead-Reitan Neuro-psychological Battery (Dodrill & Troupin, 1975; Klonoff, Fibiger, & Hutton, 1970; Matarazzo, Matarazzo, Wiens, Gallo, & Klonoff, 1976). Surprisingly, given the importance of the Wechsler Adult Intelligence Sale (WAIS) in clinical and forensic psychology and its 25-year history of more extensive utilization, relatively little has been published on the test-retest reliability of this test, one of the most frequently used assessment batteries. What little has been reported on the reliability of the WAIS has not been highlighted to an extent commensurate with the importance of the problem. As an aid, there-fore, for ourselves as well as for other clinicians working in this area, we undertook a review of the literature on the test-retest stability of the WAIS and report it here.

RETEST RELIABILITY AND STABILITY OF WAIS VIQ, PIQ, AND FSIQ

Wechsler did not carry out a study of the test-retest reliability of the WAIS and therefore no such data were included when the Manual for this instru-ment was published in 1955. However, at least seven studies reporting consis-tently high test-retest reliability values for the 1939 Wechsler-Bellevue I eventually were published (Matarazzo, 1972, pp. 237–243) and, from these, Wechsler quite likely guessed that similar future studies with the better constructed WAIS would yield equally high retest reliability coefficients.

We were able to locate, through 1980, 11 studies reporting the test-retest stability of the Verbal IQ, Performance IQ, and Full Scale IQ of the WAIS. These studies and their respective product-moment test-retest corre-lations are summarized in Table 1.

As may be seen, the subjects in these 11 studies included both young and old subjects (mean ages of 19 to 70) and normal and clinical populations. The numbers in each sample also varied considerably and ranged from 10 indi-viduals in one of the two samples reported by Kendrick and Post (1967) to 120 individuals in the study by Rosen, Stallings, Floor, and Nowakiwska (1968). The interval between test administrations also varied from one study to another, yielding a range of test-retest intervals from a low of one week (Catron & Thompson, 1979; Coons & Peacock, 1959) to a high of 676 weeks (Kangas & Bradway, 1971). Also, subjects in two studies were reexamined

tional or other life span changes) use the term test-retest *stability*. The studies here reviewed were of both types, although for ease of exposition this distinction will not always be made and we will use the terms more or less interchangeably throughout the present discussion. However, in Table 1, the true reliability studies are those by Kendrick and Post (1967), Matarazzo et al. (1973), and Catron and Thompson (1979).

TABLE 1

Test-Retest Reliabilities of WAIS VIQ, PIQ, and FSIQ

Study	Sample	Mean Age	n	Retest Interval	In weeks	VIQ	PIQ	FSIQ
Coons & Peacock, 1959	Psychiatric patients	33	24		1	.98	.96	.98
Kendrick & Post, 1967	Depressed and normal elderly	70	30	1–2	6	.90	.85	–
	(each patient was examined 3 times)			2–3	6	.95	.76	–
				1–3	12	.89	.66	–
	Brain damaged elderly	70	10	1–2	6	.81	.94	–
	(each patient was examined 3 times)			2–3	6	.82	.90	–
				1–3	12	.87	.90	–
Rosen et al., 1968	Mentally retarded	24	120		130	.87	.92	.88
Klonoff et al., 1970	Chronic schizophrenics	47	42		416	.80	.58	.71
Kangas & Bradway, 1971	Normal adults	42	48		676	.70	.57	.73
Matarazzo et al., 1973	Normal job applicants	24	29		20	.87	.84	.91
Rosen et al., 1974	Educable retardates	29	50		186	.89	.90	.91
Dodrill & Troupin, 1975	Chronic epileptics (each patient was examined 4 times)	27	17	1–2	35	.89	.71	.84
				1–3	70	.95	.78	.91
				1–4	105	.94	.74	.89
				2–3	35	.83	.74	.77
				2–4	70	.88	.78	.83
				3–4	35	.96	.92	.96
Catron & Thompson, 1979	Normal college students	19	19		1	.91	.87	.94
			19		4	.87	.79	.83
			19		8	.72	.82	.74
			19		16	.83	.85	.90
Brown & May, 1979	Psychiatric patients	44	50		100	.91	.90	.92
Matarazzo et al., 1979	Endarterectomy patients	62	17		20	.91	.85	.92
			Median			.89	.85	.90

more than once; namely, two reexaminations in the Kendrick and Post (1967) study and three additional examinations in the Dodrill and Troupin (1975) study. In these two studies the initial examination is designated by the numeral 1 and subsequent examinations are numbered serially thereafter. Thus, in Table 1, the designation 1–2 signifies the interval between initial test and first retest, whereas 1–3 signifies the interval between initial test and the second retest (namely, the third examination of the same individual), and the numbers 3–4 signify correlations between the scores obtained on the third versus fourth test administration on the same individual.

Examination of the results summarized in Table 1 indicates a remarkable high test-retest stability for the three WAIS IQ scores. Despite the fact that some of the individuals examined in these studies were clinically quite disturbed, and that a variety of pharmacologic agents were administered between test and retest in two of the studies (Klonoff et al., 1970; Dodrill & Troupin, 1975), and also that one group underwent a neurosurgical procedure (Matarazzo, Matarazzo, Gallo, & Wiens, 1979), the majority of the values shown in Table 1 are in the 80's and 90's. Specifically, 26 of the 66 r values in Table 1 fall between .90 and .98, 24 between .80 and .89, 13 between .70 and .79, and the remaining values were .66, .58, and .57. The *median r* values for VIQ, PIQ, and FSIQ taken separately are .89, .85, and .90, respectively. The lowest correlations reported for one of the three IQ scores were .70 for VIQ, .57 for PIQ, and .71 for FSIQ but, as revealed in Table 1, such low r values were the exceptions and not the rule.

The data in Table 1 support several conclusions. First, the three summary WAIS IQ values possess test-retest reliabilities which are statistically and clinically very robust. Second, this high stability obtains in both clinical and normal samples and, with one or two exceptions, is found as frequently in studies which utilized a very long test-retest interval as a very short interval. Thus the retest correlations of .87, .92, and .88 obtained by Rosen et al. (1968), who utilized a test-retest interval which spanned two and one-half years or (130 weeks), were little different from the values of .91, .87, and .94 obtained by Catron and Thompson who, in one of their samples of subjects, used a test-retest interval of only one week. Finally, in the age range covered by these 11 studies (ages 19 to 70), retest stability of the WAIS seems as high for one age level as for another.

In sum, the values in Table 1 reveal that, like its Wechsler-Bellevue I predecessor, the test-retest reliability of the three IQ values of the WAIS is very high.

RETEST RELIABILITY AND STABILITY OF THE WAIS
SUBTESTS

Only six of the 11 studies reported the test-retest stability of the 11 individual WAIS subtests and these results are summarized in Table 2. Two of these sets of r values in Table 2 were unpublished but were provided to us by Klonoff and by Dodrill. Additionally, the numbers in Table 2 are the same as those shown in Table 1, except that the Klonoff et al. data in Table 2 are for an n of 15 instead of all 42 of the subjects shown in Table 1. As may be seen in Table 2, the 121 retest coefficients of correlation for the 11 subtests, while respectable (almost all the values in Table 2 reach the .001 level of statistical significance), are lower than are the values shown in Table 1 for the three Scales to which they contribute individually.[2] Specifically, although the median values for r for each subtest range from .68 to .90, 5 of the 121 individual r values in Table 2 are below .49, 10 are in the .50's, 28 are in the .60's, 25 in the .70's, 39 in the .80's, and 14 in the .90's. The *median r* for the total group of 121 values shown in Table 2 is .76. This lower retest reliability for the subtests is not surprising, given both the fact that each subtest represents a smaller sample of behavior than does the WAIS taken as a whole, and the restriction of range problem brought about by the fact that, when the raw scores are converted into their scaled score equivalents, most WAIS subtests' scores fall (see Tables 4 and 5 for an example) into too limited a range to produce very high values of retest reliability. This methodological artifact notwithstanding, the median values as well as the 121 individual coefficients of retest stability shown in Table 2, some of which were obtained after retest intervals during which powerful drugs were administered to the patients, suggest that the 11 individual subtests of the WAIS nevertheless still possess a moderately good degree of *relative* test-retest reliability. However, as will be discussed below in relation to Table 6, caution is necessary in the interpretation of this moderately high retest reliability when one is evaluating a change in subtest score in the *individual* patient (namely, when attempting to infer absolute reliability).

RELATIVE VERSUS ABSOLUTE RETEST RELIABILITY

Statisticians, test constructors, and psychometric methodologists typically pay attention to the test-retest reliability coefficients of correlation of a test, and concern themselves less with the amount of change in absolute score for a

[2] Wechsler reported similarly smaller test-retest stability coefficients for the 12 subtests of the WISC-R relative to the higher stability values for VIQ, PIQ, and FSIQ for three samples of children used in his standardization group (Wechsler, 1974, pp. 29–34).

TABLE 2

Test-Retest Reliabilities of 11 Individual WAIS Subtests

Study		Inf.	Comp.	D Sp.	Arith.	Sim.	Voc.	P A	P C	B D	O A	D Sy
Coons & Peacock, 1959		.94	.89	.84	.94	.94	.95	.88	.87	.88	.86	.92
Rosen et al., 1968		.78	.60	.69	.69	.68	.80	.85	.81	.87	.87	.88
Klonoff et al., 1970		.79	.58	.82	.52	.63	.24	.69	.54	.91	.59	.63
Matarazzo et al., 1973		.75	.59	.73	.66	.58	.79	.70	.71	.72	.73	.87
Dodrill & Troupin, 1975	1–2	.90	.81	.75	.83	.68	.85	.27	.68	.69	.64	.87
	1–3	.90	.67	.81	.62	.88	.95	.67	.64	.72	.61	.67
	1–4	.85	.65	.61	.82	.88	.94	.72	.74	.67	.73	.74
	2–3	.90	.80	.55	.74	.70	.86	.59	.66	.63	.71	.79
	2–4	.96	.69	.44	.89	.82	.83	.38	.78	.79	.80	.80
	3–4	.94	.76	.87	.83	.81	.92	.78	.64	.82	.82	.89
Matarazzo et al., 1979		.88	.70	.57	.42	.83	.84	.64	.50	.76	.67	.67
Median		.90	.69	.73	.74	.81	.85	.69	.68	.76	.73	.80

single individual from one test administration to the next. Yet this change is exactly the datum of interest to the clinical practitioner who examines and, at a later date, reexamines a patient who is recovering from a brain injury, or has made significant clinical improvement following surgery or the administration of antidepressive or antipsychotic medication.

For example, a problem which frequently faces the clinical psychologist is whether a test-retest gain of 5 or so IQ points is mirroring actual clinical improvement, or whether such a gain is possible from a *retest* effect alone. Relative test-retest coefficients of correlation, even those as high as the ones shown in Tables 1 and 2, merely indicate that the two test scores obtained for each individual in the sample studied *maintained* their relative position, one against another. That is, if rank-ordered from lowest to highest, each subject's two scores arrayed themselves in their respective rank on retest much as they had arrayed themselves on the initial administration. Thus, for example, initial test FSIQ values for five individuals of 80, 90, 100, 110, 120 and retest values of 100, 110, 120, 130, and 140 would yield a coefficient of correlation of 1.00, despite the fact that each individual's initial FSIQ score had improved by 20 points on reexamination. Such a finding would show perfect *relative* retest reliability (*r* of 1.00) for the WAIS FSIQ, but poor *absolute* retest reliability (a change for the 5 subjects from a mean IQ of 100 to a mean IQ of 120). Thus, a clinician armed only with the report of its test-retest *r* of 1.00 could *erroneously* conclude that the WAIS would produce a score on retest identical in absolute value to the score obtained in initial test for that same individual, and be unaware from this high *r*, viewed in isolation, of the substantial gain from a *retest effect alone*.

Fortunately, clinicians have recognized this problem and, beginning with his earlier test manuals and their associated textbooks, Wechsler has consistently cautioned that a gain in IQ of about 5 points from test to retest generally should be considered a *practice* or *retest* effect rather than a clinically meaningful change in actual IQ (Kaufman, 1979, pp. 20–69; Matarazzo, 1972, pp. 241–242; Zimmerman & Woo-Sam, 1973, pp. 14–19).

RELATIVE RETEST RELIABILITY OF WAIS IQ SCORES

Fortunately, the authors of the 11 studies shown in Table 1 provided the actual *mean* VIQ, PIQ, and FSIQ scores for each test administration and these are summarized here in our Table 3. Kendrick and Post did not report either the FSIQ (Table 1) or the retest VIQ and PIQ, consequently their study is omitted in Table 3. Additionally, although Dodrill and Troupin did report the same three mean IQ scores for their third and fourth test administrations, in order to save space these additional values are omitted from our Table.

Several conclusions may be drawn from the data in Table 3. First, as

TABLE 3   453

Test and Retest WAIS VIQ, PIQ, and FSIQ Means

		Test 1	Test 2	Gain or (loss)
Coons & Peacock, 1959	VIQ	95	98	3
	PIQ	93	102	9
	FSIQ	96	101	5
Rosen et al., 1968	VIQ	70	71	1
	PIQ	71	74	3
	FSIQ	69	70	1
Klonoff et al., 1970	VIQ	97	102	5
	PIQ	91	99	8
	FSIQ	94	101	7
Kangas and Bradway, 1971	VIQ	111	117	6
	PIQ	107	118	11
	FSIQ	110	118	8
Matarazzo et al., 1973	VIQ	116	122	6
	PIQ	118	123	5
	FSIQ	118	124	6
Rosen et al., 1974	VIQ	74	76	2
	PIQ	79	81	2
	FSIQ	75	77	2
Dodrill and Troupin, 1975	VIQ	101	96	(5)
	PIQ	95	91	(4)
	FSIQ	98	94	(4)
Catron and Thompson, 1979	VIQ	117	122	5
	PIQ	116	127	11
	FSIQ	118	126	8
	VIQ	120	121	1
	PIQ	114	123	9
	FSIQ	118	124	6
	VIQ	117	120	3
	PIQ	118	127	9
	FSIQ	119	124	5
	VIQ	119	120	1
	PIQ	116	124	8
	FSIQ	119	123	4
Brown and May, 1979	VIQ	93	95	2
	PIQ	86	89	3
	FSIQ	90	92	2
Matarazzo et al., 1979	VIQ	101	103	2
	PIQ	96	101	5
	FSIQ	99	102	3
Median	VIQ			2
Median	PIQ			8
Median	FSIQ			5
Median	39 r values			5

previously suggested in the Wechsler textbooks might be the case, the *median* gain on retest in one or another of the three IQ scores shown in the 39 values in Table 3 is 5 points. The corresponding *mean* gain is 4.2 points. The *median* gains for VIQ, PIQ, and FSIQ separately were 2, 8, and 5 IQ points, respectively; and the corresponding *mean* gains[3] were 2.38, 6.08, and 4.08, respectively. Second, although most of the gain scores shown in Table 3 are at or around this median value of 5 points, the actual gain or loss in the means from one study to another ranges from −5 to +11 IQ points. Third, the one report which showed a loss in mean IQ on first retest was the 1975 study with seizure disorder patients by Dodrill and Troupin and which was designed to study (and only for the retest interval between their first and second examination) the effects of powerful chemical compounds on the cognitive functioning of such patients. However, even in that study (although not shown in our Table 3) the corresponding mean VIQ, PIQ, and FSIQ values obtained on the third and on the fourth examinations were 98, 96, and 97, respectively, and 102, 100, and 101, respectively. Thus, there was a gain in the means of 1, 5, and 3 IQ points, respectively, between the first and fourth WAIS administrations even in that Dodrill and Troupin study.

ABSOLUTE RETEST RELIABILITY OF WAIS IQ AND SUBTEST SCORES

The values reproduced in our Table 3 are *group means* and their corresponding gains or losses for the various samples studied. What the practicing clinician also needs is some idea of the stability (absolute reliability) from test to retest in the three IQ scores for a *single individual*. To our knowledge, only two sets of such individual data have been published to date. Matarazzo, Wiens, Matarazzo, and Manaugh (1973) published (see their Table 1) the *individual* test and retest VIQ, PIQ, and FSIQ scores for each of their 29 normal young adult job applicants. To that initial pool of IQ scores Matarazzo et al. (1979) added (see their Table 5) the comparable *individual* VIQ, PIQ, and FSIQ test and retest IQ scores for their sample of 17 sixty-two-year-old patients who underwent carotid endarterectomy. As a further aid to the clinician, in this second publication Matarazzo et al. (1979) published the *individual* test and retest scores of the 17 patients on each of the eleven WAIS subtests (see their Tables 6 and 7).

However, to our knowledge the comparable individual test and retest scores for the WAIS *subtests* on a sample of normal subjects has not been published to date. Yet it is just such retest data from a large and *normal*

---

[3] These mean retest gains are not dissimilar to the comparable values of 3 1/2, 9 1/2, and 7 points, respectively, reported by Wechsler (1974, p. 31) for the WISC-R.

sample of individuals (e.g., the 1,700 *individuals* used in the standardization of the WAIS) which would be highly useful to the practitioner. Such normative data would provide a useful baseline or yardstick on a sample of individuals receiving *no* intervention against which to evaluate the changes, if any, which take place between test and retest for a single patient being evaluated by the clinician.

In the absence to date of any such published test-retest data, and in order to provide the clinical practitioner with one admittedly small sample of such normative data, we present here in Tables 4 and 5 the previously unpublished individual test and retest scaled scores on each of the 11 WAIS subtests for the 29 young normal adults from the Matarazzo et al. (1973) study. To save space, the comparable and equally highly instructive individual test and retest subtest scores of the 17 carotid endarterectomy patients are not reproduced here although, as mentioned above, the interested clinician will find them in Tables 6 and 7 of Matarazzo et al. (1979). Also, the interested clinician will find the *individual* VIQ, PIQ, and FSIQ test and retest values for the same 29 healthy adults published in Table 1 of the Matarazzo et al. (1973) study.

Several conclusions may be drawn from an examination of the pairs of test-retest WAIS subtest scores for the 29 normal individuals (with an initial FSIQ of 118) shown here in Tables 4 and 5. The first is that, after a 20-week test-retest interval, most of the WAIS subtest scores change remarkably little. In fact, the *mean* change in individual scaled score for each of the 11 subtests was 0.24 (Inf), 1.93 (Comp), 0.41 (Arith), 0.90 (Sim), 1.00 (D Sp), 0.90 (Voc), 1.41 (PC), 0.76 (BD), 0.17 (PA), 0.69 (OA), and 1.00 (D Sy) points. As shown in Tables 4 and 5, many of the individuals had the identical subtest score on test and retest. To demonstrate this latter finding and thus offer the practitioner some normative data, albeit from only one small sample (the data of which, fortunately, are *fully representative* of those used by Field, 1960; Fisher, 1960; and McNemar, 1957, in deriving their tables from the full WAIS standardization sample), we tabulated the gain or loss on each of the 11 subtests for each of these 29 subjects and here present the results in Table 6. Table 6 also presents the frequencies of gains or losses, for the *individual* VIQ, PIQ, and FSIQ of the same 29 subjects, and which we tabulated from the corresponding individual test-retest scores previously published in their Table 1 by Matarazzo et al. (1973) and here publish for the first time in the form of a frequency distribution.

Table 6 reveals that, of the 174 individual test-retest gain or loss difference scores produced by the 29 subjects on the six Verbal subtests, and computed by us from the pairs of scores shown here in Table 4, a total of 110 (or 63%) fell between plus one to minus one point. For the test-retest differences in the five Performance subtests computed from the pairs of scores shown in Table 5, 78 (or 54%) fell between plus one and minus one point. Correspondingly,

TABLE 4
Individual Test and Retest WAIS Verbal Subtest Scaled Scores on a Sample of 29 Young Normal Males

S	Information			Comprehension			Arithmetic			Similarities			Digit Span			Vocabulary		
	I	II	Gain/loss	I	II	Gain/loss	I	II	Gain/loss	I	II	Gain/loss	I	II	Gain/loss	I	II	Gain/loss
1	10	10	0	15	15	0	10	11	1	12	12	0	12	6	-6	11	11	0
2	11	13	2	9	9	0	8	10	2	12	15	3	9	11	2	10	12	2
3	14	13	-1	14	15	1	13	12	-1	12	14	2	10	11	1	13	12	-1
4	13	12	-1	12	12	0	11	12	1	13	13	0	6	6	0	11	11	0
5	11	12	1	10	13	3	10	12	2	10	12	2	12	11	-1	11	12	1
6	14	13	-1	10	11	1	10	10	0	15	13	-2	12	14	2	13	17	4
7	11	11	0	16	18	2	11	10	-1	12	13	1	10	14	4	10	11	1
8	13	14	1	12	13	1	15	15	0	8	9	1	12	15	3	12	13	1
9	13	12	-1	11	15	4	15	17	2	11	12	1	15	15	0	10	11	1
10	12	11	-1	16	12	-4	11	12	1	13	14	1	12	10	-2	12	13	1
11	11	11	0	11	15	4	14	16	2	11	13	2	14	16	2	12	13	1
12	13	14	1	11	14	3	14	17	3	12	13	1	14	15	1	13	13	0
13	13	14	1	13	19	6	11	14	3	12	13	1	10	10	0	12	13	1
14	12	13	1	15	14	-1	12	16	4	12	12	0	16	16	0	13	12	-1
15	14	14	0	14	18	4	17	16	-1	15	17	2	12	10	-2	13	14	1
16	11	14	3	11	15	4	13	12	-1	13	13	0	9	11	2	12	13	1
17	14	14	0	11	11	0	16	17	1	13	13	0	14	15	1	13	13	0
18	13	13	0	10	17	7	14	12	-2	14	13	-1	12	14	2	12	13	1
19	12	13	1	16	18	2	15	16	1	12	11	-1	11	15	4	13	13	0
20	15	14	-1	15	18	3	12	15	3	14	13	-1	7	7	0	14	15	1
21	14	15	1	15	15	0	17	15	-2	12	15	3	11	16	5	16	17	1
22	14	14	0	14	17	3	15	17	2	13	14	1	14	15	1	12	14	2
23	15	15	0	12	13	1	14	15	1	13	15	2	14	14	0	12	15	3
24	14	13	-1	11	11	0	15	14	-1	14	15	1	11	16	5	14	13	-1
25	13	14	1	14	15	1	13	13	0	15	15	0	16	16	0	12	15	3
26	14	13	-1	12	17	5	15	12	-3	14	13	-1	12	16	4	14	18	4
27	16	16	0	16	18	2	17	14	-3	15	15	0	16	16	0	16	15	-1
28	15	16	1	17	18	1	12	12	0	13	14	1	14	15	1	17	19	2
29	13	14	1	15	19	4	12	12	0	17	16	-1	14	15	-1	18	17	-1
Mean	13.0	13.3		13.1	15.0		13.3	13.7		12.8	13.7		12.0	13.0		12.8	13.7	
S.D.	1.5	1.4		2.3	2.8		2.4	2.2		1.7	1.8		2.5	3.1		2.0	2.2	
r	.753***			.592***			.665***			.580**			.732***			.787***		

Significance values at the .001 and .01 levels are shown by *** and ** respectively.

TABLE 5

Individual Test and Retest WAIS Performance Subtest Scaled Scores on a Sample of 29 Young Normal Males

S	Picture completion			Block design			Picture arrangement			Object assembly			Digit symbol		
	I	II	Gain/loss	I	II	Gain/loss	I	II	Gain/loss	I	II	Gain/loss	I	II	Gain/loss
1	11	11	0	12	12	0	7	10	3	9	11	2	10	10	0
2	13	11	-2	9	10	1	12	10	-2	16	15	-1	11	12	1
3	9	10	1	8	11	3	11	12	1	7	9	2	10	10	0
4	13	12	-1	15	12	-3	9	9	0	10	10	0	11	11	0
5	11	13	2	14	14	0	8	11	3	13	9	-4	14	15	1
6	11	12	1	10	9	-1	11	12	1	9	10	1	14	14	0
7	9	12	3	9	10	1	10	11	1	16	16	0	13	13	0
8	11	14	3	11	14	3	11	8	-3	12	12	0	13	14	1
9	9	12	3	15	17	2	9	9	0	11	13	2	12	15	3
10	12	14	2	11	8	-3	10	12	2	10	14	4	13	15	2
11	14	18	4	11	12	1	17	17	0	12	15	3	11	12	0
12	11	14	3	12	14	2	13	14	1	12	15	3	11	12	1
13	18	18	0	11	14	3	14	14	0	7	12	5	15	16	0
14	12	12	0	12	15	3	10	11	1	13	12	-1	14	14	1
15	13	14	1	13	13	0	10	16	6	13	12	-1	11	12	2
16	14	16	2	16	13	-3	12	11	-1	11	13	2	10	11	2
17	14	14	0	12	14	2	17	18	1	17	16	-1	14	16	-1
18	12	12	0	17	17	0	13	15	2	12	14	2	12	14	2
19	11	14	3	17	15	-2	16	12	-4	14	12	-2	12	12	-2
20	11	13	2	15	17	2	13	12	-1	13	13	0	12	15	0
21	14	18	4	12	14	2	17	18	1	16	17	1	11	13	3
22	13	16	3	12	17	5	13	13	0	14	14	0	15	16	2
23	11	12	1	17	17	0	15	15	0	17	18	1	10	12	1
24	14	18	4	15	17	2	14	10	-4	16	16	0	12	11	-1
25	14	16	2	17	15	-2	15	15	0	18	16	-2	12	12	0
26	18	16	-2	17	17	0	13	15	2	14	13	-1	13	13	0
27	13	13	0	15	16	1	15	14	-1	9	14	5	18	18	0
28	12	14	2	14	17	3	11	8	-3	16	15	-1	15	19	0
29	14	14	0	17	17	0	13	12	-1	16	17	1	14	16	2
Mean	12.5	13.9		13.3	14.1		12.4	12.6		12.9	13.6		12.4	13.4	
S.D.	2.2	2.3		2.8	2.7		2.7	2.8		3.1	2.4		1.9	2.4	
r	.709***			.718***			.695***			.729***			.872***		

Significance values at the .001 level are shown by ***

TABLE 6

Frequency of Different Magnitudes of WAIS Gain or Loss in Scaled
Score from Test to Retest for 29 Young Normal Adults on Each of
the 11 Subtests and 3 IQ Measures

	Frequency of Occurrence		
Gain or Loss	Verbal Subtests	Performance Subtests	VIQ, PIQ, and FSIQ
−7	0	0	1
−6	1	0	1
−5	0	0	1
−4	1	3	1
−3	2	5	1
−2	7	7	2
−1	23	13	1
0	39	38	3
1	48	27	7
2	22	26	7
3	14	17	4
4	13	5	4
5	2	3	10
6	1	1	9
7	1	0	6
8	0	0	6
9	0	0	6
10	0	0	5
11	0	0	2
12	0	0	4
13	0	0	5
14	0	0	1
15	0	0	0
Total	174	145	87

very few individuals changed their *subtest* scaled score by more than one or
two points.

IMPLICATIONS FOR CLINICAL PRACTICE

This latter point notwithstanding, the Verbal and Performance subtest data in
Table 6 suggest an important caution for the clinician who is attempting to

interpret a change in subtest score from initial test to retest for one of his or her own patients. Namely, as revealed in Tables 4, 5, and 6, *even without intervention of any kind*, and due either to motivational or related differences in the subject's test-taking ability on the two occasions, or the less than perfect reliability of the subtests themselves, or a practice or retest effect, or the random error of measurement associated with any assessment instrument, or some other as yet undiscovered factor, some *normal* individuals change as much as 3, 4, 5, 6, or 7 points in subtest scaled score from test to retest over a 20-week retest interval. In fact, as reviewed elsewhere (Matarazzo, 1972, pp. 243–244 and pp. 389–390), several authors (Field, 1960; Fisher, 1960; and McNemar, 1957) have published tables showing the probabilities of finding differences in scores from one subtest to another (intra-test) in normal subjects which appropriately could be applied to test-retest changes (inter-test) in the same subtest. Clearly, any clinical significance attributed to a change in a subtest score should be *corroborated* by other assessment and clinical data instead of relying exclusively on such a change in one or more single subtest score.

The importance of this caution is discussed in detail by Matarazzo et al. (1979) in their review of several recent studies which purported to show an increase in cognitive functioning based on slight improvements on retest in WAIS subtest and IQ scores in patients who were examined before and after having openings reinstated surgically in their carotid arteries, thereby increasing blood flow to the brain. Clinicians frequently see and document massive improvement (or loss) in cognitive functioning in individual patients. However, as the VIQ, PIQ, and FSIQ change data in Table 6 make clear, and until more and better normative data of the type shown in Tables 3 and 6 are published, the caution provided in an earlier publication (Matarazzo, 1972, pp. 389–390) that a Verbal IQ minus Performance IQ difference should in most cases be at least 15 points before it becomes clinically suspect and the basis for further analysis and clarification also would seem to hold in the interpretation of a *test-retest change* in one of the three IQ scores in the *individual* patient. As the last column of Table 6 reveals, IQ test-retest increases of 5 to 14 points in that sample were not unusual (*even without clinical intervention* of any kind). Furthermore, the published probability tables cited below provide information based on much larger samples of subjects which corroborate the fact that differences of the type shown in our Table 6 are not unusual in *normal* samples. For additional background on these important issues, the clinician working in this area will find invaluable the general discussions of test-retest reliability, as well as the clinical significance of intra-test subtest difference scores obtained during a single examination, provided by the following authors: Fields (1960), Fisher (1960), Matarazzo (1972, pp. 243–244; 389–390), Wechsler (1974, pp. 31–35), Kaufman (1979, pp. 20–69), and Zimmerman and Woo-Sam (1973, pp. 14–19). The extensive discussion offered by Kaufman (1979) is especially recommended.

A conservative rule of thumb for the clinician dealing with an individual patient who has been tested and later retested might be that, generally speaking, a change of 3–5 points in a subtest score and a change of 15 points[4] or more in an IQ score in the functioning of any given patient ordinarily may be interpreted as *potentially* clinically important and worthy of further analysis and clarification. Furthermore, unless other corollary clinical or behavioral evidence *also* is available to corroborate that patient's change in WAIS score(s) of the magnitudes indicated by these rules of thumb, the burden of proof that the change is mirroring a clinically significant effect quite likely has not been met. That is, in the absence of other behavioral or clinical corroborative data, even a change of more than 3–5 scaled score points or 15 IQ points, *in isolation*, is not robust proof that a true change has occurred. The skeptic should study Tables 4, 5, and 6 in the present report, or the published probability tables which were derived from the WAIS standardization data cited earlier, to evaluate the practical utility of this rule of thumb. Finally, the findings in the Dodrill and Troupin (1975) study which, using a drug intervention in one of the test-retest intervals, showed a *loss* in IQ on that retest permit the highlighting of an additional point. Namely, that any loss (or gain) on retest should first be "corrected" for the expected gain of 5 points due to a retest effect alone. Thus, a *loss* on retest of 7 points is quite likely a "true" loss of 12 points, if other corroborative information is available, as in the Dodrill and Troupin study.

Psychologists who testify in court cases on individuals on which they have obtained test and retest WAIS subtest and IQ scores quite likely already have learned that testimony based on actuarial or other published findings provides a more reassuring platform than does refuge into clinical experience when one is under intense cross-examination regarding change in scores. The practice of clinical psychology has matured considerably during the past decade, in no small part due to the increasing base of scientific knowledge from which it draws. Accordingly, the number of requests from our legal and medical colleagues that we *buttress* our proferred clinical opinions with citations to the published literature quite likely will increase rather than decrease. The literature reviewed here, while far from an ideal data base for the important decisions clinical neuropsychologists must make daily, is a step above what was available to us even five years ago.

[4] This suggestion is merely a rule of thumb and should be treated as such inasmuch as there will be individual cases when a smaller change than these can be shown to be validly mirroring a clinically significant improvement or decline. Furthermore, when dealing with *group* rather than *individual* scores, a difference in *means* considerably smaller (or larger) than these suggested values may be both statistically and clinically meaningful.

REFERENCES

Brown, H. S. R., & May, A. E. A test-retest reliability study of the Wechsler Adult Intelligence Scale. *Journal of Consulting and Clinical Psychology*, 1979, *47*, 601–602.

Catron, D. W., & Thompson, C. C. Test-retest gains in WAIS scores after four retest intervals. *Journal of Clinical Psychology*, 1979, *35*, 352–358.

Coons, W. H., & Peacock, E. P. Inter-examiner reliability of the Wechsler Adult Intelligence Scale with mental hospital patients. *Ontario Psychological Association Quarterly*, 1959, *12*, 33–37.

Dodrill, C. B., & Troupin, A. S. Effects of repeated administrations of a comprehensive neuropsychological battery among chronic epileptics. *Journal of Nervous and Mental Disease*, 1975, *161*, 185–190.

Field, J. G. Two types of tables for use with Wechsler's intelligence scales. *Journal of Clinical Psychology*, 1960, *16*, 3–7.

Fisher, G. M. A corrected table for determining the significance of the difference between verbal and performance IQs on the WAIS and the Wechsler-Bellevue. *Journal of Clinical Psychology*, 1960, *16*, 7–9.

Kangas, J., & Bradway, K. Intelligence at middle age: A thirty-eight year follow-up. *Developmental Psychology*, 1971, *5*, 333–337.

Kaufman, A. S. *Intelligent testing with the WISC-R.* New York: John Wiley & Sons, 1979.

Kendrick, D. C., & Post, F. Differences in cognitive status between healthy, psychiatrically ill, and diffusely brain-damaged elderly subjects. *British Journal of Psychiatry*, 1967, *113*, 75–81.

Klonoff, H., Fibiger, C. H., & Hutton, G. H. Neuropsychological patterns in chronic schizophrenia. *Journal of Nervous and Mental Disease*, 1970, *150*, 291–300.

Matarazzo, J. D. *Wechsler's measurement and appraisal and adult intelligence. Fifth and enlarged edition.* New York: Oxford University Press, 1972.

Matarazzo, J. D., Matarazzo, R. G., Wiens, A. N., Gallo, A. E., Jr., & Klonoff, H. Retest reliability of the Halstead Impairment Index in a normal, a schizophrenic, and two samples of organic patients. *Journal of Clinical Psychology*, 1976, *32*, 338–349.

Matarazzo, R. G., Matarazzo, J. D., Gallo, A. E., Jr., & Wiens, A. N. IQ and neuropsychological changes following carotid endarterectomy. *Journal of Clinical Neuropsychology*, 1979, *1*, 97–116.

Matarazzo, R. G., Wiens, A. N., Matarazzo, J. D., & Manaugh, T. S. Test-retest reliability of the WAIS in a normal population. *Journal of Clinical Psychology*, 1973, *29*, 194–197.

McNemar, Q. On WAIS difference scores. *Journal of Consulting Psychology*, 1957, *21*, 239–240.

Rosen, M., Stallings, L., Floor, L., & Nowakiwska, M. Reliability and stability of Wechsler IQ scores for institutionalized mental subnormals. *American Journal of Mental Deficiency*, 1968, *73*, 218–225.

Wechsler, D. *Manual for the Wechsler Adult Intelligence Scale.* New York: Psychological Corporation, 1955.

462

Wechsler, D. Manual for the *Wechsler Intelligence Scale for Children-Revised*. New York: Psychological Corporation, 1974.

Zimmerman, I. L., & Woo-Sam, J. M. *Clinical interpretation of the Wechsler Adult Intelligence Scale*. New York: Grune & Stratton, 1973.

Journal of Clinical Neuropsychology
1984, Vol. 6, No. 4, pp. 351-366

Base Rate Data for the WAIS-R: Test-Retest Stability and VIQ-PIQ Differences

Joseph D. Matarazzo
Oregon Health Sciences University

and

David O. Herman
The Psychological Corporation

ABSTRACT

The data analyzed were the 14 WAIS-R scores from each of the individuals who comprised the WAIS-R standardization sample. Examined was the individual VIQ-PIQ difference from only the initial examination of each of the 1880 subjects, as well as the test-retest change in each of the 14 WAIS-R scores for each of the 119 subjects who were retested. The results revealed that, although the WAIS-R has excellent psychometric reliability as reflected in its standard error of measurement of a VIQ-PIQ difference and its impressively high test-retest Pearson r values, the actual magnitudes of the differences between the VIQ and PIQ assessed in a single examination, or the magnitudes of gain or loss in the 14 scores on retest, for some of these normal individuals were sufficiently high that such *base-rate* data should be routinely considered by clinical neuropsychologists and other practitioners.

Since their introduction in 1939 the Wechsler scales have been one of the most frequently employed assessment tools in the practice of the professional psychologist and, in fact, constitute a central component of the tools in the armamentarium of today's clinical neuropsychologist. However, despite the almost universal use of these Wechsler Scales in today's neuropsychology batteries, research showing the *stability* of the Wechsler (or other neuropsychological test) scores obtained from test to retest for a single individual has been relatively scarce. Given the costs, both human and financial, involved for the examiner and examinee the dearth of such retest studies is not surprising. Nevertheless, the accelerating increase in the frequency of retests of the same individual using the Wechsler scales by clinical neuropsychologists requires that certain base-rate information relative to the Wechsler scales be available to these practitioners. The need for such base rates, hopefully derived over time from many clinical as well as normal samples of individuals, becomes clear to a reader from the differences in perceptions one will discern in the differing interpretations offered by investigators who have addressed the meanings of the *same* test-retest changes in WAIS scores in patients who have had a carotid endarterectomy. From their review of the published literature, one group of practitioners (Matarazzo, Matarazzo, Gallo, & Wiens, 1979; Matarazzo, Carmody, & Jacobs, 1980) concluded that the sparse literature available today suggests that nonpatient controls (normal individuals), without intervention of any kind, have about the same average increase in IQ from test to retest as do patients who undergo carotid endarterectomy and, thus, the benefits of this surgical procedure on IQ are yet to be demonstrated. Review of that same literature by Shatz (1981) led him to suggest that this conclusion of lack of effect was premature and that the base rates for test-retest changes in neuropsychological assessment which led to that conclusion might be differentially affected by such variables as patient versus nonpatient status, a patient's age, type of brain lesion and its location and chronicity, and severity of the presurgery cognitive deficit. One subsequent study with carotid endarterectomy patients (Parker, Granberg, Nichols, Jones, & Hewett, in press), using two well-selected control groups, took into account some of the variables identified by Shatz (1981) but, nevertheless, concluded that the increases in WAIS Verbal, Performance and Full Scale IQs obtained at 6 months follow up in the carotid endarterectomy patients in this better controlled study were no different from the comparable retest effects found in their two groups of controls and thus could not be attributed to the surgical intervention.

The differing interpretations given to the same finding (an increase on retest) reported in these endarterectomy studies, and in the other related studies cited in R. Matarazzo (1979) and J. Matarazzo (1980), have made it clear that clinical neuropsychologists will continue to practice under a handicap unless a considerable amount of actuarial base-rate information is collected and published on the variables associated with the stability (or its lack) of single scores as well as group averages on the Wechsler and other scales using subjects from both normal and patient samples who are examined before and after undergoing a wide range of interventions.

METHOD

As a contribution to such a needed data base, the purpose of the present communication is to report the actual magnitudes of change in the WAIS-R which occurred from initial to second testing in each of the two subsamples which were retested without investigator intervention during the standardization of the WAIS-R. The two test-retest samples (Wechsler, 1981, pp. 31-32) consisted of 71 of the 300 community living subjects in the 25-34 year age group who were reexamined after a 2- to 7-week retest interval and 48 of the 250 subjects in the 45-54 age group whose second examination came after a 2- to 5-week retest interval. The aggregate of the *n*s in these two test-retest subsamples totalled 119 of the 1880 subjects used in the standardization of the WAIS-R. Although relatively small, this *n* of 119 upon which the present analysis of test-retest changes is based, may serve as a useful reference group from which to derive base-rate information until the results from other such samples are published.

RESULTS

Data of considerable use to practitioners for detailed examination and study would include the actual pairs of the test and the retest scores of each of the 119 individuals in the two samples, with each pair of test-retest scores shown separately for all three IQs and all 11 subtests. Limitations of journal space, however, preclude publishing such complete raw data, although the interested reader will find the publication of columns of such actual pairs of the 14 scores obtained with the earlier WAIS on a sample of 29 young normal adults (age 24) and a sample of 17 older (age 62) adults on whom a carotid endarterectomy was performed during the test-retest interval in Matarazzo et al. (1973, 1979, and 1980). Accordingly, the present report includes analyses of only the frequencies of differing magnitudes of the *gains* and *losses* between the first and second testing of the 119 individuals examined in the two WAIS-R test-retest samples. It is important to note that for the analyses reported below the two subsamples were combined into a single sample of 119 subjects after inspection of the different frequencies of gains and losses between the younger and older of these two subsamples revealed no discernible effect due to their age difference.

Table 1 presents the frequency of different magnitudes of gain or loss from test to retest separately for the WAIS-R Verbal, Performance, and Full Scale IQs. For ease of interpretation these *same* data are presented in three histograms in Figure 1. It should be noted parenthetically that, except for very slight rounding off errors, the mean changes from test to retest shown at the bottom of Table 1 (and also bottom of Tables 2 and 3) are those which also may be derived from the pairs of test and retest means for each of the WAIS-R scores for these same 119 subjects which are published in Table 11 of the WAIS-R Manual (Wechsler, 1981, p. 32).

The data in Tables 2 and 3 are comparable to those in Table 1 and present for the same 119 subjects the frequency of different magnitudes of gain or loss from test to retest separately for each subtest of the WAIS-R Verbal Scale (Table 2) and WAIS-R Performance Scale (Table 3). Although histograms comparable to the ones shown in Figure 1 would facilitate the interpretation of the test-retest data for each subtest shown in Tables 2 and 3, lack of space also precluded including such Figures in the present report.

DISCUSSION

Study of the data presented in Table 1 and Figure 1 yields the following important observations which should be of help in the clinical use of the three WAIS-R IQ measures. First, the *mean* change upon retest after 2 to 7 weeks for the 119 subjects is a *gain* of the order of 3 points in VIQ, 8 points in PIQ, and 6 points in FSIQ. These WAIS-R gains are almost identical to the *median* gains of 2, 8 and 5 points, respectively, derived in an earlier literature review of 10 published test-retest

Table 1: Frequency of Different Magnitudes of Gain or Loss in VIQ, PIQ, and FSIQ from Initial Test to Retest for 119 Adults in the WAIS-R Standardization Sample

Gain or Loss	Verbal IQ		Performance IQ		Full Scale IQ	
	n	%	n	%	n	%
−12	1	.8	1	.8	1	.8
−11	0	0	0	0	0	0
−10	1	.8	0	0	0	0
−9	0	0	0	0	0	0
−8	0	0	1	.8	0	0
−7	0	0	0	0	0	0
−6	0	0	0	0	0	0
−5	3	2.5	2	1.7	1	.8
−4	3	2.5	1	.8	2	1.7
−3	4	3.4	1	.8	2	1.7
−2	4	3.4	1	.8	1	.8
−1	8	6.7	3	2.5	1	.8
0	7	5.9	3	2.5	5	4.2
1	7	5.9	8	6.7	6	5.0
2	15	12.6	5	4.2	7	5.9
3	10	8.4	7	5.9	7	5.9
4	10	8.4	9	7.6	13	10.9
5	9	7.6	4	3.4	6	5.0
6	4	3.4	7	5.9	9	7.6
7	13	10.9	4	3.4	8	6.7
8	8	6.7	6	5.0	7	5.9
9	4	3.4	4	3.4	13	10.9
10	1	.8	6	5.0	8	6.7
11	2	1.7	5	4.2	9	7.6
12	2	1.7	4	3.4	3	2.5
13	2	1.7	4	3.4	3	2.5
14	0	0	12	10.1	2	1.7
15	1	.8	3	2.5	1	.8
16	0	0	4	3.4	1	.8
17	0	0	1	.8	1	.8
18	0	0	2	1.7	0	0
19	0	0	1	.8	1	.8
20	0	0	3	2.5	1	.8
21	0	0	2	1.7	0	0
22	0	0	0	0	0	0
23	0	0	1	.8	0	0
24	0	0	1	.8	0	0
25	0	0	0	0	0	0
26	0	0	1	.8	0	0
27	0	0	1	.8	0	0
28	0	0	1	.8	0	0
Total	119	100	119	100	119	100
Mean	3.3		8.4		6.2	

Test-Retest Changes in WAIS-R

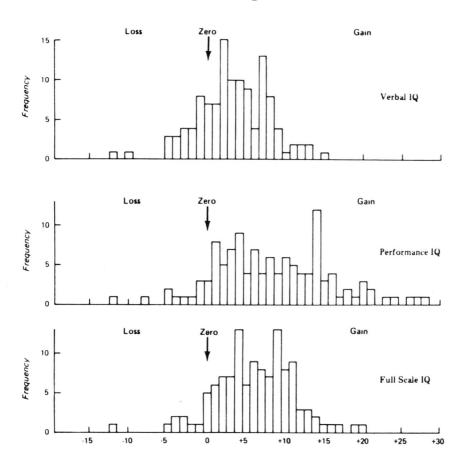

Fig. 1. Frequency of different magnitudes of gain or loss in VIQ, PIQ, and FSIQ from initial test to retest for 119 adults in the WAIS-R standardization sample.

Table 2

Frequency of Different Magnitudes of Gain or Loss in Scaled Scores on the Verbal Subtests From Test to Retest For 119 Adults in the WAIS-R Standardization Sample

Gain or Loss	INF n	INF %	DSP n	DSP %	VOC n	VOC %	ARITH n	ARITH %	COMP n	COMP %	SIM n	SIM %
−9												
−8												
−7												
−6	0		0		0		0		1	.8	0	
−5	0		1	.8	0		0		1	.8	0	
−4	1	.8	0	0	0		0		2	1.7	1	.8
−3	1	.8	3	2.5	2	1.7	2	1.7	3	2.5	0	0
−2	2	1.7	9	7.6	6	5.0	11	9.2	9	7.6	3	2.5
−1	10	8.4	14	11.8	17	14.3	12	10.1	22	18.5	23	19.3
0	50	42.0	37	31.1	50	42.0	36	30.3	34	28.6	33	27.7
1	35	29.4	26	21.8	29	24.4	24	20.2	21	17.6	20	16.8
2	12	10.1	18	15.1	10	8.4	18	15.1	11	9.2	18	15.1
3	5	4.2	9	7.6	5	4.2	11	9.2	10	8.4	9	7.6
4	1	.8	2	1.7	0	0	3	2.5	4	3.4	9	7.6
5	2	1.7	0	0	0	0	1	.8	0	0	2	1.7
6	0	0	0	0	0	0	1	.8	1	.8	1	.8
7												
8												
9												
Total	119	100	119	100	119	100	119	100	119	100	119	100
Mean	.6		.4		.2		.6		.2		.9	

studies utilizing the WAIS reported by Matarazzo et al. (1980, p. 96). Second, and as easily seen in Figure 1, with the exception of 7 subjects who showed *no* (zero) change in VIQ, 3 subjects in PIQ, and 5 subjects in FSIQ, each of the remaining 112 showed a change in the three IQ scores from test to retest. The range of these individual changes was greatest in PIQ where the changes on retest spanned a range of −12 to +28 points, was least for VIQ (−12 to +15) and, as would be expected, was intermediate for FSIQ (−12 to +20). Furthermore, although the majority of the 119 *increased* their score on retest, the practicing clinician cannot help but notice in Figure 1 that the scores of some individuals *decreased* from first to second testing. Specifically, and omitting the slight rounding off of errors in one or another line of Table 1, the numbers out of the 119 individuals who showed a *loss* were 24 (20.2% of the sample) in VIQ, 10 (8.4%) in PIQ, and 8 (6.7%) in FSIQ. Although only one or two of these subjects showed a decrease of more than 5 points, the fact that any of the 119 showed a loss at all is a critically important item of information for the

Table 3

Frequency of Different Magnitudes of Gain or Loss in Scaled Scores on the Performance Subtests From Test to Retest For 119 Adults in the WAIS-R Standardization Sample

Gain or Loss	PC		PA		BD		OA		DSY	
	n	%	n	%	n	%	n	%	n	%
—9										
—8										
—7										
—6										
—5	0		1	.8	0		1	.8	0	
—4	0		1	.8	0		2	1.7	0	
—3	3	2.5	4	3.4	2	1.7	0	0	2	1.7
—2	2	1.7	3	2.5	6	5.0	3	2.5	4	3.4
—1	5	4.2	15	12.6	13	10.9	7	5.9	9	7.6
0	39	32.8	21	17.6	32	26.9	21	17.6	30	25.2
1	25	21.0	25	21.0	41	34.5	21	17.6	41	34.5
2	26	21.8	14	11.8	13	10.9	17	14.3	14	11.8
3	14	11.8	11	9.2	8	6.7	21	17.6	14	11.8
4	2	1.7	12	10.1	2	1.7	11	9.2	2	1.7
5	2	1.7	6	5.0	2	1.7	8	6.7	2	1.7
6	1	.8	5	4.2	0	0	5	4.2	0	0
7	0	0	0	0	0	0	1	.8	1	.8
8	0	0	1	.8	0	0	1	.8	0	0
9										
Total	119	100	119	100	119	100	119	100	119	100
Mean	1.1		1.3		.7		1.9		.9	

practitioner, especially in view of the "practice effect" shown by the group as a whole as reflected in the increases in the three mean scores shown at the bottom of Table 1. Whereas the entire set of data in Table 1 is relevant, the fact that a *loss* in VIQ, PIQ, and FSIQ occurred in 20.2%, 8.4% and 6.7% respectively, of the individuals in this nonpatient, presumably healthy sample of community-living subjects provides the clinician with heretofore unavailable data for constituting a baseline of actuarial probability from a *normative* sample against which to evaluate a change of any magnitude (especially a gain) shown by one's own patient. Obviously, comparable studies of various types of *patient* samples will provide important additional base rate information. Until such studies are published, however, the frequencies of *retest* losses and gains shown in Table 1 and in Figure 1 provide a yardstick against which, by inference, to evaluate the "band of probable error" which surrounds an IQ score when such an IQ is obtained only in a *single* examination.

Nevertheless, it also is of importance for us to underscore for the practitioner the fact that, despite the variability from test to retest shown so clearly in Figure 1, the test-retest coefficients of correlation provided in the WAIS-R Manual for each of the three IQ measures (Wechsler, 1981, Table 11, p. 32) are in fact impressive, ranging from .89 to .97 for the two reliability subsamples. Therefore, what the actual frequencies of different magnitudes of gain or loss shown in Table 1 and Figure 1 contribute to clinical practice is to underscore the distinction between *relative* (or psychometric) reliability versus *absolute* reliability made in earlier discussions of this same issue (Matarazzo, Wiens, Matarazzo, & Goldstein, 1974; Matarazzo, Matarazzo, Wiens, Gallo, & Klonoff, 1976; Matarazzo et al., 1979; and Matarazzo et al., 1980). Namely, that such high *relative* retest reliability (a Pearson *r*) of a test, while an important datum, is not synonymous with a high *absolute* retest reliability (the presumed absence of a *clinically* meaningful change, in contrast to psychometric change, in relative position from test to retest for each of the three individual IQ scores of *each* of the subjects in the sample) on that same test. That is, the data presented in Table 1 and Figure 1 make quite clear that, although an instrument like the WAIS-R has high psychometric reliability (as assessed by the Pearson *r* and also implied by the very modest changes in the *means* for the group as a whole from initial test to retest shown at the bottom of Table 1 and which suggest an insignificant change on retest for the average subject), the magnitudes of the gain or loss from test to retest for one of the three scores for any given *individual* in this normal standardization sample are high enough at the upper and lower levels of each range to suggest that, until patient norms are found to be different, such actual *base-rates* as shown in Figure 1 might be used with profit by the practitioner as a yardstick against which to evaluate test-retest change obtained in a single clinical case (or in a group of such cases). The reader interested in specific examples of discrepancies which could occur in clinical practice will find these in our earlier publications on the test-retest reliability (stability) of the actual scores for any single *individual* on each of the tests, including the Wechsler scales, which make up the Halstead-Reitan Battery.

As an important contribution to this slowly accumulating but critically needed literature, Shatz (1981, pp. 174-176) has suggested that, in assessing the clinical significance of an increase or decrease in retest score, one should take into account, among other variables, the *age* of the individual who was examined. As stated above, data from the present study suggest that the age of a subject (in the range 25-35 versus 45-54) in the WAIS-R standardization group did *not* appear to influence his or her retest gain or loss. Additionally, the individual test-retest WAIS data earlier published in Matarazzo et al. (1973, 1979, and 1980) on 29 normal subjects whose mean age was 24 and on 17 patients who underwent carotid endarterectomy (mean age 62), when added to the WAIS-R data shown here in Table 1 for the present two groups whose mean ages fell between these two WAIS samples, indicate that subjects in *each* of the four WAIS and WAIS-R samples show retest changes across a rather wide range. Specifically, although admitting such an analysis provides only a single, early, and isolated finding, our study of the *percentages* of subjects in these four samples who showed retest gains or losses of each magnitude failed to suggest the presence of a differential age effect on these magnitudes. Nevertheless, if the practice of psychology is to be built upon increasingly firm scaffolding, actuarial base rates should be developed from different samples, of sufficient size, which differ on such potentially important variables such as age and the other variables identified by Shatz and other writers.

One other point regarding the findings in Table 1 needs to be underscored for the practitioner. The data presented here indicate that the single IQ score of any given *individual* is a bit less stable than may be implied by the high *median* Pearson *r* value of .94 which one may compute from the six values provided by Wechsler for the three pairs of WAIS-R IQ scores (Wechsler, 1981, p. 32). In fact, the potential variability ("unreliability") of any single IQ score as reflected in Figure 1 underscores a point made often by the first author. Namely, that such a test finding as a change in a Wechsler score from *test to retest* which *appears* to the practitioner to be clinically significant (or a difference found in a *single examination* in an individual's VIQ versus PIQ of 15 or more points which also suggests that it may be clinically significant) must be *corroborated* by non-test-based findings in the school, work, interpersonal, or medical history, or in the physical or laboratory findings, *in order for that test datum to be deemed clinically robust*. Additionally, if it is a truly meaningful finding, it typically also will be corroborated in one or more of the other neuropsychological tests which were administered to this patient.

The results presented in our Tables 2 and 3 for the WAIS-R subtest scores further underscore these points. As is the case with the three WAIS-R IQ values, the data reported in the Manual (Wechsler, 1981, p. 32) reveal that each of these 11 WAIS-R subtests possesses quite acceptable psychometric reliability. Specifically, the Pearson *r* values for the 11 subtests for the subsample of 71 retested adults aged 25-34, reading from left to right in Table 2 and continuing in Table 3, were as follows: .88, .89, .93, .80, .79, .82, .86, .69, .91, .72 and .86, for a *median* value of .86. For the slightly smaller sample of 48 adults aged 45-54 the corresponding values of *r* were: .94, .82, .91, .90, .82, .86, .89, .76, .80, .67, and .82, for a *median* value of .82. In addition, as shown in the bottom rows of Tables 2 and 3, the *mean* gains for the group of 119 subjects taken as a whole was quite small, ranging from a gain of 0.2 to only 1.9 scaled points. Added together, and as also was indicated was the case for the three IQ scores, these relatively high Pearson *r* values and very small changes in the means (and thus in the retest score of the average subject) from test to retest constitute a high relative (psychometric) reliability. Furthermore, the numbers and percentages shown in the row for zero (no) change from test to retest in Tables 2 and 3 also are impressively large. As shown, a full 42% of the 119 subjects earned exactly the same Information and Vocabulary subtest scaled score on retest as on the initial test. At the other end of the stability-instability range, a still impressive number of the 119 (17.6%) earned the same scaled score on retest on the Picture Arrangement and Object Assembly subtests.

Nevertheless, as the frequencies of different magnitudes of retest losses and gains in subtest *scaled* scores which occurred from test to retest which are shown in Tables 2 and 3 also make clear, the corresponding *absolute* reliability of a single subtest scaled score (its "variability" and thus inferential actuarial band of error) for any given individual is less robust than may be implied by these values of Pearson *r* or these small retest changes for the *average* subject considered in isolation.

Therefore, for those clinicians who have tended to impute important clinical significance to relatively small differences between one Wechsler subtest scaled score and another without utilizing considerable extratest corroborative evidence, the data in Tables 2 and 3 (and, of course, also in Table 1) reveal the potential danger of such a practice. Specifically, 1 person out of 119 (0.8%) *lost* a full 4 scaled score points on the Information subtest on retest and, at the other end, 2 out of the 119 *increased* their comparable Information scaled score by a full 5 points. It is highly improbable that an *individual* would ever fluctuate across this whole band of instability on retest which was *actually observed* in these 119 subjects used in the standardization. That clinical opinion not withstanding, the data (—40 to +5) in Table 2 show a range of *potential* change in any given individual's scaled score on the Information subtest. Corresponding percentages are shown for different magnitudes of gain or loss for each of the other 10 subtests. As is seen in Tables 2 and 3, not 1 of the 11 subtests showed what one could infer to be an actuarially persuasive high *clinical* reliability ("invariance") which would permit one to feel highly confident regarding the stability of a Wechsler subtest score which is determined only once. In fact, Tables 2 and 3 reveal that the magnitude of change which *actually* occurred in the scaled scores in this normative sample ranged from —5 to +8 for two subtests (Picture Arrangement and Object Assembly) at the high end, down through such ranges as from —5 to +4 for the changes which actually occurred in the Digit Span score, to the range of —3 to +3 for the Vocabulary subtest, at the lowest (most stable) end of observed change.

In an earlier extensive review of the literature of studies which had used the individual Wechsler subtests to construct profiles of the 11 subtests for differential diagnosis in psychopathology (Matarazzo, 1972, chapter 14), or for determining a ratio consisting of "hold" or "don't hold" subtests which might be useful in the diagnosis in psychopathology (Matarazzo, 1972, Chapter 14), or for determining a ratio consisting of "hold" or "don't hold" subtests which might be useful in the diagnosis of brain injury (Chapter 13), the first author of the present paper scores on the 11 subtests *in isolation.* By inference to the potential instability of a subtest score obtained in only a single examination, the data presented here in Tables 2 and 3, unfortunately not available previously in this form for the WAIS, quite likely constitute one of the main reasons these hundreds of studies which were conducted on the utility of "profile analysis" of the Wechsler scales in differential diagnosis yielded negative results. The present first author (Matarazzo et al., 1980, pp. 101-103) therefore suggested that, as a rule of thumb, a change of 3 to 5 scaled score points from test to retest in a single subtest score and also, by inference, a difference of the same size between two subtest scores in only a single administration, each constitutes adequate clinical potential for the practitioner *to begin to search for extratest corroborative evidence* of pathology. The empirical data presented in Tables 2 and 3 provide additional support for this clinical rule of thumb. The comparable rule of thumb regarding a difference between the VIQ and PIQ of an individual who is examined only once was that a discrepancy of 15 points likewise constitutes a datum which should stimulate the clinician to search for *corroborating,* extratest diagnostic evidence of pathology in the *clinical or social history* (Matarazzo, 1972, pp. 389-390; 426-427; 506-507). However, it also is critically important to underscore that exceptions to these rules of thumb are commonplace and have been discussed elsewhere (Matarazzo, 1972, pp. 389-390; Matarazzo et al., 1980, pp. 101-103; and Matarazzo & Herman, in press).

BASE-RATE DATA: WAIS-R VIQ-PIQ DIFFERENCES

The present authors recently completed a set of companion analyses on the WAIS-R standardization data which, as will be discussed below, also provide useful additional base-rate information for the practitioner (Matarazzo & Herman, in press).

METHOD

The work involved a detailed analysis of the frequencies of varying magnitudes of the *difference* in VIQ versus PIQ which actually occurred for *each* of the 1880 subjects of the total standardization sample. Except for the 119 subjects represented in the three first Tables and Figure 1 of the present report, the vast majority of these 1880 subjects were *not* retested. Nevertheless, the VIQ versus PIQ discrepancy score tabulated for *each* of these 1880 used in the WAIS-R standardization provides additional highly useful base rate information, albeit from only a single examination.

RESULTS

The interested reader will find in the Matarazzo and Herman (in press) chapter, tables of actual frequencies and percentages of the 1880 subjects who showed a VIQ-PIQ difference of *each* magnitude from —30 to +30 points presented separately both for three of the different age groups utilized by Wechsler and for five different subgroups which differed in their FSIQ. Those tables will not be reproduced here. Instead, we present here in Figure 2 a summary frequency distribution of the VIQ versus PIQ discrepancies for the total sample of 1880, not broken down be age or by FSIQ.

474

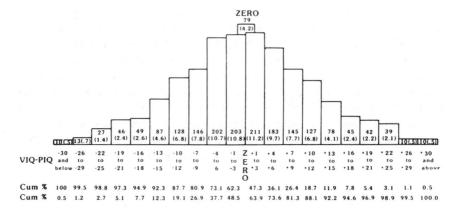

	-30 and below -29	-26 to -25	-22 to -21	-19 to -18	-16 to -15	-13 to -12	-10 to -9	-7 to	-4 to -3	-1 Z E R O	+1 +3	+4 +6	+7 +9	+10 +12	+13 +15	+16 +18	+19 +21	+22 +25	+26 +29	+30 and above
VIQ-PIQ																				
Cum %	100	99.5	98.8	97.3	94.9	92.3	87.7	80.9	73.1	62.3	47.3	36.1	26.4	18.7	11.9	7.8	5.4	3.1	1.1	0.5
Cum %	0.5	1.2	2.7	5.1	7.7	12.3	19.1	26.9	37.7	48.5	63.9	73.6	81.3	88.1	92.2	94.6	96.9	98.9	99.5	100.0

Fig. 2. Frequencies (and Percentages) of Differences between VIQ and PIQ in WAIS-R Standardization Sample.

A number of features of these VIQ versus PIQ differences actually demonstrated by these healthy, community-living subjects in this standardization sample are noteworthy. First, as is clear in Figure 2, the individual 1880 VIQ versus PIQ discrepancies are approximately *normally* distributed. Furthermore, statistical analyses revealed that the *mean* of these 1880 VIQ-PIQ differences was almost exactly zero (namely, —0.10) with a standard deviation of 11.12 and a standard error of 0.26. Second, Figure 2 reveals that the *range* of these VIQ-PIQ differences (—30 to +30) in these 1880 healthy subjects is considerably larger than what many clinicians might have anticipated. (Although abbreviated in Figure 2 the actual range was —43 to +49). Accordingly, because of the potential importance of these normative base rate VIQ-PIQ differences in the practice of clinical neuropsychology, we decided to list here in Table 4 the percent of the 1880 subjects who showed a discrepancy at each of a number of different magnitudes of gain and loss. Thus, as is shown graphically in Figure 2 but tabulated for easier visualization in Table 4, 4.2% of the 1880 subjects had a VIQ-PIQ difference of zero (0) points, 11.2% of them had a difference which fell between +1 and +3 points, and a corresponding 10.8% of them had a difference which fell between —1 and —3 points. The first of these values (4.2) is shown in the bottom row of Table 4, and the values of 11.2 and 10.8% are tabulated in the *row* just above it. The rest of Table 4 presents the comparable percentages which were observed for each of a number of other magnitudes of VIQ versus PIQ discrepancies.

Table 4

Cumulative Percentage Distributions Across All Ages of the Differences (Regardless of Sign) Between WAIS-R VIQ and PIQ

Size of Difference Between VIQ and PIQ	% V > P (+ Difference)	% P > V (— Difference)	Sum of + and — Differences	WAIS-R Cumulative Percentage**
30 and above	.5	.5	1.1*	100.0
26-29	.5	.7	1.2	98.9
22-25	2.1	1.4	3.5	97.7
19-21	2.2	2.4	4.7	94.2
16-18	2.4	2.6	5.0	89.5
13-15	4.1	4.6	8.8	84.5
10-12	6.8	6.8	13.6	75.7
7-9	7.7	7.8	15.5	62.2
4-6	9.7	10.7	20.5	46.7
1-3	11.2	10.8	22.0	26.2
0	—	—	—	4.2

* The percentages in this Table do not sum exactly due to "rounding off" errors
** Percent at or below the larger of the two numbers in column 1

DISCUSSION

The data in the last column in Table 4 would appear to be of special importance to the neuropsychologist or other practitioner of psychology. As described above, the percentages shown in that column reveal how often a VIQ-PIQ difference of varying magnitudes *actually occurred* in the 1880 seemingly healthy, normal, community-living subjects who constituted the WAIS-R standardization sample. Thus, for example, a reader who wishes to determine how frequently a VIQ-PIQ difference of any of the magnitudes which are shown in the extreme *left* hand column of Table 4 occurred need only read across to the column at the extreme right of the table to obtain that information. As examples, among the 1880 subjects 4.2% had a VIQ-PIQ difference of zero (0), 26.2% of 3 points or less, 75.7% of 12 points or less, and 98.9% of 29 points or less. (Using the obverse of these figures by substracting each from 100% reveals that 95.8, 73.8, 24.3, and 1.1% had a VIQ-PIQ discrepancy that was larger than zero, 3, 12, and 29 IQ points, respectively.) Use of the actual percentage at *each* point shown in Figure 2 instead of the ranges of points shown in the extreme left column of Table 4 permitted us to compute the VIQ-PIQ differences which *actually occurred* in the standardization sample 1 time in 100 subjects, 5 times, 10 times, and also 15 times in 100 subjects. These VIQ-PIQ differences are presented in the last column of

Table 5. By comparing these figures in the last column of Table 5 with the actuarial frequency data (which in effect amount to actually observed *p*-values) in the first column of that same table, one is able to discern how frequently (in how many subjects) in terms of the *p*-values usually used by investigators (first column) a VIQ-PIQ discrepancy of different magnitudes (last column) actually occurred in these 1880 subjects. Thus, regardless of its plus or minus sign, the last column of Table 5 reveals that a VIQ versus PIQ difference of 16, 19, 23 and 30 points actually occurred with a probability value of .15, .10, .05 and .01, respectively.

The importance of the actuarial data shown in the last column of Table 5 becomes clear when one examines the much *smaller* VIQ-PIQ differences in magnitudes which are needed at these same *p*-values to demonstrate that such a difference is significantly different from zero in the statistical sence, as determined by using the *standard error of measurement* of the VIQ-PIQ difference.

Until Kaufman (1976, 1979) made the same point in relation to the WISC-R standardization sample, many practitioners had mistakenly equated the data shown in the middle column of our Table 5 (the probability that such a difference is significantly different from zero) with those shown in the last column (the actual frequency of occurrence of such differences, or their actuarially determined probability). Such practitioners tended to overlook in their work with an individual patient that *p*-values based on how large a VIQ-PIQ difference must be to be significantly different from zero at the .01 or .05, etc. levels of statistical confidence tells us nothing about *how often* such VIQ-PIQ differences actually occur in a sample of normal subjects. Thus, using WISC-R data like the WAIS-R data in our Table 5, Kaufman summarized this critically important point by reference to an example (a boy with a 12 point VIQ-PIQ difference) not infrequently seen when one examines children in the schools. Kaufman next went on to add that, although such a VIQ-PIQ difference of 12 points on the WISC-R is statistically significantly different from zero at the .05 level of probability, his analyses of the WISC-R data revealed that such a 12-point difference *actually was*

Table 5

Statistically Reliably Different and Actually Empirically Different Magnitudes of VIQ and PIQ Discrepancies (Regardless of Sign) Across All Ages in the WAIS-R Standardization Sample

p value	Magnitude of VIQ versus PIQ Difference Required to be Statistically Reliably Different from Zero	Magnitude of VIQ versus PIQ Difference Actually Empirically Observed at Each Level of Probability
.15	7	16
.10	8	19
.05	10	23
.01	13	30

shown by 30% of the 2200 normal youngsters on whom the WISC-R was standardized. He thus cautioned the practitioner that an administrative action labelling a school child emotionally disturbed on the basis of this .05 level of statistical significance would be a professionally unsupportable act despite its appearing to be based on a scientific foundation (namely, a *p* of .05). The clinical neuropsychologist will see some similarity between that conclusion and the many implications which are suggested in the data presented here in Tables 4 and 5 and Figure 2 and which are discussed in considerable detail in the chapter devoted to these WAIS-R VIQ-PIQ differences in Matarazzo and Herman (in press). As but one example, whereas a WAIS-R VIQ versus PIQ difference of 13 points is shown in the *middle* column of Table 5 (on the basis of its standard error of measurement) to be significantly different from zero with a probability value of .01, the empirical data in the last column of Table 4 (or in Figure 2) reveal that such a 13-point (or greater) difference actually occurred in 11.9% of the cases in the plus direction and in 12.3 (100-87.7)% of the cases in the minus direction, for a total of 24.3% of the time in the 1880 individuals in the standardization sample. (This figure of 24.3% also is obtainable from the figure given five lines up in the last column of Table 4, namely, 100-75.7%, for the cumulative percentages, for a VIQ-PIQ discrepancy which is *over* 12 points.) A clinician thus must ask how pathognomonic or otherwise clinically meaningful is a *statistically* significant difference of 13 points (*p* of .01) if it *actually occurs* in 24.3% of normal, community-living American adults? Matarazzo and Herman (in press) discuss a number of variables worthy of further examination which accumulating research suggests may have the potential to produce or otherwise be associated with a VIQ-PIQ difference in any given individual, including those in the WAIS-R standardization sample. The interested reader is referred to that chapter for a detailed discussion.

REFERENCES

Kaufman, A. S. (1976). Verbal-Performance IQ discrepancies on the WISC-R. *Journal of Consulting and Clinical Psychology, 44*, 739-744.

Kaufman, A. S. (1979). *Intelligent testing with the WISC-R*. New York: Wiley-Interscience.

Matarazzo, J. D. (1972). *Wechsler's measurement and appraisal of adult intelligence* (5th and enlarged ed.). New York: Oxford Press.

Matarazzo, J. D., Carmody, T. P., & Jacobs, L. D. (1980). Test-retest reliability and stability of the WAIS: A literature review with implications for clinical practice. *Journal of Clinical Neuropsychology, 2*, 89-105.

Matarazzo, J. D., & Herman, D. O. (in press): Clinical uses of the WAIS-R: Base rates of differences between VIQ and PIQ in the WAIS-R standardization sample. In B. B. Wolman (Ed.), *Handbook of intelligence: Theories, measurements, and applications.* New York: John Wiley & Sons.

Matarazzo, J. D., Matarazzo, R. G., Wiens, A. N., Gallo, A. E., Jr., & Klonoff, H. (1976). Test-retest reliability of the Halstead Impairment Index in a normal, a schizophrenic, and two samples of organic patients. *Journal of Clinical Psychology, 32*, 338-349.

478

Matarazzo, J. D., Wiens, A. N., Matarazzo, R. G., & Goldstein, S. G. (1974). Psychometric and clinical test-retest reliability of the Halstead Impairment Index in a sample of healthy, young, normal men. *Journal of Nervous and Mental Disease, 158*, 37 - 49.

Matarazzo, R. G., Matarazzo, J. D., Gallo, A. E., Jr., & Wiens, A. N. (1979). IQ and neuropsychological changes following carotid endarterectomy. *Journal of Clinical Neuropsychology, 1*, 97-116.

Matarazzo, R. G., Wiens, A. N., Matarazzo, J. D., & Manaugh, T. S. (1973). Test-retest reliability of the WAIS in a normal population. *Journal of Clinical Psychology, 29*, 194-197.

Parker, J. C., Granberg, B. W., Nichols, W. K., Jones, J. G., & Hewett, J. E. (in press). Mental status outcomes following carotid endarterectomy: A six-month analysis. *Journal of Clinical Neuropsychology*.

Shatz, M. W. (1981). WAIS practice effects in clinical neuropsychology. *Journal of Clinical Neuropsychology, 3*, 171-179.

Wechsler, D. (1981). *Manual for the Wechsler Adult Intelligence Scale-Revised.* New York: The Psychological Corporation.

The Clinical Neuropsychologist
1989, Vol. 3, No. 3, pp. 265-273

V-C

Test-Retest Reliability of the Halstead-Reitan Battery and the WAIS in a Neuropsychiatric Population

Gerald Goldstein and John R. Watson
Highland Drive VAMC, Pittsburgh, PA
and University of Pittsburgh

ABSTRACT

Data are presented concerning the test-retest reliability of the Halstead-Reitan battery and the WAIS in a heterogeneous neuropsychiatric sample of 150 patients. Relative reliability or stability of results was evaluated through use of Pearson r correlation coefficients, while absolute reliability, or sensitivity to change in clinical condition, was evaluated with paired sample t tests. Subgroups of alcoholic/trauma, schizophrenic, and vascular disease patients were extracted from the total sample in order to examine for the possibility of different reliability levels among different clinical groups. It was found that most of the components of the Halstead-Reitan battery had psychometrically satisfactory relative reliability levels. However, schizophrenics exhibited significantly lower levels of reliability than did the other subgroups. Differences in absolute reliability were characterized by a greater incidence of improved performance on second testing in the alcoholic/trauma subgroup than in the other subgroups.

Test-retest reliabilities of neuropsychological tests have been difficult to establish because there are often substantial clinical changes in patients between the two testings. Clark (1986), among others, has pointed out that reliability is compromised when nuisance experimental or environmental variables intervene between testing occasions. Many neuropsychological tests do not readily lend themselves to alternative methods of establishing reliability, notably the alternate forms and split-half methods, although the split-half method has been used to determine the reliability of the WAIS (Wechsler, 1955) and the Halstead Category Test (Shaw, 1966). Other tests in the Halstead-Reitan battery (HRB) would be more amenable to having reliability established by the test-retest method.

Indebtedness is expressed to the Veterans Administration for support of this research.

In clinical assessment, the term reliability has been used in two senses. In the more traditional psychometric sense, reliability has to do with stability of responses over testing occasions. Indeed, Cronbach (1960) refers to the test-retest reliability correlation coefficient as the coefficient of stability. The other sense in which the term is used has to do with whether or not a test reliably describes changes in the clinical condition of the patient. Matarazzo, Carmody, and Jacobs (1980) have described these two definitions as relative reliability in the first case and absolute reliability in the second. The present study deals primarily with relative reliability, but absolute reliability was also considered. Absolute reliability may also be viewed as a form of validity in that it provides an index of the sensitivity of a test to changes in clinical condition. Ideally, tests should be reliable in the sense of accuracy of measurement as well as sensitive to fluctuations in clinical status. Relative test-retest reliability is generally evaluated with the Pearson r correlation coefficient. Because of that, high reliabilities may be obtained despite substantial changes in test scores between testing occasions as long as the ranking of scores remains relatively constant between testings. However, evaluating changes in performance levels may be readily accomplished through comparing mean scores for the two testings.

Test-retest reliability studies of the HRB have been conducted with normal adults or stable patients by Matarazzo, Matarazzo, Wiens, Gallo and Klonoff (1976), Matarazzo, Wiens, Matarazzo, and Goldstein (1974) and Matarazzo et al. (1980). While these studies all reported satisfactory levels of reliability coefficients, as indicated, they were all done with normals or clinically stable patients. The present study assessed the extent to which the various components of the HRB and the WAIS retain psychometric stability in patients who may have a fluctuating course of illness, or patients who are thought to typically produce unreliable test performances. Head injured and alcoholic patients would represent the first type, while schizophrenics would represent the second. We also performed a separate analysis for a subgroup of patients with diffuse cerebral vascular disease in order to compare our findings with those of Matarazzo et al. (1976) who also did test-retest reliability studies of the Halstead Category test and the Halstead Impairment Index with such a group and with a group of schizophrenics. Thus, test-retest reliabilities within these subgroups were computed separately in addition to the computations performed for the entire sample of neuropsychiatric patients.

METHOD

Subjects. The sample consisted of 150 cases tested with the HRB and the WAIS on more than one occasion. These cases were drawn from a collection of several thousand patients tested over a period of 23 years at two VA medical centers. The sample consisted mainly of chronic neuropsychiatric patients who were tested initially as inpatients and retested as outpatients, readmitted inpatients, or during the course of long-term inpatient hospitalization. Therefore, most of the subjects were in continued treatment or observation appropriate to their illnesses. Most notably, the majority of the schizophrenic patients were being maintained on psychoactive medications over the period of their two testings. The diagnoses are presented in Table 1.

Table 1. Diagnoses of 150 Subjects

Schizophrenia	33
Alcoholism/Trauma	54
Vascular Disease	16
Congenital Brain Malformation	10
Neoplasm	4
Multiple Sclerosis	3
Neuronal Degenerative Diseases	7
Toxic Disorders	5
Infectious Diseases	5
Epilepsy	16
Other Neurological Disorders	6

Note: Total adds to more than 150 because of multiple diagnoses.

The diagnostic groups selected for separate analyses were the alcoholics, schizophrenics, head trauma patients, and patients with vascular disorders. Head trauma and alcoholic patients were treated as a single subgroup because of the high prevalence of their coexistence in the present sample. There were also additional instances in which the association between head trauma and alcohol use was unclear, as in the case of the intoxicated individual who sustains head trauma in an accident. The remaining cases, representing a variety of neuropsychiatric disorders, were not analyzed as separate groups, but were included in the computation of reliability coefficients for the total sample of 150 cases.

The mean age for the total sample was 42.67 years (SD=12.42), and the mean level of education was 11.67 years (SD=3.19). The three subgroups did not differ from each other with regard to age ($F(2,85)$=2.88, $p > .05$) or education ($F(2,85)$=1.19, $p > .05$). All subjects were male. In all cases, diagnoses were established independently of the neuropsychological test results. State-of-the-art methods were used but, because of the length of time over which the data were collected, the methods used for establishing diagnoses were not always the same. Additionally, the alcoholic and schizophrenic patients were diagnosed utilizing DSM-II or DSM-III criteria, depending upon the time of testing.

Procedure. Pearson r test-retest correlations were computed for the full sample of 150 cases and for subsamples of alcoholic, head trauma, schizophrenic, and vascular disease patients. As indicated above, alcoholic and head trauma patients were combined. For purposes of evaluating level of performance changes between first and second testings, paired sample t-tests were employed.

RESULTS

Intertest Intervals. The mean intertest interval for the total sample was 105.9 weeks (SD=100.55). The intervals ranged from 4 to 469 weeks. The mean intertest intervals for the alcoholic/trauma, schizophrenic, and vascular subgroups were 93.21 (SD=86.25), 97.18 (SD=87.13), and 99.42 (SD=84.80) weeks, respectively. The differences among length of intertest intervals were not statistically significant ($F(2,85)$=.03, $p > .05$).

Relative Reliability. The test-retest correlations for the total sample and for the subgroups within it are presented in Table 2. It can be seen in the results of the total sample that the coefficients tend to be reasonably high, never falling below .48. The correlations obtained in the alcohol/trauma group are roughly comparable to those obtained for the total sample. However, there was a substantial number of low correlations in the schizophrenic data, notably in the cases of the WAIS Picture Arrangement subtest and the Trail Making Test, Part A. Their correlation for the Average Impairment Rating was lower than that of the other subgroups.

In order to determine whether the correlation coefficients of the schizophrenic patients were significantly lower than those of the other subgroups a one-way analysis of variance was computed with the correlation coefficients as the dependent measures and subgroup membership as the independent variable. The result was statistically significant ($F(2,81)$ = 17.66, $p < .01$). A Scheffé test indicated that the schizophrenics had significantly lower coefficients than did the other subgroups; the other groups did not differ significantly from each other.

Regarding comparisons with the Matarazzo et al. (1976) paper, both studies yielded exceptionally high coefficients in the vascular disorder subgroups for their respective versions of the impairment index (Halstead Impairment Index and Average Impairment Rating (r=.82 and .81) and for the Category Test (r=.96 and .94). There were, however, differences between the two studies in the case of the schizophrenics. Matarazzo et al. reported a coefficient of .83 for the Halstead Impairment Index and .72 for the Category test. Our corresponding correlations in the schizophrenic subgroup were .63 for the Average Impairment Rating and .53 for the Category Test.

Absolute Reliability. Means, standard deviations and paired-sample t-test results for the total sample and for the subgroups were computed in order to evaluate absolute reliability (i.e., actual changes in test scores over testing occasions). In the case of the total sample, significant changes in the direction of improvement

Table 2. Test-Retest Reliability Coefficients for the Total Sample and Alcoholic/Trauma, Schizophrenic and Vascular Disorder Subgroups.

Test	Total	Alcoholic/ Trauma	Schizophrenic	Vascular Disorder
	(n = 150)	(n = 61)	(n = 33)	(n = 16)
WAIS Information	.87	.84	.82	.94
WAIS Comprehension	.74	.79	.61	.82
WAIS Arithmetic	.74	.75	.67	.76
WAIS Similarities	.78	.80	.75	.70
WAIS Digit Span	.67	.74	.64	.85
WAIS Vocabulary	.86	.82	.88	.83
WAIS Digit Symbol	.68	.79	.38	.84
WAIS Picture Completion	.67	.72	.59	.69
WAIS Block Design	.63	.66	.41	.73
WAIS Picture Arrangement	.57	.69	.28	.76
WAIS Object Assembly	.68	.80	.48	.84
WAIS Verbal IQ	.89	.92	.81	.91
WAIS Performance IQ	.74	.84	.44	.92
WAIS Full Scale IQ	.83	.89	.64	.93
Category Test Errors	.69	.73	.53	.94
TPT-Time	.66	.72	.71	.74
TPT-Memory	.59	.61	.46	.73
TPT-Location	.48	.69	.32	.36
Speech Sounds Perception Test-Errors	.77	.80	.71	.88
Seashore Rhythm Test-Errors	.57	.50	.53	.68
Trail Making Test-Part A-Secs.	.69	.66	.36	.94
Trail Making Test-Part B-Secs.	.66	.66	.63	.86
Finger Tapping-Dominant-Taps	.67	.64	.73	.66
Finger Tapping Nondominant-Taps	.81	.84	.70	.87
Aphasia Screening Errors	.71	.69	.52	.75
Average Impairment Rating	.71	.75	.63	.81

Abbreviation: TPT = Tactual Performance Test.

were noted for WAIS Picture Completion, Object Assembly, Performance IQ, and Full Scale IQ, and for the Average Impairment Rating. In the alcoholic/trauma group, significant improvement was found for WAIS Comprehension, Vocabulary, Picture Arrangement, Object Assembly, Verbal IQ, Performance IQ, Full Scale IQ, the Category Test, and the Memory component of the Tactual Performance Test; significant decrement was found for WAIS Vocabulary. Significant improvement was only found for WAIS Picture Completion and Object Assembly in the schizophrenic group, and for the Category Test in the vascular disorder group.[1]

It is noteworthy that the alcoholic/trauma subgroup exhibited many more significant changes than did the other subgroups. It would appear that, while patients with fluctuating histories may show many absolute changes on neuropsychological tests relative to patients with more stable conditions, those changes do not appear to exert a considerable influence on the relative reliability of those tests.

DISCUSSION

These findings would suggest that the reliabilities, in the sense of stability, of the HRB and WAIS are relatively high in heterogeneous patient groups. Stability, or relative reliability is, however, less robust among schizophrenics than among patients with neurological and other neuropsychiatric disorders. This finding would be consistent with the widely held clinical view that the performance of schizophrenic patients tends to be unreliable. We might comment, however, that the reliability coefficients obtained for the schizophrenic subjects on many of the tests were quite comparable to those found in the other subgroups. Substantial unreliability was only noted among the schizophrenics for certain tests, notably those involving psychomotor speed (e.g., WAIS Digit Symbol and Trail Making Test, Part A) or visual perceptual abilities (e.g., WAIS Picture Completion and Picture Arrangement subtests). Furthermore, the issue of whether or not the unreliability noted is a function of the schizophrenia itself or of associated factors such as medication status or additional diagnoses could not be addressed in the present study.

The results also indicate that stability can be maintained in the face of changes in absolute reliability. The alcoholic/trauma subgroup, in particular, demonstrated several significant changes on retesting, but the reliability coefficients were generally comparable to those obtained for the vascular disorder group, which only had one signficant change. Conversely, relative reliability can be low in association with high absolute reliability. For example, in the schizophrenic subgroup there were only two significant changes in test performance between testing occasions but, as indicated above, the reliability coefficients tended to be

---

[1] A complete set of quantitative data may be obtained from the senior author.

low relative to the other subgroups. The implication of this set of findings would appear to be that changes in test performance may be noted over time on tests in which the relative ranking of subjects across testing occasions is well preserved.

These findings would suggest that scores from most of the components of the HRB and the WAIS change on retesting in a relatively stable way. That is, they are reasonably reliable from a psychometric standpoint. It is noteworthy that the sample consisted of a heterogeneous but relatively representative group of neuropsychiatric patients, and that the average test-retest interval was about 2 years. Different results might be obtained for patients with more rapidly resolving or deteriorating disorders, but the present findings would appear to be relevant to clinicians working with relatively chronic, stable patients.

The one exception to the high stability found would appear to be in the case of schizophrenic patients on certain tests. Our findings are not entirely consistent with those of Matarazzo et al. (1976) who found a greater degree of stability in their schizophrenics than we did. With regard to absolute reliability, it was noted that patients with stable vascular disorders showed substantially fewer statistically significant changes on retesting than did patients with histories of alcoholism and/or head trauma. We viewed these latter conditions as having the potential for fluctuating courses of illness.

The fact that the great majority of significant changes were in the direction of improvement is difficult to interpret. One major consideration would be practice effects, and it is possible that those components that showed changes are those most amenable to such effects. That is, the changes may not reflect actual clinical improvement. The present study cannot answer that question since it did not involve consideration of clinical outcome data. However, the finding that there were more improved scores in the alcoholic/trauma subgroup than in the vascular and schizophrenic subgroups would not be entirely consistent with a practice effect rationale. Alcoholism and trauma are conditions in which recovery is more probable than is the case for chronic vascular and schizophrenic disorders.

There seems little question, however, that absolute reliability studies are best accomplished when objective outcome data are available. In that regard, we would note that objective outcome data are preferable to clinical prognoses. In an earlier stage of this research we obtained prognostic ratings concerning outcome from clinicians, but found those ratings to be of questionable value because of poor interrater reliability.

REFERENCES

Clark, C.M. (1986). Statistical models and their application in clinical neuropsychological research and practice. In S.B. Filskov & T.J. Boll (Eds.), *Handbook of clinical neuropsychology* (Vol. 2, pp. 577-605). New York: John Wiley & Sons.

Cronbach, L. J. (1960). *Essentials of psychological testing.* New York: Harper & Brothers.

Reitan, R.M., & Wolfson, D. (1985). *The Halstead-Reitan neuropsychological test battery: Theory and clinical interpretation.* Tucson, AZ: Neuropsychology Press.

Matarazzo, J. D., Carmody, T.P., & Jacobs, L. D. (1980). Test-retest reliability and stability of the WAIS: A literature review with implications for clinical practice. *Journal of Clinical Neuropsychology, 2,* 89-105.

Matarazzo, J.D., Matarazzo, R. G., Wiens, A.N., Gallo, A. E. Jr., & Klonoff, H. (1976). Retest reliability of the Halstead impairment index in a normal, a schizophrenic, and two samples of organic patients. *Journal of Clinical Psychology, 32,* 338-349.

Matarazzo, J.D., Wiens, A.N., Matarazzo, R.G., & Goldstein, S.G. (1974). Psychometric and clinical test-retest reliability of the Halstead impairment index in a sample of healthy, young, normal men. *Journal of Nervous and Mental Disease, 158,* 37-49.

Shaw, D. J. (1966). The reliability and validity of the Halstead Category Test. *Journal of Clinical Psychology, 22,* 176-180.

Wechsler, D. (1955). *Wechsler Adult Intelligence Scale Manual.* New York: Psychological Corporation.

Journal of Clinical and Experimental Neuropsychology
1989, Vol. 11, No. 4, pp. 423-428

WAIS-R Test-Retest Reliability
in a Normal Elderly Sample*

William G. Snow and Mary C. Tierney
Sunnybrook Medical Centre

Maria L. Zorzitto, Rory H. Fisher, and David W. Reid
Department of Extended Care
Sunnybrook Medical Centre

ABSTRACT

We examined the 1-year test-retest reliability of WAIS-R Verbal, Performance, and Full-Scale IQs in a sample of 101 older normal individuals (mean age = 67.1). The respective Pearson rs were .86, .85, and .90. The median retest reliability coefficient for the WAIS-R subtests was .71. The test-retest reliability for the Verbal-Performance Discrepancy was .69. These data indicate that IQ scores are reliable in older normal individuals for this retest interval, but less confidence can be placed in the reliability of subtest scores and the Verbal-Performance Discrepancy.

In assessing the intellectual functioning of the elderly, the retest reliability of the tests one uses is of crucial importance. An individual's decline in intelligence in later life may be a sign of a dementing process. Such decline may also be associated with an increased risk of mortality (see, e.g., Siegler, 1980, pp 183-187). Tests which are unreliable may either fail to detect intellectual decline in those who are truly experiencing cognitive deterioration or, alternatively, give evidence of such deterioration where no real intellectual decline is present.

The Wechsler Adult Intelligence Scale (WAIS) is the most popular measure of intellectual functioning in the United States (Lubin, Larsen, & Matarazzo, 1984). However, in spite of its popularity, there is surprisingly little data about the test-retest reliability of any of the versions of the Wechsler adult intelligence scales (that is, Wechsler Bellevue, WAIS, or WAIS-R) with geriatric subjects.

* This paper is based in part on a paper presented in the symposium *Issues in the neuropsychological application of information from the WAIS-R* (K. M. Adams, Chair) at the annual meeting of the American Psychological Association (1986, August), Washington.

This research was supported by the Ontario Ministry of Health, the Gerontology Research Council of Ontario, the Canadian Geriatric Research Society, and the Sunnybrook Medical Centre Research Fund.

The first such study was conducted by Berkowitz and Green (1963) who reported test-retest correlations of .93 for VIQ, .86 for PIQ, and .92 for FSIQ for 184 hospitalized male VA patients (mean age 65 years at reassessment) who were retested with the Wechsler-Bellevue (Form I) an average of 8.6 years after their initial assessments.

Kendrick and Post (1967) examined test-retest coefficients for WAIS VIQ and PIQ in a sample of 30 depressed and normal individuals and 10 brain- damaged individuals (mean age for the entire sample - 70.5 years) retested at either 6 or 12 weeks after their first assessments. For the depressed and normal individuals, VIQ test-retest coefficients ranged between .89 and .95 across the retest intervals. The PIQ retest coefficients for these two groups were slightly smaller, ranging from .66 (12-week interval) to .85 (6-week interval). For the brain-damaged subjects, IQ test-retest correlations ranged from .81 to .87; PIQ test-retest correlations ranged from .90 to .94.

Consistent with the sparsity of research on the test-retest reliability of the WAIS is the lack of any published studies with any of the Wechsler scales which have examined test-retest reliability with *normal* older adults. Given the abiding interest in longitudinal studies of intelligence in older individuals, this is particularly remarkable.

The purpose of this paper is to examine the 1-year test-retest reliability of the WAIS-R in normal elderly individuals. In addition, since many psychologists are interested in the potential diagnostic utility of the discrepancy between VIQ and PIQ values, we also report the test-retest reliability for that discrepancy score over this same period. It was hoped that these analyses would provide an index of the stability of this measure which would be of interest to clinicians and researchers alike.

METHOD

As part of a prospective study of Alzheimer's Disease and other dementias, we reassessed a group of noninstitutionalized normal elderly volunteers 1 year after they had initially been tested with the Wechsler Adult Intelligence Scale-Revised (Wechsler, 1981). Each of these individuals had undergone medical examination at the time of both the initial assessment and the reassessment and had been classified as neurologically normal at both assessments. These individuals were volunteers, most of whom had been recruited through an advertisement on a local radio station. A few of the volunteers were relatives/ spouses of the demented patients who were tested as part of the larger study or were volunteers who were members of the local Alzheimer's society.

There were 101 patients in this sample (41 males, 60 females). Information on patient age, education, and test performance is presented in Table 1. Subjects were retested an average of 1.1 years after their first assessment (range = .9 to 2.0 years). All but eight of the subjects were retested by a different examiner in the second year.

Of the 101 subjects, 14 were not readministered the Object Assembly subtest for reasons of time constraints. For those subjects, Performance Scale and Full Scale IQ's were duly prorated according to the instructions in the manual.

Table 1

Demographic variables

	M (SD)	Range
Age at first assessment	67.1 (7.7)	50-84
Education (In years)	15.0 (3.1)	6-23
Year One:		
VIQ	117.0 (9.4)	86-135
PIQ	110.7 (13.2)	74-142
FSIQ	116.0 (11.4)	81-140
Year Two:		
VIQ	118.3 (9.9)	81-136
PIQ	112.2 (12.7)	72-152
FSIQ	117.8 (11.6)	77-150

RESULTS

Retest reliability (Pearson r) over this period was .86 for VIQ, .85 for PIQ, and .90 for FSIQ. The respective standard errors of estimation (Knight, 1983; Lord & Novik, 1968) were 3.25, 4.73, and 3.45. The reliability of the Verbal-Performance Discrepancy was $r = .69$, with a standard error of estimation of 2.88. Information on the test-retest reliability of the various subtests is presented in Table 2.

While these test-retest data provide an index of the relative stability of test scores over the interval in question, they do not indicate how much IQ scores varied in a practical sense from one year to the next. We therefore tabulated the proportion of the population showing changes of different magnitudes over one year. Table 3 indicates the percentage of subjects who show changes of less than or greater than 10 points over this time period. (This range was chosen because it was presumed that the average clinician would be concerned by changes of this magnitude over a 1-year period). Table 4 presents data on the change in magnitude of the Verbal-Performance Discrepancy from Year 1 to Year 2. It also indicates the percentage of subjects in each year who obtained Verbal-Performance Discrepancy scores of a given magnitude and direction.

DISCUSSION

For normal healthy elderly individuals in the present study, the reliability of the three major measures of intellectual functioning was high over a 1-year interval. The figures obtained were not as high as those reported by Wechsler (1981) for younger subjects, but his retest interval was much shorter.

Most of the subtest scaled scores were also relatively stable over the period in question, although the magnitude of the test-retest correlations was lower than those for the IQ scores. The median test-retest correlation for the 11 subtests in

Table 2

Retest Reliability of WAIS-R Subtests

Information[a]	.81
Digit Span	.66
Vocabulary	.71
Arithmetic	.72
Comprehension	.51
Similarities	.65
Picture Completion	.65
Picture Arrangement	.74
Block Design	.84
Object Assembly	.71
Digit Symbol	.91

[a] All $ns = 101$ except Object Assembly which is 87.

Table 3

Percentages of Normal Subjects Showing IQ Test Score Changes
of Different Magnitudes at One-Year Retest

IQ Range	VIQ	PIQ	FSIQ
< -10	1.0	5.0	1.0
-10 to -1	39.2	31.7	31.7
0	10.8	6.9	6.9
$+1$ to $+10$	47.0	46.5	55.4
$> +10$	2.0	9.9	5.0

the present sample was .71. In Wechsler's (1981) older sample, the median test-retest correlation was .82. Given the differences in test-retest intervals between his sample and the present, a difference of such a magnitude is hardly surprising. The only anomalous finding in the present study was the unexpectedly low test-retest reliability of the Comprehension subtest. The reason for the low test-retest reliability of this measure in this sample is unclear.

In terms of magnitude of change, Table 3 indicates that more patients did better on reassessment than did worse. Much of the variation seen was obviously trivial, however. For VIQ and FSIQ values, fewer than 10% of the sample showed changes of 10 points or more either way. There was slightly more fluctuation in PIQ values with almost 15% of the subjects showing variation of similar magnitudes.

As expected, given that the reliability of a difference score is constrained by the reliability of the test scores on which it is based, the reliability of the V-P discrepancy was less adequate. This was particularly the case for the more extreme discrepancy scores in this sample. Thus, the data in Table 4 indicate that, of the three individuals whose PIQ was 15 or more points greater than their VIQ at Year 1, only one had such an extreme value at Year 2. Of the 21 who had

Table 4

Percentage of Patients Obtaining Verbal-Performance Discrepancy Scores
of Different Magnitudes in Years 1 and 2

		Year 2					
		<-14	-14 to -10	-9 to 0	$+1$ to $+9$	$+10$ to $+14$	$>+14$	Total
Year 1	<-14	.99	.99	.99	0.00	0.00	0.00	2.97
	-10 to -14	0.00	0.00	1.98	1.98	0.00	0.00	3.96
	-9 to 0	.99	2.97	6.93	4.95	0.00	0.00	15.84
	$+1$ to $+9$	0.00	1.98	4.95	24.75	7.92	2.97	42.57
	$+10$ to $+14$	0.00	0.00	.99	7.92	2.97	1.98	13.86
	$>+14$	0.00	0.00	0.00	5.94	2.97	11.88	20.79
	Total	1.98	5.94	15.84	45.54	13.86	16.83	

a discrepancy score of similar magnitude, but in the reverse direction (i.e., with VIQ greater than PIQ), only 12 had discrepancy scores of that magnitude at retest. While one may have relative confidence in the stability of intellectual measures in the elderly over this time period, greater caution should be exercised when interpreting the Verbal-Performance Discrepancy.

REFERENCES

Berkowitz, B., & Green, R. F. (1963). Changes in intellect with age: I. Longitudinal study of Wechsler-Bellevue scores. *Journal of Genetic Psychology, 103,* 3-21.

Kendrick, D. C., & Post, F. (1967). Differences in cognitive status between healthy, psychiatrically ill, and diffusely brain-damaged elderly subjects. *British Journal of Psychiatry, 113,* 75-81.

Knight, R. G. (1983). On interpreting the several standard errors of the WAIS-R: Some further tables. *Journal of Consulting and Clinical Psychology, 51,* 671-673.

Lord, F. M., & Novik, M. R. (1968). *Statistical theories of mental test scores.* Reading, MA.: Addison-Wesley.

Lubin, B., Larsen, R. M., & Matarazzo, J. D. (1984). Patterns of psychological test usage in the United States: 1935-1982. *American Psychologist, 39,* 451-454.

Siegler, I. C. (1980). The psychology of adult development and aging. In E. W. Busse & D. G. Blazer (Eds.), *Handbook of Geriatric Psychiatry* (pp. 169-221). New York: Van Nostrand Reinhold.

Wechsler, D. (1981). *WAIS-R manual.* New York: Psychological Corporation.

Journal of Clinical Neuropsychology
1981, Vol. 3, No. 2, 171-179.

WAIS Practice Effects in Clinical Neuropsychology

Mark W. Shatz

Henry Ford Hospital

ABSTRACT

A recent review (Matarazzo, Carmody, & Jacobs, 1980) has focused attention on the issue of WAIS practice effects in clinical practice. Available literature suggests that WAIS practice effects in many samples of patients with neuropsychological dysfunction are minimal. Data relevant to this hypothesis are reviewed. Practical guidelines for the interpretation of test-retest changes on the WAIS in neuropsychological assessment are proposed, and the importance of considering the impact of WAIS practice effects in neuropsychological research is addressed.

This paper examines the issue of practice effects on the Wechsler Adult Intelligence Scale (WAIS) as they relate to the interpretation of test-retest IQ changes in neuropsychological evaluation. Current literature suggests that practice effects on the WAIS are substantial (Matarazzo, 1972). This paper develops the hypothesis that the practice effects typically seen on retesting healthy subjects with the WAIS may not occur in as reliable or robust a fashion in populations with known cerebral dysfunction. A model of WAIS practice effects in neuropsychological evaluation is proposed. This model recognizes age, brain state, and pattern of brain change as relevant variables. The interaction of these factors is considered to be critical in determining the presence, absence, and extent of practice effects. Further, it will be argued that WAIS practice effects in neuropsychological testing are potentially measurable and reliable and, consequently, may be useful and valid variables in the evaluation of neuropsychologically impaired patients.

In a recent paper, Matarazzo, Carmody, and Jacobs (1980) have presented a review of the influence of practice effects on test-retest evaluation of WAIS scores. They issued caveats with regard to interpretation of test-retest IQ changes, and presented "rules of thumb" for assessing these changes. Matarazzo et al. reviewed a heterogenous group of studies in which mean age of subjects ranged from 19 to 70 years and test-retest interval ranged from one week to over 10 years. Briefly, Matarazzo et al. concluded that a mean practice effect of +5 IQ points is to be expected on retesting with the WAIS. They further suggest that, as an isolated finding in the case of any given patient, a retest improvement would have to be at least 15 IQ points in order to reach a level of potential clinical significance. Our review of their reasoning, and the samples of patients on which it was based, suggests that the application of these rules may not be appropriate in many populations of neuropsychological interest. It must be pointed out here that Matarazzo and his associates (1980) do specifically recognize the possibility that smaller IQ changes, when mirrored by similar changes in other measures, may be clinically meaningful.

With the exception of three studies (Dodrill & Troupin, 1975; Kendrick & Post, 1967; Matarazzo, Matarazzo, Gallo, & Wiens, 1979), which will be discussed below, Matarazzo et al. (1980) cite data representing populations not likely to be exposed to repeated neuropsychological evaluations (e.g., normal adults, college students, chronic schizophrenics, etc.). The validity of the proposed five-point practice effect thus depends upon the degree to which these findings, which are based on samples with no clear-cut CNS damage, generalize to populations of patients with confirmed brain damage. Careful reading of the literature suggests that, in many cases, this generalization does not hold.

Subject selection factors must not be ignored. Practice effects may differ greatly in magnitude and time course when neurologically normal subject populations are compared to populations of subjects with cerebral dysfunction. If this is true, then application of the Matarazzo et al. rules of thumb to retest changes in patients with cerebral dysfunction is likely to be misleading. In order to assess the generalizability of the WAIS practice effect, the next section reviews test-retest studies which use patient samples with cerebral impairment.

Practice effects in brain-impaired samples. Kendrick and Post (1967) administered the WAIS three times to brain-damaged, depressed, and normal elderly subjects (mean age = 70 years), with a test-retest interval of six weeks. In this study, only the normal and depressed elderly subjects (*n* = 30) showed Verbal IQ (VIQ) and Performance IQ (PIQ) increases with repeated testing. The elderly subjects with chronic Organic Brain Syndrome (OBS) (*n* = 10) did not show any practice effect on the WAIS (see Table 1), even though retesting was repeated three times in the span of 12 weeks.

The findings of this study illustrate the potential clinical utility of intergroup differences in the magnitude of WAIS practice effects. If elderly depressed patients show a practice effect on the WAIS in a reliable fashion, and if elderly patients with OBS do not show WAIS practice effects, then it may be possible to differentiate patients with depressive pseudodementia from those with organic dementia. The distinction would be based on presence versus absence of practice effects with repeated testing.

TABLE 1

Test-Retest Means and Standard Deviations on WAIS
VIQ and PIQ (Kendrick & Post, 1967)

		Test 1	Test 2	Test 3
Combined Sample of	VIQ M	108.40	111.67	111.67
Depressed and Normal	SD	13.58	16.00	17.20
Elderly	PIQ M	101.67	105.23	106.93
n = 30	SD	11.20	11.52	14.30
Diffusely Brain-	VIQ M	96.00	96.70	96.00
Damaged Elderly	SD	10.90	9.81	12.50
n = 10	PIQ M	79.50	80.20	79.40
	SD	7.47	9.86	11.17

Dodrill and Troupin (1975) examined the effects of repeated testing on a sample of chronic epileptics. These patients were younger (mean age = 27 years) and suffered from major seizure disorders. On initial evaluation, the mean Halstead Impairment Index fell in the brain-damaged range ($M = .60$). These subjects showed actual mean IQ losses (VIQ —5, PIQ —4, FSIQ —4) at the 6- to 12-month follow-up. Matarazzo et al. imply that, since some of the subjects in this study had been placed on an experimental anticonvulsant medication (Sulthiame), this performance decrement may have been a medication effect. However, Dodrill and Troupin (1975) themselves are careful to point out (p. 188) that both the one-half of their sample taking this experimental drug as well as the one-half of their sample maintained on diphenylhydantoin or diphenylhydantoin and phenobarbitol at both the initial and follow-up testings showed an IQ decline. The FSIQ decline was larger in the experimental group than in the nonexperimental group (—6.44 vs. —2.25). However, the fact that both groups declined certainly limits the utility of the medication effect interpretation. Dodrill and Troupin followed these patients through a total of four battery administrations over the course of 18 to 29 months. It was not until the fourth administration of the WAIS that significant improvements from baseline emerged. Thus, this epileptic sample showed a practice effect only after three prior exposures to the WAIS items, and no practice effect was seen on the first retest.

The neuropsychologically relevant study cited in Matarazzo et al. (1980) is that of Matarazzo et al. (1979) who report the results of repeated neuropsychological testing at a 20-week interval of patients with angiographically-confirmed cerebrovascular disease. This group of patients showed a 3-point FSIQ gain at follow-up. Matarazzo and his associates (1979, 1980) interpret this gain as reflecting a practice effect. However, these patients all had undergone carotid endarterectomy during the test-retest interval, and the possibility that the observed IQ score increase represents a treatment effect rather than a practice effect cannot be excluded. This would seem to be an especially important consideration in that carotid endarterectomy is a surgical procedure specifically designed to improve the flow of blood to the brain and to prevent future cerebrovascular insult and associated behavioral decline (Thompson & Talkington, 1974). As such, this procedure might be expected to lead to improved neuropsychological function in patients with cerebrovascular disease. Several, but not all, studies of this procedure have, in fact, shown post-surgical improvement in functioning on neuropsychological tests (see Asken & Hobson, 1974, for a review, also Kelly, Garron, & Javid. 1980).

The results of a second carotid endarterectomy study are germane to both the general hypothesis (that patients with neurologic dysfunction do not show substantial practice effects on the WAIS) and to the interpretation of the 3-point postoperative IQ increase in the Matarazzo et al. (1979) endarterectomy study. Duke, Bloor, Nugent, and Majzoub (1968) reported the results of a pretest-posttest study which employed a nonsurgical control group with angiographically-demonstrated carotid artery disease. Theirs is the only study in the carotid endarterectomy literature to report WAIS test-retest data on such a control group. Although the degree of arteriosclerotic disease was not as great in the control group as in the operated group, this study still provides a sound basis for evaluating the course of patients with carotid artery disease who do not receive surgery. Duke et al. found that their sample of nonsurgical controls with carotid artery disease did not show a practice effect on the WAIS at 18-month follow-up. In fact, an actual FSIQ decline of one point was seen (mean pretest FSIQ = 95.44, mean posttest FSIQ = 94.25), although of course this was not statistically significant. The implication of this finding is clear: Patients with cerebrovascular disease who do not receive endarterectomy do not show practice effects on retesting with the WAIS.

The consistent failure of these samples of patients with preexisting cerebral dysfunction may relate directly to improved cerebral functioning rather than to the practice effects typically seen in normal controls. While patients with known brain FSIQ increases on posttreatment retesting in patients with known cerebral dysfunction may relate directly to improve cerebral functioning rather than to the practice effects typically seen in normal controls. While patients with known brain damage clearly comprise the population most likely to be exposed to serial neuropsychological assessment, elderly patients, because of their base rates for cerebral dysfunction, represent another population in which repeated neuro-psychological testing occurs with some frequency. Thus, we now turn to a review of test-retest changes in WAIS performance in the elderly.

Practice effects in geriatric samples. Examination of WAIS test-retest results with samples of elderly patients also suggests an exception to the Matarazzo et al. interpretive rules of thumb. The length of time between test and retest appears to be a relevant variable. Care must be taken in interpreting long-term test-retest IQ studies since, over long time spans, subjects in these designs frequently cross from one age reference group at initial testing to another at follow-up. This generally mandates an examination of raw or scaled scores as opposed to age-weighted IQ scores when examining an individual's or a group's performance over time.

Rhudick and Gordon (1975) report on WAIS test-retest data in a sample of 86 normal elderly adults. Mean age was 72 years at the initial testing and 76 years at follow-up, with test-retest intervals ranging from one to eight years. Thirty-five of the subjects were retested within two years, 30 at from two to six years, and 21 were retested at six to eight years. The mean baseline IQ of these subjects was 122. The one- to two-year follow-up group showed an actual mean decline on the Verbal scale and a mean 2.485 point increase in Performance scaled score. In the study as a whole, these healthy, intelligent, elderly subjects showed mean scaled score increases of one point in VSS and one point in PSS after four years.

Jarvik, Kallman, and Falek (1962) report a one-year follow-up of 48 subjects with a mean age of 67.5 years. Performance on the WB-I Digit Span, Similarities, and Block Design subtests each increased .2 scaled score points. Digit Symbol decreased by .2 scaled score points, and their Stanford-Binet Vocabulary score increased by only 1.0 raw score point. The findings of this study suggest that practice effects on intelligence tests in geriatric subjects may not be very robust.

Test-retest data on 182 elderly subjects who participated in the Duke Geriatric Project are reported by Eisdorfer (1963). After a 39-month test-retest interval, a sample of 47 subjects with a mean age of 65 years and initial IQs in the 85 to 115 range showed a gain of only .91 total scaled score points. A sample of 41 subjects with similar initial IQs and mean age of 74 showed a decrease of 1.05 total scaled score points at 39-month follow-up. Since many of the subjects in these groups crossed into an older reference group during the three-year test-retest interval, analysis of IQ scores rather than scaled scores would have given the impression of 7- to 8-point increases. Clearly, such artifacts of test norming should not obscure the remarkable stability of raw scores seen across test sessions.

The Kendrick and Post (1967) study cited by Matarazzo et al. (1980) suggests that elderly patients without evidence of brain impairment do show WAIS FSIQ practice effects (Table 1) at least after brief test-retest intervals. As shown above, studies with long test-retest intervals are less conclusive.

Taken as a whole, these studies suggest that, although there probably is a practice effect on the WAIS in normal elderly individuals, the magnitude of this effect is considerably smaller than the five-point improvement in younger subjects suggested by Matarazzo et al. (1980). The data from the studies reviewed here suggests that, with long test-retest intervals, two points would seem to be a reasonable estimation of the practice effects in elderly individuals; this may be exceeded if the test-retest interval is brief.

DISCUSSION AND CONCLUSIONS

We do not mean to propose that there are no practice effects on the WAIS. Rather, it is suggested that these effects simply do not occur to the same extent in all populations. Matarazzo and his associates (1980) have taken a very important step by focusing attention on this issue. The specific criteria which they propose for measuring change appear to be appropriate for use in general clinical populations but not for populations with known brain lesions, since these groups appear to show considerable variability in WAIS practice effects with only a single retest.

Any satisfactory model of WAIS practice effects in neuropsychologically impaired patients must take this variability into account. Such a model would allow the clinical neuropsychologist to compare performance changes in the individual patient with those seen in other individuals who are equally susceptible to practice effects.

The studies reviewed above suggest that age is probably an important variable. The length of test-retest interval appears to have little impact on practice effects in younger individuals. However, in elderly subjects, it appears that practice effects may be inversely proportional to length of test-retest interval.

Lesion type and course are also likely to influence WAIS practice effects. Thus, patients with chronic, static lesions, such as Dodrill's sample of epileptics (Dodrill & Troupin, 1975), may be more likely to show a WAIS practice effect than would patients with a progressive lesion, such as the nonoperated cerebrovascular disease patients reported by Duke et al. (1968). Patients with resolving lesions may show yet another pattern of practice effects on the WAIS.

In any case, it has been shown repeatedly (Reitan, 1964; Reitan, 1966) that patterns of neuropsychological test performance can be used to separate patients who differ in terms of lesion type, location, and chronicity. Thus, it would seem arbitrary to assume on an a priori basis that diverse patient populations will show equivalent WAIS practice effects. Researchers must be encouraged to collect and publish test-retest data in different samples of patients with known cerebral dysfunction. Only then will the necessary empirical foundation for the evaluation of WAIS practice effects in neuropsychological assessment be established. We anticipate that the accumulation of such data would reveal that WAIS practice effects vary as a function of age, severity of deficit, and type and progression of lesion.

We recognize, of course, that this model is currently speculative, and must be subjected to empirical validation. The presently available data do not permit the degree of differentiation that is ultimately desirable. With this in mind, the following tentative conclusion is offered: Patients with cerebral dysfunction are generally not expected to show practice effects on the WAIS with a single retesting. This conclusion leads to recommendations for the interpretation of WAIS test-retest changes in neuropsychologically impaired patients that differ substantially from those offered by Matarazzo et al. (1980).

The following model for interpretation of WAIS test-retest changes is proposed as relevant specifically for use in neuropsychological settings.

1. *Research.* In populations with known cerebral dysfunction, test-retest changes in mean IQ of sufficient magnitude to reach statistical significance must also be seen as systematic, treatment-related effects and, thus, of potential clinical significance. This obtains because, as our review shows, such an increase could not be explained as a practice effect. It then follows that the use of nonimpaired control or comparison groups may actually obscure true improvement in a brain-impaired experimental group. Due to the differential susceptibility of the groups to practice effects, this will occur when the magnitude of the practice effect in the nonimpaired comparison group is equal to the magnitude of the treatment effect in the brain-impaired experimental group.

Neuropsychologists designing studies to evaluate the behavioral effects of rehabilitation techniques and neurosurgical interventions must be particularly sensitive to this problem, since randomization is often impractical, thus necessitating the use of intact groups. Unless care is taken to match control and experimental groups on susceptibility to practice effects, potentially promising treatments may be mistakenly discarded as "not significantly different from control".

2. *Intraindividual test-retest changes.* An appropriate yardstick for significant retest improvement in the individual case is the standard error of measurement (S_{em}). The S_{em} can be used to set up confidence intervals around an individual patient's WAIS score. Strictly speaking, the confidence intervals should be set up around the patient's estimated true score (Nunally, 1967). However, using the observed score provides an acceptable estimate of the true confidence interval. When evaluating IQ increases on retesting, this procedure will err in the conservative direction in individuals with initial observed IQs above 100. When the initial observed IQ is below 100, this procedure will err in the liberal direction. The magnitude of error is proportional to the degree of divergence from 100 of the originally observed IQ. When retest IQ scores fall outside the established confidence interval, one can assume (within the probability established by the alpha level and the limits imposed by the caveat above) a systematic, treatment-related effect.

It seems inappropriate to assume comparability of standard deviations and reliabilities between brain-damaged populations and the WAIS standardization sample. Therefore, the S_{em} provided in the WAIS manual (Wechsler, 1955) should not be used. As an aid to the clinical neuropsychologist, we have computed several different S_{em} values based on the standard deviations and reliabilities of several studies reviewed above. These S_{em} values are appropriate to their own parent populations. However, we recognize that the sample size in several of these studies is smaller than would be optimal. They are presented in Table 2 and were computed using the following formula:

$$S_{em} = SDx \sqrt{1-r_{xx}}\,(\text{Magnusson, 1967, p. 80}).$$

TABLE 2

Standard Error of Measurement and Test-Retest Reliability
in Neuropsychological Samples

Source	Sample		FSIQ	VIQ	PIQ
Dodrill & Troupin	17 chronic epileptics	S_{em}	4.85	4.53	5.91
(1975)	Mean age = 27 yrs.	r_{xx}	.84	.89	.71
Kendrick & Post	30 normal and depressed	S_{em}		4.29	4.34
(1967)	elderly	r_{xx}		.90	.85
	Mean age = 70 yrs.				
	10 diffusely brain-damaged	S_{em}		4.75	1.83
	elderly	r_{xx}		.81	.94
	Mean age = 70 yrs.				
Matarazzo et al.	17 carotid endarterectomy	S_{em}	2.66	3.30	3.44
(1979)	patients	r_{xx}	.92	.91	.85
	Mean age = 62 yrs.				

Inspection of Table 2 suggests that, generally speaking, there is a two-out-of-three chance that a 4- to 5-point IQ change on retesting in a patient with brain impairment is clinically significant. An 8- to 10-point change probably defines the 95% confidence interval for significant individual change. Of course, it would be most desirable for the individual neuropsychologist to compute a S_{em} based on the particular retest sample in his/her setting.

The relative absence of practice effects on the WAIS in patients with cerebral dysfunction is, in a sense, not surprising. Although brain damage is certainly not a unitary construct, a factor common to successful performance on many of the "general indicator" tests of cerebral dysfunction, such as the Category Test or the Location score on the Tactual Performance Test (Reitan & Davison, 1974), is the ability to learn. If a disruption of learning ability is common to disparate types and loci of brain damage, then the failure of patients with "brain damage" to learn the WAIS, i.e., show a practice effect, must be seen as a direct manifestation of the underlying cerebral pathology.

Matarazzo (1980) and his collegues have performed a valuable service by focusing attention on the issue of WAIS practice effects in clinical evaluation. Their charge to clinicians to exercise caution and prudence in the interpretation of test-retest changes must not be overlooked. We hope to append to their review the further caveat that the evaluation of test-retest changes must not take place in isolation; rather, it must reflect the sample characteristics of the population at hand. The weight of the evidence presented here suggests that, in populations of neuropsychological interest, WAIS practice effects may be severely attentuated.

REFERENCES

Asken, M. J., & Hobson, R. W. Intellectual change and carotid endarterectomy, subjective speculation or objective reality: A review. *Journal of Surgical Research*, 1977, *23*, 367-375.

Dodrill, C. B., & Troupin, A. S. Effects of repeated administrations of a comprehensive neuropsychological battery among chronic epileptics. *Journal of Nervous and Mental Disease*, 1975, *161*, 185-190.

Duke, R., Bloor, B., Nujent, R., & Majzoub, H. Changes in performance on WAIS, Trail Making Test and Finger Tapping Test associated with carotid artery surgery. *Perceptual and Motor Skills*, 1968, *26*, 399-404.

Eisdorfer, C. The WAIS performance of the aged: A retest evaluation. *Journal of Gerontology*, 1963, *18*, 169-172.

Jarvik, L., Kallmann, E., & Falek, A. Intellectual changes in aged twins. *Journal of Gerontology*, 1962, *17*, 289-294.

Kelly, M. P., Garron, D. C., & Javid, H. Carotid artery disease, carotid endarterectomy and behavior. *Archives of Neurology*, 1980, *37*, 743-748.

Kendrick, D. C., & Post, F. Differences in cognitive status between healthy, psychiatrically ill, and diffusely brain-damaged elderly subjects. *British Journal of Psychiatry*, 1967, *113*, 75-81.

Magnusson, D. *Test theory*. Reading, Mass.: Addison-Wesley, 1967.

Matarazzo, J. *Wechsler's measurement and appraisal of adult intelligence*. Fifth edition. Baltimore: Williams & Wilkins, 1972.

Matarazzo, J. D., Carmody, T. P., & Jacobs, L. D. Test-retest reliability and stability of the WAIS: A literature review with implications for clinical practice. *Journal of Clinical Neuropsychology*, 1980, *2*, 89-105.

Matarazzo, R. G., Matarazzo, J. D., Gallo, A. E., Jr., & Wiens, A. N. IQ and neuropsychological changes following carotid endarterectomy. *Journal of Clinical Neuropsychology*, 1979, *1*, 97-116.

Nunally, J. C. *Psychometric theory*. New York: McGraw-Hill, 1967.

Reitan, R. Psychological deficits resulting from cerebral lesions in man. In J. M. Warren & K. Akert (Eds.), *The frontal granular cortex and behavior*. New York: McGraw-Hill, 1964.

Reitan, R. A research program on the psychological effects of brain lesions in human beings. In N. R. Ellis (Ed.), *International review of research in mental retardation*. Vol. 1. New York: Academic Press, 1966.

Reitan, R. M., & Davison, K. A. (Eds.), *Clinical neuropsychology: Current status and applications*. Washington, D.C.: V. H. Winston & Sons, 1974.

Rudhick, P. J., & Gordon, C. The age center of New England study. In L. Jarvik, E. Eisendorfer, & J. Blum (Eds.), *Intellectual functions in adults*. New York: Springer, 1973.

Thompson, J., & Talkington, C. Carotid endarterectomy. *Annals of Surgery*, 1976, *184*(1), 1-15.

Wechsler, D. *Manual for the Wechsler Adult Intelligence Scale*. New York: The Psychological Corporation, 1955.

Journal of Clinical and Experimental Neuropsychology
1989, Vol. 11, No. 4, pp. 461-470

Neuropsychological Improvement Versus Practice Effect Following Unilateral Carotid Endarterectomy in Patients Without Stroke*

Joseph E. Casey, Gary G. Ferguson, Doreen Kimura, and Vladimir C. Hachinski

University Hospital, London, Canada

ABSTRACT

Patients who were admitted to hospital for a recent transient ischemic attack were entered into one of three groups based on medical and surgical characteristics; those with an abnormal neurological examination or a focal abnormality on CT Scan were omitted from the study. The two surgical groups (12 patients each) underwent either a left or right endarterectomy for a symptomatic atheroma of the ipsilateral carotid artery. The control group consisted of 12 patients who either demonstrated minor or nonexistent carotid abnormalities or a TIA distribution that was contralateral to what would otherwise have been a surgically treatable lesion. Patients were tested before surgery and again 6-8 weeks later with the WAIS, WMS, and other neuropsychological measures. Significant improvement on some measures at follow-up was strictly equivalent across all groups and was attributed to practice effects.

More than 30 years have passed since Cooley, Al-Naaman, and Carton (1956) described the first successful resection of an atheromatous plaque from the inner lining of the carotid artery as a preventative treatment against future thrombo-embolic stroke. Although the efficacy of this procedure has been questioned recently (Barnett, Plum, & Walton, 1984; Warlow, 1984), the increasing popularity of carotid endarterectomy (Dyken & Pokras, 1984) coupled with the early anecdotal reports of improved mental status postoperatively has prompted investigators to examine its effect on cognitive abilities in a systematic fashion. Since the first objective evaluation of the psychological concomitants of endarterectomy was published (Williams & McGee, 1964), there have been numerous conflicting studies concerning the nature of the intellectual and neuropsychological changes that follow surgery.

The majority of studies to date have concluded with varying degrees of

*This research was supported in part by a grant from the University Hospital Pooled Research Trust Fund to Drs. Ferguson and Hachinski.

conviction that endarterectomy contributes to the postoperative improvement in cognitive functions when such improvement occurs (e.g., Bennion, Owens, & Wilson, 1985; Bornstein, Benoit, & Trites, 1981; Goldstein, Kleinknecht, & Gallo, 1970; Haynes, Gideon, King, & Dempsey, 1976; Hemmingsen, Mejsholm, Boysen, & Engell, 1982; Hemmingsen et al., 1986; Horne & Royle, 1974; Kelly, Garron, & Javid, 1980; Perry, Drinkwater, & Taylor, 1975; Williams & McGee, 1964). However, merely comparing the number of studies reporting positive results with the number reporting negative ones is an unsatisfactory approach in addressing this issue for at least two reasons. First, studies with positive results are more likely to be published and, second, this approach ignores the quality and sample characteristics of the individual studies (Asken & Hobson, 1977). Many of the earlier reports were subject to the methodological and statistical criticisms raised by Asken and Hobson (1977), such as the absence of control groups, inappropriate statistical designs, a failure to recognize the effects of practice on test scores with repeated assessments, inconsistent retest intervals, inappropriate use of test scores, and incomplete testing.

While more recent research has reflected a greater sensitivity to these methodological concerns, a number of important problems still remain. One of the major difficulties inadequately addressed in this literature concerns the degree to which the natural amelioration of deficits due to a resolving stroke may be responsible for the cognitive improvements seen in endarterectomy patients at follow-up. If patients with stroke are included in the endarterectomy sample under study, then appropriate controls to account for the confounding influence of spontaneous recovery must be instituted.

Unfortunately, many of the studies published have not reported the percentage of stroke patients in their endarterectomy and control samples (e.g., Boeke, 1981; Duke, Bloor, Nugent, & Majzoub, 1968; Goldstein et al., 1970; Haynes et al., 1976; Horne & Royle, 1974; Williams & McGee, 1964). Of those that have done so, only one attempted to balance the incidence across the groups examined and it concluded that endarterectomy had no effect on mental status 6 months postoperatively (Parker, Granberg, Nichols, Jones, & Hewett, 1983). In contrast, the only study to exclude patients with stroke altogether found that those undergoing endarterectomy showed significant postoperative improvement on more cognitive measures than did a peripheral vascular surgery control group (Kelly et al., 1980).

The exact influence of previous stroke on cognitive changes following endarterectomy is difficult to ascertain. Two studies compared *post hoc* the test performance of endarterectomy patients who had strokes versus those who presented with only transient ischemic attacks (TIAs). One found no differences between the groups (Hemmingsen et al., 1982) whereas the other found that the patients with stroke improved on a significantly greater number of psychometric measures than did those with TIA only (Bornstein et al., 1981). Moreover, Bornstein et al. found that their right endarterectomy group, which had the highest incidence of stroke patients (65%), improved on significantly more measures compared to the other groups, i.e., left endarterectomy (40%), bilateral endarterectomy (58%), cerebrovascular control (50%), and surgical controls with no stroke. However, complicating the issue is the fact that the latter four groups, who varied in their incidence of stroke, improved on an equal number of tests postoperatively.

To control for the potential influence of a resolving CNS lesion on neuropsychological measures, we evaluated the pre- and postoperative performance of TIA patients who were without stroke. In addition, the present study employed procedures to deal with some of the other problems raised by Asken and Hobson (1977) that have continued to make generalizations difficult. These include the use of a control group matched on presenting problem (i.e., TIA), a statistical design appropriate for repeated testings in which group differences can be evaluated in the context of potential practice effects, and an adequate description and control of demographic, medical, and surgical variables to permit more definitive conclusions.

If re-establishing the patency of the carotid artery has a beneficial effect on cognitive functioning in patients without stroke, then one would predict that such patients would demonstrate greater increments on psychometric measures at postoperative follow-up as compared to a similar group of nonsurgical patients. In the present study, this would be represented statistically by significant Groups x Trials interactions. Furthermore, one would predict lateralized effects whereby left endarterectomy patients would improve to a greater extent on sensorimotor measures of the right side of the body as compared to right endarterectomy patients whereas the latter would show greater improvements than the former on sensorimotor measures of the left side of the body.

METHOD

Subjects

The final subject pool comprised 36 patients who were admitted to hospital for investigation of a recent hemispheric and/or retinal TIA, or in the case of two patients, a reversible ischemic neurological deficit (RIND). Patients with abnormalities on neurological examination or who revealed a focal abnormality on CT Scan were excluded from the study. All patients except two controls underwent four-vessel cerebral angiography as part of their medical investigation. Of the two exceptions, one underwent a bilateral carotid ultrasound examination; the other, cerebral digital intravenous angiography. The degree of carotid stenosis was represented by the percent reduction in luminal diameter at the site of maximal stenosis and was estimated by the attending neurosurgeon in collaboration with the neuroradiological team.

The subjects were entered into one of three groups based on medical and surgical characteristics. The two operative groups comprised patients who underwent either a left (LCE) or a right (RCE) carotid endarterectomy for symptomatic carotid artery disease as a prophylaxis against future TIAs or stroke. Separating the surgical sample into left and right endarterectomy groups permitted each to serve as the other's control for tests thought to measure functions primarily subserved by systems within one of the two hemispheres. All operations were performed by clamp procedure under general anesthesia (see Ferguson [1982] for surgical details). The control group (CON) consisted of patients who did not demonstrate any significant carotid atheroma and hence did not undergo surgery. Therefore, a control patient was one who presented with TIA and who showed minor or nonexistent carotid artery abnormalities, or whose TIA distribution was contralateral to a potential surgical site. Patients were added to the study until each group accumulated 12 subjects, six males and six females. All were right-handed.

Procedures

Each patient was assessed twice, once while in hospital prior to surgery (but after angiography) and again approximately 8 weeks following the baseline assessment. Most of the surgical patients were tested within 1 or 2 days before surgery ($M = 2.6$, $SD = 3.6$); the control patients, just prior to discharge ($M = 1.8$, $SD = 3.8$). All surgical and 75% of control patients were discharged on antiplatelet therapy which was continued until at least the follow-up assessment. During the course of the study, six patients who met criteria for participation were replaced: Three either refused to or could not return for follow-up, two suffered myocardial infarction (one of whom died 3 days postoperatively), and one obtained a raw score on the Wechsler Memory Scale that was beyond the upper value for a Memory Quotient conversion.

With one exception, identical test forms were employed both pre- and postoperatively. The tests were administered by well-trained psychometrists and graduate students in neuropsychology who were paid for their service. Psychometric intelligence was measured using the Wechsler Adult Intelligence Scale (WAIS), and with one patient, the Wechsler-Bellevue II. During the baseline assessment, Form I of the Wechsler Memory Scale (WMS) was administered to one-half (3 males, 3 females) of each group; the other half received Form II. Each patient received the alternate form at follow-up. During each assessment, a second (delayed) recall of the Logical Stories, Paired Associates, and Visual Reproduction subtests of the WMS was requested to determine the percentage of verbal and figural information retained after a 45-min delay. The verbal score was based on a sum of the mean recall for the two stories (verbatim scoring) plus the number of correctly recalled items on one trial of the Paired Associates subtest (Milner, 1975). Delayed recall of verbal and figural information have been shown to be sensitive measures of memory impairment and are associated with lateralized brain damage of the left and right hemispheres, respectively (Milner, 1966, 1975; Russell, 1975).

The Modified Knox Cubes Test, Finger Tapping Test, Two-point Discrimination Test, and Visual Search Test were administered as measures of visual attention span, psychomotor speed, tactile sensation, and visual scanning, respectively. Briefly, in the Knox Cubes Test the patient was required to tap out a sequence of five blocks following the examiner's demonstration. The test comprised two conditions of 10 trials each. In the immediate condition, the patient proceeded to tap immediately following the examiner's demonstration; in the delayed condition, the patient tapped following a 5-s interval during which time the blocks were hidden from view. The score was the total number of correct trials. The score on the Finger Tapping Test was based on the mean of two 10-s trials. Two-point discrimination thresholds were measured in mm across the palm using a Weinstein two-point aesthesiometer (Corkin, Milner, & Rasmussen, 1970). Finally, in the Visual Search Test, patients faced an array of 86 line drawings randomly arranged on a vertically positioned board. The examiner presented a series of pictures centrally and the patient was required to point, as quickly as possible, to the identical match within the array. The number of items found within the left and right visual fields (maximum 20 each) and the mean response time to locate these items within each visual field were recorded (Kimura, Barnett, & Burkhart, 1981). See Kimura (1986) for a detailed description of the administration and scoring of the tests employed.

Preoperative group comparisons of means were based on one-way analyses of variance. All other statistical comparisons on test data were also parametric, using 3 x 2 analyses of variance (Groups x Trials) with repeated measures on the second factor.

RESULTS

Demographic, medical/surgical, and preoperative IQ and MQ data are presented in Table 1. The groups were fortuitously well matched and did not differ significantly in mean age, years of education, follow-up interval, or baseline measures of psychometric intelligence or memory. The frequency of preoperative TIAs across the three groups ranged from 1 to approximately 70, with the majority of subjects in each group presenting with less than 10 TIAs. In three cases, the onset of the most recent TIA could not be determined. Of the remaining 33 cases, 26 (79%) experienced their most recent TIA between 1 and 16 weeks prior to the initial assessment ($M = 4.9$; $SD = 4.5$). The surgical groups, by definition, demonstrated a greater degree of internal carotid artery stenosis on the surgical side, as compared to the nonsurgical side and to the control subjects. The LCE and RCE groups were similar in the degree of ipsilateral and contralateral stenosis and in the amount of time the operated artery was clamped. In all surgical cases, the etiological source of the TIAs was considered to be the ipsilateral carotid artery. For the control group, the source was considered to be the carotid artery in two cases, suspected to be the carotid artery in four cases, suspected to be embolic from the heart in three cases, and of unknown etiology in the remaining three cases.

Table 2 presents the preoperative and postoperative data on measures of intelligence, memory, and attention. A significant main effect for trials, indicating improvement on second testing, was found on the Wechsler measures of Verbal IQ, $F(1, 33) = 6.07$, $p < .05$, Performance IQ, $F(1, 33) = 45.40$, $p < .0001$, Full Scale IQ, $F(1, 33) = 30.65$, $p < .0001$, and Memory Quotient, $F(1, 33) = 4.94$, $p < .05$. However, there was no significant groups effect or Groups x Trials interaction. In addition, no significant effects for groups, trials, or Groups x Trials interaction was found in the percentages of verbal and figural

Table 1
Baseline Demographic and Medical Characteristics

	LCE	RCE	CON
n	12	12	12
Age - years	66.0 (5.3)	63.4 (6.0)	59.2 (13.3)
Education - years	10.0 (2.1)	10.2 (2.5)	9.7 (2.3)
Follow-up interval - days	59.8 (12.3)	60.7 (9.8)	59.1 (13.6)
Full Scale IQ	105.7 (9.6)	103.2 (11.6)	104.4 (11.3)
Memory Quotient	108.5 (14.4)	103.8 (13.3)	107.8 (11.6)
n with < 10 TIAs	9	10	10
n with stenosis $\geq 90\%$[a]	8/2	7/1	0/0
Clamp time - minutes	38.7 (9.1)	39.8 (8.7)	

Note. LCE = left carotid endarterectomy group; RCE = right carotid endarterectomy group; CON = control group; ( ) = standard deviation. [a]-carotid artery ipsilateral/contralateral to the surgical side.

Table 2
Mean Pre- and Postoperative Performance on Measures of Intelligence,
Memory, and Attention

		LCE	RCE	CON
Verbal IQ	pre	106.5 (11.5)	101.6 (12.1)	105.3 (12.8)
	post	107.9 (12.8)	107.1 (13.4)	106.3 (15.2)
Performance IQ	pre	103.7 (9.1)	104.5 (12.7)	103.1 (11.4)
	post	107.8 (9.6)	111.4 (13.7)	111.2 (12.2)
Full Scale IQ	pre	105.7 (9.6)	103.2 (11.6)	104.4 (11.3)
	post	108.3 (10.2)	109.6 (13.4)	108.9 (13.3)
Memory Quotient	pre	108.5 (14.4)	103.8 (13.3)	107.8 (11.6)
	post	112.0 (9.6)	110.2 (17.1)	108.3 (14.3)
% Verbal Recall	pre	72.9 (12.0)	75.4 (17.3)	80.8 (20.1)
	post	74.7 (18.3)	68.3 (22.1)	82.7 (17.8)
% Visual Recall	pre	67.5 (36.6)	68.6 (25.3)	74.0 (28.6)
	post	94.6 (82.0)	77.2 (19.5)	78.3 (23.6)
Knox Cubes Test	pre	11.0 (4.1)	10.3 (4.4)	9.3 (5.7)
	post	12.8 (4.7)	11.0 (5.4)	9.5 (6.2)

Note. pre = preoperative or baseline assessment; post = postoperative or follow-up assessment.
[a]One patient in the LCE group was not administered the delayed recall of Logical Stories and Paired Associates, therefore, $n = 11$. [b]Two patients in the LCE group were not administered the delayed recall of Visual Reproduction, therefore, $n = 10$.

information recalled after a 45-min delay. Also presented in Table 2 are the results of the Knox Cubes Test. Again, no significant effects for groups, trials, or Groups x Trials interaction were found. Therefore, based on these measures, the three groups did not demonstrate a differential change in psychometric intelligence, memory, or visual attention span performance postoperatively.

Test results providing lateralizing information based on measures of performance on the left and right sides of the body are presented in Table 3. The only significant finding was an overall decrease in the time used to locate items in the left visual field collapsed across all groups at follow-up, $F(1,33)=5.66$, $p<.05$, perhaps suggesting the development of a left-to-right scanning strategy. It is clear that the surgical groups did not improve to a greater degree than did the control group. Furthermore, there was no lateralizing pattern to suggest that LCE patients improved to a greater extent than did the RCE patients on sensorimotor measures typically associated with functions of the left hemisphere and vice versa for RCE patients.

Table 3
Mean Performance on Measures of Psychomotor Speed,
Two-Point Discrimination, and Visual Search

		LCE	RCE	CON
Finger Tap - RH	pre	42.7 (7.2)	42.1 (7.7)	43.7 (10.6)
(# of taps)	post	44.5 (7.0)	43.2 (6.4)	42.4 (7.1)
Finger Tap - LH[a]	pre	41.1 (5.6)	41.6 (6.7)	38.2 (7.4)
(# of taps)	post	42.6 (5.7)	41.1 (7.6)	37.5 (8.3)
2-Pt Disc - RH	pre	9.3 (4.7)	9.3 (3.5)	9.4 (3.3)
(mm)	post	10.0 (2.0)	9.3 (2.0)	8.1 (2.6)
2-Pt Disc - LH	pre	10.1 (3.7)	11.2 (3.8)	8.6 (3.5)
(mm)	post	9.5 (2.5)	10.6 (7.2)	9.1 (2.3)
VSIF - RVF	pre	10.0 (1.5)	9.9 (2.0)	10.0 (2.1)
(# of items)	post	9.8 (1.6)	10.4 (2.2)	9.8 (1.4)
VSIF - LVF	pre	9.8 (1.7)	9.7 (2.3)	9.9 (2.1)
(# of items)	post	9.9 (1.8)	9.3 (2.2)	10.3 (1.4)
VST - RVF	pre	8.0 (3.3)	6.5 (2.3)	5.7 (6.6)
(sec)	post	7.3 (2.3)	7.0 (4.6)	7.2 (3.8)
VST - LVF	pre	9.0 (4.4)	8.4 (6.1)	7.3 (2.5)
(sec)	post	7.4 (3.9)	6.8 (4.0)	5.9 (2.4)

Note. RH = right hand; LH = left hand; RVF = right visual field; LVF = left visual field;
VSIF = number of items found on the Visual Search Task for the visual field indicated,
maximum score possible per visual field is 20; VST = mean number of seconds to find the
objects in the indicated visual field on the Visual Search Task.
[a]Due to a congenital malformation of the left index finger in one patient, $n = 11$ for the
LCE group.

DISCUSSION

The present study found that all groups, taken together, showed a statistically
significant increase in performance at follow-up on five of the measures
employed, viz., VIQ, PIQ, FSIQ, Memory Quotient, and search time for the left
visual field. However, the absence of significant Groups x Trials interactions on
these measures indicates that the degree of improvement exhibited by the
surgical groups was no greater than was that of the control group. In addition,
neither of the surgical groups demonstrated a pattern of postoperative
neuropsychological changes that would suggest a specific improvement of
functions ordinarily associated with the cerebral hemisphere supplied by the
operated artery: This was the case for more primary sensorimotor functions and
for more complex cognitive functions such as those reflected in the Verbal and
Performance Scales of the WAIS. These findings support the conclusions of
Matarazzo, Matarazzo, Gallo, and Wiens, (1979) and Parker et al. (1983) that
the postoperative improvements observed in endarterectomy patients are
probably not attributable to carotid surgery itself, but rather to the normal

effects of practice.

A number of factors may have contributed to the discrepancy of the present findings with many of those reported in the literature. First, the exclusion of stroke patients from the present investigation permitted an evaluation of the neuropsychological outcome of surgery that was independent of a potentially resolving cerebral lesion. Second, the use of a control group well matched on several demographic factors considered to be important in clinical neuropsychological research, such as age and education (Parsons & Prigatano, 1978), may have minimized the amount of extraneous variability that would have otherwise confounded the results. Interestingly, Kelly et al. (1980) found that those endarterectomy patients who demonstrated improved performance postoperatively were significantly younger and better educated than were those who did not show improvements. Unfortunately, the same comparison was not reported for the peripheral vascular surgery control group; this would have addressed the issue of whether the observed changes were due to age and education alone or to their interaction with cerebrovascular surgery.

The appropriateness of the present control group is further enhanced by the fact that these patients were admitted to hospital with the same presenting problem as did those who underwent surgery, had a similar history of TIA frequency, were followed over the same interval, and exhibited equivalent baseline levels of intelligence and memory. While the control group included a few patients whose TIA source was suspected to be embolic from the heart, this group was, in effect, similar to the surgical groups in every other way except for the degree of carotid artery disease and the treatment prescribed (i.e., surgery). The importance of a control group matched for demographic and medical variables is underscored by the evidence that test-retest changes, at least on the WAIS, may vary according to age and the neurological condition in question (Shatz, 1981).

Finally, given that practice effects are likely to occur on some measures, the statistical design employed herein enabled us to test for a significant interaction between the group and testing-session factors. If present, it would have meant a differential improvement in one or two of the groups over and above that which might have occurred on the basis of a practice effect alone. Analysis by t tests for correlated samples, common in the endarterectomy literature, does not allow for such a direct evaluation.

The present findings do not exclude the possibility that certain other subgroups of endarterectomy patients may demonstrate significant cognitive improvements following surgery (e.g., TIA patients who present with minor stroke and its attendant neurological and neuropsychological impairments; or perhaps those with severe multiple-vessel cerebrovascular disease and global cerebral dysfunction -- the so called "low perfusion syndrome"). Obviously, the design of the present study did not lend itself to an evaluation of these possibilities, each of which is deserving of investigation in its own right.

In summary, the results of the present study indicate that carotid endarterectomy does not improve neuropsychological functioning in patients without stroke. Postoperative increases in test performance, when observed, paralleled those of the control group, suggesting that these gains merely represent normal practice effects. It is suggested that future neuropsychological research evaluate potential postsurgical changes in specific subgroups of carotid endarterectomy patients.

REFERENCES

Asken, M. J., & Hobson, R. W. (1977). Intellectual change and carotid endarterectomy, subjective speculation or objective reality: A review. *Journal of Surgical Research, 23,* 367-375.

Barnett, H. J. M., Plum, F., & Walton, J. N. (1984). Carotid endarterectomy - An expression of concern. *Stroke, 15,* 941-943.

Bennion, R. S., Owens, M. L., & Wilson, S. E. (1985). The effect of unilateral carotid endarterectomy on neuropsychological test performance in 53 patients. *Journal of Cardiovascular Surgery, 26,* 21-26.

Boeke, S. (1981). The effects of carotid endarterectomy on mental functioning. *Clinical Neurology and Neurosurgery, 83-4,* 209-217.

Bornstein, R. A., Benoit, B. G., & Trites, R. L. (1981). Neuropsychological changes following carotid endarterectomy. *Canadian Journal of Neurological Sciences, 8,* 127-132.

Cooley, D. A., Al-Naaman, Y. D., & Carton, C. A. (1956). Surgical treatment of arteriosclerotic occlusion of common carotid artery. *Journal of Neurosurgery, 13,* 500-506.

Corkin, S., Milner, B., & Rasmussen, T. (1970). Somatosensory thresholds: Contrasting effects of postcentral-gyrus and posterior parietal-lobe excisions. *Archives of Neurology, 23,* 41-58.

Duke, R. B., Bloor, B. M., Nugent, G. R., & Majzoub, H. S. (1968). Changes in performance on WAIS, Trail Making Test and Finger Tapping Test with carotid artery surgery. *Perceptual and Motor Skills, 26,* 399-404.

Dyken, M. L., & Pokras, R. (1984). The performance of endarterectomy for disease of the extracranial arteries of the head. *Stroke, 15,* 948-950.

Ferguson, G. G. (1982). Extracranial carotid artery surgery. *Clinical Neurosurgery, 29,* 543-574.

Goldstein, S. G., Kleinknecht, R. A., & Gallo, Jr., A. E. (1970). Neuropsychological changes associated with carotid endarterectomy. *Cortex, 7,* 308-322.

Haynes, C. D., Gideon, D. A., King, G. D., & Dempsey, R. L. (1976). The improvement of cognition and personality after carotid endarterectomy. *Surgery, 80,* 699-704.

Hemmingsen, R., Mejsholm, B., Boysen, G., & Engell, H. C. (1982). Intellectual function in patients with transient ischaemic attacks (TIA) or minor stroke: Long-term improvement after carotid endarterectomy. *Acta Neurologica Scandinavica, 66,* 145-159.

Hemmingsen, R., Mejsholm, B., Vorstrup, S., Lester, J., Engell, H. C., & Boysen, G. (1986). Carotid surgery, cognitive function and cerebral blood flow in patients with transient ischemic attacks. *Annals of Neurology, 20,* 13-19.

Horne, D. J., & Royle, J. P. (1974). Cognitive changes after carotid endarterectomy. *The Medical Journal of Australia, 1,* 316-317.

Kelly, M. P., Garron, D. C., & Javid, H. (1980). Carotid artery disease, carotid endarterectomy, and behavior. *Archives of Neurology, 37,* 743-748.

Kimura, D. (1986). *Neuropsychological test procedures* (5th ed.). DK Consultants, London, Ontario.

Kimura, D., Barnett, H. J. M., & Burkhart, G. (1981). The psychological test pattern in progressive supranuclear palsy. *Neuropsychologia, 19,* 301-306.

Matarazzo, R. G., Matarazzo, J. D., Gallo, Jr., A. E., & Wiens, A. N. (1979). IQ and neuropsychological changes following carotid endarterectomy. *Journal of Clinical Neuropsychology, 1,* 97-116.

Milner, B. (1966). Amnesia following operation on the temporal lobes. In C. W. M. Whitty & O. L. Zangwill (Eds.), *Amnesia* (pp. 109-133). London: Butterworths.

Milner, B. (1975). Psychological aspects of focal epilepsy and its neurosurgical management. In D. P. Purpura, J. K. Penry, & R. D. Walter (Eds.), *Advances in neurology: Vol. 8. Neurosurgical management of the epilepsies* (pp. 299-321). New York: Raven Press.

Parsons, O. A., & Prigatano, G. P. (1978). Methodological considerations in clinical neuropsychological research. *Journal of Consulting and Clinical Psychology, 46,* 608-619.

Parker, J. C., Granberg, B. W., Nichols, W. K., Jones, J. G., & Hewett, J. E. (1983). Mental status outcomes following carotid endarterectomy: A six month analysis. *Journal of Clinical Neuropsychology, 5,* 345-353.

Perry, P. M., Drinkwater, J. E., & Taylor, G. W. (1975). Cerebral function before and after carotid endarterectomy. *British Medical Journal, 4,* 215-216.

Russell, E. W. (1975). A multiple scoring method for the assessment of complex memory functions. *Journal of Consulting and Clinical Psychology, 43,* 800-809.

Shatz, M. W. (1981). WAIS practice effects in clinical neuropsychology. *Journal of Clinical Neuropsychology, 3,* 171-179.

Warlow, C. (1984). Carotid endarterectomy: Does it work? *Stroke, 15,* 1068-1076.

Williams, M., & McGee, T. F. (1964). Psychological study of carotid occlusion and endarterectomy. *Archives of Neurology, 10,* 293-297.

Journal of Clinical and Experimental Neuropsychology
1986, Vol. 8, No. 3, pp. 190-200

V-C

Fifteen-Year Stability of Some Neuropsychological Tests in Learning Disabled Subjects With and Without Neurological Impairment*

Francine F-A. Sarazin and Otfried Spreen

University of Victoria

ABSTRACT

The stability of the WISC/WAIS-R and seven other commonly used neuropsychological tests over a period of 15 years was investigated in 133 learning-disabled subjects, and for subgroups with hard neurological signs, soft neurological signs, and without neurological findings. Results showed high and significant correlation coefficients between time 1 (mean age 10 years) and time 2 (mean age 25 years), even though for some tests a change from the children's to the adult version occurred. Using a repeated-measures multivariate design, the three subgroups did not differ on this limited test battery. The correlation coefficients for the three subgroups provide an estimate of the range of stability in three different samples.

Follow-up studies of children with learning disabilities have been concerned with specific effects of treatment (Bradley, Battin, & Sutter, 1979; Gottesman, Belmont, & Kaminer, 1975; Hardy, 1968; Koppitz, 1971), emotional and/or behavioral adjustment problems (Balow & Blomquist, 1965; Peter & Spreen, 1979), academic achievement (Howden, 1967; Preston & Yarington, 1967; Robinson & Smith, 1962), occupational outcome (Bruck, 1985; Hardy, 1968; Preston & Yarington, 1967; Robinson & Smith, 1962), intelligence and socioeconomic status (Howden, 1967; Rawson, 1968; Robinson & Smith, 1962), specific deficits, improvements, as well as presence or absence of brain dysfuntion/damage (Kaste, 1971; Spreen, 1982). The purpose of most of these studies was to examine whether the children with learning disabilities "grow out of" associated symptomatology in adolescence and/or early adulthood. Two extreme positions arise from the results: (a) one supporting a favorable outcome in adulthood (Birch, 1964; Bruck, 1985; Klebanoff, Singer, & Wilenski, 1954; Laufer & Denhoff, 1957; Rawson, 1968;

* This study was supported by the Medical Research Council and the National Health Research and Development Program of Canada.

Robinson & Smith, 1962); and, (b) one suggesting persisting deficits (Kaste, 1971; Mendelson, Johnson, & Stewart, 1971; Silver & Hagin, 1964). For a comprehensive review, see Spreen (1982). Although the reports discuss their findings in view of one or the other outcome, they often neglect to indicate the degree of change over time in quantified measures. On the other hand, if mean scores of initial and/or follow-up tests are reported, they often correspond to different tests from one assessment to the other.

Earlier follow-up studies usually employed nonstandardized methods such as interviews, questionnaires, and rating scales of unknown reliability and validity in assessing adult outcome (Balow & Blowquist, 1965; Carter, 1964; Hardy, 1968; Hermann, 1959; Howden, 1967; Preston & Yarington, 1967; Rawson, 1968; Robinson & Smith, 1962; see Herjanic & Penick, 1972 for a review). Only a few studies have used and repeated the same objective tests at follow-up. Test-retest stability has rarely been the focus of discussion in follow-up studies so far.

Silver and Hagin (1964) were the first to retest their subjects as adults by means of the same comprehensive battery of psychological tests that had been administered to them as children, 10 to 12 years before. However, their data were only reported in terms of change scores over time, describing the persistent deficits and improvement of functions. Smith (1978) reported the stability of WISC-R subtest profiles for children in learning-disabled classrooms over a 7-month test-retest interval. His purpose was to replicate the findings of a unique subtest profile previously reported by Smith, Coleman, Dokecki, and Davis (1977). Koppitz (1971) reported stable levels of the IQ score for each group of pupils who remained between 1 to 5 years in special classes for learning-handicapped children. However, she also limited the analyses of her data to the measure of gain scores.

Dykman and his colleagues (Dykman, Peters, & Ackerman, 1973) followed up a subgroup of children diagnosed with minimal brain dysfunction (MBD) after an interval of 3 to 6 years later, and included test-retest stability correlations for only a limited number of measures (WISC IQs, the Gray Oral Reading Test, and neurological scores) although a few others were available for comparison (Bender Motor Visual Gestalt Test, Simple Reaction Task, and Differentiation Task). In an attempt to obtain retest information on well-standardized academic achievement tests on a group of boys who were diagnosed during elementary school as having specific reading disability, Trites and Fiedorowicz (1976) computed the correlations between selected achievement, IQ, vocabulary, and perceptual measures. Although two measures – Wide Range Achievement Test (WRAT) and Peabody Picture Vocabulary Test (PPVT) – were repeated at a 3-year follow-up, test-retest correlations for these two tests were not presented.

While long-term stability was not a primary focus of Kaste's dissertation (1971), she did provide test-retest correlations on 50 subjects over a 10-year follow-up period in an appendix. These correlation coefficients ranged from .35 on the Comprehension subtest to .66 on the Similarities subtest, and from .74 on the Performance IQ to .81 on the Full Scale IQ of the WISC and WB-II. Correlations were also computed for two other tests: the Bender Gestalt score ($r = .52$) and the WRAT Reading test ($r = .60$).

In summary, while considerable effort has been spent to determine the adult consequences of a childhood learning disability, follow-up research has generally not used the same measures repeatedly over time to provide a consistent assessment of outcome, and thus failed to evaluate test-retest stability of the test measures. The present study was designed to offer such information by comparing test-retest stability of a selection of well-standardized neuropsychological tests on three groups of learning-disabled children with and without neurological impairment over a period of 15 years.

METHOD

Subjects:

One hundred and seventy five young adults who had been seen for neuropsychological testing and educational counselling because of learning problems at the University of Victoria Neuropsychology Laboratory between the ages 8 and 12 were followed up between 9 and 17 years later. All subjects were a minimum of 1 SD below expected grade level on the WRAT in reading, spelling, and/or arithmetic. At the time of original assessment (time 1), three diagnostic groups were defined on the basis of the neurological examination performed at time 1, as follows:

(1) those with definite neurological indications of brain damage ("hard" signs such as hemiparesis, athetosis, hydrocephalus, ataxia, EEG delta activity, etc.), labeled as BD ($n = 67$);

(2) those with minimal brain dysfunction as indicated by one or more "soft" signs (e.g., EEG dysrhythmia, hyperreflexia on one side or other, asymmetry of motor control or sensation, tremor, nystagmus, dyspraxia, etc.), labeled as MBD ($n = 73$); and,

(3) those learning disabled children without any neurological indication of brain dysfunction, labeled as LD ($n = 35$).

Children with mental retardation, primary emotional disorders, or brain damage acquired late during childhood were excluded from the three clinic-referred groups at follow-up (time 2). All subjects had to achieve a VIQ or PIQ of at least 70 to be included in the study.

Representativeness of the follow-up (time 2) and original assessment (time 1) samples was evaluated to verify that no selective attrition had occurred. A 2 (presence/absence at time 2) x 3 (group) multivariate analysis of variance compared the subjects missing at time 2 to the remaining participating subjects. There were no significant differences on all tests except for the IQ scores which tended to be slightly higher in the subjects who dropped out. The proportion of retest scores available differed from one test to another, and ranged from 78.05% to 89.89%.

Tests

At the time of original assessment (time 1), the subjects were administered a battery of selected neuropsychological tests, including widely used measures of intelligence (Wechsler Intelligence Scale for Children - WISC), academic achievement (Wide Range Achievement

Test - WRAT; Jastak & Jastak, 1965), concept formation (Category Test - Shortened Intermediate Form; Kilpatrick, 1969), immediate verbal memory (Sentence Repetition; Spreen & Benton, 1969), spatial body-orientation (Right-Left Orientation; Benton, 1959), lateralization (Lateral Dominance; Harris, 1947); and, motor grip strength (Dynamometer; Reitan & Davison, 1974). All tests were readministered at follow-up; two were replaced by the appropriate age-equivalent forms (Wechsler Adult Intelligence Scale-Revised - WAIS-R; and Category Test - Shortened Adult Form, Labreche 1982). All tests followed standard order and instructions of administration.

Statistical Analyses:
Pearson Product Moment correlations between time 1 and time 2 were computed for each test across all subjects and for each learning disabled group; these constituted the measures of stability over time. Time effect and group differences were analyzed by means of multivariate analyses of variance, MANOVA, (2 times of assessment x 3 groups).

RESULTS

A total of 133 subjects was available for test-retest comparison, although not all subjects had taken all tests at time 1. Pearson correlation coefficients for all tests administered on both occasions are summarized in Table 1. In general, the correlation coefficients were high and significant. Bloom (1964) suggests that correlation coefficients of .5 or better are indicators of good long-term stability.

Measures of lateral dominance (hand, eye, and foot preference) appeared to be the most stable over time, followed by IQ tests, academic achievement, handedness (writing only), and sentence repetition. Lower stability coefficients were found for the Category Test, grip strength, and Right-Left Orientation. No consistent pattern of the magnitude of correlations emerged across the three groups. However, there was a trend for the BD group to show the highest correlations, with relatively lower correlations in the MBD group, and comparatively low correlations in the LD group. It appears that the LD group was the least stable group on this battery of neuropsychological tests.

Since psychometric intelligence may be an important factor in the outcome of many different areas of adult achievement and adjustment, the three groups were equated for IQ (mean IQ = 96 for all groups) by eliminating some subjects. Correlations for IQ-matched groups (Table 2) were not substantially different from those shown in Table 1.

Correlation coefficients were also computed for the 30 subjects who took all tests at both times (see $Total_1$, Table 1). The results remained essentially the same. The only significant difference between the correlation coefficient of $Total_1$ and $Total_2$ was found for the Handedness measure, where $Total_2$ (n = 133) produced a lower r (.71) than $Total_1$ (n = 30, r = .94).

A 3 (group) x 2 (time) MANOVA was conducted and revealed a significant overall time effect (F (13, 15) = 54.03, p < .001), which allowed for the

Table 1

Correlation Coefficients for Corresponding Tests Given At
Mean Age of 10 and 25 Years in Learning Disabled Subjects

Tests	Total$_1$ Ssa	n	Total$_2$ Ss	n	BD	n	MBD	n	LD	n
Category Test	.41	30	.47	64	.47	26	.55	30	.59	8
Sentence Repetition	.58	30	.58	124	.65	50	.46	52	.44	22
Lateral Dominance	.93	30	.87	105	.75	42	.92	41	.89	22
Handedness	.94	30	.71	133	.56	55	.87	52	.94	26
Dynamometer-Right Hand	.17	30	.36	111	.66	43	—.03	45	.36	23
Dynamometer-Left Hand	.17	30	.36	111	.53	43	.11	45	.40	23
Right-Left Orientation	.27	30	.27	97	.25	35	.34	44	.14	18
WRAT Reading	.75	30	.74	80	.76	33	.81	33	.57	14
WRAT Spelling	.76	30	.73	80	.78	34	.87	32	.50	14
WRAT Arithmetic	.74	30	.65	80	.74	34	.57	32	.49	14
WISC/WAIS-R VIQ	.73	30	.79	124	.86	48	.72	55	.69	21
WISC/WAIS-R PIQ	.68	30	.73	121	.78	45	.69	55	.51	21
WISC/WAIS-R FSIQ	.70	30	.79	118	.83	44	.78	54	.65	20
Information			.68	119	.80	48	.50	50	.61	21
Comprehension			.58	113	.62	44	.57	50	.39	19
Arithmetic			.49	120	.57	49	.46	50	.40	21
Similarities			.62	118	.60	48	.55	49	.71	21
Vocabulary			.64	116	.75	46	.50	50	.60	20
Digit Span			.66	110	.65	41	.74	48	.23	21
Picture Completion			.55	118	.63	47	.33	50	.56	21
Picture Arrangement			.52	109	.51	42	.46	46	.36	21
Block Design			.63	120	.60	48	.69	51	.48	21
Object Assembly			.58	90	.60	34	.57	38	.46	18
Coding/Digit Symbol			.50	115	.43	42	.64	51	.29	22

Note. Using Fisher's Zr transformation, significant differences between correlation coefficients for the BD and MBD groups were found on the Lateral Dominance ($p < .01$), the Handedness ($p < .01$), the Right-Hand Dynamometer ($p < .01$), and the Left-Hand Dynamometer ($p < .05$). For the BD and LD groups, correlation coefficients were different for the Handedness measure ($p < .01$). For the MBD and LD groups, correlation coefficients differed on the WRAT Spelling score ($p < .05$). Total$_1$ and Total$_2$ were found to have different correlation coefficients on the Handedness measure ($p < .01$).
Ss = subjects; BD = definite neurological signs; MBD = 'soft' neurological sings; LD = no neurological signs.
a Reduced sample size including only those subjects who received all tests at both testing times.

interpretation of univariate analyses of variance (ANOVA) on each dependent variable (Hummel & Sligo, 1971). Significant time effects were obtained for the WISC/WAIS-R VIQ ($F (1, 121) = 44.24$, $p < .001$); the WISC/WAIS-R PIQ ($F (1, 118) = 31.09$, $p < .001$); the WISC/WAIS-R FSIQ ($F (1, 129) = 63.13$, $p < .001$); the Category Test, Intermediate/Adult ($F (1, 61) = 182.82, p < .001$); the Handedness ($F (1, 130) = 6.36, p < .013$); the left hand Dynamometer ($F (1, 108)$

Table 2

Correlation Coefficients for Corresponding Tests Given At
Mean Age of 10 and 25 Years in LD Subjects Matched for IQ

Tests	Total Ss	n	BD	n	MBD	n	LD	n
Category Test	.48	57	.60	20	.50	29	.83	4
Sentence Repetition	.21	97	.60	30	.49	45	.21	22
Lateral Dominance	.90	83	.83	25	.92	37	.89	21
Handedness	.83	99	.72	31	.86	44	.94	24
Dynamometer-Right Hand	.34	84	.24	24	.40	38	.36	22
Dynamometer-Left Hand	.31	84	.20	24	.09	38	.40	22
Right-Left Orientation	.19	79	.11	22	.31	39	.14	18
WRAT Reading	.75	59	.78	17	.81	29	.55	13
WRAT Spelling	.69	59	.75	18	.85	28	.45	13
WRAT Arithmetic	.59	59	.69	18	.58	28	.48	13
WISC/WAIS-R VIQ	.62	105	.82	31	.67	50	.48	24
WISC/WAIS-R PIQ	.76	104	.65	30	.64	50	.69	24
WISC/WAIS-R FSIQ	.71	104	.74	30	.73	50	.67	24
Information	.58	93	.73	29	.41	43	.61	21
Comrehension	.46	90	.50	28	.45	43	.39	19
Arithmetic	.34	93	.30	29	.38	43	.40	21
Similarities	.57	92	.54	29	.51	42	.71	21
Vocabulary	.59	92	.77	29	.41	43	.60	20
Digit Span	.62	86	.58	24	.75	41	.23	21
Picture Completion	.43	89	.60	27	.27	42	.52	20
Picture Arrangement	.41	83	.37	24	.48	39	.30	20
Block Design	.65	91	.62	28	.72	43	.57	20
Object Assembly	.52	67	.54	19	.54	31	.46	17
Coding/Digit Symbol	.44	89	.29	25	.62	43	.39	21

Note. Ss = subjects; BD = definite neurological signs; MBD = 'soft' neurological signs; LD = no neurological signs.

$= 623.46, p < .001$); the right hand Dynamometer ($F(1, 108) = 707.59, p < .001$); the Right-Left Orientation ($F(1, 94) = 47.23, p < .001$); the Sentence Repetition ($F(1, 121) = 349.78, p < .001$); the WRAT Reading ($F(1, 77) = 398.92, p < .001$); the WRAT Spelling ($F(1, 77) = 162.39, p < .001$); and the WRAT Arithmetic ($F(1, 77) = 140.62, p < .001$). The VIQ and PIQ ratings were slightly lower at time 2, as compared to time 1, for all three groups. A decrease in scores on the Category Test was also in evidence. There was an increase in scores on all other measures. Table 3 summarizes the means and standard deviations of tests administered at referral and follow-up for all three groups.

The overall group effect did not reach significance in the MANOVA ($F(13, 15) = .95, p < .56$), although group differences were noted on 4 univariate ANOVAs: the WISC/WAIS-R VIQ ($F(2, 121) = 3.11, p < .048$), the WISC/WAIS-R PIQ

Table 3

Means and Standard Deviations of Selected Neuropsychological Tests
At Time of Referral (Time 1) & at Follow-up (Time 2), 15 Years Later

Tests:		Time 1			Time 2		
		BD	MBD	LD	BD	MBD	LD
Category Test	M	65.7	55.4	59.8	28.7	32.4	23.3
No. errors (80) a	SD	19.1	21.0	25.3	13.6	14.4	14.4
Sentence Repetition	M	10.4	11.3	11.9	13.9	14.8	15.0
No. correct (22) a	SD	2.7	2.0	2.1	2.6	1.9	1.4
Lateral Dominance	M	10.8	11.5	11.0	11.6	12.0	11.5
No. right side (14) a	SD	2.9	4.0	3.4	3.0	4.3	3.3
Handedness	M	1.3	1.2	1.2	1.2	1.2	1.2
1 = R, 2 = L, 3 = A	SD	.7	.5	.5	.4	.4	.4
Dynamometer-Right Hand	M	12.1	14.0	13.1	35.1	35.8	38.0
No. kilograms	SD	4.5	3.5	3.7	14.3	13.0	14.6
Dynamometer-Left Hand	M	11.1	13.4	12.0	32.0	35.0	35.3
No. kilograms	SD	4.9	3.8	4.2	13.8	13.0	16.0
Right-Left Orientation	M	20.9	21.5	22.1	27.3	27.8	28.1
No. correct (32) a	SD	8.9	8.4	8.4	6.1	5.9	6.2
WRAT Reading	M	3.6	4.1	4.2	7.3	7.4	8.0
Grade Score	SD	2.3	2.2	2.3	2.6	2.0	1.6
WRAT Spelling	M	3.3	3.4	4.0	6.1	5.6	6.2
Grade Score	SD	2.2	1.5	2.7	2.9	2.2	2.2
WRAT Arithmetic	M	3.0	3.4	3.9	5.1	5.0	5.5
Grade Score	SD	1.6	1.2	1.4	2.1	1.4	1.6
WISC/WAIS-R VIQ	M	88.9	94.4	99.8	85.3	88.4	90.8
	SD	16.3	13.5	14.6	14.9	11.1	12.3
WISC/WAIS-R PIQ	M	88.5	96.7	102.0	83.5	91.9	92.6
	SD	16.3	14.2	14.9	14.9	13.0	11.5
WISC/WAIS-R FSIQ	M	87.8	94.8	102.2	83.2	88.6	91.8
	SD	15.4	13.2	14.0	14.3	12.1	11.1

Note. Pairwise comparison of group means, using a critical ratio (difference between two means / standard error of the difference between two sample means), revealed significant mean differences (at time 1) between the BD and MBD groups on the Right-Hand Dynamometer ($p < .05$), the Left-Hand Dynamometer ($p < .05$), the WISC/WAIS-R PIQ ($p < .01$), and WISC/WAIS-R FSIQ ($p < .05$). The BD and LD groups showed significant mean differences on the Sentence Repetition ($p < .05$), the WISC/WAIS-R VIQ ($p < .01$), the WISC/WAIS-R PIQ ($p < .01$), the WISC/WAIS-R FSIQ ($p < .01$). The MBD and LD group means were significantly different on the WISC/WAIS-R FSIQ ($p < .05$).

At time 2, significant differences between the BD and MBD group means were found on the WISC/WAIS-R PIQ ($p < .01$) and the WISC/WAIS-R FSIQ ($p < .05$). The BD and LD groups showed significant mean differences on the Sentence Repetition ($p < .05$), the WISC/WAIS-R PIQ ($p < .01$), and the WISC/WAIS-R FSIQ ($p < .05$).

BD = definite neurological signs; MBD = 'soft' neurological signs; LD = no neurological signs; R = right; L = left; A = ambidextrous.
a Maximum total score.

(F (2, 118) = 7.09, $p <$ .001), the WISC/WAIS-R FSIQ (F (2, 129) = 7.20, $p <$ .001), and Sentence Repetition (F(2, 121) = 4.23, $p <$ .017). These tests suggested a linear trend with the lowest score in the BD group and the best score in the LD group. The other test measures tended to follow the same trend.

The MANOVA produced an overall significant interaction effect (F(13, 15) = 2.20, $p <$ .02), with the univariate ANOVAs revealing significant time by group effects for the Category Test (F(2, 61) = 4.69, $p <$ .013), and the WISC/WAIS-R FSIQ (F(2, 129) = 3.34, $p <$ .038). The Category Test displayed a quadratic trend at time 2 which was the reverse of that at time 1. That is, the MBD group achieved a lower mean score than the BD and LD groups at time 1, while at follow-up the MBD group obtained a greater error score than the two other groups. As for the WISC/WAIS-R FSIQ, there was a linear trend at both times of assessment, with the highest IQ score pertaining to the LD group, and the lower to the BD group.

DISCUSSION

The retesting of learning-disabled subjects provides an opportunity to investigate the longterm stability of a limited number of tests. The correlation coefficients for the three groups give an estimate of the range of stability in three different samples. Overall, test results for the BD group appeared to show the highest stability, while those for the LD group were less stable. Psychometric intelligence does not seem to be a significant prognostic indicator of stability in scores since the less stable group (LD) was the one with the best intellectual levels (FSIQ time 1 = 102, 95, 88, time 2 = 92, 89, 83, for LD, MBD, and BD groups, respectively). On the other hand, the presence/absence of soft neurological signs may prove to be a more critical factor: While neurological signs in the BD and MBD groups persisted over the follow-up period, the LD group was free of neurological signs at time 1 but revealed a number of soft signs at time 2 (Hern & Spreen, 1984), indicating more change or lack of stability in this respect as well.

The results may also be viewed as an indication of longterm persistence of neuropsychological deficits as the child matures from middle childhood to adulthood. The children with "minimal brain dysfunction" (MBD) showed poorer outcome as compared to those without any evidence of brain damage (LD), but generally better outcome than the group with definite neurological impairment (BD) (Spreen, 1982). The results reported here (Table 3) also support persistent deficits over time, and do not support the maturation hypothesis which claims that, as the child matures, many disabilities tend to diminish or disappear (Birch, 1964; Klebanoff et al., 1954; Laufer & Denhoff, 1957). Rather, our findings are consistent with the report that subjects with organic deficits show less improvement and persistent difficulties into later life (Hinton & Knights, 1971; Kaste, 1971; Silver & Hagin, 1964). This is also supported by data on life and occupational adjustment in our subjects (Spreen, 1984).

Nevertheless, there were significant time effects on several tests. These reflected an increase in scores consonant with the sequential acquisition of the measured skills with age. For example, academic skills and hand grip strength, as measured with the WRAT and dynamometer respectively, improve steadily with age (continued instruction, practice, and maturation). VIQ and PIQ scores were slightly lower at time 2, as compared to time 1, for all three groups. This may represent a genuine minor reduction in intellectual abilities, but it is more likely the result of administering the recently revised adult intelligence scale (WAIS-R) with the newly standardized norms. Wechsler (1974) found IQ shifts (about 6 points) for 16-year-olds tested with the WISC-R (standardized in the early 1970s) compared to the 1955 WAIS. Similar IQ shifts (7-8 points) were reported between the WAIS and WAIS-R (Wechsler, 1981).

The change in error scores on the Category Test for all three groups reflects differences between the shortened two versions of the test for children and adults. While the maximum scores in both tests is 80, the mean error score for normal children of the same age is 49.00, $SD = 18.63$ (Kilpatrick, 1969), and for the normal adults it is 19.55, $SD = 7.78$ (Labreche, 1982). Compared to these norms, our participants at both ages made more errors than the normative groups. Using standard (z) scores, their performance at time 1 was at $+0.6$ SD from the normative mean, while at time 2 it was at $+1.3$ SD. A group of young adults who had been normal learners in school and who were age-matched with the LD groups, obtained a mean of 19.32 ($SD = 12.67$).

Using this limited battery of neuropsychological tests, differences between LD children with definite, suggested, or without indication of brain damage were not found on a repeated measures multivariate design. However, these results do contribute to group discrimination if treated in a multivariate manner, without the time factor, and together with other results (Spreen, 1984).

REFERENCES

Balow, B., & Blomquist, M. (1965). Young adults ten to fifteen years after severe reading disability. *The Elementary School Journal, 66,* 44-48.

Benton, A. L. (1959). *Right-left discrimination and finger localization: Development and pathology.* New York: Hoeber-Harper.

Birch, H. G. (1964). *Brain damage in children, the biological and social aspects.* Baltimore: Williams & Wilkins.

Bloom, B. S. (1964). *Stability and change in human characteristics.* New York: John Wiley & Sons.

Bradley, P. E., Battin, R. R., & Sutter, E. G. (1979). Effects of individual diagnosis and remediation for the treatment of learning disabilities. *Clinical Neuropsychology, 1,* 25-32.

Bruck, M. (1985). The adult functioning of children with specific learning disabilities: A follow-up study. In: I. E. Sigel (Ed.), *Advances in applied developmental psychology, Vol. 1* (pp. 91-129). Norwood, NJ: Ablex.

Carter, R. P. (1964). A descriptive analysis of the adult adjustment of persons once identified as disabled readers. Unpublished Doctoral Dissertation, University of Indiana, Bloomington.

Dykman, R. A., Peters, J. E., & Ackerman, P. T. (1973). Experimental approaches to the study of minimal brain dysfunction: A follow-up study. *Annals of the New York Academy of Sciences, 205*, 93-108.

Gottesman, R., Belmont, I., & Kaminer, R. (1975). Admission and follow-up status of reading disabled children referred to a medical clinic. *Journal of Learning Disabilities, 8*, 642-650.

Hardy, M. I. (1968). Clinical follow-up study of disabled readers. Unpublished Doctoral Dissertation, University of Toronto, Canada.

Harris, A. J. (1947). *Harris Tests of Lateral Dominance, Manual of Directions for Administration and Interpretation.* New York: Psychological Corporation.

Herjanic, B. M., & Penick, E. C. (1972). Adult outcome of disabled child readers. *Journal of Special Education, 6*, 397-410.

Hermann, R. (1959). *Reading disability.* Springfield, IL.: Charles C. Thomas.

Hern, A., & Spreen, O. (1984, February). Persistence and incidence of neurological findings in learning disabled and normal learning subjects from age 10 to early adulthood. Paper presented at the annual meeting of the International Neuropsychological Society, Houston, TX.

Hinton, G. C., & Knights, R. M. (1971). Children with learning problems: Academic history, academic prediction, adjustment, 3 years after assessment. *Exceptional Children, 37*, 513-519.

Howden, M. E. (1967). A nineteen-year follow-up study of good, average and poor readers in the fifth and sixth grades. Unpublished Doctoral Dissertation. University of Oregon, Eugene.

Hummel, T. J., & Sligo, J. R. (1971). Empirical comparison of univariate and multivariate analysis of variance procedures. *Psychological Bulletin, 76*, 49-57.

Jastak, J. F., & Jastak, S. R. (1965). *The Wide Range Achievement Test Manual.* Wilmington, DE: Guidance Associates.

Kaste, C. M. (1971). A ten-year follow-up of children diagnosed in a child guidance clinic as having cerebral dysfunction. Unpublished Doctoral Dissertation. University of Minnesota.

Kilpatrick, D. L. (1969). Revision of the intermediate version of the Halstead Category Test. Unpublished Master's Dissertation. University of Victoria.

Klebanoff, S. G., Singer, J. J., & Wilenski. H. (1954). Psychological consequences of brain lesions and ablations. *Psychological Bulletin, 51*, 1-41.

Koppitz, E. M. (1971). *Children with learning disabilities. A five year follow-up study.* New York: Grune & Stratton.

Labreche, T. M. (1982). Revision of the Halstead Category Test. Unpublished Doctoral Dissertation. University of Victoria.

Laufer, M. W., & Denhoff, E. (1957). Hyperkinetic behavior syndrome in children. *Journal of Pediatrics, 50*, 463-474.

Mendelson, W., Johnson, N., & Stewart, M. (1971). Hyperactive children as teenagers: A follow-up study. *Journal of Nervous and Mental Diseases, 153*, 272-279.

Peter, B. M. & Spreen, O. (1979). Behavior rating and personal adjustment scales of neurologically and learning handicapped children during adolescence and early adulthood:

522

Results of a follow-up study. *Journal of Clinical Neuropsychology, 1,* 75-92.

Preston, R. C., & Yarington, D. J. (1967). Status of fifty retarded readers eight years after reading clinic diagnosis. *Journal of Reading, 11,* 122-129.

Rawson, M. B. (1968). *Developmental language disability: Adult accomplishment of dyslexic boys.* Baltimore: Johns Hopkins University Press.

Reitan, R. M. & Davison, L. S. (1974). *Clinical neuropsychology: Current status and applications.* Washington, DC: V. H. Winston & Sons.

Robinson, H. M., & Smith, H. K. (1962). Reading clinic clients - Ten year after. *The Elementary School Journal, 63,* 22-27.

Silver, A. A., & Hagin, R. A. (1964). Specific reading disability: Follow-up studies. *American Journal of Orthopsychiatry, 34,* 95-102.

Smith, M. D. (1978). Stability of WISC-R subtest profiles for learning disabled children. *Psychology in the Schools, 15,* 4-7.

Smith, M. D., Coleman, J. M., Dokecki, P. R., & Davis, E. E. (1977). Intellectual characteristics of school-labeled learning disabled children. *Exceptional Children, 43,* 352-357.

Spreen, O. (1982). Adult outcome of reading disorders. In: R. N. Malatesha & P. G. Aaron (Eds.), *Reading disorders: Varieties and treatments* (pp. 473-498). New York: Academic Press.

Spreen, O. (1984) A prognostic view from middle childhood. In: M. Levine & P. Satz (Eds.), *Middle childhood: Developmental variations and dysfunction* (pp. 405-432). New York: Academic Press.

Spreen, O., & Benton, A. L. (1969). *Neurosensory Center Comprehensive Examination for Aphasia.* Victoria, B.C.: Neuropsychological Laboratory, Department of Psychology, University of Victoria.

Trites, R. L., & Fiedorowicz, C. (1976). Follow-up study of children with specific (or primary) reading disability. In: R. M. Knights & D. J. Bakker (Eds.), *The neuropsychology of learning disorders. Theoretical approaches* (pp. 41-50). Baltimore: University Park Press.

Wechsler, D. (1981). *Manual for the Wechsler Intelligence Scale for Adults-Revised.* New York: The Psychological Corporation.

Wechsler, D. (1974). *Manual for the Wechsler Intelligence Scale for Children-Revised.* New York: The Psychological Corporation.

The Clinical Neuropsychologist
1989, Vol. 3, No. 2, pp. 157-161

CLINICAL ISSUES

Stability of Children's Neuropsychological Profiles: Comparison of McCarthy Scales and WISC-R

Joan E. Backman and Anne Cornwall
Izaak Walton Killam Hospital for Children

Mary L. Stewart
University of Windsor

Joseph M. Byrne
Izaak Walton Killam Hospital for Children
and
Dalhousie University School of Medicine

ABSTRACT

The power of the McCarthy Scales of Children's Abilities (MSCA) to predict WISC-R performance was examined in a sample of children referred for neuropsychological assessment. Thirty-two children were administered the MSCA and given the WISC-R on follow-up an average of 2 years later. In contrast to previous findings, no significant differences were found between the mean MSCA General Cognitive Index (GCI) and WISC-R Full Scale IQ (FSIQ) scores. Significant correlations were found between GCI and FSIQ, Perceptual-Performance Scale and Performance IQ, and Verbal Scale and Verbal IQ. However, the variance of the Verbal IQ accounted for by the Verbal scale of the MSCA was less than 40%. Furthermore, when dividing the data into three intelligence classifications, the classification of verbal ability made by the MSCA Verbal Scale was as likely to change as it was to stay the same upon retesting with the WISC-R. These findings are discussed with reference to predicting later patterns of neuropsychological test performance.

Portions of this paper were presented at the meeting of the International Neuropsychological Society, New Orleans, February, 1988.

524

In the practice of child neuropsychology, clinicians are often asked to assess the cognitive abilities of preschool children, and to make predictions about their later levels of functioning. The McCarthy Scales of Children's Abilities (MSCA; McCarthy, 1972) has become a popular instrument for assessing neuropsychological functioning of preschool children, since it is comprised of scales assessing Verbal, Perceptual-Performance, Quantitative, and Memory skills. Studies examining concurrent validity of the MSCA and the Wechsler Intelligence Scale for Children-Revised (WISC-R; Wechsler, 1974) in "learning disabled" children have suggested that the MSCA General Cognitive Index (GCI) tends to be significantly lower than the WISC-R Full Scale IQ (FSIQ; e.g., Goh & Youngquist, 1979; Kaufman & Kaufman, 1977b). Differences between the two measures have been found to fall consistently between 8 and 11 points. However, the degree to which the MSCA predicts later WISC-R performance in a sample with a wider range of neuropsychological problems has not been evaluated.

In the present study, the value of the MSCA in predicting WISC-R performance was examined in a sample of children referred for neuropsychological assessment. The MSCA was administered when the children were approximately 6 years of age; the WISC-R was administered during clinic follow-up, approximately 2 years later. This allowed us to examine a related issue: whether discrepancies between Verbal and Perceptual-Performance Scales on the MSCA predict similar patterns of performance on the WISC-R. It was our clinical impression that, while the GCI and FSIQ agree quite well, the MSCA and WISC-R Verbal Scales do not. It was our hypothesis that the MSCA would estimate higher levels of verbal ability than the WISC-R, possibly reflecting the heavy reliance on rote memory and verbal associative abilities on subtests comprising the MSCA Verbal Scale. Some children, for example, might do well on tasks involving rote associative skills, but lack the higher order conceptual abilities required on several subtests of the WISC-R, and thus would score relatively higher on the MSCA Verbal Scale than on the WISC-R Verbal Scale.

METHOD

Thirty-two subjects were selected from psychology files in a regional pediatric teaching hospital. These children were referred for assessment of suspected or known neurodevelopmental disorders. These included delays in language, motor or general cognitive development (n = 23), phenylketonuria (n = 2), Williams Syndrome (n = 1), Down's Syndrome (n = 1), myotonic dystrophy (n = 1), closed-head injury (n = 1), seizure disorders (n = 2), and porencephalic cyst secondary to neonatal intraventricular hemorrhage (n = 1). All children who had been administered the MSCA (M age = 6 years, SD = 12.6 months, range = 47 months) and were subsequently tested with the WISC-R (M age = 7 years, 9 months, SD = 16 months, range = 75 months) were chosen for this study.

RESULTS

Pearson product-moment correlations were computed between the MSCA and the WISC-R scales. Significant correlations ($p < .001$) were obtained on all comparisons: GCI and FSIQ [$r(30) = .72$], Perceptual-Performance Scale score and PIQ [$r(30) = .71$], and Verbal Scale score and VIQ [$r(30) = .62$]. The means and standard deviations for the MSCA and WISC-R are presented in Table 1. In contrast to previous findings, there was no significant discrepancy between the GCI and FSIQ [$t(31) = 0.19$, ns].

Table 1. Means and Standard Deviations for MSCA and WISC-R Scales.

	MSCA		WISC-R	
	M	*SD*	*M*	*SD*
GCI/FSIQ	80.34	(15.56)	79.94	(16.63)
Verbal Scale/ VIQ	43.25[1]	(10.49)	84.25	(16.08)
Perceptual- Performance Scale/ PIQ	37.38	(9.57)	78.44	(18.78)

Note: For Verbal and Perceptual Performance Scales: $M = 50$ and $SD = 10$.

While the correlations obtained suggest a statistically significant association between these measures, a more relevant clinical issue is whether or not results from each Scale lead to similar clinical classifications with regard to level and pattern of functioning. Therefore, a series of classification analyses were undertaken. The MSCA GCI and WISC-R FSIQ scores were divided into three ranges of functioning: Average and Above (≥ 90), Borderline/Low Average (70-89), and Cognitively Impaired (≤ 69). Similar ranges of functioning were demarcated for MSCA and WISC-R Verbal and Performance abilities. Even though the MSCA has a standard deviation of 16 and the WISC-R has a standard deviation of 15, the descriptive classification of ability level for each scale is based on the same numerical values (see Kaufman & Kaufman, 1977a; McCarthy, 1972; Wechsler, 1974).

In terms of FSIQ and GCI, 24 of the 32 children (75%) were classified into the same categories by the two scales. In the eight cases where there was disagreement, the MSCA classified six of them in a higher category (75%). A similar degree of agreement was observed on the Performance Scales. The two instruments classified the children in the same category in 22 of 32 cases (68.7%). Of the 10 cases where the two scales disagreed, there did not seem to be any consistent pattern of overestimation or underestimation; in five of the cases, the MSCA classification was higher (50%). A lower degree of agreement was observed on the Verbal scales. Eighteen of the 32 children were classified in the same category by the two measures (56.2%). In the 14 cases where there was a disagreement, the MSCA classified 10 of the children in a higher category (71.4%).

Tests for significance of difference between two proportions were conducted to determine whether or not children were receiving similar classifications by each measure (Bruning & Kintz, 1977). There was a significantly larger proportion of children obtaining similar classifications for both overall cognitive ability (.75 vs .25; $z = 2.53$, $p < .05$) and performance abilities (.69 vs. .31; $z = 2.01$, $p < .05$). However, there was not a significant difference in the proportion of children obtaining the same verbal classification when compared to the proportion of children obtaining a different verbal classification (.56 vs .44; $z = .67$, ns). Thus, a youngster's verbal classification was as likely to change as it was to stay the same from one measure (MSCA) to the other (WISC-R).

DISCUSSION

In this fairly typical clinical sample of children referred for neuropsychological assessment, there was good correspondence in terms of both correlation and clinical classification between the MSCA GCI and WISC-R FSIQ over a period of approximately 21 months. The underestimation of WISC-R FSIQ by the MSCA General Cognitive Index, observed in previous studies where the children were assessed concurrently, was not observed in this study. In fact, when disagreements in FSIQ/GCI and Verbal Scale score/VIQ comparisons were noted, the MSCA was usually higher (75% and 71.4% of disagreements, respectively).

This discrepancy with previous findings may reflect the limitations of the instruments used. When children with learning difficulties are assessed with both the MSCA and the WISC-R at age 7 (as in Goh & Youngquist, 1979, Kaufman & Kaufman, 1977b), they may be scoring near the ceiling of the MSCA, while scoring near the floor of the WISC-R. This may result in an underestimation of their cognitive abilities by the MSCA, and an overestimation of their true abilities with the WISC-R. However, in the present sample, children were observed longitudinally over an average of 21 months, and at age ranges perhaps more suitable to the instruments themselves. This may have yielded a greater degree of correspondence. Whether or not this level of agreement is maintained for older children should be examined. In addition, these findings should be replicated with samples having a greater range of intelligence, as the level of agreement may differ in children with higher (or lower) ranges of intellectual ability. Nonetheless, the overall low average level of ability in this sample is not felt to be at all atypical of children referred to pediatric neuropsychology services and, as such, the range of intellectual ability relates to the clinical imperatives at hand.

In regard to specific subscales, the results of this study would suggest that the MSCA Verbal Scale was not a good predictor of later WISC-R VIQ. This was reflected in both the lower correlation and the lower degree of agreement in classification of intellectual functioning between the two instruments. The present study confirms our clinical observation that the MSCA Verbal Scale may not be an accurate estimate of later verbal ability, as assessed by the WISC-R. This may reflect, in part, the fact that the MSCA Verbal Scale taps different verbal abilities than does the WISC-R. Therefore, these preliminary findings suggest that, although the MSCA GCI is a fairly reliable predictor of later general intelligence, the instrument should be used cautiously to predict later patterns of neuropsychological ability, particularly subsequent verbal functioning as assessed by the WISC-R.

REFERENCES

Bruning, J. L., & Kintz, B. L. (1977). *Computation handbook of statistics* (2nd Ed.) Glenview, IL: Scott, Foresman, and Company.

Goh, D., & Youngquist, J. (1979). A comparison of the McCarthy Scales of Children's Abilities and the WISC-R. *Journal of Learning Disabilities, 12,* 64-68.

Kaufman, A. S., & Kaufman, N. L. (1977a). *Clinical evaluation of young children with the McCarthy Scales.* New York: Grune and Stratton.

Kaufman, A. S., & Kaufman, N. L. (1977b). Research on the McCarthy Scales and its implications for assessment. *Journal of Learning Disabilities, 10,* 30-37.

McCarthy, D. (1972). *McCarthy Scales of Children's Abilities.* New York: Psychological Corporation.

Wechsler, D. (1974). *Wechsler Intelligence Scale for Children-Revised.* New York: Psychological Corporation.

The Clinical Neuropsychologist
1989, Vol. 3, No. 4, pp. 353-368

Reliability of Tests and Measures Used in the Neuropsychological Assessment of Children

Sandra J. Brown
Henry Ford Hospital

Byron P. Rourke
University of Windsor

Domenic V. Cicchetti
West Haven VA Medical Center and Yale University

ABSTRACT

Reliabilities of the tests that comprise Reitan's neuropsychological batteries for children, as well as other allied tests of neuropsychological functioning used in the assessment of children, were examined. A heterogeneous sample of 248 youngsters who had been evaluated more than once over an average of 2.6 years was drawn from a population of 3600 children referred for neuropsychological assessment. Pearson and intraclass correlation coefficients were calculated on the data provided by these children. The results demonstrated a high degree of reliability for many of the 50 variables studied. A hierarchy of reliability coefficients is presented as is a discussion of the pattern of consistency and stability in evidence.

The reliability of the tests that comprise the Halstead-Reitan Neuropsychological Battery for Adults has been reasonably well studied in various populations (Bornstein, 1982; Bornstein, 1983; Dodrill & Trupin, 1975; Eckardt & Matarazzo, 1981; Goldstein & Watson, 1989: Klonoff, Fibiger, & Hutton, 1970; Matarazzo, Matarazzo, Wiens, Gallo, & Klonoff, 1976; Matarazzo, Wiens, Matarazzo, & Goldstein, 1974; Morrison, Gregory, & Paul, 1979; Shaw, 1966). Despite the research using adult populations, there are no published accounts of the reliability of the tests incorporated in the Reitan Neuropsychological Battery for Children (Reitan & Davison, 1974).

However, Sarazin and Spreen (1986) have provided some estimate of the reliability of various neuropsychological measures used in the assessment of children. Some of the tests they examined are included in Reitan's tests while others are independent achievement and/or neuropsychological tests. In their investigation, Sarazin and Spreen (1986) examined a sample of children described as learning diasbled at the time of their initial assessment who were then reevaluated 9 to 17 years later as adults. The results of this investigation indicated that the most psychometrically reliable tasks in this population were measures of lateral dominance, followed by IQ tests, scholastic achievement measures, handedness surveys (writing only), and a sentence repetition test; lower reliability coefficients were observed for the Category Test, Grip Strength Test, and Right-Left Orientation Test. Correlation coefficients ranged from $r = .87$ (all subjects) on the test of lateral dominance to $r = .27$ (all subjects) on the measure of right-left orientation. Although the protocols of children were used at one point in the evaluation, the reliability coefficients were generated partly on the performance of adults, as the subjects had matured to adulthood by the time of the second assessment. In addition, not all of the usual Reitan tests for children were studied and, in at least one instance (i.e., the Category Test), an alternate form of a Reitan measure was used (Shortened Intermediate Form of Kilpatrick, 1969).

The current study is an effort to explore the reliability of the Reitan Neuropsychological Battery for Children as well as other allied measures of neuropsychological functioning used in the assessment of youngsters (Rourke, Fisk, & Strang, 1986). A reliability analysis of Reitan's Neuropsychological Battery for Children is important as these tests are (a) the most widely used measures in the evaluation of youngsters, (b) well standardized, (c) sensitive to brain functioning, and (d) familiar to most neuropsychologists (Reitan & Davison, 1974). A heterogeneous sample of youngsters was chosen for this study for two reasons: (1) diagnostically mixed groups are more representative of populations evaluated in many children's clinics, and (2) investigating reliability in a mixed group of children reduces the attenuation of reliability estimates caused by homogeneity of variance. As this study was exploratory in nature, as opposed to an hypothesis-testing effort, no expectations about the relative magnitude of the reliabilities of the various tests studied were formulated prior to the analysis of the results of the study.

METHOD

Subjects

The neuropsychological protocols of 3,600 children who had been assessed at a large, urban children's clinic specializing in the assessment of neuropsychological functioning served as the data base for this project. These youngsters had been referred for evaluation because they demonstrated some type of perceived impairment in perception, learning, language, information processing, and/or behavior, that was thought to be due to cerebral dysfunction. From within this large pool of subjects, only those children who were assessed at least twice ($n = 248$) were included in this study. The children were between the ages of 5 to 14 years at the time of both the first and second assessments.

Table 1. Diagnostic Criteria for the Learning-Disabled, Mentally Retarded, Brain-Damaged, Emotionally Disturbed, and Environmentally Deprived Subjects.

Learning-Disabled	Subgroup 01:	WISC FSIQ > 85
		one WRAT subtest centile score < 30
	Subgroup 00:	if above criteria are not completely met
Mentally Retarded:	Subgroup 01:	WISC FSIQ 70-84 inclusive
	Subgroup 02:	WISC FSIQ 55-69 inclusive
	Subgroup 03:	WISC FSIQ < 55
	Subgroup 00:	WISC FSIQ > 85
Brain-Damaged:	Subgroup 01:	no clear evidence but has had questionable neurological exam
	Subgroup 02:	unequivocal evidence of injury – no seizures
	Subgroup 03:	suggestion of neurological dysfunction – no seizures
	Subgroup 04:	epilepsy suggested only by medication data and evidence of intervention
	Subgroup 00:	no evidence of brain lesion
Emotionally Disturbed:	Subgroup 01:	diagnostic statement that child is in need of psychotherapeutic intervention
	Subgroup 02:	neuropsychological evidence that child has socioemotional disorder
	Subgroup 00:	no evidence of emotional disturbance
Environmentally Deprived	Subgroup 01:	evidence of environmental deprivation
	Subgroup 00:	no evidence of environmental deprivation

The children comprising this study could be categorized into five groups: (1) learning-disabled, (2) mentally retarded, (3) brain-injured, (4) emotionally disturbed, and (5) environmentally deprived. We present this categorization scheme, not as an analytic variable, but rather to indicate to the reader the composition of the sample. The diagnostic criteria for inclusion into these groups are spread in Table 1. Each child's protocol was rated as to the presence or absence of all characteristics within each major diagnostic category. For example, every youngster was judged as to whether there was clear medical evidence of a brain lesion and whether there was evidence of emotional disturbance or environmental deprivation. The classification of these children is depicted in Table 2. Although a total of 248 children were included in this study, the subject census in each diagnostic category, as reflected in Table 2, does not necessarily reflect that figure due to missing data in some categories.

As shown in Table 2, the average age of the 248 children at their first assessment was 8 years; the average age at the time of retest was 10.6 years. The mean test-retest interval was 2.65 (SD = 1.74) years. This sample of youngsters was primarily male and primarily right-hand dominant. The majority of children were categorized as having evidence of a learning disability, brain injury, or mental retardation.

Test Measures

The children were administered the tests included in the Reitan Neuropsychological Test Battery for Children as well as other measures of neuropsychological functioning (e.g., Auditory Closure Test). However, only those tests that are common to both age groups (the 5- to 8-year-old youngsters and the 9- to 14-year-old children) and that are administered in the same fashion (e.g., Finger Tapping) were considered in the analyses. For example, the younger children (ages 5-8 years) are not assessed on the Trail Making Test, and the Category Test

Table 2. Characteristics of the Sample

	First Assessment	Second Assessment
Age	8.0 years	10.6 years
	(*SD* = 1.7)	(*SD* = 2.3)
Gender	Male: 203 (81.9%)	
	Female: 45 (18.1%)	
Handedness		
Right:	199 (80.2%)	204 (82.3%)
Left:	45 (18.1%)	45 (16.9%)
Unclassified:	4 (1.6%)	2
Learning-Disabled	FSIQ 85 and one WRAT centile	
	score 30: 109	132
	Do not meet complete criteria: 133	115
Mentally	FSIQ 85: 155	161
Retarded	FSIQ=70-84: 65	64
	FSIQ=55-69: 22	16
	FSIQ= 55: 3	6
Brain-Damaged	No clear medical evidence of brain lesion: 205	212
	Questionable neurological findings: 6	6
	Unequivocal evidence of brain injury: 7	6
	Suggestion of brain injury: 12	8
	Seizure disorder: 15	16
Emotionally	No evidence: 214	203
Disturbed	Evidence of need for psychotherapeutic	
	intervention: 31	44
Environmentally	No evidence: 244	243
Deprived	Some evidence: 2	3
Test-Retest		2.65 years
Interval		(*SD* = 1.74)

used with this younger age group contains a different number of items and qualitatively different items than does the Category Test used with older children. The reliability of these tests, therefore, was not examined in this study. Fifty variables were available for analysis, including measures of psychometric intelligence, academic achievement, language skills, memory, and sensory-motor skills and abilities. Complete descriptions of the various test measures are available elsewhere (Reitan & Davidson, 1974; Rourke, Bakker, Fisk, & Strang, 1983; Rourke et al., 1986).

Procedures
The 50 variables in this study were examined for both their consistency and their stability of measurement. Consistency reflects the extent to which the rank order and relative distance between subjects is maintained from one assessment to the second; this was investigated using the Pearson product-moment correlation coefficent. Stability addresses the question of whether there is a significant difference in the means of one test given twice; this was examined through application of the intraclass correlation coefficient (ICC). This technique, which is based on the analysis of variance model, is an index of stability; significant differ-

ences between the means of two scores attenuate the magnitude of the intraclass r. The formula used to calculate the ICC is described by Shrout and Fleiss (1979) as Model III.

[*A Note on Reliability*. Reliability is herein defined in what we take to be the correct sense of extent of interchangeability or agreement between independently derived, paired measurements, within the specific context of controlling adequately for the extent of paired agreement expected on the basis of chance alone. This chance-corrected level of paired agreement is obtained by application of the appropriate model of the intraclass correlation coefficient (Ri), in our case Model III of Shrout and Fleiss (1979). This chance-corrected level of test-retest agreement is also to be distinguished from the more usually obtained, albeit incorrect, assessment of test-retest reliability provided by exclusive evaluation via the standard Pearson product-moment correlation (Rp). The problems with Rp are numerous: (1) The statistic measures the extent to which independently derived pairs of measurement covary in the same order *regardless* of the extent to which the pairings are in agreement. Thus, the WISC full scale IQ scores (FSIQ) of three children might be 85, 100, and 115 at the first assessment and 75, 85, and 100 at the second assessment. In such a case, Rp will produce a coefficient of +1.00, falsely indicating "perfect agreement" between the two testings. Ri, on the other hand, will produce a much lower value of .61 because this statistic measures level of paired agreement, while Rp does not. (2) Ri corrects for chance, whereas Rp does not. (3) Various models of Ri will adjust for the fact that different pairs of examiners may have made the assessments rather than the same two examiners throughout. (4) Ri can provide an overall measure of test-retest agreement when the number of assessments exceeds two, whereas Rp cannot.]

The raw scores for the 50 variables were converted to standard scores in terms of the Knights and Norwood (1981) and other (e.g., Wechsler, 1949) age-based norms available for these tests. This was done in order to facilitate comparisons across the age spectrum for the reliability analyses. This approach to the measurement of reliability afforded the opportunity to compare the classical model of reliability to the more recent generalizability stance proposed by Cronbach, Gleser, Nanda, and Rajaratnam (1972). The majority of these correlations was calculated with all subjects included in the data analysis. However, the correlations for the motor and sensory variables were determined on subgroups of the children based on hand dominance. Therefore, the reliabilities of the motor and sensory variables reflect the performances of the right-handed children separate from the left-handed children.

RESULTS

The means and standard deviations of the 50 test variables are presented in Table 3. In general, the absolute values of scores that were expected to change as a function of skill acquisition or developmental maturity did so; that is, there was an increase in the absolute mean value at the time of the second assessment. For example, scores on the Finger Tapping Test (right hand) improved from a mean value of 26.3 taps per 10s. period at the first examination to an average of 33.3 taps at the time of the second assessment. Scores that were expected to remain relatively constant, e.g., age-corrected scaled scores on the WISC, did remain reasonably consistent between the two examinations. However, whereas the mean standard score on the Reading subtest of the WRAT stayed constant, the mean standard scores on the Spelling and Arithmetic subtests were significantly lower ($p < .05$) at the time of the second evaluation. The mean standard score on the Spelling subtest dropped from an initial mean value of 82 to a mean of 78 at the second assessment; the mean standard score on the Arithmetic subtest exhibited a corresponding drop from an initial value of 84

Table 3. Descriptive Statistics of Test Variables

Variable	First Assessment		Second Assessment	
	M	SD	M	SD

Psychometric Intelligence

* FSIQ	88.2	14.5	88.7	14.9
VIQ	87.6	14.6	86.4	12.6
* PIQ	90.9	15.4	93.3	17.5
Information Scaled Score	6.9	2.4	6.7	2.3
* Comprehension Scaled Score	8.8	3.2	8.1	2.9
* Arithmetic Scaled Score	7.3	2.7	7.0	2.4
* Similarities Scaled Score	8.3	3.5	9.3	3.0
Vocabulary Scaled Score	8.5	3.2	8.3	2.8
Digit Span Scaled Score	7.4	2.8	7.4	2.6
Picture Completion Scaled Score	9.2	2.9	9.4	3.1
Picture Arrangement Scaled Score	8.4	2.8	8.6	3.1
* Block Design Scaled Score	9.0	2.9	9.3	3.2
* Object Assembly Scaled Score	9.2	3.2	9.9	3.7
* Coding Scaled Score	7.4	3.0	7.7	3.0

L:anguage

PPVT IQ	93.1	17.0	92.9	15.2
* Auditory Closure (correct)	7.1	4.3	11.2	5.2
* Fluency (correct)	3.5	3.0	5.9	3.2
* Speech-Sounds (correct)	14.9	6.9	19.2	6.5

Academic Achievement

* WRAT Spell Standard Score	82.6	15.2	78.8	12.6
WRAT Read Standard Score	82.5	17.2	82.4	14.2
* WRAT Arithmetic Standard Score	84.0	14.5	80.6	10.3

Memory

* Sentence Memory (correct)	8.4	3.3	11.0	3.3
* Target Test (correct)	9.4	5.2	13.0	4.9

Motor

* Finger Tap (R) taps/10"	26.3	6.4	33.3	7.5
* Finger Tap (L) taps/10"	25.0	6.3	31.3	7.5
* Grip (R) kg.	9.9	4.7	16.0	7.9
* Grip (L) kg.	9.3	4.4	14.9	7.4
Name (R) time (secs.)	23.6	15.4	20.9	15.0
Name (L) time (secs.)	32.6	20.3	29.4	17.6
* Maze Time (R) (secs.)	13.9	10.9	7.4	7.7
* Maze Counter (R) errors	70.3	42.2	40.0	34.3
* Maze Speed (R) (secs.)	100.7	30.4	108.9	34.2
* Maze Time (L) (secs.)	19.3	12.4	12.4	11.2
* Maze Counter (L) errors	87.1	38.1	60.7	41.5
* Maze Speed (L) secs.)	98.4	28.6	105.5	35.1

table continues

Table 3 (continued)

	First Assessment		Second Assessment	
	M	SD	M	SD
* Foot Tap (R) taps/10 (secs)	22.8	6.2	28.0	7.9
* Foot Tap (L) taps/10 (secs).	21.5	5.9	26.9	7.5
Sensory-Perceptual				
* TPT (Dom) time (mins.)	6.7	3.6	4.9	3.0
* TPT (NDom) time (mins.)	5.3	3.7	3.4	2.6
* TPT (Both) time (mins.)	3.1	2.6	1.9	1.7
* TPT (Memory) correct	3.0	1.7	4.1	1.5
* TPT (Location) correct	1.4	1.6	2.2	1.8
* Tactile (R) errors	1.6	2.0	.76	1.4
* Tactile (L) errors	1.0	1.6	.61	1.4
* Agnosia (R) errors	3.1	3.0	1.8	2.5
* Agnosia (L) errors	3.2	2.8	2.0	2.7
Auditory (R) errors	.30	.88	.24	.79
Auditory (L) errors	.34	.84	.28	.77
Visual (R) errors	.64	2.0	.45	1.3
Visual (L) errors	.57	1.6	.52	1.5

* significant at $p < .05$

to a mean of 80 at the time of the second examination. These lower scores on the Spelling and Arithmetic subtests of the WRAT provide some evidence that children with learning diabilities do more poorly over time, at least on achievement measures, rather than demonstrating improvement in their performance as a function of age and extended educational exposure. However, it should be borne in mind that declines in the order of 4 standard score points are of doubtful clinical significance. Lastly, the lowest mean scores from among the WISC variables, at both the first and second evaluations, were those that comprise the ACID pattern on the WISC (Arithmetic, Coding, Information, and Digit Span subtests), a profile often associated with learning disability (Joschko & Rourke, 1985).

Reliability Analysis
The Pearson and intraclass correlation coefficients for the 50 variables in this study are depicted in Table 4. The reader will be struck by the high degree of similarity between values of Rp and Ri.

The variables are categorized in a fashion similar to Reitan's conceptualization of the ability domains represented by the test measures in the Reitan Neuropsychology Battery for Children. He derived this schema based on the face validity of the measures rather than by empirical or statistical methods (Reitan & Davison, 1974). The classification schema has been modified to include additional test measures not

Table 4. Rank Order of Tests Based on Magnitude of Correlation (Pearson *r*)

Variable	Pearson *r*	Intraclass *r*	
Psychometric Intelligence			
VIQ	.82	.81	
FSIQ	.82	.82	
PIQ	.75	.75	
Vocabulary Scaled Score	.66	.65	*Excellent*
Object Assembly Scaled Score	.61	.60	
Information Scaled Score	.60	.60	
Block Design Scaled Score	.60	.60	
Digit Span Scaled Score	.56	.56	
Similarities Scaled Score	.52	.52	
Picture Arrangement Scaled Score	.52	.51	
Arithmetic Scaled Score	.52	.52	*Good*
Picture Completion Scaled Score	.51	.51	
Coding Scaled Score	.48	.48	
Comprehension Scaled Score	.46	.46	
Language			
PPVT IQ	.71	.71	*Excellent*
Auditory Closure (correct)	.60	.59	
Fluency (correct)	.54	.54	*Good*
Speech Sounds (correct)	.48	.47	
Academic Achievement			
WRAT Spell Scaled Score	.58	.57	
WRAT Read Scaled Score	.57	.56	*Good*
WRAT Arithmetic Scaled Score	.51	.47	
Memory			
Sentence Memory (correct)	.71	.71	
Target Test (correct)	.69	.69	*Excellent*
Motor Tests: *(R) Hand Dominant*			
Maze Time (R) (s)	.70	.64	
Grip (R) kg	.70	.62	
Maze Counter (R) errors	.68	.64	
Grip (L) kg	.67	.60	*Excellent*
Maze Time (L) (s)	.o7	.67	
Tapping (L) taps/10 (s)	.60	.60	

table continues

536

Table 4 (continued)

Variable	Pearson r	Intraclass r	
Tapping (R) taps/10 (s)	.58	.57	
Maze Counter (L) errors	.57	.57	
Foot Tap (L) taps/10 (s)	.56	.54	*Good*
Foot Tap (R) taps/10 (s)	.51	.49	
Maze Speed (R)	.39	.39	
Name (L) speed (s)	.32	.32	*Fair*
Maze Speed (L) (s)	.30	.29	
Name (R) speed (s)	.18	.18	*Poor*
(L) Hand Dominant			
Maze Time (R) (s)	.72	.71	
Foot Tap (R) taps/10 (s)	.69	.68	
Foot Tap (L) taps/10 (s)	.66	.62	
Tapping (R) taps/10 (s)	.64	.62	*Excellent*
Tapping (L) taps/10 (s)	.63	.61	
Maze Counter (R) errors	.63	.62	
Grip (R) kg	.58	.52	
Grip (L) kg	.58	.51	*Good*
Maze Counter (L) errors	.56	.56	
Name (R) speed (s)	.30	.27	
Maze Time (L) (s)	.27	.26	
Name (L) speed (s)	.22	.21	*Poor*
Maze Speed (L) (s)	.19	.18	
Maze Speed (R)	.02	.02	
Sensory-Perceptual Tests: *(R) Hand Dominant*			
TPT (Location) correct	.48	.48	
TPT (Both) time (s)	.44	.40	*Good*
TPT (Memory) correct	.43	.43	
Finger Agnosia (L) errors	.39	.38	
TPT (NDom) time (s)	.38	.36	
Tactile (R) errors	.43	.32	*Fair*
Finger Agnosia (R) errors	.33	.31	
Auditory (R) errors	.31	.29	
TPT (Dom) time (s)	.29	.29	
Tactile (L) errors	.25	.24	*Poor*
Auditory (L) errors	.22	.22	
Visual (R) errors	.15	.15	
Visual (L) errors	.14	.14	

table continues

Table 4 (continued)

Variable	Pearson r	Intraclass r	
(L) Hand Dominant			
Finger Agnosia (L) errors	.69	.69	
Finger Agnosia (R) errors	.62	.62	*Excellent*
Auditory (R) errors	.46	.42	
TPT (Dom) time (s)	.42	.41	*Good*
Tactile (R) errors	.45	.38	
Visual (R) errors	.45	.35	*Fair*
Tactile (L) errors	.33	.19	
Visual (L) errors	.29	.29	
TPT (Both) time (s)	.29	.22	
TPT (NDom) time (s)	.28	.26	
TPT (Memory) correct	.26	.26	
TPT (Location) correct	.22	.21	*Poor*
Auditory (L) errors	.02	.02	

Abbreviations for Tables 3 and 4: R = Right; L = Left; Dom = Dominant; NDom = Nondominant

incorporated in Reitan's assessment procedures (Rourke et al., 1983; Rourke et al., 1986). The ability dimensions represented in this classification are as follows: (1) psychometric intelligence; (2) language; (3) memory; (4) achievement; (5) motor skill; and (6) sensory functioning. The tests are (with one exception) presented within each content area according to the rank order of the Pearson r.

Within the categories of psychometric intelligence and memory, the summary indices and subtest standard scores of the WISC, the Target Test, and the Sentence Memory Test are presented. The correlation coefficients for these measures were among the largest observed in this study. The VIQ and FSIQ had r values equal to .82, with the PIQ at $r = .75$. The correlations for the subtest standard scores ranged from .66 on Vocabulary to .46 on Comprehension. There was no apparent pattern among the WISC subtest correlations, as the Verbal subtests were intermingled in the rank ordering with the Performance subtests. The reliability of the variables that comprise the ACID pattern on the WISC were as follows: Arithmetic $r = .52$, Coding $r = .48$; Information $r = .60$, and Digit Span $r = .56$. The Target Test had a Pearson r and ICC equal to .69; these values were .71 for the Sentence Memory Test.

Correlations for measures in the category of language ranged from a Pearson r value of .71 for the Peabody Picture Vocabulary Test (PPVT) to $r = .48$ on the Speech-Sounds Perception Test. The Auditory Closure and Verbal Fluency Tests had r values of .60 and .54, respectively.

The three standard scores from the WRAT comprise the domain of achievement. The correlations for Spelling ($r = .58$), Reading ($r = .57$), and Arithmetic ($r = .51$) achievement were very similar.

Correlations for the motor and sensory tests were calculated in two stages. The first analysis was based on the right-hand dominant children, and the second was based only on the sinistral youngsters. Considering the right-handed children first (a maximum $n = 190$), correlation coefficients ranged from .70 (Maze Time, right hand; Grip Strength, right hand) to .18 (Name Writing, right hand) on tests within the motor domain. Essentially, within this right-handed population, there was no evident pattern exhibited in the reliabilities of the tests. Correlations for the right (dominant) hand were slightly larger than were correlations for the left (nondominant) on some measures (Grip Strength; Maze Time; Maze Counter; Maze Speed). Correlations for the left hand were slightly larger than were those for the right hand on other tests (Finger Tapping; Name Writing; Foot Tapping). The motor tests from the Reitan Battery for Children were among the most reliable with $r = .70$ and .67 for Grip Strength, right and left hand, respectively, and $r = .58$ and .60 for Finger Tapping, right and left hand, respectively.

The Pearson r for the left-handed children (a maximum $n = 43$)on the motor tests ranged from a high of .72 (Maze Time, right [nondominant] hand) to a low of .02 (Maze Speed, right [nondominant] hand). In contrast to the right-handed children, correlation coefficients for the sinistral youngsters were of greater magnitude on tests involving the right (nondominant) side of the body; there was one exception: i.e., the Maze Test, speed component. The differences in the correlations for the right and left hand were generally small, though also quite consistent.

Thus, for the right-handed children, there was no particular pattern evident in the reliability of right- and left-handed performance across the motor measures. However, for the left-handed youngsters, correlations for the right (nondominant) hand were generally somewhat larger than were those for the left (dominant) hand.

The sensory-perceptual tests yielded somewhat lower correlation coefficients than did the motor tests for the right-handed population. The Pearson r values ranged from .48 on the Location variable of the Tactual Performance Test (TPT) to .14 on Visual imperception and suppression (left). The variables from the TPT were among the most reliable "sensory-perceptual" measures for the right-handed children, with most correlation coefficients in the range of .48 to .38; the only exception to this was the correlation for TPT dominant hand time ($r = .29$). Only two measures among the sensory-perceptual variables contrasted right-and left-hand performances: i.e., the TPT dominant and nondominant time and Finger Agnosia. For both measures, the left (nondominant) hand performance yielded larger r values than did the right (dominant) side score.

Among the sinistral youngsters, the sensory-perceptual measures had Pearson r values ranging from .69 (Finger Agnosia, left) to .02 (Auditory imperception and suppression, left). The reliability of TPT in the sinistral sample was somewhat lower than in the right-handed sample, with r values in the range of .29 to .22 for the left-handed sample; the only exception to this was the correlation for TPT (dominant hand) time ($r = .42$). The left- and right-hand performance on Finger Agnosia was very reliable among the sinistral children: $r = .69$ (left); $r = .62$ (right).

Finally, it is important to evaluate the *clinical* significance of these reliability coefficients. One scheme for so doing has been developed by Cicchetti and Sparrow (1981); the criteria employed in this method of assigning levels of clinical significance are similar to those proposed by Fleiss (1981). In the Cicchetti and Sparrow scheme, the following clinical descriptors are designated for different ranges of reliability coefficients: less than .40 = Poor; .40 to .59 = Fair; .60 to .74 = Good; .75 to 1.00 = Excellent. These designations were offered for test-retest reliability periods of the more usual range (e.g., a few days or weeks, 2 to 3 months). In view of the average test-retest interval of 2.65 years that obtained in the present study, we felt that the following scheme of designations would be more appropriate. (For the data under consideration, it was decided that both the Pearson *r* and the intraclass *r* must be within the limits specified): less than .30 = Poor; .30 to .39 = Fair; .40 to .59 = Good; .60 to 1.00 = Excellent. These designations are indicated in Table 4.

DISCUSSION

The opportunity to measure the consistency and stability of the tests examined in this study was provided by the reassessment of a heterogeneous sample of children who, for a variety of behavioral and academic reasons, required a second evaluation. The correlation coefficients obtained for the 50 variables give an estimate of the magnitude and pattern of their reliabilities for this group of youngsters.

With respect to magnitude, the results indicated that a large number of tests were highly reliable over time while a smaller number, mainly motor and sensory measures, were less consistent and stable. However, the principal finding of this study is that there appears to be a hierarchy of reliability coefficients for these test measures. Among the more cognitively demanding tasks, the most reliable tests were the summary indices from the WISC, two "memory" tests (Sentence Memory Test and Target Test), and the Peabody Picture Vocabulary Test IQ score. This finding supports the commonly held clinical impression that "general intellectual" and mnestic abilities are relatively stable and enduring facets of individual children over time. The subtest scaled scores for the WISC, as well as for the remaining test measures incorporated within the language and achievement domains, were somewhat less reliable but still fell within the "Good" range. Performance on these tasks may be relatively less impervious to external factors such as treatment effects, educational experiences, and remediation than are those tests rated as "Fair" or "Poor". It is important to note that these tests were quite reliable despite potential threats to reliability.

In general, correlations for the motor and sensory-perceptual tests examined in this study were somewhat variable. Among the motor tests, some of the most reliable tasks were measures of force and gross motor speed: e.g., Grip Strength Test and

Finger and Foot Tapping Tests. In addition, two components of the Maze test, the time and counter variables, also had relatively large correlation coefficients; these measures reflect fine motor coordination. The remaining tests (which were less reliable) included within the motor domain were Name Writing (right and left) and the speed component (both right and left hands) from the Maze Test. These measures may reflect lower reliabilities due to practice effects (name writing) and even differences in level of compliance with instructions (speed component of the Maze Test). While performance on measures of strength and gross motor speed appear to be quite consistent in this sample, scores on tests of fine motor skill were generally less so. It may be that the time and counter variables from the Maze test are the most reliable of the tasks capturing fine motor skill.

The consistency and stability of the sensory-perceptual tests (with the exception of Finger Agnosia and the Tactual Performance Test) were probably limited by the small range of scores. For example, since the mean number of errors for Auditory inperception and suppression (right) was .3 at the first assessment, the children who made even as few as one or two errors at the subsequent evaluation would dramatically alter the relative rank ordering of the subjects. This relatively minor variation in scores would then substantially affect the test-retest correlation coefficient of the sensory-perceptual measure. Therefore, even though the r values for these measures were somewhat low, this finding would not, per se, suggest that the tests are not reliable for the individual child. Rather, these lower correlations probably reflect the relatively restricted range of scores obtained in this study (and in standard clinical practice).

Correlations for the components of the Tactual Performance Test tended to be in the range of .4 to .2. However, familiarity with this task, garnered from the first exposure to it, is likely to alter performance for some children during a repeated administration. Although knowledge of the test stimuli should facilitate subsequent performance on the task, this may not be a universal phenomenon. Therefore, it should not come as a surprise that scores for this test may be less stable.

It should be noted that the reliability analyses were considered from the standpoint of both the classical model of reliability and the generalizability approach. The magnitudes of the Pearson and intraclass r were nearly identical for each measure. In the event of any differences, which were always very small, the Pearson r was the greater of the two correlations. (This is always the case since the Pearson r sets the upper limit for the size of intraclass r for a given set of data.) There would seem to have been virtually no differences in the consistency and stability of the 50 variables examined in this study.

Aside from the reliability analyses, it is interesting to note that the lowest mean scores from among the WISC variables, at both the first and second evaluations, were those that comprise the ACID pattern on the WISC (Arithmetic, Coding, Information, and Digit Span). This profile has often been associated with learning disability (Joschko & Rourke, 1985). Further, the mean scores on both the WRAT Spelling and Arithmetic subtests declined over the time period between the first and second assessments. The drop in the mean standard scores for these two achievement subtests was small but statistically significant. These two findings, i.e., poorer performance on the ACID subtests and lowered scores on the WRAT Spelling and Arithmetic subtests, suggest the possibility that specific patterns of information-processing deficits may persist over time.

The youngsters who yielded the data upon which this study is based differed from the population from which they had been drawn by virtue of having been evaluated more than once. They continued to display behavioural or academic difficulties that were deemed severe enough to warrant reevaluation. Although the children were not entered randomly into the study, they represent the subpopulation of youngsters whom clinicians are asked frequently to reexamine. Their scores reflect the reliability of these neuropsychological measures as they are applied in the clinic setting, particularly for the assessment of children with continuing problems. Therefore, the correlation coefficients generated on the data of these youngsters have more practical value for daily clinical activity than would correlations based on the data of children chosen at random.

Rp-Ri Comparisons, the Standard Error of Measurement, True Variance vs. Error Variance. The fact that Rp and Ri values were similar in our study indicates only that there were no consistent increases or decreases in children's test performance from one test assessment to the next. It does not indicate that the two statistics will always produce the same or similar results (as our example above indicates). Another way of putting this, which is also mentioned in our report, is that Rp sets the upper limit that Ri can achieve for any given data set. This means that, whenever there are systematic increases or decreases in test scores from one testing to another, Rp will overestimate the extent of agreement whereas Ri will not. As an example of the implications of these differences, note that the smallest differences (virtual identity) between Rp and Ri in the present study are observed for the IQ scores (i.e., scores that are age-corrected), while the largest differences +/- .06 to +.14 were observed on non-age-corrected variables, such as Maze Time, Grip Strength, Tactile Perception, and Tactual Performance Test, both hands.

Although not of central importance for the interpretation of the data reported in this study, the interested reader may wish to know about reliability as it relates to the expected variation in test performance from one assessment to the next. Such data are readily available for most well-standardized instruments, especially those focusing upon a cognitive measure such as the WISC. In this specific area, the test-retest variability in FSIQ scores is usually considered, in "ball-park" terms, as approximately between +/- 5 standard score units. Given this guideline, we find that the average test-retest difference for WISC FSIQ (88.2 - 88.7 = -0.5, Table 3, first entry) is essentially negligible. Note also that the same obtains for WISC VIQ and PIQ and for the various WISC subtests.

With regard to the technical issue of the reliability of "true" variance and "error" variance components, our views regarding this matter are the same as those of Shrout, Spitzer, and Fleiss (1987) who recently stated their position regarding "true" and "error" variance as these apply to Ri and Kappa. The interested reader may wish to consult the Shrout et al. paper for an extended discussion of this topic.

CONCLUSIONS: CLINICAL APPLICABILITY

It should be emphasized that the set of reliability coefficients presented in this study constitutes a kind of "worst case" scenario vis-à-vis the issue of the reliability of the tests in question. This is so for the following reasons: (1) there was no plan to have the same examiner test the child on both occasions, although this was often the case; (2) the test-retest interval was an average of 2.65 years; developmental changes during this period for the children within this age range would be expected to be significant; (3) those retested were a clinic sample of children thought to be suffering from brain impairment; in almost all cases, they were retested because they were thought to require such a second examination in view of the fact that their program of habilitation/rehabilitation was not proceeding as well as might be expected.

These threats to reliability are, to say the least, significant. Thus, the absolute levels of the reliability coefficients cited in this study should be viewed as lower-bound estimates of the clinical reliability of the tests and measures in question. At the same time, these reliability coefficients were obtained within the frame in which clinical neuropsychological practice with children ordinarily proceeds: that is, children being retested by different examiners over a test-retest interval of approximately $2^1/_2$ years because the remedial needs of these children are not being met in an optimal fashion.

With respect specifically to the results of the present study, it should be pointed out that we are well aware of the uncontrolled sources of variation that impact on our results. These are part-and-parcel of clinical samples. This represents what we have referred to as "threats to reliability". In view of these, we are firmly of the opinion that the reliability data we present are, if anything, underestimates of the "true" reliabilities of the measures in question. In the best designed reliability study (i.e., using nonclinical samples) there will always be sources of uncontrolled or error variance. The best that investigators can do is to control as much as is feasible for these sources (e.g., we used the same well-trained examiner in most of the cases), and then to eventually compare levels of reliability as a function of different settings under which the data were collected.

In closing, as the principal concern of the practicing clinical neuropsychologist vis-à-vis this paper relates to the relative reliabilities for the prototypic test-retest situation described herein, we have felt it advisable to deal in detail with certain definitional and methodological issues that relate to this situation. It is hoped that this careful explication and supporting data will be useful to the reader.

REFERENCES

Bornstein, R.L. (1982). Reliability of the Speech Sounds Perception Tests. *Perceptual and Motor Skills, 55*, 203-210.

Bornstein, R.L. (1983). Reliability and item analysis of the Seashore Rhythm Test. *Perceptual and Motor Skills, 57*, 571-574.

Cicchetti, D.V., & Sparrow, S.S. (1981). Developing criteria for establishing the interrater reliability of specific items in a given inventory: Applications to assessment of adaptive behavior. *American Journal of Mental Deficiency, 86*, 127-137.

Cronbach, L.J., Gleser, G.C., Nanda, H., & Rajaratnam, H. (1972). *The dependability of behavioral measurements.* New York: Wiley.

Dodrill, C.B., & Trupin, A.S. (1975). Effect of repeated administrations of a comprehensive neuropsychological battery among chronic epileptics. *Journal of Nervous and Mental Disease, 161*, 185-190.

Eckardt, M.J., & Matarazzo, J.D. (1981). Test-retest reliability of the Halstead Impairment Index in hospitalized alcoholic and non-alcoholic males with mild to moderate neuropsychological impairment. *Journal of Clinical Neuropsychology, 3*, 257-269.

Fleiss, J.L. (1981). *Statistical methods for rates and proportions* (2nd ed.). New York: Wiley.

Goldstein, G., & Watson, J.R. (1989). Test-retest reliability of the Halstead-Reitan Battery and the WAIS in a neuropsychiatric population. *The Clinical Neuropsychologist, 3*, 265-272.

Joschko, M., & Rourke, B.P. (1985). Neuropsychological subtypes of learning-disabled children who exhibit the ACID pattern on the WISC. In B.P. Rourke (Ed.), *Neuropsychology of learning disabilities: Essentials of subtype analysis.* (pp. 65-88). New York: Guilford Press.

Kilpatrick, D.L. (1969). Revision of the intermediate version of the Halstead Category Test. Unpublished master's thesis, University of Victoria, Victoria, BC.

Klonoff, H., Fibiger, C.H., & Hutton, G.H. (1970). Neuropsychological patterns in chronic schizophrenia. *Journal of Nervous and Mental Disease, 150*, 291-300.

Knights, R.M., & Norwood, J.A. (1980). *Revised smoothed normative data on the neuropsychological test battery for children.* Ottawa: Author.

Matarazzo, J.D., Matarazzo, R.G., Wiens, A.N., Gallo, A.E., & Klonoff, H. (1976). Retest reliability of the Halstead Impairment Index in a normal, a schizophrenic, and two samples of organic patients. *Journal of Clinical Psychology, 32*, 338-349.

Matarazzo, J.D., Wiens, A.N., Matarazzo, R.G., & Goldstein, G.S. (1974). Psychometric and clinical test-retest reliability of the Halstead Impairment Index in a sample of healthy, young normal men. *Journal of Nervous and Mental Disease, 158*, 37-49.

Morrison, M.W., Gregory, R.J., & Paul, T.J. (1979). Reliability of the finger tapping test and a note on sex differences. *Perceptual and Motor Skills, 48*, 138-142.

Reitan, R.M., & Davison, L.A. (1974). *Clinical neuropsychology: Current status and applications.* Washington, DC: V.N. Winston & Sons.

Rourke, B.P., Bakker, D.J., Fisk, J.L., & Strang, J.P. (1983). *Child neuropsychology: An introduction to theory, research, and clinical practice.* New York: Guilford Press.

Rourke, B.P., Fisk, J.L., & Strang, J.D. (1986). *Neuropsychological assessment of children: A treatment-oriented approach.* New York: Guilford Press.

Sarazin, F.A., & Spreen, O. (1986). Fifteen-year stability of some neuropsychologic tests in learning disabled subjects with and without neurological impairment. *Journal of Clinical and Experimental Neuropsychology, 8*, 190-200.

Shaw, D.J. (1966). The reliability and validity of the Halstead Category Test. *Journal of Clinical Psychology, 22*, 176-180.

Shrout, P.E., & Fleiss, J.L. (1979). Intraclass correlations: Uses in assessing rater reliability. *Psychological Bulletin, 86*, 420-428.

Shrout, P.E., Spitzer, R.L., & Fleiss, J.L. (1987). Quantification of agreement in psychiatric diagnosis revisited. *Archives of General Psychiatry, 44*, 172-177.

Wechsler, D. (1949). *Wechsler Intelligence Scale for Children: Manual.* New York: Psychological Corporation.

CHAPTER VI

General Conclusions and Future Directions

This text provided a number of approaches designed to expand our understanding of brain-behavior relationships, based upon state-of-the art research in clinical neuropsychology, as published in two major journals in the field. As such, the articles chosen represent a rather wide range of clinical assessment problems, research design issues, data-analytic strategies, and discussions of the meaning of obtained results. However, it is the editors' joint consensus that, no matter how diligent the effort, any attempt to present a thorough treatment of such complex and varied material within the confines of any single text cannot, in and of itself, be fully successful. The best that can be accomplished is to present as complete a treatment as possible and then to provide an array of additional reading material to enrich, enhance, and bring up to date what has already been presented. We, as editors, have made every attempt to accomplish this particularly challenging goal, despite the rapidity with which new developments are published in any given area of scientific inquiry. Toward this continued goal, there are several important issues that need to be discussed.

As noted in the Introduction, the first is the audience toward whom the text is directed. This would include psychologists, neurologists, psychiatrists, and other health professionals who have had at least one undergraduate course in statistics so that the basic univariate parametric approaches (e.g., chi square(d), t test, one-way analysis of variance) are part of one's repertoire.

The methods described in this volume require a sound education in the philosophy of science, experimental design and statistics, and - in some cases - computer literacy. These are essential areas of study for most graduate curricula training researchers at the university level. Interestingly, successful understanding and use of most of the methods herein does not require the investigator to be a professional mathematician or computer programmer. Rather, the curiosity and creative potential of the user of these techniques are the most important predictors of successful mastery. Put another way, if researchers *want* to use these "cutting edge" methods, they can learn them. Help to do this can be found at most institutions of higher learning and in many research settings.

Given this minimal background, it is suggested that the interested and advanced student further supplement the knowledge presented in this text by exposure to important sources for understanding the following: (1) effects of violations of assumptions underlying the appropriate application of basic parametric tests such as: the t test and the analysis of variance (Petrinovich & Hardyck, 1969), and the appropriate circumstances under which to apply given multiple-range tests (e.g., Cicchetti, 1972, and more generally, Toothaker, 1991).

Finally, when the violations of assumptions is such that parametric tests are no longer appropriate, we would suggest that one consider the most valid parametric approach available for a particular application. Here, the text by Leach (1979) has much to recommend it. In a rather ingenious approach to unification of the myriad of nonparametric statistics that are available, Leach (1979): (a) argues convincingly about which procedure is most appropriate to which class of research questions; and (b) ties together the various statistics by utilizing an element common to all of them, namely, the calculation of S which has its definition in the simple difference (ab-cd) in the cross-products of the cell frequencies in a two-by-two contingency table. Here, as previously discussed by Cicchetti (pages 417-434), the diagonal (agreement) cells are designated as a and d, while the off-diagonal (disagreement) cells are designated as c and d. Generalizing the basis S procedure, Leach is able to show mathematical relationships between numerous nonparametric statistics (e.g., between the familiar Fisher exact-probability test and the more esoteric Jonckheere test of trend).

Given the information presented in the text, the introductory, category, subcategory, overall comments, and additional readings, the instructor has considerable latitude to design a number of possible syllabi depending upon objectives. Among many others, these would include the following: (1) a course aimed at teaching students how to become better consumers of research (e.g., learning how to read critically any given research article in clinical neuropsychology); (2) a basic text for multivariate analysis of neuropsychological variables; (3) a basic primer in methodologic approaches to clinical neuropsychological research; and (4) a major source for obtaining required information for designing future studies in clinical neuropsychology at a Master's, doctoral, and post-doctoral level.

To the extent that this volume has succeeded, the serious student of neuropsychology will have seen how important the present set of papers is for the understanding of the science and practice of brain-behavior relationships. The limiting factor for progress in neuropsychology is the methods available to researchers and clinicians to design and execute studies. In turn, the effectiveness of individual investigators will depend on their understanding of the alternative methods for investigation and their command of the skills needed to use them wisely.

The paradigms and techniques described and demonstrated in this volume have varying strengths and liabilities in relation to various research questions. Merely becoming adept with the single-case study or learning cluster analysis will not meet all the researcher's methodological needs. It will become increasingly important for the successful neuropsychological researcher to follow developments in research techniques and to be alert for new ways to utilize these methods to shed light on theoretical and practical issues. As the reader can see, there are a number of examples in this volume where the investigators have done just that.

Future directions in neuropsychological research are likely to encompass all of the techniques described herein as well as incorporating additional ones. To gain some perspective on this, one need only think back to the beginning of the last decade. Few people in neuropsychology would have predicted the widespread and successful use of techniques such as cluster analysis, canonical correlation, or confirmatory factor analysis in the 1980's. Advances in sampling theory, randomization, and alternative distributional methods promise to make the next decade equally exciting.

The increasing costs of doing research are also likely to increase the prevalence of collaborative research and require the investigator to use methodology that extracts a maximum of information from data at a minimum of cost. This will mean that designs will need to pay closer attention to sampling, cross-validation, and generalization. Neuropsychologists will likely become serious students of epidemiology as well.

The computer will continue to evolve as a powerful research tool for the investigator. Actual improvements in the man-machine interface are likely to improve to the point where some data acquisition will be directed through transducers, rather than recorded manually and entered by keyboard.

Statistical programs and paradigms will improve continuously for the consumer, presenting a tremendous array of analytic and graphic programs for use. Simulation will become increasingly important as a tool for research, and software to accomplish this type of activity will be made more amenable to neuropsychological applications. Investigators will be able to see the effects of various choices of statistical approach directly, and they will also be able to pose "what if" kinds of questions and get answers with a level of complexity and speed unthinkable just 20 years ago.

Further information about possible future directions for research in clinical neuropsychology can be found in Rourke (1991). Perhaps the most overarching conclusion that can be drawn from the various prognostications that have been made is that future research will be characterized by an ever-increasing trend toward multi-disciplinary collaboration in the field of clinical neuropsychology, whether at the level of teaching or research endeavors. As a result, a science which is defined by the interface between clinical psychology and neurology, will continue to be further enhanced by the collaboration from scientists in many other fields, such as psychiatry, genetics, biochemistry, biostatistics, and computer science. These trends suggest strongly that future publications in the field will not be restricted solely to neuropsychological publication outlets, though the nucleus of such new information will remain within the confines of these primary and fundamental sources of knowledge in the field. All in all, future developments in clinical and experimental neuropsychology can be expected to excite the interest of scientists across a wide range of biomedical and biostatistical subspecialty areas.

Finally, the neuropsychological community itself will become more methodologically adept and sophisticated as graduate programs increasingly update their aims, curricula, and faculty. They will prepare students for the years ahead as innovative methods become available to study questions old and new. The editors and authors hope that this volume has provided the reader with some sense of this promise and excitement.

REFERENCES

Cicchetti, D.V. (1972). Extension of multiple-range tests to interaction tables in the analysis of variance: A rapid, approximate solution. *Psychological Bulletin, 77,* 405-408.

Leach, C. (1979). *Introduction to statistics: A nonparametric approach for the social sciences.* New York: Wiley.

Petrinovich, L.F., & Hardyck, C.D. (1969). Error rates for multiple comparison methods: Some evidence concerning the frequency of erroneous conclusions. *Psychological Bulletin, 71,* 43-54.

Rourke, B.P. (1991). Human neuropsychology in the 1990s. *Archives of Clinical Neuropsychology, 6,* 1-14.

Toothaker, L.E. (1991). *Multiple comparisons for researchers.* Newberry Park, CA: Sage Publications.

INDEX